VERMONT COLLEG[

MONTPELIER, VERMO

W9-BUD-749

GARY LIBRARY
VERMONT COLLEGE
MONTPELIER, VT.

WITHDRAWN

THE
CAMBRIDGE ANCIENT HISTORY

VOLUME I
PART 1

THE CAMBRIDGE ANCIENT HISTORY

THIRD EDITION

VOLUME I

PART 1

PROLEGOMENA AND
PREHISTORY

EDITED BY

I. E. S. EDWARDS F.B.A.
Keeper of Egyptian Antiquities, The British Museum

THE LATE C. J. GADD F.B.A.
*formerly Professor Emeritus of Ancient Semitic Languages and Civilizations,
School of Oriental and African Studies, University of London*

N. G. L. HAMMOND F.B.A.
Professor of Greek, University of Bristol

CAMBRIDGE
AT THE UNIVERSITY PRESS
1970

Published by the Syndics of the Cambridge University Press
Bentley House, 200 Euston Road, London N.W.1
American Branch: 32 East 57th Street, New York, N.Y.10022

© Cambridge University Press 1970

Library of Congress Catalogue Card Number: 75-85719

Standard Book Number: 521 07051 1

Printed in Great Britain
at the University Printing House, Cambridge
(Brooke Crutchley, University Printer)

R
930
C 178
v.1 pt.1

CONTENTS

CHAPTER I

THE GEOLOGICAL AGES

by D. L. LINTON
Professor of Geography in the University of Birmingham

and F. MOSELEY
Senior Lecturer in Geology in the University of Birmingham

CHAPTER II

PHYSICAL CONDITIONS IN EASTERN EUROPE, WESTERN ASIA AND EGYPT BEFORE THE PERIOD OF AGRICULTURAL AND URBAN SETTLEMENT

by K. W. BUTZER
Professor of Anthropology in the University of Chicago

14959

CHAPTER III

PRIMITIVE MAN IN EGYPT, WESTERN ASIA AND EUROPE IN PALAEOLITHIC TIMES

by DOROTHY A. E. GARROD, F.B.A.
Formerly Disney Professor of Archaeology in the University of Cambridge

IN MESOLITHIC TIMES

by J. G. D. CLARK, F.B.A.
Fellow of Peterhouse and Disney Professor of Archaeology in the University of Cambridge

CHAPTER IV

THE EVIDENCE OF LANGUAGE

by W. F. ALBRIGHT
W. W. Spence Professor Emeritus of Semitic Languages in The Johns Hopkins University

and T. O. LAMBDIN
Associate Professor of Semitic Philology, Harvard University

CONTENTS vii

CHAPTER V

THE EARLIEST POPULATIONS OF MAN IN EUROPE, WESTERN ASIA AND NORTHERN AFRICA

by D. R. HUGHES

Head of the Physical Anthropology Section, Human History Branch, National Museum of Canada

and D. R. BROTHWELL

Senior Scientific Officer in the Sub-Department of Physical Anthropology, British Museum (Natural History)

CHAPTER VI

CHRONOLOGY
I. EGYPT—TO THE END OF THE TWENTIETH DYNASTY 173

by the late W. C. HAYES

Formerly Curator of the Department of Egyptian Art in the Metropolitan Museum of Art, New York

II. ANCIENT WESTERN ASIA

by M. B. ROWTON
Assistant Professor at the Oriental Institute, University of Chicago

CHAPTER VIII

THE DEVELOPMENT OF CITIES FROM AL-'UBAID TO THE END OF URUK 5

by Sir Max MALLOWAN, F.B.A.

*Fellow of All Souls College, Oxford, and Emeritus Professor of Western
Asiatic Archaeology in the University of London*

CHAPTER IX

(*a*) PREDYNASTIC EGYPT

by ELISE J. BAUMGARTEL

(*b*) PALESTINE DURING THE NEOLITHIC AND CHALCOLITHIC PERIODS

by R. DE VAUX, O.P.

École Biblique et Archéologique Française de Jérusalem

(c) CYPRUS IN THE NEOLITHIC AND CHALCOLITHIC PERIODS

by H. W. CATLING

Senior Assistant Keeper, Department of Antiquities of the Ashmolean Museum in the University of Oxford

CHAPTER X
THE STONE AGE IN THE AEGEAN

by S. S. WEINBERG

Professor of Classical Languages and Archaeology in the University of Missouri

BIBLIOGRAPHIES

CONTENTS

MAPS

TABLES

TABLES

TEXT-FIGURES

PREFACE

WHEN the decision to publish this new edition of the first two volumes of the *Cambridge Ancient History* was taken, it was apparent that it would not be possible to revise the former edition and that the volumes must be entirely re-written. The new volumes, which are about twice as long as their predecessors, are divided into two parts in order to key in with the numbering of the later volumes. This substantial increase in size is to be ascribed mainly to fresh knowledge which has been acquired during the past forty-five years as a result of more and more intensive efforts to discover the past. Perhaps the most notable advances have been made in our knowledge of the very early phases of man's existence in settled communities: excavations at Çatal Hüyük in Anatolia have disclosed a city, dated to the seventh millennium B.C., which extends at least over an area of thirty-two acres, while smaller towns or villages of approximately the same date have been found in the Jordan valley at Jericho, in Iraq at Jarmo, in the foothills of Kurdistān, on the north Syrian coast at Ras Shamra, in Cyprus at Khirokitia and at Argissa in Thessaly. Settled communities presuppose the domestication of animals and the cultivation of crops, landmarks in social evolution which are now believed to have been reached between the tenth and the eighth millennia B.C. Behind these achievements lay perhaps more than 40,000 years of human development, if the dates obtained by carbon-14 determination for the Palaeolithic Age are reliable. This invaluable aid to the archaeologist, which we owe to the American scientist Professor W. F. Libby, is still lacking in precision, but improvements in technique and in the interpretation of results can hardly fail to come in time. However remote from the present day such dates as have been obtained by this method for the Palaeolithic Age may seem they are recent in comparison with the earliest evidence of primitive life in Cambrian rocks, which are believed to be 600 million years old and thus to date from nearly 4,000 million years after the earth came into existence.

Chronology, the subject of chapter VI in this volume, has always presented difficult problems to the ancient historian, and it must be admitted that complete agreement has not yet been achieved, in particular for the third millennium B.C. The adoption of a uniform system is, however, vital in a book of this kind which

deals with many different civilizations spread over a wide
geographical area. In order to achieve as high a degree of consistency as possible the editors sought the assistance of three of the
leading authorities on the chronology of the ancient world, the
late Dr W. C. Hayes, Dr M. B. Rowton and Dr F. H. Stubbings,
and the dates given in the tables at the end of each volume are
the results of their deliberations. Other contributors were invited
to express, if they so wished, their own views on the dates adopted
in the footnotes to their chapters; the instances in which this
invitation was accepted proved to be gratifyingly few.

While every effort has been made to avoid incorrect renderings
of personal names and place-names no rigid system of transcription has been adopted. As a rule the accepted and familiar
spellings have been used for well-known names and for a number
of small archaeological sites in Western Asia, since alteration
would only cause confusion. Egyptian royal names are given, if
possible, in the forms found in the writings of the Greek historians.
For geographical names in Egypt the spellings in B. Porter and
R. L. B. Moss, *Topographical Bibliography*, with the omission of
the diacritical marks, have generally been used. In Western
Asiatic names, however, the diacritical marks are normally
included. An exception has been made for the consonants transcribed from cuneiform as *ḫ* and *š*. These, accepting the risk of a
somewhat old-fashioned appearance, have been rendered as
kh and *sh*, so as to agree with the forms adopted in Egyptian
proper names. When, as sometimes happens, *ḫḫ* occurs, it has
usually been rendered by the plain letters *hh*. The forms given
are, whenever possible, those indicated by standard works such
as G. Le Strange, *The Lands of the Eastern Caliphate* (Cambridge,
1905), F. M. Abel, *Géographie de la Palestine* (3rd ed. Paris,
1967), the *Encyclopaedia of Islam* and the lists of place-names
issued by the Permanent Committee on Geographical Names of
the Royal Geographical Society (1925–37). Turkish names are
rendered according to the official transcription. The lengths of
vowels are often indicated but not in common geographical names
which are still in use. Ancient names of places in the Aegean area
have been rendered in the Latin form; where -us and -os are
equally possible, we have preferred -us for mainland places and
-os for island names. Modern Greek place-names are transliterated in accordance with the usual convention.

The publication of every chapter, in the first instance, as a
separate fascicle made it possible to put each contribution in the
hands of students within a few months of its completion. An

important consideration in choosing this method was the knowledge that many of the authors, fifty-seven in number, had already undertaken other tasks before agreeing to participate in the preparation of these volumes, and it was clear that the Editors could expect neither an early delivery of their scripts nor a regular flow of chapters in their proper sequence. Six years have indeed elapsed between the appearance of the first and the last fascicles, a far longer interval than was envisaged, and small revisions and additions have in some cases become necessary. We are grateful to the Syndics of the Cambridge University Press for their decision to invite contributors to make such changes in the texts as were necessary to bring them up to date. In two instances (volume I, chapters x and xvi) plans, which were not included in the fascicles, have been added in this edition.

Detailed references to the sources of information given in the text are an innovation in these volumes, and it is hoped that the method adopted will commend itself to readers. The references are placed in footnotes. They are in code form for the sake of conciseness and they are related to the sections of the bibliographies which are given at the end of each part. Thus §iv, 15, 10 means the fourth section of the bibliography for the chapter, the fifteenth book in the section and page 10 in the book. Instead of the Roman numeral preceded by § either the letter G or the letter A may be given, the former referring to the general section which precedes the numbered sections in some bibliographies and the latter referring to the addenda at the end of a bibliography, which were not included in the chapter when it appeared in fascicle form.

Four contributors to the present volume have expressed a desire to record their thanks to colleagues who have given them assistance. Professor K. W. Butzer is indebted to Mr Charles A. Read and Mr David Ward for reading his script and to Dr K. S. Sandford for several helpful suggestions. Professor M. B. Rowton has discussed problems of chronology with his colleagues in the Oriental Institute of the University of Chicago and wishes to acknowledge his debt to them. Dr E. Baumgartel is grateful to Professor H. W. Fairman for reading her script and making several valuable suggestions. Professor Weinberg is particularly indebted to Professor J. D. Evans and the editors of the *Annual of the British School at Athens* for providing photographs and for allowing him to use, before they were published, the proofs of Part I of the Cnossus report, to Professor John L. Caskey for providing photographs and an advance account of his excavations in the Kephala cemetery on Ceos in 1963, to Mr Robert J.

Rodden for photographs and advance reports on the 1963 excavations at Nea Nikomedeia, to Mr Roger Howell and Mr T. W. Jacobson for advance notes of Neolithic sites located in their surveys of Arcadia and Euboea respectively, and to Miss Gloria Saltz Merker for preparing the three maps in his chapter.

The Editors wish to acknowledge with gratitude the help which they have received from several sources in the preparation of this volume for publication. Professor Anis Freyha, of the American University of Beirut, and Mr G.M. Meredith-Owens, of the British Museum, have given valuable advice on the spelling of place-names in the Arab countries and in Iran. Mrs L. Copeland has located many obscurely situated and obscurely named excavations in Palestine and the Lebanon mentioned in the early chapters of this History. Mr Frank Brand, formerly on the staff of the Cambridge University Press, has kept constant watch on consistency in the spelling of proper names, a service which, in the case of some of the first fascicles to appear, was rendered by Miss Margaret Munn Rankin and Mrs Guy Evans, both of whom were unable to continue because of other demands on their time. Translations into English of chapters written in French have been made by Mrs Elizabeth Edwards (chapter IX, §§ V–VIII and chapter XV) and by Mr C. E. N. Childs (chapters XVII, § II and XXI, §§ I–IV), and Mr Guy Evans has translated chapter XXIII from German. The staff of the Cambridge University Press have been unfailingly helpful at every stage and the editors are especially grateful to them for the understanding which they have always shown when problems have arisen. Lastly the editors wish to place on record their thanks to the whole body of contributors, both for their ready co-operation and for their patience during the double operation of preparing scripts for fascicle form and subsequently for the bound volumes.

I. E. S. E.
C. J. G.
N. G. L. H.

CHAPTER I

THE GEOLOGICAL AGES

I. INTRODUCTION

THE perspective of history begins with the origin of the earth, and develops through geological time until the stage is ultimately set for human evolution. The age of the earth, so long a matter of grave controversy, is now fairly reliably known as the result of the development of delicate methods of measurement that make use of the radioactive properties of certain naturally occurring elements, and is of the order of 4,500 million years. For much of this period there was apparently no life upon the earth, and certainly any life that existed left no traces that have yet been recognized as such. Yet year by year records of primitive life are announced from older and older rocks, until now there are claims going back more than 2,000 million years. Nevertheless, complex life forms that have left abundant traces as fossils are not found in rocks older than those of the Cambrian system, which may be accepted as having been laid down about 600 million years ago. This dividing line between Cambrian and Pre-Cambrian rocks, between those with abundant fossil remains and those to all intents and purposes without any is clearly of paramount importance to the palaeontologist studying the forms of organic evolution, and to the stratigraphical geologist who depends so importantly upon his labours. The greater part of all geological writing is thus concerned with Cambrian and Post-Cambrian time, but the non-geologist must be careful to avoid the inference from this that little of importance occurred before the Cambrian. More than four-fifths of the history of our earth was over before the fossil record opens.

From that moment, however, it is clear that the evolution of life was both multifarious and rapid. The remains preserved in the Lower Palaeozoic systems (Cambrian, Ordovician and Silurian)[1] are all of marine organisms; land plants and land animals did not appear until the Upper Palaeozoic, in the Devonian and Carboniferous, respectively. The giant reptiles flourished in the era represented by the Mesozoic systems (Triassic, Jurassic and Cretaceous). Mammals made a slow start with Triassic or even

[1] See Table 1 overleaf.

Table 1. Geological ages and events

Age (millions of years)	Era	System	Evolution of life	Eurasia	Tethys	Afrasia
–2	CAINOZOIC (or TERTIARY)	Pleistocene (= Quaternary)	Decline of mammals continues. Most present-day species come into existence, including man	Glacial and interglacial phases alternate	Changes of sea level due both to crustal movements and to formation and melting of ice-caps. Some vulcanicity until today	Pluvial and dry phases alternate. Palestinian rift formed. Final volcanic activity
–12		Pliocene	Most present-day genera in existence. Mammals declining but more diverse than today	Outline of continent recognizably modern. Lakes and inland seas north of mountain belt. Pannonian, Dacian, Meotian, Aralo-Caspian	Major elevation of mountains, Alps to Himalayas, with some renewed folding. Formation of deep basins, Aegean, Pontic and Caspian	Volcanic outpourings (basaltic) in Arabia, Ethiopia and Central Sahara. Extension of Red Sea rift to Mediterranean
		Miocene	Nummulites extinct. Acme of mammals. Present-day mammal families in existence. Primitive anthropoid appears (Proconsul)	Temperate climate. Brackish water sea (Sarmatian Sea) 15° to 65° E. Vulcanicity in France and Central Europe	Continued folding and elevation of mountains with concurrent reduction by erosion and accumulation of molasse sediments. Opening of eastern Mediterranean	Beginning of volcanic activity. Widespread shallow-water limestones
–25		Oligocene	Widespread grasslands and herbivores. Horses, elephants and primates evolving	Warm-temperate to sub-tropical marine and fresh-water basins. Uplift of intervening land areas	Main orogenic phase of Alps. Extinction of Tethys and folding of contained sediments	Continued limestone deposition
–40		Eocene (including Palaeocene)	Nummulites (large Foraminifera) important. Land vegetation of modern aspect. Mammals attain dominance with extinction of dinosaurs	Marine regression exposes land with sub-tropical climate and vegetation. Seas shallow and restricted. Plateau basalts of Iceland, Hebrides, etc.	Folding of Pyrenees, Apennines, etc. Continued accumulation of sediments including flysch	Widespread limestone deposits in shallow-shelf seas
–70	MESOZOIC	Cretaceous	Angiosperms develop. Large reptiles (dinosaurs) dominate land fauna	Transgression of the Chalk Sea. Most of continent submerged. Marine regression	Folding of Carpathians following flysch deposition	Plateau basalts of Yemen and Ethiopia. Opening of Gulf of Aden and Arabian Sea rifts. Marine transgression and deposition of Nubian sandstone
–135		Jurassic	Early reptile-like birds. Cycads and conifers important	Marine transgression. Local shallow epicontinental seas	Continuous and locally very thick sedimentation in the Tethyan geosyncline with limestone the dominant lithology	Mostly continental lowland with local basins of deposition in Arabia
–180		Triassic	Evolution of reptiles	Tropical deserts with dune sands and saline lakes		
–225	PALAEOZOIC — Upper	Permian		Destruction of mountains by erosion. Hercynian (= Variscan) orogeny	Initiation of the Tethyan geosyncline	No deposits over vast areas of continental lowland—part of the 'supercontinent' Gondwanaland
		Carboniferous	Early land animals develop (amphibians)	Tropical swamps. Tropical coral seas	Unknown	
		Devonian	Early land plants	Old Red Sandstone deserts		Marine deposits in North and West Africa only
–400	PALAEOZOIC — Lower	Silurian / Ordovician		Caledonian orogeny. Caledonian geosyncline in N.W. Europe. Quiet shelf seas on Russian platform		
		Cambrian	Earliest abundant fossils (marine arthropods)			
–600 / Greater than 3600	PRE-CAMBRIAN	Many complex systems difficult to correlate	Rare remains of primitive soft-bodied animals and plants; oldest found may be 2000 million years old. Oldest rocks so far dated by radioactive properties	Basement complex formed during successive orogenies. Exposed in Baltic shield and Ukrainian swell. Deeply buried in Russian platform		Continental cover sediments resting on basement complex of Africa and Arabia

Permian origins, and did not rise to dominance until Tertiary (= Cainozoic) times. The genus *Homo*, one of the latest additions to the mammalian fauna, appeared less than two million years ago, and *Homo sapiens*, our own species, has been present on earth in only the last fiftieth of that period.

These developments have taken place upon an ever-changing earth; ever-changing in the sense that nothing in its geography, the disposition of land and sea, mountain and plain, torrid and frigid zones, dry and rainy belts, has remained fixed during geological time. Not that there was ever a time, at any rate since the Cambrian period, when any of these features of our familiar earth was not present. Nor does the record of the rocks suggest that there were climates hotter or colder, wetter or drier, than those found somewhere on the globe today. But in pattern and extent of development of all these features the world has seen great changes. Indeed, anyone who examines the reconstructions by stratigraphers of the geographies of the world at different epochs in geological time (palaeogeographic reconstructions) will tend to gain the impression that almost any change that it is possible to imagine has actually occurred. This, however, is not so. Certain elements in these reconstructions are not essential but reflect changes in the concepts of the nature of the earth's crust advanced by geophysicists. Others, however, are common to all reconstructions and have been accepted as fundamental facts of the earth's palaeogeography. As such they have made their own contribution to our ideas about the character and evolution of the crust.

Two basic generalizations about the terrestrial crust must here be kept in view. The first is that continents and oceans are physically distinct and not interchangeable elements of the crust. Old notions of foundered continents, such as the popular Atlantis and many a scholarly palaeogeographic invention, must be forgotten. Modern geophysical work has shown that of the two the continental crust is thicker, reaching 30–60 km., while that below the oceans is limited to 6, 10 or 15 km. In both cases the base of the crust is revealed by a sharp rise in the velocity of transmission of earthquake waves known as the Mohorovičić discontinuity (or Moho). The passage from continent to ocean floor is thus marked by a steep topographic descent that averages 3–5 km. and a sharp rise of the Moho through an interval many times as great. With the change in thickness goes a change in composition. The ocean floors are mantled by a relatively thin layer of sediment that is largely unconsolidated. Beneath this is a layer of approximately the density and probably the composition of basalt that extends down to the Moho. The continental crust has a more complex structure made up of three distinctive layers rather than two. The uppermost of these, as in the oceanic crust, is a layer of sediments; in places this layer may be missing; just as commonly it is very thick; generally the sediments have been consolidated and uplifted and often they have been folded. Below the sediments is a layer 10–15 km. thick whose bulk physical properties resemble those of granite, of which rock it is seen to be largely composed in areas where the sedimentary cover is absent. Below this again the third layer has measurable properties that correspond with those of the basaltic layer beneath the oceans; it is, however, much thicker than that layer and continues down to the Moho. This distinction between continents and oceans is one that underlies much of the account that follows, but to it we have to add an important generalization about the make-up of the continents themselves.

All continents reveal that they are constituted of areas of two contrasted kinds. On the one hand large tracts may be characterized as relatively stable and termed 'platforms', while on the other are regions of great and geologically recent disturbance that we may term folded belts or orogenic zones. Investigation of the folded belts reveals that they arise from areas of prolonged and thick sedimentation known as geosynclines, which, after a depositional history a hundred or more million years long, may be crushed together and converted into a zone of mountainous relief and highly complex internal structure. Platforms, on the other hand, are often covered by immense sheets of flat-lying sediments that have clearly suffered little disturbance since deposition other than the broad uplift that has converted marine sediments into dry land that may be many hundreds of feet above sea level. Beneath such sedimentary layers is a rigid basement. Where it can be investigated, it has a highly complex character, comprising deformed and metamorphosed sediments extensively invaded by huge irregular intrusions of granitic rocks. It is in fact part of the granitic layer of the continental crust. In detail many of its structural features are those revealed in the more deeply eroded parts of orogenic zones, and the conviction has been widespread for a generation or more that in the basement complex of the rigid platforms we see traces of the orogenic belts of Pre-Cambrian times. Further, there has been fairly general acceptance of the views of H. Stille[1] that in relation to the orogenic belts of today

[1] §1, 1.

portions of the older, yet Post-Cambrian, orogenic belts have behaved as though they had become parts of the rigid platform. For these platforms incorporating remnants of past orogenic belts Stille invented the term 'kraton', of obscure etymology but considerable convenience, and spoke of the platforms being enlarged by kratonization.

The bearing of these ideas upon our thinking about the ancient world is immediately apparent when we state the broadest generalization that can be made about the structural relations of the region that is the subject of this volume. This area owes its most fundamental traits to the fact that it is built of three distinctive crustal units. The most northerly is part of the world's largest rigid platform—the Eurasian kraton. The most southerly comprises Africa, Arabia and the Deccan of India, three portions of a disrupted Afrasian kraton. Between these is part of the mid-world orogenic belt that can be traced from Gibraltar to Singapore. This was created during Tertiary times (and most importantly in a powerful orogenic spasm in later Oligocene and early Miocene times, 25–35 million years ago) from the sediments accumulated in the Mesozoic era in the great mid-world sea between the Eurasian and Afrasian land masses that E. Suess called 'the Tethys'.[1] The problems involved in elucidating the history of the Tethys, its conversion into the mid-world orogenic belt and the relations of both to the bordering platforms are among the most challenging in all geology and have engaged some of the finest minds in the science for most of a century. No finality of view on these matters is yet in sight, but the imaginative vistas that have been opened up are so large that some consideration of them here seems a proper prelude to the man-focused story that follows. We shall therefore review in turn some salient episodes in the history of the two rigid masses and the intervening Tethys, and some of the views on the drastic changes of Tertiary time that have provided the framework of the present relief.

II. THE AFRASIAN PLATFORM

The basement complex in Africa emerges at the surface almost continuously from the west coast, through the Guinea lands and on all sides of the Congo basin, to the lake regions and the east coast in Mozambique. In the north-eastern sector of the continent the outcrops of the Nile–Congo divide continue northwards into

[1] §1, 2.

the western Sudan; they appear in Kordofan and again in all the Nubian desert and the mountainous border of the Red Sea. East of that sea are outcrops no less extensive from Sinai to the Gulf of Aden. Not all this country is geologically well known and much fundamental research remains to be done. Yet a late Pre-Cambrian orogenic belt (650–600 million years old) has been recognized running south-eastwards from the northern end of the Red Sea into central Arabia, and granites associated with this folding episode build the rugged desert mountains south of Mecca and in Sinai.

There is reason to believe that much of Africa has been a land mass for a thousand million years. Where the ancient basement is covered by sediments, these are 'continental deposits'—thick accumulations of detritus derived from the more upstanding parts of the land mass and laid down in such basins as that of the Congo. Only in the north did the Palaeozoic seas overlap onto the surface of the platform, and that only temporarily. Marine Silurian and Devonian strata are known in the Algerian Sahara (where they build plateaux with south-facing escarpments north of the crystalline Ahaggar massif), and in Libya, Egypt and Arabia. But continental conditions returned. The Siluro-Devonian rocks are surmounted in the striking tabular reliefs of Ennedi and the Gilf el-Kebīr by continental sandstones—the so-called lower Nubian sandstones of probably Carboniferous age—and marine deposition was not generally resumed in northern Africa for a very long interval, in fact not until Upper Cretaceous times.

Here we must take note of the remarkable evidence concerning climatic environments that is available for the Carboniferous, Permian and Triassic periods. In Great Britain, as in much of continental Europe and the eastern United States, warm clear seas in which corals flourished in Lower Carboniferous times were succeeded by swampy land areas with tropical vegetation (the source of the European and Appalachian Coal Measures) in Upper Carboniferous times. These areas then became true hot deserts, as is witnessed by the breccias, fan gravels, dune sandstones, and lake deposits with evaporites of the Permian and Triassic systems. Western Europe and eastern America evidently experienced, first, a humid tropical and, then, an arid tropical climate. Quite other is the evidence from the great series of continental deposits that were being laid down in central and southern Africa at the same time—the Karroo Series. In the Republic of South Africa thousands of square miles are underlain by tillite (ancient deposits of glacial origin), leaving 'no doubt whatever that large tracts were formerly covered by a gelid carapace'.[1] This tillite is often very thick, and is known to rest in many places on an ice-smoothed and scratched surface of older rocks. It is of late Carboniferous age and is succeeded first by dark unfossiliferous shales laid down in cold-water lakes, and then by shales and coals made of the remains of plants regarded as constituting a cold temperate flora (the famous *Glossopteris* flora).

Taken together, the evidence from Europe and Africa makes two things very clear: first, that in Carboniferous and Permian times the earth possessed climatic zones ranging from equatorial to glacial, just as it does today; and, secondly, that if the climatic zones were disposed (as we must assume) then as now in latitudinal belts from equator to poles, the continents of Carboniferous and Permian times must have occupied positions very different in latitude from those they occupy today. This was an important part of the evidence that led the climatologist Alfred Wegener in 1915 to put forward his famous hypothesis of 'Continental Drift'.[2] Some of the points he made were soon discredited and geophysicists in the 1920s and 1930s dismissed the hypothesis as inconsistent with what they knew of the mechanics of the earth's crust. Geological evidence to which the hypothesis gave rational explanations, however, continued to be assembled in formidable array, especially by du Toit.[3] It has long been known that the South African glacial deposits, and the whole overlying Karroo sequence, have an exact parallel in the Gondwana sequence of Peninsular India, and indeed Suess had proposed the name 'Gondwanaland' for the supposed land on which these and the corresponding deposits of South America, Madagascar and Australia were laid down. Nowadays it is not possible, in the face of meteorological and geophysical knowledge, to assume either that a single ice-cap could ever have covered all the areas in which Upper Carboniferous and Lower Permian glacial deposits are now found or that large parts of a former continuous continent could have foundered beneath the oceans without trace. On both counts therefore it is preferable to assume that the several portions of 'Gondwanaland' were once closely adjacent to each other and that they have drifted apart and across the latitudinal climatic zones. For this last assumption there is independent support in the recent findings of palaeomagnetism.[4] On such assumptions the sundered fragments of 'Gondwanaland' have been re-assembled by L. C. King.[5] In this re-assembly Madagascar is placed in the

[1] §ii, 2, 41.   [2] §ii, 5.
[3] §ii, 4.   [4] §ii, 1; §ii, 3.   [5] §ii, 2, fig. 17.

broad re-entrant of the African coast off Tanganyika and Kenya, and the straight east coast of Madagascar is bordered on its eastern side by the similarly straight west coast of the Deccan. East Antarctica in turn bordered the east coast of the Deccan, and on its other side and to the 'east' of both lay Australasia. The east coast of South America abutted against Africa from the Gulf of Guinea to the Cape.

Africa throughout Palaeozoic and much of Mesozoic time was thus part of a 'super-continent' and was washed by the sea only on its northern flank, and it is only on this margin, as we have seen, that any marine deposits are recorded. Continental deposits occupy basins on all the Gondwana continents and imply erosion of the surrounding higher ground. By Jurassic times Africa appears to have been worn down to a plain of little relief, and remnants of this surface are claimed to be recognizable in the higher parts of southern and central Africa today.[1] In mid-Jurassic times the fragmentation of 'Gondwanaland' was beginning and the sea was penetrating from the north between East Africa and India: the dissection of the Jurassic land surface and the accumulation of coastal marine sediments were thus initiated. In Saharan Africa enormous areas were overspread at this time (late Jurassic–early Cretaceous) by great thicknesses of sands that now constitute the plateaux of Nubian sandstone in the east and the *formation continentale intercalaire* in the west, formations that often rest directly on the crystalline basement and are highly important as aquifers. Nearer the Tethys, marine incursions took place. The Jurassic 'basin' of Sinai, for example, received more than 1,500 m. of sediment, mostly limestone, and Jebel Tuwaiq, an escarpment more than 800 km. long in central Arabia, is made of Jurassic limestone and represents an extension of the sea from the north-east. But the first widespread marine transgression onto Afro-Arabia took place in Upper Cretaceous times. Limestones, marls and sandstones were widely deposited and at their southern margins interdigitated with the fresh-water Nubian Sands. At the close of the Cretaceous period little land waste was reaching the sea, and limestones were the characteristic deposits and continued to be so into the ensuing Eocene. Today these limestones build the plateau of Cyrenaica and are revealed in the deep gorges of the Wādi Derna and the escarpments at Cyrene. In Egypt they form the high escarpment and flat barren plateaux west of the Gulf of Suez, and in Palestine they underlie the wilderness of Judaea. They have great extension in the Syrian desert and in Mesopotamia. On the

[1] §II, 2, fig. 119.

southern side of Arabia similar limestones are seen in the precipitous walls of the Wādi Ḥadhramaut.

An important event at this time was the outpouring in Ethiopia and southern Arabia of great quantities of basaltic lava. Rising through fissures in the continental crust and spreading out over thousands of square miles, flow succeeded flow to build up thicknesses of lava that in some places are known to exceed 3,000 m. (e.g. Dhala, Aden Protectorate). It is difficult not to associate this evidence of crustal tension with the completed separation of the Afro-Arabian and Indian portions of 'Gondwanaland', for on the other side of the widening Indian Ocean rift similar occurrences were responsible for the outpouring of the well-known 'Deccan Traps' over an area as large as France and to a maximum thickness of 2,000 m.

III. THE EURASIAN PLATFORM

The best known of all the world's areas of the basement complex is that which emerges in southern Norway, most of Sweden, all Finland, Karelian Russia and the Kola Peninsula. This Baltic Shield is some 1,200 km. long by 500–800 km. wide, and within it Finnish and Russian geologists have recognized traces of as many as five ancient orogenic episodes. The oldest of these may have occurred as much as 3,600 million years ago; the youngest, which the Russians term the Baykalid orogeny and date as being 700–500 million years old, has left traces along the northern margin of the Shield in northernmost Norway and the Timan Hills of North Russia.

The Baltic Shield, however, represents only a small part of the platform area, even in Europe. Unlike the Afro-Arabian mass, which has been dry land for much of geological time, the European platform has been repeatedly and extensively transgressed by shallow epicontinental seas. As a result, although the basement complex is known to exist beneath most of European Russia, it is deeply buried beneath thick layers of sediment. Boreholes and geophysical investigations have shown that this sedimentary cover thickens generally toward the Caspian, where it is fully 3 km. thick. Between Moscow and the Urals thickness is less, averaging about a kilometre, and the surface of the basement is thrown into broad undulations. West and south of Moscow these undulations become much more powerful. A great rise brings the basement up to sea level in the region of Kursk and Voronezh before it

plunges steeply to depths of 2 km. in a long trough that stretches
for 1,200 km. from the Pripet marshes to the lower Don and
includes the great Donbas coal region (see Fig. 1 and Map 1).
South-west of this buried trough the basement rises in the central
Ukraine and over wide areas is either exposed at the surface or
covered only by thin Cainozoic sediments that are cut through by
all the larger valleys of the region. This Ukrainian swell is about
800 km. long and reaches almost to the Sea of Azov. For much
of its course the Dnieper is cut into it and runs parallel to its axis,
as the Donets does that of the Donbas trough, but it must be
emphasized that neither of these great structural features makes
the slightest difference to the level skylines of the dissected plains
of southern Russia.

Intimately associated with the European platform are three
orogenic belts that developed in Palaeozoic time and have become
firmly soldered onto it. To the north-west, along what is now the
Atlantic border of Europe, a geosyncline running through Norway, Scotland and Ireland was converted into a mountain belt
about 420 million years ago. These mountains were called the
Caledonides by Eduard Suess. They were worn down and, in
Ireland at least, partly submerged by Carboniferous seas. To the
east of the Russian platforms the Upper Palaeozoic sediments
thicken greatly into another geosyncline, and from this the orogenic belt of the Urals was produced. This belt is a good deal
broader than the Ural Mountains of today and also extends a
good deal farther south beneath the dry plains of the River Emba.
There the folded structures disappear beneath the modern sediments of the Aral Sea depression but it is possible that they reappear in the Kara Tau and Nura Tau ranges that spring from
the great Tien Shan system. The third orogenic belt borders the
European platform to the south and south-west. It too was created
from a thick succession of Upper Palaeozoic sediments about
270 million years ago and is approximately contemporary with
the Urals. Its mountains have long since been worn away but
their stumps remain in a zone that can be traced from the Atlantic
coast in southern Ireland, Cornwall and Brittany through France
and the Rhinelands to central Germany and southern Poland.
The mountains of this belt are most generally termed the Hercy-
nides.[1] They are believed to have continued along the southern

---

[1] Suess recognized two mountain arcs in this belt, calling the western one *the
Armorican Arc* (§1, 2, vol. II, 105) after the Gaulish province of that name, and the
eastern one *the Variscan Arc* (*ibid.* p. 111) after the Germanic tribe of Varisci. But
he assimilated both to his *Altaides*, a name not now in use in either Russia or Europe.

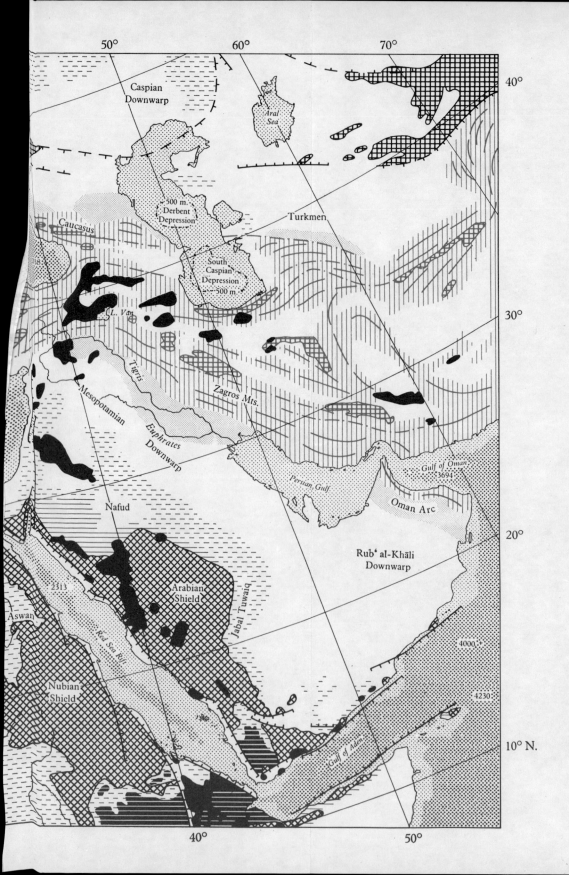

Caspian
Downwarp

Aral
Sea

─ 500 m.
Derbent
Depression

Turkmen

South
Caspian
Depression
─ 500 m.

Caucasus

385

L. Van

Tigris

Mesopotamian

Euphrates

Zagros Mts.

Downwarp

Nafud

Gulf of Oman
3694

Persian Gulf

Oman Arc

Rubʻ al-Khāli
Downwarp

2313

Arabian
Shield

Jabal Tuwaiq

Aswan

Red Sea Rift

4000

Nubian
Shield

4230

Gulf of Aden

50°   60°   70°   40°   30°   20°   10° N.

40°   50°

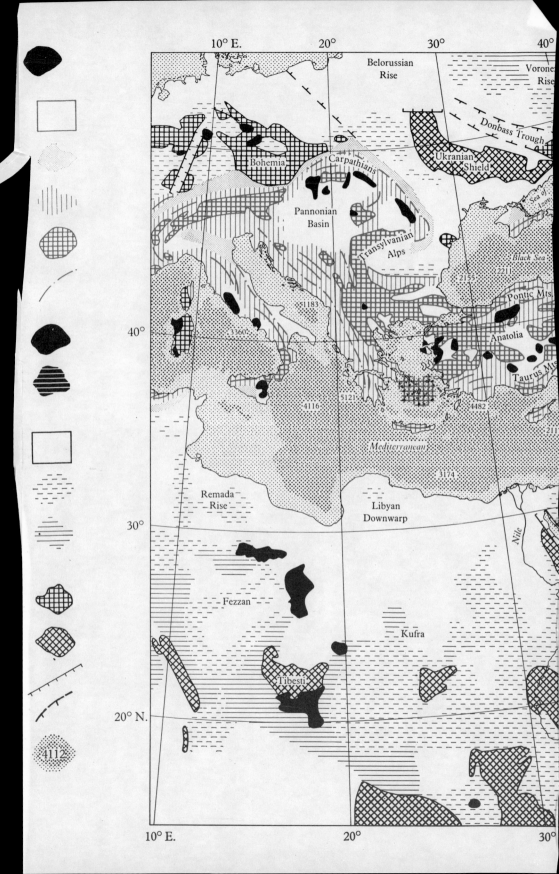

LEGEND

I. ALPINE FOLD BELT

1. Tertiary to present-day volcanic rocks.
2. Post-tectonic (Tertiary to present-day) sediments of intermontane depressions.
3. Marginal troughs to the Alpine fold belt. Accumulation of great thicknesses of sediment, Tertiary to present-day.
4. Regions of Alpine folding showing generalized fold alignment (usually corresponding with alignment of mountain ranges).
5. Median masses, etc. Mostly crystalline rocks of Hercynian, or earlier, deformation
6. Discontinuities between tectonic zones.

II. CONTINENTAL PLATFORMS

A. Volcanic rock
7. Tertiary to present-day volcanic rocks, mostly basaltic.
8. Mesozoic volcanic rocks, mostly basaltic.

B. Sedimentary cover rock of variable thickness, mostly with near-horizontal stratification
9. Tertiary to present-day sediments. There is a wide variation in lithology, including recent unconsolidated sand, silt and clay, firmly cemented sandstone, and massive sharp-forming limestone.
10. Mesozoic, mostly limestone and sandstone.
11. Palaeozoic rocks of variable lithology but generally indurated, and locally moderately folded.

C. Basement rock forming the continental surface beneath the blanketing sediment.
12. Hercynian massifs, mostly of crystalline metamorphic and igneous rock.
13. Pre-Cambrian shields; metamorphic rocks belonging to ancient orogenic episodes.
14. Major fractures (faults) and flexures.

III. SEAS AND LAKES

15. Maximum depths are shown in metres. The darker areas are deeper than 1,000 m.

```
100   0   100  200  300  400  500 miles

  0   200   400   600   800 km
```

Map 1. Main structural features of the mid-world fold belt from the Alps to Afghanistan and of adjoining parts of the Eurasian and Asian platforms.

LEGEND

I. ALPINE FOLD BELT

1. Tertiary to present-day volcanic rocks.

2. Post-tectonic (Tertiary to present-day) sediments of intermontane depressions.

3. Marginal troughs to the Alpine fold belts. Accumulation of great thicknesses of sediment, Tertiary to present-day.

4. Regions of Alpine folding showing generalized fold alignment (usually corresponding with alignment of mountain ranges).

5. Median masses, etc. Mostly crystalline rocks of Hercynian, or earlier, deformation.

6. Discontinuities between tectonic zones.

II. CONTINENTAL PLATFORMS

A. *Volcanic rocks*

7. Tertiary to present-day volcanic rocks, mostly basaltic.

8. Mesozoic volcanic rocks, mostly basaltic.

B. *Sedimentary cover rocks of variable thickness, mostly with near-horizontal stratification*

9. Tertiary to present-day sediments. There is a wide variation in lithology, including recent unconsolidated sand, silt and clay, firmly cemented sandstone, and massive scarp-forming limestone.

10. Mesozoic, mostly limestone and sandstone.

11. Palaeozoic rocks of variable lithology but generally indurated and locally moderately folded.

C. *Basement rocks forming the continental surface beneath the blanketing sediments*

12. Hercynian massifs, mostly of crystalline metamorphic and igneous rock.

13. Pre-Cambrian shields, metamorphic rocks belonging to ancient orogenic episodes.

14. Major fractures (faults) and flexures.

III. SEAS AND LAKES

15. Maximum depths are shown in metres. The darker areas are deeper than 1,000 m.

```
100   0   100  200  300  400  500  miles
 |----+----+----+----+----+----|
      0    200   400   600   800  km.
```

Map 1. Main structural features of the mid-world fold belt from the Alps to Afghanistan and of adjoining parts of the Eurasian and Afrasian platforms.

margin of the Russian platform where remnants are found in the Dobrudja of Romania and the Mangyshlak peninsula east of the Caspian Sea. By the end of Triassic times they had been eroded to the condition of a hot desert lowland with shallow saline lakes, and in the ensuing Jurassic period much of this plain was overspread from the south by the waters of the Tethys. Parts of the mountain belt, like the Paris Basin, subsided sufficiently to receive considerable thicknesses of sediment. In late Jurassic and early Cretaceous times the sea withdrew and in parts of Europe wide expanses of fresh water provided a habitat for the giant reptiles of the period.

This interesting episode came to an end in late Cretaceous times when the sea once more transgressed from the Tethys far and wide over Europe. The continent was almost completely inundated from the Hebrides to the Urals, and over most of the submerged area very substantial thicknesses of pure soft limestone accumulated—the familiar chalk of both sides of the English Channel. The absence of terrigenous matter from almost all these deposits and the presence, in the Scottish chalk at least, of wind-rounded and polished sand grains give much colour to the suggestion that the land area of northern Europe was at this time a riverless desert lowland.[1] In Hercynian Europe almost all the upstanding areas had by now passed under the sea. The Bohemian upland was covered by shallow-water sandstones, and shallow-water deposits covered part at least of the Armorican and central plateau areas of France and the Meseta of Spain. It is likely that there was encroachment on the upland area of the Rhodope and the Greek archipelago, and that in Podolia the western end of the outcrop of basement complex in the Ukrainian swell passed under the sea for the first time. Beyond the Urals the Upper Cretaceous seas spread over the Turanian depression into western Siberia, and across the site of later mountains into what is now the Tarim Basin. As we have already seen, it was at this same time that the Tethys overflowed its southern shores widely into Saharan Africa and Arabia. It is literal truth to say that at this time the waters of the Tethys reached their high-water mark, and, since much of the Americas and Australia was then under the sea also, it may

French geologists, following Marcel Bertrand, have consistently used the term *Hercynian* (from *Hercynia Silva*) to denote all the late Carboniferous mountains of Europe, and M. V. Muratov, in the *Fiziko-Geograficheskiy Atlas Mira*, has extended this usage to the whole world. It is therefore followed here, but it should be noted that in the *Notice explicative pour la carte tectonique internationale de l'Europe au 1/5,200,000*, also published in Moscow in 1964, the preferred term is Variscan.

[1] §III, 1.

well be that at no other moment in Post-Cambrian time have the continents been so reduced in area by inundation.

Whether the great Upper Cretaceous transgression from the Tethys onto both its borderlands was occasioned by a subsidence of those lands along their Tethyan margins with compensating elevations elsewhere, or whether some event took place within the Tethys itself that reduced its volume and spilled its waters upon the lands, we do not yet know. L. C. King speaks of the Gondwanaland surface being 'flexed downwards during the Cretaceous period' in North Africa and Arabia,[1] while in north-west Europe there must have been some uplift and tilting at the end of the Cretaceous since the highest stages of that system are locally missing. Moreover, in a fashion that offers a striking parallel to the plateau basalts of Ethiopia, Yemen and the Deccan, great outpourings of basalt now occurred on the margins of the widening North Atlantic. In Greenland they are stratigraphically dated as latest Cretaceous and early Eocene,[2] and in Iceland, the Faeroes, Scotland and Ireland there is evidence that points in the same direction. These massive and approximately synchronous transfers of basaltic magma from the lower layers of the crust to the surface both north and south of the Tethys are clear evidence of major readjustments in the earth's crust. There is also evidence of adjustment within the Tethys itself and to this aspect we must now turn.

IV. THE TETHYS AND THE MID-WORLD FOLD BELT

It would be natural to suppose that the waters of the Tethys which spread over parts of the Eurasian and Afrasian platforms may also have covered an intervening tract in which the crustal structure was of oceanic type. Such is believed by some to be the nature of the deep parts of the Mediterranean today,[3] and Glangeaud at least supposes the Tethys to have possessed such intercontinental areas.[4] Moreover, for half a century at least, geologists generally have recognized among the sediments of the Tethys deposits that were laid down in very deep water—in the so-called axial zone of the geosyncline. These are uniform, unbedded, dark plastic clays; they are associated with cherts and jaspers that were laid down as siliceous organic oozes and with basic and ultrabasic igneous rocks. Such assemblages are known in the *Argille Scagli-*

[1] §II, 2, 261.   [2] §III, 2, 29.   [3] See Map I, facing p. 10.   [4] §IV, 1; §IV, 5.

ose of the northern Apennines, in the *schistes lustrés* of the Pennine Alps, in the Pindus Mountains, in the Zagros Mountains of Iran and elsewhere. Nowhere are such beds seen in their original form or with their original relationships, and room for doubt about their interpretation is bound to exist. Especially is this true of the Pennine Alps, where associated granite gneisses have been interpreted both as portions of an underlying (Hercynian) continental basement and as intrusions belonging to the Alpine orogenesis itself.

However this may be, it is clear that the great bulk of the Tethyan sediments were laid down on continental foundations which became so deeply buried that in effect they were depressed to depths comparable with those of the oceans. This is the situation that has been revealed by oil-drilling and geophysical exploration beneath the continental shelf east of the United States of America. But in that case the sediments are largely clays and sands supplied by the numerous rivers of a well-watered temperate land of considerable relief. The lands bordering the Tethys, by contrast, were neither bold nor well watered. L. C. King's reconstruction[1] of the Mesozoic positions of North Africa, Arabia and India shows the two former to have lain in much their present latitudes. Very little sediment seems to have reached the Tethys from either area and it seems reasonable to suppose that both were essentially hot arid lowlands. Organic limestones make up most of the succession, especially in the later Cretaceous and Eocene periods. Limestones were important also on the Eurasian side, and particularly thick sequences characterize the Trias and Rhaetic of the Alps (the Dolomites, Julian Alps, Bavarian Alps and Salzkammergut), and the Jurassic and Cretaceous of Dalmatia (the Velebit Mountains and high karstic plateaux), and parts of the Apennines. Many of the limestones contain abundant corals and coral reefs, and it is evident that the waters of the Tethys were for long periods both clear and warm.

During Cretaceous and still more in Eocene times, however, sedimentation of a new kind began in many areas. Thick monotonous sequences were laid down in which grey unfossiliferous muds, abundantly charged with tiny fragments of pre-existing sedimentary rocks, alternate with micaceous sands. Such rocks were first described in Switzerland in 1827 by B. Studer, who called them by a local word *flysch*, said to mean 'slippery earth'. Later they were recognized as important in the Carpathians and Apennines and elsewhere and it was accepted that the onset of

[1] §ii, 2, fig. 20.

sedimentation of *flysch* type occurred at different times in different regions. In the Carpathians it begins in the Lower Cretaceous, elsewhere usually in the Upper Cretaceous, but in some areas not till Eocene times. *Flysch* deposition is now associated with the uprise of individual fold belts within the geosyncline. Material eroded from the rising ranges is rapidly deposited at a great variety of depths without ever having been sorted by stream or wave action. Much of it has been deposited from great sub-marine mud-flows or 'turbidity currents' on the steepening geo-synclinal slopes. These deposits are thus the precursors of folding. In the Carpathians Lower Cretaceous *flysch* heralds the important pre-Upper Cretaceous movements: in the Apennines Eocene *flysch* heralds the main phase of movement which occurred in this range at the end of Eocene times: in the Swiss Alps the *flysch* is Upper Eocene and Lower Oligocene and was followed by the drastic Middle Oligocene deformations.

Once the folds had been erected into mountain ranges erosion by rain and rivers immediately set about destroying them. This fact, too, is recorded in the sedimentary record by deposits of distinctive character—the so-called *molasse*—essentially bed-loads of streams, laid down as sands or pebble beds on land or in shallow water. Such deposits were first named and described from the northern border of the Swiss Alps, where they are particularly characteristic of the later Oligocene and Miocene periods, but nowadays the term is applied to post-orogenic deposits of the marginal troughs of fold ranges everywhere. There are several instances in which *molasse* deposits have accumulated in thick-nesses up to 2 km., and not a few in which the earlier have been tectonically disturbed and eroded (e.g. in Andalusia and India) before being overlain unconformably by the later.

It goes without saying that much effort has been devoted by geologists to elucidating the nature and history of the structures of the mid-world orogenic belt in Europe and the more accessible parts of South-west Asia. These structures vary widely and we can here describe them only by sample. Particularly instructive are the structures that have been worked out by oil geologists in the region of Mesopotamia and Iran.[1] Any traverse from south-west to north-east across this region reveals successive zones of contrasted structural characteristics. To the south-west the base-ment of Arabia, widely exposed toward the Red Sea, passes under a thin sedimentary cover that dips exceedingly gently toward the Euphrates and the Persian Gulf. The cover includes rocks—

[1] §IV, 3.

largely limestone—from Jurassic upwards to the Miocene
Euphrates limestone and itself passes beneath great thicknesses
of Pliocene and later material forming the Mesopotamian Plain.
Towards the eastern margin of the plain folds occur, singly at
first, and in some cases entirely overlain by the river alluvium.
Farther east they occur in bundles and build the ranges of
Bakhtiari and the Pusht-i-Kuh. They include important oil-pro-
ducing structures. These folds affect all rocks up to the Pliocene
and are thought to be surface expressions of fractures in the basement 2 or 3 km. beneath. They are succeeded eastwards, in the
Zagros Mountains, by a zone in which the folds are characteristically broken or replaced by faults. This in turn gives way to a
zone that has been recognized over a distance of 1,200 km. from
Kirmānshāh to the Gulf of Oman, in which a series of 'nappes'
or horizontally displaced rock sheets have been successively driven
from north-east to south-west. Proceeding north-eastward the
following nappes are encountered in turn, each being visibly
overlain by the one behind it: (i) with fossiliferous and unmeta-
morphosed Palaeozoic rocks overlain by Cretaceous and Tertiary
beds; (ii) with shales associated with radiolarites and basic and
ultrabasic igneous rocks; (iii) with massive and strongly folded
Cretaceous limestones; and (iv) with regionally metamorphosed
Palaeozoic and older rocks together with some infolded limestones that may be Cretaceous. It is clear that these different rock
successions cannot all originally have been laid down in a belt of
country now less than 150 km. wide and that some form of
'crustal shortening' is involved.

Beyond the zone of nappes we enter the interior of Iran with its
great enclosed depressions and desert plains. Geologically this
country is still inadequately explored but we may be certain that
it is tectonically quite different from the region just noticed.
Palaeozoic rocks are known in places resting on more ancient
rocks, but neither they nor the Cretaceous rocks that overlie them
unconformably are greatly disturbed. This appears to be a region
of relative stability. Its tectonic unity is emphasized by the fact
that in Eocene times there were volcanic outbursts and ash
accumulations on all its margins from Tabrīz in the north-west to
the Afghan frontier. Within this volcanic girdle the great basins,
the Dasht-i-Kavīr, the Dasht-i-Lūṭ, and others, became relatively
depressed and received great thicknesses of Miocene and later sediments—in places up to 3,000 m. As the basins subsided to receive
these heavy loads, there was some folding in the marginal zones,
inward toward the centre, and some renewed volcanic activity.

North of the great interior basins are the lofty ranges of Azar-bāyjān, the Elburz, Ala Dağ and Kopet Dağ of Khurāsān, and the Paropamisus of Afghanistān. These are reported to have complex folded and thrust structures with displacement towards the north and north-east. Beyond them again lie the deep basin of the southern Caspian and the Kura and Atrak lowlands that extend it to west and east. And beyond the Kopet Dağ are the vast Turkmen plains.

It will be seen that there is an evident symmetry in this arrange-ment. This was used by Kober,[1] forty years ago, to provide a plausible model of what is involved in the production of an oro-genic zone. In his view the active agents are the stable blocks that he called forelands—in this case the Turkmen plains under-lain by an inferred Hercynian block on the one hand and Arabia on the other. These forelands, he supposed, move toward each other, crushing the intervening geosynclinal region with its sedi-ments, so that the latter are forced upwards and outwards over the forelands, while a central region between may remain relatively undisturbed. In this way two series of marginal ranges (*Rand-ketten*) would arise with their structures and displacements directed towards the forelands, leaving between them a median mass (*Zwischengebirge*) in which such structures are lacking. The model appears to serve elsewhere. The Himalaya and Kunlun with out-wardly directed displacements toward the Gangetic Trough and Tarim Basin, with the lofty Tibetan plateau as median mass, are a case in point. The plateaux of Anatolia bordered by the Pontic and Taurus overlooking the deeps of Black Sea and Mediterra-nean are a second. A third is furnished by the middle Danube region, where the Dinaric Alps are thrust south-westward toward the Adriatic, the Carpathians are literally thrust over the adjoining Podolian foreland and the great Pannonian plain appears to be a sunken block between them with extensive volcanic outpourings on its Carpathian margin (Fig. 1). In the Balkans the pattern varies. A cross-section through Macedonia[2] would pass through the median mass that is partly expressed by the Rhodope moun-tain block, with the Balkan ranges to the north showing displace-ments toward the Wallachian plain. To the west matters are more complex, and successive zones of basic volcanic rocks, bathyal sediments, and neritic limestones, recalling the zone of nappes in Iran, appear to be displaced towards and over a zone of folded autochthonous sediments in Epirus; an unfolded foreland is pre-sumed to exist beneath the flat-bedded limestones of Apulia. In

---

[1] §IV, 6.   [2] §IV, 2, fig. 20, and §IV, 5, fig. 8.

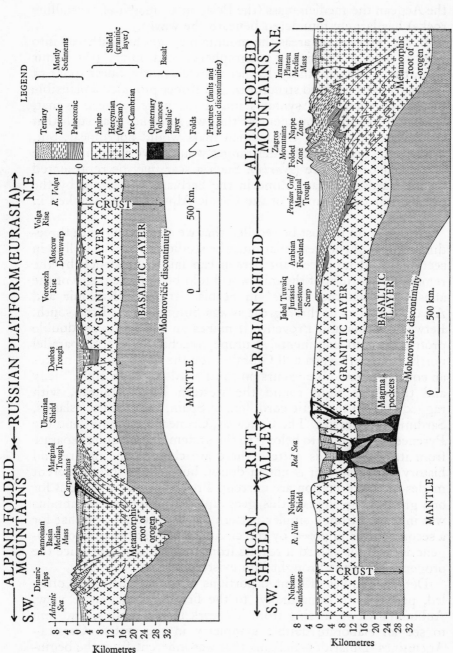

Fig. 1. Generalized sections from the Adriatic to the Volga and from the Sudan to Iran to illustrate the contrasted crustal structure beneath the mid-world fold belt and beneath the Eurasian and Afrasian platforms to north and south of it.

the Aegean the median mass (the Pelagonian massif of crystalline rocks) has largely foundered beneath the waves.

In the intervening areas the mountain ranges are gathered into what an older generation of geographers called 'knots' (the Pamir knot, the Armenian knot). Rather more elegantly, Suess spoke of 'syntaxis' of the folded structures, and Kober provided a plausible picture of what such syntaxis might mean by suggesting that, where the relative movement of the two forelands was such that they came in contact, the median mass would not appear, but, instead, the two sets of border ranges would have a common zone of contact or cicatrice (*Narbe*). Such a scar may be represented by the Vardar–Morava Zone in the Serbian syntaxis, or by the great linear disturbances of the Carnic Alps and Karawanken in Austria.

At this point it must be recalled that we are dealing with three-dimensional phenomena that must be studied in plan as well as in section. And no observant person can fail to be struck by the remarkable pattern of the mid-world fold belt on the pages of the atlas. Between the 'knots' in Serbia, Armenia, Kashmir and Assam it ranges in three great swags bulging toward the south. Between Serbia and Provence it makes an extraordinary double protrusion into continental Europe, reaching the 50th parallel north. Between Genoa and Gibraltar, on the other hand, it makes an equally remarkable excursion southwards through Italy, Sicily and the Atlas right round the western Mediterranean, with ragged ends in the Betic cordillera of Spain, the Balearic Islands, Sardinia and Corsica. The Caucasus, Crimean mountains and the Pyrenees are known to belong to the system, but lie quite separate from it. That in this pattern there are clues to the nature and history of the system is not in doubt, but at least three different modes of interpretation are current. Broadly, we may say that for one group of geologists this geographical pattern of mountains was inherited from a similar pattern of geosynclinal troughs; for a second it was imposed by the circumstances at the time of orogenesis; and for a third it results from changes wrought since the orogenic zone was brought into existence.

Detailed studies of limited portions of the fold belt have often led, perhaps not unnaturally, to the first or conservative view. Aubouin's views, arising from his work in the Pindus, lead him to see an elaborate double symmetry in the system Corsica–Apennines–Dinarides–Balkans that was inherent from the beginning of Tethyan sedimentation,[1] and de Sitter's picture of the

---

[1] §IV, 2, fig. 20.

development of the Alps envisages separate Pennine, Austrian and Apennine geosynclines with approximately their present geographical relationships as early as Jurassic times.[1] Such views may serve well to explain limited sets of facts. But it is hard to see how they will lead to explanations of the features of the fold belt as a whole.

Quite other was the highly imaginative synthesis put forward in 1922 by Emile Argand.[2] Before the ideas of Alfred Wegener had become known to English and American geologists, Argand had seized the idea of continental displacement and utilized it to explain the tectonics of Asia, and incidentally of Europe, in a single grand scheme. For him the whole mid-world fold belt was created as the result of the northward movement of the Afrasian block against the Eurasian land-mass crushing the Tethyan sediments between in the manner envisaged by Kober. What may truly be called a salient feature of Argand's views is that the form assumed by the fold belt in plan is a direct result of the actual geographical shape of the Afrasian land-mass where the interaction took place. He postulates that it had three great northward projections—his African, Arabian and Indian promontories. The first is inferred to have been in the region of the present Adriatic (the Apennines being at this stage much further west); the exposed (?Hercynian) massif of Calabria and la Sila, and the inferred (?Hercynian) foundations of Apulia, eastern Sicily and possibly Venetia are claimed as its remnants. It is supposed to have driven across the Tethys and deeply into Europe, tearing the Dinarides from their continuations in the Atlas and crushing them against and upon the Alps. The Arabian promontory impinged against the fold belt at a point that may reasonably be related to the Armenian knot. Most striking of all is Argand's view of the function of the Indian promontory. This, he suggested, not merely impinged against the fold belt but actually underran it. Detached from Africa and Arabia, the Indian block became tilted up at the southern extremity, whilst its northern passed beneath the Tethyan sedimentary accumulation. In this way a working hypothesis is offered both of the remarkable compression and inflexion of the fold belt at the Afghan and Burmese borders, and of the unparalleled elevation of the Tibetan plateau. Nor is this all. Argand perceived that these impacts had repercussions beyond the fold belt in the body of the Eurasian mass itself. North of Tibet the Asiatic kraton is broken into great arcuate slices that have been driven against each other and elevated to form the

[1] §IV, 7, 386–7, figs. 261 *a*, *b*.   [2] §IV, 1.

ranges of central Asia. These Argand calls 'folds of the base-
ment'. The Kopet Dağ, the Caucasus and the mountains of the
Crimea can be included here, and possibly also the Pyrenees.
Between the Black Sea and the Bay of Biscay the kratonized
Hercynian region reacted differently. Parts of it were already
deeply depressed beneath heavy loads of sediment and these
reacted by developing 'folds of the covering'. Such are the Jura
Mountains, the folded ridges of Provence, and those of the Paris
Basin and the English Weald. Other parts were more upstanding
and were displaced *en bloc*. Yet they appear to have influenced
the patterns of the developing fold belt, as may be judged by
noting the relation of the Jura arcs to the buttresses of the Central
Plateau and the Black Forest, or the constraining influence of the
Bohemian block on the Viennese Alps and the Little Carpathians.
In view of the even greater inflexions near Genoa and the Danube
gorges it is natural that suggestions should have been made that
these reflect the influences, respectively, of a massif beneath the
Wallachian plains that is exposed only in the Dobrudja, and of a
massif that once existed where the Ligurian Sea now is, whose
remnants survive in the Massif des Maures of the Côte d'Azur
and in Corsica.

Argand's views early came in for criticism, partly because the
geophysical evidence appeared then to negative the possibility of
major horizontal movements of the continents, and partly because
his conception of orogenesis as motivated by the relative approach
of two continental land masses in later Mesozoic and early Cainozoic time appeared ill fitted to explain the very varied timing of
orogenic manifestations in different parts of the orogenic zone.
Nor are Argand's views well attuned to the ideas of crustal
mechanics now in fashion. Yet they have left a lasting impress on
the subject and revealed the importance of the problems implicit
in the pattern in plan of the mountain belt.

An attack on these problems that is of an entirely different kind
was made by S. W. Carey,[1] who investigated some of the consequences of assuming that the fold belt was originally of simple
plan and has suffered lateral flexing to produce the changes of
direction that we now see. Such flexing, however caused, he
terms an 'orocline', and among the oroclines that he examines
is the one at the head of the Arabian Sea which turns the mountain
belt from its north-west–south-east course in Iran to an almost
south-to-north course in Pakistān. Associated with this Baluchi-
stān orocline Carey notes three facts: (i) the triangular form of

[1] §IV, 4.

the Arabian Sea with its vertex in Balūchistān and with oceanic-type crust intervening between the continental masses of Arabia and the Deccan; (ii) the southward displacements of the thrusts and folds of the Himalayan front; (iii) the high-standing Tibetan plateau with a width that diminishes from some 1,100 km. on the 90th meridian to small values in Kashmir, and beneath which the continental crust must be of double thickness. He further points out that, if the Balūchistān orocline and the associated Punjab orocline be imagined to be straightened out by the rotation of India through some 60° and its translation southwards, (a) India 'comes out' from beneath Tibet and the overthrust Himalayas, (b) the Arabian Sea closes up, and (c) the fault coastlines of Somaliland and Muscat lie opposite those of the Deccan as part of the great East African tension rift system. These, it may be agreed, are highly suggestive relationships.

Carey recognizes six oroclines in the orogenic belt in Europe and to them also he applies the process of imagining the consequences of straightening them out. The consequences are indeed striking and in Carey's own words 'the great Tethys emerges' on his maps and 'makes palaeographic sense for the first time'. But the requirements in rotation or translation of the continental masses are not examined, and the reconstruction is suggestive rather than compelling.

V. ORIGINS OF THE MODERN SEAS, RIVERS AND MOUNTAINS

In all the preceding discussion the use of place-names has been essentially to locate, in terms of a modern geography, areas where events were taking place, or where rocks that provide significant evidence may now be seen. In no instance have we described the events directly responsible for the visible features of the modern landscape. We have discussed the shaping of the continents and of the great Tethyan intercontinental and epicontinental sea in which the mid-world mountain belt had its origin. But of the mountains themselves, of actual rivers and seas, we have said nothing, since all these features belong wholly to the latest periods of geological time—the Miocene, Pliocene and Quaternary, which together have occupied only some 30 million years.[1] To these features we must now give some consideration, and clearly first among them must come the Mediterranean Sea.

[1] See Table 1, p. 2.

Since the dark argillaceous deposits associated with radiolarites and basic igneous rocks that have been generally interpreted as originating in the deepest parts of the Tethys are now found in the heart of the mountain belt in the Pennine Alps, the Pindus, the Taurus or the mountains of Luristān, it would seem that the Tethys was effectively extinguished, and Eurasia and Afro-Arabia soldered firmly together, by the crustal disturbances of Eocene and especially Middle Oligocene time. The Mediterranean and associated seas are thus features younger than the main orogenic spasm. Yet, as Fig. 1 shows, we are dealing with basins whose floors penetrate deeply into the crust—as much as 5 km. in the eastern Ionian Sea. Almost certainly this means that the granitic layer of the continents is thin or even absent. Argand imagined that such a state of affairs implied a phase of crustal stretching following the phase of maximum compressive stress and resulting in a series of 'disjunctive basins'.[1] The passage of more than forty years has not produced a better hypothesis.

The first of Argand's disjunctive basins is the largest and deepest, the eastern Mediterranean. It occupies a position tectonically similar to that of Mesopotamia, since both lie just outside the Pindus–Taurus–Zagros fold belts and on the marginal parts of the Afro-Arabian foreland. But there are differences. The Arabian platform is gently tilted north-eastwards and passes gradually under a sedimentary cover that thickens to as much as 5,000 m. Africa breaks off short and there are 3,700 m. of water just off the Libyan coast. The eastern limit of the basin against the hills of Judaea and the Lebanon is obviously tectonic, and the abrupt western end against Sicily and the Maltese platform hardly less so. Argand[2] pictures this area opening up from tensional rifts in the Upper Oligocene to basin form in the Lower Miocene (Aquitanian). At this time, he suggests, there were tensional openings further west that grew in the succeeding Burdigalian age into the Tyrrhenian and Balearic Basins. These speculations involve considerable lateral displacement of the Apennines after folding, and a good deal else about which there is no general agreement. These matters need not detain us here, though we may note that the problem is particularly difficult. Carey has a neat reconstruction[3] of the pre-orogenic relations of the fold belts of the western Mediterranean but he is unable to place the Apennines convincingly in it, and even de Sitter, making a much more conservative approach, envisages that the curvature and compression of the Alps themselves may be due to an already

[1] §IV, I, fig. 22.   [2] §IV, I, fig. 22.   [3] §IV, 2, fig. 21.

folded Italian peninsula being driven against them 'as if it were a beam'.[1]

In some form, then, the main eastern basin of the Mediterranean and perhaps a proto-Tyrrhenian were opened up in early Miocene time, but the Aegean and Black Seas did not arise until much later. The early Miocene sea, however, spread onto the European landmass and for a time surrounded the primitive Alps, which supplied it with conglomeratic deposits of *molasse*. In one of these, near Turin, boulders of gneiss, gabbro and serpentine testify to the torrential nature of the transporting streams as well as to the fact that the zone of *schistes lustrés* with its basic igneous rocks had already been exposed by erosion. Away from the Alps conditions were very variable in both space and time. Widespread deposits of grey mud (the *Schlier* of Austria) implying rather quiescent and uniform conditions were followed by renewed *molasse* deposition as the Alps and Carpathians were re-elevated, and in some cases overthrusting of Cretaceous or Eocene rocks over the *molasse* and *Schlier* has been observed. A remarkable feature of Eurasian geography in the Upper Miocene was the flooding of an immense tract from Bohemia and Hungary through Galicia and the Ukraine, across the site of the Sea of Azov and Black Sea, on both sides of the Caucasus, to the Caspian and Aral Seas by the brackish waters of the 'Sarmatian Sea'. This sheet of water extended southwards to the Sea of Marmara, and its deposits now form the cliffs and hillsides on both sides of the Dardanelles. It reached the north-east corner of the Aegean but no farther: from Persia to the Balkans and Carpathians the mountains of the orogenic belt separated it from the Mediterranean, and its fossil fauna bears witness to this. The fauna of the Sarmatian Sea is impoverished, but least so in the Ukrainian–Galician region, and it is surmised that from here it had connection with the North Sea. In southern Poland the normal deposits of the Sarmatian Sea give way to the immense salt deposits which have been mined for centuries and are known to be dislocated and overridden by thrust rock masses forming part of the advancing Carpathian front.

In Persia beds of approximately the same age—the thick Fars group—are white or red marls with limestones and mudstones and both salt and gypsum beds. They are widely developed and are involved in the strong folding east of the Mesopotamian Plain.[2] Overlying these beds and involved with them in the folding is a Pliocene series of sandstones, silts and conglomerates

---

[1] § IV, 7, p. 392.   [2] See above, p. 15.

—the Bakhtiari formation—which in places may exceed 3,000 m. in thickness. Its thick, but local, conglomerates imply that the anticlines were both rising and being eroded. Some of them yield pebbles of red cherts from strata now exposed in the zone of nappes, or of Eocene limestones (or even limestones of the Lower Fars group) exposed more locally. Moreover, the effect of erosion on the folded country was often to separate the outcrops of the more resistant strata into discontinuous sheets and masses that, as elevation continued, began to move under their own weight and were mightily assisted by the plastic nature of the underlying salt-bearing Fars group.[1] The rather fantastic structures that result from this 'gravitational gliding' are not confined to this region or to Pliocene rocks. The complexities of the limestone ridges of Provence are largely due to such gliding induced by the mid Oligocene movements on a sequence already folded in late Eocene time and considerably dissected by early Oligocene erosion.[2] More complex still are the Apennine structures induced by gliding on the *Argille Scagliose*,[3] and, most famous and most grandiose of all, the migration of the Helvetian nappes of Switzerland down the northern flank of the Aar massif into the *molasse* depression.[4]

Middle and later Miocene time also witnessed one of the important formative phases in the scenery of central Europe. Hans Cloos long ago traced a connexion here between up-arching of the crust and rifting and vulcanicity.[5] In three areas—the Central Plateau of France, the Rhinelands, and Bohemia—there is a long Mesozoic history of upward movement complementary to the downward movement of the sediment-filled depressions of Swabia and the Paris Basin. In later Oligocene and Miocene times this upward movement was enhanced but in all three regions was associated with fracturing and down-dropping of strips of the up-arched mass—la Limagne and le Velay, the Rhine rift valley, and the Eger trough of Bohemia—and with this down-dropping went considerable volcanic activity. The great structures of the Cantal and Mont-Dore were erected in France: the Vogelsberg, Meissner, and Rhön in Germany, and the Dupovské Hoři and Středo Hoři in Bohemia. Erosion has greatly reduced some of them and almost destroyed their lesser associates, but they still dominate their respective landscapes. Farther south-east within the encircling arc of the Carpathians the subsidence of the Pannonian area that let in the middle Miocene sea was similarly associated with vulcanicity. In Slovakia there were great outpourings south of the Tatra in the Ore Mountains. In Hungary are the

[1] §v, 2. [2] §v, 4. [3] §v, 6. [4] §iv, 7, 279 ff. [5] §v, 1.

Hegyalia, the Matra, the volcanic massif cut through by the Danube above Budapest, and a number of striking volcanic residuals north and west of Lake Balaton. Volcanic rocks form practically the whole inner margin of the Ruthenian Carpathians, the great mountain masses of Calimani, Gaighiu and Hargitta in Transylvania, and occur extensively in the southern Bihor. Further occurrences south of the Balkan ranges of Bulgaria and in Macedonia form a link with others in western Anatolia.

The end of Miocene times saw the regression of the sea from almost the whole of Europe. The great Sarmatian Sea that had stretched across 3,000 km. from Vienna to the Turkmen plains lost its connection with the North Sea and became progressively less salt as it shrank into a series of lakes—an Aralo-Caspian Basin, a Meotian Basin whose deposits are widely recognized on the Russian but unknown on the Turkish shores of the Black Sea, a Dacian Basin, and a Pannonian Basin. There was partial communication between the eastern basins, but the Pannonian Basin now received the drainage of southern Germany by way of the Danube and itself overflowed the mountain belt of western Rumania to establish the course that later became incised to give the gorges of the Iron Gates. Other freshwater lakes are known by their deposits—the Levantine Beds—to have existed in the Balkans, on the site of the present Aegean and inner Anatolia. Evidently there was still no connexion between the Mediterranean and Black Seas, but it seems likely that about the beginning of Pliocene times the deep southern basin of the Black Sea must have been created. Today it has depths exceeding 2,000 m., but whether it may be considered, as it was by Argand, a disjunctive basin owing its depth to thinning of the continental granitic layer, or whether it has subsided like the Pannonian area, or whether it is a severely downwarped area of the crust between upfolded ranges, we can still only speculate. Certainly its southern shore is bordered by the sympathetically curving Pontic ranges, and we can reconstruct a Balkan–Crimean–Caucasian arc to the north. Perhaps it is significant that these Pontic–Armenian and Crimean–Caucasian lines approach in Georgia but do not join. There is through passage between the apex of the little triangular lowland of the Rion draining to the Black Sea and the Kura valley leading down to the extensive alluvial plain and the southern basin of the Caspian, almost 1,000 m. deep. In fact the waters of the western and eastern basins were more than once united by this route during and after the epoch of the Sarmatian Sea.

Possibly we may associate downwarping of these two basins

with the upwarping that was, at last, to carry the mountains of Eurasia to their present heights. Two phases of activity have been recognized. The first, or Rhodanic, evicted the sea from the Rhone Valley, only to create the depression that allowed it to return as far as Lyon in early Pliocene times. Its effects are known elsewhere from the Pyrenees to Greece. The second or Wallachian phase belongs to late Pliocene or even early Quaternary time. Elevatory movements of this phase were widespread, but in the Romanian Carpathians they were responsible for the latest over-thrusts. Comparable features are known from the Siwalik ranges in front of the Himalaya.

It is appropriate here to note the views of L. C. King regarding the condition of the mid-world mountains at the end of Tertiary times.[1] Of the Himalaya he affirms that they 'had been demolished under erosion and their debris redistributed along the old mountain front. The stage was then set for the stupendous appearance of the modern Himalaya.' Again he states, in regard to the Alps, that 'each of the Cainozoic orogenic phases was followed by an interval wherein denudation reduced most of the country to low relief; and it was these Pliocene lowlands, mightily uplifted at the close of the Cainozoic era, that formed the initial arched surface from which most of the Alpine peaks and valleys were carved'.[2] Similar views are expressed regarding the Balkans, Anatolia and Iran. They may be held both to be a gross oversimplification and to express an essential truth. Tectonically King's thesis is an over-simplification since the distinction that he wishes to draw between an early Tertiary period of orogenic movement (folding and thrusting) and a late Tertiary or Quaternary period of cymato-genic movement (broad-arched uplift) cannot always be upheld. In Iran, as we have seen,[3] quite intense folding movements affected the Pliocene Beds, as is also the case in both the Car-pathians and Himalaya. Moreover, the actual timing of folding differs widely in different parts of the fold belt and may be repeated in any one area. Geomorphologically the overstatement resides on the one hand in the fact that no demonstration is to hand that the ranges of Iran have even been base-levelled, and on the other that in some of the most striking cases of summit planation this feature is early rather than late Cainozoic. Thus in the Transyl-vanian Alps, where the main orogenesis was Middle Cretaceous, the main planation surface recognized by de Martonne[4] (the *Boresco*) is dated as Eocene.

[1] §II, 2, 474.
[2] §II, 2, 529.
[3] See above, pp. 23 and 24.
[4] §v, 5, part 2, figs. 171 and 176.

But more important than these criticisms is the essential truth of King's view. The mountains we see are only rarely the mountains created by the fold movements that gave them their complex internal structures. The immense destructive achievements of Tertiary erosion must not be underestimated. Even where fold movements succeeded each other at intervals too short for base-levelling to be accomplished, it is becoming clear that the course of the later folding and the nature of the mountain structures that we see today were greatly influenced by the fact that the older folds had been largely eroded away and the original continuity of the more competent strata had been destroyed in the interval. Where, as was usually the case, the interval extended from mid Oligocene to later Miocene time, we must appreciate that it was of the order of twenty million years, a period quite long enough to permit the reduction of mountains to low relief. We must therefore accept that in general the mountains of the first generation were reduced to subdued forms. Emmanuel de Martonne remarks in a telling phrase that by the beginning of Pliocene time 'l'édifice alpin était menacé de décadence'.[1] The Banat and Transylvanian Alps that had been base-levelled once already in Eocene times had suffered a second period of erosion to produce the Miocene surface of Rīu Ses. The Balkan Mountains generally carry extensive remnants of base-levelled surfaces uplifted to summit levels, as the descriptions of the Belashitza Planina and other Macedonian mountain blocks by Ogilvie[2] well exemplify. Even the isolated Mount Olympus reveals the contrast of forms, between the old subdued surface of the summit and the steep flanking slopes due to Plio-Pleistocene rejuvenation, that is widespread from the Adriatic to the Levant. Nor is the evidence confined to form. In the limestone Alps of Austria well-known siliceous gravels (*Augensteine*) occur at high levels: they have been derived from the Tauern Mountains by rivers that flowed northward across the line of what is now the great trench of the Enns and the Salzach. Evidently the gravels relate to an old topography quite different from that of today. Again in the Rhodope Mountains river gravels 20 m. thick are reported to have been uplifted to heights of 1,000–2,000 m. Levantine freshwater-lake marls are found in the island of Cos at 330 m., and on the mainland fluviatile conglomerates believed to be of this age are encountered at 900 m. in the mountains of Locris and may reach 1,500 m. in the Peloponnese. There can be no doubt that King is substantially correct in ascribing the present general high

[1] §v, 5, part I, p. 26.   [2] §v, 7.

altitude of so much of the fold belt, in Tibet, Afghanistān, Iran,
Armenia, Anatolia, Greece and Yugoslavia, and in the Alps, to
crust movement no older than Pliocene or even early Pleistocene.
Whether the movement was all of the broadly arched nature that
he calls cymatogenic is another matter. Some of it is almost
certainly associated, in some mechanism of crustal and sub-crustal
adjustment, with the growth of the deep sea basins from the
southern Adriatic to the Gulf of Oman. And in Macedonia,
Anatolia and northern Persia, where massive uplands alternate
with enclosed basins filled by Pleistocene and recent sediments,
or still holding lakes (e.g. Ochrid, Prespa, Eğridir, Beyşehir, Tuz,
Vān, Gökça and Urmia), the pattern is one of disturbed crustal
blocks, some uplifted and some depressed. Moreover, there is
evidence from the drainage system that much of the latest uplift
has been, not in the axial portions of the fold belt, but in its
marginal zones, the *Randketten*.[1]

This point is one of much interest. From the Himalaya to the
Danubian region an astonishing number of streams cut their way
through ranges that rise to elevations greater than those of their
sources, and are believed to do so because they first took their
present courses before the ranges rose across their paths. They
are for this reason termed antecedent rivers. Most famous of all
such instances are the stupendous crossings of the Himalaya by
the Brahmaputra and the Indus below the peaks of Namcha
Barwa and Nanga Parbat, respectively 7,755 and 8,125 m. Better
documented, and fully discussed by L. R. Wager,[2] is the case of
the Arun that flows first in a shallow valley on the upland of Tibet
at 4,000 m., then cuts through the main range beside Mt Everest
in a profound gorge to reach the Hindustān plain. Farther east
the Subansiri of Assam and the Manus of Bhutān imitate the
Arun, and farther west the Karnali and the Sutlej equal or excel it.
Both Wager[2] and A. Holmes[3] have pointed out that the carving
of valleys such as these appreciably lightens the load of rock to be
borne locally by the crust and can lead to an isostatic response that
elevates the remaining peaks to higher levels. No small part of
the great altitude of the Himalaya, therefore, may be ascribed to
crustal readjustments actually provoked by river erosion. Almost
certainly this is true of the great line of peaks that runs westward
from Everest through Cho Oyu, Himalchuli and Annapurna to
Dhaulagiri; they have become severed alike from each other and
from the Tibetan plateau by the rivers that rise in the plateau and
trench their way southward to the low valleys of Nepal. Almost

---

[1] See above p. 16.   [2] §v, 8.   [3] §v, 3, 576 and 599.

certainly, also, the principle can be applied to strongly dissected marginal ranges elsewhere.

In the arid lands west of the Indus the phenomenon is modified and many rivers may be said to *find* their way rather than *cut* their way from interior depressions through the border ranges to the lowlands beyond. Such are the Zhob and the Narechi in the Sulaimān region, the Hingol, Dasht and Chil rivers of the Makrān coast, the Shūr, the Mund and the Kārūn of Fārsistān, the Diz and Shirvān in the Zagros. In all these cases there may be reason to think that the rivers found their way round and between the rising folds of Pliocene time rather than across them. But the Great Zab and other headstreams of the Tigris cut their way from the plateau between peaks that rise a mile above them, and the Euphrates carries the drainage of a large part of inner Anatolia out through its gorges in the marginal ranges. From the back-slopes of the Anti-Taurus and Taurus water is carried through these ranges to the sea by the Semanti and the Gök.

On the northern side of the fold belt are other instances. From the same interior valley in northern Afghanistān water passes out both to the Indus plains by the Kābul river and to the plains of the Amū Daryā. The Harī Rūd, after flowing for 300 miles along the southern side of the Paropamisus range, turns northward and cuts its way to the Turkmen lowland. Even the mighty Elburz range is completely transected by the Sefīd Rūd, whose furthest headwaters rise on ranges on the Iraqi border. The Aras (Araxes) carries the drainage of the interior depression north of Lake Urmia, and behind it much of the plateau back to Erzerum, out between peaks exceeding 3,400 and 3,600 m., while along the Black Sea coast the Çoruk, the Yeşil Irmak, and the Kızıl Irmak all make spectacular transections of the main Pontic range. Beyond this the Bağali and the Sakarya continue the sequence, with the latter draining substantial interior basins and avoiding two remarkable lowland routes to the Marmara. It is difficult not to include in this sequence the Bosporus itself as having once carried the waters of the Marmara Basin and most of the classical Mysia through the Istranja Dağ into what is now the Black Sea but must at first have been a Pontic lake.

In Bulgaria the Tundzha cuts southward successively across the Sarnena Gora and the continuation of the Istranja to enter Turkey, while the Isker transects the main Balkan range to connect the basin of Sofia with the Danubian lowland. This famous case is of particular interest since the rising of the mountains is known to have continued long enough to arch upwards the terraces of the river. Further north-west the Balkans are again transected by the Timok and at their eastern end there is a curious crossing by the Kamchiya. The great gorges of the Iron Gates may be accepted as having originated by overflow of the Pannonian Lake, and the straight trough that leads north from Orsova is a true rift valley with Miocene deposits on its floor. But the Transylvanian Alps are crossed by the Jiul in the west, the Oltul in the centre and the Buzàul in the east, while further north the folded Carpathians are crossed by the Bistriţa from the volcanic slopes of Calimani inside the range to the plains of Moldavia outside. In Macedonia and Serbia some river gorges may have arisen as overflows from enclosed basins, but the gorge of the Piva through the culminating range of Durmitor in Montenegro and that of the Neretva through the lofty Čvrsnica in Hercegovina are clearly not of this class. They must represent old stream-courses of the Miocene landscape incised into what have since become the loftiest parts of the region. That movements of elevation continued to affect the periphery of the Mediterranean until Quaternary times is shown by such evidence as the elevation of the Lower Pliocene limestone known as the Piano Zancleano to as much as 1,200 m. in Aspromonte, or the occurrence of older Pleistocene marine beds 500 m. above the shores of the Peloponnese. Marine sands, clays and limestones attributed to the lowest Pleistocene are found in the island of Rhodes up to 300 m. above present sea level and rest on beds of the Levantine fresh-water lakes. Similar relations are known from Cos and the Cyclades and it is evident that subsidence of the Aegean was permitting ingress of Mediterranean waters. Recent vulcanicity in the Aegean is concentrated along a curved line that runs from Aegina, Methana and Poros in the Saronic Gulf, through Melos and Thera (Santorin) to Nisgros in the Dodecanese. Possibly it was movement along this line that both initiated the vulcanicity and led to the subsidence and submergence of the area south of it. At a later stage Mediterranean waters passed this line and spread over the whole of the present Aegean. The great depth of the northern Aegean and the Sea of Marmara (more than a thousand metres) and the rectilinear nature of the southern boundaries of the deep basins suggest that both were opened up by tensional rifting. Certainly, when the Mediterranean waters spilled over the watershed into the river valley that is now the Dardanelles, they descended to a Marmara Basin that was already depressed and flooded, and had communication by a drowned Bosporus with the brackish Pontic lake and shared its special fauna. This fauna was abruptly killed by the arrival of the salt Mediterranean water and survives today only in the brackish coastal limans and river mouths of southern Russia.

Tensional rifting, subsidence and submergence were also occurring on the African side of the Mediterranean. We have already seen[1] that in Ethiopia and Yemen great outpourings of lava occurred in late Cretaceous times and we associated this with the rifting that separated India from Afro-Arabia and created the Arabian Sea. Doubtless these movements extended into the Gulf of Aden, and possibly the first initiation of the Red Sea rift may have occurred as early as this. But the important disturbances came later and like those of central Europe were associated with doming. Hans Cloos recognized a single major dome,[2] but present-day photogeological knowledge of Arabia makes it both more accurate and more helpful to recognize two. The more southerly includes the highlands of the Yemen, Somaliland and Ethiopia and has its axis along the Gulf of Aden. It is split into three by the Y-plan of the rifts with the downdropped block of Danakil in the angle, overlooked by some of the greatest elevations. The doming has here lifted the Cretaceous plateau basalts to great heights and the copious monsoon rains of Ethiopia have carved them into impressive mountains. The second dome is not separated from the first but has its axis along the Red Sea to Sinai and broadens greatly in the region of the Tropic. On the Arabian side the effects of doming reach eastward to Riyadh, and it is this upland bulge of central Arabia that separates the two great sand-filled depressions—the Nafūd to the north and the Rub' al-Khāli to the south. On the Nubian side the doming is less pronounced but its effects may be traced as far as the Nile at Dongola. Hereabouts also the Red Sea deepens in a long narrow central trench to more than 2 km. Doming and the beginnings of rifting are essentially middle and later Tertiary. Recent geological exploration has revealed great thicknesses of sediment, possibly exceeding 6,000 m. and of Miocene or later age, in the southern or Eritrean portion of the rift. Further north the earliest beds laid down within the rift are Pleistocene. At its northern end, where the rift forks on either side of Sinai, it is very young indeed. Here rifting invaded an area that had been overspread by the Mediterranean of Miocene times, and deposits of that age are faulted down beside the Gulf of Suez at the foot of the Red Sea Hills. Not only so, but the breaching of the Egyptian-Sinaitic upland is complete. Even today the fauna of Eritrean and Indian Ocean affinities

[1] See above, p. 9.   [2] §v, 1.

flourishes as far north as the Great Bitter Lake in the Mediterranean lowland. Old shorelines at higher levels show that for a time there was free communication between the two seas, but a small rise of the land relative to the sea permitted the growth of the Nile delta to effect their separation.

East of Sinai in the Gulf of 'Aqaba old shorelines with corals have been claimed to occur as much as 230 m. above present sea level. This is (presumably quite coincidentally) only a few metres lower than the rock sill that leads into the southern end of El-Ghor, the Palestinian rift that holds the Dead Sea and the Sea of Galilee, some 350 km. long, 15–20 km. wide, with a rock floor that descends more than a kilometre below the rim on either side. As everyone knows, most of the floor lies far below sea level, but it is clear that the sea has never gained access to it. The only deposits in it are of Recent alluvium.

Associated with this late Tertiary and Quaternary rifting were further outpourings of basalt. They are found widespread in Ethiopia, and in Arabia from the Yemen northwards to the Syrian desert, where they occur extensively on the north-east side of the long, linear and possibly tectonic depression of the Wādi Sirḥān, in the Jebel Druz and the Ḥaurān. Yet others cover large areas on both sides of the Syrian-Turkish border. Vulcanicity of the same period but of a different kind has added some of the most striking landscape features to the fold belt in Turkey in the form of major volcanic cones. Melendiz and Erciyas rise 1,500 m. or more above the Anatolian plateau beyond the Taurus; Nemrut, Sūphan, Ai Adag and Ararat (5,165 m.) form a remarkable aligned sequence north of Lake Vān, while Haram and Savalan dominate all the country between Lake Urmia and the Caspian. Demavend (5,655 m.), rising above the Elburz 40 miles north-east of Tihrān, carries permanent snows, as does its companion Kuh-i-Nizwa, 60 miles to the east. Far to the south-east on the borders of Balūchistān another line of volcanic peaks occurs, of which Kuh-i-Taftan is the most notable. Farther to the east vulcanicity is absent, but on the northern margin of the fold belt Elburz (5,633 m.) and Kazbek (5,047 m.) form the culminating peaks of the Caucasus, and in Mediterranean Europe we have already noted the Aegean volcanoes and need hardly mention the volcanic line that stretches north and north-west from Etna to the extinct volcanoes of Latium.

Here we conclude. We have traced the evolution of that portion of the terrestrial crust that was to become the Ancient World in terms of the knowledge and ideas current among geologists today.

It is the history of two great land masses, Afrasia and Eurasia, and an intervening mid-world sea, the Tethys. From their inter-action has come the great and complex mid-world belt of moun-tains, and the group of seas, geologically of very different origins and relationships, that are so closely associated with it. In two places these seas transgress on the fold belt, so that Africa and the eastern Mediterranean are connected on the one hand by Aegean, Marmara, Black Sea and Azov to the steppes of Russia, and on the other by the Sicilian straits and the western Mediterranean to Pyrenean France. It is tantalizing that geological science can as yet throw so little light on the causation of these patterns of land and water that have so much importance for pre-history and history, but, in geological as in human history, elucidation of the nature and succession of events must precede speculation about causes. Our account has, of course, not been without its recourse to speculation but has naturally become fuller as the dawn of history is approached. Its time scale is not constant but elastic and has been more and more extended as it approaches the present. In the end it overlaps with pre-history, and the most recent events we have described—for example the separation of the waters of the Mediterranean from those of the Red Sea—were unwittingly witnessed by tool-using man.

The earlier part of our sketch depicts a time when the relation of the land masses Eurasia and Afrasia to the climatic zones of humid and arid tropics was very different from that of today, but in the later part—the 60 million years of Tertiary time—this relationship was much as it is now, though there was perhaps more warmth in all latitudes. The last part of our sketch has laid stress on the very recent origin—only three to five million years ago—of our mountain ranges as positive relief features. The climatic importance of this fact cannot be overestimated. Only from this time could the distribution of rainfall with wet windward mountain slopes, and rain shadows in intermontane valleys and leeward plains, that is such an essential feature of the environmental geography of the Ancient World, come into existence. Only with their elevation into the altitudinal zone of regular rains or winter snow and summer melting could the mountains of the region give birth to and nourish some of its most significant rivers. Particularly where the mountains of the fold belt abut against the lowlands of the arid tropical zone or against the dry interior plains of Asia does this relationship become prominent. Finally, we may note how two of the most recent of geological events—the downwarping of the foreland in front of the Zagros Mountains to let the waters of the Persian Gulf into the Mesopotamian region, and the in-breaking of the Red Sea till it joined for a brief time the eastern Mediterranean— have provided 'water bridges' across the great zone of aridity that, everywhere west of Makrān, cuts off the mountain zone from the Indian Ocean. And even the third 'water bridge', whose history we have not attempted to follow here, the Nile, was not un-influenced by those same events. For the zone of the cataracts that separates the Nile of Egypt from the region of the former Lake Sudan is the zone of influence of the Nubian-Arabian up-warp that was certainly active in Pleistocene times and may possibly be still moving today.

CHAPTER II

PHYSICAL CONDITIONS IN EASTERN
EUROPE, WESTERN ASIA AND EGYPT
BEFORE THE PERIOD OF AGRICUL-
TURAL AND URBAN SETTLEMENT

I. THE NATURAL, EARLY POSTGLACIAL
ENVIRONMENT

T H E elements of the physical geography of the Near East and the Middle East are characterized by considerable regional diversity and colour no less rich and varied than the present cultures and peoples of this area. Whether we contrast the warm, parched plains of the Libyan Desert with the cool, foggy slopes of the high Caucasus, or the humid, fertile tract of riverain Mesopotamia with the bleak shores of the northern Caspian, the manifold variations in the natural environment are ever obvious. In the course of millennia races of diverse religions and cultures have modified the physical landscape of plain and mountain, steppe and forest, impressing upon it the features of a cultural landscape. This new pattern has in places obscured the basic physical features; elsewhere it has emphasized more vividly the preexisting distinctions and distributions.

The Near and Middle East presented a somewhat different aspect in pre-Neolithic times from that of today. Topography and landforms, it is true to say, have not changed perceptibly, but vegetation and soils have suffered severely at the hand of man. Forests have given way to fields, or have been reduced to barren scrub by fuel-gatherers and browsing goats. Extensive grasslands have been ploughed up or impoverished by overgrazing. Desolate steppe or the few isolated pines or oaks preserved in a Muslim cemetery may be the only evidence of a once luxuriant forest. These are changes due to the intervention of man. Climatic changes have also taken place which, by reason of their effect on the composition and character of natural vegetation, have significantly modified conditions of human habitation.

The following sketch of the major physical aspects of the natural environment before the advent of villages and farming communities, of towns and cities, must necessarily be incomplete; it need not, however, be either speculative or hypothetical. Prehistoric geography is essentially a physical science founded on factual evidence which is provided by such studies as geology, geography, botany, zoology, meteorology and archaeology; no attempt will be made to discuss or evaluate here the various methods of research and classes of evidence employed.

Topography and terrain are fundamental factors in biological distribution. The Eurasian and the Afrasian steppes, the broad intervening expanse of mountain systems and the intermontane valleys or plateaux constitute three zones of climatic and biological phenomena. Geologically and topographically also this threefold division is applicable, as follows:

(a) *The Northern Plains and Tablelands.* Tectonic stability and a dominance of horizontally bedded sedimentary rocks are characteristic of European Russia, a great geotectonic province. Relief is largely limited to deeply incised, widely spaced river valleys or ravines.

(b) *The Mountain Belt.* The central zone in the Balkans, Asia Minor, the Caucasus and Iran reflects the complex folding and faulting associated with the alpine phase of mountain-building. This type of terrain is one of high and low mountain-chains with interspersed alluvial valleys or intermontane plateaux.

(c) *The Southern Hills and Plains.* To the south of the mountain belt, the territories of northern Africa, Arabia and the Fertile Crescent are built of horizontal or moderately warped, somewhat eroded and dissected, sedimentary rocks on an ancient crystalline shield. The diversified topography varies from flat or irregular plains and tablelands to hills or even low mountains.[1]

These landforms have a direct bearing upon human settlement. Agriculture in mountain areas was strictly limited to the confined basins, while only sheep or goat herding may have been practicable on the steeper slopes. Communication with other areas was often difficult; as a result cultural and political isolation may have occurred within the regions and traffic between neighbouring fringes was hindered. On the whole, the central mountain belt was a mosaic of densely and sparsely inhabited areas, with a multitude of ecological niches on ridges, foothills and valley-floors; possibly, but not necessarily, it constituted an impediment to cultural and commercial exchange between north and south. In contrast, settlement in the open areas of the Eurasian and the

[1] The classification of landform types by E. H. Hammond (§1, 1) has been applied to the areas shown in Map 2.

Afrasian plains was governed mainly by the distribution of water. Communications of all kinds were good and the easier conditions facilitated the movements of peoples and the maintenance of large political organizations.

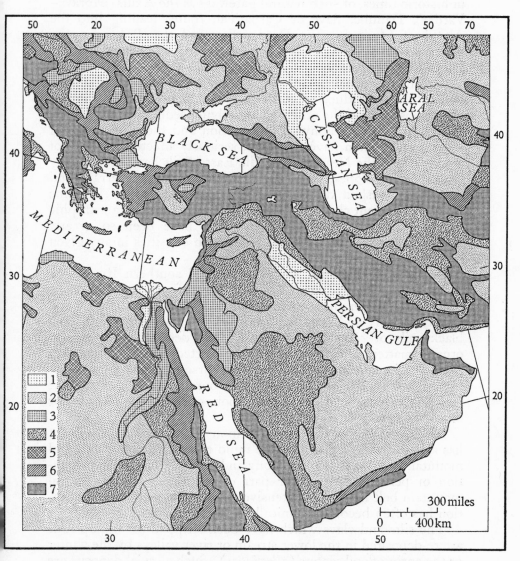

Map 2. Distribution of terrain types (after Hammond, see §1, 1; modified in detail). 1, Level plains; 2, undulating and rolling plains; 3, hill lands; 4, plains studded with hills or mountains; 5, tablelands and plateaux; 6, low mountains; 7, high mountains.

Terrain as a controlling factor was thus limited to the Mountain Belt. The best localities for settlement, such as the Hungarian Plain or the Aegean Basin, need no detailed description. Nor is it necessary to stress the obvious importance, both in prehistoric and in historic times, of such natural gateways as the Axius (Morava–Vardar), Danube, Save or Carpathian routes leading into the Alföld of Hungary, the Dardanelles and the Bosporus, the Cilician Gates, the Halys–Euphrates–Araxes routes or the Diyālā–Zagros passes.

The natural qualities of the various soils—the backbone of agriculture—are due, on the one hand, to prehistoric climatic conditions and, on the other, to underlying sediments or bedrock as well as to topography. Deforestation and the destruction of vegetation by man have, however, seriously affected the soils of large parts of the Near and Middle East. Soils have been widely eroded on hill slopes, particularly in areas of rougher terrain, and have been washed down into the alluvial lowlands. In some centres of ancient civilization the effects have been so catastrophic and the natural resources of the land have been so greatly modified that past and present population densities in any given region need by no means correspond.

In lowland Romania, the Ukraine and southern Russia the dominant surface sediment is a thin sheet of ancient wind-borne dust or loess. In the climate of the area the loess has a good mineral supply and produces the world's most fertile soils. The black soils or *chernozems* are many feet deep and are rich in organic matter. They have not been subjected to erosion, nor have they deteriorated appreciably in the course of time. Good aeration and drainage render loess unfavourable to forest growth; loess in the Danube Basin suited a more open vegetation, a factor of importance to early farmers.

On the steeper slopes of mountainous terrain soil development has always been retarded by the rapid run off of rain water, and mountain soils are naturally stony and poor (*lithosols*). Deforestation of perhaps the greater part of the slopes of the central mountain belt has led to extensive soil erosion so that re-forestation has often become technically difficult.

The silts and clays which have been stripped off the uplands are re-deposited in the lower stream or river valleys by the winter or the spring flood-waters (*alluviation*). Such alluvial deposits are frequent in the basins of the central mountain belt, in the larger river valleys such as Mesopotamia and Egypt, on coastal plains, and in some oases. Where these loamy or clayey soils are suffici-

ently fine (i.e. without much sand and gravel), they are highly
fertile by reason of their structure and of the repeated replenish-
ment of their minerals. If, however, salt is present in the bedrock of the catchment area salinization of soils may take place, as
in some interior basins or in the low Mesopotamian plain, where
large quantities of slightly salty water have evaporated (particularly where water has been dammed back by irrigation works).
Accelerated alluviation has occurred in historical times as a
result of man-induced erosion in the upper reaches of rivers;
major changes have followed, most strikingly in the coastal plains
of the Aegean Basin and in the Orontes Valley.

The greatest transformation has taken place on the moister uplands of the Mediterranean littoral and on the hilly flanks of the
Fertile Crescent. Originally this undulating country was covered
by a mantle of rich red loams (*terra rossa*), which generally do not
form afresh under present climatic conditions. *Terra rossa* is an
easily erodible sediment, and the combined effects of early deforestation, agricultural decline during the Byzantine period and
overgrazing by the herds of pastoral peoples have removed the
greater part of the soils on this type of terrain. Evidence that
such soils cannot be replaced is provided by the denuded limestone hills of the Peloponnese and Syria.

In the arid parts of the southern hills and plains the poor sandy
or stony soils are due to the dry climate which impedes the
biological and chemical processes of soil development. The
deserts may consist of angular rock rubble (rocky desert or
hammada), gravel wastes (*serir*), or mobile or fixed sand dunes of
various types (sandy desert or *erg*). The borders of the hill
country and the dried-up river systems are dominated by *serir*,
hammada being more characteristic of upland or tableland
surfaces, such as the Syrian Desert. Areas of *erg* occur sporadically
in lowland basins, often in association with alluvial salt flats
(*sabkhas*), in eastern and southern Arabia, in north-western India,
in the deserts of Turkestan, and on the northern shores of the
Caspian Sea.

Natural vegetation, inasmuch as it consists of specific regional
plant associations, is the outcome of the sum total of local climatic
factors. Indeed one of the basic principles of plant geography is
that vegetation is a function of the climate and is determined by
it. Accordingly, Map 3 shows the modern climatic zones, with
latitude or elevation, more effectively perhaps than would
charts of temperature or of rainfall distribution. This map of the
natural—as opposed to the man-induced—vegetation of the Near

and Middle East simultaneously provides a fairly accurate picture
of the distribution of vegetation and of climates during the Post-
glacial Period, before the first agricultural and urban settlements.

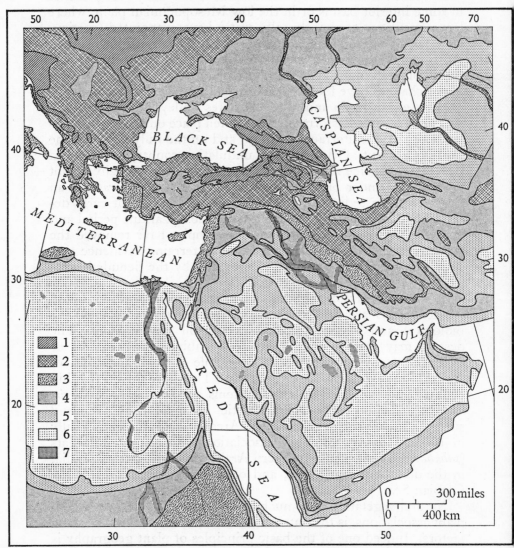

Map 3. Natural, postglacial vegetation belts before agricultural colonization (i.e.
c. 8000–5000 B.C.). 1, Cool-temperate, predominantly coniferous forest; 2, warm-
temperate, deciduous or mixed forest; 3, subtropical, evergreen and coniferous woodland (including tropical scrub and thorn forest in south); 4, semi-arid grasslands and
parklands (steppe); 5, semi-desert, shrub and grass; 6, desert; 7, subtropical, galeria
woodland along exotic rivers and at ground-water oases.

The salient features and elements of the vegetation belts in Map 3 may be briefly described. The cool temperate forests experience moderate to abundant moisture throughout the year; they have long, cool winters and at least 120 days of frost per annum. Although some of the winter-dormant, deciduous trees are present, several species of spruce, pine, and fir form a dominantly needle-leafed coniferous forest. This is the case in the Armenian–Kurdish highlands, the Caucasus and some of the higher ranges of south-eastern Europe. In the warm-temperate forests winters are less severe; the annual number of days of frost varies from 30 to 120 and a moderately dry season occurs. In south-eastern Europe and the Caucasus, where rains are most frequent in summer, hardwood forests with oak, ash, lime, elm and maple are typical, whereas black pine, juniper and evergreen oak are more abundant in the summer-drought areas of northern Greece, Asia Minor and north-western Iran. These areas have all been affected by deforestation and overgrazing in various degrees.

Southwards of the warm-temperate forests lies the classical Mediterranean woodland with its subtropical, evergreen and drought-resistant elements. With less than 30 days of frost annually the effect of winter is negligible, but summers are conspicuously dry. Along this belt, which rises to an altitude of 2500–3000 ft. and extends from the Aegean Basin and Coastal Anatolia to the Levant and the uplands of the Fertile Crescent, open woodlands of evergreen oak were probably once predominant. Subtropical pines and the wild olive tree are also important. However, as the result of deforestation, goat-browsing and soil erosion, a secondary scrub or brush vegetation known as *maquis* has replaced the arboreal elements with species such as the strawberry bush, heather, myrtle, pistachio, and stunted evergreen oaks. These characteristic Mediterranean types, originally confined to poorer soil and rocky terrain, have thus occupied wide stretches through the agency of man, replacing the more ornamental higher elements. In many areas a second stage, a climax of impoverishment, has been reached, in which only a steppe-like shrub vegetation with several thorny species (*garigue*) has been able to resist the effects of over-grazing.

Throughout much of the Near and Middle East tree growth is impeded by intense periodic or even chronic drought. In the loess belt of the northern plains the exceptionally well-drained subsoil and the vegetation growth during the season of greatest evaporation place the steppe tree-limit near the line of 20 in. annual rainfall. Elsewhere with normal soil conditions and winter rains this limit is about 12 in. Consequently grasslands with occasional stands of trees dominate southern Russia and extend as a series of enclaves along the loess of the Romanian and the Hungarian plains up into Central Europe. Similarly the inner margins of the Fertile Crescent and large parts of Iran and western Turkestan are by nature characterized by a grassland vegetation. The moister grasslands are still accessible to dry farming, that is to agriculture without irrigation.

A continuous mat of herbaceous or grass vegetation is no longer possible where there is more than a certain intensity of drought. Below the average rainfall limit of 6 to 8 in. semi-desert is found and economic use is confined to nomadic pastoralism. The vegetation is restricted to isolated tufts of grass, shrubs and low bush. When the average interval between such scattered plants exceeds some 50 yards the term 'desert proper' is employed. The line of climatic division lies somewhere between 2 and 4 in. of rainfall. This kind of desert is of little use even to the nomadic pastoralist.

A conspicuous exception to the quasi-sterility of the arid zone is the oasis, whether fed by ground-water springs or by exotic streams (streams which derive their waters from a different climatic region) carrying waters from distant humid lands. Such are the fertile and well-watered alluvial flood-plains of the Nile and of the Tigris and the Euphrates. Within the range of these flood or river waters—on the surface or below it—there grows a combination of lush subtropical forests and seasonal grasslands known as galeria woodland. To some extent perennial swamps are present, but the greater part of such alluvial flats is only seasonally inundated. Such habitats and their vegetation will be discussed in detail for Mesopotamia and Egypt below.[1]

Just as the main physiographic units in the area under consideration are divided into three almost latitudinal belts, so are some of the most distinctive climatic regions. Obviously it is impossible to speak of 'climatic controls' in a deterministic sense, but certain climatic factors do definitely set broad limits to human efforts unless special pains are taken to offset them. This is particularly the case where more primitive populations have a less efficient technology. The lack of sufficient rainfall makes dry farming impossible, while irrigation agriculture is practicable only in certain selected areas. A further lack of rainfall will eventually impose a similar restriction on a pastoral economy. With less than 4 in. of rainfall human existence outside the oases

[1] See Sects. III and IV.

or galeria woodlands was distinctly marginal, and this line may be taken as a kind of practical 'arid limit' (Map 4).

Severe or repeated frosts set northern and southern limits to a variety of cultivated plants such as citrus fruits, date palms,

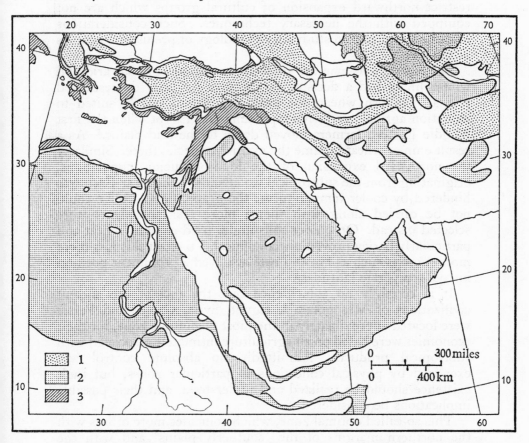

Map 4. Some climatic zones. 1, Areas with more than 30 days of frost annually; 2, areas with less than 4 inches average precipitation, excluding oases; 3, most favourable Mediterranean climates defined by distribution of olive cultivation and wild habitat of *Olea sativa*.

olives and eventually even the grape vine. An ecologically significant limit is given by the criterion of 30 days of frost annually, which coincides approximately with the 32° F. isotherm for the coldest month (January). The present-day cultural landscape as well as the natural vegetation indicates notable changes or transitions in this critical zone, which divides areas with and without an effective winter, in the sense of a cold season. This limit can also be used to differentiate the temperate zone from the subtropics. It is likely that this 'winter limit' had its implications for prehistoric peoples. Intense cold can be counteracted only by effective clothing and artificial heating, and may thus restrict northward expansion of cultural groups which are not equipped with the necessary techniques. Such considerations must be significant in studying the ecology of prehistoric peoples in the area.

But not only to man are such limits crucial. Similar arid and winter limits had a decisive significance for early domesticated plants. Einkorn wheat, for example, proved poorly suited to irrigation agriculture in Mesopotamia and Egypt when the first Middle Eastern farmers moved down to the arid plains.[1] As a result emmer wheat became the exclusive species there. Similarly the northward expansion of the food-producing populations, originating from the subtropical woodlands of the Near East, was hindered by cooler temperatures: the grape, fig and olive could not be carried along with them; more resistant plants were selected instead. On poorer soils under hard climates wheat and particularly barley proved uneconomical. To offset this loss more modest crops such as rye and oats achieved a prominent position in cool-temperate latitudes.

It is certainly no coincidence that the foci of the ancient civilizations of Mesopotamia, Egypt, Syria, Greece and Persia were located approximately in the most favourable zone, for their economies were based on an agriculture intimately associated with subtropical products. Admittedly no absolute control was exercised by physical conditions in particular zones, but their existence should be realized and understood, and their possible implications be considered.

This so-called optimal zone, which coincides more or less with the northern margins of the 'southerly plains' and with the southern peripheries of the 'central mountain belt', coincides also with the natural distribution of wild plants which archaeology has identified as the first to be domesticated. By far the majority of the plants, known from palaeo-ethnobotany to have been first domesticated in the earliest ('western')[2] Neolithic cultural sphere,

---

[1] Geographical aspects of early plant domestication are described with further references in §1, 2.

[2] Reference is made here exclusively to what is known as the Middle Eastern nuclear or hearth area, in which western civilizations had their first roots. Early, and probably independent, first cultivations of numerous other species must be assigned to other areas such as South-East Asia, Central America and the tropical Andes.

had their wild distribution here. Hans Helbaek has been able to show that the earliest plants shown by archaeology to have been cultivated and domesticated were emmer wheat and two-rowed barley, probably grown in association. The areas of distribution of the respective forms *Triticum dicoccoides* and *Hordeum spontaneum* overlap only on the slopes of the Fertile Crescent at altitudes of 2000–4300 ft. (Map 5). The first steps towards the

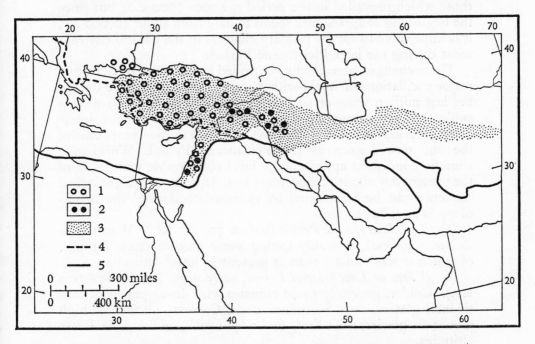

Map 5. Some biological zones. Native habitats of: 1, *Triticum aegilopoides* (wild prototype of einkorn); 2, *Triticum dicoccoides* (wild prototype of emmer); 3, *Hordeum spontaneum* (wild prototype of barley), after Helbaek, see §1, 2; 4, northern limits of citrus fruits; 5, northern limits of date palm (*Phoenix dactylifera*).

domestication of plants within the Middle Eastern cultural area may therefore have taken place in that region, or at least within the native habitat of either of the two wild wheats. Equally important are the subtropical cultures of olives, dates and grapes. All three were widespread and ubiquitous in the cultural landscape before 3000 B.C. The native habitat of the wild olive tree (*Olea sativa*) coincides with the limits of olive cultivation indicated in Map 4. The grape also seems to have originated in the Fertile Crescent, but the early history of the cultivated date palm is obscure.

The areal focus of transition from food-gathering to food-producing economies and the establishment of the earliest farming communities can be better understood if the relevant physical factors are appreciated. Indeed the vital intellectual and economic transition associated with the first domestication has been attributed by several authorities to changes of physical environment. The physical conditions previously described were those which prevailed in the period *c.* 8000–5000 B.C., but since the beginning of agriculture seems to date from about 10,000 B.C. it is imperative to survey primary changes in the natural environment during the later Pleistocene Period.

These changes were chiefly controlled by climate. In fact many major oscillations of world-wide climate have taken place during the last million years or so. Higher middle latitudes have been subjected to an alternating series of glaciations and warmer, interglacial, periods, the series covering at least a million years during the age now known as the Pleistocene Period. World-wide climatic conditions approached a level comparable with those of the present day about 10,000 years ago. In so far as the geological sequence can be ascertained by radiocarbon dating[1] the chronology is as follows.

(*a*) *Last Interglacial Period* (before 70,000 B.C.). Warm conditions universal, probably lasting some 30,000 years, for part of which it was moister than at present in lower latitudes.

(*b*) *Würm or Last Glacial Period, early stages* (70,000–28,000 B.C.). Colder, generally moist climates with development of continental glaciers over Scandinavia and Canada, advance of high mountain glaciers. At first, moist 'pluvial' conditions in lower latitudes.

(*c*) *Interstadial Phase* (28,000–26,000 B.C.). Cool-temperate interval, with temporary recession of world glaciers.

(*d*) *Würm or Last Glacial Period, main and late stages* (26,000–8000 B.C.). Cold, generally dry climates with maximum advance of glaciers, *c.* 18,000 B.C., followed by intermittent retreat and last glacial relapse, *c.* 9000 B.C.

(*e*) *Postglacial or Recent Period* (8000 B.C. to present day). Approximately modern conditions of temperature and precipitation; higher latitudes experienced their maximum temperatures with greater moisture in most latitudes, *c.* 5500–2500 B.C.

[1] See §1, 3, which gives the most recent analysis and detailed commentaries by specialists as well as an extensive bibliography of the subject in general.

II. PHYSICAL CONDITIONS IN SOUTH-EASTERN EUROPE DURING THE LAST GLACIAL PERIOD

The Postglacial environment of the Balkan Peninsula and southern Russia was, from all available evidence, more or less identical with the conditions described as 'natural' above. A slight advance of the forest at the expense of the steppes is recorded in the Ukraine, contemporaneously with the Atlantic phase, c. 5500–3000 B.C. For greater contrasts in physical conditions in this zone it is necessary to turn to the environment of the Last Glacial Period.

The climate in south-eastern Europe was decidedly cold during the Last Glacial Period. Small glaciers were present in the eastern and southern Carpathian mountains, the Balkan ranges and the Peloponnese (above levels of about 6000 ft.), and particularly in Yugoslavia (above 4000 ft.). All the high and low mountain country was reduced to the conditions of the alpine meadow or scrub zone, while wind-borne loess sediments were deposited over a vast area which covered all southern Russia, the Rumanian and Bulgarian lowlands and the Hungarian plain. Natural conditions on the loess plains long retained a special significance for prehistoric man during Postglacial times as has already been shown.

At the time of its deposition during the main and late glacial stages the loess belt had a dry steppe vegetation, while the foothills of the higher country carried a forest–tundra vegetation. True woodlands of boreal type occurred in eastern Bulgaria and the southern Crimea, and of mixed deciduous type along the Greek and Yugoslav littoral. Permanently frozen subsoil, such as is now found in northern Siberia, was present in the Hungarian Plain and the greater part of the Ukraine. These areas, together with the higher terrain of the Balkan Peninsula, had annual mean temperatures lower than 28° F. (today over 50° F.) and mean July temperatures in the 50's (today in the 60's).[1] These conditions were reflected in the fauna, which consisted of large herds of woolly mammoth, wild horse and reindeer as well as woolly rhinoceros, wild cattle and various cervids.[2]

The early glacial periods however were moist and not so severe climatically as is indicated by tree pollen in many of the later steppe areas as well as by geomorphic phenomena.

The vegetation belts of south-eastern Europe during the main glacial period are shown in Map 6 according to a reconstruction

[1] §II, 3; §II, 1, 276 f.   [2] §II, 4, chs. 8 and 12.

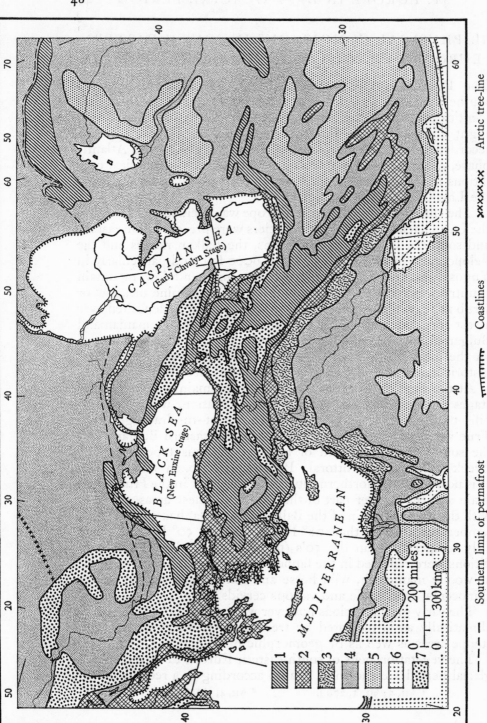

Map 6. Vegetation belts during the last (Würm) glacial (representing temperature conditions of the glacial maximum and moisture conditions of the pluvial maximum). 1, Cool-temperate and sub-arctic forest; 2, warm-temperate forest; 3, subtropical woodlands; 4, semi-arid grasslands and parklands, in Europe tundra with sub-arctic scrub or with loess deposition; 5, semi-desert; 6, desert; 7, mountain tundra (alpine meadows or scrub) and isolated glaciers. Galeria woodlands omitted. (Modified from Frenzel, §II, 2, and Butzer, §II, I.)

– – – Southern limit of permafrost   Coastlines   xxxxxx Arctic tree-line

by B. Frenzel[1] on the basis of pollen, geological features and fauna. Map 6 includes both south-western Asia and Egypt; here we rely partly on Frenzel's work and partly on other reconstructions[2] which, being dependent on geological data, are less trustworthy for the areas south of the mountain belt. The overall reconstruction does, however, give a fair picture of physical conditions in the Würm or Last Glacial Period.

III. PREHISTORIC GEOGRAPHY OF SOUTH-WESTERN ASIA

Here we must confine our attention to the last glaciation and the first half of the Postglacial Period. Abundant evidence of at least two cold phases is available from the highland areas and of several pluvial or moister periods from the drier lowlands. It should, however, be borne in mind that much of the evidence in many areas has been obtained from inadequate field studies, so that it must be used selectively; it is, moreover, often open to different interpretations.

In the naturally rougher and well-wooded highlands of Anatolia, the Caucasus and Iran two geomorphic processes, now restricted to the highest peaks, were of some significance. These are glaciation and frost-climate weathering such as is found above the timber line in the high alpine zone. Permanent ice and snowfields are of very little importance here at the present time and even at the climax of the last glaciation they were limited to cirque glaciers and a few isolated valley glaciers. These phenomena, recent and fossil, have however been the best studied of all geomorphic features in the area. By contrast, those of the alpine zone, which are frost-climate agencies responsible for patterned ground and for the slow flow of water-saturated muds over impermeable, frozen subsoil (solifluction), have been but little studied.[3]

At the present time the climatic snowline—below which as much snow melts as falls per annum—lies between 10,000 and 15,000 ft. Only a few of the highest peaks in eastern Anatolia and northern Iran still harbour glaciers, but they are more numerous in the high Caucasus. During the last glaciation the existing glaciers increased in size and advanced to form tongues of ice protruding downhill into adjacent valleys. Those of the Caucasus

---

[1] §II, 2.   [2] § III, 4.

[3] The materials of this section are summarized in §II, 4, ch. 12 and §III, 4, ch. 4.

extended to a maximum of some 40 miles on the northern flanks
and of 25 miles on the southern. New glaciers also formed at
lower elevations in the same areas and throughout many lower
ranges of central and western Anatolia, Kurdistān and the
southerly Zagros ranges of Iran. The climatic snowline responsible for these glaciers is estimated to have been 2000–2700 ft.
lower than that of the present day.

The rather scanty evidence of glacial age solifluction at least
suggests that the alpine tree-line also stood proportionately lower.
This seems to put the unglaciated parts of the Caucasus and the
greater part of the Armenian and Kurdish plateau into the inhospitable climate of the alpine zone (see Map 6). The implication of this for palaeo-ecology is greater than the spatial extent of
these areas might suggest. That the snow-line and the tree-line
together stood so much lower implies that the temperature levels
were correspondingly lower throughout the highland belt. Such
a depression by 2000–2700 ft.[1] when we interpret it in terms
of the modern average upper air lapse rate (1° F. per 300 ft.)
suggests that the entire area was some 7–8° F. cooler on the
average than it is today. This estimate is confirmed by palaeo-
temperature measurements obtained from deep sea cores from
the eastern Mediterranean. A section of sediment dated to
28,000–10,000 B.C. indicates that surface water temperatures
were some 9° F. colder than at present.

The significance of these cooler conditions for Palaeolithic man
is difficult to assess. There appears to have been no human
occupation at Shanidar Cave in Iraq (at 2200 ft.) during the time
from about 24,000 to 10,000 B.C., which corresponds with the
glacial maximum. No contemporary cultures have yet been
discovered elsewhere in the region at similar elevations.[2] It
remains possible, if doubtful, that great parts of the highland belt
were largely unoccupied by man during the second half of the last
glaciation. As the transitional Natufian and Karīm Shahr-Zawi
Chemi[3] cultures with the beginnings of food-production date back
to 9000 B.C. cultural progress in those early crucial millennia may
have been limited to south-east and south-west of the high
Taurus and of the Zagros. Palaeolithic surveys of the interior of
Anatolia and Iran are absolutely essential if an answer is to be
given to this problem.

Pollen cores which were taken recently in western Iran may

---

[1] §III, 15, 131ff. maintains that a lowering of 6000 ft. occurred in north-eastern
Iraq, a somewhat anomalous situation possibly related to greater precipitation but
certainly requiring further investigation.   [2] §III, 2.   [3] Ibid.

elucidate the Late Glacial and Postglacial climatic history of the highlands, of which very little is known at present. The only detail available is that the Würmian glaciers retreated from their maximum extent (perhaps 20,000 years ago) in stages, probably making a last minor re-advance during the final glacial relapse *c.* 9000 B.C. The snow-line during the latter stage was lowered to about half the maximum extent of the Würmian glaciers, and this reduction may suggest an average temperature which was lower by 4° F. It has been conjectured that some existing ice fields disappeared temporarily during the warmer parts of the Postglacial Period, but convincing proof of this suggestion is not yet forthcoming. By about 8000 B.C. temperatures probably approached those of the present day.

In the interior basins of the central mountain belt of southwestern Asia,[1] as well as in the arid Aralo-Caspian Depression,[2] palaeo-ecological conditions during the Würm glaciation and in part during the early Postglacial Period differed not only in terms of temperature but also in humidity. Moisture fluctuations in semi-arid country are very significant for all biological elements. The lowering of mean temperatures in these areas by some 8° F. can be safely assumed, and would—if all other factors such as wind velocities and cloudiness remained constant—result in a reduction of evaporation from open stretches of water by at least 25 per cent. This would mean that more moisture would percolate into the soil and be absorbed by plants so that the density of vegetation and the discharge of rivers would be increased. Inland lakes and seas with no outlets would retain a greater volume of water, and in some cases they were actually able to overflow into adjoining basins.

Chronologically, however, these high interior lake levels, which can be more precisely dated, fall within about the first quarter of the last glaciation, when the continental glaciers of the Early Würm epoch were advancing. The lowering of temperatures suggested above was certainly not experienced at this time; a different explanation must be sought in terms of primary changes in the general circulation of the atmosphere. As an example the Caspian Sea, which during the Early Würm epoch had a long enduring level at 240 ft. above that of the present day (or 148 ft. above sea level), overflowed over the Manych Depression into the Black Sea. The area ('Early Chvalyn Sea') was approximately twice that of the present day. Some 75 per cent of the waters of this sea are now derived from the Volga Basin in

[1] Cf. §III, 4, chs. 3 and 5.   [2] Cf. §II, 2, vol. 2, sect. I, 7.

central Russia.[1] Today the sea-level fluctuations reflect primarily the summer temperatures in the Volga Basin. A more maritime climate with cooler, wetter summers would considerably augment the volume of water in the Caspian Sea and also feed the advancing glaciers further north.

As we have indicated briefly above, other geological evidence confirms that eastern Europe in the earliest parts of the last glaciation experienced a cooler, wetter climate, considerably more oceanic in character. Greater rainfall extended in varying degrees to all the areas under consideration.

The Aral Sea stood 40 ft. higher than at present during the Early Chvalyn stage, but was deprived of most of the Oxus (Amū Daryā) waters at a later date. Lake Balchash expanded, joining with the Sasyk and Alakol. The Tarim Depression probably contained a large lake, ancestor to the present Lop Nor pan. Along these lakes and their tributaries grew galeria forests with oak, alder, hornbeam, pine, birch and spruce.

In Iran the great salt pans, or *kavīrs*, harboured considerably more water than at present, although it is not possible to say in what part of the Pleistocene Age were formed the terraces suggesting a lake some 200–250 ft. deep in the Great Kavīr. In the Nama Kavīr of the Lūṭ Desert there is some probability that the younger basin deposits (contradictory reports give 65 or 800 ft. of lacustrine sandstone, sands and clays) are of the Last Glacial Age. The Hamun Lake of the Irano-Afghan border was at the same date probably some 25 ft. deeper and ten times as large as it is today. Further westwards Lake Urmia or Riẓā'iyeh at the Turkish border, which is today only 50 ft. deep, expanded to about twice its size and had a depth of some 200 ft. during the Last Glacial Age.

In Anatolia the existing lakes expanded, while new lakes were created in several depressions. Most important in the latter category was Lake Konya covering roughly 2000 square miles. If we mention two only of the other lakes still in existence, the salt pan Tuz Gölü (which now varies between 0 and 7 ft. in depth) was a broad, flat lake some 17 ft. deep, and Lake Burdur had a level higher by 250 ft., which caused the lake to overflow. Other evidence from each of the above areas includes river terraces, massive spring deposits and so forth.

There is little doubt that ecological conditions in the climatically less harsh lowlands were particularly favourable in the early part of the Last Glacial Age. But after perhaps 30,000 B.C.

[1] §III, 5, 129 f.

moisture conditions were reduced to about those which prevail at present, and the lower temperatures were sufficient to account for a Caspian Sea level some 90 ft. higher than at present, although it had no outlet. Aeolian activity became significant in the Turkestan and Iranian Basins, and wind-borne loess sediments were widely deposited in treeless or sparsely wooded steppes between perhaps 30,000 and 10,000 B.C. The natural environment of the second half of the Last Glacial Age was comparatively harsh and not particularly attractive. This period corresponds with the Upper Palaeolithic cultures, which have so far not been recorded in the interior of Anatolia. However, well-adapted hunting populations on the northern and western fringes of the Aralo-Caspian Depression lived on herds of reindeer, woolly mammoth and wild horse. An advanced Upper Palaeolithic culture found in the Devis-Chvreli cave of Georgia includes a fauna of boar, cave bear, brown bear, reindeer(?) and deer.[1] The apparent setting of this locality is woodland.

In early Postglacial times climate and ecology assumed their modern patterns in this area. Two radiocarbon dates indicate that loess deposition had ceased by about 9000 B.C. The Postglacial Period was uneventful except for a drier interval, indicated by apparent aeolian activity along the Caspian shores; this belongs to the Bronze Age (second millennium B.C. ?). Conditions may have been similar in central Turkestan. Evidence of occasional moister interludes in the areas under consideration is problematical and not very convincing.

In the hill country of the Levant—Palestine, the Lebanon and Syria, the Syrian Desert, the Mesopotamian lowlands and the Taurus–Zagros foothills—modern conditions range from desert in the centre to subtropical forests in the peripheral high country. The earliest geological work directed at the Pleistocene history of the area recognized evidence of greater moisture rather than of greater cold, but there is little doubt to-day that moister periods of geological significance known as 'pluvials' have affected the Fertile Crescent on several occasions. Traces of them are strongest on the Mediterranean littoral, and decrease rapidly towards the interior. They were caused by more frequent depressions over the eastern Mediterranean, with more numerous rainstorms passing eastwards. These pluvials were probably associated with more frequent torrential rains during the transitional seasons while the summers were certainly no less dry than at present.

The most reliable or most applicable data come from the

[1] §III, 12, 228 ff.

Mediterranean littoral, from a sequence of cave deposits and from littoral sediments.[1] Along the shores of Palestine and the Lebanon there are, as along the coasts of other seas, innumerable indications of fluctuations of world sea level. Such glacio-eustatic oscillations, as they are called, reflect changes in the actual volume of ocean waters. Their origin is as follows. The water content of the continental glaciers of the Pleistocene Age was ultimately derived from the oceans, and during the various glaciations many million cubic miles of ocean waters were stored up in continental ice masses so that the sea level around the world fell to more than 350 ft. below that of the present day. During the warmer interglacial periods the present glaciers of Greenland and Antarctica were possibly reduced in size, thus contributing in part towards higher sea levels than at present. Consequently, geological indications of falling or lower sea levels (regressions) or rising or high sea levels (transgressions) can be used as chronological tools. Evidence of a regression implies a glacial date, of transgression an interglacial date.

The Levantine deposits of the regression corresponding with the Last Glacial Age show a uniform pattern. When there was a drop in sea level, masses of alluvial gravels were transported and deposited by streams now inconspicuous. The early regressional phase marked the maximum moisture of these pluvial phases. Later regressional deposits consisted of coastal dunes, interbedded with smaller gravel horizons or lake beds. This is the general picture of moisture reduction in the middle of the glacial phases, so that after perhaps 20,000 B.C. conditions were no moister, perhaps even drier, than at the present time.

Inland, the excellent stratigraphy, both in terms of geological deposits and in terms of Palaeolithic industries, makes caves like the Mount Carmel group, Jabrud,[2] Jebel Qafzah, 'Irq el-Aḥmar, Umm Qaṭafah,. Ksar Akil, Abu-Halka and 'Adlūn as instructive as those of the French Dordogne. Geological interpretation of the cave sediments and study of the rich faunal associations provide a picture of a moist, cool early glacial period with Middle Palaeolithic industries, a midway warmer interval, and a final, intense cold phase corresponding with the Upper Palaeolithic occupation of the area. Table 2[3] gives a more vivid impression of the natural environment of the Levant.

Of the other sources of evidence with regard to the Last Pluvial

---

[1] See §III, 8, for the most adequate summary.
[2] More correctly Yabrūd. See p. 78, n. 1, below (Ed.).
[3] The basic sources are §III, 6, vol. I; and §III, 11.

Table 2. Mammalian fauna in the Levant

	Herbivores			Carnivores	Rodents and small mammals
	Predominantly woodland	Predominantly steppe	Aquatic		
Late Middle Palaeolithic Fauna (Early Würm Period)	Elephant, rhinoceros, deer (fallow, red and roe), wild cattle, boar	Horse, onager, antelope, gazelle	Hippopotamus	Brown bear, wolf, fox, jackal, spotted hyena, leopard	Vole, mole rat
Upper Palaeolithic Fauna (Main and Late Würm Period)	Deer (fallow, red and roe), wild cattle, boar	Horse, onager, antelope, gazelle	—	Brown bear, wolf, fox, spotted hyena, leopard	Mole rat, marten, hare, hedgehog

Note. Among the Upper Palaeolithic fauna the elephant, rhinoceros and hippopotamus are not recorded and may not have tolerated the cooler environment; the jackal is not recorded locally.

Period, inland lakes are few in this area. The only example available is the Dead Sea, which probably reached a level some 300 ft. higher at this time, as compared with 650 ft. during a more ancient Pluvial Period. Further evidence, unfortunately undated, comes from innumerable alluvial deposits (silts, river gravels, etc.) throughout the area in question.

Nothing has yet been said about the temperature. The evidence for greater cold is limited to indirect indications, although there is every reason to assume that a lowering of temperature of some 7–8° F. also characterized this zone. As we have suggested above, the record of the fauna of the Levant may reflect increasing cold during the Last Glacial Age. This is substantiated by the presence of the crocodile in Palestine during the Last Interglacial Age, and again—apparently after an interval—in Postglacial times.

In a few caves there are also deposits of flattish, angular limestone rubble which is generally attributed to frost-shattering. Lastly, plant impressions found in the Lebanon mountains and thought to date from the Last Glacial Age record only temperate woodland species such as oak, beech, elm and hazel, but none of the subtropical genera there at the present time.

The evidence at present available from the northern and eastern sections of the Fertile Crescent implies that modern conditions of moisture have persisted for some 15,000–20,000 years, and modern temperature conditions since at least 8000 B.C. The fauna of the final Palaeolithic cultures of Iraq, dated by radiocarbon to 10,000 B.C., is not unlike that to be expected under natural conditions today.[1] Neither the contemporary recessional moraines probably recorded in the youngest glaciological material from the highlands nor the thermoclastic deposits (due to strong variations in temperature) of contemporary cave levels in the Levant permit of the assertion that ecological conditions were 'modern' before 8000 B.C.[2]

The zone of the southern Levant experienced a slightly moister climate in about 9000 B.C. during the period of early Natufian occupation. The gazelle, a creature characteristic of open country, was surprisingly rare at this level in the Mount Carmel caves, and several species of the genus disappeared in Palestine. By far the most abundant species of the time was the fallow-deer, a woodland animal. Moreover, the hedgehog and a species of hyena became extinct locally.[3] To supplement the evidence of the fauna there is archaeological material which indicates fishing in the wādis of the Judaean highlands. This shows the presence of

[1] §III, 13.   [2] §III, 4, 104 ff.   [3] §III, 6; §III, 1, 418–33.

possibly stagnant, yet permanent, pools of water throughout the year. The existence of hunting populations, as indicated by the presence of plentiful Natufian flints, in the Negeb and Sinai deserts also supports this conclusion. Geologically there are several comparatively recent, high strand lines along the Dead Sea. These younger, unfortunately undated, shore lines rise to 165 ft. above the present level.[1] Some of them are certainly not more than 12,000 years old.

Another, later, moist interlude is indicated, but only in the same area of the southern Levant. The fauna at a Neolithic level of the Abu-Uṣbuʿ Cave on Mount Carmel suggests an annual rainfall of 28–32 in. precipitation as compared with 22–24 in. at the present time.[2] There is no precise dating for this or for the many other, albeit less coherent, pieces of geological information. From the Egyptian sequence a date in the fifth and fourth millennia may apply locally. This moister phase probably cannot be left out of account in Palestine, but the present state of knowledge about it is very rudimentary.

Beyond the material mentioned here, there is no clear evidence that the average ecological conditions during the last ten millennia differed greatly from those possible today. This does not exclude the irregular occurrences of sequences of 'good' or 'bad' years, but, seen as a long-term condition, climate in the better watered parts of the Fertile Crescent has not fluctuated significantly during Postglacial times. This need not, however, apply to the desert margins, where minor changes can easily be of ecological but not geological significance.

Our understanding of the late prehistoric environment is imperfect, however, unless we discuss the physical geography which is relevant to the possibilities of early settlement.

The lower Mesopotamian lowlands, downstream of Ramadi on the Euphrates and beyond the Tigris bend below Sāmarrā, represent the flood-plain of those two rivers—a combination of natural river embankments or levees and seasonally inundated alluvial flats. Annual high water on these rivers occurs in May and June when the melted snow waters from Armenia and the spring rainfall maximum in Turkey coincide. Thus, depending on the synchronization and the character of the winter snowfall and the temperature conditions in the high country, there may be appreciable floods. These floods are, however, irregular in character; they vary in time and extent and are not dependable. So despite an overall similarity with the Nile flood-plain of

[1] §III, 4, 106. [2] §III, 4, 114–15, with references.

Egypt, there are certain peculiarities. The deposition of silt is also not as great as in the case of the Nile, so that archaeological remains are very much more accessible and often quite visible, something unimaginable in the lower flood-plain of the Nile. The last major difference is the presence of salts in the Mesopotamian waters, which, when concentrated through repeated evaporation in alluvial basins or irrigated flats, lead to salinization. This hazard is not present in Egypt except in the coastal marshlands of the Delta.

Given such a system with ground water available throughout the year along the river banks and in swampy parts of the alluvial flats, these areas naturally support a woodland vegetation. Today this is largely composed of date palms. In the natural state tamarisk (*Tamarix articulata*) and aspen (*Populus euphratica*) were probably characteristic trees of the river levees, together with oleander, burning bush (*Rubus sanctus*), acacias and *Ziziphus* species. The seasonally flooded flats would be desiccated by late summer, permitting only a brush and herbaceous vegetation to thrive. Finally, on the desert uplands or ancient river terraces, only a desert or semi-desert vegetation is possible.

The first agricultural settlement of the lowlands was no easy step for prehistoric man. The agricultural settlements of the Hassunan (perhaps 5900–5400 B.C.) and Halafian–Sāmarran (perhaps 5400–4300 B.C.) Periods generally made use of the winter rains in the foothill country of the Fertile Crescent. Further expansion in the plains was impossible without irrigation; in fact it is most interesting to find that these older settlements actually lie somewhat beyond modern dry-farming limits. The difficulty was not so much one of using ground-water moisture, as was certainly done at some earlier riverain sites, but of ecological adaptation to a summer-growing cycle, making use of the flood waters of late spring and early summer rather than the winter rains. Not all the winter grains and orchard species were successfully adapted, as we know. The other difficulty was to organize flood-plain irrigation in a simple technical sense.

Possibly this difficulty explains why actual settlement of the lowlands by agricultural populations may not have proceeded downstream from the older sites between the Diyālā and the middle stretches of the Tigris and Euphrates, but rather upstream from the estuary. To understand this it is necessary to explain simple basin irrigation as practised in Mesopotamia and Egypt before the installation of perennial irrigation by dams and barrages. Owing to the presence of natural ridges of abandoned levee embankments, and of small distributary branches, abandoned stream channels and the like, the alluvial flats are divided into irregular natural basins. According to their elevation these drain off successively as the river recedes after the flood has reached its maximum. But, if the waters are held back by dams, dry season reservoirs can be created and the waters can be released into the fields as required. Water was later also lifted by means of the Archimedean screw or by the *sāqiya* driven by animals.

A plausible interpretation of the successive stages of colonization has been advanced by P. Buringh[1] on the basis of distinct physiographical units which have been observed in the Mesopotamian lowlands. Buringh divides them into five major units as follows.

The estuary. In the lowest portions of the river, annual flow variations are subordinate to or obliterated by the tidal movements of the Persian Gulf. Throughout this area along the Shaṭṭ el-'Arab the waters rise and fall to a maximum of 6 ft. twice daily. Low levee embankments and small basins are dominant, and these are automatically irrigated or irrigable with this diurnal rhythm of the waters. To judge by soil profiles, the shores of the Persian Gulf did not deviate appreciably from the modern coastline. Buringh believes that this zone was the most suited to the earliest form of agricultural settlement, because cultivation could be adequately performed by the efforts of individual families. There is, however, no archaeological evidence available to prove this theory.

The marsh. In the marsh areas, in the confluence zone of the Tigris and Euphrates, levees are low and weak, while the groundwater table is high. As this, however, appears to be an area of repeated recent subsidence[2]—without which the swamps would have silted up long ago—it is not possible to be sure exactly how conditions were at the time in question.

The delta. The interior 'delta' of the two rivers consists of broad expanses with innumerable shifting channels and minor branches. The levees are of moderate size and basins are of limited extent owing to countless distributaries. The latter condition has the great advantage that smaller basins can be managed with limited organization and technical skill. The delta zone is generally inundated by annual floods, although these are not regular or as reliable as those of the Nile. But the destructive character of the floods, as manifested further upstream, is largely eliminated by the spreading out of the waters and the reduction of

---

[1] §III, 3.   [2] §III, 10.

their velocity. Although eminently suitable for basin irrigation this area requires more organization and communal effort to function efficiently than does the estuary. Buringh believes that this area was occupied in a second stage of colonization of the flood-plain.

The river-plain. In this zone where the Euphrates, Tigris and Diyālā converge, floods are violent and often disastrous, and the levees correspondingly high. The basins are large in extent and more difficult to control, and they run dry more rapidly in the summer when, however, they provide fine grazing country. Buringh suggests these areas were occupied in a third stage.

The river terraces and desert uplands. These lands between the terrace banks are elevated above the flood-plain, out of range of the annual inundations, and high above the ground waters percolating from the streams. Water would have to be lifted some 30 ft., which requires a rather elaborate system of lift-irrigation. This was not available until historic times. Buringh thus explains the absence of agricultural settlement on the river terraces before Assyrian times, when the fourth stage in his progression of colonization began.

Buringh also makes the deduction that the advance in technology would enable the bulk of the population to shift from south to north. Simultaneously this shift would be aided by progressive salinization of the soils, proceeding upstream.[1] This process had probably already affected the Babylon area in the time of Herodotus.

In practice, the archaeological and historical picture of this period seems to support this theory. The earliest settlement known in the southlands was probably at Eridu, the foundations of which antedate the 'Ubaid Period (c. 4300–3500 B.C.). It is located on the desert edge of the delta zone, just like Merimda or the sites on the shores of the Faiyūm in Egypt at about the same time.[1] The 'Ubaid culture itself was characterized by towns springing up everywhere in this delta and the source of their origin was apparently either in the estuary or from the edge of the desert at Eridu. The archaeological evidence supports the suggestion that irrigation farming involved only the breaching of the natural embankments of streams and made use of uncontrolled local flooding. Large-scale networks are later than the 'Ubaid Period.[2] The delta area remained the centre of agricultural activity and urban life in Iraq until the second millennium B.C. (Map 7). Meanwhile the river-plain area was occupied by semi-

[1] §III, 9.   [2] See, however, below, p. 363.

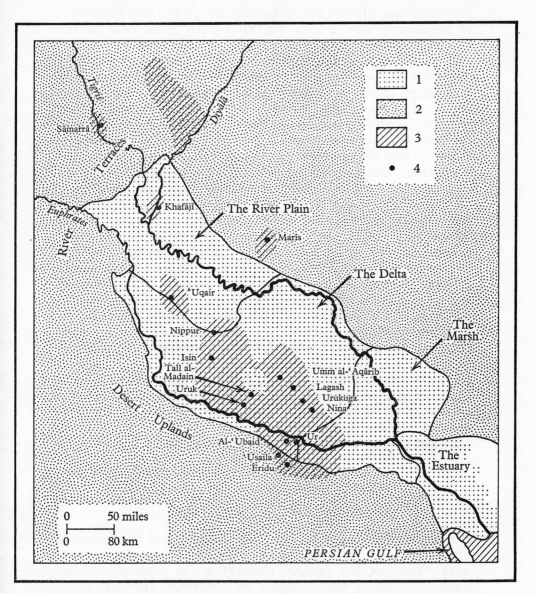

Map 7. Geomorphology and early settlement in lowland Mesopotamia. (Physio-graphic units adapted from Buringh, §III, 3, archaeological data from Stier *et al*. §III, 14.). 1, Modern flood-plain of the Tigris–Euphrates; 2, river terraces, uplands and highlands; 3, major areas under cultivation before 3000 B.C.; 4, villages and towns founded before 3000 B.C.

pastoral Semitic tribes, the Akkadians, by *c.* 2370 B.C. The centre of population moved into the river-plain zone only in the nineteenth century B.C. at the earliest, so that it can be assumed that agricultural use of the land in the river-plain achieved a dominant position some 1500 years later than it had in the delta area. Agricultural occupation of the river-terrace zone did not begin before about 1100 B.C.

Many parallels can again be drawn with Egypt; in particular the Nile delta and the flood-plain of the Nile valley have strong analogies with the delta and river-plain areas of Iraq. It has been conjectured that agricultural colonization in Egypt also moved upstream; if so the centre of gravity shifted very much earlier.

Arabia plays a key role in numerous archaeological, cultural and ethnological theories of relationships between Asia and Africa, but its archaeology and its prehistoric ecology are virtually unexplored. Frequent reference is made to the great extinct drainage system of fairly ancient date running west to east across the breadth of the Peninsula. The Wādis Ḥaurān, Bāṭin-Rummah and As-Sahbā' once emptied their waters into the Persian Gulf,[1] while the Wādi Dawāsir cannot be traced beyond the Rubʿ al-Khāli sands, which incidentally have buried fossil bones of hippopotamus. The moister highlands of the Yemen and Ḥadhramaut experienced pluvial periods on a scale perhaps comparable with Egypt, but these areas are of only marginal importance here and probably raise more problems than they solve. It is perhaps decisive that no part of this area, except possibly the southwestern highlands, has ever offered more than a distinctly marginal environment for non-pastoral cultures.

IV. PREHISTORIC GEOGRAPHY OF EGYPT AND THE NILE VALLEY

During the Pleistocene Period Egypt experienced a sequence of pluvial episodes, while during the Post-Pleistocene Period there were numerous, but modest, changes in the physical environment. Geological, archaeological and historical material in this country is exceptionally rich, so that the evidence in many ways possesses a reliability seldom found in western Asia. The land of Egypt consists of three major features: the alluvial lands of the valley and the delta, the low desert bordering these lands on both flanks, and, beyond, the desert uplands. Each of these units has

[1] §III, 7.

had a different significance for settlement or habitation in the course of time. During the pluvials the entire country appears to have been sparsely, but more or less uniformly, inhabited, whereas during other periods, as indeed today, only the river-valley was capable of supporting life. In other periods, as for example the 'Neolithic' Sub-pluvial (c. 5500–2350 B.C.), considerable parts of the low desert and of the higher desert uplands were occupied by a varied fauna as well as by hunting or pastoral peoples.

During several phases of the Pleistocene Period Egypt experienced a fairly moist climate; both the Nile and its tributaries were able to transport great masses of gravels and sands, eroded from the desert hills.[1] Soils which have developed on these terraces suggest that there was an appreciable vegetation and considerable moisture. Mineralogical investigations of Nile deposits indicate that the Ethiopian waters, which now contribute some 80 per cent of the Nile flow in Egypt, were less significant and possibly provided a much smaller proportion of the Nile waters. To-day the summer rains (May–September) of the Ethiopian highlands lead to a flood-crest in August. North of the Sudanese border, occasional light rains now fall mainly in the winter. If this boundary between the summer monsoonal and the winter cyclonic rains was the same in prehistoric times, the flood waters which were responsible for the widespread erosion and sedimentation in the desert wādis of Egypt would have come in winter, when the Nile was low. Although Nile flood deposition (due to sub-Saharan rainfall) and wādi deposition (due to local rainfall) were going on at the same time[2] they did not occur at the same season. These are some of the imponderable complications involved in seeking to explain the Pleistocene Period in Egypt.

The last major phase of wādi-activity led to the deposition of the 10–15 ft. gravels of Upper Egypt. Most of the wādis south of Asyūt have well-bedded deposits of flint and limestone gravels, which contain a Late Levalloisian industry,[3] and also are graded on to a higher Nile flood-plain. There are no proven contemporary gravels north of Asyūt, probably because the lower river was in the process of deepening its bed. This seems to represent the Early Last Glacial regression of as long as 60,000 years ago. The climate was semi-arid. Middle Palaeolithic surface finds are by no means scarce in the Egyptian deserts.

During or immediately after the 10–15 ft. gravel stage a massive influx of Ethiopian waters and silts took place each

---

[1] §IV, nos. 13, 15, 16, 17; §IV, 14; §IV, 3; §IV, 8.
[2] §IV, 9.   [3] §IV, 10, 57 ff.

summer and early autumn, leading to the deposition of sands, silts and clays. This is our first record of a seasonally inundated flood-plain such as now characterizes the Egyptian Nile valley. Previously, during the earlier stages of the Pleistocene Period, the Nile seems to have flowed over a pebbly bed on at least several occasions, with a more balanced regime of Ethiopian flood waters in summer and of wādi-influx in winter.

The Late Pleistocene alluviation of the Nile valley took place in three stages. The earliest is represented by fine 25 ft. gravels and silts in Lower Egypt and by the 112 ft. Faiyūm lake deposits, both with an Upper Levalloisian industry. In Lower Nubia this same stage built up a flood-plain 110 ft. higher than that of the present day; the local wādis were quite active at the same time. Middle Palaeolithic populations also occupied this area.

The Second Late Pleistocene stage of alluviation followed a lowering of the river bed; related silts can be found up to 100 ft. above the present flood-plain in Lower Nubia, although their level drops rapidly to the north of Aswān. The Egyptian climate was probably arid during much of this time.

After renewed lowering of the river bed the final Late Pleistocene alluvial stage began some 17,000 years ago, lasting through about seven millennia during which local wādi-influx again resumed some of its former importance. The flood-plain sands and silts lie 65 ft. above the present Nile valley in Lower Nubia diminishing to 40 ft. at Sebīl and Kōm Ombo, where a number of Late or Upper Palaeolithic (Sebīlian) groups inhabited the luxuriant vegetation along a number of high Nile channels now abandoned.

This then is the geological picture of the Late Pleistocene Period in Egypt. How did man utilize the flood-plain environment established at this time? Distribution of Upper Palaeolithic artefacts seems to have been concentrated in the neighbourhood of the Nile, so that it can be suggested that man inhabited the flood-plain area, where he could hunt the endemic aquatic and woodland game, as well as the species of the steppe, which came down to drink. Certainly the faunal remains in the later silts, which were largely bone refuse from encampments, indicate a combination of galeria and open-country forms.[1] The Sebīl beds contain hartebeest, isabella gazelle, wild ass, ostrich and spotted hyena as examples of the latter category, while the various species of wild cattle, water buffalo, hippopotamus, crocodile, fish and tortoise reflect the former. The Qāw beds con-

[1] §IV, 4, 20–2.

tain isabella gazelle, bubal and horse in the one category, and
boar, cattle, hippopotamus, crocodile, tortoise and fish in the
other. Both fish and fresh-water molluscs could be readily
obtained in shallow pools after the recession of the flood-waters,
and the Middle Sebīlian sites are already veritable kitchen-
middens. The sites in Nubia and the Faiyūm suggest that fishing
was an important part of the economy of one part of the population in the earliest Neolithic times.

Like the Tigris and Euphrates of Mesopotamia, the Nile
moves across an alluvial flood-plain north of Aswān. After the
onset of the summer monsoon in Ethiopia, the Nile rises and
leaves the low water bed it has cut in the sedimentary plain. The
coarser and hence heavier load, namely the fine- to middle-grained
sands, are deposited, first of all, immediately on the river banks
where the currents and transporting capacity are strongest. The
velocity of the waters diminishes rapidly as the floods spread out
over the alluvial flats, so that transport ability is also reduced.
Only the finer silts and clays are carried beyond the river banks,
where they too are gradually deposited. Hence deposition along
the banks is more rapid and forms levees, which then rise some
5–10 ft. above the general level of the flood-plain.

When the flood-waters begin to recede, these levees are
immediately left dry, while the low-lying basins of the alluvial
flats remain inundated for many months. Only sporadically do
the lowest sections harbour perennial waters in the back swamps.
The ground-water table is quite deep under the levees during the
low-water Nile, whereas it lies above the surface in the area of the
back swamps on the outer margins of the flood-plain. The simple
picture of a natural flood-plain is fundamental to understanding
the possibilities of settlement in the later prehistoric Egypt, and
convincing modern analogies can still be obtained from such
African rivers as the Chari, Logone or Senegal, where man-
made conditions do not obliterate the natural processes involved
in seasonal flooding.

In the Nile delta the pattern is a little more complicated,
because the waters spread out in a broad fan and are distributed
over countless minor branches, which reduce gradient and
current so that the heavier materials are no longer transported.
The levees are appreciably lower and smaller, while the basins
are so low that they often deteriorate into perennial swamps or
lakes. The latter become important at the mouths of the delta,
where they merge into brackish lagoons. These lagoons are cut
off from the sea by sand bars and spits deposited as barriers by

the westerly longshore drift. The interior Nile delta has, however, innumerable coarse sand ridges of variable size, known as 'turtle-backs', which represent remnants of ancient river deposits and provide large expanses of dry, un-inundated country among the maze of distributaries and swampy alluvial flats.

The characteristics of the flood-plain are thus quite distinct from the primitive conditions found in the Sudd swamps of the Bahr el-Ghazal, a comparison which many Egyptologists have tended to accept. The Sudd basin does not have a similar high- and low-water regime, since its waters are not obtained from the monsoon rains of Ethiopia but from the region of the Central African lakes. The flooded area is therefore perennially inundated, with a correspondingly distinct physiography and vegetational association.

The Sudd represents a former lake which is now reduced to a vast marsh; it is not a river flood-plain. This marsh continues to fill up with organic and inorganic sediments, and so the floating islands and the papyrus swamps have become its characteristic features. Levees are poorly developed and there are no seasonally flooded basins, which were the decisive distinguishing marks of the natural flood-plain of the Nile in Egypt at c. 5000 B.C.

The extent of the perennial swamps and lakes in the Nile valley was limited in early settlement times, and the greatest part of the plain consisted, as it does today, of seasonally inundated basins.[1] Woods of Nile acacia, tamarisk (*Tamarix nilotica*, *T. articulata*) as well as sycomore (*Ficus sycomorus*) and Egyptian willow (*Salix safsaf*) crowned the levees. These levees were at all times distinctly inviting to settlement, being submerged for only very short periods of several days at the crest of the flood. The greater number of modern villages, which stand several metres above the plain on the cultural debris of centuries or millennia, were probably at first located on active or abandoned river levees. From the very beginning man could take up his abode on the levees or upon the low desert margins, and after the floods had receded, throw the seeds of his crops upon the wet mud of the basin floors or graze his cattle and other herds on the lush herbaceous and brush vegetation which flourished there. By the time that the waters rose once more, the harvest had been gathered and the livestock could be pastured on the levees or on the desert margins of the alluvium.

The presence of the turtle-backs in the delta area rendered physical conditions there equally good, and indeed the myth of a

[1] § IV, 4, 27–36; abridged translation in §IV, 5, 43 ff.; §IV, 12, 77–152.

delta rapidly expanding seawards in historical times is as unfounded as that of the postulated jungle swamps of the Nile
valley. Numerous bore profiles indicate that the delta coastlines
have shifted very little for at least 8000 years, and the greater part
of the saline flats or central lagoons were probably drained
throughout pre-Moslem times except for a millennium or so in
the Predynastic Period. It is important to remember that the
papyrus swamps and quiet expanses of stagnant water, with the
Egyptian and the blue lotus, sedge and reeds, which were in-
fested by hippopotamus, crocodile and a host of aquatic birds,
constituted only a very small portion of the ancient land of
Egypt.

Ecological conditions outside the Nile flood-plain were comparatively favourable in Neolithic and predynastic times and also
in dynastic times until the Sixth Dynasty. A number of distinct
and culturally dated geological deposits leave no doubt as to the
increased discharge and rubble transport of the desert streams.[1]

Tree roots of acacias, tamarisks(?) and sycomores have been
found on the low desert, well beyond the range of flood-waters or
riverain ground water between Khawālid and Deir Tāsa, and also
at Armant. These are dated between the Badārian Period and the
Fourth Dynasty. Definite confirmation is found on the Fifth and
the Sixth Dynasty reliefs (in the tombs of Ptahhotpe and Mereruka at Saqqara and of Djau at Deir el-Gabrāwi, and in the temples
of Sahure and Nyuserre at Abusīr) which show characteristic,
irregular low desert terrain with acacia and sycomore trees as well
as typical desert shrubs and succulents, and possibly even halfa-
grass. There was then a sparse growth of sycomore, acacia and
tamarisk in an open parkland association with grass tufts and
desert shrubs, which made up an 'acacia desert–grass savanna'
vegetation due to infrequent, but ecologically important rains.
Just as with the acacia scrub of the eastern desert today, such
copses would have been concentrated near or within the wādis,
where accessory ground moisture would have been available.[2]

A third line of evidence is the fauna of the eastern desert, the
Nile valley, the Dākhla area and the Gilf el-Kebīr–Uwaynāt, as
well as the other highlands of the central Sahara. The rock
drawings of these areas show a magnificent array of animals
ranging from elephant, both species of African rhinoceros, giraffe,
oryx, ibex, hartebeest, various gazelles, barbary sheep, wild
donkey to cattle, fallow deer, various larger cats, hyena and

[1] §IV, 4, 48–54; §IV, 5 with references.
[2] §IV, 4, 44–8 with references.

ostrich. The traditional objection to using these drawings as evidence of habitat is that these animals were not actually present in the areas where they are drawn. For each of the Saharan groups (western Tibesti, eastern Tibesti, Uwaynāt–Gilf el-Kebīr and Dākhla-Khārga) there can be little doubt that the autochthonous ethnic groups with individualistic local styles were more or less isolated in their respective regions, leaving little room for itinerant artists. Similarly, the oldest drawings of the 'earliest hunters' in the eastern desert belong to a desert folk with no immediate access to the Nile valley. The boats, hippopotami and crocodiles depicted in the Wādi Hammāmāt are no contradiction, because they are stylistically the work of the Naqāda II culture which had commercial routes to the Red Sea hills. Such 'aquatic' elements are the product of Nile dwellers, who drew familiar scenes from the valley. Another objection is that such drawings are thought to be limited to the sandstone areas. There are, however, a number of sites in the limestone mountains northwest of Luxor.

In the light of this pictorial evidence, which in some instances has been verified palaeontologically, an attempt can be made to draw a sketch of living conditions as reflected in the contemporary distribution of individual species and current rainfall. It has been suggested that the Red Sea hills formerly experienced 4–6 in. of rainfall (compared with a maximum of 0·8 in. today) and the Uwaynāt–Gilf el-Kebīr region 2 in. (instead of the present 0·4 in.). The latitudinal shifts of semi-desert and grassland belts of the north and south are reckoned to have a scope of 50–150 miles, together with a contraction of the axis of the Sahara. The absolute change involved was trivial but of great ecological significance locally. A meagre pastoralism or food gathering existence was thus temporarily feasible over wasteland now uninhabitable.[1] These environmental circumstances also provide a reasonable explanation of the wide distribution of Neolithic implements in the eastern and Libyan deserts of Egypt.

Temporary worsening of conditions is indicated between the Naqāda I and the Naqāda II Periods. Between the First and the Fourth Dynasties, the second and major faunal break, characterized by the disappearance of the rhinoceros, elephant, giraffe, and gerenuk gazelle in Egypt, culminated in the modern aridity by the time of the Sixth Dynasty. Dunes invaded the western margins of Middle Egypt; a series of documents of the First Intermediate Period refers to famines resulting from low Niles

[1] §IV, 1; §IV, 5, 36–43, 54–67.

(rather than from human negligence), and Old Kingdom records indicate a progressive lowering of the Nile flood levels.[1] The period c. 2350–500 B.C. was thus exceptionally unfavourable climatically, but thereafter conditions became more or less those which obtain to-day.

As a last consideration the peculiarities of settlement location[2] in the Predynastic Period can be reviewed very briefly. First, the known predynastic sites from the low desert margins have particular geomorphic situations, which suggest that the apparent settlement gap in Middle Egypt may be adequately explained on the ground of the poor preservation of the sites. Secondly, there was deliberate choice of location on fine-textured unconsolidated sediments, probably for the purpose of sunken-dwelling construction. Thirdly, the population indicated by numerous early cemeteries without corresponding settlement sites, as well as the low population density suggested by known sites, makes it imperative to assume that the majority of villages were located within the flood-plain from the very beginning of agricultural colonization. This then is the pattern of environment and settlement which immediately preceded the dawn of the historical era in Egypt.

[1] For details of evidence and interpretation see §IV, 4, 67–74; §IV, 2; §IV, 6.
[2] §IV, 7.

CHAPTER III

PRIMITIVE MAN IN EGYPT, WESTERN ASIA AND EUROPE

PALAEOLITHIC TIMES

I. EGYPT

THE earliest record of man's presence in Egypt is written in the ancient gravels and silts of the Nile. The pioneer work of Sandford and Arkell in this field,[1] together with that of Caton-Thompson and Gardner in the Faiyūm,[2] set a standard which remains substantially unchallenged, though supplemented by later work—in particular that of Ball[3] and Little.[4]

The Nile valley was already excavated nearly in its present form by the end of the Miocene, but the high sea-level of the Pliocene brought the Mediterranean flooding into the depression, transforming it into a long narrow gulf, reaching as far south as Kōm Ombo in Upper Egypt. Into the southern end of this flooded inlet the Nile and its tributaries continued to pour detritus, until by the end of the Pliocene it was filled almost to water-level. In the Lower Pleistocene the sea withdrew to the north, and the river began to erode its bed in conformity with the falling base-level, with pauses marked by gravel terraces at heights ranging from 90 m. to 45 m. above the present stream. These high-level gravels, which can be traced at intervals from Wādi Halfa to Cairo, contain no traces of man. The first stone implements are found in the 30 m. terrace, the gravels of which have yielded bifaces of Abbevillian and Acheulean types, made from pebbles, or from small boulders of brown chert. Further down-cutting brought the river to 15 m. above its present level, and in the gravels of this stage were found ovate bifaces and discs of Middle Acheulean type, and some later Acheulean forms. Sandford considered that the deposits of the 30 m. and 15 m. terraces suggested the evenly distributed rainfall of temperate latitudes, and took the absence of windborne sand and faceted pebbles to mean that there were at that time no deserts in the region. He thought that the continued down-cutting of the river was caused by the falling level of the Mediterranean, and

[1] §1, 11 ff.   [2] §1, 7.   [3] §1, 1.   [4] §1, 10.

not by increase of volume due to a pluvial period such as is postulated for East Africa at this stage. Nevertheless, in the Khārga oasis, Caton-Thompson and Gardner found clear evidence for two major pluvials,[1] the first, without trace of human activity, corresponding presumably with the high-level gravels of the Nile, while the second, which is associated with a series of industries from the Upper Acheulean to the Levalloiso-Khārgan, covers a part of the later Pleistocene history of the river, beginning with the 15 m. terrace.

After the 15 m. stage, a period of renewed degradation was followed by deposition of gravels at 9 m. above the present stream, and from these came some bifaces of Late Acheulean type, associated with Levallois flakes. Caton-Thompson suggests that this is possibly the same industry as the Acheuleo-Levalloisian of El-Khārga,[2] which shows a similar association.

The Pleistocene history of the Nile is so far fairly straightforward, but after the 9 m. stage it is complicated by the fact that successive degradations in the northern end of its course carried the river far below its present level, with the result that the deposits of the later stages are today deeply buried beneath the modern alluvium. Meanwhile in Upper Egypt a falling-off of water-supply, first sign of a post-pluvial aridity which was later to affect the whole of the Nile valley, had initiated a local phase of aggradation, during which the river, unable to carry its load, had choked the valley with a thick deposit of silt. Without tracing in detail this rather complicated geological story, it is possible to say that at this stage the 8–9 m. aggradation gravels of Middle and Lower Egypt, in so far as they are accessible for study, contain the same flake industry, the Levalloisian, as do the 3–4 m. terrace and the basal silts of Upper Egypt. The Levalloisian is found also in the higher beaches of the Faiyūm lake, which at this time communicated with the Nile through the Hawāra Channel.[3]

The last phase in the Palaeolithic history of the Nile is marked by the appearance of a number of industries derived from the Levalloisian, which in Egypt take the place occupied by the blade-cultures in neighbouring areas (Capsian and Oranian in North Africa, Upper Palaeolithic I–VI in the Levant). Of these, the best-known is the Sebīlian of Upper Egypt, first discovered and studied by Vignard in a number of camp-sites in the plain of Kōm Ombo,[4] but present also in its earlier stages in the degradation gravels and the top of the silts of the river itself.[5]

[1] §1, 8.   [2] §1, 5.   [3] §1, 5; §1, 7; §1, 12.
[4] §1, 15.   [5] §1, 13.

The Kōm Ombo sites were grouped on the rims of dry water-channels, and clearly represent encampments on the shores of streams which were gradually shrinking during the successive Lower, Middle and Upper Sebīlian stages. The industry has clear affinities with the Levalloisian, but the cores and flakes are smaller, and progressively diminish in size, while implements are shaped by a peculiar nibbling retouch. In the Middle Sebīlian, geometric forms begin to appear, and become abundant in the Upper stage. Together with the flints there are stone querns and rubbers, but pottery is always absent. Food remains include bones of aurochs and buffalo and mounds of *Unio* shells.

The great interest of the Sebīlian sequence, as Caton-Thompson has insisted,[1] lies in the demonstration that a people possessing a flake industry which had its origin in the Middle Palaeolithic, and living in a backward area apparently cut off from outside influences, was capable of transforming its age-old culture into a microlithic flake industry with geometric forms, having obvious resemblances to the apparently unrelated microlithic blade industries of neighbouring more progressive areas.

In Lower Egypt also are found a number of industries derived from the Levalloisian, for example, the Diminutive Levalloisian of Huzayyin[2] and the Epi-Levalloisian of Caton-Thompson,[1] which are found widely distributed on the surface, and in the intermediate lake beaches of the Faiyūm. These are poorer in tool-types than the Sebīlian, and Caton-Thompson considers that they developed more or less independently from the Levalloisian, in response to similar environmental changes—changes of a nature unknown to us, but leading to a spontaneous decision that small tools were more useful than larger ones.

In spite of its outstanding part, we are not wholly dependent on the Nile valley for a knowledge of the prehistoric chronology of Egypt. The Khārga oasis, 110 miles to the west of the Nile, intensively studied by Caton-Thompson and Gardner,[3] has produced a large amount of stratified material which supplements the evidence of the river deposits. This great trough-like depression, 115 miles long, lies 400 m. below the surface of the Libyan plateau, touching sea-level at its lowest point. Palaeolithic tools were found in gravels and calcareous tufas of wādis dissecting the limestone scarp of the hollow, and in mounds thrown up on its floor by springs long extinct. The evidence from all these sources combines to make a picture of a climatic curve in which a first major pluvial, and a period of aridity, both without traces of

[1] §1, 5.   [2] §1, 9.   [3] §1, 8.

contemporary human activity, are followed by a second major pluvial covering a succession of industries from the Upper Acheulean, through an Acheuleo-Levalloisian and a Levalloisian proper, to the Levalloiso-Khārgan, which is a variant of the Epi-Levalloisian of the Nile valley with Sebīlian affinities. Following on these, in a stage of increasing aridity, come the Khārgan, which is a more diminutive form of the Levalloiso-Khārgan, and a 'foreign' industry, the Aterian, already well known from north-west Africa and the Sahara.[1] The Aterian, which like the Khārgan has a Levallois ancestry, shows much finer workmanship than do the native Egyptian cultures. Its tool-kit includes two types of projectile head, one a leaf-shaped point flaked over both faces, resembling the Solutrean 'laurel leaf' of Europe, the other a tanged point made from a triangular flake. These are the weapons of a skilful and possibly aggressive people, as is shown by their penetration to El-Khārga, 1400 miles east of their North African homeland.

The correlation of the Nile terraces with the raised shore-lines of the Mediterranean, and through them with the European glacial chronology, has given rise to much discussion and wide divergence of views.[2] Similarly the correspondence of the pluvials of the Khārga oasis with glacial advances remains uncertain. In a general way the best that can be said is that the older industries, Abbevillian, Acheulean and Levalloisian, are probably more or less contemporary with their European equivalents, while the Levalloisian derivatives, Sebīlian, Epi-Levalloisian, Levalloiso-Khārgan and Khārgan cover the time-span which in Europe is occupied by the blade-cultures of the Upper Palaeolithic.

As in the Levant, it is not easy in Egypt to fix the borderline between the Palaeolithic and the Mesolithic. We have seen that the Upper Sebīlian of Kōm Ombo presents the case of an Epi-Levalloisian industry, apparently still of Pleistocene age, evolving spontaneously towards the geometrical microlithic forms which characterize the Mesolithic over so wide an area. The Epi-Levalloisian of Lower Egypt, on the other hand, shows no such tendency,[3] but true blade-microlithic assemblages, presumed to be post-Palaeolithic and pre-Neolithic, are found in scatters on the surface in this region, and at least one of these, at Helwān, has affinities with the Mesolithic Natufian of Palestine.[4] At El-Khārga too there is an apparent break between the Khārgan and

---

[1] §1, 6.
[2] §1, 1 ; §1, 5 ; §1, 16, 232 f.
[3] §1, 5, 112 ff.
[4] §1, 9, 270, 288 ff.

the 'bedawin' microlithic, a non-geometric industry with transverse arrow-heads.[1] All this presents a rather confused picture; what is certain is that the life of the hunters and gatherers was coming to an end. The next scene in Egyptian prehistory opens with the first Neolithic settlements of the Faiyūm,[2] in which a microlithic element surviving from an earlier time is finally swamped by new kinds of artefacts and a new way of life.

No fossil human remains have yet been found in Egypt, but its cultural isolation during the Upper Pleistocene suggests the possibility that the makers of the various industries which derive from the Levalloisian may have been lingering survivors of a race having Neanderthal affinities, who were not displaced by men of modern type before Mesolithic times. This, of course, is mere speculation, which can be proved or disproved only by the discovery of skeletal remains.

II. WESTERN ASIA IN GENERAL

Western Asia today can be roughly divided into sea coast, mountain and desert, with one great fertile basin, the Valley of the Two Rivers. Anatolia is predominantly a land of mountains, from which two main branches, the coastal mountains of the Mediterranean shore, and the parallel ranges of the Zagros arc, run south-west and south-east respectively. Between the two, the northern part of the vast Arabian desert separates the Tigris–Euphrates basin from the valley of the Jordan. The River Jordan, the most remarkable single feature of the whole region, in a course of 150 miles from northern Galilee to the Dead Sea, runs for most of the way below sea-level, and the cleft which contains it can be traced southward through the Red Sea to the Zambezi. The tectonic movements which created this great rift seem to have ended, as far as Palestine is concerned, not later than the Early Pleistocene, and there has probably been little physiographical change in the whole West Asian area since the Middle Pleistocene. Variations of climate, though certain, were apparently not catastrophic. The glaciations of Northern Europe brought cool, moist periods, of which traces remain in alluvial and cave deposits, but the three Mediterranean Pluvials do not seem to have been comparable in intensity with those of Equatorial Africa.[3] Old shore-lines, which are well marked along the coasts of Syria and the Lebanon, at heights ranging from 95 m. to 6–8 m. above present sea-level, correspond with interglacial or

[1] §1, 8, 32 ff.   [2] §1, 7.   [3] §11, 3, 1 ff; §111, 18 and 19.

interstadial periods, but neither for pluvial nor for marine deposits has the correlation with European stages yet been worked out with complete certainty.[1] Semi-arid regions, such as Palestine, must have enjoyed a better water-supply and more trees than they do today, while the presence of stone implements widely scattered on the surface of the North Arabian Desert testifies that a part at least of this rocky waste was then more or less habitable.[2]

From the prehistoric point of view Western Asia can be divided into four regions, which must be considered separately. These are the coast and coastal ranges of Syria–Lebanon–Palestine,[3] the mountains and high plateau of Anatolia, the North Arabian Desert (which politically is divided between Syria, Jordan and Iraq), and the mountains of southern Kurdistān. In the Tigris–Euphrates basin any Palaeolithic remains which may exist are buried so deep that they have not so far been recovered, and the terraces of the Jordan between the Sea of Galilee and the Dead Sea have yielded no traces of early occupation.

III. SYRIA–LEBANON–PALESTINE

The oldest industry so far known in this area comes from Jisr Banāt Ya'qūb, in Upper Galilee, and was revealed by drainage work carried out in the bed of the Jordan between Lake Ḥūleh and the Sea of Galilee between 1933 and 1950.[4] The bed of the river was dug to a depth of 5·50 m., and four layers of clay and soil were found between an upper and a lower gravel. The oldest soil (Bed V) yielded a large number of basalt hand-axes and cleavers of Lower Acheulean type, associated with bones of elephant (probably *Elephas trogontherii*). Beds IV and III contained flint bifaces of Middle Acheulean type, also with *E. trogontherii*, and Bed II, Late Acheulean bifaces with bones of horse. Finally in Bed I, the Upper Gravel, came Levallois flakes and cores. The Lower Acheulean of Bed V is the oldest industry so far found in a stratified deposit in the Levant, and its interest is increased by its association with a characteristic fauna. Apart from Jisr Banāt Ya'qūb, and a rather sparse Middle Acheulean from the slope breccia of the +45 m. shore-line at Ras Beirut,[5] the early biface industries are known only from surface finds, or from alluvial deposits of uncertain age, as in the wādis around

[1] §II, 3, 3 ff.   [2] §II, 3, 6 f.
[3] For convenience, the traditional name is used throughout for the country west of Jordan, in place of actual political divisions.
[4] §III, 22.   [5] §III, 3.

Gaza, or the gravel beds of Rephāīm-Biqā', near the Jerusalem railway station.[1]

Only slightly younger than the Middle Acheulean is an industry of choppers, chopping-tools and rough flakes, very like the Tayacian of Europe. This has been found in abundance in the *cordon littoral* which marks the beginning of regression from the + 45 m. shore-line at Ras Beirut (?Tyrrhenian I),[2] while a scanty flake industry found in relation with the + 45 m. level at Bahsas, in the North Lebanon, probably belongs to a slightly later stage of the same regression.[3]

Signs of the Levallois technique of flint working are already visible in the Tayacian, and following on the *cordon littoral* at Ras Beirut the ancient sub-aerial deposits of the + 45 m. terrace contain several stages of the Lower Levalloisian.[2] A more evolved Levalloisian industry occurs in the beach deposits of the + 15– 18 m. shore-line (?Tyrrhenian II) both at Ras Beirut[2] and in the Bay of Shakkah in the North Lebanon.[3] In the sub-aerial deposits of the same terrace, the Levalloisian shows an evolution towards the Levalloiso-Mousterian, or Mousterian of Levallois facies, which is the most widespread of the Middle Palaeolithic industries of the Levant. In this, the prepared flint cores and resulting flakes are of Levallois type, but the secondary retouch and shaping of the implements are typically Mousterian. The Levalloiso-Mousterian is above all an industry of the caves, but it is known from open-air sites, and along the coast it occurs in fossil dunes which are certainly later than the + 6–8 m. shore-line, for example, in the coastal ridge at 'Atlīt, in North Palestine[4] and in the sands of Ras Beirut.[2]

At this point we must turn to the many caves, which in this region are particularly rich in prehistoric remains. The oldest industry so far found in a cave is a Tayacian characterized by small irregular flakes, the majority with plain striking-platform. The edges are often broken by use, but seldom intentionally retouched. This industry has been found in two Palestinian sites, the Ṭābūn cave of the Wādi el-Maghārah group on Mount Carmel,[5] and the cave of Umm Qaṭafah in the Judaean desert.[6] At the Ṭābūn, the Tayacian deposits had been sucked down into a swallow-hole in the rock, and at Umm Qaṭafah also they were contained in dissolution cavities in the cave floor. In both cases, animal remains at the base of the deposits were reduced to a few fossilized millipedes, but in the Upper Tayacian horizons of

[1] §III, 21.   [2] §III, 3.   [3] §III, 26.
[4] §III, 10.   [5] §III, 9, 89 f.   [6] §III, 16, 29 ff.

Umm Qaṭafah, Neuville found bones of horse (*Equus* cf. *mauritanicus* Pomel), gazelle, red deer and fallow deer. This is the fauna which, with some additions and variations, was to persist until the closing stages of the Middle Palaeolithic in the Levant. Neuville considered the Tayacian of Umm Qaṭafah to be contemporary with that of Bahsas, and to date from the end of the Interpluvial which preceded Pluvial B of the East Mediterranean.

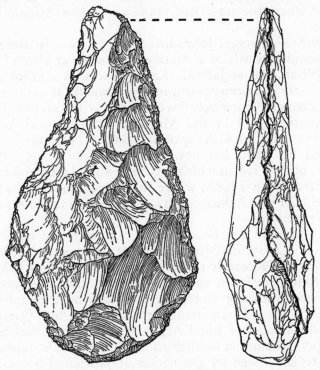

Fig. 2. Late Acheulean biface, Jabrud. Re-drawn after Rust (1/2).

The Ṭābūn industry, which shows more secondary retouch and a larger number of definite tool types, appears to be more recent, and Neuville places it at the end of Pluvial B. Clark Howell,[1] however, pointing out that there are no clear indications of the damp climate originally postulated by Garrod and Bate,[2] prefers a last Interpluvial age.[3]

[1] §ɪɪ, 3, 9 f.   [2] §ɪɪɪ, 9.
[3] The opinions of Neuville and Howell are not shared by Vaufrey, an extreme supporter of a short chronology, who would place the entire cycle of deposition of the Palestinian caves in the last Glaciation, §ɪɪɪ, 25.

Next in the cave succession comes a Late Acheulean with pear-shaped bifaces (Figs. 2 and 3), which is present at Jabrud[1] in Western Syria, in a rock-shelter facing towards the desert from the eastern slope of the Antilebanon, at Umm Qatafah[2] and at the Ṭābūn.[3] At Umm Qatafah *Rhinoceros merckii* Jaeger first appears in this horizon, whereas in the Ṭābūn it arrives only in the succeeding Jabrudian. This industry is probably more recent than the Upper Acheulean from Bed II of Jisr Banāt Yaʿqūb,[4] where the associated fauna suggests a Middle Pleistocene age.

The following stage, Jabrudian (Fig. 3), was discovered more or less simultaneously in a stratified sequence at Umm Qatafah, in the Ṭābūn, and at Jabrud. Later, it was recognized that the same industry had been present in a rock-shelter at ʿAdlūn,[5] in the South Lebanon, tentatively investigated at the end of the nineteenth century, and in the Maghārat ez-Zuttīyah[6] in Lower Galilee, in association with the Galilee skull.[7] The name Jabrudian, first used by Rust, has now been generally adopted for this industry, but the site in which it is most abundantly and typically represented is the Ṭābūn, where the Jabrudian deposits (originally labelled Final Acheulean) had a maximum thickness of more than seven metres.

The Jabrudian has little in common with the more widely distributed Levalloiso-Mousterian. It is characterized by an abundance of elaborately retouched scrapers on thick flakes with plain striking-platform, and both in technique and typology it has affinities with the European Mousterian facies now sometimes described as Charentian. At Zuttīyah, Umm Qatafah and the Ṭābūn, bifaces of Final Acheulean type are associated with the scrapers, though in smaller numbers, whereas at Jabrud there appears to have been an alternation of Jabrudian horizons with and without bifaces. An important feature is the presence at Jabrud and the Ṭābūn, in the upper half of the Jabrudian, of a blade industry of definite Upper Palaeolithic aspect, Rust's 'pre-Aurignacian', characterized by a fine 'nibbled' retouch of the edges (Fig. 4). At Jabrud, where the number of flints at all levels was relatively small, it was possible to distinguish two well-marked pre-Aurignacian layers, unmixed with Jabrudian, but in the Ṭābūn, although the blade-tools appeared at definite

---

[1] §III, 20. More properly Yabrūd, but the form with initial J seems to have established itself (Ed.).

[2] §III, 16 and 17.   [3] §III, 9.   [4] §III, 22.

[5] §III, 27 and 28.   [6] §III, 24.   [7] §III, 24.

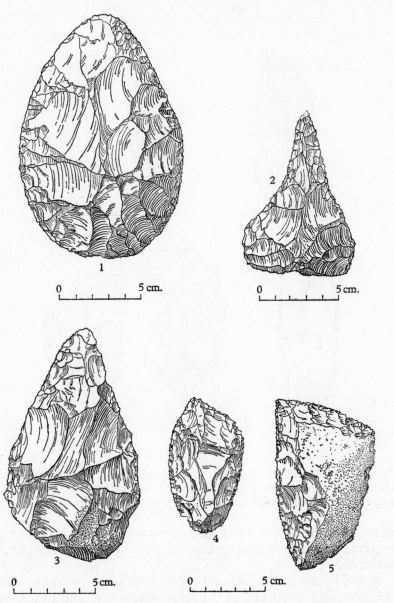

Fig. 3. No. 1, Late Acheulean biface, Ṭābūn; nos. 2, 3, Jabrudian bifaces, Ṭābūn; nos. 4, 5, Jabrudian scrapers, Ṭābūn. Re-drawn after Garrod.

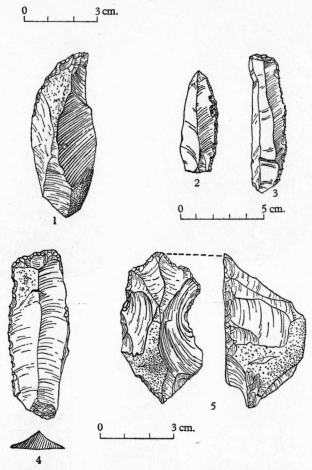

Fig. 4. Upper Palaeolithic Stage 0 (Pre-Aurignacian): no. 1, blunted-back knife, Jabrud; nos. 2, 3, nibbled blades, Ṭābūn; no. 4, nibbled blade, Jabrud; no. 5, steep scraper, Jabrud. Re-drawn after Rust (1, 4, 5) and Garrod (2, 3).

levels, they could not be separated from the mass of Jabrudian implements which surrounded and obscured the pre-Aurignacian horizons.[1]

Neuville, on geological and palaeontological grounds, placed the Jabrudian at the end of the Last Interpluvial and in the early stages of the Third Pluvial, that is, in the Last Interglacial and the beginning of Würm I.[2] Recent excavations in the Abri Zumoffen at 'Adlūn have provided a tie-up with the Lebanese shore-lines which tends to confirm this dating.[3] The pre-Aurig-

[1] §III, 8; §III, 9, 67, 81 ff.   [2] §III, 16, 261.   [3] §III, 12.

nacian was found in a land-surface intercalated in a fossil beach
at + 1 2 m. above present sea-level, and on the surface of the same
beach. Overlying the pre-Aurignacian horizons was a Jabrudian
with bifaces, which must belong to the early stage of the regression from the + 1 2 m. shore-line. The exact relation of the 'Adlūn
beach to the + 1 5 m. shore-line (? Tyrrhenian II) is not yet clear, but
Zeuner does not hesitate to place it late in the Last Interglacial.

The Jabrudian is confined to a small number of sites in the
Levant, and it disappears as suddenly as it arrives. The temptation to look for origins farther east has been somewhat strengthened by recent finds at the oasis of Qaṣr el-'Azraq, in the western
fringe of the North Arabian Desert,[1] but there is so far no trace
of this industry in Iraq or in Iran.

At the Ṭābūn, the massive Jabrudian deposits were covered
by another 1 4 m. containing four stages of Levalloiso-Mousterian.[2] The relative position of the two industries is thus firmly
established, and is confirmed at Jabrud,[3] although Rust's very
complex nomenclature rather obscures this fact.

The Levalloiso-Mousterian (Fig. 5) has been divided into
Lower and Middle, or Lower, Middle and Upper stages, by
different excavators, but its essential features—Levallois flaking
technique, combined with Mousterian retouch and typology—
are the same all through. The nature of the deposits in several
caves, together with indications from the fauna, suggest that the
whole of the Levalloiso-Mousterian falls within the early stage of
the Last Pluvial, therefore most probably in the early Würm.[4]
Recent excavation of a cave at Ras el-Kelb,[5] to the north of
Beirut, has confirmed that a Levalloiso-Mousterian for which a
carbon-14 date of more than 5 2,000 years (Groningen 2 5 5 6) has
been obtained, is posterior to the + 6–8 m. shore-line (? Tyrrhenian III).

Between 1 9 2 7 and 1 9 3 5 remains of a hitherto unknown race
of fossil man were found in four Palestinian caves. The Galilee
skull, the first to be discovered,[6] belongs almost certainly to the
Jabrudian, and is of a slightly more archaic type than the others,
all of which date from the Levalloiso-Mousterian.[7] Two caves
of the Wādi al-Maghārah group, the Maghārat es-Sukhūl, and
the Ṭābūn, yielded remains of eleven individuals, four nearly
complete, all buried intentionally.[8] The bodies lay in various
positions, on the back, side or face, but always with the legs

---

[1] §v, 4, 8 f.   [2] §iii, 9.   [3] §iii, 20.
[4] §ii, 3, 18–24.   [5] §iii, 11.   [6] §iii, 24.
[7] See below, ch. v.   [8] §iii, 9; §iii, 15.

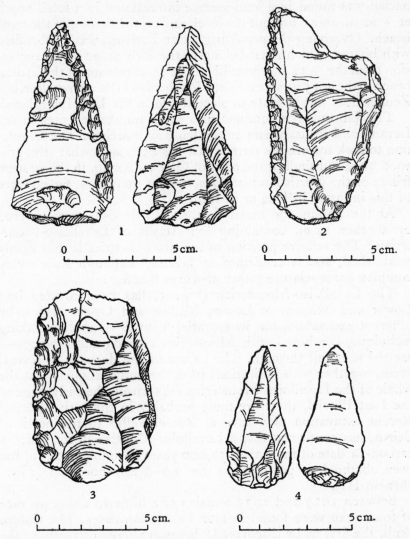

Fig. 5. Nos. 1–3, Levalloiso-Mousterian, point and scrapers, Ṭābūn; no. 4, Upper Palaeolithic Stage 1, Emīreh point, Maghārat el-Wād. Re-drawn after Garrod.

flexed. One man held in the crook of his arm the jawbone of a wild pig, probably a food-offering. All the Wādi el-Maghārah bodies come from the Lower or Middle Levalloiso-Mousterian, as do five fragmentary skeletons, still unpublished, from the Jebel Qafzah cave, near Nazareth.[1]

[1] §II, 2.

These people belong to a type intermediate between Neanderthal and modern man, and they show marked variations from individual to individual. The majority have the heavy Neanderthal brow ridges, though with a higher skull, and in most cases with a well-marked chin. The stature on the whole is greater than in Neanderthal man, and with few exceptions the long bones are of modern type. Keith and McCown considered the Carmel race to be 'in the throes of evolutionary change';[1] others have preferred the theory of hybridization between a Neanderthaloid and a modern type of man.[2] A quarter of a century after the discoveries on Mount Carmel this question is still in debate, but the theory of hybridization has been weakened by the fact that we still have no trace of the pure races of *Homo neanderthalensis* and *Homo sapiens*, whose existence side by side would be required if intermarriage were to take place.

Whether Carmel man be regarded as an evolutionary or a hybrid type, it is interesting to note that the industries made by him also show a certain mixture of characters, and that the passage from the Middle to the Upper Palaeolithic is more gradual in the Levant than in Western Europe. We have first the very early appearance of a blade industry, the pre-Aurignacian, and although this has a relatively short life, blade-tools persist in fair numbers all through the Levalloiso-Mousterian, until in the first stage of the Upper Palaeolithic we reach a definite transitional industry.[3] Even in the later Upper Palaeolithic stages there is a persistence of Levalloiso-Mousterian tools and flakes, though in dwindling numbers as time goes on.[4]

In contrast with Egypt, the Upper Palaeolithic industries of the Levant have European affinities, and attempts have been made to identify them with various European stages. But in spite of resemblances, in particular with the Aurignacian, the two sequences are very different, and for the present it seems better to adopt Neuville's non-committal classification, in which the blade industries of Syria–Lebanon–Palestine are simply numbered Upper Palaeolithic Stages 1–6.[5] This also makes it possible to use the label Upper Palaeolithic o for the awkwardly named pre-Aurignacian.

The only site in which the Upper Palaeolithic sequence appears to be complete is the rock-shelter called Ksar Akil, near Anṭilyās, in the Lebanon.[6] The oldest industry is Upper Leval-

[1] §III, 15.   [2] §II, 2.   [3] §III, 5 ; §III, 7 ; §III, 13.
[4] §III, 6.   [5] §II, 1 ; §II, 3 ; §III, 16.
[6] §III, 1 ; §III, 2.

loiso-Mousterian, and above this an important transitional horizon introduces a long series of Upper Palaeolithic occupation levels. Good sequences, though less complete, were found at the Maghārat el-Wād,[1] and the Kabārah cave,[2] on Mount Carmel, at 'Irq el-Aḥmar in the Judaean Desert,[3] and at Jabrud.[4]

Upper Palaeolithic Stage 1, the transitional horizon mentioned above, for which Emiran, from the Emīreh cave in Galilee, is a possible alternative name, contains a flake and core element which is identical with that of the Upper Levalloiso-Mousterian, associated with blades and blade-cores and curved knife-blades with blunted back which resemble those of the Chatelperronian.

Stage 2 has been found only in a very few sites, where it is poorly represented, and its separate existence is not absolutely certain. Neuville describes it as having blunted-backed blades intermediate between the Chatelperron and La Gravette types;[5] the Levallois element is still present, but the proportion is smaller than in Stage 1.

Stages 3–4 (Fig. 6) have fairly close affinities with the Aurignacian, more marked in 4 than in 3. They have typical carinated and rostrate scrapers, beaked burins, and profuse secondary retouch of the edges of flake and blade tools. Characteristic of 3 are bladelets with fine sharpening retouch at the tip. The Levallois element is still present in 3, but falls off in 4. For these two stages the name Antelian (from the Cave of Anṭilyās where they were first described) has been suggested, and may eventually be adopted.

Stage 5 is a very specialized development of Stage 4, known only from two sites, the Maghārat el-Wād,[6] where it was originally described under the name of Atlitian, and the shelter of el-Khiām in the Judaean Desert.[7] Steep scrapers and prismatic burins far outnumber all other tools.

Stage 6 marks a definite change. The characteristic tool is a small, very narrow, sharply pointed blunted-backed blade; this is accompanied by burins and scrapers in small numbers, but the characteristic Aurignacian forms have disappeared. At Kabārah, where it was first identified,[8] this industry was named Kabaran. It is present, with local variations, at Ksar Akil,[9] at Jabrud, where Rust has named it Nebekian,[10] at El-Khiām,[11] and on the western border of the North Arabian Desert at Wādi Dhubay[12] and in a rock-shelter near Petra.[13]

[1] §III, 9.   [2] §III, 6.   [3] §III, 16.
[4] §III, 20.   [5] §III, 16.   [6] §III, 9.
[7] §III, 16.   [8] §III, 23.   [12] §V, 7.   [9] §III, 1; §III, 2.
[10] §III, 20.   [11] §III, 16.   [13] §V, 5.

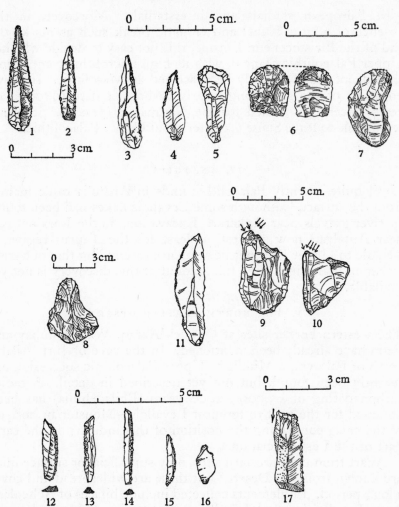

Fig. 6. Upper Palaeolithic Stages 3–6. U.P. 3: nos. 1–4, points, Jabrud (1, 2), Maghārat el-Wād (3, 4); nos. 5–7, scrapers, Maghārat el-Wād. U.P. 4: no. 8, rostrate scraper, Maghārat el-Wād. U.P. 5: nos. 9, 10, prismatic scrapers; no. 11, blunted-back knife, Maghārat el-Wād. U.P. 6: nos. 12–15, microlithic blades; no. 16, micro-burin; no. 17, burin, Jabrud. Re-drawn after Garrod (3–11) and Rust (12–17).

The evidence for climatic conditions in various sites is conflicting,[1] and at present it does not seem possible to say more than that the Upper Palaeolithic in the Levant falls within the second half of the Last Pluvial, without attempting a closer correlation

[1] §II, 3.

with European stadials and interstadials. Moreover, in the absence of a clear faunal and climatic break such as marks the end of the Pleistocene in Europe, it is not easy to decide whether Upper Palaeolithic Stage 6, with its high microlithic component, should not more properly be described as Mesolithic. In view, however, of the surprisingly early carbon-14 date (9800±240 years) recently obtained for the Natufian of Jericho,[1] it seems reasonable to leave Stage 6 as a terminal Upper Palaeolithic.

IV. ANATOLIA

Until quite recently Palaeolithic finds in Anatolia came mainly from the surface,[2] although some Levallois flakes had been found in river gravels near Ankara.[3] Excavations in the Kara'in cave, near Antalya,[4] now suggest, at least for the Taurus region, a Middle to Upper Palaeolithic sequence resembling that of Syria–Lebanon–Palestine, but a full account of this discovery is not yet available.

V. THE NORTH ARABIAN DESERT

The western border sites at Qaṣr el-'Azraq, Wādi Dhubay and Petra have already been mentioned. In the cave of Jurf 'Ajlah,[5] north of Palmyra, a Middle to Upper Palaeolithic succession has recently been found, but not yet described in detail. A radio-carbon dating of 43,000 ± 2000 years (Philadelphia) has been obtained for the next to topmost Levalloiso-Mousterian horizon of the cave, confirming the position of this industry in the early part of the Last Glaciation.[6]

Apart from these western sites, only superficial or surface finds are known from the Desert,[7] but these are widespread and cover a long period. Implements collected include bifaces of Acheulean type, Levalloisian and Levalloiso-Mousterian flakes and cores, and some Upper Palaeolithic steep and rostrate scrapers. The bulk of the desert material is, however, post-Palaeolithic, probably Mesolithic or later.

VI. SOUTHERN KURDISTĀN

In Iraq and western Iran Palaeolithic finds up to the present are confined to the foothills and middle slopes of the mountains which build up the Zagros arc. At Barda-Balka,[8] in the Chamchamāl

---

[1] §III, 14. [2] §IV, 2; §IV, 4; §IV, 5; §IV, 6. [3] §IV, 1.
[4] §IV, 3. [5] §V, 2. [6] §V, 2; §III, 2, 23.
[7] §V, 1; §V, 3; §V, 6. [8] §VI, 9.

plain, a gravel bed dated to the Last Pluvial contained an assemblage with worked river-pebbles, flake tools and a few bifaces on flakes, which seems to represent a local Mousterian facies, differing from that of the caves. Higher up in the mountains a number of caves have yielded stages of the Middle and Upper Palaeolithic, the oldest industry being Mousterian. The latter is known from four caves, Hazār Mard,[1] near Sulaimaniyyah, where it was first discovered, Shanidar,[2] in the region of Ruwāndiz, Babkhal,[3] on the edge of the Diyana plain, and Bīsetūn,[4] just over the Iranian frontier. Upper Palaeolithic industries have been found at Zarzī,[5] Pawli-Gawra and other caves in the Sulaimaniyyah area,[6] and at Shanidar.

The Mousterian of southern Kurdistān is characterized by narrow subtriangular points, heavily retouched, and narrow scrapers (Fig. 7). Although a fair proportion of the implements and flakes have faceted striking-platforms, this is not an industry of Levallois facies. A Groningen radio-carbon dating for the upper part of the Mousterian deposits at Shanidar gives 50,000 ± 3000–4000 years, with a 10 per cent possibility that it is older than 60,000 years.[7] This corresponds well with the older stage of the Levantine Levalloiso-Mousterian. Three human skeletons were found fairly deep in the Mousterian at Shanidar; these have not yet been published in detail, but it appears that they are, on the whole, of the same type as Mount Carmel Man.[7]

The older stages of the Upper Palaeolithic are known only from Shanidar,[8] where the 9 m. thick Mousterian deposit was followed by 3 m. containing a rather poor blade industry. The implements comprise polyhedric and angle-burins in fair numbers, notched flakes and blades, small, rather rough core-scrapers, but very few blade-scrapers. This is quite unlike the Upper Palaeolithic of the Levant, and it has been given a distinctive name, Baradostian, after the Baradost mountain in which the cave lies. Two radio-carbon dates are available for the Baradostian; the first (Washington) gives more than 34,000 years for the lower part, and 29,000 ± 1500 years for the upper, the second (Lamont) gives 32,300 ± 3000 years for the lower, and 26,500 ± 1500 years for the upper. The two are in substantial agreement, and place the Baradostian in the main stage of the Last Glaciation.[9]

Between the Baradostian and the final Upper Palaeolithic, the

[1] §vi, 4.   [2] §vi, 5–8.   [3] §vi, 2.
[4] §vi, 3.   [5] §vi, 4.   [6] §vi, 1.
[7] §vi, 8.   [8] §vi, 5 to 7.   [9] §vi, 5 to 7; §ii, 3, 28.

Zarzian, there is a gap attested by the unconformity of the two layers at Shanidar, and by the radio-carbon datings (Washington) which give 12,000 ± 400 years for the lower part of the Zarzian

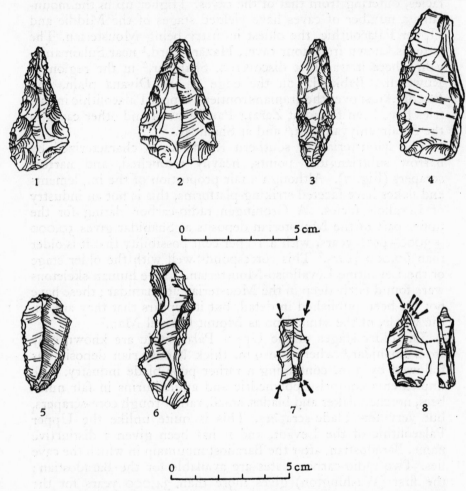

0   5 cm.

0   5 cm.

Fig. 7. Southern Kurdistān. Mousterian: nos. 1, 2, points; nos. 3, 4, scrapers, Shanidar. Baradostian: no. 5, end-scraper; no. 6, notched blade; nos. 7, 8, burins, Shanidar. Re-drawn after Solecki.

deposit, and about 10,650 years for the upper.[1] Howell suggests that the hiatus may correspond with the Late Glacial,[2] when there would be a maximum extension of mountain glaciation in the Zagros. Other sites do not throw any light on this question,

[1] §vi, 6 and 7.   [2] §ii, 3, 29.

as, with the exception of a scatter on the surface of the Mousterian at Hazār Mard,[1] and possibly at Babkhal,[2] the Zarzian is found in isolation.

The Zarzian is a rather elegant industry, with abundant notched blades, round and steep scrapers, shouldered arrow-points and Gravette-like blunted-back knives. All these imple-ments are small, and there are also some true microlithic lunates and triangles.[1] The notched blades form a link with the larger and rougher specimens of the Baradostian, and it is just possible there may be an evolutionary connexion, but there is nothing in the older industry which foreshadows the Gravette blades and shouldered points. The radio-carbon dates show that the Zarzian is older than the Natufian and it is therefore almost certainly approximately contemporary with Stage 6 of the Upper Palaeolithic of the Levant.

VII. WESTERN ASIA: CONCLUSIONS

For the region of Western Asia which has so far been most extensively explored, that is, Syria–Lebanon–Palestine, we are now able to present a more or less complete succession, from Middle to Upper Palaeolithic, with geochronological evidence, and a small number of radio-carbon dates. Next in importance comes southern Kurdistan[3], first tested in 1928, and more closely explored since 1950. Enough has now been recovered to give a picture, less complete than that of the Levant, but in which something more than a rough outline is visible, and with an important set of radio-carbon dates. If the two regions are com-pared, it becomes clear that we are dealing with two distinct culture areas. The contrast is less marked between the Levalloiso-Mousterian and the Mousterian of Kurdistan than between Upper Palaeolithic Stages 1–6 and the Baradost–Zarzi group of industries. Stages 1 and 2 of the Levant look like a native blade industry, developed on the spot from the Levalloiso-Mousterian, but after this an outside influence appears, definitely Aurignacian, and probably derived from Central Europe.[4] In southern Kur-distān, the Baradostian has no close affinity with any known blade industry, least of all with the Aurignacian, but in the Zarzian, the shouldered points and Gravette blades suggest the possibility— no more—of a contact with the Eastern Gravettian, presumably by way of southern Russia, through the Caucasus and along the valleys of the Zagros arc.[5]

[1] §vi, 4.   [2] §vi, 2.   [3] See Fig. 7.
[4] §ii, 1, 35; §ii, 3, 42.   [5] §ii, 1, 22; §ii, 3, 43.

MESOLITHIC TIMES

VIII. NEOTHERMAL ENVIRONMENT AND ITS IMPACT

The Mesolithic hunter-fishers,[1] who occupied Europe, much of
the Mediterranean strip of North Africa and extensive tracts of
Western Asia between the end of the Ice Age and the progressive
establishment of Neolithic culture based on farming, stemmed
directly or indirectly from the Upper Palaeolithic peoples whose
territories extended from the Atlantic Ocean to the mountain
backbone of Inner Asia. Their economy and general way of life
show this, as well as many details of their technology, and in some
cases there is even a high degree of continuity in the actual choice
and occupation of settlement sites.

Yet although, in some territories more markedly than in others,
the Mesolithic peoples were in essence epi-Palaeolithic, they
developed a number of features peculiar to their particular phase
of prehistory. Beyond a doubt the most important factors
involved were the complex changes in the physical environment
that marked the onset of Neothermal conditions at the close of
the Ice Age and the adjustments to these made by the hunter-
fishers themselves. In the temperate zone the onset of Neothermal—and specifically Post-glacial—times is conventionally
defined by the withdrawal of the Scandinavian ice-sheet from its
final (Fenno-Scandian) moraines, an event dated by counts of the
clay varves deposited in its melt-waters and substantially confirmed by radio-carbon dating, at c. 8300 B.C.[2] During the final
phases of the Late-glacial period higher temperatures temporarily
prevailed on more than one occasion before the final melting, the
last being named after the Danish locality of Allerød where
evidence for it was first recognized. Traces of this Allerød oscillation (c. 10,000–8800 B.C.) form a convenient marker,[3] since
they have not only been recognized in Europe as far west as
Ireland and as far south as the Pyrenees, but even have their
counterpart in the Two Creeks stage of North America. The
final cold (Younger Dryas) phase immediately following the
Allerød, though well defined in temperate Europe, apparently
had no equivalent fluctuation in the semi-tropical zone, where
Neothermal conditions seem to have set in at the time of the
Allerød oscillation. During the Anathermal phase of Post-glacial
climate temperatures rose steadily from a mean July reading of
c. 8° C. to c. 14° C.[4] Thereafter during Altithermal times they

[1] §VIII, 2.   [2] §VIII, 7.   [3] §VIII, 7, 9.   [4] §IX, 5.

reached some $2\frac{1}{2}°$ C. above that prevailing today in the same part of the world. The increase of temperature during Post-glacial times must have encouraged settlement in the open, but more important were its indirect results.

Table 3. The course of ecological change in the West Baltic area since 10,000 B.C.

B.C.			CLIMATE (Blytt-Sernander)	(Godwin)	(Jessen)	VEGETATION	BALTIC PHASES (Munthe)
	POST-GLACIAL	MEDI-THERMAL / ALTI-THERMAL / THERMAL					
500			Sub-Atlantic	VIII	IX		IV
			Sub-Boreal	VIIb	VIII	Progressive clearance of	Litorina III Sea II
3000						OMF : farming	I
5000			Atlantic	VIIa	VII	Alder, oak-mixed-forest (oak, elm,	
					VI	lime)	Ancylus
	ANA-THERMAL	THERMAL	Boreal				Lake
					V	Pine, hazel	
						Pine, birch, willow	
			Pre-Boreal		IV	Birch, pine, willow	Yoldia Sea
			Retreat from Fenno-Scandian moraines				
8300	LATE-GLACIAL		Younger Dryas		III	Tundra/Park tundra	Ice-dammed
8800							lake
			Allerød		II	Park tundra/Birch	
10,000			Older Dryas		I	Tundra	

The Pleistocene ice-sheets had already shrunk notably, so that their continued retreat from their last moraine merely emphasized processes which had already been long in train, notably the iso-static recovery of land-masses locally depressed by ice-sheets and the world-wide eustatic rise of sea-levels. At the beginning of Post-glacial times sea-levels in north-western Europe were still something like 150 feet lower than they are today, so that the greater part of the North Sea was still dry land, even if much of it was occupied by extensive fens ;[1] and Jutland, the Danish islands and South Sweden formed part of the continental land-mass. At the same time most of the Scandinavian peninsula remained iso-statically depressed, so that sea-levels, especially towards the heads of the fjords, were higher than today ; yet before long middle Sweden rose high enough to cut off the waters of the Baltic which was thus converted from a branch of the sea (Yoldia Sea) into a lake (the Ancylus lake). As temperatures rose

[1] §VIII, 6.

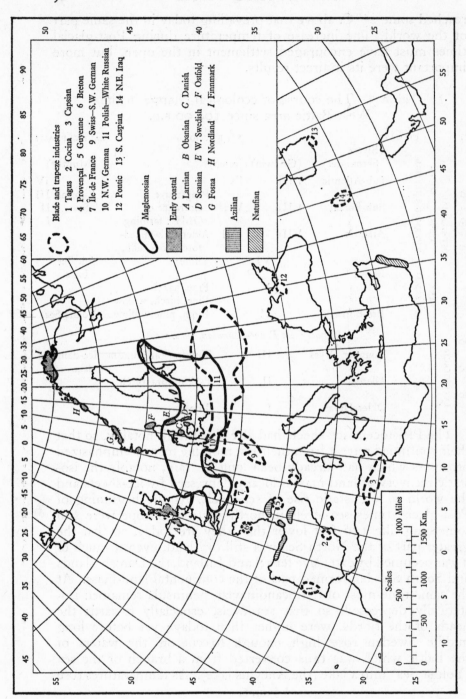

Map. 9. The principal Mesolithic cultures of Europe and proximate parts of North Africa and Western Asia.

progressively faster and accelerated the melting of the ice-sheets, the sea rose eustatically, transgressing low land on the Atlantic shore-line, flooding over the North Sea bed, insulating Britain, cutting the Belts between Jutland, the islands and Denmark, and converting the Baltic once more into a sea (the Litorina Sea); indeed at the height of Altithermal times sea-levels generally must have risen higher than they stand today.

The Post-glacial rise of temperature also affected powerfully, and in a way that affected early man profoundly, the nature of vegetation and animal life. The most obvious and dramatic change in temperate Europe was that forest trees were able to expand from their refuge areas and colonize the relatively open spaces of the Late-glacial landscape.[1] They did so in successive waves as the temperature rose sufficiently to allow fresh species to spread, first the birch and willow, then the pine and, only as climate entered on its Altithermal phase, the hazel and the deciduous trees, alder and the components of the oak-mixed-forest. By means of pollen-analysis the main phases of Neothermal forest history have been established, at least for much of temperate Europe west of the Vistula, providing a basis of relative chronology and illuminating the ecological background of the period during which Mesolithic cultures flourished in this part of the world. The ecological transition from zones III to IV was evidently a sharp one;[2] and this is consistent with the speed with which the ice-sheet withdrew from the Fenno-Scandian moraine —according to the varve-counts the ice-margin contracted by over 300 miles in a period of 1500 years—and the rate at which ocean-levels rose during the earlier part of Post-glacial times. Conversely, climate did not become favourable enough for agriculture and a Neolithic way of life to spread to north-western Europe until deciduous trees had established dominance in zone VII. The duration of the Mesolithic phase in north-western Europe was thus of the order of 5000 or even 5500 years. Over much of central and south-eastern Europe, on the other hand, Neolithic societies were able to establish themselves up to three thousand years earlier and the duration of the Mesolithic phase was correspondingly reduced.

Although it is common to speak of the change from Late-glacial to Post-glacial climate as though this was necessarily favourable—and even to speak of the peak of the Altithermal as marking a Climatic Optimum—it by no means follows that increasing temperature was any advantage to the European hunting

[1] §VIII, 4 and 5.   [2] §VIII, 10.

peoples. Indeed the reverse seems to have been the case. The late Magdalenians and their counterparts on the North European Plain were adapted to hunting animals, and in the latter case a particular animal, the reindeer,[1] that grazed on a Late-glacial vegetation, a vegetation richer and more varied than that existing today in any one ecological zone.[2] The abundance of game animals, including herds of reindeer, bison and horse, and the outstanding development of particular forms—for instance the Giant Irish Deer (*Megaceros giganteus*)[3] attained an antler span of up to eleven feet—emphasize how favourable grazing conditions must have been.

The onset of Post-glacial climate can have been little less than catastrophic. To quote a leading Danish palaeobotanist :[4] 'The rich late-glacial flora was severely reduced in the beginning of the post-glacial period. Some plant species were eradicated by the climatic change itself. . . . The great majority . . . however, succumbed in the shade of the post-glacial forest; light, not temperature, being the decisive factor. . ..' The spread of forest not only brought about a change in the species of game animal available to the hunter, red and roe deer, aurochs and wild pig replacing the Late-glacial herbivores ; it reduced the density of grazing animals and meant that instead of being hunted in herds they had to be taken individually in the forest. Reduction in the supply of larger game led to an intensification of methods : the bow came into much more general use and the microlith used to barb and tip arrows became a veritable symbol of the Mesolithic phase ; and the appearance for the first time of the domestic dog also made hunting more effective. The food quest was also more diversified : many more kinds of animal were hunted ; plant foods were gathered with more assiduity ; and, especially as the level of the ocean rose and encroached on the former land-area, more attention was devoted to the coast as a source of food.

It was only in the far north that the Post-glacial warmth brought incontestable advantages. The contraction of ice-sheets and the isostatic recovery of formerly depressed land-masses made possible a dramatic expansion of settlement, a process made more practicable by boats. In the British Isles settlement was extended to Scotland and northern Ireland. In Scandinavia the expansion was even more notable : traces of Mesolithic settlement are found discontinuously the whole way up the Atlantic and Arctic coasts to Finnmark, a range of some 1200 miles, and even to the White Sea coasts, a distribution that can be explained only

[1] §IX, 6, 22.   [2] §VIII, 9.   [3] §VIII, 11.   [4] §VIII, 9, 108.

in terms of movements by people habituated to hunting and
fishing at sea from boats, that must in this case have been of
skin.[1] Farther east again, hunter-fishers moved along the river
and lake systems and occupied a larger tract of Eurasia than their
Palaeolithic forbears.

Detailed investigation by modern methods of the ecological
history of the Mediterranean basin and West Asia is only now
seriously beginning. The prevailing hypothesis, that the arid zone
of sub-tropical climate is likely to have shifted northward as the
temperate zone itself encroached on the shrinking areas of glacial
and peri-glacial climate, has recently been subjected to some
questioning,[2] and this in itself has helped to stimulate the kind
of palaeontological research that alone can provide a valid answer.
Already it begins to appear that the onset of Neothermal conditions in this part of the world around 10,000 B.C. was in fact
accompanied by some measure of desiccation. Thus at the 'Cueva
del Toll' near Moya[3] in the coastal zone of eastern Spain between
Barcelona and the Pyrenees, the onset of Neothermal climate has
been shown to coincide with the beginning of a warm, dry phase
marked by low values for pine. At the Haua Fteah in Cyrenaica,
again, the Neothermal was marked in level X of the cave, dated
by radio-carbon to the ninth millennium B.C., by the onset of a
dry phase with a decline of pine and a corresponding increase of
Bos at the expense of the *Caprini*.[4] Farther east again, Palestine
can show strong evidence for a marked dry period at the time of
the Mesolithic Natufian settlement: this is reflected both in the
mollusca and in the fact that gazelle predominated over fallow
deer more strongly in this than in any other level in the caves of
the Wādi el-Maghārah ;[5] again, the Natufian level near the spring
at the base of Tell es-Sulṭān, Jericho, was marked by an over-
whelming proportion of gazelle among the animal remains.[6] Evidence that the climate turned warmer and drier during the ninth
millennium B.C. in northernmost Iraq has recently been obtained
from the Valley of Shanidar.[7] Lastly, preliminary examination of
the fossil pollen from sediments by Lake Marivān[8] in north-west
Iran suggests a dry phase in the region beginning around 9000
B.C. and continuing until the middle of the fourth millennium B.C.

The ecological changes, which in different ways affected and
in some cases even transformed the territories occupied by
Advanced Palaeolithic man, did far more than mark a formal

[1] §IX, 6. [2] §XII, 2. [3] §VIII, 3.
[4] §VIII, 8. [5] §VIII, 1. [6] §XII, 7.
[7] §VIII, 13. [8] Information from Dr van Zeist.

end to an archaeological phase. The coincidence between the passing of Late-glacial and Late-pluvial climate and the emergence of Mesolithic societies is more than merely temporal : it must surely have been causal, even if the precise links are not always apparent. Traditions formed under ecological conditions that had passed away had either to disappear or to undergo the modifications needed to accommodate them to new ones. Over almost the whole territory the basic economy of Advanced Palaeolithic societies persisted, although with a varying degree of emphasis; but in parts of Western Asia it looks as though desiccation may have created conditions sufficiently different to have forced a more radical readjustment. Indeed, the indications are that the Neothermal transformation which in more northerly territories brought about the modifications in hunting and gathering, and in the equipment used for these activities, that we recognize as Mesolithic, created in parts of south-west Asia conditions under which the domestication of animals and plants and the adoption of Neolithic culture provided a way of escape from the limitations that necessarily afflict societies lacking a knowledge of food-production. The progress of research in Western Asia, and especially the early dates now being obtained for the beginnings of domestication, make it appear that the inventions underlying farming were in fact made by Mesolithic communities very early in Neothermal times. On the other hand, the more usual role of the Mesolithic peoples was to provide a medium through which the new economy infiltrated over everbroader territories.

IX. THE MESOLITHIC SETTLEMENT OF NORTHERN EUROPE

The inhabitants of the North European plain refute the notion that the hunter-fishers of the Neothermal era were merely epi-Palaeolithic, perpetuating an old way of life into a new age, and lacking in distinctive attributes. Certainly the Mesolithic populations must have stemmed originally from their Upper Palaeolithic predecessors : the Maglemosians may have originated from such Late-glacial groups as Tjonger and Rissen ; the coast-dwellers, who spread ultimately as far north as arctic Scandinavia, may have stemmed from the Bromme-Lyngby[1] or Ahrensburg[2] people. Yet it is after all the new developments that claim our attention.

The inhabitants of the uninterrupted European plain reacted

[1] §IX, 24.   [2] §IX, 22.

positively to the new forested environment. Already in Pre-Boreal times, as we know from Star Carr in Yorkshire,[1] they had devised equipment for felling and shaping timber. By means of adzes and axes chipped from nodules and thick flakes of flint and sharpened by striking off burin-like flakes transversely to the main axis they felled trees, which must have been attacked by oblique strokes working down to a frequently renewed ring or kerb cut into the trunk.

The spread of forest trees transformed the conditions under which hunting was conducted. Whereas the Late-glacial hunters pursued herds of reindeer in a predominantly open landscape, those of the Neothermal era had different problems. Some hunting dodges were of course common to both, among them the trick of wearing masks to attract male animals within easy range, a practice fully documented from Star Carr, as well as from Berlin-Biesdorf and Hohen-Viecheln in North Germany.[2]

Among novel features was the dog, which occurred already at Star Carr from the mid-eighth millennium B.C.[3] The first certain evidence for the bow in Northern Europe dates from the final phase of the Late-glacial in Schleswig-Holstein.[4] As the forests thickened archery came more and more into its own. In Mesolithic Denmark the bows (Fig. 8, no. 1) were made roughly of the size of a man and of elm, the best wood then available in this area; they had well-defined rectangular grips and relatively broad limbs that tapered to pointed nocks, a type which significantly persisted during the Neolithic phase in Northern Europe. The arrowshafts (Fig. 8, no. 2) were often longer than those in use with the medieval long bow, sometimes exceeding a metre in length, and were fletched near the nock. The Maglemosians armed their arrows by mounting triangular or lance-shaped microliths (Fig. 8, nos. 3–7) at the tip and simpler forms lower down the shaft with the sharp edge outermost for cutting.[5] With such arrows they were able to shoot animals as large as the aurochs (*Bos primigenius*). They also hunted elk, red deer, roe deer and wild pig for meat; and brown bear, fox, beaver and squirrel for furs as well as flesh. Many kinds of bird were taken and some of these, as well as of the smaller fur-bearing animals, were doubtless shot by the wooden bird-bolts found on Maglemosian sites.

A special feature of the food-quest was the stress laid on fishing[6] in the lakes and rivers which attracted the main weight

[1] §IX, 7.   [2] §IX, 23; see Plate I.   [3] §IX, 12.
[4] §IX, 9.   [5] §IX, 3; 5; 7; 9; 11.   [6] §IX, 6.

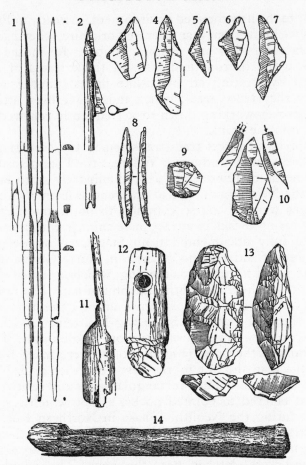

Fig. 8. Maglemosian equipment: no. 1, yew bow from Holmegaard, Denmark (1/15); no. 2, arrow from Loshult, Sweden (1/3); nos. 3–7, microliths from Star Carr, England (2/3); no. 8, flint awl from Star Carr, England (4/9); no. 9, flint scraper from Star Carr, England (4/9); no. 10, scraper-burin from Star Carr, England (4/9); no. 11, wooden paddle from Duvensee, Germany (2/9); no. 12, flint adze in antler holder, Svaerdborg, Denmark (2/9); no. 13, flint adze and sharpening-flake, Broxbourne, England (1/3); no. 14, dug-out canoe, Pesse, Holland (c. 1/45).

of Maglemosian settlement. Among the gear used were fish-hooks[1] that were commonly made by drilling a hole towards one end of a carefully shaped bone plaque and working out from this. Pike, one of the most important fish taken in northern waters, could have been caught on hook and line using live bait, but

[1] See Plate 2.

during the spring spawning it would not have been difficult to spear them in shallow water, and it must be significant that bone spearheads barbed on one edge have been found sticking into pike skulls or backbones. Although netting was used by Advanced Palaeolithic people in connexion with head-ornaments, its employment for taking fish[1] is first documented on Maglemosian sites: the nets were made from threads of bark fibres and knotted in the same manner as those later used by the Neolithic peasants in the Swiss lakes; they functioned as seine nets and must have been operated by a small team, one end being kept on shore, the other taken out by boatmen, drawn round in a sweep and pulled ashore close to the first.

The role of plant-food is not easy to estimate, but it may be noted that many of the plants represented at Star Carr were used for food in later times. They include water-lilies; swamp and marsh species, such as common reeds and bog-beans; several from open communities including species of *Polygonum*, *Chenopodium*, *Rumex*, *Galeopsis*, *Stellaria* and *Urtica*; and woodland plants, including mountain ash (*Sorbus aucuparis*), the dried berries of which were eaten in parts of Europe down to modern times.

The distribution of the Maglemosian culture was more or less coterminous with the North European plain, as we are forcibly reminded by the barbed spearhead dredged from a depth of between 19 and 20 fathoms between the Leman and Ower Banks some twenty-five miles off the coast of Norfolk.[2] Low-lying areas were preferred, especially those on the margins of former lakes and in river valleys. Thus in England the low-lying parts of East Yorkshire, the vale of Pickering, Holderness and the Hull Valley were favoured together with the Thames and its tributaries, notably the Kennet, Colne and Lea. In France and the Low Countries, the region between the Somme and the Scheldt was occupied, but not the sandy heaths of Holland. The rivers and lakes of North Germany and Poland between the Weser and the Niemen were also settled, but the main focus lay in Denmark and the contiguous part of South Sweden.[3] An eastern variant of the same culture is known from either side of the Gulf of Finland[4] and from as far east as Perm.

Little is known about the nature of the sites themselves, beyond the fact that they were small—no larger than would be necessary for groups of three or four biological families—and apparently re-occupied seasonally. At Star Carr we seem to have traces of

[1] See Plate 2.　　[2] §IX, 5 and 6.　　[3] §IX, 1.　　[4] §XI, 15.

a brushwood platform laid directly on the reed swamp, but the only remains of actual floors are those from the Danish site of Holmegaard[1] made up of rectangular slabs of tree bark, the fire-place resting on a sand patch. Later descendants of the Magle-mosians in southern England occupied irregular huts with sunken floors and, presumably during the summer, tent-like shelters of light construction.[2] That the Mesolithic peoples were able to move about easily on inland waters is shown by the wooden paddles (Fig. 8, no. 11) from a number of sites, ranging from Star Carr to Holmegaard in Zealand, and a dug-out boat (Fig. 8, no. 14) about 3·5 m. long from Pesse in Drenthe, Holland.[3]

The main components of the flint-work of the Maglemosians comprised axes and adzes, microliths, which in the later industries included more regular geometric forms, scrapers and the burins or graving tools needed for working antler and bone. Great use was made of these latter materials for spears, mattocks, axe-hafts, netting-needles, leather-working tools and fish-hooks.[4] The Star Carr people made their mattocks from elk antler (Fig. 8, no. 12) and their axe-hafts presumably from wood, which left stag antler available for making their spearheads, but the later Maglemosians of Zealand were short of elk antler and needed stag antler for mattocks and hafts, so they had to make their spearheads from metapodials or ribs.

That the Maglemosians had established a satisfactory working relationship with their environment is suggested by the care they were able to give to ornamentation. For personal wear they perforated animal teeth, lumps of amber, and thin stone pebbles as beads, as well as lengths of bird-bone to serve as spacers.[5] In the central and richest area, notably in Denmark and South Sweden, they decorated objects made from bone and antler, as a rule by delicate incision, but quite often by drilling small pits (Fig. 9, nos. 2–4). The commonest motifs were geometric, comprising varieties of barbed line, shaded band, chevron, triangle, and lozenge, and these were often arranged in parallel lines separated into lengths by gaps or transverse lines. Other designs clearly reflect the influence of nets. Animal designs, more or less schematic, occasionally appear in engraving, but more often in the form of carved amber lumps. A feature of the art is the use of anthropomorphic designs. These may appear singly on amber pendants or amulets, the perforation taking the place of the head (Fig. 9, no. 5). Sometimes they appear singly

[1] §ix, 3.   [2] §ix, 10 and 15.   [3] §ix, 27.
[4] §ix, 3; 5; 6; 11.   [5] §ix; 3; 5, 11. See Plate 2.

or repetitively on the same objects as geometric patterns; but in one instance, on an aurochs metapodial from Ryemarksgaard, Zealand,[1] a row of four figures is shown assisting in an enigmatic scene, one, the only one shown with free arms, apparently triumphing over the others.

Traces of another group of hunter-fishers are known to us from coastal sites at present submerged by the sea or buried under old sea-banks, like Carstensminde and Bloksbjerg respectively, and very occasionally, as at Kongemose in Zealand, from sites in the interior.[2] Some elements remind one of the Maglemosian, notably axes and adzes chipped down from flint nodules and stag-antler mattock-heads, but others are distinctive. Among these are a style of ornamenting antler objects, much more deeply incised than was practised by the Maglemosians, pecked stone axes with ground edges, harpoon-heads, bull-roarers, bone points slotted on either side for the insetting of flint micro-flakes, flint blades with controlled parallel flake-scars and rhombic arrowheads made from sections of these. The last two, which occur with great regularity and abundance, point to the Ahrensburgian Late-glacial culture as a main source of origin; again a bone bull-roarer and certain geometric motifs from Kongemose find almost exact parallels at Stellmoor. It looks as though the Early Coastal people, though they shared certain forest adaptations with the Maglemosians, may have originated during the break-up of the Late-glacial environment through the adaptation of Ahrensburgian reindeer-hunters to a coastal mode of life. The relatively more complete coastal sequence on the western and northern coasts of Scandinavia supports this (see p. 104).

Disappointingly little is known of Mesolithic burial customs in the north.[3] Disarticulated human remains are known from Maglemosian settlements and remains of what may have been a burial were dug up from a deposit of zone V age at Koelbjerg near Odense on Funen; also two extended burials found in a shell-bank of Ancylus Lake age at Stångenäs in West Sweden were probably Maglemosian. From the Early Coastal culture a good example of an extended burial is known from Korsør Nor in Zealand, the skeleton, accompanied by a pointed flake with exceptionally regular flake-scars, being apparently enveloped in bark, which was stiffened by wooden poles at the sides and by tapered wooden slats across the top. Seated burials were also known, including one in a pit of 60 cm. diameter and c. 120 cm. depth at Bäckaskog in Scania, accompanied by a bone chisel and

[1] See Plate 2.   [2] §IX, 3 and 16.   [3] §IX, 3.

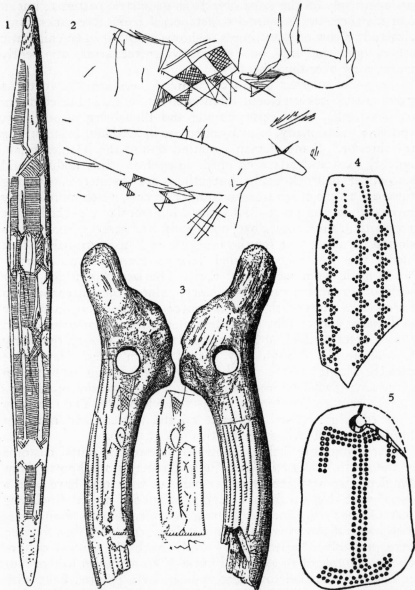

Fig. 9. Maglemosian art : engravings and pit-ornament : no. 1, netting-needle from Travenort, Holstein, Germany (2/3); no. 2, fine engraving on antler mattock, Ystad, Sweden (5/9); no. 3, anthropomorphic and geometric designs on perforated antler, Podejuch, Kr. Greifenhagen, East Germany (1/3); no. 4, pit-ornament on bone, Pernau, Esthonia (5/6); no. 5, amber pendant with anthropomorphic design in pit-ornament, Denmark (5/6).

a slotted bone point.[1] The lower part of a comparable burial is known from Janisławice near Skiemiewice in Central Poland ;[2] in this case the grave-goods comprised microliths of late Maglemosian type, stag-tooth beads, knives of boar's tusk and sundry pieces of shaped animal bone. The physical type represented by the northern burials is basically Nordic, tall, well built and having a lofty, dolichocephalic skull.

Coastal settlement was greatly intensified during Altithermal times. The flooding over of the North Sea bed, and the formation of the Belts, converting the Ancylus Lake into the Litorina Sea, must have intensified pressure on local resources, a pressure which may be reflected in the reduction in the numbers of aurochs and elk and which could be relieved only by migration or by a more effective exploitation of local resources. One way of doing this was to intensify coastal gathering, hunting and fishing, and the other was to adopt farming as at least an ancillary occupation.

At the height of Altithermal times sea-levels in the northern parts of Denmark actually rose during four periods above those prevailing today.[3] From a study of stratified finds it is possible to detect certain broad trends in development between the Early Coastal or Carstensminde stage and the 'classic' Ertebølle that first appeared at the time of the third Litorina transgression. Thus pecked-stone axes and deep engraving dropped out early ; rhombic arrow-heads gave place to chisel-ended, transverse ones ; and side-blow flake axes gained progressively over core ones. The 'classic' Ertebølle stage is marked by the acquisition of stock-raising, cereal-growing and pot-making, as well as by the appearance of flat flaking on flake axes and radial flaking on core axes, and by the manufacture of antler mattock heads having sockets formed by the stumps of tines.[4] At this time kitchen middens composed of discarded shells eaten for food, together with other refuse,[5] became common on the Litorina shores, monuments to a sedentary form of life, in which land and sea hunting, fishing, fowling, shell-gathering and collecting were combined to varying degrees with stock-raising and cereal-growing, an economy which persisted well into Middle Neolithic times in Denmark. A feature of the Ertebølle culture well represented at Dyrholmen is unmistakable evidence for cannibalism,[6] comprising fine cut marks on cranial bones, human long bones split open in precisely the same way as those of food-animals, the lower

[1] §IX, 1.   [2] §IX, 4.   [3] §IX, 19.
[4] §IX, 25.   [5] §IX, 18.   [6] §IX, 13.

margins of human jaw-bones removed in the same manner as those of stag and roe deer bones and evidence that human bones were gnawed by dogs.

The colonization of the western and northern coasts of Scandinavia should be viewed as an alternative response to the flooding over of living-space in the regions immediately to the south. Evidence for coastal settlement is relatively complete in the Scandinavian peninsula[1] because the old strand-lines have been left exposed above modern sea-levels. The makers of stone industries, named after the ancient Norwegian province of Fosna, on the west coast south of the Trondelag, and Mount Komsa in Finnmark, date from a time after the formation of the Portlandia strand and in fact the earliest dated artefact from Norway, a heavy tanged flake, recalling those of Late-glacial age in Denmark, from Christiansund, dates from the Pholas phase. By the time the sea had come to rest at the Tapes strand, equivalent in age to the Litorina phase of the Baltic, the Fosna–Komsa settlement had ended. The discontinuity of settlement—isolated finds have been made between Fosna and Finnmark, in the Ostfold and on the west coast of Sweden[2]—and its coastal nature suggest colonization and contact by boat and an economy in which fishing played an essential part. The distribution suggests a spread from the West Baltic area. This impression is confirmed by a study of the stone industries themselves. Although the settlement continued up to the time of the classic Ertebølle culture in the south, an earlier beginning is suggested by the presence, especially prominent in south-west Norway, of a distinctive element of tanged points, including heavy tanged flakes, like the specimen from Christiansund, and lighter ones, some of which approach the rhombic form. In fact, there are signs that the first groups to occupy the strands of southern Norway stemmed, like the Early Coastal people of Denmark, from the break-up of the Late-glacial environment, the movement being given added impetus by the impact on the richly occupied West Baltic area of rising ocean levels.

Further evidence for the expansion of settlement to remote areas can be cited from the British Isles, where Scotland and Ireland were first settled comparatively late in Neothermal times. The eastern part of Scotland was occupied as far north as Morayshire[3] by people whose only trace consists of flint and stone industries in which geometric microliths (triangles, crescents) play a key role, industries of the kind that flourished over a large part

---

[1] §IX, 2, 14.   [2] §IX, 14.   [3] §IX, 17.

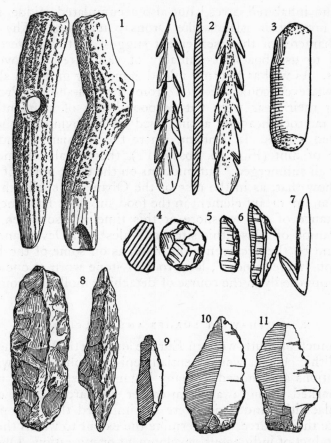

Fig. 10. Obanian (nos. 1–7) and Larnian (nos. 8–11) equipment: no. 1, mattock-head of stag antler, Meiklewood, Stirling (2/9); no. 2, harpoon-head of antler, MacArthur's Cave, Oban (4/9); no. 3, stone 'limpet-scoop', Cnoc Sligeach, Oronsay (1/3); no. 4, flint scraper from Risga, Argyll (2/3); nos. 5–6, microliths from Risga (2/3); no. 7, bone fish-hook from Risga (2/3); no. 8, flint adze, Larne, Antrim (4/9); no. 9, microlith, Cushendun, Antrim (2/3); nos. 10–11, flakes worked at butt end, Cushendun (4/9).

of the highland zone of England and Wales from the final phase
of the Boreal climatic phase.[1] South-west Scotland and north-east Ireland on the other hand were settled by people whose flint
and antler (Fig. 10, nos. 1–7) and bone work owes something
ultimately to Maglemosian and possibly even to Azilian sources,
but whose culture was adapted to life around the Irish Sea and
the coasts of the western Highlands. The Obanians of western

[1] §ix, 8.

Scotland inhabited caves,[1] but also accumulated middens in the open, notably on islands like Oronsay and Risga. The pattern and character of their settlement suggest that they were accustomed to use boats, presumably of skin stretched over light frames. As well as hunting inland game they gathered shell-fish and whatever could be won from the sea-shore. Prominent among their gear were flat harpoon-heads of stag antler and heavy mattock-heads of a kind used for removing blubber from stranded whales. In Antrim, where the Larnians found a rich source of flint (Fig. 10, nos. 8–11), the actual settlements are nearly all submerged,[2] but middens on the coast north of Dublin Bay show that, as in the case of the Obanians, shell-fish contributed an important element in the food supply.[3] Evidence of the importance of the sea-shore at this time is also given by the distribution of Mesolithic sites in Wales[4] and Devon and Cornwall and by the occurrence on these, as on some of the Larnian sites, of 'limpet-scoops', long rods of stone worn at one or both ends supposedly in the course of detaching molluscs from rocks.

X. SOUTH-WEST EUROPE AND NORTH AFRICA

Over much of south-western Europe and North Africa the earlier Mesolithic peoples were essentially epi-Palaeolithic, showing few innovations and indeed in many instances displaying a more or less marked falling away from earlier standards. Most of these epi-Palaeolithic industries were so simplified that it is not easy to trace their sources or determine the extent to which they were the product of indigenous development or migration. One of the few cultures of which the origin is well established is that named after Mas d'Azil in the Ariège.[5] The flint industry (Fig. 11) alone would not tell us very much in this respect, though it is worthy of note that the burins, scrapers and battered back points were all small. On the other hand, the harpoon-heads clearly suggest an origin in the Late Magdalenian. Geographically the correspondence between the Azilian and Late Magdalenian is closely displayed in the Cantabric region of northern Spain, where every Azilian site overlies a level with Magdalenian harpoon-heads and three-quarters of the sites with Magdalenian harpoon-heads were later occupied by Azilians; even in France, where the Azilian is concentrated on the northern slopes of the Pyrenees and in the Dordogne and Lot, about half the Azilian

[1] §IX, 17.   [2] §IX, 21.   [3] §IX, 20.
[4] §IX, 26.   [5] §X, 15 and 24.

occupations overlie Late Magdalenian ones. Given the sharpness
of the ecological break, symbolized by the change from reindeer
to red deer antler as the material for harpoon-heads, the degree
of continuity is indeed striking. Signs of impoverishment in

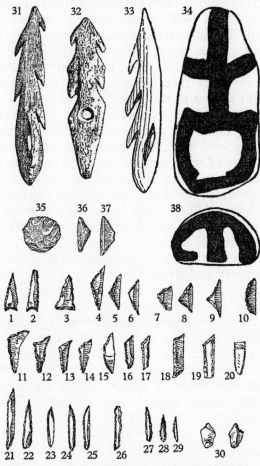

Fig. 11. Azilian (nos. 31–8) and Sauveterrian industries: nos. 1–29, 36, 37,
microliths (2/3); no. 30, 'micro-burin' (2/3); nos. 31–3, harpoon-heads of stag
antler (1/2); no. 35, flint scraper (2/3); nos. 34, 38, painted pebbles (2/5).

relation to the Magdalenian include the smallness of the flints
and the lack of variety and poorer finish of much of the bone and
antler work: one of the few technical innovations seems to have
been the modification of the harpoon-head to allow it to swivel
toggle-fashion when embedded in the victim.[1] Again, the only

[1] §x, 24.

traces of art consist of schematic designs painted in red on river pebbles (Fig. 11, nos. 34, 38) which must presumably have served some cult purpose. A few of the more elaborate designs are clearly anthropomorphic in intent and in this resemble ones from the central Maglemosian territories and from southern Italy.

There is evidence in Provence and eastern Spain, notably in Tarragona,[1] of flint industries resembling the Azilian but lacking its distinctive enrichments. Similarly, there is evidence from Italy of the closely similar epi-Palaeolithic industries in some respects poorer than their predecessors, notably from a layer dated by radio-carbon to the seventh millennium B.C., and over-lying a Grimaldian deposit in the cave of La Porta at Positano near Salerno.[2] The food refuse of Positano suggests that the collection of shell-fish had grown greatly in importance as a source of food. In North Africa the Oranian, first recognized in Algeria and Morocco,[3] but since identified in the Jebel Akhdar of Cyrenaica,[4] provides another close analogy : the flint-work pre-serves a uniform dullness ; the bone-work is even poorer ; and there is no trace of art. The human skeletal material associated with the Oranian belongs to the type first identified at Meshta el-Arbi and noteworthy for the prominence of its brow-ridges and mastoid processes and generally for the strong development of muscular markings. The frequency with which the upper incisor teeth have been removed suggests some rite, perhaps connected with fertility, but widespread indications of dental caries and abscesses, arthritis, osteitis, rheumatism, exostosis and suppurat-ing sores, emphasize that these Oranians were as miserable physically as they were culturally. The homogeneity of the Oranian over the whole of North Africa suggests that it had some common origin. The absence of any basis of Advanced Palaeolithic culture in the north-west, where the Aterian pro-longed an essentially Middle Palaeolithic tradition, leads one to seek an origin in the Dabba culture of Cyrenaica, a region where the Oranian seems to have appeared by c. 12,000 B.C., that is some two thousand years earlier than in Morocco.

Traces of quite a different culture, marked by geometric micro-liths made from narrow bladelets by a special process that involved the production as by-products of the so-called 'micro-burin', are known from France and neighbouring parts of Europe. At Sauveterre-la-Lémance itself[5] it overlay an Azilian deposit, but there seems no reason to doubt that the Sauveterrian, like the

---

[1] §x, 26.   [2] §x, 21.   [3] §x, 3.
[4] §x, 14.   [5] §x, 9.

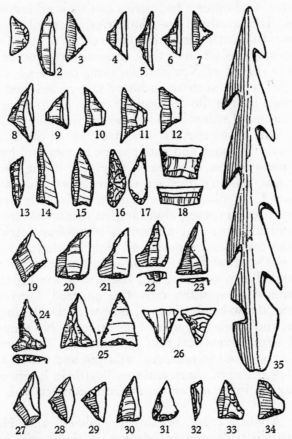

Fig. 12. Blade and trapeze industries of south-western and central Europe: nos. 1–12, microliths from La Cocina, Spain (nos. 1–3 upper, nos. 4–7 middle, nos. 8–12 lower) (8/15); nos. 13–18, microliths from north-west Germany (2/3); nos. 19–26, microliths from Tardenoisian of inland France (nos. 19–21 lower, nos. 22–4 middle, nos. 25–6 upper) (2/3); nos. 27–34, microliths from Ensdorf, South Germany (2/3); no. 35, harpoon-head of stag antler, Falkensteinhöhle, Hohenzollern, South Germany (2/3).

Azilian itself, stemmed from an Upper Palaeolithic source, especially since geometric microliths and 'micro-burins' (Fig. 11, no. 30) had already appeared in the Mediterranean area in Magdalenian[1] and Grimaldian levels.[2]

In south-western France the Sauveterrian industry was succeeded by one characterized by regular blades and by trapeze-shaped arrow-heads made from sections of these by means of the

[1] §x, 4.   [2] §x, 18.

'micro-burin' technique. Industries of this kind are widespread
in France, Iberia, the Low Countries, Central and Eastern
Europe, part of North Africa and large tracts of south-west Asia,
and throughout this territory they immediately precede and overlap with the spread of Neolithic farming cultures.[1] One of the
first localities where such an industry was recognized was Fère-
en-Tardenois in the Île-de-France,[3] and for this reason it is
generally termed Tardenoisian in France and some neighbouring
countries. One of the most striking facts about the Tardenoisian
is its poverty. The bone and antler work is poor and monotonous
and art is non-existent. The leading element in the flint industry
(Fig. 12, nos 19–26), the arrow armatures, shows a certain
development.[4] In phase I the armatures include symmetrical
and asymmetrical trapezes, right-angled forms (*pointes de Vielle*),
a few rhombic forms and numerous broad-based triangles; in
phase II the trapezes are nearly all right-angled and new types
appear in the spurred form (*à base recurrent*) and the transverse
or chisel-ended arrow-heads; and lastly in phase III the trapeze
element almost disappears, only the spurred form surviving,
chisel-ended arrow-heads abound, now with flat flaking invading
either face, and crescentic microliths appear. No remains of elk
and few of large bovids occur on Tardenoisian sites, and hunting
was mainly restricted to red deer, wild pig and the smaller forest
game. A few traces of sheep and small cattle in layers of phases I
and II may be intrusive or result from contact with Neolithic
farmers.

On the Atlantic coast, notably at Téviec[5] and Hoëdic,[6] at
present small islands, but in Mesolithic times still part of the
coastal zone of Morbihan, the Tardenoisians, while still hunting
forest animals in the interior, drew substantially on what they
could obtain from the sea-shore. Shell-fish were gathered, occasional fish were taken from the rocks and some effort was made
to secure sea-birds, including the hapless Great Auk. Although
resembling that of the interior the flint industry of the midden-
dwellers differed in some respects, notably in lacking right-angled
forms and spurred points and in possessing microlithic triangles.
Objects of antler and bone were slightly less scarce than in the
interior and even display slight traces of ornamentation, as for
instance in the criss-cross incisions on a large fish-mandible and
in bunches of transverse cuts on bone cloak-pins.

Many hearths were observed in the midden but no huts were

[1] §x, 4.   [2] §x, 8.   [3] §x, 10.
[4] §x, 11.   [5] §x, 16.   [6] §x, 17.

recovered. It is evident that no attempt was made to dispose of the dead in separate cemeteries. The bodies were apparently buried clothed and wearing their personal ornaments: bone pins, presumed to have been used for fastening skin cloaks, were worn at the base of the throat; and perforated shells were strung together to form necklaces, bracelets and in one case a head-dress,

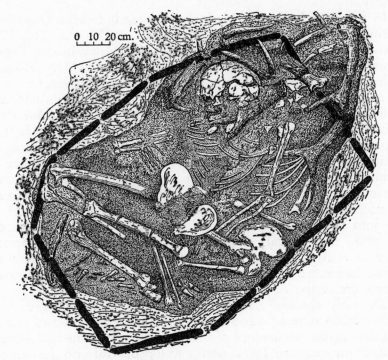

0 10 20 cm.

Fig. 13. Tardenoisian burial, Téviec, Morbihan, France.
Note stag antlers over skull.

large numbers being used for single individuals. The corpses were normally contracted, the legs being flexed, the hands placed on the sides and the heads slightly raised. Some people were buried singly, but others were interred successively in collective graves, and, though they generally rested directly on the soil or on previous burials, they were generally protected by stone slabs. The most impressive burial at Téviec comprised six persons: at the bottom there was a man of between twenty and thirty who had evidently been killed by an arrow mounted with a triangular microlith, and above five more burials, including those of two men, two women and a girl, the whole surmounted by a heap of stone incorporating what appears to have been a ritual hearth. Two symbolic practices are worth noting. Both the Téviec people and those of Hoëdic followed the ancient custom of sprinkling red ochre over the body of the dead man; and they frequently heaped stag antlers over the heads of the buried people (Fig. 13), as if to endow them with the vitality inherent in the emblems of virility.

In Iberia, as in France, blade and trapeze industries flourished during the latter part of the Mesolithic settlement. The best documented sites are the shell-middens of Muge in the Tagus estuary[1] and the stratified cave of La Cocina, Dos Aguas, Valencia,[2] the other side of the peninsula. The middens, between 60 and 70 km. from the existing mouth of the Tagus, incorporate numerous hearths and burials. At one of the sites, Moita do Sebastião, the excavator distinguished settings of stake-holes that appeared to define the sites of semicircular huts. The burials were noticeably poorer than those of Morbihan, lacking protective stone structures and having either no or at most very meagre ornaments. The flint industries, which resemble those from Morbihan more than the Tardenoisian of the French interior, fall into two groups: in one of which (Arruda and Moita do Sebastião are typical) trapeziform arrow-heads were normal; whereas at Armoreira the leading forms were triangles, many of which had more or less prominent spurs, and to a much lesser degree crescents.

The only absolute date we have for the Muge middens is a radio-carbon date of 5400 B.C. ± 350 for Moita do Sebastião,[3] but the regular occurrence of blades and trapezes in chalcolithic contexts in southern Iberia points to its survival into the second millennium B.C. The vigour and duration of the blade and trapeze tradition in this region is doubtless due to the late introduction of husbandry by metal-working people from overseas: there seems to have been nothing comparable in Iberia to the long-lasting colonization by Neolithic cultivators such as we know from Central Europe. The people who adopted elements of the exotic higher culture were essentially Mesolithic hunters. This is demonstrated in the first place by the fact that the flint-work from the megalithic and contemporary tombs is basically of the blade and trapeze tradition with some infusion of the exotic mitre-shaped arrow-head having shallow flaking on either face;[4] and in the second by the occurrence, impressed on pottery and

[1] §x, 6; 22; 23.   [2] §x, 19; 20; see Fig. 12, nos. 1–12.
[3] §x, 23.   [4] §x, 7; 13.

painted on the slabs of megalithic tombs,[1] of art motifs clearly
stemming from the schematic paintings found on the walls of
rock-shelters over a large part of southern Iberia and manifestly
relating to the indigenous hunting population.

The Mesolithic rock-paintings of Iberia display a wide diversity of style,[2] ranging from the naturalistic group in the Levant,
at one time ascribed to the Upper Palaeolithic, to the schematic
representations which, from their content alone, can sometimes
be seen to have continued into the period of metallurgy. By

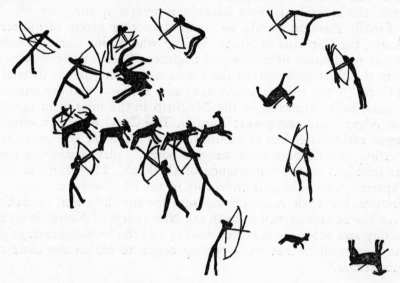

Fig. 14. Mesolithic rock-painting, Cueva de la Araña, Castellón, East Spain,
showing bowmen closing in on ibexes.

comparison with the Franco-Cantabric cave art even the liveliest
ones, like Alpera and Minateda, are small in size and lacking in
modelling, human figures are much more common and scenes
are frequently depicted. These confirm that the bow was the
main weapon used and show that hunting was a highly organized
activity (Fig. 14).

The middens of Morbihan and the Tagus estuary each produced a substantial body of human skeletal material.[3] Some of
their most striking characteristics were probably due to poor
nourishment. Both were poorly built and short in stature, the
males from each averaging only 1·60 m. (5 ft. 3 in.) and the

[1] §x, 12 and 15.   [2] §x, 1 and 2; see Fig. 14.   [3] §x, 16.

females 1·50 m. (4 ft. 11 in.); and two-fifths of those from the Tagus estuary and three-fifths of those from Morbihan suffered from platycnemia or transverse flattening of the shin-bone. The skulls of both groups were high-vaulted and inclined to be long; those from Morbihan were more keeled than the Tagus ones; and the former were on the whole a little shorter (dolicho-mesocephalic rather than dolichocephalic) and had a slightly smaller capacity. The faces of both groups were rather large and the lower portions projected (sub-nasal prognathism). Both had rather broad (mesorhine) noses and both had large teeth, the individuals from Morbihan invariably so.

Finally mention should be made of another group of hunter-fishers, the Capsians of North Africa,[1] whose flint work is based on the production of blades and trapezes. Their middens, which form the chief memorial of the Capsians, abound in the districts of Gafsa (hence the name Capsian) and Tebessar and the culture is most fully displayed in the Maghrib in the interior of north-east Algeria and north-west Tunisia. The Capsian culture, which began rather later but ran alongside the Oranian, was based on hunting, but digging stick weights point to plant-gathering and the middens to the importance of shell-fish. The origin of the Capsians, who belonged physically to the Mediterranean race, is obscure, but their role as a medium for the diffusion, probably from the Sahara as well as from the Nile valley, of Neolithic technology and economy is not in doubt; and the rock-engravings of the area confirm that stock-raising began to enrich the basis of subsistence.[2]

XI. CENTRAL AND EASTERN EUROPE

Here again there are signs of epi-Palaeolithic cultures emerging from indigenous Upper Palaeolithic ones. Examples so far identified include the Fürsteiner culture of the Swiss Mittelland, named after a morainic hillock near the Burgäschisee where it was first recognized, a culture which had already emerged by the end of the ninth millennium B.C. (B. 16: 8250 ± 200) and evidently stemmed from the local Late Magdalenian.[3] Epi-Palaeolithic flint industries have been recognized both in Hungary, notably at Szekszard (8400 B.C. ± 500),[4] and in Poland, in the central part of which the Witów culture emerged[5] and where the Swiderian, a Late-glacial group comparable with the Ahrensburgian farther west, continued into Neothermal times; and

---

[1] §x, 3 and 25.   [2] §x, 25.   [3] §xi, 26.
[4] §xi, 24.   [5] §xi, 5 and 6.

similar manifestations are known from South Russia.[1] A feature
of all these industries is that, while retaining the leading characteristics of their Upper Palaeolithic prototypes, they reveal a
tendency to smaller types of flint, including in the case of
Szekszard[2] scrapers of thumb-nail size and microliths of geometric
triangular and crescentic forms.

Over the territory as a whole the Mesolithic settlement is
represented mainly by flint industries marked by various forms
of trapeze and bridging the transition to the Neolithic of the
region. What happened during the intervening period is still
obscure in most parts of the territory. Switzerland is one of the
few areas to show something closely akin to the French Sauveterrian in the form of microlithic industries that include geometric forms :[3] such are known, for example, in the Wauwilermoos, in the neighbourhood of Robenhausen, and in the lower
levels of a small cave at Birsmatten near Nenzlingen in the Jura,[4]
dated by radio-carbon analysis to the late sixth millennium B.C.
(level 5, B. 238 : 5510 B.C. ± 160; level 3, B. 236 : 5020 B.C.
± 120).

Much more is known of the final phase of the Mesolithic
settlement corresponding with the French Tardenoisian and more
or less contemporary with the first or Danubian I phase of
Neolithic colonization.[5] Clusters of irregular hollows marking
the sites of artificial shelters have been observed by the Wauwilermoos in Switzerland and at Tannstock by the Federsee in
Württemberg.[6] On the other hand, the most important Tardenoisian find in Switzerland is without doubt the Birsmatten cave,[7]
the upper levels of which, dating from c. 3300 to 3400 B.C.,
yielded a flint industry with long and right-angled trapezes made
from sections of regular blades, together with stag antler harpoon-
heads of a type previously known from the Wachtfelsen, near
Grellingen, Bern,[8] and one which, although resembling Azilian
ones in many respects, differs in the arrangements made for
securing the line.

Similar flint industries occur over much of Germany south of
the Main, being distinguished by a greater abundance of broad-
based points and broad isosceles triangles (Fig. 12, nos. 27–34).[9]
In two caves in Hohenzollern, the Falkensteinhöhle and the
Bernaufels near Tiergarten,[10] similar flint industries were accom-

[1] §xi, 4 and 10.   [2] §xi, 24.   [3] §xi, 27 and 28.
[4] §xi, 1.   [5] §xi, 8.   [6] §xi, 3 and 19.
[7] §xi, 1.   [8] §xi, 23.
[9] §xi, 8; 11; 12; 16; 21.   [10] §xi, 18.

panied by antler harpoon-heads (Fig. 12, no. 35) identical with those from Birsmatten, together with antler leather-working tools and beads, made from perforated snail-shells, and deer-, fox- and fish-teeth. To this population probably belong the remarkable series of skull-burials at Ofnet and Kauftersberg near Nördlingen, Bavaria,[1] and at Hohlestein, Lonetal,[2] near Ulm. At Ofnet there were two nests, one of twenty-seven, the other of six skulls, resting in depressions in the underlying Late Magdalenian deposits ; this and the fact that all the perforated teeth found with the skulls were of red deer rather than reindeer confirms their Post-glacial age. The fact that the top two or three neck vertebrae adhered to the skulls shows that they must have been severed from the bodies soon after death, and the absence of cut marks on the skulls indicates that they were deposited with the skin still attached. The way in which the skulls in the middle of the nests had been to some extent damaged, whereas those on the periphery were intact, argues that the deposits were made successively. How can we interpret these finds ? Evidently there was some kind of skull cult, but can we infer head-hunting ? In any case, the presence of large numbers of perforated snail-shells and animal teeth suggests that the skulls, which included only four males as against nine females and twenty children, were buried with reverence. Physically they included some dolichocephalic skulls of a type peculiar to Ofnet, dolicho-mesocephalic ones resembling some from the Morbihan middens, and three brachycephalic, the only ones of the kind from Mesolithic Europe.[3]

In the Middle Danube area we find a microlithic flint industry, notably at Sered in south-west Slovakia,[4] dating from Late Boreal or Early Atlantic times, which is distinguished from the much earlier one at Szekszard only by the appearance of the long trapezes, a type which appears at this time over wide expanses of Europe and could well have spread among communities of indigenous origin. Microlithic industries combining geometric microliths and long trapezes are also distributed on the northern margins of the German highlands from Saxony to the Teutoburger Wald ;[5] and analogous ones, enriched by asymmetric points with pressure-flaking on parts of either face of the type termed 'mistletoe leaf' points by Belgian prehistorians,[6] occur in the extreme west of North Germany and in the neighbouring Low Countries. In Poland two main microlithic industries with triangles and crescents exist in the Polish dunes, one including

[1] §XI, 20. [2] §XI, 25. [3] §X, 16.
[4] §XI, 2. [5] §XI, 21. [6] §XI, 17.

points of the type found in the underlying Swiderian,[1] the other
trapezes, mainly long ones, but also in a few cases closely
resembling the French *pointe de Vielle*.[2]

Industries of broadly Tardenoisian type extend as far east as
the upper course of the Dnieper and the valley of the Desna,[3]
and there is a well-defined Pontic Mesolithic, best studied in the
stratified rock-shelters of the Crimea.[4] Although a single tradition runs through the flint-work, three main phases can be
recognized, during the last of which the culture had been
transformed by the adoption of Neolithic arts.

	Key sites and levels			
Stages	Murzak-Koba	Tash-Air I	Shan-Koba	Fatma-Koba
Neolithic	—	5	1	—
Late Mesolithic				
(Murzak-Koba)	x	6, 7	2, 3	1–4
Early Mesolithic	—	8, 9	4, 5	6

During the Shan-Koba stage the climate was still in an
Anathermal phase, but forests were already established. The
larger animals killed for food comprised in the main forest forms
like red deer, roe deer, wild pig and bear, and the hunter was
already assisted by dogs. The flint industry comprised flakes and
blades, scrapers, burins and microliths, the latter predominantly
of triangular and crescentic form but already including a few
long trapezes. During the Murzak-Koba stage Altithermal conditions prevailed and the deciduous forest was dominant. During
this time settlements became more numerous and snails, the shells
of which were found in large numbers in special pits, became
important for food. The flint-work is marked by a greater regularity of blade-production and by the much greater importance
of four-sided forms, mainly trapezes, but including a few rhombic
forms. In the uppermost levels remains of domestic cattle, pigs,
sheep and goat supplemented those of wild animals, pottery made
its appearance, and trapezes were modified by a flat retouch and
supplemented by bifacially flaked arrow-heads. Burials included
the internment on their backs in the same grave of a tall, long-
headed man and a woman at Murzak-Koba and of a man buried
in a crouched position under a heap of stones at Fatma-Koba.

[1] §xi, 13.   [2] §xi, 22.
[3] §xi, 7.   [4] §xi, 10, 14; see Fig. 15, nos. 21–6.

XII. SOUTH-WEST ASIA

The initial phases of the social transformation that resulted in
the emergence of Neolithic village communities and in due course
of metal-casting urban dwellers ran parallel in Western Asia with
the transformation in Northern Europe of reindeer hunters into
tree-felling Maglemosians; and the people who initiated the
transformation of human society in the Old World were on the
same kind of material plane as the Mesolithic peoples of peripheral regions. They were both hunter-fishers and their material
equipment was analogous and in some respects identical. Two
main groups of Mesolithic hunter-fishers may be distinguished
in Western Asia, those of the highlands comprising the Iranian
plateau and its outliers, and the more localized groups of the
East Mediterranean zone between the Nile valley and South
Anatolia.

The Mesolithic flint industries of the former region stem from
the local Advanced Palaeolithic tradition, well represented at the
cave of Zarzī near Sulaimaniyyah,[1] Kurdistān, the flint industry
of which comprised burins, backed blades and scrapers, with in
the upper level an addition of microlithic triangles, crescents and
rods. In the rock-shelter of Pawli-Gawra between Zarzī and Sulaimaniyyah,[2] this microlithic element is further developed and now
includes trapezes. Flint industries of this kind, in which the
'micro-burin' technique is freely used, extend as far afield as the
Iranian plateau, the Caspian shore and Turkmenistān and span
the transition from a hunting and gathering to a stock-raising
and cereal-growing economy.

The inhabitants of the Pawli-Gawra shelter (Fig. 15, nos. 1–8)
lived predominantly by hunting animals like gazelle, onager (?),
ox, red and roe deer and pig, helped out by bird-catching and
fishing, and they do not appear even to have possessed dogs. A
similar form of economy was associated with a flint industry of
Pawli-Gawra type dated to c. 10,000 B.C. by radio-carbon in
level B 2 of the cave of Shanidar in the same part of Kurdistān,[3]
and in the lower levels of the Belt Cave[4] near the eastern end of
the southern shore of the Caspian, dating from the tenth to the
seventh millennia B.C.

Historically, however, the significance of the Kurdistān and
Caspian caves differs profoundly. The Belt Cave was marginal
to the innovating region, and the hunting culture with the Pawli-

[1] §xii, 5.   [2] §xii, 2.
[3] §xii, 10.   [4] §xii, 3; 4; see Fig. 15, nos. 15–20.

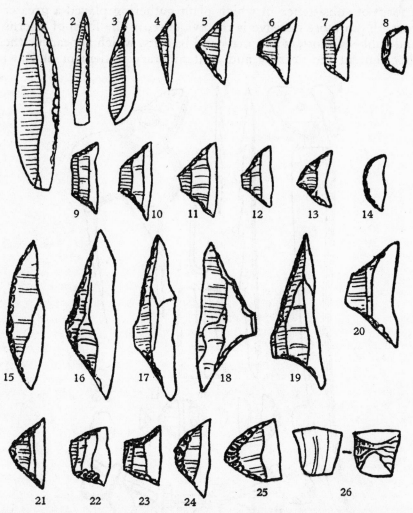

Fig. 15. Blade and trapeze industries from the Crimea and Western Asia: nos. 1–8, Pawli-Gawra; nos. 9–14, Jarmo, Kurdistān; nos. 15–20, Belt Cave, North Iran; nos. 21–6, Tash-Air, Crimea (no. 21 lower, nos. 22–4 middle, nos. 25–6 upper).

Gawra-type industry persisted until replaced around 6000 B.C. by a farming one replete with domestic ox and pig, sickle-blades, polished stone axes and pottery. At Shanidar, on the other hand, there is evidence for a gradual transition in economy within a basic continuity of culture: in level B 1, dated by radio-carbon analysis to the ninth millennium B.C., and containing a Pawli-Gawra type of flint industry, there is evidence for a shift towards a form of subsistence in which plant gathering played a greater part. Even more decisive is the evidence, in the form of querns and rubbers, mortars and mats and baskets, which appear for the first time at the near-by and contemporary settlement of Zawi

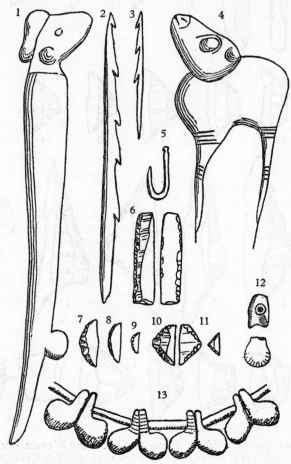

Fig. 16. Equipment of the Natufian Culture, Mount Carmel, Palestine: nos. 1–3, Maghārat el-Kabārah; nos. 4–13, Maghārat el-Wād. (Scales: 1 (c. 1/3); 6–12 (4/9); 2, 3, 5 (1/2); 4, 13 (2/3).)

Chemi Shanidar, that man had begun to practise an elementary type of farming as long ago as 8900 B.C.[1] When we turn to Jarmo,[2] an open village settlement in the same area a little farther south, with a more mature farming economy evidenced by the

[1] §XII, 10.   [2] §XII, 2; see Fig. 15, nos. 9–14.

cultivation of emmer, spelt, two-rowed barley and peas, and a fauna in which wild animals amounted to no more than 5 per cent, we find essentially the same microlithic industry associated with reaping-knife blades and reinforced by polished stone axes and after a time by pottery.

The richest and most distinctive manifestation of Mesolithic culture in Western Asia, the Natufian, so-called after the Wādi en-Naṭūf in Palestine,[1] is confined to a territory within forty miles or so of the Mediterranean between the Nile and Beirut with a possible extension in simplified form into southern Anatolia, exemplified by the site of Beldibi near Anṭalya.[2] The Natufians settled both in caves and in the open. They were keen hunters, especially for gazelle, and tipped their arrows with crescentic microliths the backs of which might be blunted by steep flaking from either face. Their bone-work (Fig. 16, nos. 1–3, 5) was richly developed and included barbed spear-points and fish-hooks. Reaping-knife handles slotted to receive flint blades, many of which show the diffuse lustre resulting from the harvesting of cereals, and pestles and mortars, including some cut out of the living rock, point to the importance of plant food and specifically of cereals, though whether these were wild or to any degree cultivated is a matter of debate in the absence of botanical determinations. The lack of domestic animals and the fact that the heads of wild ones were carved even on the heads of reaping-knives suggests strongly that the Natufian economy was still predominantly a wild one. However this may be, the size and character of the cemeteries in the rock-shelters—that of El-Wād (Fig. 16, nos. 4, 6–13) comprised eighty-seven burials, six of them adult—and the round tomb of monumental character constructed in the open at ʿEynān[3] suggest that the Natufians had already begun to achieve a certain fixity of settlement. On the evidence of radio-carbon dating it is plain that the Natufian territory was marginal to the earliest centres of food-production in the highlands of Kurdistān, and it seems likely that it was thence that the idea of the reaping-knife reached the Natufians. In relation to the beginnings of agriculture in the Mediterranean zone, however, there seems little doubt that the Natufian culture, at least in its early stage, was antecedent to the rise of settled farming communities and in this respect their encampment round the spring at the base of the *tell* at Jericho about 7800 B.C. is surely decisive evidence.[4]

[1] §XII, 6; 8; 9.   [2] §XII, 1.   [3] §XII, 9.   [4] §XII, 7.

CHAPTER IV

THE EVIDENCE OF LANGUAGE

I. LANGUAGE AND HISTORY

WHILE it is difficult to establish a close relationship between language form and the racial or cultural characteristics of its speakers, an intimate relationship does exist between culture and language content.[1] The study of language content needs no special justification, since the written records of antiquity are our most valuable source of information concerning the peoples and civilizations which form the object of historical investigation. But language as a formal structure, like the tools and institutions of a society, represents a kind of transmitted organism and as such falls into the category of data which can be ordered in typologically related sequences. Thus, for the historian, who is interested primarily in tracing interacting continuities, the study of the history and development of a language, apart from its use as a vehicle for oral and written traditions, provides useful and sometimes unique evidence of otherwise undiscernible ethnic and cultural affiliations.[2]

LANGUAGE CHANGE

The evolution of a language through time is most conveniently described in terms of two distinct but related features: function and form. Limiting ourselves for the moment to spoken language, we may define the primary function of language as communication. It is virtually axiomatic that a language, in order to serve the communication needs of a given community effectively, must keep pace with cultural changes within that community. That one is static implies that the other is also static, a generally unlikely situation. The ever-changing communication needs of a community will thus be reflected in its language, and mainly in lexical content rather than in form.[3] It is more or less irrelevant whether such changes are internal (evolutionary) or caused by some impetus from outside the community in question.

The changes which take place within the form of a language are of a very different sort and are to a great extent self-generated. The structure of a language may be described as a complex inter-

---

[1] §I, 13, 207 ff.   [2] §I, 15.   [3] §I, 14, 89 ff.

locking set of systems, the analysis of which may be approached at several levels. Although traditional divisions into phonology, morphology, and syntax are no longer recognized as adequate, this tripartite breakdown is still at the basis of the more elaborate modern analyses. But emphasis is placed not only on descriptions of the various isolatable entities that make up a language, but also on their systemic identification and function, as well as on the more complex relationships that exist among the various subsystems.[1] Regardless, however, of the technical level of synchronic description, linguistic change may be defined in more general terms for our present purpose.

Within a given linguistic community the complex nature of language makes it highly improbable that any two speakers use precisely the same form of the language. This results from imprecision arising from imperfect transmission and memory and from slight differences in the connotations of words and structures, a natural consequence of individual experience. To say that a community is linguistically homogeneous is to rise above this idiolect (or individual language) difference and to recognize a composite norm to which all speakers conform within accepted degrees of tolerance. Change in the form of a language is easily understood within this context: there is a precarious balance between the centrifugal force of idiolect deviation (individual 'error') from the norm and the centripetal force arising from the need to conform for effective communication. Thus, most deviations are cancelled out by conformist correction, but those which are accepted and imitated for one reason or another may gradually bring about a permanent change in the language.

Fortunately, linguistic change is not a random process. While changes are more or less independent of cultural influence, either internal or external, they are limited and conditioned by the structural patterns of the language itself.[2] Even more generally, linguistic change is amenable to classification, regardless of the language involved, and from the vast amount of material already studied there has emerged a set of principles sufficiently coherent to provide a foundation for an empirical science such as historical linguistics.[3]

LANGUAGE RELATIONSHIPS

There are four ideal situations which may be represented as models illustrating the types and degrees of relationships existing among languages of a given family. It must be remembered, however,

[1] §I, 5, 2.   [2] §I, 9.   [3] §I, 5, 365 ff.; §I, 2, 346 ff.; §I, 8.

that actual historical situations are usually much more complicated than any simple model and can be reconstructed only by any and all combinations and repetitions of these basic concepts.

First there is the simple *linear* relationship, in which a linguistically homogeneous community remains isolated and coherent over a span of time long enough for significant changes to occur in the language. The languages of the earlier and later periods are said to be linearly related.

Secondly, there is the ideal situation of *divergence in isolation*. If a language community splits into two or more groups which are subsequently and immediately isolated from one another, the language of each group will continue to evolve. But because there is no fixed direction for linguistic change, these languages will gradually diverge from one another in both form and content, until, after a suitable time, they will have become quite distinct. Some parallel development may occur as the result of inherited structural features, but this will prove negligible in the long run.

The *dialect continuum*,[1] our third model, begins with the same relatively small linguistically homogeneous community, but which, in the course of time, because of population growth or some other non-linguistic factor, spreads over a geographical area so great that the stabilizing effect of the core community is no longer strong enough to exert corrective conformity on the dialects of the outlying regions. In such a situation linguistic sub-communities are formed, each of its own norm. As long as there is some degree of linguistic coherence throughout the area and there is at least some mutual influence between contiguous sub-communities, we may describe the total as a dialect continuum. It is well to note here that there is no accepted definition of a dialect as opposed to a new language; there is no absolute, measurable differential by which a dialect deviating from some other one in the continuum is automatically labelled a different language. Although we have described this model in terms of geographical spread, it is equally applicable to dialect differentiation among the various strata of a given society or to the divergences that arise between spoken and written forms of a language which continue to influence one another.

The fourth model cannot be defined so precisely as the foregoing. A language community is often subjected to *interference* in a wide variety of ways.[2] A model situation in language can be represented at best only as an indefinite variable; the nature and degree of interference is determined by the extent of contact,

---

[1] §1, 5, 471 ff.; §1, 2, 321 ff.   [2] §1, 16.

ranging from the most casual cultural interchange to actual bilingualism. Historically, these may represent the contacts between an indigenous group and an immigrant group, between a subject people and its conquerors, or even the mutual interference between two dialects (geographical or social) of a single community. It is obvious that each of the preceding models is capable of being disturbed by the phenomenon of interference. If the two languages brought into contact are structurally distinct, the task of sorting out intrusive elements may not be too difficult. But when there is mutual contamination between two or more closely related languages, the resulting situation may defy analysis. Most language interference is visible in the lexicon, while, in general, widespread bilingualism would appear to be necessary to effect changes in structure. The term *substratum* is often applied to the special instance of this model in which an indigenous population exerts an influence on the language of an immigrating group.

METHODS OF HISTORICAL LINGUISTICS

The science of comparative linguistics has its origin in the last decades of the eighteenth century, when the new knowledge of Sanskrit awakened European scholars to the realization that long-cherished ideas about the perfection and elegance of the classical languages had to be abandoned and that long-held views on the more or less static relationship among languages should be replaced with one based on historical process.[1] The nineteenth century was characterized by vast enthusiasm, a century of search and discovery in both practical and theoretical directions, abetted by parallel interests in the concepts of evolution and naturalism.[2] The present century has seen the rise of descriptive and structural linguistics with new and important techniques of analysis and presentation, including the increasingly important use of statistical measurement and concomitant employment of the computer.

The comparative method in its simplest application is an attempt to reconstruct a parent language from the data of two or more derived languages.[3] The reconstruction proceeds along accepted lines in accordance with (1) the general principles of linguistic development and (2) the basic situations and their compounds, as described in our models. More specifically, reconstruction begins with a thorough study of cognates and recurring correspondences in form, for without the presence of both of these in

[1] §1, 1, 133 ff.   [2] §1, 12.
[3] §1, 2, 297 ff.; §1, 5, 485 ff.; §1, 7, 119 ff.

some degree a genetic relationship among the languages in question would not be suspected in the first place. While absolute limits cannot be established and 'intuition' still plays an important role in preliminary investigations, cognates may be defined as a set of lexical items similar in meaning and form in the various languages involved; the ultimate goal of the linguist is to discover a set of rules or relationships true of these words, which will allow him to generate from a hypothetical parent word all the forms attested in the derived languages. If it were not for recurring correspondences on the phonological and morphological levels, there would have to be as many rules as there are cognates. Such a demonstration would, needless to say, be regarded as a failure, since there must be a significant difference between the number of derived forms and the number of rules necessary for deriving them.

The method known as internal reconstruction is limited both in application and value.[1] Careful examination of a language always reveals certain systemic imbalances, such as sharp limitations or conflicts in the distribution of certain sounds or the presence of small groups of irregular forms as opposed to a dominant group of regular ones. Since it is known from the study of controlled situations that such variations *may* be the result of historical change from a more uniform earlier stage of the language, it is possible to approach any given language from this point of view and to reduce the existing imbalance to a uniform hypothetical progenitor coupled with a set of rules for deriving the subsequent forms. Although internal reconstruction can lead to greater insight into the structure of a given language, the lack of external controls and the absence of theoretical backing detract much from its value as a tool in historical linguistics. There is also the remote possibility that a supposed earlier form so reconstructed may be more readily identified as being related to some other language.

The comparative method itself has serious limitations. These arise from the fact that a certain degree of coherence must exist in the empirical data before the method can be applied. If the divergence is too great, reconstruction is impossible, in spite of obvious genetic relationships deduced from a larger number of cognates and recurring correspondences than chance would allow. This sort of impasse cannot be considered as a condemnation of the comparative method, but it does emphasize the need for other acceptable methods of evaluating historical relationships when the data are too sparse for conventional treatment.

[1] §1, 6; §1, 5, 461 ff.

A recent and different approach to this problem is based on a statistical examination of vocabularies. The method is known generally as lexicostatistics,[1] and in a more specialized form, as glottochronology.[2] Two basic assumptions are made, neither of which has firm theoretical support: (1) that a diagnostic list can be established, for each item of which a single word can be found in any given language; (2) that the words in such a list will, over a given time, suffer replacement (attrition) at a constant rate. Transferred into mathematical formulae, these two assumptions are now in wide use for determining the degree of relatedness between two languages. While this is not the place to enter into a detailed discussion of this theory, it must be noted that objections have been raised which are so serious as to vitiate the results claimed for this method.[3] The first assumption suffers from the naïveté of assuming discrete universals of perception and expression. The second, when reduced to the formulae now in use, does not measure accurately what it claims, since any two languages which diverge from a common parent may well retain a similar proportion of the parent vocabulary, but compared with one another the range of comparable items will depend on which items have been replaced. The time measurement, computed between the two possible extremes (from identical replacement in the two languages to completely different replacements) is too vague to have any real significance. That lexicostatistical measurements may prove of historical value is undeniable, but results claimed by current practitioners cannot be assessed without much more refinement and correction in the method itself.

BORROWING, DIFFUSION, AND INTRUSION

As we have stated, cultural interchanges of even a slight degree may leave their traces on the languages of the affected communities in the form of loanwords or, less commonly, of borrowed grammatical features. The detailed study of loan material serves, therefore, to corroborate the existence of cultural contacts which are indicated by other data and, in those cases where other indications are lacking, to suggest contacts which would otherwise be unknown. Linguistic corroboration of this sort is quite valuable, for example, in the study of the Sumerian and Semitic components of Mesopotamian civilization during the third millennium, where the mutual influence of the languages on one another sheds light on the relevant technical and institutional aspects of the two ethnic

[1] §1, 10.   [2] §1, 11.   [3] §1, 3.

groups.[1] Similar examples may be cited: the mutual influence of Persian and Aramaic during the Achaemenid period and, in the east, later; the large admixture of Greek in Coptic; the diffusion of Hurrian elements in certain phases of Akkadian.

The analysis of personal names has proved to be a powerful tool for identifying various ethnic elements that constitute an otherwise homogeneous population. One of the most striking examples of this is the detection of Indo-Aryans in Syria and Palestine during the Late Bronze Age. Indo-Aryan personal names, reflecting a language closely akin to Vedic Sanskrit, show up clearly in the fifteenth-century documents from Alalakh IV and are attested in the south for approximately the same period in the Taanach Letters. The continued presence of these Indo-Europeans is well documented in the Amarna Letters of the fourteenth century, where they actually make up a majority of the non-Semitic rulers mentioned. Other examples of similar ethnographic information provided by onomastic analysis include the large number of Semitic (mostly Amorite and Canaanite) names found in Egyptian records from the Middle Kingdom and later, and the Aramaic names in late Assyrian and Babylonian sources.

We are often dependent on personal and place names as our only source for a language. An excellent example is afforded by Amorite, a north-west Semitic language of the second millennium. All of our information about Amorite, including proof of its existence, comes from the analysis of personal names in cuneiform sources from Mesopotamia (especially Mari) and Syria-Palestine, augmented by a considerable number from Egyptian documents. These names supply many details of Amorite phonology, morphology, and vocabulary, all of vital importance for reconstructing the linguistic and historical picture in this complex area of investigation. Similar indirect analysis has been used with the Canaanite Amarna Letters. In many of these letters the deviation from the Middle Babylonian norm in which they were ostensibly written furnishes us with our most valuable source for the local Canaanite dialects of the period.

THE MAJOR LANGUAGE FAMILIES

In sections II and III of the present chapter we shall present a detailed survey of the two large and well-attested language families whose members play a dominant role in the early history of

[1] See below, pp. 147 ff.

western civilization: Hamito-Semitic (or Afro-Asian) and Indo-European (or Indo-Hittite). Section IV will include a discussion of some important isolated (i.e. non-affiliated) languages of early history, such as Sumerian, Hurrian, and Elamite. The other recognized major families of Eurasia and Africa are relatively unimportant at this stage since their earliest attestations are mostly recent and their history in the pre-Christian period is conjectural. But because relationships between these families and the languages mentioned in this work have been suggested, but never convincingly demonstrated, we list them below for purposes of general orientation and reference.[1]

(a) Eurasian

Finno-Ugrian, in north-eastern Europe and north-western Asia, includes Finnish, Hungarian, Cheremissian, etc., and more remotely Samoyed.

Caucasian, in the area of the Caucasus, is used of languages which are not Indo-European or Turkic in origin, and whose ancestral speakers found refuge there at different times in the past. Divided generally into three main ethno-geographical groups—south-west Caucasian (including especially Georgian and Mingrelian), north-west Caucasian (including Circassian), north-east Caucasian (including Chechen and Avar)—there is still no accepted comparative linguistic classification.[2] Georgian was reduced to writing in the fifth century A.D.

Altaic, a name of doubtful coherence, which always includes the Turkic languages, spoken over a vast area extending from the region of the upper Irtysh River, west of Outer Mongolia to European Turkey. The once popular grouping of Turkish with Mongolian and Manchurian has become more and more doubtful, in view of the differences in structure, which suggest that the common elements of vocabulary are the result of long periods of close political and cultural ties.[3] There is no solid evidence for considering the ancestral Turks as Mongoloid. The Old Turkish Orkhon inscriptions go back to the early eighth century A.D.

(b) Asian

Sino-Tibetan, including the Tibeto-Burman and the Chinese groups.

Mongolian, Manchu and others (see above, on Altaic).

[1] §I, 4.
[2] The speculations of N. Marr and his followers were politically oriented.
[3] §IV, 4; 5; 27.

Japanese and Korean, each an isolated language.

Kadai, limited to south-east Asia, includes Thai-Laotian and others.

Dravidian, now limited chiefly to southern India (Tamil, Telugu, etc.) and Balūchistān (Brahui). The Dravidians almost certainly occupied much of northern India and especially the Indus Valley, before their conquest by the Indo-Aryans about the eighteenth century B.C.[1]

Malayo-Polynesian, now covering a vast area, from Madagascar to the islands of the eastern Pacific.

The preceding list includes only major families of languages in Eurasia, northern Africa and the Pacific. It does not include the so-called Chari-Nile family (Nubian, Sudanic, etc.), whose relationships are often obscure, nor the Bantu and other true Negro families and groups of languages, nor the Khoisan (Hottentot and its congeners). It also excludes the Australian and Papuan languages of New Guinea and the Melanesian islands, as well as all the many apparently unrelated linguistic families of the American Indians. Of course, many isolated and as yet unclassified languages are known in all the areas concerned.

It is now becoming more and more probable that spoken languages were already well developed at least 100,000 years ago—probably as early as the functionally superb stone tools fashioned by the craftsmen of Lower Palaeolithic (Abbevillian, etc.) in Western Europe.[2] After all, languages are as much tools of communication as artefacts are tools for making articles of wood, bone and stone, used for a large variety of purposes by primitive man. Even without this obvious parallel, the fact that such different animals as bees and dolphins are now known to have most elaborate communication patterns should give us pause. Besides, the pre-glacial Australopithecines of East and South Africa seem to have been far ahead of modern chimpanzees as adapters and even as inventors of tools—and we are rapidly learning not to despise the cleverness of the latter.

Not only is human language exceedingly ancient, but the mobility of primitive languages can scarcely be exaggerated. An

[1] See below, pp. 154 f.

[2] See the fully documented presentation of the present chronological situation, resulting from the Urey-Emiliani correlation, and a defence of the latter against the impossibly high chronology of Curtis and Evernden in *The World History of the Jewish People*, 1 (ed. E. A. Speiser, Tel-Aviv, 1964), 67 ff. and 353 ff. The probable *appearance* of language is dated there (p. 67) '150,000–200,000 years ago—perhaps considerably more'.

excellent illustration is furnished by the peopling of America, which began not less than 20,000 years ago and brought groups of many racial origins and radically divergent linguistic stocks across seas and oceans to occupy every habitable part of the hemisphere. Just as beginnings are now being made in locating Old World sources of elements in Palaeo-American and more recent cultures, so we may expect that a few, at least, of the presumptive sources of language will also be identified. We must, to be sure, expect that most of the putative Old World cognates have become extinct or have been transformed beyond recognition. As recently as 10,000 years ago such far-ranging families as Afro-Asian and Indo-Hittite may have been severely limited in geographical extension, while now isolated tongues like Basque and south Caucasian may have spread over wide areas. Even structures may change quite rapidly. Though Egyptian and the Semitic languages of Asia share a host of diagnostic phenomena, there are too few common words to make glotto-chronological methods applicable with significant results. Yet Egyptian, as a language of sedentary folk, transformed its basic verbal structure twice between predynastic times (before the late fourth millennium B.C.) and Coptic (about A.D. 300). The consistent extension of the triconsonantal pattern to biconsonantal verbs by developing weak stems, was substantially completed in parent Semitic no later than the fourth millennium in all probability; it was never completed in Old Egyptian and in later times lost ground again because of phonetic decay. On the other hand, in view of the close parallelism between the prefixed conjugations of the other Hamitic languages and the corresponding Semitic patterns, it seems certain that Egyptian once possessed prefixing conjugations, which were lost before the end of predynastic times, at latest. The general shift to verbal forms related in structure to the Egyptian participles, which may themselves have originated in 'gerundive' use of the infinitive, was certainly completed by our oldest inscriptions. In New Egyptian this structure began to yield ground to increasingly wide use of periphrastic clauses and phrases prefixed to a simple verbal form, which ended by giving Coptic a strangely agglutinative appearance. That this structural transformation should have taken place in an inflected language is a warning as to the possibilities of apparently basic change in supposedly crystallized linguistic structures. On the other hand, Classical Arabic about A.D. 500 was in many ways more primitive in structure than Akkadian at the beginning of its career as a sedentary language (not later than c. 2500 B.C.). In short, we must be prepared to find great mobility, rapid increase or decline in populations, and a high differential rate of change, caused in large part by different social structuring.

II. THE AFRO-ASIAN (HAMITO-SEMITIC) FAMILY

The Hamito-Semitic language family has until recently been rather poorly defined. Already in the last century the study of a number of North African languages had brought to light enough common lexical and grammatical items to suggest a common origin. But the term Hamitic, used to denote this language stock, was unfortunately applied also to various racial and ethnic characteristics, so that as a linguistic term it lost in precision. The languages as a group also have many elements in common with the Semitic languages, originally spoken outside of Africa; the combined designation 'Hamito-Semitic' gained general acceptance in spite of the lack of clear internal classification. Only recently has careful attention been directed toward this problem, the most systematic survey being that of J. H. Greenberg, whom we shall follow here.[1] It must be emphasized, however, that the last word concerning the affiliations of many African languages is far from being said, and the next decade or so will undoubtedly see important modifications.

Five co-ordinated subgroups may be recognized: (1) Semitic, (2) Ancient Egyptian, (3) Berber, (4) Cushitic, and (5) Chadic (Hausa). Only the first two are clearly attested in antiquity, both from the early third millennium onward. The Berber dialects are currently spoken in the vast area extending from the Siwa Oasis westward to the Atlantic and southward to the Niger River.[2] Whether the language of the so-called Libyan inscriptions, dating from the Roman Period in North Africa, is an early form of Berber or not remains problematical.[3] A similar situation prevails with reference to the strongly Egyptianizing Meroitic inscriptions from the long-lived kingdom in Nubia (Cush), centred first at Napata (c. 1000–300 B.C.) and then at Meroe (to c. A.D. 400). The Meroitic language cannot be related confidently to any known family, but is often classified uncritically with Hamito-Semitic.[4] The ancient forerunners of Cushitic[5] and Chadic,[6] both represented by many languages and dialects in present-day north-

---

[1] §II, 24, 42 ff.   [2] §II, 6, 38.   [3] §II, 6, 47.
[4] §II, 26.   [5] §II, 43, 118 ff.   [6] §II, 47, 153 ff.

east and north-central Africa respectively, are unknown. It should be noted that the present classification of Hamito-Semitic excludes several language groups formerly assigned to it, such as Fulani in West Africa,[1] the Nilo-Hamitic (*sic!*) languages in north-east Africa,[2] and Hottentot (Khoisan) in the extreme south.[3]

The language of ancient Egypt, attested from early in the third millennium with the beginnings of hieroglyphic inscriptions during the Early Dynastic Period, is now sufficiently well understood to permit serious study of its genetic relationship with other members of the Afro-Asian family and with the Semitic languages in particular. Although Egyptian is not to be placed within the Semitic family, there are few grammatical features which can be considered alien to that group.[4] A close genetic relationship is thus indicated and accepted; only on details is there a divergence of scholarly opinion. The total loss in Egyptian, for example, of prefix verbal conjugations, a common feature not only of Semitic but also of Berber and other African members of the Afro-Asian family, points probably to early separation from the parent stock. Then too, much of the ordinary vocabulary of Egyptian finds no convincing cognates in Semitic, and many of the items which have been compared suggest, by the irregularity of their phonetic correspondences, a long and complex prehistory whose details cannot be reconstructed without more evidence than is currently available.[5]

The recognized phases and written forms of Egyptian are as follows:

(1) Old Egyptian, attested in hieroglyphic texts from *c.* 3100–2160 B.C.[6]

(2) Middle Egyptian, a standard literary form evolved from late Old Egyptian and employed not only during the Middle Kingdom (*c.* 2160–1780 B.C.) but in slightly modified forms for monumental purposes down through the first millennium.[7] It is at the beginning of this period that the hieratic script, a cursive adaptation of hieroglyphic for use on papyrus and ostraca, begins an ever-increasing divergence from its parent form.

(3) Late Egyptian, a second standard form which came into wide use at the end of the Eighteenth Dynasty (*c.* 1370 B.C.) for literary and everyday uses, mainly in hieratic script.[8] It differs considerably from Middle Egyptian, owing to the incorporation of many new features from the spoken language of the period.

---

[1] §II, 24, 25 ff.   [2] §II, 24, 43 ff.   [3] §II, 24, 66 ff.
[4] §II, 1, 41.   [5] §II, 11.   [6] §II, 15.
[7] §II, 20.   [8] §II, 16.

(4) Demotic, a third standard form, evolved during the first half of the first millennium B.C., distinct in grammar, orthography, and script from the preceding phases of the language.[1]

(5) Coptic, the last standard form of the language from the early Christian era, written in a modified Greek alphabet.[2] The dialectal divisions known from Coptic, i.e. Sahidic, Bohairic, Faiyumic, and Akhmimic (*inter alia*) were of course present to some extent in the older stages of Egyptian, but it is only rarely that these differences show through the highly standardized earlier writings.

Geographical, ethnic, and linguistic criteria are employed simultaneously in most classifications of the Semitic languages, with the result that imprecision, vagueness, and controversy persist.[3] But such disputes, largely terminological, are common to the problem of linguistic classification, and since they rely on scholarly consensus, they will probably never be completely resolved. The geographical distribution of the languages in antiquity is a convenient starting-point and will suffice for our purposes.

North-east Semitic is represented by the dialects of Akkadian, attested from the middle of the third millennium to the beginning of the Christian era. Prior to *c.* 2000 B.C. the evidence is too sparse to support dialectal distinctions; this phase of the language is referred to simply as Old Akkadian. After 2000 B.C. there is an increasingly clear differentiation into Assyrian and Babylonian, in the north and south respectively, and within each of these dialects successive phases such as Old, Middle, and New are established. The following sketch includes the more important of these subdivisions with their approximate dates.

Old Akkadian (*c.* 2500–2000), in which three periods are recognized: Pre-Sargonic, Sargonic, and Ur III.[4]

Old Babylonian (*c.* 2000–1500), the classical form of the language, associated primarily with Hammurabi and the First Dynasty of Babylon.[5]

Old Assyrian (*c.* 2000–1500), the contemporary phase of the northern dialect, best known from texts discovered at the Assyrian merchant colony of Kanesh (Kültepe) in Cappadocia.

Middle Babylonian and Middle Assyrian (both *c.* 1500–1000).[6]

Literary Babylonian, a standard form of the language having its origins in the Middle Babylonian period but used for a wide variety of literary and technical works down to *c.* 500 B.C.

Neo-Babylonian refers to the actual spoken language during

---

[1] §II, 30.   [2] §II, 40, 42.   [3] §II, 32; 3 ff., 46.
[4] §II, 22.   [5] §II, 45.   [6] §II, 5.

the first millennium, with the term Late Babylonian reserved for the latest phases, from about 600 B.C. on.

Neo-Assyrian designates the contemporary dialect in the north down to the fall of Assyria c. 600 B.C.

Akkadian is written in a cuneiform script borrowed from the Sumerians. During most of the second millennium Akkadian was the *lingua franca* of the entire civilized Near East, excepting Egypt. Several important corpora of texts in Akkadian have been recovered from areas outside of or bordering on Assyria and Babylonia proper, such as the Nuzi tablets, showing strong Hurrian influence, the Mari tablets, with Amorite influence,[1] and the Amarna letters, exhibiting strong Canaanite and Hurrian substrata.

Before the turn of the present century the limited number of speech forms known from the north-west Semitic area was small enough for simple classification. Of the two main branches, Canaanite included Biblical Hebrew and a few Hebrew inscriptions, none predating the tenth century, Phoenician, and the poorly attested Moabite; Aramaic constituted the other main branch. The convergent original form of these languages could be projected backward into the then relatively undiscovered second millennium B.C. So far as these languages are concerned, the discoveries of the present century have produced no change in status or classification; to be sure, the number of early inscriptions recovered has in each case increased significantly and the interpretation of this early material has progressed substantially. It is the enormous amount of new data from the second millennium, however, that has complicated the classification of languages in this general area. The recovery of cuneiform tablets at sites from northern Mesopotamia to the Mediterranean, mostly in Akkadian, has provided us with hundreds of different personal names whose components reflect the languages of the local populations during the first half of the millennium. Whatever dialectal differentiation existed is considered minimal and the terms East Canaanite[2] and Amorite[3] have been applied to this material as a whole. From after the middle of the millennium come the Ugaritic texts discovered at Ras Shamra in Syria.[4] These texts are of two types: (1) epic and religious texts whose composition must certainly be projected back into the first half of the second millennium, and (2) letters and administrative documents whose language must be considered contemporary with the finds them-

[1] §II, 17.
[3] §II, 21, 28.
[2] After T. Bauer, §II, 7.
[4] §II, 23.

selves, i.e. from the fourteenth and thirteenth centuries. Also to the fourteenth century belongs the extremely important corpus of letters discovered in Egypt at El-Amarna, representing the correspondence between kings of the Eighteenth Dynasty and their representatives and vassal rulers in Syria and Palestine. Although these letters are in Akkadian, the language of the local rulers has so influenced their style and grammar that they provide a valuable source for the local dialects of this period.[1] A corpus of early alphabetic material extending from about the middle of the millennium, or perhaps slightly earlier, supplements the data just described. The most important of these are the Proto-Sinaitic inscriptions (*c.* 1500), a series of rather crudely inscribed texts discovered at Serābīt el-Khādim, an Egyptian turquoise and copper mining site in the Sinai Peninsula.[2] These texts are important both for the early history of the alphabet and for the linguistic picture in general. The development of the north-west Semitic languages may be sketched briefly as follows:

(1) *c.* 2000 (and earlier) to *c.* 1750: A dialect continuum (Amorite) extending from northern Mesopotamia westward into Syria-Palestine. Contemporary data are insufficient for dialect divisions.

(2) *c.* 1750–1400: There are enough data to justify a general division between Early Canaanite in Syria-Palestine and Amorite to the east. In view of the divergences attested immediately after this period, we may assume that distinctive dialectal differences separated the languages of the northern Canaanite area from the southern. The epic language of Ugarit would belong chiefly to the northern group, though it had become generalized, like Homeric Greek. Some scholars would recognize a closer tie between North Canaanite and Amorite than between North and South Canaanite at this time.

(3) *c.* 1400–1000. Contemporary data and extrapolations from the later situation support clear dialectal distinctions in the Canaanite area, leading to a clean break by the end of this period between Hebrew and Phoenician.[3] The absence of relevant material from areas later inhabited by the Aramaeans hinders us in our attempt to determine with any precision the specific locales in which this branch of north-west Semitic had its origins, but Proto-Aramaic must have reached a recognizable form during or even before this period.[4]

(4) *c.* 1000 and after. Hebrew,[5] Moabite, Phoenician,[6] and

---

[1] §II, 31; see *C.A.H.* II³, ch. xx, sect. I. [2] §II, 2. [3] §II, 25.
[4] See *C.A.H.* II³, ch. xxxiii, sect. IV. [5] §II, 10. [6] §II, 18.

Aramaic[1] are attested as distinct inscriptional languages. Evidence for minor dialects (e.g. Byblian Phoenician) survives from early in the millennium, but in general standard forms of these languages prevail by the middle of the millennium. The subsequent history of each of these languages is complicated by the persistence of standard written forms fixed during their early phases beside naturally developing and divergent forms, with inevitable mixing of the two. Hebrew has continued in use until today. Phoenician, after the early period of colonization, beginning in the tenth and ninth centuries, split into two types developing concurrently: Phoenician in the homeland proper and Punic in the colonial cities, especially Carthage. Both languages died out early in the Christian era after the third century A.D. Aramaic, well attested through most of the millennium, survived after the Christian era in two dialectally distinct groups: Western Aramaic, including Nabataean,[2] Palmyrene,[3] the various dialects of Jewish Palestinian Aramaic,[4] Samaritan Aramaic, Christian Palestinian Aramaic,[5] and scattered modern survivals; Eastern Aramaic, including Syriac,[6] Babylonian (Talmudic) Aramaic, Mandaean,[7] and a rather extensive modern form known as 'Assyrian'.

South-west Semitic comprises North Arabic and its antecedents. North Arabic appears as a literary language in pre-Islamic poetry, as preserved by a later tradition, and in the Quran. These works served as a basis for the standard literary Arabic of the medieval period, systematized by several generations of grammarians and altered by various dialectal influences. The spread of Islam carried the Arabic language to the borders of China in the east and to the Atlantic in the west. The present-day extent is somewhat less, but attested in many dialects in a zone ranging across northern Africa, dipping deeply into the Sudan, spanning the Arabian peninsula, most of Syria and Palestine, stretching across Mesopotamia and into mainland Asia. The antecedents of Quranic and classical Arabic are obscure; it would appear to be based on a poetic *koinē* widely used in the immediately preceding pre-Islamic period.[8] Also classified as North Arabic are the more ancient inscriptions known as Thamudic, Lihyanite, and Safaitic, dating from about 500 B.C. to 300 A.D.[9]

South-east Semitic (or, according to others, a branch of south-west Semitic)[10] is well attested in an ancient form by the inscrip-

[1] §II, 8, 19, 4. [2] §II, 13. [3] §II, 12.
[4] §II, 14. [5] §II, 39. [6] §II, 33.
[7] §II, 34. [8] §II, 37. [9] §II, 48.
[10] §II, 32, 13; §II, 29.

tions originating in the kingdoms of South Arabia from the eighth century B.C. to the sixth A.D. Recognized dialects are Sabaean, Minaean, Qatabanian, and Ḥadramī.[1] Modern descendants of this same family survive in Mehrī and Shaḥrī, spoken along the southern coast, and in Soqoṭrī, spoken on the off-shore island Soqoṭra. The major survivors of this important branch of Semitic come from Ethiopia, however, where South Arabian merchant colonies were founded no later than the fifth century B.C.[2] A large Christian literature is extant in Ge'ez (classical Ethiopic), following the Christianization of the country in the fourth century. Modern spoken languages include Amharic, the official language, Tigré, Tigriña, Harari, Gafat, Argobba, and the dialect group known as Guragé.

III. THE INDO-HITTITE FAMILY

It is now a century and a half since Franz Bopp published his first treatise on the relationship of Sanskrit to Greek, Latin, Germanic and Persian (1816). Ever since, there has been a sustained scholarly attack on Indo-European problems, thanks to which the state of our knowledge has been enlarged and deepened to an extent nowhere even remotely approached in other areas of linguistic research, although the standard treatises from the early part of this century have seldom been replaced by publications of equal authority.[3] The discovery of a set of proto-Indo-European 'laryngeal' sounds and the widening of horizons resulting from the decipherment of the Anatolian languages and Tocharian have made it possible to continue research along the old lines, while descriptive and structural approaches to comparative linguistics are diverting scholarly attention to completely new lines of investigation. As a model of rigorous analysis Indo-European remains unique in the general area of linguistics and seems likely to hold this place for some time to come.

Indo-European has been divided into two main groups—a European and a Eurasian. The former includes chiefly Greek, Italic, Germanic and Celtic; the latter comprises Balto-Slavic (Lithuanian, etc., and the Slavonic languages), Indic (Sanskrit) and Iranian (Avestan and Old Persian, etc.). We omit Albanian

---

[1] §II, 9.   [2] §II, 44.

[3] The second edition of K. Brugmann's *Grundriss der vergleichenden Grammatik der indogermanischen Sprachen* (1897–1916) still remains basic, though a great deal of valuable work has since been devoted to individual languages and linguistic phases.

and Armenian at this point since they are not yet clearly located in the Indo-European or the larger Indo-Hittite group; there are only some four hundred words in each of them which belong to the original language, all others being loanwords. As we shall see below, the Armenian language appears to be a late offshoot of Hittite. The first four languages mentioned above are conventionally called *centum* languages because they still preserve the old velar ('palatal') stops without changing them to sibilants. It is still uncertain whether the 'Tocharian' languages, discovered at Turfan in Central Asia early in this century, are really *centum* or are simply unpalatalized Indo-Hittite; Tocharian has points in common with Hittite. In the Balto-Slavic, Indo-Aryan and Iranian groups palatalization is carried through with fair consistency. There has been much debate as to the original home of the Indo-Europeans, but this matter does not concern us here.[1]

The southward irruption of the Greek-speaking peoples into mainland Greece took place no later than the eighteenth century B.C., and may perhaps have fallen a century or so earlier; the Indo-Aryan irruption into India can now also be dated no later than the late eighteenth century B.C., and the Iranians migrated into Iran some centuries later. The question when the main diffusion eastward and westward took place is at present unanswerable. It should be said, however, that there is no solid basis for the hypothesis of long-range weather cycles such as the 800-year cycle which is defended by some historians of climate today. For instance, it is thought that there was one prolonged period of drought to be dated roughly between the twenty-first and eighteenth centuries B.C. This is quite superfluous as an explanation for the movement of peoples from Europe southward. In the first place, not only do we lack evidence for any such hypothesis in the Near and Middle East, but the European evidence is quite inadequate for the structure built upon it. The ideas of Caetani and Ellsworth Huntington have long since been disproved and there is no good reason to revive them in a new form today. In the second place, any succession of five to ten dry years may bring about very serious famine conditions and may start mass movements on the part of hungry peoples. From prehistoric times on there was a strong tendency to increase population by improving the production of food, both through use of new tools and methods of cultivation, and through the spread of important food plants and animals. As a result peoples living in marginal areas became more vulnerable to famine conditions. It is also erroneous to say

[1] See *C.A.H.* I³, ch. XXVII.

that during the third millennium the Indo-Europeans were nomad horsemen—or in Central Asia nomad cameleers.[1] Both assumptions are based on false *a priori* hypotheses and misdated stratigraphic finds. Even today the chronology of central Europe and even more of central Asia in the Neolithic, Early and Middle Bronze periods is almost hopelessly confused. Until archaeological chronology has been clarified, and the exact level in stratified sites, at which remains of domesticated horses and camels are found, has been fixed, it is idle to speculate about equine nomads as bearers of early Indo-European migratory movements.

We have, in fact, increasingly strong evidence for a long period of slow Indo-European development, as well as for the existence of groups which have long since disappeared, such as the Anatolian group of Indo-European languages.[2] The recovery of this linguistic group is the direct result of the decipherment of 'cuneiform' Hittite in 1915. To it belong most of the languages of Asia Minor during the second millennium B.C., as well as their congeners of the second and first millennia. It is now quite certain that the Anatolian group of languages was closely related to Indo-European.[3] There are some differences which point to a considerable age for the separation between them. For example, among early Anatolian peoples with Hittite affinities there is no trace of *Ablaut* (shift of vowels in the principal parts of the verb and noun) in the verb, though we do have some *Ablaut* in the noun (for example, *watar*, 'water', genitive *wetenas*).

It is often supposed that the Indo-Hittites migrated into Asia Minor at the beginning of the second millennium shortly before their first appearance in cuneiform and other texts. This is, however, an extremely doubtful assumption. For we find Hittite sharply defined and quite different from Indo-European by the sixteenth century B.C.[4] and perhaps considerably earlier (as the official language of the Old Hittite empire). In fact there is clear evidence from proper names, both names of places and names of persons, that these differences went back well before the earliest records of the Assyrian merchant colonies in Cappadocia about

[1] It is now certain that large-scale horseback-riding did not come into use until late in the second millennium, and that chariots with spoked wheels remained unknown until well after the beginning of the second millennium. After this type of chariot had been invented, it spread over the Near and Middle East like wildfire because of its military and sporting significance: contrast §III, 16, 12, n. 2. On the chronology of the domestication of the Bactrian (two-humped) camel see Reinhard Walz in *Z.D.M.G.* 104 (1954), 45 ff.   [2] §III, 16.

[3] §III, 16, 47 ff.; §III, 7; §III, 25. The literature is now very extensive.

[4] Or seventeenth, following the usual chronology.

the nineteenth century B.C.—though these undoubtedly went back to the late third millennium for their foundation. In these records we already find Luwian and Hittite names at the beginning of the second millennium B.C.[1]

In recent years the work of many scholars has demonstrated beyond any possible doubt that the languages of south-western and southern Asia Minor in the Iron Age, including the dominant tongues used in Lydia, Caria, Lycia, Pamphylia, Pisidia, Isauria, Lycaonia and Cilicia, were offshoots of the older Anatolian languages of the second millennium.[2] Moreover, we find in the Hittite inscriptions clear evidence that the Luwian names of that time were already specifically Lycian and Cilician in type. A recent discovery has added to our direct information, proving that a Lycian held a post at the court of the prince of Byblos about 1800 B.C.[3] The name, *Kuk(k)un(is)* and national origin are both given in a mortuary stele mentioning the name of the prince of Byblos in question, Abi-shemu. Since the same name appears in Lycia in the Hittite period (fourteenth century B.C.) and is also found in the Lycian inscriptions of the sixth to fourth centuries B.C., we have a particularly clear example of the existence of daughter dialects of Luwian at about the time when the Luwians are supposed by some scholars to have entered Asia Minor. It has long since been pointed out that the suffixed elements *-nthos* and *-ssos*, with variants, appear all over Greece and the Aegean islands as well as throughout south-western, southern and south-eastern Anatolia. As long ago shown by Blegen, these place names are frequently associated with Early Bronze archaeological deposits, indicating clearly that by far the easiest hypothesis in the circumstances is to recognize that the Luwian occupation of southern Anatolia probably went back to the middle of the third millennium B.C. or even earlier.[4] We know now that Lydian was closer in some respects to Hittite than to Luwian.[5] Since Lydia was located at the end of the central highland of Asia Minor, the Lydians participated in Aegean cultures as well as in the plateau civilization which the Hittites led. Similarly we know today that hieroglyphic Hittite was an offshoot of Luwian used in the inscriptions of southern and south-eastern Asia Minor as well as northern Syria between the twelfth and the seventh centuries B.C.[6]

[1] §III, 12; §III, 13, 73.
[2] In addition to previous references note especially G. Neumann, *Untersuchungen zum Weiterleben hethitischen und luwischen Sprachgutes in hellenistischer und römischer Zeit.* Wiesbaden, 1961. [3] §III, 2, 33 f., corrected in §III, 3, 46 f.
[4] §III, 6. [5] §III, 7. [6] §III, 13, 18, 22.

We may, therefore, set up the following probable relative chronology. There were three cognate tongues called respectively *Nasi-* (Hittite), *Lū(w)i-* (commonly called Luwian), and *Pala-* (the native home of which in Asia Minor is not yet known).[1] The speakers of these tongues had almost certainly moved into Asia Minor from the north not later than the middle centuries of the third millennium and had been pushed southward by subsequent invaders of quite unknown origin, perhaps including the so-called Proto-Hittites, called *Ḫatti* by the 'Hittites'. The Proto-Hittites certainly founded the ethno-political aggregation in which their language was ultimately displaced by cuneiform Hittite (*Nasi-*). In other words the former may have occupied Cappadocia after the latter and have established a group of city-states which were finally absorbed by the native Nasi, much as the Franks occupied and founded France but were finally absorbed by the older population and language. Proto-Hittite became the sacred language of the later 'Hittites', but does not seem to have been well known to them and is still very obscure; though we do know, for example, that it stressed prefixes but also possessed suffixes. Since most of the 'Hittite' royal names in later Cappadocia belong to this stratum, it is virtually certain that it had established itself in Asia Minor at a comparatively early date, probably no later than the twenty-fourth century B.C., which is about the date of the so-called royal tombs of Alaca. But the mere presence of a dominant Proto-Hittite stratum in Cappadocia suggests, as we have seen, that the Hittite-Luwian stratum had entered earlier and had been pressed farther to the south and east by the new invaders.

With the Phrygian occupation about 1200 B.C. (though the movement may, of course, have begun centuries earlier) we have the first true Indo-European language in Anatolia (outside of previous Greek occupation of parts of the western coast and the adjacent islands). Our knowledge of Phrygian is probably less than often supposed, because of the paucity of inscriptions and the fact that even less is known about ancient Thracian than about its Phrygian sister. The usual view that the Phrygians, in their movement eastward into southern Armenia in the late twelfth century B.C., were able to settle and ultimately to hand on their language in modified form to the Armenians is probably without any basis. We have no evidence in either Assyrian or Urarṭian inscriptions for supposing that any substantial number of Phrygians remained behind after their thorough defeat by Tiglath-pileser I.

---

[1] See *C.A.H.* II[3], ch. VI, sect. II.

It was pointed out a number of years ago by Austin[1] that Armenian shares so many grammatical and lexical elements with Hittite that it is much more reasonable to suppose that Armenian developed naturally from the Hittite-Luwian dialects of Armenia Minor west of the upper Euphrates. We have ample historical evidence that the Armenians tended to move eastward as they spread, rather than westward. It was suggested long ago by Jensen that the Armenian national name, *Haik*, stands for older *Hati-k*, in accord with the phonetic regularities of Armenian. The so-called *satem* character of Armenian, as contrasted with the *centum* character of Hittite, may most easily be explained in the same way as a similar phenomenon in hieroglyphic Hittite, namely by palatalization of the Indo-Hittite velar stops. This is a familiar phenomenon in a great many languages and is no argument at all for a *satem* origin of Armenian. Actually there are so many characteristics of Armenian which remind one of Hittite (for instance, its lack of grammatical gender), that it is highly improbable that they can be separated.

Nor is the similarity in Hittite and Armenian physical type irrelevant. While it is, of course, quite true that physical type and language are not necessarily related, at the same time it is rather remarkable that of all the populations of modern Anatolia and neighbouring areas to the east and south-east, the Armenians have best preserved the well-known 'Armenoid' form of Hittite crania. It was no idle combination which made von Luschan give the name 'Armenoid' to this brachycephalic, or even hyper-brachy-cephalic type with large noses and often receding chins. The original cradle of the Armenian nationality and culture is pre-cisely the area of greatest use of hieroglyphic Hittite script. Less than a century and a half separates the latest Hittite inscriptions from the first mention of Armenia as a name of the country in question (in the inscriptions of Darius Hystaspes). Nor is it irrelevant to recall that Luwian personal names survived into the Hellenistic and Roman periods all through southern Anatolia as far as eastern Cilicia and Cappadocia.[2] In fact the native Isaurian dialect is said to have been spoken as late as Byzantine times.

One of the least expected results of the Boğazköy excavation in 1907 was the discovery that Indo-Aryan was spoken in south-western Asia during the second millennium B.C. Our evidence for the Indo-Aryans in the Near East now comes not only from Hittite texts but also from the Amarna, Nuzi and Alalakh tablets, and from Middle-Assyrian inscriptions—as well as from mis-

[1] §III, 5; cf. §III, 24, 40 f. for a divergent view.   [2] §III, 25; see above, p. 141, n. 3.

cellaneous sources. They worshipped specifically Vedic gods, as
has been proved conclusively by Paul Thieme,[1] and they employed
specifically Indic forms of the numerals (for instance, 'one' is
written *aika*, like Sanskrit *eka*, and not **eva*, like Iranian *aiva*).
There are many common nouns connected directly and indirectly
with horse-breeding and training, as well as with chariot-racing,
which are in large part specifically Indo-Aryan in origin.[2] Furthermore, there are well over a hundred personal names dating between *c.* 1700 and 1250 B.C. which are certainly or probably
Indo-Iranian.[3] Some of them are pure Vedic, like *Indrota* for
older **Indrauta*, which appears as *Indaruta* in the Amarna tablets.
Owing to the inadequacies of cuneiform writing it is often very
hard to tell just which one of several etymological possibilities
should be adopted in any given case. However this is not too
serious a difficulty, since the evidence is increasing all the time.
While a few of these names *might* be Iranian, there does not seem
to be a single doubtful case where Indic origin is not equally
possible.[4] The earliest of these Indo-Aryan names belongs to
Zayaluti, a Manda chief who played an important role in the
political and military affairs of Syria about the middle of the
seventeenth century B.C.[5] Not long afterwards we find a group of
'Khurri' chieftains with certain or probable Indo-Aryan names,
and the founder of the royal dynasty of Mitanni, Kirta,[6] about
the sixteenth century, like his successors down into the thirteenth
century B.C., bears an Indo-Aryan name. Many of these names
have to do with horses and chariots, as might be expected from
the extraordinary popularity of the then quite recently invented
chariot wheel with spokes, which made possible much greater
speeds than had been known before.

Since our new evidence from Mesopotamian inscriptions of
the dynasties of Akkad, Ur III, and the following centuries make
it clear that the final ruin of the Indus valley civilization took
place somewhere between the end of Ur III and the eighteenth
century B.C., we are justified in attributing the destruction of this
civilization to the Indo-Aryan invasion, whether or not it was
hastened by natural catastrophes.[7] It follows, therefore, that the

---

[1] §III, 26.   [2] §III, 17; §III, 19, 83 ff.; §III, 20, 144 f.
[3] See especially §III, 23, 149 ff.; §III, 19; 20; 21.
[4] §III, 26; §III, 21, 456 f.   [5] §III, 1, 31 f.
[6] So read, with B. Landsberger, instead of the previous [ ]-*di-ir-ta*. P. E. Dumont
has pointed out (unpublished) that the name *Kirta* is good Indo-Aryan. Incidentally,
I have long been connecting the name (possibly the person) with the hero *KRT*
('Keret') of Ugarit, who is represented as founder of a dynasty.
[7] §IV, 23. See also the last footnote to this chapter.

old date about 1800 B.C. or perhaps a little later, is very satis-factory for the first irruption of the Indo-Aryans into India. It appears that when the Indo-Aryan nomads came down from Transcaspia about that time, they divided north of the central desert of Iran, one branch going eastward through Bactria to the upper Indus valley, and the other going westward through the Zagros into Mesopotamia and Syria. This invasion had nothing to do with that of the Iranians, who were also charioteers but had by the time of their irruption learned to domesticate the two-humped camel and to depend on it largely for livelihood.[1] Since our earliest evidence from cuneiform sources for Iranian invaders comes from the ninth century B.C., by which time they were already well settled in Media, it seems to follow that they must have come in at some time toward the end of the Late Bronze Age or the beginning of the Iron Age—roughly between 1300 and 1000 B.C. as earliest and latest probable dates.

IV. SUMERIAN, HURRIAN, URARŢIAN, ELAMITE

Sumerian is the oldest known literary language of mankind, sur-passing even Egyptian in age; the earliest known inscriptions come from the late fourth millennium, perhaps a century or two before the earliest Egyptian inscriptions, and the oldest now known literary texts date from about the twenty-sixth century B.C. (Shuruppak and Tell Abu Ṣalābīkh).[2] As the language of the first known high culture, it ultimately influenced the West far more than Egypt could.[3] It became extinct as a spoken language, for all practical purposes, soon after the close of the Ur III Dynasty, at the end of the third millennium, but was intensively cultivated by scribes down into the second century B.C., if not even later. Thanks to the extraordinary efforts of the Akkadian scribes, from Old Babylonian to Hellenistic times, we have a wealth of trans-

---

[1] As is now well known, many hymns of the Avesta are pre-Zoroastrian. In any case, the '600 years' before his time attributed by Xanthus of Lydia (middle of the fifth century) to Zoroaster (accepted by Eduard Meyer) may have been based on calculation by generations, in which case the Iranian prophet might have lived about the ninth century B.C. The 'official' date in the sixth century is more and more difficult to accept.

[2] For Shuruppak (Tell Fārah) see W. G. Lambert in *Bull. A.S.O.R.* 169, 63 f.; for Tell Abu Ṣalābīkh (near Nippur) my information comes from Dr Robert D. Biggs, who has been working on the tablets recently excavated there.

[3] §IV, 18, 20.

lations and school texts of all kinds. Specialists can now master most unilingual texts from the third and early second millennium B.C., thanks to these unique helps to study.[1]

Sumerian was an agglutinative, semi-incorporating language with no known relatives. Morphemic complexes, grouped around nouns and verbs, are often incorporated into single closely knit structures. Breaking the transcribed Sumerian chains into their formative elements, we may analyse three selected examples from the Gudea texts as follows:

(1) *alam-Gudea-ensi(-k)-Lagaša(-k) lu-E-ninnu-in-du-a-k-e*. An approximate analysis of these elements in English translation would be: 'statue-Gudea-viceroy(-of)-Lagash(-of) who-house-of-Ninnu-he-it-built-(participial ending)-of-(subject suffix)'. Put into intelligible English this would become: 'The statue of Gudea, viceroy of Lagash, who built the house of Ninnu.'

(2) *uru-a ama-lu-tur-ak-e a-silima(-k) garr-am*... In literal English translation this would yield: 'city-in mother-man-ill-of-(subject affix) water-health(-of) put-(transitive participial ending)...'. In English prose this would become: 'In the city the mother of the sick man has set water of health...'

(3) *Gudea...ensik-e uru-na lu-aš-gim na-ri ba-ni-gar ki-Lagaša-(-k)-e dumu-ama-aš-a-gim ša-mu-na-aš-e*. Literally translated, we have something like this: 'Gudea...viceroy-the (subject), city-his-for, man-one-like, jubilee-he-it(there)-made, territory-Lagash(-of)-the, son(s)-mother-one-of-like, mind-he-him-for-uniting.' In intelligible English this would be: 'Gudea... the viceroy, arranged a general celebration for his city; the territory of Lagash, like children of one mother, becoming of one mind toward him.'[2]

There are in particular many verbal prefixes and infixes which were employed for elaborate distinctions between direction in which, direction from which, and other shades of local and objective/subjective meaning. There was also a remarkable breakdown in the phonetic structure of individual words and compounds which often led to a situation quite comparable to that which now exists in Chinese, where we have many syllables containing the same articulatory elements which appear to us as homonyms but which are distinguished by the use of 'tones' or other similar modes of differentiation. We must remember, however, that (as proved by Bernhard Karlgren) ancient Chinese had more elaborate phonetic structures before they were broken down in the course

---

[1] §IV, 26, 9.
[2] The foregoing examples have been adapted to our purposes from §IV, 9. We have rendered na-ri-gar 'make a purification' as referring to a consecration or a jubilee.

of the last two millennia, so that there were not nearly as many superficially homonymous words in ancient Chinese as are found in the modern dialects of China. We cannot be sure that there were tones in Sumerian, but it is very difficult to see how its speakers could otherwise have distinguished meanings of so many monosyllabic words with only two phonemes. Such phenomena may be quite secondary, as in Swedish. In modern linguistics it is recognized that every practicable means of differentiation, including gestures, may be used to clarify meaning.

Sumerian is also known to have had half a dozen or more 'dialects', which we cannot clearly distinguish geographically or historically. For instance, the so-called Emesal dialect was certainly used in much Sumerian religious poetry, but we are still unsure of its proper location or period. To judge from Semitic loanwords and phonetic considerations, it would seem that it split off from ancestral Sumerian quite early and developed in northern Babylonia.

It is often held today that Sumerian was a newcomer in Babylonia, which the Sumerians are supposed to have occupied in comparatively recent times, between the end of the 'Ubaid period and the beginning of Early Dynastic.[1] Today many scholars are inclined to think that the Semites were there as early as the Sumerians and that they may have exercised as much influence on the latter as the latter on them.[2] This goes, however, much too far, in view of often neglected facts to the contrary. If it were true we should scarcely expect to find that all known divine names used in the context of early Sumerian inscriptions are Sumerian; a case such as *Sin*, the Moon-god, is no exception. *Sin* is sometimes declared to be Semitic because it is used to translate Sumerian *Nanna(r)*. The earliest form of the name was *Zuen* or *Zuin*, which is found in Old Assyrian inscriptions from the nineteenth century B.C. *Zuin* was later contracted and the sibilant shifted until the name became *Sin*, following normal principles of phonetic development. Since in early Sumerian inscriptions the order of elements in phonetic as well as in 'logographic' writing was irregular, a sign which we should place second often precedes a sign which we should place first. Thus the Sumerian logogram EN.ZU should be read *Zuen*, from which the other forms are normal derivatives.

[1] §IV, 14, 261 ff. offers an extreme view; §IV, 20, 42 ff. states a somewhat more moderate position.
[2] In addition to the foregoing note see §IV, 8, 246 ff.; for Landsberger's views on the pre-Sumerian source of Mesopotamian civilization see §IV, 20, 40 f. Contrast especially §IV, 10, 310 ff.

Similarly, a name which has sometimes been taken to be Semitic in origin, that of the Sumerian water god Ea, is certainly Sumerian and not Akkadian. We should read *Ae* (or *'A$_x$-a* without transposition) instead of *Ea*, as is proved by the facts that in Hurrian and Hittite the name of the god is spelt *Aya-*, and that the later Greek transcription is *Aos*.

Strong evidence for early date of Sumerian penetration into Mesopotamia is found in the names of rivers and streams, which are not likely to have been introduced after the building of towns had begun. Among such names are those of the Euphrates and Tigris, of the Khabur and Balīkh, as well as probably the names of a number of minor tributaries. If any of these names were Semitic we should have much more reason to assume that the Semites had entered Babylonia before or about the same time as the Sumerians. There is, however, no such evidence. Just as in most parts of the Old World where we can control our data, in ancient Mesopotamia the names of rivers belong to the earliest known phase of linguistic occupation. Note especially the following river names:

Sumerian *Buranun-* (Euphrates) > **Burann-* > Akkadian **Purantu* (with typical feminine ending) > *Purattu*; Hurrian *Puranti-* is derived from an older Akkadian form. *Buranun-* contains the same element, *bur*, that we have in *Ḫabur*, and probably means 'mighty water-source' (Delitzsch) or the like.[1]

Sum. *Idigna* (Tigris) > Akk. *Idiqlat*. *Idigna* was probably derived from **Id(i)gina*, 'running river' (Delitzsch).[2]

Akk. *Ḫabur* (Arab. *Ḫābūr*), 'source of fertility', from Sumerian *ḫe(n)-bur*; cf. *ḫenbur* > *ḫabbūru*, 'flowering stalk', and Sum. *Ḫubur*, name of the river of fertility in the underworld (*Ḫubur* for **Ḫabur* is like *dumu* for *damu*, 'son').

Akk. *Balīḫ* (Arab. *Balīḫ*) is the river god *Baliḫ* (written in the same way, both phonetically and logographically, as the name of Etana's son in different copies of the King List).[3]

Some insist that the lack of clear—or even of any—phonetic relationship between many names of early Sumerian cities and the Sumerian reading of the logograms with which these names are usually expressed proves that the latter are older than the entrance into the country of the Sumerians, who gave them logographic names, most of which have to do with shrines and temples of the

---

[1] §IV, 6, 70. Note that not only the names of the two great rivers, but also the oldest Akkadian names of countries, *Subartu* (< Sum. *Subir*) and *Elamtu* (< Sum. *Elam*) have feminine endings attached to the Sumerian base.

[2] §IV, 6, 21.   [3] §IV, 16, 80 f. and n. 76.

gods.[1] Just to illustrate, there is no obvious connexion between the logographic EN.LÍL^{KI} and the phonetic *Nibru* (properly **Nibur ⟩ Nippur*). But since Enlil (⟩ Ellil) was the chief god of the most important cultic centre in central Babylonia, such a writing is in no way strange. This entire point of view is very much exaggerated. In the first place there is no reason whatever to doubt that there has been some phonetic change in really old names like those of *Uruk* (Biblical *Erech*) which was *Unu(g)* in late Sumerian. *Uruk* for *Unug* is very possibly influenced by the ordinary word *uru* for city. It can also be explained in other ways. The name of Ur, which is written logographically URÍ.UNU(G)^{KI} (which may also be transcribed URÚ.UNU^{KI}), was pronounced with final *m* (*Urum* or *Urim*), which may have been taken as mimation in Akkadian, leaving only *Uru* (⟩ *Ur*) as Semitic nominative. On the other hand, we cannot explain a name like *Larsa(m)*, for possible **(A)rar-za(m)*, from the logographic spelling UTU.-UNU(G)^{KI} meaning 'shrine of the sun-god'. The name of the ancient sacred city of Eridu in the extreme south of Babylonia was written two ways: (1) URU.DÙ(G), probably the direct source of *Eridu*, since URU also had the value *eri*, perhaps in one of the dialects; (2) NUN.KI, literally 'Place of the Prince', *Enki* or *Ae* (*Ea*).

There are several points to be considered which are usually neglected in such sweeping judgements as the supposed non-Sumerian origin of most Sumerian place-names. The first point is that we must reckon with much shifting of dialects and different pronunciations in different periods as well as with the fact that the Akkadian forms of later times were taken over from Sumerian at various stages and from different dialects of Sumerian. Secondly we seldom possess a phonetically written name of an important Sumerian city dating from the third millennium B.C., so there is often no means of knowing how a unilingual Sumerian actually pronounced the name of his native town. A good illustration of the sort of thing that happens is found when we compare the many different writings of a canal name such as *Iturungal* with minor and even major variations.[2] A third difficulty is caused by the use of undoubtedly different names for the same place in different circumstances and in different periods, just as we find three different names of Memphis in Egypt: *'Ineb-ḥedj*, 'White Wall',

---

[1] The names in question may also have been applied primarily to the fortified temple around which a town was built; parallels in Egypt and Palestine are very numerous.

[2] §IV, 17, 177.

which was the oldest known name of the city; its monumental name, *MEN-NEFER*, Hebrew *Moph* and Akkadian *Mempi*; and thirdly its sacred name, belonging primarily to the shrine of Ptaḥ, chief god of Memphis: *Ḥekuptaḥ* (*ḥwt-kʒ-PTḤ*), whence Ugaritic *Ḥekupta* (*ḥkpt*) and Greek *Aiguptos*.

Sometimes there can be reasonable doubt as to whether the Sumerian or Semitic name is older. It is held by some that *Bābili(m)* (Hebrew *Bābel* and Greek *Babylōn*) was originally Sumerian KÁ.DINGIR.RA^KI, 'Gate of God', as the name was written logographically. In this case the Hurrian and Cossaean *Pabil* or *Pabal* confirms the antiquity of the Semitic name. In another case we have a logographic writing BÀD.URUDU.-NAGAR^KI, pronounced *Bad-tibira*, 'Wall of Copper Worker(s)', as we know from early phonetic writings and especially from the corrupted Greek name *Pantibibla* (formerly the name was read as Semitic: *Dūr-gurgurri*). Since Bad-tibira was one of the ante-diluvian cities in the Babylonian lists, its Sumerian origin is certain.[1] Another name with the same formation is Borsippa, the oldest known logogram of which is BÀD.SI.(A).AB.BA^KI. The Akkadian form of the name was Barsip, which is a transparent Semitic corruption of the Sumerian form—probably at an early period, antedating inscriptional evidence; the name appears on the upper Euphrates in early times as *Barsip* (later *Til-Barsip*). Still other names, such as Dilbat and Aratta, are obviously abbreviations of longer names with cultic meanings. The logo-gram UNU is also used for phonetic *ab* as well as for phonetic *un(u)*: witness spellings like *Udab* or *Adab* for UD.UNU^KI.

We can also make the Sumerian origin of most Babylonian place-names clear by simply comparing their phonetic structure with that of common Sumerian words.[2] For example, many ordi-nary Sumerian words have suffixed *g* or *k*, often identical with the genitive *ak*. Thus with names like *Šurup(p)ak*, *Larak*, *Akšak*, we may compare words like *ḥursak* (*ḥursag*), *nisak* (*nisag*), *isak* (for older *ensik*), *santak* and the like. With names ending in *r*, which are particularly common in Sumerian, we may compare *agar*, *ingar*, *amar*, *engar*, *ubar*, *babbar*, *gišimar*, *dupsar*, and so on. With names ending in *ir* we may compare *esir*, *egir*, *bap(p)ir*, *gigir*, *dingir*, *tibir*, etc. Furthermore, the structure of words is often parallel. For instance, *Agade*, Semitic *Akkadû* for **Akkade'u*, may be compared with many equally composite Sumerian words ending

---

[1] §IV, 16, 70 ff.

[2] §IV, 1, 61 f. Naturally this is antiquated, but the principle remains sound; a thorough study would yield very interesting results.

in *e*, for example, *unuge, ade, gude*. The ending *ua*, which we find in *Gudua, Ninua*, appears also in *indua, narua*, and so on. Similarly the archaic form of later *Aššūr*, which appears in an Assyrian seal from the Akkad Dynasty as *Anšur*, reminds one of the Sumerian *banšur*, etc. With *Nibru* (undoubtedly a dialectal variant of **Nibur*, which became normal *Nippur* in Akkadian), we may compare such place-names as *Girsu*, and such common nouns as *ildu, amaru, abzu, geštu*, etc. In short, there is no reason whatever to derive the place-names of early Babylonia from some otherwise unknown northern or eastern language—preserved only in a few place-names.

It has been argued repeatedly that there was a sharp break in the cultural continuity of Babylonian life, which must somehow be connected with the entrance of the Sumerians. This Sumerian invasion is supposed to have taken place in the latter part of the fourth millennium, after the end of the ʿUbaid period proper, or in the early third millennium, after the Uruk and even the Jamdat Nasr period.[1] Recent archaeological work in Babylonia has proved that settlement there went far back to before the ʿUbaid period, and that there is no real discontinuity of culture after that.[2] The fact is that changes in pottery and building styles do not necessarily mean a change in ethnic identity or language. For example, in Greece we now know that Late Helladic pottery was used in most of the country by a population that spoke and wrote Greek. The following superficially quite different Geometric culture was still Greek, and so were the phases of Corinthian pottery and of black-figured and red-figured ware which followed in historical order from *c.* 700 to the middle of the fourth century B.C.

General continuity of physical type is traceable in Mesopotamia back to the earliest times for which we so far have evidence. Cranial types were all about the same, with a similar mixture of dolichocephaly and brachycephaly in all known ages.

During the century since the discovery of Sumerian no valid cognate has been recognized, in spite of indefatigable efforts. Possibly the closest in structure among known Eurasian languages is Turkish, which possesses a host of suffixes, whereas in Sumerian we have a semi-incorporating structure, built up with nominal suffixes and with verbal prefixes and infixes, as well as some suffixes. It is impossible in a case like this to utilize the few similar morphemes or separate words which occur, because we know too little of their original meaning and structure. For example, Turkish *tengri* (Ottoman *tanrı*), 'god', has often been quoted as an illustra-

---

[1] See above, p. 147, n.1.
[2] §IV, 22, 44 ff. The archaeological evidence is set out below, pp. 343 ff.

tion of possible relationship between Sumerian and Turkish. In Sumerian the word for 'god' is *dingir*, or *dim(m)er*, or *tiḫer*, in different dialects. The effort has sometimes been made to connect Sumerian with Finno-Ugrian[1] or Hurrian. In both we have a proliferation of suffixes with noun and verb, but agglutination or semi-incorporation of verbal or morphemic elements does not prove kinship. The once accepted hypothesis of genetic relationship between Finno-Ugrian and Turkish (supposed to belong to a single Ural-Altaic family), has now been given up by many specialists.[2] As for Hurrian (see below), the fact that we can trace it back to about 2400 B.C. in south-western Asia without finding any signs of kinship to Sumerian, makes it doubly improbable that any common origin will be found. In short, it seems probable that Sumerian will prove refractory to any yet known method of comparative linguistic analysis.

Since the first—and still the most important—Hurrian tablet was discovered among the Mitanni letters from Amarna published in 1889, texts and documents in this language have multiplied. We now have written Hurrian material extending over approximately a millennium, from the time of Tisari (or Tisatal), king of Urkish in the eastern Khabur basin (Akkad Dynasty)[3] to the fourteenth-thirteenth century B.C. Our texts come chiefly from Boğazköy, Ugarit and Mari, while Akkadian documents from Nuzi, Alalakh and many other sites furnish a vast storehouse of Hurrian personal names.[4] Curiously enough, most of these texts are literary and scholastic in nature, yielding examples of genres as far apart as myths and epics, divinatory tablets and bilingual vocabularies (Sumerian and Hurrian). Since the Hurrian texts are transcribed into different forms of Mesopotamian cuneiform as well as into different scripts, and since they exhibit both diachronic and synchronic differentiation according to successive phases and contemporary dialects, their linguistic interpretation has proved to be very difficult; it has best been accomplished by Speiser, whose analysis retains most of its value after a quarter of a century.[5]

Hurrian was an agglutinative language, with chains of suffixes invariably placed after substantives and verbal stems. According to Speiser, as many as ten suffixes may be distinguished.[6] This situation reminds one of Finno-Ugrian, but there is no evidence for an historical connexion. Since word units and complexes are

---

[1] This view was held by a distinguished Finnish Assyriologist, the late Harri Holma, but most of his work was never published.

[2] See above, p. 129, n. 3.   [3] §IV, 25.   [4] §IV, 13.

[5] §IV, 29.   [6] §IV, 29, 69.

separated from one another in most Hurrian texts (especially in the Mitanni letter, where we find careful spacing, and in the Ugaritic texts, where word dividers are used), there is a solid basis for morphological and syntactic analysis.

As we have seen, Hurrian first appears on our geographical horizon in the extreme north of Mesopotamia. No Hurrian names appear at Nuzi (then called *Gasur*) in the twenty-fourth to twenty-third centuries B.C., whereas they became dominant there in the fifteenth-fourteenth centuries. No Hurrian names are found in the Egyptian Execration Texts dealing with Palestine and southern Syria in the twentieth-nineteenth centuries, but they became common in the fifteenth-fourteenth centuries. Evidently the Hurrians accompanied the Indo-Aryans in their advance westward and southward. It would seem that the Hurrians, who tended to be strongly Armenoid in physical type, had long been occupying the northern mountain ranges, but details escape us completely.[1]

On the other hand there must have been a close cultural relationship between the Hurrians and the Urarțians who followed them in the mountains and plateaux of Armenia Major (east of Armenia Minor), where the still later Armenian ethno-geographical unit developed.[2] This close relation appears in borrowed names of divinities and in similar vocables, which may either be loanwords from Hurrian or originally related words. Because of the limited extent and specialized character of the Urarțian texts, which are nearly all royal building or triumphal inscriptions, it is difficult to analyse their structure adequately for comparative purposes.[3] Yet it may be seen that the language was prevailingly suffixal, though no such long chains are yet known as we find in the Mitanni letter. It is also clear that there is a penchant for a passival concept of the transitive verb, as in Hurrian. According to Goetze and most students, Urarțian is simply a 'younger Hurrian dialect'.[4] According to Dyakonov Urarțian is, however, more archaic than Hurrian in phonology and less archaic in morphology.[5] In spite of the resemblances it cannot be denied that the personal names are quite different, and that both vocabu-

---

[1] The physical type is inferred from monuments of the Mitanni region in the second millennium, which show the same type as we find on the Hittite monuments, as well as from the tendency to replace dolichocephaly by brachycephaly in cemeteries of the Middle Bronze Age in Syria and Palestine.

[2] §IV, 2; §III, 13, 187 ff. See above, p. 143.

[3] §IV, 11.   [4] §III, 13, 194.

[5] §III, 24, 41 (in the title given to Dyakonov's contribution, 'Hittite' should be 'Hurrite').

lary and syntax diverge widely. The safest view at present seems
to be that there is kinship, but that it is remote. Nothing can
obscure the fact that there was a sharp break between the Hurrian
cultures known from personal names and cultural tradition down
to the late second millennium, and the Urartian which followed
almost immediately.

The last of the languages which we shall discuss is Elamite,
which has been known since the early nineteenth century as the
third language of the trilingual Achaemenian royal inscriptions
of the late sixth to early fourth centuries B.C.[1] Thanks to several
decades of French excavation at Susa and other sites in Susiana,
Elamite can be traced back to the early third millennium, when
it was written in a pictographic script (Proto-Elamite) with
Sumerian analogies.[2] The pictographic script was followed by an
apparently unconnected linear script which was partly deciphered
by Walther Hinz in 1961.[3] In the Akkad period it began to be
written in Babylonian cuneiform, which gradually developed a
special syllabary of its own. Meanwhile Elamite continued in use
as the actual language of Susiana, though it was already filled
with Old Persian loanwords by the late fifth and early fourth
centuries B.C.[4] There is no reason to doubt that Elamite continued
to be spoken as *Khōzī* until the tenth century A.D., if not later.[5]

Elamite was also a suffixing language, though the extent to
which it can be called 'agglutinative' must await the discovery
and interpretation of letters and literary texts, which generally
tell us much more about linguistic structure than the formal
inscriptions and administrative texts on which we largely depend.
It was certainly agglutinative in the sense that morphemic elements
are much more loosely 'bound' in a chain than would be true of
inflectional families like Indo-Hittite and Afro-Asian. There was
also a tendency to treat transitive verbs passively, as in Hurrian
and Urartian; it must, however, be emphasized that this phenomenon may also be considered as an isogloss rather than as an
indication of genetic relationship.

Since there is absolutely no evidence for a migration of Elamite-
speaking people from the northern mountains, there is a strong
possibility that Elamite is related through Brahui, still spoken
in Balūchistān (south-western Pakistān) to the Dravidian tongues
of southern India, which exhibit a somewhat similar structure.

---

[1] On the Elamites and their background see particularly *C.A.H.* I³, ch. xxiii
and II³, chh. vii, xxix, xxxii.

[2] *C.A.H.* I³, ch. xxiii, sect. iv.   [3] §iv, 15.   [4] §iv, 3, 40 ff.

[5] Arabic *Khūzistān* means, of course, 'Khōzī-land'.

This frequently suggested connexion has gained plausibility in recent years, after the recovery of the Indus Valley civilization of Harappā and Mohenjo Daro. Today it is ethno-geographically even more plausible, since Harappā ports have been discovered some 400 miles west of the mouth of the Indus, at the Iranian frontier,[1] while Indian archaeologists have located nearly a hundred sites between the Rann of Kutch on the Indian frontier south-east of Karachi and a site some 150 miles north of Bombay.[2] In other words, the entire coastal area of Indus valley civilization was perhaps occupied by Dravidians, who have left their linguistic imprint west of the lower Indus valley and within 400 miles of the southernmost now known outpost of the Harappā culture in question. Among common features are the relatively simple suffixing structure in nouns and verbs, which is agglutinative rather than inflexional, and a tendency toward passival treatment of transitive verbs. It is interesting to note that M. Andronov has lately employed glottochronology to estimate the approximate time at which Brahui may have separated from its Dravidian sisters in India, arriving at a plausible date in the early fourth millennium B.C.[3] Needless to say, this is not a precise calculation, but it is quite reasonable in the light of our archaeological and cuneiform evidence, which fixes the final destruction of the Indus valley culture by the Indo-Aryan invaders somewhere between c. 1950 and 1750 B.C.[4] Further research in comparative Dravidian linguistics, which seems to be a most likely area for scientific exploration, has now become an urgent necessity.

[1] See George F. Dales, 'Harappan Outposts on the Makran Coast', *Antiq.* 36 (1962), 86 ff.

[2] See S. R. Rao, 'Excavation at Rangpur and Other Explorations in Gujarat' in *Ancient India*, nos. 18–19 (1963).

[3] §III, 4.

[4] §S. R. Rao, *op. cit.*, Plate LII, opposite p. 200, places the end of Harappā culture proper about 1500 B.C., with its height about 2000, but the dates are too low even for the low Babylonian chronology, and B. B. Lal, *Ancient India*, nos. 18–19, pp. 208 ff., basing himself on radiocarbon datings, now wishes to raise the date of the end of Harappā culture in its proper sense 'by about a couple of centuries' (p. 219), 'to c. 1700 B.C.'. See above, p. 144.

CHAPTER V

THE EARLIEST POPULATIONS
OF MAN IN EUROPE, WESTERN ASIA
AND NORTHERN AFRICA

I. AUSTRALOPITHECINES AND
PITHECANTHROPINES

DURING the course of human evolution, three major phases of morphological change can be distinguished (Table 4). These divisions belong to the realm of palaeontological convenience and are not an actual fact, for hominid development consisted of the cumulative effect of micro-evolutionary changes giving rise in time and space to a complex mosaic of physical change. These changes were dependent upon such factors as mutation, selective pressures, size of population, and—more important in man than any other creature—upon cultural development such as tool making, language formation, and transmission of complex information.

The earliest group of hominids, described now in some detail, may be considered together under the general title of Australopithecines.[1] They may be briefly characterized by a brain capacity of about 400–800 c.c.; dental features showing considerable variability, but generally showing closer affinities with the human dentition than pongid teeth; a foramen magnum placed more forward; a remarkably human pelvis and probably a fairly upright posture. Even allowing for marked sexual dimorphism, it is still obvious that more than one species demands recognition. There is wide agreement that this group represents the beginning of human differentiation from a more basic 'proto-hominid' stock. There is still some debate as to what fossils should and should not be regarded as Australopithecines, and clearly palaeontological divisions of this kind must include specimens of a 'marginal' or 'intermediate' nature.

The Australopithecines were widespread in Africa and if, as some suggest, related forms were present in South-east Asia, they could well have occurred in the eastern Mediterranean area at

[1] §1, 3. See Fig. 17.

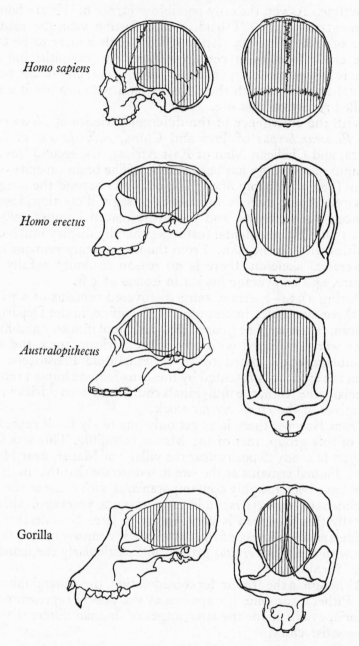

Homo sapiens

Homo erectus

Australopithecus

Gorilla

Fig. 17. Facial change and endocranial expansion at the three major levels of hominid evolution (and in comparison with gorilla). After Weidenreich, §1, 4 (and others).

some time. As yet, the only possible evidence of this are hominid fragments from Tell 'Ubaidīya in Palestine near the southern shore of Lake Tiberias. Although the tools appear to be of the same crude form as at certain African Australopithecine sites, there is still some doubt as to the contemporaneity of the human skeletal fragments with the deposits, and we must await a more detailed report on this site.

With the emergence of the different varieties of *Homo erectus* (i.e. *Pithecanthropus* of Java and China, *Atlanthropus* of North Africa, and Chellean Man of East Africa), the second 'level' of hominid morphology has been reached. The brain capacity of this group (being probably 800–1200 c.c.) was beyond the range for the Great Apes; there is an absence of sagittal cresting, less pronounced nuchal crests, and forwardly placed foramen magnum (Fig. 17). Oral and dental features generally display much closer affinities with recent man. From the fragmentary remains of the post-cranial skeleton, there is no reason to doubt a fully erect posture, and an average height in excess of 5 ft.

During 1954–5, Arambourg discovered remains of a parietal and three mandibles in a sandpit at Ternifine, in the Department of Oran, Algeria.[1] The generalized early tool industry and human bones were associated with a typically African fauna, the whole assemblage being dated to an early Middle Pleistocene date. From the evidence presented by these inadequate human remains, especially the teeth, the individuals could have been African representatives of the *Homo erectus* stock.

From Europe, there is as yet only one likely fossil representative of this group, that of the Mauer mandible. This was found in 1907 in sandy deposits near the village of Mauer, near Heidelberg. Faunal remains at the site demonstrate that this individual must have been roughly contemporaneous with some of the other specimens of *Homo erectus* and lived c. 400,000 years ago. Although dentally this specimen is very similar to later Neanderthal man, in size and robustness of the mandible it compares more favourably with the *Homo erectus* group, and particularly the mandibles from Ternifine.

Although in the area under consideration, the Australopithecine and Pithecanthropine groups are as yet poorly represented, the material available for the later stages of human differentiation is more satisfactory.

[1] §I, I.

Table 4. The three major morphological levels of hominid evolution, together with representative examples

(Fossils within the area under review are in bold type.)

Hominines	Homo sapiens sapiens			
				'Classic' Neander-thalers (Tābūn, Gibraltar, Shanidar, Le Moustier)
	Jebel Qafzah **Sukhūl** **Fontechevade** (?)Kanjera	**Saccopastore** **Ehringsdorf** **Krapina**		
		Montmaurin **Steinheim** **Swanscombe**		
Pithecanthropines	Choukoutien			
				Ternifine (Atlanthropus) Chellean Man
	Sangiran Trinil Modjokerto		**Heidelberg (Mauer)**	
Australopithecines	Homo habilis Telanthropus			Zinjanthropus Paranthropus
	(?) **'Ubaidīya**	Australopithecus Plesianthropus		(?)Meganthropus

←————Tentative assessment of morphological similarity————→
(*within*, but not between, the three stages)

II. 'HOMO SAPIENS'

The date of the emergence of *Homo sapiens* is still a controversial matter, mainly because palaeoanthropologists are not agreed on the precise morphological criteria that serve to delimit the fossil representatives of this human species. Even more uncertain is the place of origin of our species. The evidence of the Swanscombe and Steinheim cranial remains, if their owners may be regarded as being early representatives of *Homo sapiens*, suggests that this emergence may well date back in Western Europe at least as far as the Second, or Mindel–Riss Interglacial Age. There are as yet in the area under discussion no other finds of human remains even tentatively assignable to *Homo sapiens* which are of comparable antiquity.

The Swanscombe remains, comprising an occipital and two parietal bones, are probably those of a young female adult; they were found in well-stratified deposits forming part of the 100 ft. terrace of the Thames river gravels. In direct association with the human remains were a Mindel–Riss (or 'Hoxnian') Inter-glacial fauna, and a Middle Acheulean hand-axe and flake in-dustry. Fluorine analysis and other relative dating methods have demonstrated that the human and animal bones are of similar antiquity.[1] While the chronological position of the Swanscombe remains may therefore be considered as being beyond doubt, their inclusion within the species *Homo sapiens* cannot be demonstrated as clearly. In general, a dichotomy exists with regard to the taxo-nomic status of the Swanscombe remains between those who seek to differentiate specifically between *Homo neanderthalensis* and *Homo sapiens*, and those who consider such a taxonomic division to be confusing and superfluous. Thus, those who believe in the specific differentiation of Neanderthal man prefer to stress the way in which certain features of the Swanscombe remains foreshadow later Neanderthaloid characters; those who regard the distinction as being genetically invalid prefer to consider the Swanscombe remains as foreshadowing the full emergence of *Homo sapiens* in Europe.[2] One practical compromise which has been suggested is that this important but fragmentary find should be placed in the taxon created for the better-preserved Steinheim cranium, i.e. *Homo steinheimensis*, but that this taxon itself be de-moted to subspecific status, i.e. *Homo sapiens steinheimensis*. (See Fig. 18.)

Where there may be said to be virtual unanimity, however, is that the Swanscombe cranial remains, mainly by reason of their estimated cranial capacity and expanded upper vault area, lie outside the known morphological range for *Homo erectus (Pithe-canthropus)*. In particular, this assessment is supported by the estimates of height and biparietal breadth of the cranium, and the lack of the facial portion of the cranium does not detract from it.

The Steinheim cranium was discovered in a gravel pit at Stein-heim an der Murr in Württemberg, about 12 miles north of Stuttgart. Almost the entire cranium was recovered; it is probably that of an adult female, although the assessment of the sex of fossil human remains is notoriously unreliable.[3] The associated faunal evidence points to a warm period within the Mindel–Riss Interglacial Age. The cranium has been considerably distorted by earth pressure, and although allowance has been made for this in metrical studies, the cranial length, breadth, height and

[1] §II, 10.   [2] §II, 11.   [3] §II, 7.

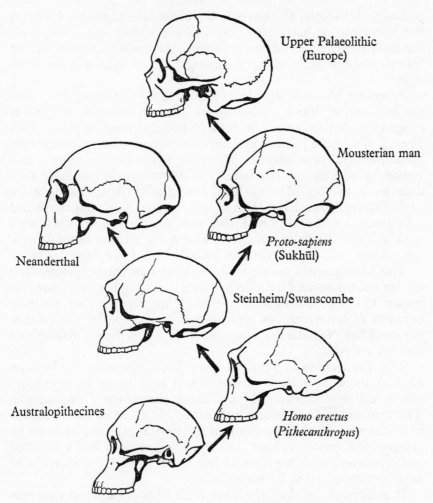

Upper Palaeolithic
(Europe)

Mousterian man

Neanderthal

Proto-sapiens
(Sukhūl)

Steinheim/Swanscombe

Australopithecines

Homo erectus
(*Pithecanthropus*)

Fig. 18. Morphological changes in the human skull during the one and a half million years of man's evolution. (Modified from Le Gros Clark, §1, 2.)

capacity do not differentiate very convincingly between the Steinheim remains and those of the Java and Pekin forms of *Homo erectus*. Here the resemblance ends, however, as almost all other morphological details of the cranium recall *Homo sapiens*, although certain features such as the strongly developed brow ridges would appear to presage the Neanderthaloid subspecies.

One isolated find that may bear some relationship to these early representatives of *Homo sapiens* is that of the occipital bone found in a cave near Carotta, Quinzano, in the Verona commune of Italy. Its shape, thickness and dimensions resemble those of the Swanscombe occipital. The faunal evidence associated with the find, however, indicates a more recent age than that of either Swanscombe or Steinheim, i.e. during the Riss–Würm Interglacial Age.

After the Mindel–Riss Interglacial Age, the skeletal remains attributable to *Homo sapiens* grow more numerous, and their geographical distribution widens to include western Asia. Two French sites have yielded evidence that may point to a relatively greater antiquity, namely Montmaurin, in the Haut-Garonne, and Fontechevade, in the Charente. The Montmaurin mandible may date back to the Mindel–Riss Interglacial Age, but is more probably from the Riss–Würm Interglacial Age. A calotte and a fragmentary frontal bone found at Fontechevade are associated with a Tayacian flake industry and a warm climate fauna, corresponding to the last, Third, or Riss–Würm Interglacial Age.

The Montmaurin mandible is robustly constructed, exceeding in size most known Neanderthal mandibles, and, mainly for this reason has been considered to occupy an intermediate position between *Homo erectus*, as represented in Europe by the Mauer jaw, and the Neanderthal varieties of Europe, North Africa and south-west Asia.

The Fontechevade remains have been carefully studied by H. V. Vallois, and he is unconvinced that there is any morphological characteristic differentiating them from *Homo sapiens*. The remains of both individuals resemble those of Swanscombe in thickness with the exception of the frontal portion. It must be emphasized, however, that the larger fragment is badly crushed and distorted, and the frontal fragment cannot be considered with any certainty to be fully adult.

It is difficult to place the next finds of fossil man in any precise chronological order. They come from Saccopastore (Italy), Ehringsdorf and Taubach (Germany), Gánovce and Krapina (Czechoslovakia) and Monsempron (France). They all belong to the Early Upper Pleistocene, being attributable to the last, Third, or Riss–Würm Interglacial Age. The people represented by the fossil remains from Mount Carmel, according to Zeuner, may also have lived through the last Interglacial Age and on into the first phase of the Würm Glaciation. The possibility that the two Mount Carmel populations, i.e. those of Maghārat es-Sukhūl and Maghārat eṭ-Ṭābūn, may be separated by a gap of some ten thousand years or so cannot however be excluded.[1]

[1] §11, 9.

This group of fossil human finds is customarily, though not very satisfactorily, considered to be a fairly homogeneous early Neanderthal group exhibiting 'more generalized' or 'less specialized' morphological features than the chronologically later 'classic' or 'specialized' Neanderthals, who are associated, in the main, with the first phase of the Würm glaciation and the subsequent interstadial.

The remains of at least eighty-three of these Würm I Neanderthalers, from forty-three sites, have now been recovered. Relatively few of these finds have been described, however, so that there are difficulties in making an adequate survey, or in drawing any but tentative conclusions. The main sites are listed in Table 5. Sites of minor importance, such as have yielded only isolated teeth or bone fragments, have been omitted.

Table 5. Sites with Neanderthal finds attributable to Würm I or a later date (see Fig. 19)

Germany	Neanderthal (near Düsseldorf)
Belgium	Bay-Bonnet, Engis (near Liège); La Naulette, Spy (near Namur)
France	La Chapelle-aux-Saints (Corrèze); La Ferrassie, Le Moustier, Peyzac, Pech de l'Azé, Sarlat, Regourdou (Dordogne); Malarnaud, Montseron (Ariège); La Quina (Charente)
Spain	Bañolas (Catalonia); Cova Negra de Belus (Valencia); Piñar (Granada)
Gibraltar	Forbes Quarry; Devil's Tower
Greece	Petralona
Italy	Circeo (near Rome)
U.S.S.R.	Kiik-Koba (Crimea); Starosel'e (Crimea); Teshik-Tash (Uzbekistan)
Iraq	Shanidar
Palestine	Maghārat eṭ-Ṭābūn, Maghārat es-Sukhūl (Mount Carmel); Maghārat ez-Zuṭṭīyah (Galilee); Jebel Qafzah (Nazareth); Shukbah (Wādi en-Naṭūf); Amud Cave (Lake Tiberias)
Lebanon	Ksar Akil (near Beirut)
Libya	Haua Fteah

The morphological features of the skulls of these later and 'classic' Neanderthals are very distinctive and serve to emphasize the homogeneity of the group (Fig. 19). Cranial capacity was large by hominid standards, the range for the six best-preserved, and possibly male, crania being from 1525 to 1640 c.c., the average capacity of female crania being about 200 c.c. less. Thus on the basis of this sample the 'classic' Neanderthals appear to have had a larger endocranial volume than the 'early' or 'less specialized' groups from pre-Würm times. The 'classic' Neanderthal has a

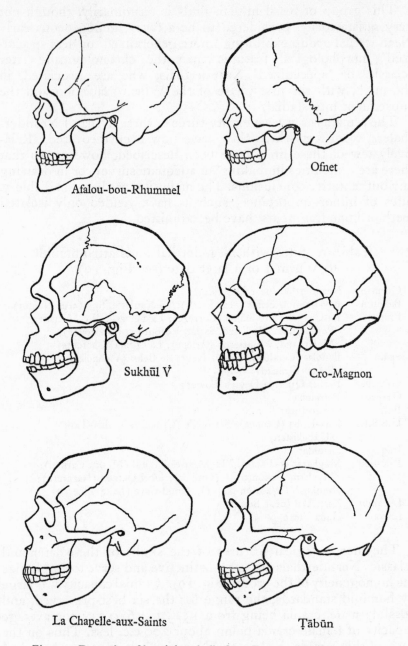

Afalou-bou-Rhummel

Ofnet

Sukhūl V̇

Cro-Magnon

La Chapelle-aux-Saints

Ṭābūn

Fig. 19. Examples of hominine skulls from Europe, Western Asia,
and North Africa.

large, broad-based, low-vaulted skull, often characterized by a globular or bun-shaped projection in the occipital region. The forehead is sloping rather than upright; the facial part of the skull projects forward markedly, with a 'puffed out' appearance; the brow ridges above the orbits are usually salient; the orbital and nasal apertures are larger than is normal in modern man. The large wide nose of the 'classic' Neanderthal may have been an adaptation to climatic extremes of cold, but in general the pattern of the skull cannot be said to demonstrate further adaptation to cold very convincingly. What is now known regarding the post-cranial skeleton of Neanderthal man is sufficient to dismiss earlier suggestions (mainly based upon faulty skeletal reconstructions) of a bent posture and shambling gait, with the head hanging forwards from the neck.

The conundrum concerning the evolutionary fate of the Neanderthals continues to exercise the controversialists.[1] If, however, the inclusion of this group as a subspecies of *Homo sapiens* is acceptable the evidence of progression from Neanderthaloid features to those of contemporary Europiforms that is apparent, for example, at Krapina, suggests either a cline of morphological features, indicative of successful evolution, or the possibility of local hybridization between Neanderthaloid groups and groups that, morphologically speaking, might be considered as already more advanced.

In the European area during the period beginning approximately in 40,000 B.C. and ending in *c.* 26,000 B.C. (mid-Würm I to the end of the Interstadial Phase), significant cultural and biological changes occurred. During the course of this period it is considered, on a basis of both artefactual and skeletal evidence, that there was a replacement of Neanderthal varieties by Upper Palaeolithic people more nearly resembling modern Europeans. Such new peoples may indeed have been represented, somewhat earlier, by certain of the remains at Maghārat es-Sukhūl and Jebel Qafzah.[2] The apparent abruptness of this replacement, however, has led to explanations couched in terms of populational catastrophism, but it is more likely that the replacement process was a gradual one, and explicable in the ways that have been mentioned above.

The sites of the finds of skeletal evidence of Upper Palaeolithic men are numerous and extend over most countries of western and eastern Europe and into western Asia and northern Africa. The distribution pattern that is revealed, however, is very similar to that of the earlier Neanderthals of Würm I. The inference to

[1] §II, I. [2] §II, 4.

be drawn from this is that almost certainly the regions in Europe where life was tolerable were geographically much the same throughout the successive cold phases of the Würm glaciation. It is only to be expected, too, that some of these individuals are occasionally found to exhibit morphological traits reminiscent of the preceding Neanderthal population.

Over 160 sites of skeletal finds have been listed, but the remains of only about twenty-five Upper Palaeolithic individuals have been described in any adequate fashion. The range of distribution of these sites is from western Europe (where there is a concentration in France), eastwards across Europe as far as Czechoslovakia and north-western Hungary. The evidence from western Asia is much sparser. It is virtually confined to scanty remains of inhabitants of the Hūtū Cave, Iran, and of the Natufian inhabitants of Mount Carmel.

These Upper Palaeolithic people were of average height by modern standards, the mean stature of males being 5 ft. 8 in., and that for females 5 ft. 1 in., these estimates being based upon samples of twelve and five individuals respectively. They had long, broad, well-fitted skulls of modern European proportions, except for a greater facial breadth measured between the cheekbones. Attempts to identify evidence pointing to the differentiation of the modern races, however, can only be regarded as dubious because the samples are small and criteria, other than osteological, are lacking. The scanty evidence from Hūtū Cave, Iran, and from the Natufian inhabitants of Mount Carmel,[1] does not offer any valid distinction between western Asian and European men of the Upper Pleistocene.

Skeletal evidence from a number of sites in North Africa has also been interpreted as indicating that contemporary peoples in that area resembled, to some extent, those found in Europe. For example, parts of some fifty individuals have been recovered from Afalou-bou-Rhummel, near Bougie in Algeria, associated with an Ibero-Maurusian (Capsian) culture.[2] Parts of some thirty individuals, associated with an Ibero-Maurusian (Oranian) culture, have been recovered from Meshta-el-Arbi,[3] near Constantine in Algeria. There are only minor differences between the cranial and facial structure of these African peoples and that of the Cro-Magnon people of Europe. Other sites of importance are Wādi Halfa,[4] within the borders of the Sudan, and Taforalt in Morocco.[5]

Through adaptation, selection and hybridization, these men of

[1] §II, 6.   [2] §II, 12. See Fig. 19.   [3] §II, 2 and 3.
[4] §II, 8.   [5] §II, 5.

the Upper Pleistocene Age were to evolve into the Mesolithic and Neolithic villagers and into the various tribes of the Bronze and Iron Ages. It is reasonable to assume that such evolutionary change did not proceed everywhere throughout the region at the same rate, and it is only to be expected that such different rates of evolutionary change were reflected in slight morphological differences.

Although the differences between the people of the Mesolithic Period and their Upper Pleistocene predecessors are small, two morphological trends stand out, viz. towards shorter stature and rounder heads. These trends can be seen in Mesolithic remains from Muge, Portugal, from Téviec, Brittany, and also from Meshta-el-Arbi in North Africa. They are further substantiated, to some extent and in so far as head shape is concerned, by the cranial remains from the Ofnet cave in Bavaria.

The ecological changes initiated during the Mesolithic Period continued into the Neolithic Period, which is characterized by the adoption of agriculture and animal husbandry. As the glaciers continued to shrink northwards into Scandinavia, so the well-watered grasslands moved in response, so that areas such as Iran and Afghanistān became desiccated, and the fertile Nile valley became swampy and inimical to man. One result of these ecological changes was the migration of peoples, a movement that had begun in Mesolithic times but which now received fresh impetus from newly learned agricultural techniques. Palestine, North Africa and southern Europe were the first areas to feel this immigration, Neolithic farmers eventually spreading over most of Western Europe and reaching Britain. Such migration came from the south and from the east, and these immigrant populations were to form the basis from which the present populations of Europe are descended.

Also relevant at this stage of human evolution is a tendency towards population units of larger size, a concomitant of a more settled way of life, and a progression leading eventually to concentrations of people into towns and cities, e.g. such as in early Jericho. One important result of this may have been to change the nature of the epidemiology of the peoples of these times. Infectious diseases, for example, may have received an impetus in these early urban aggregates of peoples, an impetus largely absent perhaps in the case of smaller nomadic groups whose way of life centred upon hunting and collecting. Such epidemiological differentials may have affected the composition of the gene pools of these newly-emerging and larger urban populations, if the analogy with modern populations is a valid one.

By the time when the Neolithic culture was firmly established in Europe, the population responsible for its introduction into the continent was widely distributed but somewhat heterogeneous in so far as this may be gauged from cranial morphology. The traits held in common by most of these Neolithic people were long heads of medium size, vertical orthognathous facial profiles, and noses of narrow or medium width. There are many localized exceptions, e.g. the somewhat round-headed Danish Neolithic people. No doubt there were pigmentary and other genetically determined differences between many of these Neolithic groups, but in osteological terms and with only minor exceptions there is little gross difference demonstrable between the Sumerians of Mesopotamia, the predynastic Egyptians, and the Neolithic inhabitants of Switzerland, except perhaps in stature. The Badārian series of crania from Upper Egypt is the earliest of any length to have been recovered, and demonstrates a variability no less than that of many modern populations. They were a small, gracile people, with fairly broad noses and protruding jaws, although negroid affinities would seem to be contradicted by the hair samples that have been preserved. The Badārians were succeeded in Upper Egypt by people who are usually grouped together as the predynastic Egyptians, and who are well represented by the Naqāda cranial series. The Naqāda people were taller than the Badārians, had wider faces and heads, narrower noses and less jaw protuberance. The predynastic population of Lower Egypt, however, differed from that of Upper Egypt in having broader heads, longer faces and narrower noses. The subsequent racial history of Egypt was to be that of a gradual replacement of the Upper Egyptian type by that of Lower Egypt—a history amply documented by the numerous well-preserved series of crania from predynastic times and extending to Ptolemaic times.

Neolithic crania from Europe and western Asia are not nearly so numerous. There are fairly small cranial series from Spain and Portugal, some of which are claimed to resemble metrically those of the predynastic Naqāda series from Egypt. This skeletal evidence appears to confirm suggestions, based upon archaeological evidence, that the Iberian peninsula was an entry point for Neolithic peoples from North Africa—peoples who also moved into the upper valley of the Nile in predynastic times.

Access to Europe through the Mediterranean littoral must have been practicable in Italy and Greece, but the osteological evidence is scanty. The route from Anatolia over the Bosporus into the Balkans is similarly almost devoid of Neolithic human remains. The lack of such evidence does not necessarily preclude population movements along this route. North of the Black Sea, however, there is skeletal evidence of Neolithic peoples, resembling those known elsewhere in Europe, from such sites as Anau near the eastern shore of the Caspian Sea, and Mariupol near the Sea of Azov. In the Late Neolithic cemeteries of Kiev a taller, more narrow-headed and high-vaulted population is found, and is claimed to resemble metrically the earliest Sumerian skulls from Al-'Ubaid.

The Neolithic agriculturalists of the Danube shores, although scantily represented by skeletal remains, are essentially the same kind of people as are exemplified by the Neolithic human remains from Spain and the U.S.S.R.

In Britain, the remains of Megalithic or Long Barrow peoples represent the periphery of the Neolithic population expansion. They were larger in body, stature and skull dimensions than most other Neolithic people, and their morphological homogeneity may be accounted for by a persistent genetic isolation following their arrival in Britain by sea.

There is a resemblance, however, between these British Long Barrow people and certain of the French Neolithic people, for example, those represented by the remains from the corridor tomb of Vaudancourt, Oise.

In France too, and in Belgium, there is scattered evidence of an intrusive group of broad-headed Neolithic people, and yet another broad-headed group, but with possibly Mongoloid traits suggestive of an Asian origin, appears amongst the Neolithic populations of Scandinavia.

The coming of the Metal Age with the introduction of Bronze into the area under discussion was only gradually effected, and the cultural stage called the Bronze Age varied in duration from place to place. The interval between stone and iron extended over fifteen hundred years in Mesopotamia and Egypt, but rarely exceeded a few hundred years in Europe, except in some peripheral regions like Britain. Within this culturally defined span of time, however, there were to be shifts of population comparable in extent with those of the preceding Neolithic period.

One of the best-known groups involved in these shifts is that of the Bell Beaker people who arrived in Britain from northern Europe and who buried at least some of their dead in round barrows that are clearly distinguishable from the long barrows of the earlier Megalithic peoples of these islands. The skulls of these Beaker people are large, and high vaulted, although variable in shape, being both long and broad headed. It is not yet known, however, whether this variability is the result of hybridization with indigenous Neolithic peoples in Britain or of hybridization on the continent before immigration into Britain. The Beaker people chose to occupy the same areas as the Long Barrow people, and, as is only to be expected, evidence of some degree of hybridization is forthcoming.

In western Asia, there is skeletal evidence from Alişar Hüyük and Hisarlik, in Asia Minor. This points again to a broad-headed element in the population, presumably having come from farther east. A similar intrusion is noted in the Bronze Age remains from Cyprus. Skulls found in Crete, and attributable to the Bronze Age Minoan periods, may be indicative of some degree of genetic isolation from the hybridization going on elsewhere in the Mediterranean region. Such hybridization is apparent in crania recovered in Greece, Italy, Sicily, and Sardinia.

The distinctive group of mankind which is seen for the first time in any number during the Bronze Age, was a tall, round-headed people with a prominent vertical profile to the back of the head—a flattened occiput. They had salient narrow noses, and triangular-shaped faces. This was the group that was to become a recognizable element of subsequent populations of Europe, and it first appeared about 2000 B.C. in Asia Minor, Palestine and Cyprus, spreading through Central Europe to Spain and across the North Sea to England and Scotland.

By the close of the Bronze Age, the racial history of Europe, western Asia and northern Africa may thus be said to have consisted of the gradual infiltration into an initial stratum of long-headed Mediterranean peoples, widespread in distribution in Late Neolithic times, of round-headed varieties of man. The custom of cremation in the late Bronze Age cultures impedes the study of the subsequent population history until the beginning of the Iron Age, two or three hundred years later on.

It has been suggested that the genesis of the Iron Age accompanied the fall of the Hittite Empire at the beginning of the twelfth century B.C. With the downfall of the Hittites came the dispersion of their technological knowledge of iron-working, first to Palestine, and then through Anatolia, or Syria, to Greece and eventually to western Europe.

In the early stages of the Iron Age, burials were still of the ashes of the dead, often in urns that have given their name to the so-called Urnfields people and their culture; they first appeared in the Late Bronze Age. Whilst very little can be reconstructed that illuminates the physical characteristics of this cremated population, its geographical distribution is well documented and extended across Europe into France and Spain.

It was not until the Hallstatt phase of the Iron Age—a phase named after an extensive Austrian burial ground—that the custom of cremation was replaced by normal interment, about 700 B.C. The people buried at Hallstatt were of moderate stature and long headed. Many similar crania dated to this period have been recovered in Germany, Czechoslovakia and Switzerland. Cranial evidence of the Celtic peoples also found in Central Europe at this time is much scantier, but is characteristically of a round-headed people. More sizeable Celtic samples have been recovered from France and Britain but it is difficult to find any truly homogeneous group. This is only to be expected in a period of considerable population movement and consequent gene flow and exchange. In general, the cranial evidence from Britain and France indicates a moderately round-headed population, with sloping foreheads, long faces and prominent noses. It should be emphasized, however, that almost any Celtic sample selected for examination will show a proportion of aberrant individuals, representing survivals of older populations, accretions of emerging populations other than Celtic ones, and hybridization.

The tendency towards round-headedness, or brachycephaly, becomes more and more prominent through the Iron Age in Europe and cannot be explained away entirely by reference to round-headed immigrants from the east. Whilst the mechanism involved must have been adaptation and genetic selection, the advantage conferred by this particular cranial trend is still obscure. There is no increase, for example, in brain size. By the advent of modern times, most of the peoples of France, Switzerland, Southern Germany and Austria, the Balkans, and that part of western Asia lying near the Mediterranean had become round-headed. This tendency was not apparent, however, in the peoples of northern Europe, the Mediterranean littoral, and most of western Asia.

In view of the increasing size of the Iron Age populations in the area under present discussion, and the inherent uncertainty attaching to estimates of similarity based upon small cranial samples and upon a few recorded metrical traits, it is of little utility to look for precise genetical affinities between many of these peoples. There was little standardization of metrical techniques in many early inquiries, and comparative studies based upon their results are, in many cases, of doubtful utility. Until an up-to-date and comprehensive review of this accumulation of skeletal material has been undertaken, it is probably wiser to limit estimates of affinities to the inferences that are possible from the abundant archaeological and linguistic evidence which is available for study, and wiser to restrict comparative studies of cranial samples and of post-cranial bones to the elucidation of empirical problems.

CHAPTER VI

CHRONOLOGY

I. EGYPT—TO END OF TWENTIETH DYNASTY

THE most significant advance made in the study of ancient Egyptian chronology in recent years is the repudiation by Neugebauer and others of an astronomical origin for the Egyptian civil calendar[1] and, as a corollary, the elimination of the so-called Sothic Cycle[2] as a factor in dating the earliest periods of Egyptian history. It is thus unnecessary to associate the inauguration of the calendar, and all that is implied therein, with the beginning of such a cycle in 4241 B.C.;[3] the beginning of Egyptian history may now be lowered to about the end of the fourth millennium B.C., a date which agrees far better with the body of historical and chronological evidence available than do the much higher figures once favoured by some leading scholars.[4] It does not, however, entitle us to disregard this evidence and arbitrarily telescope the earlier periods of Egyptian history to allow for synchronisms with the admittedly fluid chronologies of neighbouring lands or merely to gratify an intuitive feeling that such eras as the Early Dynastic Period and the Old Kingdom 'could not' have been as long as our ancient sources indicate that they were.[5]

For the fixing in time of the Egyptian Middle Kingdom and the periods preceding it the key date is the seventh year of the

---

[1] §1, 23; *J.N.E.S.* 1, 396–403; §1, 37; Scharff and Moortgat, *Ägypten und Vorderasien im Altertum*, 30–1; §1, 25, 51 ff.

[2] The interval of approximately 1460 years between coincidences of the heliacal rising of the bright star Sothis (our Sirius) and the beginning of the 365-day Egyptian civil year. See §1, 19, 17–31; §1, 4, vol. 2, 10–35; §1, 25, 32 ff., 51 ff.; §1, 26

[3] Eduard Meyer's 'erste sichere Datum der Weltgeschichte' (§1, 19, 38–41, 45). According to Censorinus (21, 10) a coincidence of the type described in the preceding footnote occurred in the second year of Antoninus Pius, A.D. 139–40. The beginnings of the three preceding Sothic cycles fell, accordingly, in 1321–1317 B.C., 2781–2773 B.C., and 4231 (not 4241) B.C. Since the civil calendar was evidently in use before 2781 B.C. Meyer concluded that it must have been introduced at the start of the preceding Sothic cycle, a date far back in Egyptian prehistory.

[4] 3400 B.C. (Breasted, *A History of Egypt* [ed. 2, 1927], 14, 597); 3500(?) B.C. (Hall, *C.A.H.*[1] vol. 1 [ed. 2], 173, 656, 661); 4056 (±175–265 years) B.C. (Borchardt in §1, 4, vol. 2, 117); 5546 B.C. (Petrie, *A History of Egypt*, 1 [ed. 11, 1924], 7, 10).

[5] Cf. §1, 16, 82 n. 1; §1, 44, 103; Scharff and Moortgat, *op. cit.* 37.

reign of King Sesostris III of the Twelfth Dynasty. In this year
a heliacal rising of the star Sothis (our Sirius) was recorded on
16. VIII of the 365-day civil calendar, a fact which, thanks to
the regular displacement of this calendar in relation to the true
astronomical year, allows the year in question to be placed between 1876 and 1864 B.C., with every probability favouring
1872 B.C.[1] Since the reigns of Sesostris III's predecessors of the
Twelfth Dynasty amount to a total of 120 years, and since the
Turin Canon of Kings[2] (confirmed in part by surviving monuments of the time) gives 143 years as the duration of the Eleventh
Dynasty, it is possible, with only a negligible margin of error, to
date the founding of this dynasty to 2133 B.C. It is generally
accepted that the Heracleopolitan Tenth Dynasty was contemporaneous with the first two-thirds of the Eleventh Dynasty;[3]
it is also evident that the Ninth Dynasty, only two of the rulers
of which have left inscribed monuments, was of very brief
duration—two or three decades at the most. We shall, then, not
be far wrong in placing the end of the Eighth Dynasty and, with
it, the end of the Old Kingdom at about 2160 B.C.

Here the Turin Canon (IV, 17) comes to our aid with a total
figure of '955 regnal years and 10 (+ ?) days' for the interval
separating the end of the Eighth Dynasty from the accession of
King Menes, the founder of the First Dynasty. Since the interval
in question comprised eight dynasties which followed one another
without any apparent overlapping (co-regencies, with one exception, are unknown at this period), and the years referred to
represent successive periods of 365 days each, we have no choice
but to accept the figure at its face value and place the founding of
Egypt's first historic dynasty at about 3114 or, in round numbers,
3100 B.C.

Fortunately, the information available on the composition and
duration of Dynasties I–VIII tends to confirm this dating.

The reigns of the kings of the First and Second Dynasties

---

[1] §1, 9; §1, 25, 66.

[2] A fragmentary hieratic papyrus acquired with Bernardino Drovetti's first collection in 1824 by the king of Sardinia and now in the Regio Museo in Turin. It
appears to have been written in or near Memphis and bears on the *recto* a tax-list
drawn up in the reign of King Ramesses II of the Nineteenth Dynasty. On the
verso are preserved parts of eleven columns of a list of the kings of Egypt to the end
of the Hyksos Period, the name of each king followed by the duration of his reign
given in years, months, and days. The fragments of the papyrus were last remounted
by Hugo Ibscher in 1930–4 (§1, 11, 11). The transcription used here is that made
by Sir Alan Gardiner in 1947 and published by him in §1, 13.

[3] See below, p. 181.

were recorded year by year on the *recto* of a stone tablet of Annals carved in the Fifth Dynasty and represented today by fragments in Palermo,[1] Cairo, and London.[2] Reconstructions of the tablet (or tablets), effected chiefly by reference to the Fifth Dynasty entries on the *verso* of the 'Palermo Stone' and the largest of the four fragments in Cairo, have produced the following figures for the combined duration of the first two dynasties (Registers 2–5 of the *recto*): 453 or 419 years (Eduard Meyer in 1904 and 1925),[3] 520–545 years (Kurt Sethe in 1905),[4] 544 years (Ludwig Borchardt in 1917 and 1935),[5] 295 years (Wolfgang Helck in 1956),[6] and 444 years (Richard A. Parker in 1957).[7] Helck's estimate is low, presumably because he has chosen to start the First Dynasty (Register 2) with the reign of Aha rather than with that of his predecessor, Narmer, and has taken a forty-five-day interval between the reigns of Aha and Djer to represent a complete reign, thus reducing appreciably the reconstructed length of the second register and those preceding and following it. Otherwise, the figures obtained by four different scholars, each using a slightly different *modus operandi*, are consistent in exceeding four hundred years. The estimate of 415 years (*c.* 3100–2686 B.C.) adopted here, implies an average reign of almost twenty-four and a half years for the seventeen kings of the two dynasties. At first sight it may seem high, but it is below the average of 18.5 years established by Rowton for the throne tenure of seven generations of ancient oriental rulers.[8] A duration of four centuries for Dynasties I and II is not only reflected in the figures preserved in the Turin Canon (cols. II, III) and in the excerpts from the *Aegyptiaca* of the Ptolemaic historian, Manetho of Sebennytos,[9] but is indicated by the extensive cemeteries of the period at Saqqara, Helwān, and elsewhere and by the remarkable advances in architecture and the allied arts achieved between prehistoric times and the rise of the Old Kingdom (see below, ch. XI).

On the Annals tablets, as on the ebony and ivory labels and the inscribed vessels of the earliest dynasties, the years are not numbered, but each year is identified by reference to the most important event (or events) which occurred in it. Though the years so identified are clearly civil, not regnal, years, the events after which

[1] See Plate 25.
[2] §1, 35; §1, 15; §1, 29.
[3] §1, 19, 197; §1, 21, 68.
[4] §1, 38, 44–50, 57–8.
[5] §1, 4, vol. 1, 60; vol. 2, 115–16.
[6] §1, 16, 82 n. 2.
[7] §1, 27, 14c.
[8] §1, 32, 100–1.
[9] §1, 45.

they are named are usually associated with some activity of the reigning king.[1] As early as the First Dynasty we find a year designated as 'the first occasion' of an event which evidently occurred more than once within a single reign; and under the name of King Nynetjer of the Second Dynasty a succession of eight 'occasions' of the nationwide 'count', or inventory of taxable property, is recorded in alternate compartments of the fourth register of the Palermo Stone preceded in each case by a record of a 'Following of Horus', or royal tour of inspection. The count, originally of various kinds of property, later defined as 'the count of oxen and of all small cattle of Lower and Upper Egypt', was inaugurated in the first or second year of each king's reign and was held thereafter biennially. Each alternate year of a reign came, accordingly, to be referred to as 'the Year of the Nth Occasion of the Count' or simply as 'the Year of the Nth Occasion' and each intervening year, from the late Fourth Dynasty onwards, as 'the Year after the Nth Occasion'. Though it is evident that the Egyptians were only a step away from numbering the individual years of the reigns of their kings, this step was not actually taken until the very end of the Old Kingdom when the cattle count either became an annual occurrence or, more likely, was abolished altogether, allowing the expression 'Year of the Nth Occasion' or 'Year of Occasion N' to be used with the simple meaning of 'Regnal Year N'. In order to determine what regnal year is indicated in an inscription of the Old Kingdom and estimate the length of the reign involved, it is necessary in each case to double the number of the recorded 'occasion' and then subtract one from the resulting figure to allow for the possibility that the series of cattle counts may have begun, not in the king's second year, but in the same year as his accession.[2] Thus, if a 'Year of the 10th Occasion' is recorded for a king of Dynasties II–VI we may assign to the king in question a reign of at least nineteen years, the last of which, however, was almost certainly incomplete.

Column III (4–8) of the Turin Canon gives complete figures for the reigns of the five kings who appear to have comprised the Third Dynasty.[3] The total of the figures amounts to seventy-four years and, since this is in agreement with what can be gathered from the surviving monuments of the period, it can very reasonably be accepted as the duration of the dynasty. The Turin Canon

[1] §1, 12, 13.   [2] §1, 42, 123.
[3] The heading accompanying the name of Djoser in col. III, 5, does not indicate the beginning of a new dynasty. See §1, 16, 83–4, and below.

and the list of kings in the temple of Sethos I at Abydos[1] agree on the order of Nebka and Djoser, but the Westcar Papyrus, written in Hyksos times, unaccountably makes Nebka a successor of Djoser,[2] and this is the tradition followed in a third kings' list of the Ramesside Period, that from tomb of the architect Tjenry at Saqqara.[3] An architectural and structural comparison of the recently discovered pyramid of the Horus Sekhemkhet (King Djoser Teti?) with the corresponding elements in the pyramids of Djoser, Khaba, and Huni has led Lauer to the most convincing reconstruction of the dynasty hitherto proposed.[4]

Despite the fact that his reign appears to have included sixteen or seventeen 'occasions (of the count)' Sneferu, the founder of the Fourth Dynasty, is believed to have ruled for no more than the twenty-four years assigned to him by the Turin Canon. Under him the count seems to have been taken annually, beginning with the 7th Occasion and continuing until the end of the reign (see ch. XIV). Quarry or transport inscriptions of 'the Year of the 11th Occasion' on blocks of the boat-grave opened in 1954 beside the pyramid of Cheops[5] almost certainly belong to the reign of 23 years of that king rather than to the time of his successor, Redjedef, whose evidently short reign accords with the eight years attributed by the Turin Canon to the third ruler of the dynasty. For Chephren a 'Year of the 13th Occasion (= Year 25) is preserved on a casing block built into a mastaba near his pyramid at Giza.[6] In all probability the '[2]8 years' of Turin Canon III, 14 refers to Mycerinus. As Chephren's immediate successor this canon lists a ruler whose name and years are now lost, but who is probably to be equated with the Bicheris of Manetho's history and perhaps identified as Cheops' third(?) son, Prince Baufre. An inscription of the Middle Kingdom in the Wādi Hammāmāt[7] would seem to indicate that both this prince and his well-known brother, Hordedef, ruled as kings between the reign of Chephren and that of Mycerinus, but, in the case of the latter especially, the other evidence available militates against this interpretation.[8] It should be noted, however, that the

---

[1] Porter-Moss, *Top. Bibl.* 6, 25. See Plate 26.

[2] Erman, *Die Märchen des Papyrus Westcar*, 1, 22; 2, pl. 1.

[3] Porter-Moss, *op. cit.* 3, 192.

[4] *C.-R. Ac. Inscr. B.-L.* 1954 (1955), 368–79.

[5] Zaki Nour, *Revue de Caire*, Numéro spécial (1955), 41; Bothmer, *American Research Center in Egypt, Newsletter*, no. 14 (1954), 5.

[6] §1, 42, 128, fig. 7   [7] Drioton, *Bull. trimest. Soc. fr. d'égyptol.* 16, 41–9.

[8] Christophe, *Cahier d'histoire égyptienne*, sér. VII (Dec. 1955), 220–1; Goedicke, *Ann. Serv.* 55, 35–55.

Saqqara List names nine kings for the Fourth Dynasty[1] as against the Turin Canon's eight.[2] At the end of the dynasty may be placed Shepseskaf and an ephemeral ruler whom Manetho calls 'Thamphthis' (= Ptahdedef?)[3] and to them, respectively, may be ascribed the '4 years' and '2 years' of Turin Canon III, 15 and 16. It is apparent that the total of 115 years for the dynasty as a whole, derived from the foregoing data, must be regarded as a minimum figure and that 120 years is closer to, though perhaps still below, its actual duration. This was the figure deduced independently by Alexander Scharff, partly on the basis of a tabulation of the careers of some of the more distinguished contemporaries of the kings in question.[4]

Gardiner's demonstration that the biennial 'counts' were maintained throughout the Old Kingdom[5] requires an increase in the duration of the Fifth Dynasty from 140 years to a minimum of 150 years. The reigns chiefly affected are those of Sahure and Djedkare Isesi for whom are recorded, respectively, a 'Year after the 7th Occasion' (Year 14) and a 'Year of the 20th Occasion' (Year 39).[6] For Neferirkare the Palermo Stone mentions a year following the 'Year of the 5th Occasion', thus assuring to this ruler a reign of at least ten years.[7] Reigns of seven, seven, eight and thirty years are assigned in the Turin Canon to [Userkaf], [Shepseskare], Menkauhor, and Unas, respectively,[8] and, in view of his evident importance and the monuments which he has left us, we can probably restore the damaged year-figure following the name of [Nyuserre] as '31'.[9] No figure other than that given by Africanus exists for Neferefre (= 'Khaneferre' = 'Cheres'), but since he was able to build a sun-temple and apparently begin a pyramid at Abusīr he must have had a reign comparable at least with that of his less well-documented predecessor, Shepseskare Isi. On the number, order and identities of the kings who made up this dynasty there is, happily, a general agreement between the monuments, the Annals, the Ramesside kings' lists, and the epitome of Manetho's history.

In the Sixth Dynasty the most serious point of disagreement between the Turin Canon and our other sources lies in the reign of Phiops I ('Phios'). This important ruler, whose inscriptions

[1] Nos. 16–24 (§1, 19, pl. 1).   [2] Col. III, 9–16.
[3] Reisner, *Mycerinus*, 244–6; §1, 16, 25.
[4] §1, 36, 51 ff.; Scharff and Moortgat, *op. cit.* 58.
[5] §1, 12, 13–16. For a contrary opinion: §1, 16, 53, 57.
[6] §1, 42, 113; §1, 35, 38; *Hierat. Pap. Berlin*, 3, pl. 7, P 10523[Aw] 22.
[7] §1, 35, 40.   [8] Col. III, 17, 20, 23, and 25.
[9] Col. III, 22. See §1, 13, 16, pl. 2.

record a year after the eighteenth cattle count (Year 36), a twenty-first count (Year 41), and a twenty-fifth count (Year 49)[1] and to whom Manetho gives a reign of fifty-three years, is in the papyrus assigned only twenty years.[2] The missing years were perhaps attributed by the Canon partly to his predecessor, User-kare(?), who may have functioned with Phiops I's mother, Iput, as regent during his minority, and partly to his son and successor, Merenre I, who appears to have served as his co-regent during the last nine years of his reign.[3] This leaves for the latter an independent reign of only five years,[4] which agrees with the well-founded tradition that Phiops I's younger son, Phiops II, succeeded his brother at the age of six and died in his hundredth year after the longest recorded reign in world history. The ninety-four-year reign indicated by Manetho for Phiops II is supported by the entry, '..., years, 90 ($+x$)', in Turin Canon IV, 5, and is consistent with a number of exceptionally high cattle counts, including a '33rd(?) occasion' (Year 65),[5] Gardiner's restoration of Fragment 43 of the Turin Canon to its correct position[6] tends to confirm the Manethonian tradition that the Sixth Dynasty ended with Queen Nitocris and equates the personal name Nitokerty with the throne-name Menkare of the Abydos List (no. 41).[7] The same list names as the immediate successor of Merenre Antyemsaf II and the predecessor of Menkare (= Nitokerty?) a king Netjerykare. Allowing a year or less for this otherwise unknown ruler and two years for Nitokerty-Nitocris (Manetho's '12 years' minus 10), the total for the dynasty as reconstructed here comes to 165 years.

Since the Turin Canon (IV, 14–15) gives 187 years, 6 months, and 3 days as the combined duration of Dynasties VI–VIII there remain twenty-two and a half years for the fifteen ephemeral Memphite rulers who made up the Seventh and Eighth Dynasties and whose names are recorded, more or less accurately, in the Abydos List (nos. 42–56).[8] Of the last six of these kings (nos. 51–6) five appear to have been named also in Fragment 43 of the Turin Canon and in the two-line lacuna which follows it when it is moved

[1] *Urk.* I, 91, 209, and 95, respectively.
[2] Col. IV, 3.
[3] §1, 42, 121; Drioton, *Ann. Serv.* 45, 55–6.
[4] Hardly the '[40] +8(?) years' which would result from Gardiner's restoration of the numeral in col. IV, 4.
[5] §1, 42, 113, fig. 1. W. S. Smith is now inclined to read the numeral as '33'.
[6] Two lines higher than its former position. See §1, 13, 16, pl. 2.
[7] Cf. Newberry, *J.E.A.* 29, 54.
[8] See H. Goedicke, *Z.D.M.G.* 112 (1962), 239–54 [Ed.].

up to its proper position (IV, 9–13). It is these six kings who evidently comprised the Eighth Dynasty—though, like the Turin Canon, the Eusebius version of Manetho's Epitome represents the dynasty as made up of only five rulers. The years of their reigns, derived in part from Fragment 61 of the Turin papyrus and in part from their surviving monuments, total fourteen, leaving eight and a half years (as against Manetho's '70 [or 75] days') for the Seventh Dynasty. To this dynasty, which appears to have been omitted altogether from the Turin Canon, may be assigned the preceding nine kings named in the Abydos List, from Neferkare, 'the Younger' (no. 42), to Neferkahor (no. 50), inclusive.

If the figures obtained from the foregoing survey of Egypt's first eight ruling houses be added together the result will be found to be a well documented total of 532 years for Dynasties III–VIII and a probable grand total well in excess of 932 years for the duration of Dynasties I–VIII. The agreement between the last figure and the '955 years' given by the Turin Canon as the duration of the same eight dynasties strongly suggests that our chronology of this earliest phase of Egyptian history is fundamentally sound.

It is evident that the fifteen kings of Dynasties VII and VIII, with an average reign of one and a half years, do not represent generations of rulers, but simply the constantly shifting leadership characteristic of periods of political instability. That this was also true of the thirteen rulers of the Heracleopolitan Ninth Dynasty is indicated by the facts that only three of these kings, Meryibre Achthoes I, Neferkare, and Nebkaure Achthoes II,[1] are known from documents apart from the Turin Canon,[2] that in the provinces of Upper and Middle Egypt not more than two or, at the most, three nomarchs seem to have held office in each of the nomes between the end of the Eighth Dynasty and the expansion of Theban power early in the Eleventh Dynasty,[3] and that the relatively slight developments discernible in Egyptian art and culture during the interval in question do not suggest a period of

[1] §1, 14, vol. I, 204, 206; Hayes, *Scepter of Egypt*, I, 143, fig. 86; Vandier, *Mo'alla*, 36, 263, Inscription 16, 18 (in view of the conditions described in the Mo'alla tomb-inscriptions it is difficult to agree with Vandier that this was King Neferkare [Turin Canon, v, 6] who was a contemporary of the early Eleventh Dynasty); Newberry, *Z.Ä.S.* 50, 123.

[2] IV, 18—V, 4.

[3] See, for example, §1, 44, 12, 13, 16, 17, 67, 68, 72, 98, 99, 101; Brunner, *Ägyptol. Forsch.* 3, 87 and *passim*; 5, 38 ff.; Anthes, *Unters.* 9, 114; Porter-Moss, *op. cit.* 4–5, *passim*.

more than thirty years' duration.[1] On the other hand, since kings and nomarchs did exist between the Memphite rulers of Dynasty VIII and the Thebans of Dynasty XI and held their offices in brief, but none the less real, successions and since developments did take place in, for example, the style of tomb reliefs and inscriptions, there is no justification for eliminating the interval altogether and making the Ninth as well as the Tenth Dynasty contemporary with the Eleventh.[2]

That the Tenth and Eleventh dynasties, however, were contemporary with one another from the outset follows from a number of synchronisms which scholars have been able to establish between the kings of the two ruling houses.[3] When, for example, Wahkare Achthoes III, the third king of the Tenth Dynasty, battled for the possession of the Thinite nome his adversary was evidently the Horus Wahankh, Inyotef II, the third ruler of the Eleventh Dynasty.[4] One of Inyotef II's henchmen indeed mentions that he 'fought with the House of Achthoes on the west of This'.[5] The end of the Tenth Dynasty coincided with the final overthrow of Heracleopolis and the re-unification of Egypt under Nebhepetre Mentuhotpe II. This event, which must have taken place between Nebhepetre's 14th and 39th Years (2047 and 2022 B.C.), has been plausibly fixed by Hanns Stock at about 2040 B.C.[6]

For the Eleventh Dynasty the Turin Canon (v, 12–18) listed six kings, four of whom, Inyotef I–III and Nebhepetre Mentuhotpe (II), are represented in that order on a limestone doorjamb from the Middle Kingdom temple at Tōd.[7] Since, on a private stela in the British Museum, Inyotef III's successor is called 'the

[1] Speaking of the Eighth-Dynasty tomb of Setka at Aswān, Henry G. Fischer in his as yet unpublished *Denderah in the Third Millennium B.C.* says: 'The general style and some of the most distinctive details of the wall painting within this tomb are so like those at Moʻalla' [Dyn. IX] 'that it is hard to believe that they can be very far removed in time.'. . . 'Even assuming that *St-kʒ* built his tomb at the end of a long life, well into the Ninth Dynasty, the Ninth Dynasty would appear to have been relatively short, since the aforementioned details of orthography and so on at Moʻalla and Gebelein suggest that Dyns. X/XI are already near at hand.' See also Kees, *Or.* 21, 97.

[2] So for example, Helck (§1, 16, 82 n. 1).

[3] The fall of the Ninth Dynasty was without much doubt a result of the revolution which inaugurated the Eleventh Dynasty.

[4] Gardiner, *J.E.A.* 1, 23; Scharff, *Sitzungsb. München*, 1936, Heft 8, 51–4; §1, 44, 60, 61, 74, 75; §1, 7, 217, 218; Clère, *Cah. H.M.* 1, 650.

[5] Clère-Vandier, *Bibl. Aeg.* 10. sect. 18.

[6] §1, 44, 80, 92, 99, 103.

[7] Vandier, *Bull. Inst. fr. Caire*, 36, 101-16.

Horus Sankhibtowy, the Son of Re, Mentuhotpe',[1] it has been concluded that Sankhibtowy was the first of Nebhepetre's three Horus names, the two others, adopted in succession some time between his 14th and 39th regnal years, being Netjeryhedjet and finally, after his suppression of the Heracleopolitans, Smatowy, 'Uniter-of-the-Two-Lands'.[2] As Nebhepetre's successor the Turin Canon names Sankhkare (Mentuhotpe III) and then, at the end of the dynasty, records a hiatus, or lacuna, in its source covering a period of seven years. To this period belong, without much doubt, the brief reign of Nebtowyre Mentuhotpe IV[3] and the regency(?) of 'the God's Father Sesostris'—whose son(?), the Vizier Ammenemes, became in all likelihood the first king of the Twelfth Dynasty.[4] The Eleventh Dynasty was apparently founded by a God's Father Mentuhotpe (I), whose name appears on a statue dedicated to him by his son, Inyotef II,[5] and—preceded by the Horus name Tepya—in the Karnak list of ancestors of the Eighteenth Dynasty pharaoh, Tuthmosis III.[6]

The Twelfth Dynasty, comprising eight well-documented reigns fixed in time by the already mentioned sidereal date in Sesostris III's seventh year, presents no major chronological problems.[7] The date in question is preserved for us in a temple papyrus from El-Lāhūn and can with great probability be pin-pointed to 1872 B.C. by reference to four lunar dates contained in documents from the same archive. The co-regencies set up by Ammenemes I and three of his successors amount, in aggregate, to seventeen years. When allowance has been made for these co-regencies the duration of the dynasty is found to be 206 years, a figure comparable with that obtained for the first two dynasties and surpassed only three times in the subsequent course of ancient Egyptian history.

To achieve a harmony between the years of his reign and the years of the civil calendar it was apparently the practice through-

[1] Clère-Vandier, op. cit. §23.

[2] Meyer, Gesch. Alt. 1, 2 sect. 277; §1, 7 (ed. 1), 272; §1, 44, 77–80; Clère, op. cit. 646 ff.; Gardiner, Mitt. deutsch. Inst. Kairo, 14, 42–51.

[3] Winlock, J.E.A. 26, 116–19; §1, 44, 88–90, 92; Habachi, Ann. Serv. 55, 189; Simpson, J.N.E.S. 18, 25–8; Clère, op. cit. 649.

[4] Clère, loc. cit.; Habachi, op. cit. 185–9; Posener, Littérature et politique dans l'Égypte de la XIIe Dynastie, 50.

[5] Habachi, op. cit. 176–84.

[6] Now in the Louvre. See §1, 30, pl. 1.

[7] §1, 9; §1, 25, 63–9; Clère, op. cit. 649–50; Posener, op. cit. The evidence for a long co-regency between Sesostris III and Ammenemes III (Goyon, Nouvelles inscriptions rupestres, 22) is inconsistent and self-contradictory. See also Simpson, J.N.E.S. 18, 32–3.

out the Middle Kingdom for each ruler to make the date of this official accession to the throne coincide with the civil New Year's Day following the death of his predecessor and either surrender to that predecessor the preceding months and days or, as in Saïte and later times, retain them for himself and record them as his first regnal 'year'.[1] In the New Kingdom, on the other hand, regnal years were reckoned from the actual day of the king's accession without regard to whole calendar years—a system which must have proved as awkward to the scribes of the time as it has to the modern chronologist and historian.[2]

Following the end of the Twelfth Dynasty in 1786 B.C. the next astronomically determinable 'anchor-point' in Egyptian history is the ninth year of the reign of King Amenophis I, the second ruler of the Eighteenth Dynasty. This year, in which, according to the calendrical table of the medical Papyrus Ebers, a heliacal rising of Sothis occurred on 9. xi of the civil calendar, can be fixed with a high degree of probability at 1537 B.C.[3] If Manetho's very reasonable figure of 25–6 years for the reign of Amenophis I's predecessor, Amosis, be accepted, the beginning of the latter's reign can be set at 1570 B.C. and his expulsion of the last Hyksos ruler some three or four years later, in 1567 B.C.

Since the Turin Canon assigns to the 'great Hyksos' of the Fifteenth Dynasty alone a period of more than 100 (probably 108) years[4] and since before them the Thirteenth Dynasty ruled all Egypt for at least a century starting in 1786 B.C.,[5] it is clear that the Hyksos Sixteenth Dynasty must have been a subsidiary line of rulers more or less contemporary with the Fifteenth Dynasty and therefore of no particular chronological significance. Added to 1567, the Turin figure of 108(?) years for Dynasty XV takes the occupation of Memphis by the Hyksos Salitis back to 1674 B.C., this date also marking the defeat of the Egyptian king Tutimaios (Dudimose I)[6] and the end of the independent regime of the Thirteenth Dynasty, though not apparently the end of the dynasty itself. The initial occupation of the north-east Delta by the Hyksos forerunners of the Fifteenth Dynasty has been set at approximately 1720 B.C. on the basis of the so-called Stela of Year 400, a monument erected by Ramesses II to commemorate a visit made by his father Sethos to the temple of Seth of Avaris

---

[1] §1, 12, 16–23.   [2] *Ibid.* 23–8.   [3] §1, 8.
[4] Col. x, 21, See §1, 27, 14c; §1, 1, 17 n. 49.
[5] See below, p. 184, n. 5.
[6] §1, 45, Fr. 42, Fr. 38 n. 3; §1, 1, 15 n. 44.

on the 400th anniversary of its founding, presumably by the first Hyksos devotees of the god. The visit itself is believed to have taken place about 1320 B.C., when Sethos was serving as Vizier and Troop Commander under King Horemheb, the last ruler of the Eighteenth Dynasty.[1]

The Turin Canon (cols. VI–VIII) and the fairly numerous royal monuments which have survived from the period following the Twelfth Dynasty support the Manethonian tradition that the Thirteenth Dynasty comprised sixty kings, and if Manetho's obviously miscopied figure of '453 years' be amended to read '153 years' we shall have in all probability the correct total of their many, but for the most part very brief, reigns. At least half a dozen kings known from their monuments and from the Karnak List are not included in the Turin Canon[2] and through an understandable confusion Sekhemre Khutowy (Sobkhotpe I), the founder of the dynasty, has been made to change places with Khutowyre (Ugaf), the fifteenth or sixteenth ruler in the succession.[3] What were once thought to be group or dynasty headings here and elsewhere in the Turin papyrus have been plausibly identified by Helck[4] as merely the page-headings of a source document mechanically copied into the present list and therefore entirely meaningless. It is, in any case, reasonably certain that the rulers of the Thirteenth Dynasty followed one another in one long, continuous succession and that the date of any one of them can be roughly estimated from the existing figures for the reigns of his predecessors and successors.[5] Thus, the eleven-year reign of Khasekhemre Neferhotep I may be placed at about 1740–1730 B.C. and it may be concluded from a contemporary relief of Prince Yantin of Byblos that at this time the sovereignty of the Thirteenth Dynasty kings was still recognized not only in Lower Egypt, but also in Syria.[6] By 1720 B.C., however, the Hyksos were ensconced in the north-east Delta, and by 1674 B.C. they had

[1] Sethe, Z.Ä.S. 65, 85–9; §1, 22; §1, 1, 16; von Beckerath, Ägyptol. Forsch. 16, 38–41.

[2] E.g. Hetepibre Amu Sihornedjheryotef (§1, 7, 317 [31]; Habachi, Ann. Serv. 52, 460, 461, 469, 470); Seneferibre Sesostris IV (§1, 7, 314 [8]); Sekhemre Wadjkhau Sobkemsaf I (Hayes, Papyrus of the Late Middle Kingdom, 113, 145 n. 503); Sekhemre Sankhtowy Neferhotep III (Weill, Fin du Moyen Empire, 408, 835; Rev. d'Égyptol. 4, 218–20; Ann. Serv. 38, 625; etc.); Sewahenre Senebmiu (§1, 7, 316 [28]); Djedankhre Mentuemsaf (ibid. 317 [29]); Menkaure Senaayeb (ibid. 317 [30]); Djedhetepre Dudimose II (ibid. 317 [33]).

[3] §1, 7, 322–3; cf. von Beckerath, Z.Ä.S. 84, 81–5.

[4] §1, 16, 83–4.

[5] §1, 1, 13–16; Hayes, J.N.E.S. 12, 38.

[6] §1, 1, 13–16.

ousted the Egyptian ruler from his capital and taken over control of most of the country. The balance of the Thirteenth Dynasty, until its end about 1625 B.C., seems to have been made up of local rulers in the south and vassals of the Hyksos in the north.[1]

Following the names of these kings the Turin Canon (cols. VIII–X) lists seventy or more otherwise unknown kings who are almost certainly to be equated with the '76 kings of Xoïs' said by Manetho to have comprised the Fourteenth Dynasty and assigned by him (in the Africanus version) a total span of 184 years. A provincial ruling house evidently contemporaneous with the Thirteenth Dynasty, this group of rulers would appear to have held sway in their little west Delta kingdom from the fall of the Twelfth Dynasty in 1786 until about 1603 B.C.—less than forty years before the rise of the New Kingdom.[2]

The Hyksos 'Salitis', designated by Manetho as the founder of the Fifteenth Dynasty, is probably to be identified with the King Sharek, or Shalek, who appears in the Berlin genealogical table of Memphite priests[3] one generation before another Hyksos, King Apophis (I), and two generations before Nebpehtyre (Amosis), the first ruler of the Eighteenth Dynasty. That he is to be equated with King Mayebre Sheshi of the early Hyksos scarabs[4] is not unlikely and there can be little doubt that he and his five successors were the '6 [Hyk]sos' once listed in col. x (14–20) of the Turin Canon. Here the first king is assigned a reign of thirteen(?) years and the second (the Bnon, or Beon, of the Manethonian lists?), eight (or eighteen?) years. The fourth ruler, with a reign of more than forty years, can hardly have been other than King Auserre Apophis I, whose thirty-third year is attested on the title-page of the Rhind Mathematical Papyrus.[5] His predecessor was probably the important Hyksos ruler, Khyan (whose reign must also have been a long one), and his two successors, Aqenenre Apophis (II) and Asehre,[6] the latter presumably represented in the Turin Canon by his personal name, Khamudy. Asehre's reign was evidently brief and this must have been the case also with Aqenenre, since Apophis I is known from a stela found in 1954 at Karnak to have been a contemporary and

---

[1] §1, 43, 63–4; §1, 1, 15, 16.
[2] Winlock, *Rise and Fall of the Middle Kingdom*, 95–6.
[3] §1, 4, vol. 2, 96–112 (see especially 106–7).
[4] §1, 43, 25, 26, 45, 64–7; Säve-Söderbergh, *J.E.A.* 37, 62.
[5] Chace, Bull and Manning, *The Rhind Mathematical Papyrus*, 49, ph. 1, pl. 1.
[6] §1, 7, 318 (35, 38, 39).

antagonist of the Theban king, Kamose, the last ruler of the Seventeenth Dynasty.[1]

If the Manethonian figures given by Africanus ('518 years') and Barbarus ('318 years') be corrected to '118 years' the Sixteenth Dynasty would have begun in 1684 B.C., a decade earlier than the principal Hyksos line. This date would agree with the inclusion in the dynasty of such very early Hyksos as Anather and Semqen.[2] In the Turin Canon a group of eight kings (col. x, 22–9) listed immediately after the Great Hyksos and before the Theban rulers of the Seventeenth Dynasty may be reasonably assumed to be the Sixteenth Dynasty. Only one of their names—somewhat doubtfully read 'Seket'—is preserved in the papyrus, and it is necessary to complete the dynasty with kings' names preserved on scarabs and various small monuments of the period.[3]

The order of the sixteen Thebans of the Seventeenth Dynasty (Turin Canon, x, 30–xi, 14) was convincingly worked out in 1924 by Herbert Winlock[4] and in 1942 by Hanns Stock.[5] The list of kings at the end of this volume follows the results obtained by these two scholars with, however, some emendations derived in part from the Gardiner–Černý transcription of the Turin Canon. Interestingly enough, this document divides the rulers of the dynasty into two groups, separating the five warlike kings at the end of the dynasty from their ten (or eleven) predecessors.[6] Many of these kings have left inscribed monuments; the tombs of six of them are referred to in the tomb-robbery papyri of the Twentieth Dynasty, and the names of more than half of them can be found in the Karnak List and in several shorter Theban lists of New Kingdom date.[7] Though his name was apparently copied as 'Sewadj[en]re' by the Ramesside scribe or his source, the king of Turin Canon xi, 4, was in all probability Sankhenre Mentuhotpe (VI), the owner of two inscribed limestone sphinxes from Edfu.[8] Of interest to the chronology of the period is the fact that the grandfather of a contemporary of King Nebiryerawet I

[1] Habachi, *Ann. Serv.* 53, 195–202; *Rev. du Caire*, Numéro spécial (1955), 52–8; Hammad, *Chron. d'Ég.* 30, 198–202; Montet, *C.-R. Ac. Inscr. B.-L.* 1956, 112–20; Säve-Söderbergh, *Kush*, 4, 54–61.

[2] §1, 43, 42, 43, 46, 64, 67.   [3] *Ibid.* 43–6, 64–8.

[4] *J.E.A.* 10, 217–77.   [5] §1, 43, 75–81.

[6] Col. x, 30–col. xi, 9 and col. xi, 10–15.

[7] §1, 30, pls. 1, 3; Capart, *Recueil de monuments égyptiens*, 2e sér., pl. 86, §1, 6; Maspero, *Catalogue du Musée Égyptien de Marseille*, 3–5; Roeder, *Aeg. Inschr., Berlin*, 2, 190–2.

[8] Gauthier, *Ann. Serv.* 31, 1–4.

(*c.* 1628–1623 B.C.) is known from a Karnak stela to have lived fifty years earlier, in the time of King Merhetepre Ini of the Thirteenth Dynasty (*c.* 1677 B.C.).[1] Variant Horus names used by Kamose, the last king of Dynasty XVII, once gave rise to the unfounded supposition that there was more than one ruler of this name.[2] Allowing a substantial reign for this king because of his association with Apophis I[3] and estimating the sum of the remaining reigns on the basis of the surviving figures it is possible to reach a total for the dynasty of over eighty years (*c.* 1650–1567 B.C.).

In the Turin Canon the Seventeenth Dynasty is followed in the second half of column XI by a series of fifteen kings who must have belonged to yet another local dynasty of the Hyksos Period. Here the surviving fragments of the Canon come to an end and this invaluable document, on which so much of our knowledge of Egyptian chronology depends, affords no further assistance.

Compared with those of the older periods of Egyptian history the chronological problems of the more recent and more generously documented New Kingdom—the Eighteenth, Nineteenth, and Twentieth Dynasties—are relatively minor. For the Eighteenth Dynasty we have at the outset the date of 1537 B.C. fixed astronomically for the ninth year of the reign of Amenophis I and an inscription of one of his officials which 'makes it highly probable that' the 'king died in the twenty-first year of his reign'[4] (1526/25 B.C.). A Sothic date and two lunar dates in the reign of Tuthmosis III allow the accession of that great pharaoh to be placed at either 1504 or 1490 B.C., with the probabilities favouring the earlier of the two dates.[5] This dating would leave twenty-one years between the two rulers for the reigns of Tuthmosis I and II; we shall not be far wrong in assigning thirteen of these years (1525–*c.* 1512 B.C.) to the notable conqueror and builder, Tuthmosis I, and eight (*c.* 1512–1504 B.C.) to his short-lived son, Tuthmosis II.[6] A text at Karnak describes

[1] Lacau, *Bull. Inst. fr. Caire*, 30, 893; *Ann. Serv., Cahier* no. 13, 36.

[2] §1, 7, 331.

[3] See above, p. 186, n. 1.   [4] §1, 8, 193.

[5] §1, 28, 41 (possibilities 1 and 4). Source errors of equal gravity have to be assumed in the case of either date; a sound chronology of the later Eighteenth and early Nineteenth Dynasties, obtained from independent sources (see below), requires the earlier date. So also do the probable lengths of the reigns of Tuthmosis I and II. See e.g. Jaritz, *Mitt. Inst. Or.* 6, 199. See, however, A, 3, 317, n. 5 [Ed.].

[6] A date in 'Year 18' of Tuthmosis II, published by Daressy in *Ann. Serv.* 1, 99, is otherwise unsubstantiated and is open to serious doubt on many grounds. See Edgerton, *The Thuthmosis Succession*, 33; cf. §1, 16 and 64–66.

Hatshepsut's assumption of the kingship in Year 2 of Tuthmosis III.[1] Her disappearance from history some time between his 20th and 22nd years[2] agrees with Manetho's slightly garbled statement that after the third king of the dynasty 'his sister Amessis' ruled for twenty-one years and nine months. Scholars have generally abandoned the elaborate and unconvincing reconstruction of the early Tuthmoside succession devised by Kurt Sethe[3] and followed by James Henry Breasted.[4]

Having served as Tuthmosis III's co-regent for four months preceding the latter's death on 30. VII of his fifty-fourth year[5] (1450 B.C.) Amenophis II, according to an inscribed jar from his funerary temple, was still on the throne in his own twenty-sixth year, but probably did not attain the thirty-one years assigned to him by Manetho.[6] On the other hand, Manetho's figure (according to Josephus) of nine years and eight months for the reign of the short-lived Tuthmosis IV may be accepted as correct, since the highest recorded date for this king is Year 8[7] and there is no reason to suppose that his son and successor, Amenophis III, was not born before Tuthmosis himself came to the throne.[8] For Amenophis III we have an unbroken succession of dates extending from Regnal Year 28 to Regnal Year 38,[9] a fact which suggests that the king died either late in the thirty-eighth or early in the thirty-ninth year of his reign (1379 B.C.).

It is clear that in early Ramesside times the existence of the four 'Amarna kings'—Akhenaten, Smenkhkare, Tutankhamun, and Ay—was officially ignored and in official documents the reign of Horemheb was assumed to extend back to the death of Amenophis III.[10] Thus, a 'Regnal Year 59' of Horemheb, cited in an inscription of the time of Ramesses II,[11] must not be interpreted as an indication of the actual length of Horemheb's reign.

[1] Schott, *Nachr. Göttingen*, 1955, Nr. 6, 212 ff.

[2] *Ibid.* 216.

[3] *Unters.* 1; *Abh. Berlin*, 1932, Nr. 4.

[4] See Meyer, *Gesch. Alt.* II, 1 (ed. 2, 1928) 110 ff.; Winlock, *Bull. M.M.A.* 23 (1928), Feb., sect. II, 46 ff.; Edgerton, *op. cit.*

[5] §1, 12, 27–8.   [6] §1, 16, 66.

[7] *Urk.* IV, 1545; §1, 14, vol. 2, 292 (VII).

[8] For a discussion of the problem see §1, 7, 383–4. While it is clear that Amenophis III was the son of Tuthmosis IV and Queen Mutemweya, there is no basis for identifying the latter with the princess of Mitanni referred to in Amarna Tablet no. 29 (16–18) and nothing to show that Mutemweya and Tuthmosis IV were not already married at the time of his accession.

[9] Hayes, *J.N.E.S.* 10, 56 (fig. 16), 87–8.

[10] §1, 33; §1, 19, pl. 1. See J. R. Harris, *J.E.A.* 54 (1968), 95–9 [Ed.].

[11] Gardiner, *Unters.* 4, 11, 22 n. 72, 52.

On the other hand, it does mean that he was on the throne in 1320 B.C. and, perhaps, for a year or two thereafter. For Akhenaten, Smenkhkare, Tutankhamun, and Ay the records furnish high dates of seventeen, three, nine and four years, respectively, which suggest probable reigns of eighteen, one (plus two to three as co-regent), ten, and four to five years, and therefore a total of thirty-three or thirty-four years.[1] For Horemheb there appears to be a date in the twenty-seventh year after his actual accession.[2] The date of his accession depends on the answer to a question on which opinion is sharply divided whether Amenophis III and Amenophis IV (Akhenaten) ruled together as co-regents during the first decade or so of the latter's reign[3] or whether, as seems more likely, the younger king's reign did not start until his father's death in 1379 B.C.[4] In the first case Horemheb would have come to the throne in 1358 B.C. and reigned a hardly credible thirty-eight years, in the second he would have occupied the throne for twenty-eight years beginning in 1348 B.C. In either case his reign would have included the visit of the Vizier Sethos (later King Sethos I) to the temple of Seth of Avaris, an event recorded on the Stela of Year 400.

Thanks to a lunar date in his fifty-second regnal year and other pertinent considerations, the date of the accession of Ramesses II, the third ruler of the Nineteenth Dynasty, has been narrowed down to a choice between 1304 and 1290 B.C.; recent studies of cuneiform documents relating to the king's contemporaries or near-contemporaries in western Asia tend to indicate that the higher date, 1304 B.C., is the correct one.[5] An allowance of fourteen or fifteen years for the reign of Sethos I and one year and four months for that of Ramesses I[6] puts the beginning of the Nineteenth Dynasty (and the end of the reign of Horemheb) at 1320/19 B.C. Like that of Ammenemes I of the Twelfth Dynasty

[1] Pendlebury, *Tell el-Amarna*, 33; Fairman in Pendlebury, *City of Akhenaten*, 3, 158–9; Newberry, *J.E.A.* 14, 3–9; 18, 50–2; Gardiner, *J.E.A.* 14, 10–11; Roeder, *Z.Ä.S.* 83, 45; Engelbach, *Ann. Serv.* 40, 163–4; Seele, *J.N.E.S.* 14, 179–80.

[2] Anthes in Hölscher, *The Excavation of Medinet Habu*, 2, 107–8, fig. 90, pl. 51 c. See, however, Fairman, *op. cit.* 158; von Beckerath, *Ägyptol. Forsch.* 16, 104.

[3] Fairman, *op. cit.* 152–9; Aldred, *J.E.A.* 43, 114–17; 45, 19–33; *J.N.E.S.* 18, 116, 120; Hayes, *J.N.E.S.* 10, 37 n. 14.

[4] Helck, *Mitt. Inst. Or.* 2, 189–207; Gardiner, *J.E.A.* 43, 13, 14; Smith, *The Art and Architecture of Ancient Egypt*, 184–5; Campbell, *The Biblical Archaeologist*, 23, 7–10.

[5] Rowton, *J.C.S.* 13, 1–11; *J.N.E.S.* 19, 15–22.

[6] §1, 16, 69–70; von Beckerath, *op. cit.* 104; §1, 7, 353, 354, 631.

the accession of Sethos I was hailed in official texts of his time as the dawn of a new era called a 'Repeating of Births' and the years of his reign were sometimes numbered by reference to this Renaissance.[1] His accession in 1318 B.C. may also have coincided with the start of an 'era' described by Theon of Alexandria as *apo Menophreōs*, which began in 1321–1317 B.C. and has been identified as the last pre-Christian Sothic cycle.[2] The copiously documented sixty-seven year reign of Ramesses II was followed by that of his fourteenth son,[3] Merneptah, a man already elderly at the time of his accession, whose tenth regnal year is attested by Papyrus Sallier I (III, 4), but whose total reign probably did not exceed twelve or thirteen years.[4] Merneptah was apparently succeeded first by his nephew, Amenmesses,[5] who occupied the throne for more than three and perhaps as many as five years,[6] and then by his son, Sethos II, whose death in his sixth regnal year is reported on an ostracon from the Valley of the Tombs of the Kings.[7] The final eight or nine years of the dynasty (1209–1200 B.C.) were taken up by the partially overlapping reigns of Sethos II's widow, Tewosret, and his son(?), Merneptah Siptah, whose identity with Ramesses Siptah and whose position as a successor of Sethos II now seem established beyond a reasonable doubt. The 'Palestinian Irsu', who according to the somewhat biased testimony of Papyrus Harris I helped to bring the dynasty to an unhappy end, has been plausibly identified either as Siptah himself, who may have had a Palestinian mother, or as his powerful chancellor, Bay.[8]

Like Ramesses I, Sethnakhte, the founder of the Twentieth Dynasty, appears to have been well advanced in age at the time of his accession, and his reign, of which only the first year is recorded, probably did not exceed two years.[9] The death of his famous son, Ramesses III, in the latter's thirty-second regnal year is indicated by the opening line of Papyrus Harris I and is

[1] von Beckerath, *op. cit.* 90–1, 105; §1, 40, 4–7.

[2] von Beckerath, *op. cit.* 105–7; Cornelius, *A.f.O.* 17, 305; Rowton, *Iraq*, 8, 107–9. See, however, *C.A.H.* II³, ch. XXIII, sect. 1 [Ed.].

[3] Christophe, *Ann. Serv.* 51, 335 ff.

[4] von Beckerath, *op. cit.* 107; §1, 31, 73.

[5] Helck, *Z.D.M.G.* 105, 39; Caminos, in *Ägyptol. Studien Hermann Grapow... gewidmet*, 17–29; Gardiner, *J.E.A.* 44, 16.

[6] §1, 16, 70.

[7] Gardiner, *op. cit.* 12, 14.

[8] On the end of Dynasty XIX see von Beckerath, *Z.D.M.G.* 106, 241 ff.; Helck, *Z.D.M.G.* 105, 39–44; Gardiner, *op. cit.* 12–22.

[9] von Beckerath, *Ägyptol. Forsch.* 16, 79, 107; §1, 7, 356.

referred to on a fragment of papyrus in Turin.[1] Ramesses IV, who ascended the throne either on the day of Ramesses III's death or ten days later,[2] reigned for six years according to the unequivocal testimony of Papyrus Turin 1887.[3] The same document records the fourth year of Ramesses V and an ostracon in Cairo shows 'that the interval between year 3 (or 4 ?) of Ramesses V and year 1 of Ramesses VI could not have been very long'.[4] The identities and order of the next three rulers are based to a great extent on the lists of 'sons of Ramesses III' preserved for us in the latter's temple at Medīnet Habu.[5] For the first of these, Nebmare Ramesses VI, a high date of Regnal Year 6[6] occurs on a stela from the temple of Maat at Karnak. Ramesses Setherkhepeshef, identified by Seele, Černý and Helck[7] as Ramesses VIII, reigned for less than a year, while his predecessor, Ramesses (Itamun) VII, is known from the *verso* of another papyrus in the Turin museum's rich collection to have occupied the throne for seven years.[8] Papyrus Turin 2075 fixes the reign of Ramesses IX at nineteen years[9] and Parker has produced evidence which indicates that Ramesses X ruled for nine years.[10] The *verso* of Papyrus Abbott equates Regnal Year 19 of Ramesses XI, the last ruler of the New Kingdom, with the first year of a new Renaissance, or 'Repeating of Births', an era apparently commemorating the rise to power of Hrihor, the first of the priest-kings whose rule at Thebes was contemporaneous with the Twenty-first Dynasty.[11] An inscription at Karnak is dated to Year 7 of this era, which is the equivalent of Year 25 of Ramesses XI,[12] and a stela from Abydos mentions that the latter retained the throne for a minimum of twenty-seven years.[13] It was evidently not until his death, about

---

[1] Černý, *Z.Ä.S.* 72, 109–18.

[2] *Ibid.*; Schaedel, *Z.Ä.S.* 74, 96–104.

[3] Gardiner, *J.E.A.* 27, 60–2; Sauneron, *Rev. d'Égyptol.* 7, 53–62.

[4] Černý, *J.E.A.* 31, 42 n. 2.

[5] Seele, *Ägyptol. Studien Hermann Grapow…gewidmet*, 296–314; *J.N.E.S.* 19, 184–204; Nims, *Bi. Or.* 14, 137–8; Černý, *J.E.A.* 44, 33–7; von Beckerath, *op. cit.* 85–7.

[6] Christophe, *Bull. Inst. fr. Caire*, 37, 32 n. 1; Sauneron, *op. cit.* 56.

[7] See above, footnote 5; Helck, *An. Bi.* 12, 126–8.

[8] von Beckerath, *op. cit.* 86 n. 467, 87, 108.

[9] *Ibid.* 89 n. 485, 108.   [10] *Rev. d'Égyptol.* 11, 163–4.

[11] Černý, *J.E.A.* 15, 194 ff.; *Z.Ä.S.* 65, 129–30; Kees, *Nachr. Göttingen*, n.F. 1, 2 (1936–38), 1–20; Nims, *J.N.E.S.* 7, 157–62; von Beckerath, *op. cit.* 88 ff. See also Helck, *Mitt. Inst. Or.* 4, 176–8.

[12] Nims, *loc. cit.* Drioton and Vandier (§1, 7, 389) have evidently taken the day-date, '28', in this inscription to be the number of the regnal year of Ramesses XI.

[13] Peet, *J.E.A.* 14; von Beckerath, *op. cit.* 90 n. 488, 108.

1085 B.C., that Smendes in the north and Hrihor in the south allocated, each to himself, the titles and insignia of kingship, thereby bringing the New Kingdom to a definite end and plunging Egypt into the final tumultuous phases of her dynastic history.

The chronology of the latest periods of Egyptian history is not only beyond the scope of the present review, but depends to such an extent on the chronologies of other Near Eastern and Mediterranean lands—Assyria, Persia, Greece, and Rome—that its study is no longer within the competence of the Egyptologist alone.

For the earlier stages of Egypt's development indirect synchronisms with other civilizations of the ancient world can be recognized far back into prehistory,[1] and from the early second millennium onwards records exist of direct associations between kings of Egypt and rulers of other eastern Mediterranean lands whose names are known and whose dates can be independently determined with varying degrees of accuracy.[2] These synchronisms are occasionally of value in helping to establish points in the Egyptian chronological system on which it might otherwise be difficult to reach a decision. As an example we may cite the date of the accession of Ramesses II, whose numerous contacts with his Hittite contemporaries link him chronologically with the rulers of Assyria and other western Asiatic nations. Faced with a choice between the Egyptian chronologist's dates of 1304 or 1290 B.C.,[3] students of the cuneiform evidence have been able to produce convincing arguments in favour of the earlier date.[4]

For Egypt in the dynastic period the results so far obtained from the carbon-14, or radiocarbon, method of dating,[5] though agreeing in general with the chronological scheme adopted here, are not sufficiently precise or sufficiently consistent to contribute much of value to our reconstruction of Egyptian history. This may be attributable in part to 'contamination' of the samples

---

[1] Scharff, *Alte Or.* 41 and 42; Hayes, *Scepter of Egypt*, 1, 367–8; Vercoutter, *L'Égypte et le monde égéen.*

[2] Virolleaud, *Syria*, 3, 273–90; *L'Ethnographie*, n.s. no. 45, 3–16; §1, 1, 9–18; §1, 41, 170–1; Knudtzon, *Die el-Amarna-Tafeln;* Gordon, *Or.* 16, 1–21; Güterbock, *J.C.S.* 10, 41–68, 75–98, 107–30; Edel, *J.N.E.S.* 7, 11–24; *J.C.S.* 12, 130–3; Rowton, *J.C.S.* 13, 1–11; Desroches-Noblecourt and Krieger in Schaeffer, *Ugaritica III*, 164–226; Tadmor, *J.N.E.S.* 17, 139 ff.

[3] §1, 28, 42–3; §1, 4, vol. 2, 43.

[4] Rowton, *J.C.S.* 13, 1–11; *J.N.E.S.* 19, 15–22. Cf. Cornelius, *Arch. f. Or.* 17, 308.

[5] §1, 18. See especially pp. 77–9.

submitted through prolonged contact with organic material of more recent date in the storerooms of the expedition camps and museums from which they came.[1] In any event, the radiocarbon date of 1671 B.C. ± 180 years for Sesostris III, whose seventh regnal year fell probably in 1872 B.C., is hardly satisfactory for the purpose of the historian. Nor does the dating of Hemaka of the mid-First Dynasty (sample C-267) more than 160 years earlier than a prehistoric Egyptian of the second Naqāda culture (C-813) and the placing of King Djoser of Dynasty III (C-1) more than eight centuries later in time than his successor, King Huni (C-12), tend to inspire confidence in the results obtained from the dynastic samples examined. On the other hand, for Egyptian prehistory, where no other system of absolute dating has been developed and even the relative dating of finds has been the subject of much dispute,[2] the radiocarbon dates for the Faiyūm A,[3] Naqāda I, and Naqāda II cultures form welcome islands in a sea of uncertainty.

II. ANCIENT WESTERN ASIA

INTRODUCTION

THE chronology of every country in ancient Western Asia bristles with problems. A comprehensive survey of the whole area introduces further problems of comparative chronology. And if, as here, the intention is to deal with the subject in abridged form, a danger arises which it will be prudent to point out at the very outset. Abridged treatment necessarily means that only the more important problems can be brought into clear focus. And even these can be dealt with only by a method which is not satisfactory. Only the solution which appears to be the most probable at the moment of writing can be given, because space will not permit discussion of other possibilities. This tends to obscure the ever present element of uncertainty, and a picture emerges which is drawn in bolder and surer outline than the evidence justifies. Nor is it always possible to refer the reader elsewhere for fuller discussion. Even some of the main problems have not yet been

---

[1] §1, 5 (see especially 6–8); Ralph, *Expedition* (*Bull. Univ. Mus. Penn.*), 1, 24–5. See also Arkell, *Shaheinab*, 107; *Bi. Or.* 13, 123, 126; Leclant, *Kush*, 5, 95.

[2] Baumgartel, *Cultures of Prehistoric Egypt* (revised ed., 1955), 49–51; Arkell, *Bi. Or.* 13, 123–7; Kaiser, *Z.Ä.S.* 81, 87–109; *Archaeologica Geographica*, 6, 69–77.

[3] Arkell, *op. cit.* 126; §1, 18, 77.

adequately discussed, and a satisfactory comprehensive study is still lacking.[1]

The appearance of writing marks the end of the prehistoric period. From that point on, texts tend to become the chief chronological source. Lack of space will restrict description of chronological sources to this essential category; among those which it will not be possible to single out for special discussion are: pottery,[2] glyptic, orthography, radiocarbon chronology,[3] astronomical chronology,[4] and dating by the average throne tenure per generation.[5]

SOURCES

(a) The Assyrian eponym-lists and king-lists

In Assyria years were designated by the name of the *limmu-* official. These eponyms, whose exact functions have not yet been determined, held office for one year, and lists were kept of the eponyms.[6] In such a list no single error would normally involve more than one year. Hence the eponym-lists constitute one of the most reliable chronological sources we have.

Among the individuals of prominent status who served as eponyms were the kings. They usually held office only once during their reign, although two kings are known to have served as eponym a second time, in their thirtieth regnal year, and one held the office throughout his reign. The kings normally held office in their first or second regnal year,[7] a custom which is attested as far back as Tukulti-Ninurta I, in the thirteenth century.[8] At present the earliest identifiable king known to have held eponym office is Enlil-nirari, in the fourteenth century, though it cannot be proved during which regnal year he held the office.[9]

The interval between the year in which a given king held

---

[1] §II, 144; for Mesopotamia alone see §II, 105; 107, vol. II, 332 ff. 125; for areas other than Mesopotamia see §II, 123. For the bibliography of Mesopotamian chronology up to 1939 see the literature quoted in §II, 104, 235 ff.

[2] For a good example of the use of pottery in chronology see §II, 25.

[3] §II, 90.   [4] §II, 46 and 97.

[5] §II, 118, 100 ff.

[6] §II, 148; for additional eponyms §II, 157, 110 ff.; for the eponyms of the Old Assyrian period see §II, 4; for additional eponyms of the Middle Assyrian period §II, 160, 213 ff.; for a discussion of the eponyms of that period see §II, 30; for additional eponyms of the New Assyrian period see §II, 28 and 52.

[7] §II, 110, vol. 2, 71 ff.

[8] §II, 30, 51.   [9] *Ibid.* 41.

eponym office and the year in which his successor held eponym office we call an eponym period. This interval would equal the length of the first king's reign, on condition that both kings held office in the same regnal year of their respective reigns. Should a king postpone tenure of eponym office his eponym period would be shorter than his reign. But in that case the eponym period of his predecessor would be increased by an equivalent amount; the discrepancies would cancel out in chronological summation. And in the rare event that a king died before holding eponym office, the interval of his reign would be included in the eponym period of his predecessor.

The Assyrian scribes drew lines in the eponym-lists to mark the limits of the eponym periods, and in some cases they even added a total for the period. This indicates that most eponym lists were also meant to serve as king-lists. Indeed a king-list could be easily obtained from an eponym-list by the simple process of leaving out the names of eponyms, and listing only the eponym periods. This taken in conjunction with other pertinent evidence makes it very probable that the Assyrian king-lists are really lists of eponym periods.[1] The eponym-lists, except for one small fragment, do not reach back beyond the eleventh century B.C. But it can be shown that the original copy of the Assyrian king-list was in all probability compiled from an eponym-list in the eleventh century.[2] In that case the king-list has preserved the essential chronological content of the earlier eponym-lists, now lost.

The eponym-list which is behind the Assyrian king-list was damaged, or otherwise deficient, for the interval between Shamshi-Adad I and Adasi. There is also heavy damage to the king-list, in all three copies, for the reigns between Erishum I and Shamshi-Adad I. Before Erishum I no figures were quoted.[3] This means that the king-list is not a reliable source for the period prior to the beginning of the dynasty of Adasi. For the next few centuries we have no means of verifying its reliability, but there is no reason to believe that it contains substantial errors, particularly if it is based on an eponym-list. The earliest point at which verification becomes possible is the accession of Ashur-uballiṭ I, in or about

[1] §11, 116, 98 ff. and §11, 119, 220 ff.; for evidence of a scribe using an eponym-list to bring a king-list up to date, §11, 110, vol. 2, 78.

[2] The present writer plans to discuss the date of the Assyrian king-list in a forthcoming article.

[3] For the Assyrian king-list see §11, 44 and also Plate 4; the text was discussed earlier in §11, 110. For incompleteness of the list in the period before Adasi see §11, 159, 96 ff. and §11, 77, 31 ff. For an earlier, but badly damaged copy of the king-list see §11, 96 and 153.

1365. Measured against the Egyptian and the Hittite evidence this date is found to be closely correct, though an error of a few years cannot be excluded. This important approximate synchronism is discussed below in connexion with the chronology of the Amarna period.[1]

Apart from the main copies of the Assyrian king-list mentioned above fragments have been found of several other king-lists, both with and without figures. Some of these are probably copies of the same original king-list from which the three main lists are descended. But at least one represents an independent source; unfortunately it is without figures.[2]

There are also king-lists of a very special kind, the synchronistic king-lists, in which the Assyrian kings are listed parallel to a second column containing the Babylonian kings.[3] Most of these lists are of little value for comparative chronology. But the one which is best preserved has a system of lines by which the author intended to indicate what he considered to be genuine synchronisms between Assyrian and Babylonian kings, as against mere juxtaposition of names. This source deserves serious consideration, although it too is not free from demonstrable error.[4]

A similar category of texts, the synchronistic chronicles,[5] will not be discussed, both for lack of space, and because these texts are not primarily chronological sources. But though essentially historiographical, their contribution to comparative chronology is of outstanding importance. Where verification is possible the synchronisms in the synchronistic chronicles have so far been found correct. This should be borne in mind in evaluating the reliability of the synchronism one of these sources provides, that between Burnaburiash I of Babylon, and Puzur-Ashur III of Assyria. As we shall see below this constitutes one of the basic data in Babylonian chronology.[6]

---

[1] See below, pp. 206 f.

[2] See O. Schroeder, *K.A.V.* nos. 10–18 (no. 16 may not be a king-list). The independent source is no. 14 (VAT. 9812), also published in §11, 150, transliterated *ibid.* 6f., improved readings in §11, 77.

[3] The synchronistic king-lists are discussed in §11, 150, 10 ff. and §11, 129, 349 ff.

[4] This text is Assur 14616c., republished in §11, 152. Only the first two cols. are transliterated there, for transliteration of cols. iii and iv see §11, 150, 15 f.

[5] Chief among these are the Synchronistic History, and Chronicle P, both very inadequately published. The cuneiform text of the Synchronistic History is reliably published in *C.T.* xxxiv, pls. 38–43, but it is not available in complete and reliable transliteration and translation. Chronicle P was published by Pinches, *Records of the Past*, v, 111 ff., republished in §11, 165, 1, 297 ff.; see also §11, 12, 43 ff., and §11, 161, no. 37, but no complete up-to-date translation is available.

[6] See pp. 207 f. and 233 below.

(b) The year-lists

From the Kassite Dynasty on the Babylonians dated by regnal
year. Only the year in which a king died had a name as well as a
number. Prior to the king's death it had the number of the last
regnal year, after the accession of the new king it was named 'the
accession year' (lit. the year of the beginning of the kingship
of PN).

Before the Kassite period all years had names. The name was
announced each year by official proclamation. These names we
term date-formulae, or better year-names. The earliest attested
year-name comes from the reign of the Sumerian king, Enshakushanna,[1] c. 2400 b.c., but fuller documentation would very
probably show that the system originated earlier. At that time
various systems were in use. The kings of Lagash dated by regnal
year, as did the Kassites. The still earlier texts from Fārah suggest a system akin to the Assyrian system of dating by eponyms.
In Fārah the office corresponding to that of the Assyrian limmu
appears to have been the bala,[2] both terms embodying the concept
of 'turn of office'. Some of the Fārah texts are dated by the bala
of individuals.

Lists of the year-names were compiled.[3] These year-lists constitute as reliable a chronological source for the period before
c. 1600 b.c., as do the Assyrian eponym-lists, and the king-lists
based upon them, for the period after 1600 b.c.

Like the eponym-lists, the year-lists could also serve as king-
lists. The first full year of a king's reign was named after his
accession mu PN lugal-e 'the year in which PN became king'.
Consequently the number of year-names between two such
years corresponds with the number of years of the reign in question.
As in the eponym-lists, so in the year-lists, totals were given for
the number of year-names in each reign. In the year-lists this was
the usual practice, whereas in the eponym-lists the more usual
practice was simply to distinguish between the eponym-periods
by means of a dividing line. A list of the totals in a year-list constitutes a king-list. In one instance, in addition to the total after
each reign, the year-list includes a list of these totals appended at
the end.[4] In another instance a year-list of Larsa starts with the

---

[1] See p. 223, n. 3 below.

[2] For bala in the Fārah tablets see now J.C.S. 14, 89.

[3] See A. Ungnad, 'Datenlisten', in R.L.A. II, 131 ff., with two supplements by
E. Ebeling, 194 ff.; also §II, 93. For the main recent accretions see pp. 208, n. 7,
209, n. 3, below.   [4] R.L.A. II, 171.

totals for the reigns of the first four kings of the dynasty not included in the list.[1]

The year was usually named after an event which took place in the preceding year. If the preceding year was not marked by a propitious event, or an event deemed sufficiently important to give a name to the following year, the latter would be called *mu us-sa* YN 'the year following YN', where YN stands for the name of the preceding year. Sometimes there would be several of these *ussa*-years, as it will be convenient to call them, before a new year-name was promulgated.

The *ussa*-years constitute the main source of error in the year-lists.[2] The chief difficulty is that a year often started as an *ussa*-year, and then received a name of its own in the course of the year. When this happened the new year-name refers to an event which took place in that same year, and not in the preceding year. And though the year-lists omit most of those *ussa*-names which were subsequently changed, there is good reason to believe that the lists are not free from error in this respect. A further potential source of error is the fact that the year-names are commonly given in highly abbreviated form. Sometimes even totally different abbreviated forms were used for the same year. Thus for the thirty-second year of Hammurabi one abbreviated form in the year-lists is 'Year (of the defeat) of the army of Eshnunna', another is 'Year (of the defeat) of the army of Mankisum.' In its full form the year-name runs into more than twenty words, and mentions the defeat of several armies.[3]

(c) The Babylonian king-lists

The principal Babylonian king-list, King-list A,[4] is a late Neo-Babylonian text which covers the period from the First Dynasty of Babylon to the death of Kandalanu in 626. The list is badly damaged in parts. All of the First Dynasty is missing, except the total; there is a large gap in the Kassite Dynasty, and another in the Dynasty after it. With the later kings we are not concerned here.

There are numerous texts dated to the reigns of the later Kassite kings, and from the fourteenth to the eleventh century we also dispose of a close network of synchronisms with Assyria.

---

[1] *R.L.A.* ii, 150.

[2] For an example of this difficulty see §ii, 135; for a recent discussion of the *ussa*-years see §ii, 22, 27 ff.   [3] *R.L.A.* ii, 180, no. 134.

[4] First published in §ii, 109; republished in §ii, 81; and in *C.T.* xxxvi, pls. 24–5; latest translation in §ii, 125, 77 ff.

For that period at least King-list A is proved to be a fairly reliable source. Only two errors can be established: 6 instead of 9
for Kudur-Enlil, and omission of the seven years of Assyrian
domination under Tukulti-Ninurta I.[1] On the other hand, the
Dynasty of the Sea Country has several reigns which are grossly
exaggerated. It should be noted however that these were not
kings of Babylon.

The gaps in King-List A are partly made good by two other
king-lists. King-List B gives the reigns of the First Dynasty.
It was copied from an older source in which there was damage to
some of the figures. In King-List B there are approximate estimates in place of the figures damaged in the source. The kings of
the Dynasty of the Sea Country are listed, but without figures for
their reigns.[2] King-List C gives the first seven kings of the
Fourth Dynasty, successor to the Kassites.[3] The fact that it stops
with the seventh king suggests that it was written not long after
that reign. It therefore ranks as a source of high reliability. A
fourth king-list, the so-called Dynastic Chronicle, forms the first
part of a text which continues in the form of a chronicle.[4] The
portion which consisted of a king-list is almost totally lost. It
included the earliest Sumerian dynasties.

The period between the conquest of Mesopotamia by the
Third Dynasty of Ur and the conquest by Hammurabi, is covered
by three king-lists, two of which exist in more than one copy. The
Sumerian king-list,[5] discussed below, has as its last two dynasties
the Third Dynasty of Ur, and the Dynasty of Isin. Several
extant copies contain these two dynasties. Discrepancies in the
figures quoted range from 1 to 12 years. Another list of the kings
of these two dynasties has recently been published.[6] It represents
a source independent of the Sumerian king-list. Two copies have
been found. Compiled in about 1813, during the reign of the last
king of the Dynasty of Isin, its source is very probably a date-list.
Comparison with lists of year-names shows that it is more reliable
than most of the extant copies of the Sumerian king-list. The
third list gives the kings of the Dynasty of Larsa.[7] It is copied

[1] For latest discussion of this material see §II, 120, 5 ff. and §II, 121, 18 ff.

[2] BM 38122 (coll. no. 80-11-12, 3), for most recent cuneiform copy see §II, 114,
240, reproduced in §II, 125, pl. 4; for photograph see *Sitzungsb. Berlin* (1887),
pl. 11; for discussion of the text, and of the use in it of mathematical mean values see
§II, 111.

[3] §II, 112, in which this new list is designated as (Babylonian) King-list C.

[4] §II, 69, vol. 2, 46 ff. and 143 ff., commented vol. 1, 182 ff.

[5] §II, 60; a new fragment in §II, 73.   [6] §II, 134.

[7] Discussed in §II, 72.

out twice, on both sides of the tablet, and hence is probably a school text. It includes the first two Babylonian rulers of Larsa, and was written during the reign of Samsuiluna. Where it can be checked against the year-lists it appears to be reliable.

(d) The Sumerian King-List

Numerous copies have been found of the Sumerian King-List, some of them little more than fragments, others very substantial. This material has been collected and discussed fully by T. Jacobsen in his work *The Sumerian King List* (1939), and subsequently some additional fragments have appeared.[1] The original king-list is probably to be dated about the beginning of the Third Dynasty of Ur, that is either shortly before, or shortly after the accession of Ur-Nammu, *c.* 2113. A later date cannot be excluded, but it would be not more than a decade or so after the end of the Third Dynasty.

This dating is based upon certain linguistic criteria,[2] which a recent investigation has tended to confirm.[3] A further criterion is the presence in some copies of the king-list of entirely artificial figures for two successive dynasties, the Fourth Dynasty of Uruk and the Dynasty of Gutium. It can be shown that these were probably not present in the original king-list, and that they were inserted some time before the reign of Ur-Ninurta of Isin (1923–1896).[4]

The date of the king-list is of some importance in evaluating its reliability. On this count it comes off well. For it was probably compiled *c.* 2100 B.C.,[5] and only a few of the historical kings in it go back more than five hundred years before that date. Unfortunately there is reason to believe that estimating the exact interval between events was probably still something of a novelty at the time the king-list was compiled. If so, its author would not have felt the need to strive for precision in this respect, nor would he have been under the check of criticism for the lack of it. We have to envisage behind the king-list a period in the history of chronology when the chief factor was the sequence of events, and not the interval between them. This factor remains prominent in the building inscriptions right down to the end of Babylonian history. It has been responsible for some confusion in modern chronological research.[6] The impression one has is that the author

---

[1] § II, 73: and see Plate 3.   [2] §II, 60, 128 ff.
[3] §II, 135, 19, n. 37.   [4] §II, 122.
[5] *Ibid.* p. 162.   [6] See p. 201, nn. 2 and 3 below.

of the original king-list was not genuinely interested in exact chronology. If so, the figures he quotes should be taken with considerable reserve. More useful is the sequence of the dynasties and the kings, but we shall see that even there caution is indicated.

(e) The Tummal Chronicle

This building chronicle gives the builders of the Tummal sanctuary in the Enlil temple complex at Nippur.[1] Two sources of this chronicle, one almost certainly from Nippur, the other from Ur, have some kings in a sequence different from that of the king-list; but other examples from Ur maintain that order.

In the chronicle the father of each builder of the Tummal is also credited with important building operations in Nippur. This somewhat artificial arrangement indicates that the text must rank essentially as a literary composition. The building operations assigned to the father of each Tummal builder are therefore subject to doubt. But where the Tummal is concerned, the case is different. The Tummal is the chief subject of the chronicle, the text stems from Nippur, almost certainly from the Tummal itself, and it is a fairly early text, from the beginning of the Dynasty of Isin. Consequently the Nippur version of this chronicle should be treated as a high authority.

Now in the present writer's opinion, if we have to choose between a king-list and a building chronicle, both to some extent literary compositions, preference should be given to the building chronicle. In many building inscriptions down through the long Mesopotamian record there is reference to earlier building operations at the site in question. Almost without exception where verification is possible we find that both the identity and the sequence of the earlier builders have been recorded correctly. Building tradition ranks as a highly reliable chronological source, although it should be emphasized that reliability applies only to the identity and the sequence of the builders, and not to estimates of the intervals which separate them. In this latter respect both the Assyrian[2] and the Babylonian[3] scribes were notoriously unreliable. As mentioned above, we have the view that funda-

---

[1] *P.B.S.* v, 6, 7, and xiii, 48. For the divergent order see *T.u.M.* n.F. iii, 34, 35; §ii, 71, 62. For information upon the other Ur version I am indebted to Dr E. Sollberger. See *J.C.S.* 16 (1962), 40 ff. and *U.E.T.* viii, nos. 58–60.

[2] §ii, 118, 107 ff.

[3] The Babylonian chronological statements are discussed in §ii, 69, 11 ff., 81, 86 ff. At that time considerable importance was still attached to these statements.

mentally what mattered in Mesopotamian chronology was the sequence of events, not the magnitude of the interval between them.

(f) Hittite royal lists of sacrifices for the dead

In the absence of Hittite king-lists the lists of sacrifices constitute an important chronological source,[1] for the kings appear to be listed in chronological order. These lists confirm the sequence of kings known from the edict of Telepinush. For the very obscure period between Telepinush and Tudkhaliash II the only source we have for the sequence of kings is a list of sacrifices. A potential source of error is that these texts include, not only the kings and queens, but also other members of the royal family who certainly never held the supreme office, although they may have been rulers of vassal kingdoms.

THE CHRONOLOGY OF THE SECOND MILLENNIUM B.C.

(a) Assyria

There is firm chronological evidence for the last three centuries of Assyrian history, including a solar eclipse in 763 B.C.[2] The eponym of that year is known, so that correlation with the Assyrian eponym-lists and king-lists is possible. From that point the Assyrian king-list carries the record back to the beginning of the dynasty of Adasi, c. 1700 B.C. As already mentioned the king-list is damaged, and not very reliable, for the period before Adasi. But it does give some slight reason for tentatively dating Ushpia not far from the beginning of Ur III. The king-list puts him ten generations before Shamshi-Adad I. If this is correct Ushpia should come, either shortly before, or shortly after Assyria came under the control of Ur III. Since room has to be found for twelve other kings between the son of Ushpia, Api-ashal, and Shamshi-Adad I a date after Ur III is difficult.

Another factor is also in favour of the earlier date for Ushpia. On the whole it is unlikely that the city of Ashur came to be regarded as the city of the god, Ashur, before the first temple of the god was built. But it was regarded as the city of that god already in the reign of Amar-Sin, as the writing (d)a-šir(ki) indicates, and Ushpia is given by Shalmaneser I, and by Esarhaddon, as the founder of the temple of Ashur.[3] Shamshi-Adad, in his turn, is

---

[1] §ii, 101.   [2] See most recently §ii, 144, 7.

[3] On these inscriptions and their bearing on Assyrian chronology see §ii, 110, vol. i, 258 f. with n. 25. Note that the city bore the name Ashur already early in the

dated by an inscription to 701 years before the rebuilding of a temple by Tiglath-pileser I.[1] This may be a very nearly accurate estimate based on an eponym-list.

Most of these chronological estimates in the Assyrian building inscriptions are manifestly rough approximations, either in centuries, or in units of sixty years. One which does not belong in this category quotes 126 years between the building of the temple of Ashur by Erishum I, and its rebuilding by Shamshi-Adad I.[2] This figure may correspond closely with the actual interval between the accession of Erishum I and the death of Shamshi-Adad I— space will not permit discussion of the reasons. The date adopted here for the accession of Erishum I is based upon it, but it should be emphasized that the conclusion is tentative, and is introduced only for the lack of better evidence.

In the interval between the death of Adasi and the end of the second millennium B.C. figures are missing in the Assyrian king-list for a total of four kings. Two successive twelfth-century kings are said to have reigned *ṭuppišu*. This term very probably denotes the reign of a king who did not hold eponym office, and therefore did not figure in the eponym-lists. In chronological summation such reigns are to be reckoned zero.[3]

As the result of damage to the text figures are also lacking for two successive fifteenth-century kings, Ashur-rabi I, and his son, Ashur-nadin-ahhe I. Where succession is orderly a reasonable allowance is twenty years per reign.[4]

Not long before these two kings we have the reign of Puzur-Ashur III, important because of the synchronism with Burna-buriash I of Babylon. From the death of Puzur-Ashur III to the accession of Ashur-uballiṭ I in 1365 the Assyrian throne was held by five generations of kings. The average throne tenure for five

Sargonic period, as we know from the Old Akkadian tablets from Nuzi; see §II, 92 and §II, 110, 259 ff. But the fact that theophoric names with Ashur only begin to appear in the Ur III period suggests that the god emerged, as the deified city, much later. For the first occurrence of personal names with Ashur see most recently §II, 56, especially 225, n. 29. See *J.C.S.* 20, 113.

[1] For Shamshi-Adad I and his successors see also pp. 210, 232 below.

[2] On these various chronological statements in the building inscriptions of the Assyrian kings see §II, 118, 107 ff. For the 126-year datum see now *Arch. f. Or.* Beiheft 9, 3, iii, 16 ff. For a discussion of the difficulties which arise in connexion with a rival estimate of 159 years for the same interval by Shalmaneser I see §II, 4, 58 ff., where the writer concludes that the higher figure is preferable.

[3] Most recently §II, 119; for the opposite view see §II, 77, 111 ff.

[4] §II, 77, 40; there the two kings in question are designated by the numbers 65 and 66 following Poebel's numeration.

generations is *c.* 135 years,[1] which indicates a date close to 1500 B.C. for the death of Puzur-Ashur III. This allows just about twenty years each for the two fifteenth-century reigns missing in the king-list. Since all Assyrian dates prior to Ashur-rabi I rest on this factor, it is important that at least some measure of verification is possible. In this connexion it is worth noting that the resultant chronology is more likely to be too low than too high. The reason is that during this interval of five generations on four occasions the royal line was continued by a younger brother. And this tends to increase the average throne tenure per generation.

(b) Babylon

In the second millennium it is Assyrian chronology which provides the basis for Babylonian chronology. In the three centuries which follow the accession of Ashur-uballiṭ I (1365–1320) we have a close network of synchronisms between Assyrian and Babylonian kings.[2] And one of these synchronisms shows that the two-year reign of Ashared-apal-Ekur (1076–1075) of Assyria is entirely comprised within the thirteen-year reign of Marduk-shapik-zeri of Babylon. We know also that the reign of the former did not start before the second year of the latter.[3] And though not certain, it is at least probable that the first four years of the next Assyrian king, Ashur-bēl-kala, come before the death of Marduk-shapik-zeri. For we have the annals of the first four years of an Assyrian king who is very probably Ashur-bēl-kala,[4] and enough of the damaged text is preserved to show that the intervention of Ashur-bēl-kala in Babylonia at the death of Marduk-shapik-zeri was probably not mentioned in any of the four years covered by this text.[5]

From the above it follows that the two-year reign of Ashared-apal-Ekur very probably comes within the interval between the second and the ninth year of Marduk-shapik-zeri. Hence if we equate the two years 1076 and 1075 with the fifth and sixth year of Marduk-shapik-zeri we have a synchronism which is in all probability subject to a margin of error of only three years either way. The resultant date for Marduk-shapik-zeri, 1080–1068, constitutes the basis of Babylonian chronology in the last four

[1] Based on the average of 185 years for the throne tenure of seven generations; see §II, 118, 100 ff.
[2] See §II, 120, 7 for a table of these synchronisms.
[3] *Ibid.* 6, and §II, 121, 21.
[4] §II, 155.
[5] *Ibid.* 86.

centuries of the second millennium B.C. The margin of error has to be increased slightly for possible error of a year or two in the date of Ashared-apal-Ekur. There is therefore a basic element of uncertainty, some five years either way, which affects all Babylonian dates within that period.

During those four centuries there were at least three short periods of foreign rule in Babylonia. An interval of seven years of Assyrian rule under Tukulti-Ninurta I,[1] is followed by an interval of Elamite rule between Adad-shum-iddin and Adad-shum-nasir, under the Elamite king, Kidin-Khutran.[2] And half a century later it is probable that there was another interval of Elamite rule between the end of the Kassite Dynasty and the Second Dynasty of Isin.[3] But the probability is that no allowance need be made for chronological gaps in the Babylonian king-list. It is unlikely that on either occasion the Elamites managed to gain control of the whole of Babylonia. The Babylonian tradition has of course assigned these intervals to the native rulers who kept alive resistance to the invaders, and eventually prevailed against them. This is inferred from the chronicles and kindred sources, and these texts are sadly fragmentary. However, the chronological material points to the same conclusion. We have a complex network of synchronisms between the kings of Assyria and Babylonia covering precisely the period we are concerned with here. And these synchronisms hardly leave room for any further gaps in the Babylonian chronological record.

The text of King-List A is destroyed over a large portion of the Kassite Dynasty. Figures resume with Kurigalzu II, son of Burnaburiash II, just after the Amarna period in Egypt. Kurigalzu II came to the throne in about 1345. He was preceded by three short-lived kings, Karakhardash, Kadashman-kharbe II, and an usurper, Nazibugash.[4] These reigns are certain to have been short, since no contracts dated to them have been found, whereas in Nippur all the other reigns of this period are amply attested in the contracts. It follows that the death of Burnaburiash II can be dated c. 1350. And since the contracts prove that the latter reigned at least twenty-five years, and probably at least twenty-seven years,[5] we may date his reign c. 1380–1350.

Now we know from the Amarna correspondence that Burna-

---

[1] §II, 121, 18 ff.   [2] *Ibid.* 19.   [3] §II, 140, 137 ff.

[4] This period, like the one at the time of Tukulti-Ninurta I, is marked by invasion, revolt, and anarchy; chronology is necessarily uncertain. For detailed discussion see A, 8.

[5] Most recently §II, 65, 199.

buriash II reigned during the latter part of the reign of Amenophis III, the whole reign of Akhenaten, and part at least of the reign of Tutankhamun.[1] Since the Egyptian material yields 1379 as the approximate date of the accession of Akhenaten, and since 1380 for the accession of Burnaburiash II is only an approximate date, the measure of agreement is very satisfactory.

The combined evidence of the Hittite material and the Assyrian king-list provides an even closer synchronism which can be used to check the reliability of the Assyrian king-list. From the Hittite records we know that an eclipse of the sun very probably occurred in the tenth year of Murshilish II. The text speaks only of a portent involving the sun, but since it was a disastrous portent the probability is very high that the event was an eclipse. And since it occurred in the spring, the eclipse of March 1335 provides a fully satisfactory solution, as shown by Forrer and Schoch.[2] This dates the accession of Murshilish II in 1344.

Murshilish II was preceded by the short reign of his brother, Arnuwandash II, the latter by his father, Suppiluliumash. It is towards the end of the reign of Suppiluliumash that the Hittite records mention the death of Tutankhamun.[3] It follows that 1344 is the lowest limit for the death of Tutankhamun, hence $1344 + 9 + 18 = 1371$ is the lowest limit for the accession of Akhenaten. The latter was a contemporary of the Assyrian king Ashur-uballit I[4] who came to the throne in 1365. It follows that $1366 + 18 = 1384$ constitutes an upper limit for the accession of Akhenaten. Between 1384 and 1371 the middle date is 1378. This date for the accession of Akhenaten should be correct within a margin of error of seven years either way. The date 1379, obtained from the Egyptian chronological material, is so close that there can be little doubt the Assyrian king-list is substantially correct at least as far back as Ashur-uballit I.

The Babylonian king Karaindash concluded a treaty with the Assyrian king, Ashur-bēl-nisheshu,[5] who came to the throne in or about 1420. Burnaburiash II came to the throne before the accession of Akhenaten in 1379. This means that the interval between the death of Karaindash and the accession of Burnaburiash II can

---

[1] See §11, 70, nos. 6–9, and 11 ff. For identification of the addressee of no. 9 with Tutankhamun see §11, 19, 14 f., and p. 215, n. 5 below.
[2] See p. 216, n. 1 below.
[3] §11, 19, 14 f. and, with new material, §11, 54, 94 A iii 7, and note e.
[4] §11, 70, nos. 15 and 16.
[5] Synchronistic History, C.T. xxxiv, 38 i 1–4.

hardly have exceeded forty years by much, and was very probably less. During this interval we have the reign of the father of Burn-aburiash II, Kadashman-Enlil I,[1] as well as the unnamed father of Kadashman-Enlil I, who gave the latter's sister in marriage to Amenophis III.[2]

In the Amarna correspondence we are told that the exchange of envoys between Egypt and Babylon began under Karaindash.[3] We are also told that under Kurigalzu Babylon and Egypt were firm allies.[4] Hence in Babylon Kurigalzu comes after Karaindash. This means that in the interval of forty years between 1420 and 1380 we have part of the reign of Karaindash, the whole reign of Kurigalzu I, the whole reign of Kadashman-Enlil I, and part of the reign of his son, Burnaburiash II. It is therefore very improbable that the reign of the father of Kurigalzu I, Kadashman-kharbe I, also comes within this interval.

More probably Kadashman-kharbe I was the immediate predecessor of Karaindash, either his father or his brother. Kurigalzu I was therefore either the brother of Karaindash, or his nephew. What the relation was between Kurigalzu I and Kadashman-Enlil I we cannot as yet say. Karaindash must have died not very long after the accession of Ashur-bēl-nisheshu in 1420. Hence we may date the accession of his predecessor Kadashman-kharbe very roughly 1450.

Kadashman-kharbe was preceded by five kings who reigned, from Burnaburiash I to Agum III, in three generations. The average throne tenure for three generations is *c.* 80 years. This yields 1450 + 80 = *c.* 1530 for the accession of Burnaburiash I, who was a contemporary of the Assyrian king Puzur-Ashur III,[5] and we have seen that the latter died *c.* 1500.[6] So here too we have very close agreement between the Assyrian and the Babylonian sources. Both dates are based on entirely independent evidence, and both involve the same approximate estimate for the average throne tenure per generation.

Before Burnaburiash I comes Agum II, and 24 years before an unknown year in the reign of Agum II the First Dynasty of Babylon was brought to an end by the Hittite king, Murshilish

---

[1] Burnaburiash II was the oldest son of Kadashman-Enlil I; cf. *B.E.* 1/1, 68 i 5' and 14' f. In line 5' [. . .*r*]*i-ia-aš* certainly stands for Burnaburiash; first, there is insufficient room for the name Shagaraktishuriash, second, in 5*R.* 64, iii 31 Nabonidus gives Kudur-Enlil as the father of Shagaraktishuriash.

[2] §II, 70, no. 1 : 12.

[3] *Ibid.* no. 10 : 8 ff.   [4] *Ibid.* no. 9 : 19 ff.

[5] Synchronistic History, *C.T.* xxxiv, 38 i 5–7.

[6] See p. 204 above.

I.[1] This means that Burnaburiash can hardly have come to the throne more than about half a century after the end of that Dynasty.

The date of the First Dynasty of Babylon is based on observations of Venus made during the reign of the tenth king of that dynasty, Ammiṣaduqa. Several solutions are possible; the problem is discussed elsewhere in the present chapter.[2] The chronology suggested here is based on the solution which corresponds to the date 1595 for the end of the dynasty, which is the most probable on the evidence available at the moment of writing. Other solutions which deserve serious consideration are 1651 and 1587.

The First Dynasty is missing in King-List A; in King-List B it was copied from a damaged original, and some of the figures are wrong.[3] This deficiency is amply compensated by the lists of year-names, where the First Dynasty is exceptionally well represented.

(c) Larsa

Only one king-list of Larsa has survived,[4] but from Gungunum onwards it can be checked against the lists of year-names, and it appears to be reliable. No year-names are available for the first five reigns of that dynasty. Larsa was captured by Hammurabi in his thirtieth year;[5] this event provides the basic date.

(d) Isin

The Dynasty of Isin constitutes the last dynasty in the Sumerian king-list, and it is preserved in several copies of that text. These copies date from that dynasty, or soon after, and are therefore much more reliable for the Dynasty of Isin than for the preceding Sumerian dynasties. Recently an independent list of the kings of Ur III and Isin has been published, preserved in two copies, and also written before the end of the Dynasty of Isin.[6] The existence of two king-lists, each in more than one copy, goes a long way to compensate for the scarcity of year-lists,[7] which are particularly deficient for the middle part of the dynasty.

---

[1] §11, 42, more recently §11, 65, 207 f., §11, 118, 103, and *ibid.* note 31. Starting with the ninth king of the Kassite Dynasty, both names and sequence are uncertain for several reigns; A, 8, 97 ff.   [2] See pp. 231 ff. below.

[3] See p. 199 above.   [4] See p. 199 and n. 7 there.

[5] Most recently §11, 22, 22 ff.   [6] See p. 199 and n. 6 there.

[7] The most important recent addition to the year-lists of Isin is the list of the years of Ishbi-Erra published in *Sumer*, 4, 112 f., discussed in §11, 63, 42 ff.; for further literature see discussion in §11, 22, 24 f.

There are some discrepancies in the figures which the two king-lists provide. Most of these amount to only one year, and are doubtless due to the *ussa*-year factor, a difficulty discussed above. The only major discrepancy is twenty years instead of ten years for Shu-ilishu, and there it can be shown that the lower figure is correct.

The Dynasty of Isin was brought to an end by Rim-Sin of Larsa in his twenty-ninth year. Another valuable synchronism is provided by the defeat of Zambia of Isin by Sin-iqisham of Larsa in the latter's fourth year. As Zambia reigned only three, or possibly four years, this synchronism is a close one.[1]

The reign of the last king of Ur III, Ibbi-Sin, lasted twenty-four years. During approximately the last half of it the reign of Ibbi-Sin overlapped with the reign of the first king of the Dynasty of Isin, Ishbi-Erra.[2]

(e) Eshnunna

No king-list exists for this dynasty, and lists of year-names are available for only just over one decade.[3] The sequence of the kings of Eshnunna has been reconstructed by T. Jacobsen from inscriptions and from letters, the latter still largely unpublished.[4] Jacobsen's results have been accepted here, with one exception: the rulers Abdi-erakh and Shiqlanum have been omitted. One letter shows that at the time it was written these were not kings of Eshnunna; they may have been ruling elsewhere.[5] For the period in question we have more kings of Eshnunna than it is easy to accommodate, and no valid evidence has been hitherto adduced that these two ever ruled there. Pending evidence to the contrary it will be prudent to regard them as two of the numerous petty dynasts reigning at that time in the vicinity.[6]

The basic date in the chronology of Eshnunna is the date of the death of Shamshi-Adad I of Assyria. He is known to have died in

[1] For these and other problems see *ibid.* 18 ff., and literature quoted there. For the reign of Shu-ilishu see *Bull. A.S.O.R.* 122, 45 ff.

[2] §11, 63; §11, 135, 38 ff.

[3] See *Sumer*, 5, 34 ff. and 136 ff. for new year-names of Eshnunna and vicinity; *ibid.* 45 ff. for the lists of year names.

[4] §11, 62; §11, 22, 66 ff., 71 ff., 118 ff., 162 ff. and §11, 128, 80 ff.

[5] On this unpublished letter see §11, 59, 49 f., and §11, 62, 120 f.; also §11, 22, 119 n. 605. For a further unpublished letter which probably mentions the same Shiqlanum see §11, 59, 50.

[6] For the chronology of the lesser rulers in the vicinity of Eshnunna see §11, 58, 45 ff.

or about the twelfth year of Hammurabi of Babylon.[1] The death of Shamshi-Adad I is recorded in the year-name for the fifth year of Ibalpiel II of Eshnunna.[2] The event occurred therefore in the fourth year of that king, and this means that the first year of Ibalpiel II corresponds very closely to the ninth year of Hammurabi of Babylon, 1784. Silli-Sin of Eshnunna is known from the Mari archives to have been a later contemporary of Hammurabi.[3]

(f) Mari and Khana

Only a few rulers of Mari in the Old Babylonian period are known, and no king-list or list of year-names has been found. Most of the period covered by the archives is accounted for by eponyms or year-names,[4] but there is insufficient evidence to establish their order.

The most important ruler of Mari during this period was Shamshi-Adad I. From a city called Shubat-Enlil he reigned over Mari as well as Assyria, with a son as viceroy in each place. He died in about the twelfth year of Hammurabi, and in Assyria he was succeeded by the former viceroy, his son, Ishme-Dagan I. In that country the dynasty of Shamshi-Adad I maintained itself for at least three further reigns.[5]

In Mari the reign of Shamshi-Adad's other son, Iasmakh-Adad, was brought to an end four years after the death of Shamshi-Adad I by Zimrilim, with the help of his father-in-law, Iarimlim, king of Iamkhad.[6] Zimrilim had been driven from Mari by Shamshi-Adad I after the death of Iakhdunlim, king of Mari, his father, and had found refuge in Aleppo, at the court of Iarimlim, king of the country Iamkhad. From the Mari archives we know that Iarimlim was succeeded by a king called Hammurabi during the second half of the reign of Hammurabi of Babylon.[7] These synchronisms are of considerable importance for the chronology of Syria.

It has been generally believed that the reign of Zimrilim came to an end with the dismantling of the walls of Mari by Hammurabi of Babylon in the latter's thirty-third year. The number of

[1] See §II, 80, corrected by §II, 84, 439, n. 7.
[2] *Sumer*, 5, 45, no. 1 : 5, and 46, no. 2 : 6.
[3] For references to Silli-Sin in the Mari archives see *A.R.M.* xv, 157.
[4] §II, 17; §II, 41; §II, 4, 100 f.
[5] §II, 77, 31 ff.
[6] §II, 84, 445 ff.
[7] For a preliminary report on the relations between Mari and Iamkhad see §II, 15; much of the material is still unpublished.

year-names already attested for the reign of Zimrilim casts doubt
on the validity of this conclusion. The solution may prove to be
that after the destruction of the walls the court moved elsewhere
for greater safety. If so, the royal correspondence does not exceed
the thirty-third year, but the small group of economic texts and
contracts found in two rooms of the palace continues the record a
few years longer.

For the kings of Khana who ruled over the territory of Mari in
the period after destruction of that city no chronological sources
are available[1] and the sequence of these kings is unknown.

(g) The Sea Country

Three sources have this dynasty: King-Lists A and B, and the
Ashur Synchronistic List. Only the first of these gives figures for
the reigns, and some of these are much too high. Figures which
exceed fifty years are best not taken into account in the absence
of supporting evidence. A further difficulty is that the Ashur
List gives one king, name uncertain, x-KÀD-en, whom the other
sources do not include.[2]

The dynasty began some time during the reign of Samsuiluna
of Babylon. Its first king, Iluma-ilu, was also a contemporary of
the next Babylonian king, Abieshuʻ.[3] A further probable synchronism, between Ammiditana of Babylon and Damiq-ilishu of
the Sea Country, is suggested by the last year-name in the reign of
Ammiditana.[4] The dynasty was brought to an end by the Kassite
king, Ulamburiash.[5] Unfortunately none of these synchronisms
are close enough to provide a basic date for this dynasty.

(h) Anatolia, Syria, and Palestine in the second millennium

A colony of Assyrian merchants had their own quarter in ancient
Kanesh, the site of modern Kültepe. There are two phases in the
history of this settlement. The earlier, more prosperous one
begins in the twentieth century B.C. The Assyrian kings attested
at this level, Kültepe II, are: Erishum I, his son, Ikunum, and a

[1] §II, 50, 63 ff.
[2] See most recently §II, 77, 69 and n. 180; note also that the name of the first king
of this dynasty is there read Ili-man, not Iluma-ilu.
[3] For these two synchronisms, as well as the one relating to Ulamburiash, see
§II, 69, vol. I, 145 ff. 150 ff. and II, 19 ff.
[4] Most recently §II, 77, 68 n. 174 para. (c).
[5] See n. 3 above, and p. 233, n. 2 below.

son of Ikunum whose name, perhaps to be read Ilum-sharma, is
not found in the Assyrian king-list.[1]

During the nineteenth century B.C., the Assyrian settlement of
Kültepe II was destroyed, and some time later Assyrian merchants
reoccupied the site. This second settlement, Kültepe I b, lasted at
least till the time of the king of Assyria, Shamshi-Adad I. Texts
and a dagger from the reign of the early Hittite kings, Pitkhanash,
and his son, Anittash, probably come from this level in Kültepe,
as well as from the corresponding level in Alişar.[2] Assyrian merchants are also attested at Khattushash, modern Boğazköy. In
the lower city Assyrian texts of this period were found in level 4.
From a copy of an inscription of Anittash we know that he captured and destroyed Khattushash, since level 4 ended in massive
destruction, and it is reasonably safe to conclude that this was the
work of Anittash. Now the texts found in level 4 are dated by eponyms from the reign of Shamshi-Adad I,[3] so that if these texts
belong immediately before the destruction of the city Anittash is
to be dated to about the time of the accession of Hammurabi in
Babylon, for Shamshi-Adad I was reigning in Assyria two or three
decades before the twelfth year of Hammurabi. Of course, should
future excavation show that these eponyms of the reign of Shamshi-Adad I come a significant interval before the destruction of
Khattushash, it will be necessary to lower the date of Anittash.

After an interval of Hittite history which is still very obscure we
come to Khattushilish I, son of the brother-in-law of the previous
king, Labarnash. Early in his reign Khattushilish I destroyed
Alalakh in Northern Syria,[4] the capital of a small kingdom which
formed part of the powerful kingdom of Iamkhad whose kings
resided in Aleppo. This event in the Syrian campaigns of Khattushilish I marks the end of Level VII at Alalakh.

Murshilish I, the grandson of Khattushilish I, destroyed both
Aleppo[5] and Babylon[6] in 1595, the latter event marking the end of
the First Dynasty of Babylon. In the absence of evidence to the

---

[1] See most recently §11, 89, and note that the author reads Sharrum-ken instead of
Ilum-sharma or Ilum-sharrumma. The probability is the same kings are intended, and
that Sharrum-ken is the throne name of Ilum-sharrumma.

[2] On the chronology of the Kültepe period see §11, 4 and §11, 5, 60 ff. and note
that the author dates Pitkhanash and Anittash just after Shamshi-Adad I. See also
§11, 88; §11, 100; and §11, 113.

[3] §11, 102, especially p. 71.   [4] §11, 103, especially p. 78, n. 14.

[5] §11, 151, 82: 11 ff. and recently §11, 77, 52, n. 89.

[6] The Hittite invasion of Babylonia is mentioned in a Babylonian chronicle, cf.
§11, 69, vol. 2, 22 r. 10. It is also mentioned in the Proclamation of Telepinush, for
recent translations of which see §11, 77, 64; and §11, 66, 142.

contrary, about half a century has to be allowed for the interval between an event early in the reign of one king, and an event some time in the reign of his grandson. The approximate date for the accession of Khattushilish I is therefore c. 1650.

This estimate of about half a century between the end of Alalakh VII and the end of the First Dynasty of Babylon is borne out by the curious genealogical situation in Alalakh. In the accompanying table, the Babylonian rulers have been included for purpose of comparison. For that purpose Hammurabi I of Aleppo can be set alongside Hammurabi of Babylon. Although he was a junior contemporary of the Babylonian king, the six Babylonian kings listed here have a throne tenure which is one of the longest in ancient Western Asia for six generations.[1]

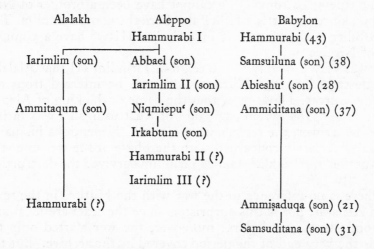

Alalakh	Aleppo	Babylon
	Hammurabi I	Hammurabi (43)
Iarimlim (son)	Abbael (son)	Samsuiluna (son) (38)
	Iarimlim II (son)	Abieshu' (son) (28)
Ammitaqum (son)	Niqmiepu' (son)	Ammiditana (son) (37)
	Irkabtum (son)	
	Hammurabi II (?)	
	Iarimlim III (?)	
Hammurabi (?)		Ammiṣaduqa (son) (21)
		Samsuditana (son) (31)

Obviously the Alalakh genealogy makes it impossible to date the death of Ammitaqum, and the destruction of Alalakh VII, a very short time before the end of the First Dynasty of Babylon. On the other hand, a date appreciably more than half a century earlier would excessively compress the five generations in Aleppo.

The two kings of Alalakh Level VII, Iarimlim, and his son, Ammitaqum, must have had very long reigns. For the reign of Iarimlim began during the reign of his brother, Abbael, in Aleppo, and the reign of Ammitaqum ended during the reign in Aleppo of Iarimlim III, very probably the great-grandson of Abbael.[2] The

[1] §II, 118, 100, no. 26 (listed are the throne tenures of seven generations).
[2] For the order and filiation of the kings of Iamkhad in the Old Babylonian period see §II, 77, 51 ff., §II, 50, 68ff., §II, 95, 109 ff. The first should be corrected for Irkabtum in accordance with §II, 50, 70, n. 181a, so also the table ibid. 69. The

number of generations we have in Aleppo, a minimum of five counting from Hammurabi I, the father of Abbael, makes it virtually certain that this Hammurabi is identical with the Hammurabi of Aleppo, known from the Mari archives to have been a younger contemporary of Hammurabi of Babylon.[1]

Ammitaqum came to the throne during the reign of Niqmiepu', the grandson of Abbael. His reign continued after the death of Niqmiepu''s son, Irkabtum, through the short reign of Hammurabi II, for whom only the accession year is attested, into the reign of Iarimlim III. The filiation of these last two kings of Aleppo is not known. But if Iarimlim III was a grandson of Niqmiepu' we would have from Abbael to himself five generations in Aleppo against only two in Alalakh. On the other hand, by the rule of patronymy he cannot have been a brother of Niqmiepu', since the latter's father also bore the name Iarimlim. The probability is therefore that in Iarimlim III we have a younger son of Niqmiepu'.

It was very probably in the reign of Iarimlim III that Alalakh was destroyed by the Hittites. This can be inferred from the Hittite sources. These show that the name of the king of Aleppo at the time of the Syrian campaign of Khattushilish I was Iarimlim.[2] Moreover, the fragmentary text which mentions his name is almost certainly concerned with the phase of the war after the destruction of Alalakh.[3] Hence Iarimlim survived the destruction of the city.

There is no reference to the war with the Hittites in the texts from Alalakh; nor is this surprising since the texts are legal and economic texts, not letters; moreover, the war started only towards the very end of the period covered by the archive. But the general, Zukrashi, who is a witness to one of the legal documents from the reign of Iarimlim III, is mentioned in the Hittite sources in connexion with the Syrian wars.[4]

These sources also mention a Hammurabi, son of a king whose name is destroyed. It is possible that reference here is to a son of

reconstruction in §11, 95 is not acceptable. It requires that Hammurabi, father of Abbael, be distinguished from Hammurabi, father of Iarimlim, king of Alalakh. But §11, 164, AT 56 : 43 f., where Abbael is followed as witness by Iarimlim, brother of the king, is a text from the reign of Iarimlim of Alalakh. And it is now confirmed by AT 456 : 31 f., in which Abbael calls Iarimlim of Alalakh his brother. For this latter text see §11, 163, 124 ff.

[1] Cf. p. 210, n. 7 above.
[2] *K.U.B.* xxxi, 5; see §11, 53, pt. 11, 93, §11, 77, 52, and *M.D.O.G.* 86, 12.
[3] I owe this information to Professor Güterbock.
[4] See §11, 77, 52 and *M.D.O.G.* 86, 60 f.

Iarimlim III campaigning alongside his father. Another possibility is that this Hammurabi is the son of Ammitaqum whom we know he appointed heir during his lifetime.[1] In that case, this Hammurabi inherited the kingdom of Alalakh after the city itself was destroyed.

From the accession of Khattushilish I to the death of Ammunash, shortly before the accession of Telepinush, we have five generations.[2] The average throne tenure for five generations is 130 years, which would indicate 1650—130 = c. 1520 for the accession of Telepinush. Of course, this kind of evidence yields only very approximate results. Here it can be taken to indicate the second half of the sixteenth century B.C. for the reign of Telepinush with the reigns of Zidantash II, Khuzziyash II, Tudkhaliash II, and Khattushilish II accounting for most of the fifteenth century.

Of key importance for the chronology of this period is the problem of the date of Saustatar, king of Mitanni. This problem is discussed elsewhere in this chapter.[3] The conclusion is that his reign falls in the first half of the fifteenth century. This in turn provides the basis for dating the kings of Level IV at Alalakh, Idrimi, his son Niqmepa, and his grandson, Ilimilimma, for Niqmepa is known to have been a vassal of Saustatar.[4]

With Suppiluliumash, the grandson of Khattushilish II, we are already in the Amarna period, that is, in the first half of the fourteenth century. In the interval from the Amarna period to the end of the Hittite empire, c. 1200 B.C., we have a series of synchronisms between the Hittite kings and their contemporaries in Egypt and Mesopotamia.

Suppiluliumash was a contemporary of Akhenaten and Tutankhamun, and perhaps also of Amenophis III, the father of Akhenaten.[5] For his son, Murshilish II, we have what is probably the only exact date in Hittite chronology, a probable solar

---

[1] See §11, 164, AT no. 6.

[2] Ammunash was the grandson of the sister of Murshilish I; cf. §11, 48, 20; and §11, 50, 55 ff. Murshilish I was the grandson of Khattushilish I; cf. §11, 151, 82 : 13.

[3] See below pp. 229 f.

[4] On the kings of Level IV see §11, 77, 53 ff. For a different view of the chronology of Alalakh, see for Level IV, §11, 132, 58 ff. for Level VII §11, 133, 173 ff.

[5] The only attested synchronisms are between Suppiluliumash and Tutankhamun; cf. §11, 138, 161 ff., §11, 19, 14 f.; §11, 54, 94 and note e). However, §11, 70, no. 41 mentions relations between Suppiluliumash and the father of the addressee; if Akhenaten and Tutankhamun were brothers, reference would be to their father, Amenophis III. See vol. 11, chap. XIX.

eclipse in 1335, in his tenth year.[1] Muwatallish, the son of Murshilish II, fought the Egyptians at the Battle of Qadesh, in the fifth year of Ramesses II. The brother of Muwatallish, Khattushilish III, concluded a treaty with Egypt in the twenty-first year of Ramesses II, and in his thirty-fourth year Ramesses married the daughter of Khattushilish. Earlier, upon his accession, Khattushilish wrote a letter [K.Bo. 1, 14], to an Assyrian king who is almost certainly Adad-nirari I, followed by another letter [K.U.B. xxiii, 102] shortly before the treaty with Egypt. A number of years after the treaty, we have [K.Bo. 1, 10] a third letter from Khattushilish III to Kadashman-Enlil II of Babylon, a text which shows that Khattushilish was also a contemporary of Kadashman-Turgu, the father of Kadashman-Enlil II.[2] Finally, other letters show that Tudkhaliash IV, the son of Khattushilish III, was reigning when Tukulti-Ninurta I of Assyria came to the throne, in 1245.[3]

There are good reasons for concluding that the interval between the death of Ammishtamru II in Ugarit and the accession, in 1245 B.C., of the Assyrian king, Tukulti-Ninurta I, cannot have amounted to more than about ten years.[4] Yet between Ammishtamru II and the destruction of Ugarit there are at least three further reigns, at least two further generations. Consequently the suggestion that Ugarit was destroyed in the first year of Tukulti-Ninurta I is hardly tenable.[5] From the Egyptian sources we know that the event comes before the eighth year of Ramesses III, c. 1190 B.C.[6] Hence the destruction of Ugarit, an event of key importance in archaeology as well as history, has to be dated very close to 1200 B.C.

---

[1] §ii, 32, ii/1, 1 ff. The text in question, K.U.B. xiv, 4, speaks only of a (sinister) omen of the sun, but this can hardly be anything else but a solar eclipse. So already §ii, 10, 306 f., and Professor H. G. Güterbock informs me that he had reached the same conclusion. For this eclipse see already p. 206 above.

[2] For a recent discussion of the above synchronisms see §ii, 120, 1 ff. and §ii, 121, 15 ff; for the royal marriage see J. H. Breasted, A History of Egypt (1912), 439.

[3] See §ii, 161, 64 ff. There is no basis for the alleged synchronism between Urkhi-Teshub, as king, and Shalmaneser I of Assyria; see ibid. 68. The chronological evidence indicates that in K.U.B. xxvi, 70, reference is to a former letter, probably appealing for help, sent by Urkhi-Teshub to Shalmaneser I some time after the deposition of Urkhi-Teshub. The importance Tudkhaliash attaches to recovering the original copy of this letter is understandable, if it could be construed as proof that Urkhi-Teshub was a traitor.

[4] For detailed discussion see A, 11, 000; see also pp. 238 and 246 below on the chronology of Ugarit.

[5] So in C.A.H. ii³, ch. xxxiii, 31.

[6] C.A.H. ii³, ch. xxiii, 28.

In spite of the paucity of Hittite chronological material this intricate network of synchronisms yields a fairly close outline of Hittite chronology, and this in turn provides the basis for reconstructing, though again only in outline, the chronology of Ugarit during that period. Texts recently excavated have yielded a number of synchronisms between the Hittite kings and their vassals in Ugarit.[1] The date of the end of the Hittite empire is still unknown. Tudkhaliash IV was followed on the throne by two sons, Arnuwandash III and Suppiluliumash II. Both these reigns, as well as the latter part of the reign of Tudkhaliash IV come after 1245, the date of the accession of Tukulti-Ninurta I.[2] Whether there were any later Hittite kings is not yet certain.[3]

About 1200 B.C., both Asia Minor and Syria were engulfed in disaster. This event, probably more complex than it appears to us at present, is known as the Invasion of the Sea Peoples. One consequence of this invasion was to cut off the supply of Mycenaean pottery which for two centuries had enjoyed considerable popularity in Syria and Palestine, in which area it constitutes an important criterion. The Mycenaean pottery found in the recent excavations at the site of ancient Hazor is particularly significant in this respect, for it has an important bearing on the chronology of the period of the Judges. This problem is discussed elsewhere below.[4] The conclusion is that Baraq should be dated to the second half of the thirteenth century.

(i) The chronology of Elam in the second millennium B.C.

The sequence of the rulers in the Elamite countries Awan, Simashki, and Elam proper, has been fully discussed by G. G. Cameron in his *History of Early Iran* (1936). The reader is referred to that work for a comprehensive discussion of the chronology of that area. Here we will confine ourselves to comment on the synchronisms by means of which these rulers can be integrated with the Mesopotamian chronological structure. A few new synchronisms have come to light since Cameron wrote, and in a few other instances additional comment is required. The discussion is of necessity confined at present to identifying the rulers, establishing the order in which they reigned, and the synchronisms between them and rulers in other countries. For no king-lists have been found, and

---

[1] §II, 98, 6 ff.   [2] See preceding page.
[3] On the main problems in Hittite chronology see §II, 79, for the problem of the last Hittite kings, *ibid*. 8–10.
[4] See pp. 237 ff. below.

in the period under consideration we do not know the length of a single reign.

E. Unger's theory that Khurpatila of Elam was for a while ruler of Babylonia[1] is devoid of foundation.[2] The synchronism between Untash-Khuban and Kashtiliash IV[3] should also be abandoned. In the relevant passage we should read [*Tup-li*]-*ia-aš*, rather than [*Kaš-ti-li*]-*ia-aš*. The text speaks of carrying off the statue of a god, and reference to the provenance of the statue is very much more probable than reference to the king whose personal god the statue was thought to represent.[4] With this synchronism out of the way, and with sixteen years instead of nine between Kashtiliash IV and Adad-shum-naṣir, we have more time in Elam for Unpatar-Khuban and Kidin-Khutran, the successors of Untash-Khuban. Kidin-Khutran may have ruled over most of Babylonia between the end of the reign of Adad-shum-iddin and the third year of Adad-shum-naṣir.[5]

In the Old Babylonian Period we have a firm new synchronism in unpublished texts from Mari.[6] These speak of Seplarpak, king of Anshan, also called *sukkal* of Elam, as well as another Elamite ruler, Kudushulush, *sukkal* of Susa. The first is certainly identical with Siwepalarkhuppak, the second with Kuduzulush I.

In the absence of king-lists Elamite chronology in the second half of the Old Babylonian Period rests on the above synchronisms with Hammurabi of Babylon, and on a synchronism over a century later between an Elamite ruler by the name of Kuknashur and the Babylonian king, Ammiṣaduqa. Unfortunately it is not quite certain whether the Elamite is the first or the second king of that name. This issue, crucial for Elamite chronology in the Old Babylonian Period, is discussed elsewhere in this chapter.[7] The conclusion is that identification should be made with Kuknashur II.

In the Sumerian period one new synchronism has come to light since Cameron's book was published. A text from the reign of Shu-Sin, of the Third Dynasty of Ur, mentions an envoy of a ruler called Ki-ir-na-me. As T. Jacobsen has shown, this is fairly certain to be Girnamme, king of Simashki.[8]

[1] *Arch. f. Or.* 10, 93c. [2] See §11, 72, 12.
[3] §11, 8, 103 f.
[4] I owe this opinion to Professor Erica Reiner.
[5] On the interval between Kashtiliash IV and Adad-shum-naṣir, and on the invasions of Kidin-Khutran see most recently §11, 121, 18 ff.
[6] §11, 16, 109. [7] See pp. 234 f. below.
[8] §11, 61, 6 ff.

CHRONOLOGY OF THE SUMERIAN PERIOD: 3500–2000 B.C.

(a) The Neo-Sumerian Period (c. 2230–2000)

The Third Dynasty of Ur (Ur III) figures in the Sumerian king-list, as well as in the independent Ur III–Isin king-list.[1] It is also fairly well preserved in the year-lists. In so far as this dynasty is concerned only minor chronological problems remain. The manner in which the *ussa*-years were treated under Ur III is one such problem, another is the problem of determining the exact year in the reign of Ibbi-Sin in which Ishbi-Erra assumed the status of king.[2]

Less than a century before Ur III we have the last *floruit* of Lagash under Ur-Baba and Gudea. How long before this we should date Shar-kali-sharri of Akkad is not clear. The anarchy which broke out at the death of Shar-kali-sharri very probably marks the end of the effective rule of the Dynasty of Akkad over Sumer. It provides a suitable conventional point for the beginning of the Neo-Sumerian Period. Between that point and the beginning of Ur III chronology is still very obscure.[3] The evidence at present available justifies no more than a provisional, tentative estimate of approximately 120 years.[4] The resultant date 2233 for the death of Shar-kali-sharri is rounded off here to 2230 so as to avoid giving the impression of unwarranted precision.

(b) The Sargonic Period (c. 2370–2230)

The Sargonic Period begins with the rise of Lugalzaggisi, and with Sargon still a cupbearer at the court of Kish. The advantage of this arrangement is that it groups in one period the first known attempts at 'empire'.

The figures which the Sumerian king-list provides for Sargon and his successors cannot be verified, as no year-lists are available prior to Ur III. There is only one major discrepancy in the various copies of the king-list, thirty-seven as against fifty-six for Naram-Sin, and there Jacobsen has shown that thirty-seven is probably correct.[5] The figure of fifty-five or fifty-six years for Sargon is

---

[1] For these texts see pp. 199 f. above.
[2] On these problems see most recently §II, 135, 38 ff.
[3] *Ibid.* 29 ff.
[4] In the main copy of the king list (W.B.) the total between the Dynasty of Akkad and Ur III is: 30 +91 +7 = 128 years, beginning with the death of Shu-Durul; see §II, 122, 156 ff. Note that the title of king is not attested for Lugalushumgal as erroneously stated there on p. 158.   [5] §II, 60, 23 ff.

taken to cover the whole of his career, beginning from the time when he left the court of Kish to become a local ruler under Lugalzaggisi. The reason is that Meskigala, *ensi* of Adab under Lugalzaggisi, was still ruling under Rimush.[1] This makes it improbable that as much as fifty-five or fifty-six years could have elapsed between the end of Lugalzaggisi and the accession of Rimush.

In synchronizing four events at the beginning of the primacy of Lugalzaggisi we are oversimplifying the problem. These events are: the capture of Lagash by Lugalzaggisi, his capture of Uruk, his assumed defeat of Kish, and finally, the accession of Sargon as a local ruler. Though it is not likely that these events lie much apart in time, some adjustment will be necessary.

(c) *The Old-Sumerian Period (c. 2800–2370)*

As defined here the Old-Sumerian Period corresponds with the following archaeological periods: Early Dynastic II, Early Dynastic III, and the ill-defined interval which in Lagash runs from Entemena to Lugalzaggisi. Close chronology goes back beyond Lugalzaggisi only in Lagash, and there only for a matter of thirteen years. The conquest of Lagash by Lugalzaggisi is preceded by two short reigns, Lugalanda seven years, followed by Urukagina eight years; the total is under fifteen years because the accession year system was apparently not yet in use.[2]

Dated texts are available from the reigns of two of the three preceding reigns. Entemena had a fairly long reign, at least nineteen years.[3] For Enetarzi only five years are attested, but he may well have reigned longer.[4] No dated texts are available from the interval between these two reigns. This suggests that it was not a long interval, though it is known to have contained at least one reign, that of Enannatum II, son of Entemena.

Information we have on the careers of several individuals who lived during this period confirms that the interval between Entemena and Urukagina was not a long one. Enetarzi himself already held the high office of *šanga* of Ningirsu under Entemena.[5]

---

[1] §II, 55, 10, re no. 26. Professor T. Jacobsen drew my attention to the implications of this datum. For this *ensi* at the time of Rimush see *P.B.S.* v, 34, col. xx, and *P.B.S.* xv, 41, col. xx.

[2] §II, 136, 129 ff.; see *ibid.* 136, n. 1 for the length of Urukagina's reign.

[3] §II, 78, 211 f. for a tablet dated 'At that time Entemena was *ensi* of Lagash, Enetarzi was *šanga* of Ningirsu—Year 19'.

[4] For a text which may be dated in his sixth year see *R.A.* 11, 61 f.

[5] See n. 3, above and n. 1 next page.

That the *šanga* is the same person as the ruler, Enetarzi, is proved by the fact that the wife of the *šanga* has the same name as the wife of the *ensi*.[1] Other individuals who are well attested during the reigns of Lugalanda and Urukagina appear already in texts from the reign of Enetarzi, and in one instance even earlier. The inspector of the smiths (*PA simug*) under Urukagina is mentioned, with the same rank, in a report addressed to Enetarzi when he was still the *šanga* of Ningirsu.[2] The possibility cannot of course be excluded that different persons are involved, but where name and function are identical it is usually safest to assume identity of person.

On the probable assumption that there are no unknown rulers of Lagash in the period from Entemena to Lugalzaggisi, the total for that interval can be formulated as follows, with x_2 standing for the reign of Enannatum II:

$$(19 + x_1) + x_2 + (5 + x_3) + 13 = 37 + x_1 + x_2 + x_3.$$

In view of the fact that the careers of Enetarzi and Dudu began already under Entemena an estimate of eighty years should be ample.

That it would be unsafe to allow appreciably less than eighty years is indicated by the evidence from Uruk. The king of Uruk, Lugalkinishedudu, concluded a treaty with Entemena.[3] He was followed by his son, Lugalkisalsi,[4] after whom we may have a gap in the sequence of rulers. But the grandson of Lugalkisalsi, Sautu, was still a ruler of Uruk, with the title *NĪG ensi*[5] and since it is unlikely that Lugalzaggisi would have left the native dynasty in power after his conquest of Uruk, Sautu probably belongs before Lugalzaggisi. Consequently, from Lugalkinishedudu to Lugalzaggisi we must reckon with a throne tenure of at least four generations, and this would hardly be less than about eighty years.

The treaty between Entemena and Lugalkinishedudu constitutes a major chronological landmark. Both Lugalkinishedudu

---

[1] The name of the wife of Enetarzi is written LÚ + ŠESSIG.TUR. She is mentioned as the wife of the *šanga*, Enetarzi (see n. 3, p. 220), and in §II, 55, 352, i, 2 f., a text from the seventeenth year of Entemena. She is mentioned as the wife of the *ensi*, Enetarzi, in §II, 78, 212 f. i, 1 ff., and in §II, 55, 347, xi, 116 ff.

[2] §II, 35, 125 ff.

[3] §II, 40, 125 f, and §II, 75, 200 f. A treaty is not explicitly mentioned, it is inferred from the date of the text: 'At that time Entemena, *ensi* of Lagash, made "brotherhood" with Lugalkinishedudu, *ensi* of Uruk.'

[4] See most recently §II, 64, 128, n. 82.

[5] §II, 142. The name is read Sá-laḫ in §II, 64, 125 n. 75.

and his son, Lugalkisalsi, bear the title king of Uruk and Ur,[1] and at least the former was titular king of Kish.[2] Neither of these kings figures in the first dynasties of Uruk, or of Ur, and it is very unlikely that kings of such importance[3] would have been omitted. Hence both Uruk I and Ur I must have come to an end before the time of Lugalkinishedudu and Entemena.

The generation represented in Lagash by Eannatum I and his brother, Enannatum I, father of Entemena, stands midway between the Early Dynastic Period, and the archaeologically ill-defined period which follows. Eannatum still uses the plano-convex brick characteristic of the Early Dynastic Period, although the brick is only slightly convex,[4] and he is the first ruler of Lagash whose inscriptions have an orthography virtually free of the archaic features which, gradually diminishing, are characteristic of the Early Dynastic epigraphic material.[5] In the earlier writing the signs are not always written in the order in which they were pronounced. The orthography is also more elliptic. The scribes did not deem it necessary to express as much of the phonetic structure of a word, as they did by the time of Eannatum.

Now the crucial point is this. These archaic features are missing in the few short texts we have from the reign of A'annipada, the son of the first king of Ur I, Mesannipada. On the other hand, they are present in the inscription of Kur-lil, an official whose statue was found in the temple which A'annipada built at the site of modern Al-'Ubaid, and who therefore was presumably either contemporaneous with A'annipada or later than he. This suggests that A'annipada belongs to the transitional period when the archaic orthography was disappearing, a period which in Lagash corresponds with the reign of Ur-Nanshe.

Between Ur-Nanshe and Entemena, both excluded, we have in Lagash three kings in two generations.[6] Between A'annipada and the end of Ur I we have at least three kings; Meskiag-Nanna, Elulu, and Balulu.[7] On this evidence the end of Ur I cannot be dated more than a few decades before the treaty between Entemena and Lugalkinishedudu. We have seen already that the end of the dynasty cannot be placed after the treaty. From which it follows that the end of the First Dynasty of Ur comes not long before

[1] §11, 57, 5.   [2] §11, 64, 134 n. 97.
[3] On the rule of these kings see *ibid.*   [4] §11, 38, 139 n. 2.
[5] *Ibid.* 128 ff.; and cf. §11, 60, 184 ff.
[6] The material for the successors of Ur-Nanshe in Lagash is listed under the articles Akurgal, Eannatum, Enannatum I, Entemena, Enannatum II in *R.L.A.*; see also p. 224, n. 3 below.
[7] For the First Dynasty of Ur see §11, 60, 172 ff.

the reign of Entemena, or less probably, early in that king's reign.

Two important rulers whose chronological location is still uncertain, are Lugaltarsi and Enshakushanna. The former, titular king of Kish, could conceivably be identical with Lugal-TAR, an *ensi* of Uruk.[1] For we know that in the period immediately before Lugalzaggisi even royal names were rendered in abbreviated form. If this somewhat doubtful identification is correct, Lugaltarsi is best inserted between Lugalkisalsi and his grandson, Sautu (or Salakh). Enshakushanna is likely to have been a king of either Ur, Uruk, or of both those cities.[2] His father, Elilina, may perhaps be identical with Elulu, the last king but one of the First Dynasty of Ur. As pointed out to me by Professor I. J. Gelb, the script of a text which is dated to Enshakushanna by the oldest known year-name is very close to the Sargonic script.[3] It therefore supports a date for Enshakushanna not long before Lugalzaggisi.[4]

A king of Kish defeated by Enshakushanna is possibly identical with the last king of Kish II, a king whose name is written *I-bi*(var. *bí*)-[. . . . .] in the king-list.[5] This could go back to Ibbi-Ishtar, misconstrued by later scribes from Inbi-Ishtar or Enbi-Ishtar, the name of the adversary of Enshakushanna.[6] This identification is tentative only; more evidence is needed. If correct it constitutes a very important synchronism since it locates the end of Kish II after Entemena and Lugalkinishedudu, and at about the time of the fourth king of the Dynasty of Akshak.

[1] §11, 14, 5 ff. and pl. 1 (= §11, 45, pl. XLII, T. G. 2065). A difficulty is that the title *ensi* is not attested in Uruk texts before the Sargonic period. But there are very few Uruk texts, and in a contemporary text, already mentioned, Lugalkinishedudu is called *ensi* of Uruk (see p. 221, n. 3 above). Note also that a Lugal-TAR is mentioned in *Collection de Clercq*, 1, 82; I owe this reference to Professor I. J. Gelb.

[2] §11, 60, 184; and §11, 64, 134. For criticism of the identification of Enshakushanna with the first king of the Second Dynasty of Uruk see §11, 73, 42.

[3] A. Pohl, *T.u.M.* v, 158 : 10 ff. For the correct reading of the personal name in this text see §11, 93, 5, no. 8.

[4] §11, 60, 171 would make Enshakushanna the unknown founder of the Second Dynasty of Uruk, and identifies the last king of Ur II with Kaku, defeated by Rimush, king of Agade, about sixty years after the beginning of the Dynasty of Agade. On the evidence of the two passages adduced in §11, 73, 42 it would seem safest to read the name of the first king of Uruk II as En-PIRIG (?)-du-an-na.

[5] See §11, 60, 169 and 183, criticized in §11, 73, 39. In the new fragment there discussed the name is written I-bí-[. . .]. The last signs cannot be read in either copy of the king-list.

[6] It should be noted however that according to §11, 73 the traces at the end of the name are not compatible with a reading *Eš₄-tár*.

For the latter, Puzur-Nirakh, is given in a late chronicle as contemporary of the mother of Puzur-Sin.[1] And since Puzur-Sin is the predecessor of Ur-Zababa, king of Kish when Sargon was a young man, Puzur-Nirakh cannot be dated much later than Entemena.

Even from this very brief discussion of the chronology of the Old Sumerian period it should be clear that with each searching step we sink deep in conjecture and uncertainty. This becomes more pronounced the further back in time one attempts to grope; the problem is simply to make the best of the very limited evidence available. For the period of a century or so before Entemena we have a fairly coherent outline only in Ur and Lagash. In Ur the information contained in the Sumerian king-list is supplemented by the Tummal chronicle. The chronicle shows that Meskiagnunna, son of Mesannipada, should be distinguished from Meskiag-Nanna. Both these kings were listed in the original copy of the king-list; the extant text is defective for Ur I.[2] Meskiag-Nanna was the son of a king variously called Ananne, Nanne, in the chronicle. The latter may be identical with A'annipada, another son of Mesannipada, whom we have already had occasion to mention. To allow for this possibility it will be safest to place A'annipada after his brother, Meskiagnunna, rather than immediately after Mesannipada.

Our knowledge of the contemporary rulers of Lagash comes in part from inscriptions dealing with border wars between Lagash and Umma. These continued, off and on, down to the time of Lugalzaggisi's final victory over Lagash. From the texts concerned with these events we also learn a little of the chronology of Umma in the period between Eannatum and Lugalzaggisi.[3]

The best known ruler before the time of Ur-Nanshe and A'annipada is Mesilim. We know that he comes before Ur-Nanshe because his contemporary in Lagash was Lugalshagengur,[4] and for the latter there is no room after Ur-Nanshe. On the other hand, it is unlikely that Mesilim reigned much before Ur-Nanshe. For he settled a border dispute between Lagash and

---

[1] §II, 53, 51 : 5 ff.; §II, 60, 106, vi, 1.

[2] For the Tummal chronicle see above pp. 201 f. and p. 235 below. For the First Dynasty of Ur in the king-list see §II, 60, 92 ff. 172 f. Note also that the writer of the name list *P.B.S.* XI/1, no. 25, was clearly thinking of the First Dynasty of Ur when he listed the sequence (m)Mes-ki-ag-[(d)Nanna], (m)Mes-ki-ag-nun-n[a], (m)Mes-an-ni-pad-da; cf. §II, 60, 94 n. 146.

[3] For the genealogy of the dynasty of Ur-Nanshe, and of the contemporary rulers of Umma see most recently §II, 23, 22.

[4] §II, 141, 160 no. 2.

Umma,[1] and this border apparently remained undisturbed until approximately the time of Eannatum, the grandson of Ur-Nanshe. It is not likely that this happy state of affairs endured more than a few generations, if we are to judge by the subsequent history of Lagash and Umma.

The earliest Sumerian ruler referred to in inscriptions which are probably contemporary with him is Enmebaragisi of Kish. He is to be dated well before Mesilim, towards the beginning of the Old Sumerian period. A votive inscription which mentions him was found in the Diyālā region in an Early Dynastic II level.[2] According to Sumerian legend which we have no reason to doubt, the son of Enmebaragisi, Agga, fought Gilgamesh, king of Uruk.[3] The Sumerian king-list locates Gilgamesh in about the middle of the First Dynasty of Uruk.[4] He is preceded by kings of a legendary—mythical character, with reigns of fantastic lengths and is followed by Ur-lugal, stated to be the son of Gilgamesh, and by six other kings for whom normal figures are quoted, and none of whom are known from legend or myth.

This raises a difficult problem. Are we to regard the connexion between the Gilgamesh section of Uruk I, and the Ur-lugal section of that dynasty as artificial? This connexion rests on the statement that Ur-lugal was the son of Gilgamesh. But in Sumerian the word *dumu* 'son' also has the meaning 'descendant'. Consequently a later king of Uruk who claimed to have been a descendant of the legendary Gilgamesh, might well have come to be enshrined in tradition as the actual son of Gilgamesh.[5] Legend dates Gilgamesh at the very beginning of the Old Sumerian period. But the Nippur version of the Tummal chronicle and one of the versions represented at Ur date Ur-lugal after Meskiagnunna, the brother of A'annipada. If this is correct there is a considerable gap between the two sections of the First Dynasty of Uruk. This solution has been rejected here, but caution is necessary for the following reason—it is easy to see that if the

---

[1] §II, 141, 24, text f; 36, text n.

[2] On these two inscriptions see §II, 24. As pointed out there the building level immediately above the level with the inscription of Enmebaragisi yielded a seal from the very beginning of Early Dynastic III. This proves only that the inscription is older than Early Dynastic III; but Professor Delougaz confirms that the Enmebaragisi inscription comes from an Early Dynastic II Level.

[3] According to a legend from the time of Shulgi, king of the Third Dynasty of Ur, the war with Gilgamesh had already begun during the reign of Enmebaragisi, cf. §II, 24, 20 ff.   [4] §II, 60, 88 ff.

[5] In the legend referred to in n. 3 above Gilgamesh is called the brother of Shulgi.

Tummal chronicle disagreed with the king-list, a text which acquired canonical authority, the chronicle would have been emended. The opposite process, emendation of the chronicle in spite of the king-list, is more difficult to assume, although a possible explanation will be suggested later.[1]

It is tempting to infer from the Nippur version of the chronicle that Gilgamesh and Mesannipada were contemporaries. But the Enmebaragisi–Gilgamesh period belongs towards the beginning of Early Dynastic II, possibly even on the fringe of Early Dynastic I; and we could not possibly date the inscriptions of Ur I so close to Early Dynastic I, if the archaic texts from Ur have been correctly placed in that level. In this connexion it should be borne in mind that the recent excavations at Nippur warn against unduly compressing the period during which writing developed.[2] At Nippur, from a level roughly corresponding with Uruk V up to the last having plano-convex brick, there are no fewer than sixteen levels. Texts of the Fārah type, close to the transition Early Dynastic II–Early Dynastic III appear only in the fourteenth of these sixteen levels.

(d) The Proto-historic Period (Uruk V–Early Dynastic I), c. 3500–2800

There can be little doubt that the only valid criterion for defining the end of the Prehistoric Age is the appearance of writing. In Mesopotamia the earliest writing hitherto discovered comes from Level IVb at Uruk.[3] Though these texts are probably not far from the beginning of writing,[4] it is unlikely that in Uruk we have stumbled upon the very earliest texts. Consequently it will be prudent to allow some slight margin beyond Uruk IVb for the very earliest texts. By setting the limit of the Prehistoric Period at the start of Uruk Level V the beginning of writing is made to coincide with the appearance of monumental architecture.[5]

---

[1] See pp. 235 ff. below.

[2] For a preliminary report see Ill. Ldn. News. 9/9/1961, 408 ff.

[3] For a description of the texts from Uruk IVb see §11, 27, 22 ff. On the possibility that these tablets may have to be dated to the end of Level IV, that is to IVa see most recently §11, 107, vol. 2, 244.

[4] Writing as a criterion for the end of the Prehistoric Period means writing used to transmit language, technically known as logography. Primitive systems of rendering ideas, pictography and ideography, may reach far back into the Prehistoric Period. On this distinction see §11, 43, 65 ff.

[5] The view is accepted here that the main transition is at the beginning of Uruk V; cf. §11, 107, vol. 2, 275 ff. The author uses the term 'Protohistoric' for the period

Writing in Mesopotamia is demonstrably a product of intensified economic growth. Hence what we may well have at the beginning of Uruk Level V is the emergence of one of the most potent and lasting factors in Mesopotamian civilization, namely the prominence of the temple in the economic life of the country.

The end of the Proto-historic Period is reached when writing becomes sufficiently intelligible, and sufficiently general in use, to justify the expectation that the documentary evidence will ultimately yield a coherent picture. Before that, writing is restricted to economic texts, usually of a very simple kind, and in several respects it is very deficient. Signs lack standardization; their order within a word is arbitrary; phonetic writing is largely confined to personal names.[1] This inefficiency of early writing, coupled with its highly restricted use, means that our picture of the period it covers is never going to be more than fragmentary. The personalities, events, and institutions of that age are destined to remain obscure, our knowledge of them gleaned, not from contemporary texts, but from legend and myth. Hence the spread of writing beyond the economic sphere, and the appearance of fully intelligible texts, marks the beginning of history proper in Mesopotamia.

The location of this landmark would appear to be midway between the archaic texts from Ur and the Fārah texts. H. Frankfort dated the former by seal impressions to Early Dynastic I;[2] with the Fārah texts we are in Early Dynastic III.[3] The inscriptions of Enmebaragisi, together with two other early texts from Early Dynastic II levels in the Diyālā region, are intermediary between Ur and Fārah.[4] Provisionally, and pending further evidence, we may locate Enmebaragisi on the threshold of the period with which history proper begins in Mesopotamia.

The dark Proto-historic Period which precedes Enmebaragisi comprises Uruk Levels V and IV, the Jamdat-Naṣr Period

which precedes Uruk V; for the period from Uruk V to Early Dynastic he suggests the term 'Predynastic.' To a historian this is quite unacceptable, since we know virtually nothing about the date of the beginning of 'dynasties' in Mesopotamia.

[1] For early Mesopotamian writing see §ii, 27, 1–68, particularly 19 ff., and 64 ff.; also §ii, 43, 61 ff.   [2] §ii, 33, particularly 337.

[3] §ii, 27, 22, would date the Fārah texts about a hundred years before Ur-Nanshe; §ii, 33, 337, puts them at the very beginning of Early Dynastic III.

[4] See §ii, 13, 291, nos. 8 and 9. These tablets were found in the main level of the Shara Temple. The content of the rooms they were found in, M 14 : 4, and L 14 : 1, is Early Dynastic II, cf. *op. cit.* 226 f., 274 f., 278 ff., and 228 n. 5. See also p. 225, n. 2 above. Note that text no. 1, as yet published only in photograph (*op. cit.* 289) comes from Level VIII of the Sin Temple, and so from Early Dynastic II.

(Uruk Level III) and Early Dynastic I. In the Sin temple at Khafājī we have as many as seven levels for Uruk III and Early Dynastic I.[1] Such an accumulation requires several centuries, and before that we have the first two levels in Uruk with monumental architecture, Uruk V and Uruk IV. For each building level we should not reckon less than about seventy years, at least not without clear evidence that a lower total is indicated. This yields roughly 600 years for a total of nine building levels.

Between the end of this span of some six centuries and the time of Eannatum, *c.* 2500 B.C., we still have two whole archaeological periods, Early Dynastic II and III, an interval during which writing passes from the hardly intelligible archaic texts of Ur to the fully developed writing of Eannatum's inscriptions. What this means is that by and large the Mesopotamian material independently confirms the evidence from Egypt which suggests a high date for Uruk III (Jamdat-Naṣr). There is a clear affinity, particularly in glyptic, between the Jamdat-Naṣr material in Mesopotamia and the Naqāda II material in Egypt.[2] And in Egypt Naqāda II comes before the First Dynasty, that is before 3100 B.C.

Now if the culture of Uruk Level III was flourishing in Mesopotamia already before 3100, the beginning of Uruk V can plausibly be dated *c.* 3500 B.C., for it would not be safe to allow appreciably less than a hundred years, on an average, for the following four phases: Uruk V, Uruk IV, the interval from the beginning of Uruk III to the contact with Naqāda II, the interval from the latter to the First Dynasty in Egypt. On the other hand, this date means that from the beginning of writing in Mesopotamia to the full development it reached under Eannatum, *c.* 2500 B.C., we have a total of about 1000 years. This is very much longer than one would have expected,[3] and in the absence of evidence to the contrary one is certainly entitled to regard a thousand years as the maximum plausible for the development of writing. This suggests that we should not go much above 3500 B.C. with Uruk V. And if we also cannot come much lower, then as a rough estimate the date 3500 for the beginning of the Proto-historic period may perhaps be not too far off the mark. With nine building levels attested for the Proto-historic period, six centuries is a somewhat conservative estimate. If we are to guess, it will be

[1] That is, from the beginning of 'Protoliterate c'; cf. table in §II, 13, 134.
[2] For the early relations between Egypt and Mesopotamia see §II, 67; and see chaps. IX and XI below.
[3] §II, 43, 62 f.

safer to allow at least a century more. The resultant date, 2800, for the beginning of the Old Sumerian Period will do as a tentative estimate pending further evidence.

(a) The Assyrian Calendar

The Assyrian calendar presents a chronological problem which is not fully ripe for discussion.[1]

Towards the end of the twelfth century B.C. the Babylonian calendar was introduced, with its system of intercalary months. Whether before that the Assyrian calendar was purely lunar, or whether it was in some way adjusted to the seasons, is not yet clear. It certainly had no intercalary month. On the other hand, if there was no adjustment to the seasons, one would expect to find evidence that the harvest moved through all the months. The limited amount of material available does not give the impression that such was the case, but this may be due to insufficient evidence. If no adjustment equivalent to intercalation existed, the calendrical year was eleven days shorter than the Julian year. In that case all Assyrian dates prior to the middle of the twelfth century will have to be reduced in the ratio of three years per century. The effect would be cumulative, and dates in the eighteenth century, for instance, would have to be reduced by some eighteen years.

(b) The date of Saustatar and Alalakh Level IV

The Hittite king Suppiluliumash came to the throne not later than Akhenaten. The Hittite domination of Northern Syria at the time of Tudkhaliash II and Khattushilish II began during the reign of Tudkhaliash II, the great-grandfather of Suppiluliumash.[2] Since we have only about half a century between the death of Amenophis II and the accession of Akhenaten, it is fairly certain that the Hittite domination of Northern Syria began before the death of Amenophis II. They were not in control of Northern Syria at the time of the Syrian campaigns of Tuthmosis III, half a century before the death of Amenophis II, for the opponent of Tuthmosis III was the king of Mitanni, not the Hittite king. Nor can we assume that the Hittite domination comes before the Mitanni domination encountered by Tuthmosis III since that would place the Hittite kings Tudkhaliash II and Khattushilish II too far from

[1] §II, 154 and §II, 156, 27 ff.; §II, 87; §II, 86, 47 ff.   [2] See §II, 151, 82 f.

Tudkhaliash III, the son of Khattushilish II. Tudkhaliash III
was campaigning with his own son, Suppiluliumash, during the
reign of Amenophis III, in the first half of the fourteenth century
B.C.[1]

From this it follows that the whole of the earlier Hittite domination of Northern Syria has to come after the Egyptian domination
under Tuthmosis III and Amenophis II. The latter successfully
suppressed a revolt in Aleppo in his third year. By his seventh
year Aleppo was free of Egyptian control,[2] but it is fairly certain
that it had not yet come under the suzerainty of the Hittites.
Amenophis II very probably reached the vicinity of Aleppo in the
campaign of his seventh year, and the Hittites are still not mentioned as his opponents.[3] By this process of bracketing we are
able to date the earlier Hittite domination of Northern Syria
approximately to the second half of the reign of Amenophis II.
It certainly did not begin before Year 4 of that king, and probably not before Year 10.[4] Thus although it may well have ended
after the reign of Amenophis II, it certainly began during that
reign. The importance of this conclusion is that it leaves no room
during the reign of Amenophis II for the domination of Northern
Syria by the kings of Mitanni, Parratarna and Saustatar.[5] In
Alalakh this phase corresponds to Level IV, during which we
have at least three kings in three generations. These are Idrimi,
Niqmepa, and Ilimilimma, and Idrimi reigned some thirty years.
Hence Alalakh IV has to be dated before the conquest of Northern
Syria by Tuthmosis III in 1473.[6]

The ceramic evidence from Alalakh supports this date for
Level IV. The imported Aegean Mycenaean pottery termed
III a, characteristic of the fourteenth century, is well attested only
in Level II. Hence between this typically fourteenth-century
level and Level IV we have the whole of Level III. The pottery
therefore suggests for Level IV a date not later than about the

---

[1] §II, 54, 119–20.   [2] §II, 20, 174.
[3] § II, 20, 148 f.

[4] *Ibid.* 136. After the account of the campaign in Year 9 it is said that, upon
hearing of the victories of Amenophis II, the rulers of Mitanni (Naharina), Khatti,
and Babylon (Sangara) hastened to send presents. This strongly suggests that none of
these kings were among the opponents of Amenophis II, either in Year 7 or in Year 9
and that it was revolt that broke the Egyptian domination.

[5] See most recently §II, 50, 66 ff.; §II, 118, 105 n. 46.

[6] The Mitannian domination in Syria under Saustatar and his predecessors was
dated before the conquests of Tuthmosis III already in §II, 99, 82, though without
stating reasons. Later §II, 77, 54, reached the same conclusion, and so also §II, 83,
276 n. 1.

middle of the fifteenth century.[1] In view of the fact that at least one of the kings of Alalakh IV is known to have had a long reign, and because that level spans at least three generations, about seventy-five years should be allowed for it. A decade or so less would be possible but could not be postulated in the absence of supporting evidence. The resultant date for Alalakh IV is c. 1550–1473.

(c) The date of the First Dynasty of Babylon (Babylon I)

The sixty-third tablet of the astrological series Enuma Anum Enlil has preserved observations of Venus made during the reign of the tenth king of Babylon I, Ammiṣaduqa.[2] These allow only a limited number of solutions for the date of that dynasty. Babylon I came to an end thirty-one years after the reign of Ammiṣaduqa, and in the discussion which follows, the solutions available from the Venus observations have been translated into the corresponding dates for the end of the dynasty.[3]

The ninth king of the Kassite Dynasty was already king in Babylon,[4] and from him to Burnaburiash II, who reigned in the first half of the fourteenth century, there are some ten reigns and at least half that number of generations. Hence on the Babylonian evidence alone a date for the end of Babylon I after 1500 B.C. is out of the question.

No solutions are available for the Venus observations which would allow a date for the end of Babylon I in the second half of the eighteenth century, and in the seventeenth century down to 1651.[5] But the ceramic evidence from Alalakh, as well as the glyptic, precludes a date for the end of Babylon I as high as 1750, for this would put the end of Alalakh VII c. 1800, during Dyn-

---

[1] §II, 167, 369 ff. A few sherds and fragments of Myc. IIIa occur in Levels IV and III. In some cases the stratification is uncertain, and only three sherds of Myc. III are positively dated earlier than Level II. The present writer would like to acknowledge use of a detailed study by G. F. Swift, Jr. On p. 34 of this unpublished thesis, Swift concludes that the Mycenaean material supports a date as early as 1400 B.C. for the beginning of Level II.

[2] J.E.O.L. 10, 414ff.; O.L.Z. 32, 913ff., also §II, 10, 296f. and §II, 11, 101, where the author attempts to show that astronomical factors exclude all solutions except the one which corresponds with 1531 for the end of the First Dynasty.

[3] For the bibliography of this problem see §II, 105, 463 ff., and §II, 118, 98, footnotes 4–9; add §II, 11, 101 ff.; §II, 83, 241 ff.; §II, 106; and §II, 146.

[4] It is now more probable that Agum II was the seventh king, and that he was omitted from the lists; see E. F. Weidner in Arch. f. Or. 19, 138; §II, 65, 228f.; §II, 118, 103. Agum II brought back the statue of Marduk twenty-four years after it had been taken from Babylon by the Hittites; §II, 42.

[5] J.E.O.L. 10, 418.

asty XII in Egypt.[1] Between 1651 and 1500, the Venus observations permit the following dates for the end of Babylon I: 1651, 1595, 1587, and 1531,[2] but the evidence at present available does not favour the two extreme dates, 1651 and 1531. Indeed this adverse evidence is almost sufficient to exclude the lowest date, 1531, against which there are three arguments.

(1) The city of Level VII at Alalakh was destroyed by the Hittite king Khattushilish I a little less than half a century before the end of Babylon I, i.e. on the lowest date c. 1575, and we have seen that the end of Level IV is to be dated not later than 1473.[3] A total of only one hundred years for the three levels, VI, V, and IV, is very improbable.

(2) The Assyrian king-list yields the date 1700 as a close approximation for the accession of Bēlu-bānī. The date 1531 for the end of Babylon I corresponds with a date 1728–1686 for Hammurabi, and the king of Assyria, Shamshi-Adad I, died in about the twelfth year of Hammurabi.[4] On this solution we have therefore only about fifteen years between the death of Shamshi-Adad I and the accession of Bēlu-bānī. Yet, in this interval we have the reigns of three descendants of Shamshi-Adad I, in at least two generations, followed by a period of anarchy during which a number of usurpers fought for the throne.

The date 1700 for Bēlu-bānī is based on an allowance of forty years for two reigns, the figures for which are missing in the Assyrian king-list. We have seen that a figure significantly lower than forty would be improbable in view of the filiation in this part of the Assyrian king-list.[5] However, reduction of some seventeen years would be indicated if the earlier Assyrian calendar had no arrangement equivalent to intercalation.[6] The lowest plausible date for Bēlu-bānī is therefore c. 1680. This would allow nearly forty years for the interval in question, a solution which is possible, though still not probable.

[1] If the texts are left out of consideration the Alalakh material can be taken to indicate a date in the second half of the seventeenth century for the end of Alalakh VII. Thus on the basis of this material §II, 1, 26 ff. dates the end of Alalakh VII to about the middle of the century; §II, 68, 158 ff., n. 22, dates it to about the end of the century.

[2] See the table in *J.E.O.L.* 10, 418; the end of Babylon I comes thirty-one years after the last year of Ammiṣaduqa. On the probability that the figure of thirty-one years assigned to Samsuditana in King-list B is correct see §II, 29, 159. Note that §II, 11, 101 n. 8, allows for the possibility of a further solution, namely a date for Ammiṣaduqa which would correspond with 1539 for the end of Babylon I.

[3] See above, pp. 229 f. [4] See above, p. 210.
[5] See above, pp. 203 f. [6] See above, p. 229.

(3) The Kassite Dynasty ended *c.* 1157. The Babylonian king-list gives its total as 576 years, and this does not include the seven years of Assyrian domination under Tukulti-Ninurta I.[1] On this evidence the appearance of the Kassites in Mesopotamia has to be dated *c.* 1740. If the First Dynasty of Babylon (Babylon I) ended in 1531 the appearance of the Kassites would have occurred during the reign of Sin-muballiṭ in Babylon, and Shamshi-Adad I in Assyria. Now from the Mari archives we have ample information on the period of over half a century following the accession of Shamshi-Adad I, and there is no mention of the Kassites. This points to a date before 1740 for the period covered by the Mari archives.

On the other hand, it is not impossible that the Kassite kings listed in King-List A include at least one king who never ruled in Babylon. This is Ulamburiash, a younger son of Burnaburiash I, of whom the chronicles say that he conquered the Sea Land, the country ruled by the Second Dynasty of King-List A. In the only inscription from his reign he is called only 'king of the Sea Land'. Since he is followed by Agum III the son of his brother, a king of Babylon,[2] it is not impossible that he was the ruler of an independent kingdom in the South, and that his kingdom never did include Babylon. In that case the date of the appearance of the Kassites in Mesopotamia would have to be reduced by at least as much as the figure which was quoted in King-List A for Ulamburiash.

Against the solution which corresponds with a date 1651 for the end of Babylon I are the very high averages it requires, simultaneously in Assyria and Babylonia, for certain reigns in the period after Puzur-Ashur III and Burnaburiash I. These two kings were contemporaries, and they cannot have come to the throne much more than half a century after the end of Babylon I.[3] This adverse evidence is by no means conclusive. All it means is that whereas the middle dates, 1595 or 1587, are in easy agreement with all the available evidence, the same cannot be said of the 1651 solution.

[1] §II, 121, 18 ff.

[2] On these kings see most recently §II, 65, 208 f., and 230.

[3] §II, 118, 102 ff. If we date the Mitannian domination of Syria under Saustatar before the conquest of Tuthmosis III, the Hittite evidence, discussed *ibid.* 105 ff., is equally compatible with the solutions 1651, 1595 and 1587, but would be difficult to reconcile with the 1531 solution.

(d) The Kuknashur problem in Elamite chronology

An Elamite ruler by the name of Kuknashur was reigning at the time of the accession of Ammiṣaduqa in Babylon.[1] The problem is whether we have here the first or the second ruler of that name. The available evidence points to Kuknashur II. The bearing this problem has on Elamite chronology in the Old Babylonian period has already been mentioned.[2]

For the purpose of comparative chronology it is important to note that in the Old Babylonian Period a much lower average should be allowed for Elamite rulers than for their Babylonian contemporaries. According to Cameron three rulers held office simultaneously during that period of Elamite history. When the senior ruler, the *sukkalmaḥ*, died, the next senior, the *sukkal* of Elam and Simashki, moved up to *sukkalmaḥ*. The junior ruler, the *sukkal* of Susa, would move up whenever the next highest office was vacated, and a new *sukkal* of Susa would be appointed.[3] There is no reason to believe that the average age of a man appointed to the junior office of *sukkal* of Susa was any lower than the average age of princes in the ancient Near East when he ascended the throne. But the former would have to serve in two different offices before assuming the highest office of *sukkalmaḥ*, and consequently the average tenure of the office of *sukkalmaḥ* would be very much shorter than the average reign.

Now it so happens that Hammurabi and his three successors have reigns with an average which is among the highest in the ancient Near East. Hence the disparity at this time would be particularly great. If we reckon about three Elamite *sukkalmaḥ* to one Babylonian king of the Hammurabi period, we would expect some twelve *sukkalmaḥ* from Siwepalarkhuppak, the contemporary of Hammurabi, to Ammiṣaduqa. This points to Kuknashur II as the contemporary of Ammiṣaduqa, since he is the twelfth or the thirteenth *sukkalmaḥ* counting from Siwepalarkhuppak.

Strong confirmation of this conclusion is provided by a letter, the writer of which states that his grandfather, his father and he himself had worked a field through a stated sequence of reigns.[4] These are: Shir⟨uk⟩dukh, Siwepalarkhuppak, Kuduzulush I,

---

[1] *V.A.S.* vii, 67, cf. *B.A.* vi/5, 2–5. The subject is a grant of land by Kuknashur, but the text is dated to the first year of Ammiṣaduqa of Babylon.

[2] See p. 218 above.

[3] Cf. §ii, 8, 71 ff. and 88, n. 60.

[4] *Mém. D.P.* 28 (1939), 14–15, no. 14.

Kutir-Nahhunte, Temtiagun, Kutir-⟨Shilkhakha⟩, and Kukna-shur I. In the first place, this confirms the rapid turnover in the highest office, seven *sukkalmaḫ* in two and a half generations. Secondly, Shirukdukh belongs before Hammurabi. Hence if we were to assume that the Elamite contemporary of Ammiṣaduqa was Kuknashur I we should have to assume that the three generations in the family of the writer of the letter cover a period of two centuries.

(e) The chronology of Uruk in the Old Sumerian Period

The Sumerian king-list gives Ur-lugal of Uruk as the son and successor of Gilgamesh. There follow six other kings with a total of 110 years, after which the primacy passed to Ur. When this happened Mesannipada was king of Ur, and he was followed by his son, Meskiagnunna.[1]

A recently published portion of the Tummal chronicle has a very different tradition.[2] There the first four builders of the Tummal sanctuary in Nippur are:

1. Agga (king of Kish), son of Enmebaragisi,
2. Meskiagnunna (king of Ur), son of Mesannipada (and therefore brother of A'annipada),
3. Ur-lugal (king of Uruk), son of Gilgamesh,
4. Meskiag-Nanna (king of Ur), son of Ananne (variant Nanne, identified by some scholars with A'annipada).

Here the information in parenthesis is not contained in the chronicle.

Now between the First Dynasty of Ur and Lugalkinishedudu there is hardly room for the Second Dynasty of Uruk and for Enshakushanna. These four kings were probably contemporaneous with the latter part of the First Dynasty of Ur. Thus if we prefer that version of the chronicle which agrees with the king-list the rival Nippur version can plausibly be ascribed to the memory of a temporary domination of Uruk over Ur after Meskiagnunna. Going a step farther the theory could even be put forward that the name of the second king in the Second Dynasty of Uruk, a name rendered Lugal-ur-e in the king-list, actually stands for the name Ur-lugal. The author of the Tummal chronicle would have confused this Ur-lugal II with the earlier Ur-lugal I, son of Gilgamesh. As already explained above,[3] it was not uncommon for the signs to be written in inverse order in the Old Sumerian Period; the *e* could be the subject element,

[1] §II, 60, 88–93.   [2] See p. 201, n. 1 above.   [3] See p. 222 above.

and not part of the name. Hence what this hypothesis really amounts to is simply that the author of the king-list found the name of Ur-lugal II written with the signs inverted in his source for the Second Dynasty of Uruk.

Date	I Kish II Lagash	Ur	Uruk
2700	*I Kish* Enmebaragisi Agga (son)		Gilgamesh Ur-lugal I (son) (30)
	II Lagash		
2650			Utulkalamma (son) (15) La-ba-'-[š]um (9) En-nun-dàra-an-na(8) MES(?)-ḪÉ (36?) Melamanna (6) Lugal-ki-tun₃(?) (36?)
2550	Ur-Nanshe Akurgal (son)	Mesannipada Meskiagnunna (son) A'annipada (brother) (= Ananne, Nanne)	 En-PIRIG(?)-du-an-na Lugal-ur-e
2500	Eannatum (son) Enannatum I (brother)	Meskiag-Nanna (son) Elulu Balulu	Ar-ga-an-de-a (7) Enshakushanna
2450	Entemena		Lugalkinishedudu

On this solution the First Dynasty of Ur, under Mesannipada, gained the primacy in Sumer from the First Dynasty of Uruk, as stated in the Sumerian king-list. But the Second Dynasty of Uruk did not attain the primacy hundreds of years later, as the king-list would have it. Instead, this dynasty represents a comparatively short interlude within the period of the First Dynasty of Ur, during which Uruk for a while regained the primacy. This interval would correspond roughly with the reign of A'annipada in Ur, and it would imply that A'annipada may have been a vassal of Uruk. There is at least one datum which independently suggests the same possibility. An official from Uruk, Kur-lil, built a sanctuary in the territory of the city state of Ur, and commemorated the event with a statue of himself. This statue he set up, without the slightest reference to the king of Ur, in the temple which A'annipada had built in Al-'Ubaid.[1]

From the strictly chronological point of view this solution also

---

[1] For the Kur-lil inscription see §11, 38, pl. XL and p. 125, also §11, 39, 49 f.

has some very substantial advantages.[1] First it provides ample room for the Second Dynasty of Uruk which cannot easily be accommodated on any other solution. Secondly, it locates Enmebaragisi, an older contemporary of Gilgamesh, about two centuries before Eannatum, i.e. *c.* 2700 B.C. This is a plausible date for the archaeological level Early Dynastic II from which the Diyālā inscription of Enmebaragisi comes. Thirdly, this solution makes it possible to keep A'annipada much closer to Eannatum, particularly if the usual identification of Ananne with A'annipada is accepted. The result is to place A'annipada less than a century before Entemena, and therefore only some twenty or thirty years before Eannatum. As already explained, this accords better with the orthographic conditions of the problem. Fourthly, it leaves room for Enshakushanna between Elulu of Ur and Lugalkinishededu, king of Uruk and Ur. This is an advantage because the father of Enshakushanna, Elilina, is not improbably identical with Elulu. Also it leaves more room for the rulers of Kish who come after the last king of the Second Dynasty of Kish, probably dethroned by Enshakushanna.

(f) The early period of the Judges in Israel

Hazor is not listed among the Canaanite cities against which Israel had to struggle long after the Conquest. Yet tradition and archaeology are in full agreement on the pre-eminence of Hazor among the cities of Palestine, and according to the Book of Judges Hazor retained this position down to the time of Baraq. Hence, when that book was edited, the tradition that Baraq's opponent was a king of Hazor, though absent from the Song of Deborah, must nevertheless have been so strong that it could not be ignored.

Mycenaean III a is the pottery of the Amarna period, and it was still in use at the beginning of Dynasty XIX. The change to Mycenaean III b coincides approximately with the turn of the century, 1300. It is more difficult to establish a lower limit for the end of Mycenaean III b. In Egypt it is rare, and it has never been found in closely datable context. A scarab of Ramesses II found with it merely proves that the ware came to an end some time after the accession of that king.[2]

Much more significant is the evidence from North Syria. It is

---

[1] In the four points which follow see, for all references, pp. 220 ff. above.

[2] For the date of Mycenaean pottery in terms of Egyptian chronology see §11, 34, 110 ff.; §11, 137, 90 ff.; §11, 167, 373 ff.; also p. 246 below.

virtually certain that Ugarit and Alalakh were destroyed by the invading Sea Peoples. A wave of these invaders had hit Egypt round the time of the accession of Merneptah, but that wave can hardly be credited with the destruction of Ugarit and Alalakh. The reasons are the following:

(i) The Hittite king, Tudkhaliash IV, was a contemporary of the Assyrian king, Tukulti-Ninurta I.[1] The latter came to the throne less than ten years before the accession of Merneptah in 1238. In Ugarit the contemporary of Tudkhaliash IV was Ammishtamru II, and after him we still have in Ugarit no fewer than three kings, in at least two further generations.[2]

(ii) A sword bearing the name of Merneptah was found in the ruins of Ugarit.[3]

The conclusion is therefore reassuringly safe that not the first but the second wave of the Sea Peoples was responsible for the destruction of Ugarit and Alalakh. This wave hit North Syria some time before the eighth year of Ramesses III, but well after Merneptah. The date is therefore not far from 1200 B.C. Now when Ugarit and Alalakh were destroyed, Mycenaean IIIb pottery was still in full use. Consequently, Furumark's lower limit for Mycenaean IIIb has to be brought down from 1230 to 1200.[4]

At Hazor level XIV was probably destroyed by Sethos I in 1318, for that pharaoh is known to have campaigned in the vicinity of Hazor in his first year, and Hazor figures in his list of captured cities. As might be expected, the Mycenaean pottery of Hazor XIV is still Mycenaean IIIa.[5] In the next level, Hazor XIII, we have Mycenaean IIIb. Consequently, the city came to an end in the thirteenth century.

Of outstanding importance for the chronology of the period of the Judges is the fact that there is no subsequent Canaanite level in Hazor.[6] Hence the Canaanite kingdom of Hazor which

---

[1] See p. 216, n. 3 above.

[2] §II, 98, 6 ff.   [3] §II, 124, 169 ff.

[4] Without knowing of the documentary evidence from Ugarit, the author of §II, 167, 373 ff. argued for bringing the date of the end of Mycenaean IIIb down to 1194 B.C. See, however, below, p. 246 [Ed.].

[5] §II, 169, vol. 1, 4 and II, 159f. Reference there is to Levels 1b and 1a in the lower city. These correspond with Levels XIV and XIII respectively in the upper city; cf. §II, 168, 14f. The characteristic Mycenaean pottery of Level 1b is Mycenaean IIIa:2, that of 1a is Mycenaean IIIb; cf. §II, 18, 64; for 1a (= XIII) correspondences with other sites are: Lachish Fosse Temple III, Megiddo VIIb.

[6] It should be emphasized that the levels in question are still largely unpublished. Firmer conclusions must await full publication.

Baraq fought against should be the city of Hazor XIII. Now the war between Israel and Hazor in Baraq's time presupposes a period during which Egyptian control of Palestine had broken down. In the vicinity of the thirteenth century we probably have three such periods: (i) before Sethos I, (ii) between about 1250 and the eighth year of Ramesses III, though during part of this interval Merneptah probably re-established Egyptian control; (iii) after 1150. Here periods (i) and (iii) are excluded by the presence in Hazor XIII of Mycenaean IIIb. Hence Baraq is to be dated to the second half of the thirteenth century.

In the present writer's opinion it would be premature to attempt a date for the Exodus. More evidence is needed to indicate whether we have to reckon with one exodus or two.[1] Very tentatively, the chronological proportions of the problem can be summed up as follows.

If there was only one exodus, some three or four generations before the time of Baraq, then in view of the above date for Baraq, the background of the Exodus should be the Amarna Period, or the aftermath of that period. In that case the Conquest really gathered impetus only some two centuries later.

If the earlier movement out of Egypt at about the time of the Amarna Period was confined to 'Josephite' elements, the 'Levitic' exodus under Moses should be dated midway in the period of the Judges, with culmination at the time when Israel was fighting the Midianites.

III. THE AEGEAN BRONZE AGE

THE NATURE OF THE EVIDENCE

THOUGH the pioneer work of Schliemann established the general truth that the Greek heroic age was a historical reality, the task of making preciser identifications of this type fairly soon gave place, and rightly, to the absolute work of archaeology in building, by its own unaided means, a history of material culture in Greece. Such history is a tale of processes of development and interaction, with only occasionally the possibility of inferring with near certainty some actual *event*—invasion or the like—without which the material record would be inexplicable. It is indeed *pre*-history, since there are no contemporary records of particular happenings. Even the Late Bronze Age in this area can still only be called *proto*-historic; for though there are contemporary

[1] On this problem see §II, 117, 46 ff., criticized in §II, 115, 196 ff.

writings preserved from Greece and Crete, and some at least (those in Linear B script) can be read, these are not historical but domestic documents; and though it is generally agreed that Hittite records refer occasionally to the activities of Mycenaean Greeks, the precise identity of these particular Mycenaeans is barely settled as yet. Again, though it is now possible, with our fuller archaeological tale of the Late Bronze Age, to return to the story of events in Greek legend and collate the two, it is not to be supposed that they will fit each other like the halves of a tally. Both have their imperfections; both are likely by their nature to be in some parts (and we cannot often tell which) out of scale with themselves.

'Absolute' chronology can be achieved only in patches, and between these there is a regrettable though as yet inevitable elasticity in the scale. For most of the Bronze Age our dates are based, as will be shown, on cross-contacts with Egypt, where datable records go back so much further. In the upper reaches of Aegean prehistory there is also the method, which is likely to be used increasingly, the method of dating by radio-carbon isotopes,[1] whether the method be applied directly to finds from Aegean sites, or to those of adjacent areas with which finds in the Aegean may be correlated. The Greek legends are not wholly dateless, as preserved by later Greece; but there are discrepancies and variations, and some dates may be extrapolated by ancient writers rather than traditional. This evidence therefore must, in chronological discussion, be subordinated. It should not, however, be ignored. If the events related are historical at all (and some are of such a kind as could not be invented) their order of sequence at least is likely to be correct. The intervals between them, however, are not reliable. Often they are expressed only in terms of generations; and it seems probable that in many cases these have been telescoped. Most of the major events of the heroic period are assigned either to the generation of heroes that fought in the Trojan War, or to that of their fathers. If for 'fathers' we read 'forefathers' and for 'children' (especially in phrases like 'children of Heracles') we substitute 'descendants', the heroic tales begin to make sense in correlation with the Mycenaean period as a whole. As with most heroic legends, the Greek legends seem to refer to periods of disruption and resettlement; the earlier 'generation' are those who first established the Mycenaean states and then struggled one with another for supremacy; the latter 'generation' are those who engaged in the Trojan War and in the warlike

_____
[1] A, 14; A, 16, especially pp. 310–12.

events of the disturbed century that followed it. True, there were ancient attempts to give preciser dates to the events of legend; our most striking surviving example is the *Marmor Parium*, a long inscription of 264/3 B.C. which lists events, with their dates, back to the time of Cecrops King of Attica in 1582 B.C.[1] Others we know only at second hand through later writers, such as Eusebius or Clement of Alexandria, of the early centuries of the Christian era. All such attempts were themselves liable to some of the same hazards that beset our own.[2]

Our own chronological table exhibits the general scheme of sequence of periods and cultures now established for the principal areas of the Aegean world, and in relation to them a few events, recorded by history or tradition (these are noted in italics) or inferred from archaeology. The dates in figures are for the Late Bronze Age perhaps never more than a few decades out; but the margin of error increases rapidly before that period. The sequence, on the other hand, may be regarded as reliable, subject to the general caution that one should not automatically treat the name of a phase of culture as transferable to an absolute chronological period. In this second Elizabethan period there are still, perhaps, some areas, certainly individual homes, that preserve a Victorian material culture: this illustrates a truth perhaps more valid amid the slower communications of prehistoric times. Again, some cultural phases, as Middle Minoan II or Late Minoan II, may be represented in limited areas only. To add a further caution against reading the tripartite divisions of Early, Middle, and Late (or their tripartite subdivisions), as representing rise, peak, and decline, should for most readers be superfluous. Nor should it be necessary to state that the transition from, say, Early Minoan III to Middle Minoan I pottery style, is not the event of a particular year but a process of growth.

The development of pottery style is, indeed, the basis on which the sequence-chronology in this age and region is founded; for pottery is the most ubiquitous archaeological material, plentiful to a degree unimagined by those who have excavated prehistoric sites in Britain only, and fortunately providing valuable links with the cultures of adjacent regions, which in turn assist in the establishment of relative chronology. Of the three main culture-sequences with which we are concerned here, the Minoan was the first to be established, as a result of Sir Arthur Evans's excavations at Cnossus.[3] *Cnossian* might indeed have been a better name, inasmuch as the sequence does not apply equally to all Cretan

[1] §III, 14; §III, 9, 50ff.   [2] §III, 9, 2-4.   [3] §III, 8.

sites, and because the king or kings named Minos belonged (if historical) mainly to the *Late* Bronze Age. Moreover a geographical name (as *Helladic* and *Cycladic*) need not be associated, as *Minoan* has tended to be, with the concept of racial and cultural continuity from start to finish. The *Helladic* and *Cycladic* terminology, whose currency we owe principally to A. J. B. Wace and C. W. Blegen, avoid these disadvantages while recognizing a broad parallelism between the principal divisions of the Bronze Age in the three areas of the Aegean.[1] Apart from the important settlement at Phylakopi in Melos, too few sites in the islands have been excavated to permit a satisfactory subdivision of Early and Middle Cycladic. (Late Cycladic really falls, culturally, within the sphere first of Minoan and then of Mycenaean [Late Helladic III] civilization.) Nor are we much better off for Early and Middle Helladic, though three phases of Early Helladic were properly distinguishable at the site Eutresis, in Phocis, excavated by Miss H. Goldman in 1924–7. This site, together with that of Korakou near Corinth (excavated by Blegen in 1915–16), long since determined the outline sequence of the cultures now called Early and Middle Helladic; but much detail remains to be filled in. For Early Helladic much has already been done by J. L. Caskey's excavation of Lerna in the Argolid,[2] for Middle Helladic the possibilities are but foreshadowed by D. Theochares' trial trenches in the important well-stratified mound of Iolcus in Thessaly.

THE CHRONOLOGY OF THE PERIODS

Of Neolithic Greece much is already known from excavations both in Thessaly and Central Greece and in the Peloponnese; but the chronologies[3] of the northern and southern areas are still difficult to relate to each other, nor is there much evidence to tie the neolithic of Crete to that of the mainland. When these neolithic series began is even more doubtful: recent estimates, based on radio-carbon dating (where available) and possible correlations with Anatolia, suggest as early as the sixth (or for Crete the fifth) millennium B.C. For the beginning of the Bronze Age in the Aegean there is general agreement on a date somewhere early in the third millennium. The pottery of the various areas which is associated with the introduction of metal shows common factors which imply that a common origin for the new cultures of all three may be sought in Asia Minor, and that the beginnings of Early

---

[1] §III, 21, 186 ff.   [2] *C.A.H.* I³, ch. xxvi (*a*).
[3] §III, 22; §III, 23; A, 16, 291 ff.

Minoan, Early Cycladic, and Early Helladic cannot lie very far apart in time. We have placed Early Cycladic somewhat before the rest because the Early Cycladic tombs in Syra show affinities with the first settlement of Troy (already a metal-using community), and the tombs of Pelos in Melos may be earlier than this Syra group.[1] The beginning of the Aegean Bronze Age seems on general grounds likely to be somewhat later than that of Egypt; but the evidence of Proto-Dynastic Egyptian stone bowls at Cnossus, formerly used for absolute dating,[2] is now known to have been illusory or misleading, and clear evidence from the Egyptian side is hardly to be obtained at present.

For the second phase of E.M., however, we are on surer ground: here we have Minoan stone vases closely imitating Egyptian types of the IVth to VIth Dynasties; and in the subsequent E.M. III phase Minoan signets bear designs almost certainly influenced by those on Egyptian scarabs of the VIIth to Xth Dynasties. The marble female figurines so characteristic of Early Cycladic (but not easily given a precise place within that period) seem to be contemporary with E.M. III in Crete, where they are sometimes imported and imitated in other materials.

Middle Minoan shows more and preciser cross-contacts with Egypt. Scarabs of Dynasties XII to XIII (and also a Babylonian cylinder-seal of the time of Hammurabi) have been found associated with M.M. Ia pottery at Platanos in the Cretan Messara;[3] a XIIth Dynasty scarab at Psychro[4] had M.M. II hieroglyphs scratched upon it; a XIIIth Dynasty scarab was at Cnossus associated with early M.M. II pottery; and a fine M.M. II vase was found in a XIIth Dynasty tomb at Abydos in Egypt.[5] None of this gives precise absolute dates, nor are there yet any historical events known, to need dating; but the general coherence is comforting. In the second city of Phylakopi in Melos M.M. II pottery and Middle Helladic grey Minyan ware were associated,[6] thus enabling us to date the introduction of Minyan (at the beginning of Middle Helladic) very roughly to the nineteenth century B.C.; and by a further remove to date the changes at Troy that mark the establishment of the sixth city to about the same period.

The beginning of M.M. III is not closely definable, chronologically, but the new features of material culture that are characteristic of this 'new era' in Crete, with their suggestions of Near

[1] §III, 23, 94; A, 16, 301 f. [2] §III, 16, 21.
[3] §III, 16, 34 f.; §III, 20, 7 ff. [4] §III, 16, 12 f.
[5] §III, 8, 267 f. [6] §III, 21, 187.

Eastern origins, may not be unconnected with the widespread disturbances which in another direction resulted in the Hyksos conquest of Lower Egypt.[1] Certainly such Egyptian objects as turn
up within M.M. III in Crete belong to the Hyksos period.[2]
The expansion of Minoan influence in the Aegean islands at this
time makes it reasonable to seek at this still early date the historical counterpart of tradition's 'thalassocracy of Minos'; and by a
slight backward extension to recognize in the myth of Europa's
transit from Syria to Crete (where she became the mother of
Minos) a remote recollection of real Near Eastern origins for the
developments of M.M. III. If such an early origin for legend is
surprising, it need not therefore be considered untrue.

Many of the Minoan sites were abruptly destroyed in the
L.M. I b phase, a disaster which may very plausibly be associated
with the last stage of the great volcanic disruption of the island of
Thera (Santorin).[3] The first stage of this cataclysm in Thera itself
is dated archaeologically by L.M. I a pottery found beneath the
resultant volcanic deposits. The absolute dates, however, have
to be based (at some removes) on the Egyptian contacts of Crete.
We have a useful equation in the representation of foreign
envoys (probably Minoans) bearing recognizably Late Minoan I b
objects as gifts to the pharoah in tomb-paintings at Thebes
executed in the first half of the fifteenth century B.C.;[4] but by this
time L.M. I is well developed, and to date the *beginning* of Late
Minoan on the same chronological level as the beginning of the
Egyptian New Kingdom, after the expulsion of the Hyksos
(c. 1570) is merely a tidy approximation or conjecture.

Nevertheless it may be right. One of the most obvious features
of the Shaft Graves culture at Mycenae, which marks the transition from Middle to Late Helladic or Mycenaean civilization, is
a vigorous surge of Minoan influence in all decorative art, and it
is equally obvious that this inspiration comes from the products of
incipient L.M. I. Thus we can firmly date the beginnings of L.M. I
and L.H. I as contemporary. As will be argued in another chapter
there is a case for inferring the arrival in Greece at this time of new
rulers from abroad, such as are indeed ascribed by legend to the
beginnings of the first heroic age. Some of these immigrant founder
heroes are of origins too improbable to be fictitious—Danaus, for
example, from Egypt; Cadmus from Syria. The only probable
juncture for such immigration which can be recognized in the
archaeological record is at the transition from M.H. to L.H.;

---

[1] §III, 8, 300, 315 f.   [2] E.g. §III, 16, 22, no. 30.
[3] A, 14, 2.   [4] §III, 11, 223 ff.

while in terms of external history no time is so likely as the period of the expulsion of the Hyksos overlords from Egypt.[1] It seems more than fortuitous coincidence that the heroic era of Athens, according to the *Marmor Parium*, begins at 1582 B.C., and that Danaus is in that document placed at least in the same century. Several, consequently, of the principal legends of the earlier heroic age may be set in relation to the archaeological history as events of the period of settlement in Greece after the first immigrations, a period of internal conflict leading ultimately to the supremacy of Mycenae.

Late Helladic II and the Late Minoan II of Cnossus represent the closest assimilation of the civilization of the two areas, to be followed by a new divergence as the mainland takes the lead (in L.H. III) after the destruction of the Cnossus palace at the end of L.M. II. The dating of this cardinal event in Aegean history about 1400 B.C. is again only approximate. The latest datable Egyptian object in Crete in a context before the destruction is a seal of Queen Tiy (consort of Amenophis III, who reigned 1417–1379 B.C.) from a chamber tomb at Hagia Triada. The earliest Egyptian cross-link *after* the destruction is a scarab of the same queen found at Mycenae with Late Helladic III pottery.[2] Our date can hardly, therefore, be more than a quarter century wrong, but until new and preciser evidence comes to light it seems idle to try to adjust the '*c.* 1400' figure by the odd decade.

Late Helladic III, which occupies the rest of the Bronze Age, is subdivided on the usual basis of the typology of the pottery, which for this era is an even better guide than usual. The importation of L.H. IIIa pots to the short-lived city of Akhenaten (El-Amarna)—1379 to 1362 B.C.—provides a valued fixed point, but dates neither the bounds of our L.H. IIIa phase nor any known events within it. That early IIIa pottery belongs to the first quarter of the fourteenth century is confirmed by its occurrence at Qatna on the upper Orontes before that site was destroyed by the Hittites *c.* 1375 B.C. For the transition from IIIa to IIIb the finds of Mycenaean pottery of this phase at Ghurāb in the Faiyūm are helpful: the associated Egyptian objects show that they cannot be much earlier than the accession of Ramesses II (1304 B.C.).[3]

The transition from Mycenaean IIIb to IIIc is more difficult to date. The figure of 1230 B.C. which has become current was first proposed by Furumark,[4] partly on the admittedly negative argument that no IIIb pottery had been found with dated objects

[1] §III, 3.   [2] §III, 16, 9, 55.
[3] §III, 17 and §III, 10.   [4] §III, 10, 114 and 118 ff. See above, p. 238 [Ed.].

later than the reign of Ramesses II (for whose death the date of 1232 B.C. was then accepted), and partly on the evidence of the pottery (a derivative of developed Mycenaean IIIc) characteristic of the Philistines, an important group of the 'Peoples of the Sea' who were originally settled in South Palestine shortly after their defeat by Ramesses III about 1191 B.C. If this ware really belongs to the earliest years of their settlements the implication is that Mycenaean IIIc style was already developed by the 1180's. But IIIb pottery was current, as an imported ware, at Tell Abu Hawwām (on the Bay of Acre) and at Alalakh and Ugarit in Syria[1] down to the destruction of these sites, which is attributed to the raids of the 'Sea Peoples' at the date already mentioned, about 1191. If this attribution is correct, the IIIc phase cannot have begun before the 1180's; and this is the view accepted for the purposes of the synchronistic table.

THE DATE OF THE FALL OF TROY

The dating of the transition from Mycenaean IIIb to IIIc is indeed a matter of great consequence, for it is developed Mycenaean IIIb pottery which 'dates' the sack of Troy VIIa as well as the destruction of a number of Mycenaean sites in the Peloponnese, including the palace of Pylus and the extra-mural buildings of Mycenae itself.

The destruction of Troy VIIa cannot but be identified with the 'Homeric' sack of Troy, about the date of which Greek tradition was more unanimous than at first appears. It can be shown[2] that the Fall of Troy was normally reckoned as having happened eighty years or two generations before the Return of the Heraclidae (the descendants of the Mycenaean dynasty which had been ousted by the Pelopids). The Return itself was dated, again in terms of generations, by the pedigree of the Spartan kings which could be traced back to it. Discrepancies arose, however, in the reckoning of the standard 'generation' and in the correlation of the Spartan pedigree with later eras, such as that of the Olympiads. Hence the dates for the Fall[3] vary from 1270 to 1135, with the mean at 1203 (*Marmor Parium* 1209). That which has been most generally accepted is 1183 B.C., the date established by the Alexandrian scholar Eratosthenes late in the third century B.C.; and the archaeological evidence now available seems fairly

---

[1] Cf. p. 237 f.   [2] §III, 9, 2, 4.
[3] §III, 5; §III, 7; §III, 13; §III, 12; §III, 6 *passim*, e.g. Bk. I, 5, Bk. XIII, I, 2, Bk. XIV, 2, 4.

compatible with such a figure. The most likely explanation of the late Mycenaean III b destructions at sites in the Peloponnese is that they are due to the southward incursions of the Dorian Greeks associated by tradition with the Return.[1] That the attackers came from the north or centre of Greece has recently been rendered more probable by the discovery that a fortification wall was constructed at the Isthmus of Corinth at this very time (towards the end of Mycenaean III b). This identification may at first seem to date the Return somewhere about 1180, and only a few years instead of two generations after the Fall of Troy. But the true explanation may well be that the Dorian invasion covered a long period; one tradition does indeed speak of an attempted Return,[2] defeated at the Isthmus, fifty or a hundred years before the final resettlement,[3] another tells of an oracle that bade the Heraclids await the third generation before renewing their attempt.[4] Whatever the uncertainty of detail, we cannot escape the main fact: the destruction at the Peloponnesian sites attested by archaeology marks for Bronze Age Greece the beginning of the end.

[1] §III, 15, Bk. III, i, 5, Bk. IV, iii, 3.   [2] §III, 15, Bk. I, xli, 3.
[3] §III, 6, Bk. IV, 58.   [4] §III, I.

CHAPTER VII(a)

THE EARLIEST SETTLEMENTS IN WESTERN ASIA

FROM THE NINTH TO THE END OF THE FIFTH MILLENNIUM B.C.

I. GEOGRAPHY, TERMINOLOGY AND CHRONOLOGY

THE scene of man's first emergence as a food-producer as opposed to the countless millennia of his existence as a food-gatherer during the Palaeolithic period, an event frequently alluded to as the 'neolithic revolution', was that part of south-west Asia which is usually described as the Near East, or in the terminology of some the Near and Middle East.

Even before the last glaciers had retreated from northern Europe, man in south-west Asia had embarked on a momentous course which was to lead slowly but inexorably to the development of civilization, a higher and more efficient form of living than had been practised during the long aeons of the Palaeolithic period. These changes towards the domestication of animals and plants, the conservation and eventually the production of food no doubt came slowly. They were not accomplished over-night, or due to a sudden discovery or the arrival of new ethnic elements bringing a higher culture from 'elsewhere'. On the contrary, they were the culmination of a process that had started long ago, we assume, with the appearance of modern man, *Homo sapiens*, at the beginning of the Upper Palaeolithic. Improved technical skills in the production of tools and weapons with which to catch and kill his quarry, the manufacture of clothing, nets and matting, the construction of tents and huts, a greater cohesion of hunting groups and the first rise of semi-permanent hunting-camps, all marked important steps forward, well in advance of his predecessor, Neanderthal man. In no single field were the changes more marked than in the field of religion; slowly art developed, first sculpture in the form of statuettes of a goddess of fecundity, next the arts of engraving and painting, to culminate in the unsurpassed cave paintings of

[248]

such sites as Lascaux, Altamira, Font de Gaume, Niaux, Pech Merle and a host of others. Upper Palaeolithic man in the later stages of the Ice Age is emerging as an individual, deeply religious, a craftsman and artist of no mean order, and a most successful hunter, but bound by his environment and utterly dependent on the food supplies available. Our knowledge of Upper Palaeolithic man is to a great extent derived from western Europe, where he left the most complete record, including the great cave sanctuaries of France and northern Spain, but there is a steadily increasing recognition that elsewhere also, as in Italy and Czechoslovakia, south Russia, the Urals and even Anatolia,[1] similar and artistically gifted hunting tribes were established. In the Near East, in general, the remains left by Upper Palaeolithic man are more modest, but it was here towards the end of the Glacial Period that he would take the next steps forward under the more favourable conditions which then prevailed.

As early as 9000 B.C. we find him established in open settlements, some seasonal, others perhaps already permanent, in round or oval huts with simple stone foundations. Zawi Chemi–Shanidar on the Great Zab river in north Iraq, 'Eynān ('Ain Mallaḥa) near the shores of Lake Ḥūleh in Israel, Jericho, and Beidha near Petra in Jordan are the best examples of such open settlements. Hunting was still the main occupation, but at Zawi Chemi there is abundant evidence for domestic sheep, the first animal to be domesticated.[2] Domestication of animals must have begun during the tenth millennium B.C., but the domestication of plants seems to have started somewhat later. Carbonized remains of domestic plants have not yet been found in any deposit of the ninth or eighth millennium B.C., but are firmly established by 7000 B.C. in three main areas of the Near East: at Hacılar in western Anatolia, at Beidha in Jordan, and at Ali-Kush in Khūzistān (Susiana).[3] By this period a certain standardization in crops grown in each of these areas is notable and evidently the result of previous experimenting over an unknown period of time. From about 9000 B.C. onwards there are a number of indications of the importance attached to vegetable food;[4] saddle querns and grinding stones unknown before, sickle blades with or without silica sheen, and storage pits all suggest the reaping and preparation of certain new foods, such as cereals (wheat and barley) or legumes (peas, lentils or bitter vetch). In

[1] §I, 1, 78 f.   [2] §II, 3, 410.
[3] Information received from Dr H. Helbaek.
[4] §II, 5, 5,

the early stage these plants need not have been domesticated, or sown, and they could have been used in their wild form, but as time went on they were gradually selected, domesticated and sown, developing larger grain sizes and thus providing more and more food. With the domestication of grain, 'man's most precious artefact', a steady supply of food was assured, and bread (and beer) have dominated man's rise as a civilized human being ever since. It assured adequate food supplies, for the yield of the wheat (and barley) fields was enormous; populations could expand and, as grain could be stored, the surplus of food relieved part of the population to engage in pursuits other than food production. With the specialization of labour, part- or even full-time specialists arose, engaged in arts and crafts, trade, government and religion. Thus were laid the bases of civilized societies which were to develop into villages and towns, city states, kingdoms, and finally empires.

The domestication of crops and animals, then, was to have unforeseen results, but why was this development confined to Near Eastern societies? The answer is an obvious one: only in the Near East do we find that combination of domesticable animals[1] such as sheep, goat, cattle and pig with the wild ancestors of wheat and barley, bitter vetch, peas and lentils upon which the 'neolithic revolution' was based. Only in the natural habitat of these particular plants and animals was this accomplished, and it is therefore possible to define the limits fairly closely. In Egypt, for example, the wild ancestors of sheep and goat are not found, nor those of wheat and barley, which are medium-altitude plants (800–1000 m. above sea level), but cattle and pig were common, as in Europe and North Africa. These areas all fall outside the central area where the 'neolithic revolution' was accomplished. The same applies to the deserts of Syria and Arabia, the Mediterranean littoral, the alluvial plains of Mesopotamia and the jungles of the eastern Black Sea and the Caspian. The area can be narrowed down considerably by observing the habitat of the wild progenitors of the cereal grasses, wheat and barley, which ranged, respectively, from the Anatolian plateau to the deserts of central Asia and from the Caucasus range to the uplands of Palestine.

In this vast area we now can recognize three or perhaps four primary centres where the domestication of plants and animals was accomplished in the first few millennia after the Glacial period: Palestine and Lebanon (?), the Zagros mountain zone of Iraq and Iran, with a possible extension up to Transcaucasia, the

[1] §1, 3, 31 ff.

south Anatolian plateau, and perhaps the eastern Elburz (Kopet Dağ) and the northern slopes of the Hindu Kush mountains.[1] In short, the highland zones of the Near (and Middle) East turn out to be the areas in which these earliest developments occurred, and those in the lowland plains date from later periods, thus reversing the old theories that Mesopotamia and Egypt were the birthplaces of civilization. Developments in Europe likewise are purely secondary, even if they clearly precede similar patterns of development in Egypt, as radiocarbon dates have now conclusively shown for Bulgaria and Greece.

Now that series of radiocarbon dates, or determinations as the sceptics prefer to call them, are offering us a coherent pattern of absolute chronology, it seems advisable to drop and eliminate the century-old traditional system of terminology, devised for Western Europe, the usefulness of which has not stood the test of recent Near Eastern research. If we then discard the traditional sequence of Mesolithic, Neolithic and Bronze Age, which in the Near East had to be enlarged and modified into Mesolithic, Proto-neolithic, Pre-pottery neolithic, Pottery-neolithic, Chalcolithic and Bronze Age, each with various subdivisions, we see no reason either to adopt an equally cumbersome and no less theoretic scheme devised by Braidwood on the basis of supposedly successive economic patterns which recent excavations have shown to be equally unacceptable.

For the purpose of correlation with earlier literature[2] the following table may be useful; it illustrates the confusion in which Near Eastern terminology has been trapped. The terms in use for one country rarely correspond with those among its neighbours. In fact, they have lost all meaning. Early chalcolithic, for example, in Anatolia no longer means that copper was then first used beside stone, but really indicates the period in which painted pottery was first widely used!

10th millennium	Mesolithic or Final Palaeolithic. Zarzian, Kebaran, Belbaşı cultures.
9th and 8th millennia	Proto-neolithic or Mesolithic cultures. Karīm Shahr, Shanidar, Natufian and Beldibi cultures.
8th millennium	
In Palestine	Pre-pottery neolithic A.
In Anatolia	Aceramic Hacılar.
7th millennium	Palestinian Pre-pottery neolithic B, Pre-pottery Jarmo, and Pottery or early neolithic Çatal Hüyük.
6th millennium	Early neolithic Byblos, neolithic Hassūnah, Pottery-neolithic Jarmo, Late neolithic Hacılar and, after 5600 B.C., Early chalcolithic Hassūnah, Hacılar, Mersin, 'Amūq B, etc.

[1] §x, 2, 3.   [2] §1, 1, *passim*.

5th millennium	Middle chalcolithic Halaf, Mersin, 'Amūq C, Can Hasan, but Late chalcolithic Beycesultan and Pottery-neolithic Palestine.
4th millennium	Late chalcolithic 'Ubaid and Uruk, Late chalcolithic Anatolia, but chalcolithic Ghassulian, etc., in Palestine.

Instead, therefore, of using such terms as mesolithic, neolithic, chalcolithic, etc., we shall try to use names of cultures or significant building levels of key sites, but it must be pointed out that consistent use of this principle cannot always be maintained.

The carbon-14 dates used in this chapter are those calculated with the higher half-life of 5730 years, which is now considered to be the more accurate one. In the Near East most scholars are now using these higher dates, even if by convention the radiocarbon laboratories continue to publish their dates with the lower half-life. Whereas in prehistory it matters very little whether a settlement was built or destroyed c. 6800 rather than c. 7000 B.C., the higher dates have the advantage of agreeing more closely with dates calculated from the king-lists in Egypt or Mesopotamia during the historical period.

The present chapter, then, deals with the prehistoric cultures of the Near East from Syria and Lebanon and Anatolia in the west to southern Turkestan in the east during the period which spans the millennia between the end of the Ice Age in Europe and the beginning of the 'Ubaid period in Mesopotamia. In absolute chronology this is a period from c. 10,000 to 4300 B.C. Research in the various regions is necessarily unequal: many new finds here included are known only from preliminary reports or notices, and the present chapter is therefore a sort of interim report, liable to change in the next few years. In archaeology this cannot be avoided, and nothing is final, and it is as well to remember that the little we know about these early developments in the Near East is nothing in comparison with what remains to be learned.

Finally, it may not be superfluous to sound a note of caution. The archaeology of the Near East is in a state of constant flux; every year new discoveries are made that may disprove long-cherished theories or suggest important modifications. A generalized picture such as is presented here is, even with the best of intentions, a subjective one, for the days are gone when a single archaeologist could hope to be familiar with all the material from Anatolia to Central Asia. In the related field of history, it has recently been suggested that it is a good thing if a scholar sometimes devotes himself to a similar study in which he is not a specialist, for, unaware of the minutiae, he is able to generalize

Table 6. Prehistoric cultures of the Near East from c. 10,000 to 4300 B.C.

Approximate dates	S. Anatolia	Palestine	Byblos	Tell Ramad	Ras Shamra	'Amuq	N. Mesopotamian plain	N. Zagros	S. Mesopotamian plain	S. Zagros	Iranian plateau	Hisar	Anau region	Tejen Oasis	N. Afghanistan and Oxiana
4300	Mersin XV	Yarmukian etc. Pottery in Palestine	L. Neolithic	IIIc	IIIb	F	N. Iraq	'Ubaid	South Iraq 'Ubaid Susiana C ←	Giyán Vc	Pisdeli / Sialk III,4	Hisar Ic	Namazga III	Göksür I	Kelteminar culture (Anal-Bokhara) ←
4500	XVI		M. Neolithic	III A–B	IIIc	E	Halaf	?	Susiana B Hajji Muhammad	Giyán VB	Dalme / Sialk III,3	Hisar IB ←	Namazga II (late)	Göksür I ←	
5000	XVII–XIX	Hiatus — Nomadism	Early Neolithic	II	IVa / IVb / c	D / C	Samarra; Hassuna V IV III II Ic Ib Ia	Samarrā; Aceramic Shemshara; Lower Matarrah	Susiana A and Eridu	Giyán VA	Sialk III,2 / III,1	Hisar IA	Namazga II (early)	Yalangach	Snake Cave and Pottery
5700	Çatal Hüyük West and Can Hasan IX–I			I	VA	B	Tell es-Sawwān	Jarmo 1–5	← Tepe Sabz → ; Muḥ. Jaʿfar	T. Gūrān S–D / T. Sarāb; Yanik Tepe (lowest)	Hajji Firūz; Sialk II		Namazga I / Anau Ib	Dashliji	Snake Cave Aceramic
6000	Çatal Hüyük East	Pre-pottery Neolith. B			VB / VC	A / ?		Jarmo (lower)	Ali-Kush	T. Gūrān V–T	Sialk I		Anau IA		?
7000	Aceramic Hacilar	Pre-pottery Neolith. A						M'lefaat Karim Shahr → ?	Bus Mordeh				Jeitun		
8000 / 8300		Natufian						Zawi Chemi Shanidar					?		
9500?		Kebaran						Zarzian					Caspian, etc. Caves 'Late Mesolithic'		Snake Cave 'Mesolithic' ←

Earlier Mesolithic (South Turkestan / Tejen Oasis, lower right).

where no specialist would tread and thus offer new views and ideas, not necessarily correct but, it is hoped, stimulating to further research.

II. THE ZAGROS ZONE OF NORTHERN IRAQ

Whereas prehistoric research in Iraq had been conducted almost entirely in the plains up to the end of the Second World War, the last two decades have marked the beginning of systematic exploration and excavation in the foothills of the Zagros range of mountains which form the border between Iran and Iraq. In a series of expeditions under the auspices of the Oriental Institute of Chicago, R. J. Braidwood, L. S. Braidwood, and B. Howe led a team of archaeologists brought together for the first time with natural scientists in order to investigate the change from food-gathering to food-production in Iraqi Kurdistān. An unsuspectedly long and interesting series of early cultures was found, from the Upper Palaeolithic to the Hassūnah period of the sixth millennium. Independently, R. S. Solecki and R. L. Solecki explored the Upper Zab river just south of the Turkish frontier and carefully investigated the now famous cave of Shanidar near Barzan and discovered at Zawi Chemi–Shanidar the earliest post-Pleistocene village site known in Iraq. Danish expeditions, led by H. Ingholt, excavated the early site of Tell Shemshāra near the Dokan dam.

After the Iraqi revolution, Americans and Danes continued their explorations in Iranian Kurdistān, the former working in the plain of Kirmānshāh, the latter in Northern Luristān (Tepe Gūrān). In the last few years another American expedition from Rice University, led by F. Hole, continued this pattern with a highly successful investigation of the Deh Luran district in the foothills of Khūzistān (Iran) to the south; and in collaboration with Istanbul University the Chicago party have moved north to south-eastern Turkey, east of the Euphrates, a territory more closely linked to Iraq and Syria than to the Anatolian plateau above.

Zawi Chemi, Shanidar, Karīm Shahr, M'lefaat and Gird Chāi. Zawi Chemi, the earliest open village site yet found in north Iraq, lies about a hundred yards from the river in the mountain valley of the Great Zab at an altitude of 425 m.[1] The surrounding mountains rise to a height of 1800 m. The site itself extends 275 × 215 m. and the early deposits are 1–2 m. deep with large

[1] §II, 5, fig. 2; §II, 3, 405.

refuse pits at the bottom cut into the natural soil. Remains of rough walling indicate circular huts with diameter of *c*. 4 m., twice rebuilt. The walls are built of river boulders, whole or broken artefacts such as querns, grinding stones, mortars, etc. Fireplaces or other domestic arrangements have not been detected and the architecture is primitive. There is good evidence to suggest that the site was occupied for a long time, and changes are found to occur throughout the deposit, at least in the tool kit. Hunting was still the most important occupation, as is shown by the enormous deposits of bones;[1] in the lowest level Red Deer was the main quarry but there was also sheep. In the upper levels a domesticated sheep is found and wild goat was hunted. The sudden appearance of numbers of tools used in the preparation of plant food, such as U-shaped querns with mullers, V-shaped quern-mortars, bone sickle-hafts[2] (but no blades with a gloss along the edge), is significant. In the absence of any carbonized grains it is, however, impossible to say whether wild cereals were reaped, or other foods such as acorns, abundant in the area and still a source of food. Snails also seem to have formed part of the diet. Zawi Chemi was not yet an established agricultural village, but the preparation of vegetable food and the early appearance of domesticated sheep foreshadow the great economic revolution which was to come. A radiocarbon date of 9217 ± 300 from the lowest level of the village and another of 8935 ± 300[3] from the contemporary B 1 layer of the cave of Shanidar, 4 km. away, place this culture roughly in the late tenth and early ninth millennia, approximately contemporary with the Natufian culture of Palestine.

The industries of Zawi Chemi (and Shanidar B 1) are a mixture of old and new techniques. The chipped flint industry (obsidian, imported from the Lake Vān area, is rare) is impoverished and probably derived from the Zarzian industry of Shanidar B 2.[4] Artefacts are rare; microliths such as backed blades and lunates are characteristic, but not dominant.[5] Among the larger tools are notched and serrated implements: borers, side scrapers, knives, angle-burins and crude core scrapers. New are the ground and pecked stone tools: querns, mortars, mullers, pounders, pestles, balls, hammer-stones, polishing stones, grooved steatite pieces, sometimes with incised decoration. Chipped celts with polished bits occur only at the end of the occupation of the site. Pottery, figurines or any objects made of clay are still unknown,

[1] §11, 3, 409 f.   [2] §11, 3, pl. 1.   [3] §11, 3, 405, 410.
[4] §11, 3, 411.   [5] §11, 5, fig. 8.

nor are there any spindle-whorls or loom-weights. Fragments of mats and baskets have been found. Bone tools are abundant: awls, flakers, chisels, knife- and sickle-handles in which blades were inserted and fixed with bitumen. Many of the bone tools bear geometric or even a few naturalistic ornaments. Luxury objects occur in small numbers, such as beads of bone, animal teeth, steatite, greenstone, native copper, limestone, marble (?), and small slate pendants bearing incised designs.[1]

Shanidar Cave may represent the winter quarters of the seasonal community which spent the summer at Zawi Chemi, and it has also yielded a cemetery of this period with burials of twenty-six individuals, mainly infants and children.[2] A flexed burial of a young woman was accompanied by red ochre, a grinding-stone and a necklace of small beads; another burial was accompanied by a knife of flint, set in bitumen in a long handle made from a rib bone.[3] Several small platforms of rough stones were found with the burials; one of them, arc-shaped, resembles the stone enclosure at Zawi Chemi. These alignments are suggestive of a funeral cult.

A few articles found in the settlement and cave suggest trade: obsidian from the Lake Vān area, bitumen from Kirkuk, native copper, perhaps from Ergani Maden north of Diyārbakr, where recent excavations at Çayönütepesi[4] have revealed another pre-pottery village site. In an upper level houses were found with stone foundations, partly equipped with buttresses and orthostats. In a lower level were remains of parallel lines of stone and mud walls. Flint and obsidian tools, as well as ground stone objects, were found, and with them fragments and beads of malachite, as well as drills or pins (?) of native copper, perhaps used as stone before the advent of pyrotechny. No dates are yet available for this early village.

Unlike Palestine, where numerous Natufian sites are overlaid by deposits of successive cultures which enable one to trace subsequent developments, as at Jericho or Beidha, there is as yet no single site in Iraq where a sequence from Zawi Chemi to Jarmo has been found. The sites of Karīm Shahr (north of Chamchamāl), M'lefaat and Gird Chāi (on the lower reaches of the Great Zab) might supply a typological link, but the series may well be incomplete. Unless the development in the southern Zagros is derivative and therefore somewhat later in date, which is by no means apparent, the similarities between the Bus Mordeh

---

[1] §II, 5, fig. 7.

[2] §II, 4, 417; §II, 5, figs. 5, 6.

[3] §II, 5, fig. 17.

[4] §II, 2, 138.

phase, dated to about 7000–6500,[1] and Karīm Shahr do not support a date for the latter culture contemporary with Zawi Chemi. On the contrary, Karīm Shahr may be considerably later, and nearer in time to Jarmo. Typologically M'lefaat is placed between Karīm Shahr and Jarmo by Braidwood, but he also places Karīm Shahr in the Zawi Chemi period, which seems too early. Even by stretching the radiocarbon dates there is a long period to fill between the end of Zawi Chemi (at latest *c.* 8500 B.C.) and the beginning of Jarmo (at the earliest *c.* 7000–6750 B.C.) and the published evidence is by no means conclusive to fill this gap.

Karīm Shahr[2] is a hilltop site with no traces of any continued occupation, and like Zawi Chemi it may be a seasonal site. A random scatter of pebbles may represent a denuded house-floor(?) or remains of inconsequential huts. Domestic animals or plant cultivation have not been reported, but there is apparently an increase in the numbers of such animals as later became domesticated, hence a selection of quarry, which may be significant. Unlike Zawi Chemi, Karīm Shahr produced some blades with sickle sheen, implying the reaping of probably wild cereals, but ground stone tools are less in evidence than at Zawi Chemi.[3] A greater emphasis is placed here on chipped tools; but here also artefacts are rare in comparison with the number of retouched pieces and waste flakes. Notched and serrated pieces are the most common types; microliths occur, but lunates are missing. The Karīm Shahr flints are better made. Stone rings and bracelets and two lightly baked clay figurines are innovations; beads and pendants continue as before.

The site of M'lefaat,[4] which may be of the late Karīm Shahr period, shows rough circular stone walls and a preponderance of ground and pecked stone tools over chipped ones. M'lefaat is said to be a mound with several occupation levels and the same animals are present as at Karīm Shahr. Gird Chāi[5] has a flint industry close to that of Karīm Shahr and M'lefaat and there is some obsidian. No further details are yet available. It is evident that more research is required to elucidate developments in north Iraq for the period between Zawi Chemi and Jarmo.

Jarmo, an agricultural village. On the edge of a deep wadi in the plain of Chamchamāl lies the now famous site of Qal'at Jarmo,[6] covering about 3–4 acres, which is small compared

[1] §III, 3, 106. [2] §II, 1, 52, 170, pls. 22 f. [3] §II, 3, 410; §I, 1, fig. 4.
[4] §II, 1, 50. [5] §II, 1, 55 [6] §II, 1, 38 ff., 170 f., pls. 14 ff.

with the 10 acres of Jericho or the 32 acres of Çatal Hüyük, its contemporaries. It probably contained not more than twenty to twenty-five houses with an estimated population of about one hundred and fifty souls. Sixteen superimposed floor-levels have been established, of which only the top five were characterized by pottery. Braidwood would allow about four hundred years for the entire sequence, which seems too short a span of time and clashes with his own chronology, which places the *floruit* of the site *c.* 6750 B.C. on the basis of a cluster of radiocarbon dates.[1] Jarmo represents something new in the prehistory of Iraq: a fully sedentary agricultural village growing (and not merely reaping) Emmer wheat, still morphologically close to the wild form, but already accompanied by Einkorn wheat, as well as hulled two-row barley (also close to the wild ancestor) at a date *c.* 6500 B.C. Lentils, field peas, blue vetchling were also grown and pistachios and acorns were still collected for their fat contents.[2] Among the animals, goat and dog (?) and perhaps pig were domesticated, but not sheep, or cattle, which were hunted together with gazelle and wild boar. Snails still formed part of the diet.[3]

These early farmers lived no longer in round huts, but had learned to build houses of rectangular plan,[4] made of irregular slabs of mud (locally known as *tauf*), but only in the latest levels set on stone foundations. The walls were plastered but not painted. The floors were likewise plastered over a basis of reeds. Reeds also served as roof cover, supported by beams and covered with a thick coating of mud. Sunk, clay-lined basins served as hearths and only in the later houses were ovens with chimneys found[5] (as at Tepe Gūrān in Iran). The rooms were small, 5–6 ft. in length, but each house consisted of a number of rooms. These houses marked a great advance over the earlier round huts and the change from circular to rectangular buildings during the seventh millennium is paralleled in Palestine.

The chipped stone industry, mainly in flint, but with a significant addition of imported East Anatolian obsidian (used mainly for microliths such as diagonally ended bladelets, triangles, trapezoids, crescents, etc.), is essentially a blade industry. Knives and sickle blades predominate and these were fixed with bitumen in wooden handles.[6] Some of the microlithic points may have served as arrowheads. Great advances were made in the ground stone industry, which now no longer produced only the articles

[1] §II, 1, 68 f.

[2] §II, 1, 99 ff, pls. 27 f.

[3] §II, 1, 170 f.

[4] §II, 1, pl. 14A.

[5] §II, 1, pl. 14B.

[6] §II, 1, pl. 17 ff.

needed for the preparation of plant food (such as grinding stones, etc.), but tools for carpentry, such as polished axes and adzes, and also door-pivots, palettes for ochre-grinding, perforated maceheads and finely ground stone bowls, beads, rings, bracelets and other items of jewellery.[1] Bone tools continued without much change; also spatulae, awls, rings, beads and pendants. New also are the first well-modelled and sun-dried or lightly baked figurines of Mother Goddess type, or portraying animals, often with marked naturalism.[2] Children's toys such as small marbles and cones were made of the same material, but pottery was not yet fashioned.

Ceramic Jarmo and Iranian relations. When pottery finally appears at Jarmo, in the top five levels, there are two successive groups, of which the earlier (levels 4–5) is the better made. This earliest pottery is painted in red on an orange-buff or reddish surface with oblique blobbed lines and is known as 'Jarmo painted ware'.[3] It appears without prototypes and was probably imported from further east, where e.g. at Tepe Gūrān it appears from level P-H, coming to an end *c.* 6000 B.C.[4] There it preceded the Tepe Sarāb ware, which is a development of it, but both wares continue to exist side by side. Braidwood considered that Tepe Sarāb represented a more advanced culture than (aceramic) Jarmo. Tepe Gūrān confirms it. Among the various wares that follow in Tepe Gūrān G–D is a red burnished ware that may be related to the crude and probably locally made pottery of the uppermost three levels of Jarmo,[5] at Ali Āghā and perhaps a little later in the bottom layers (1 a) of Hassūnah near Mosul. The Tepe Gūrān sequence then suggests that 6000 is the rough dividing point of the two ceramics at Jarmo, where the first pottery may have been introduced *c.* 6100 B.C. Aceramic Jarmo therefore ends at this date and with its eleven building levels its beginning may reach Braidwood's date of 6750 B.C. The end of Jarmo would then fall fairly soon after 6000, in any case before the beginning of the following Hassūnah culture *c.* 5800 B.C., when for the first time early farmers established permanent settlements in the alluvial plain of Mesopotamia. Some previous attempts to settle, as at Ali-Kush in Khūzistān or at Buqras on the Syrian Euphrates, settlements which were afterwards abandoned when agriculture failed, will be described below.

[1] §II, I. pl. 21. [2] §II, I, pl. 16.
[3] §II, I, 43 f., 63 f., pl. 15, 12 ff.
[4] §III, 4, 120. [5] §II, I, 43 f.

III. THE ZAGROS ZONE OF SOUTHERN IRAN

Before we can turn our attention to the rise of the first agricultural communities in the alluvial lowlands, developments in
the southern (and Iranian) part of the Zagros zone must claim
our attention, for it is not only in the north, in what was later to
become Assyria, but also in the south, the future states of Sumer
and Elam, that farmers would set out to exploit a new environment soon after the beginning of the sixth millennium B.C.

Ali-Kush. The mound of Ali-Kush, also known as Bus Mordeh,
is circular in size, with a diameter of 175 m., rising 4 m. above
the level of the steppe-like plain, a natural winter grassland.
Though situated only 650 ft. above sea level, it is overshadowed
by the Iranian plateau to the north and east rising to a height of
2700 m. and near enough to it to have an annual rainfall of
12 inches, enough for dry farming.[1] The site seems to have been
chosen *c.* 7000 B.C. by goat herders taking advantage of the
winter pastures. These intensively collected the seeds of wild
legumes and started to grow domestic Emmer wheat and two-
row barley in small amounts, grains introduced from the Zagros
mountains to the north-east.[2] Hunting still played an important
role in their economy; gazelle, onager, wild cattle and boar
were the principal quarry. Carp and catfish, turtles and clams
added to the diet. In this early 'Bus Mordeh phase' (*c.* 7000–6500
B.C.) the houses of the village were built of slabs of clay, apparently
unplastered. On the floors of these pit-houses (circular in shape?)
were found hearths and heaps of compost and a few flat-topped
and saddle-shaped querns. Crude unbaked clay figurines were
made, but pottery was yet unknown. Great quantities of chipped
flint tools, including many fine end scrapers, poorly made cores
and a few sickle blades, resemble those of the site of Karīm
Shahr in north Iraq.

The next period on this site, known as the 'Ali-Kush phase'
(*c.* 6500–6000 B.C.), saw a steady cultural advance. The domestication of the goat, and perhaps also of sheep, has been accomplished, and more intensive hunting of wild cattle and onager with
wooden or bone-tipped spears is accompanied by a development
of specialized butchering tools. Important advances are made in
agriculture: instead of a preponderance of legumes, Emmer and
some Einkorn, hulled and naked barley, are now grown, amounting to 40 per cent of domesticated plants.

The houses are better built in large mud-bricks and the walls

---

[1] §III, 3, 105 f.; §II, 297 ff.　　　[2] §III, 3, 106.

are now plastered on the inside. Burials are found below the floors; corpses are buried in seated position and accompanied by turquoise, stone and shell ornaments. The skulls show cranial deformation. Technological improvements are characteristic of this phase; there is a marked increase in grinding stones parallel with the increased importance of cereal foods. Flint is still the main material for the manufacture of tools and weapons, but imported obsidian is now found. Crescents or microliths are absent, and there is no evidence for the use of bow and arrow. The stone industry resembles that of aceramic Jarmo. New is the use of hammered native copper, which must have come from the Iranian plateau. Weaving is attested in the form of twilled mats and twined basketry. Pottery is still unknown, and does not appear until the 'Muḥammad Jaʿfar phase' (c. 6000–5700 B.C.), the last represented on this site. In this phase further developments are notable, among them a great increase of domesticated goats and sheep, a steady decline in the frequency of cultivated plants, Emmer and hulled barley, the cultivation of which seems to have come almost to a standstill in the second half of the period. This increase towards pastoralism is accompanied by the predominance of a wild plant, *Prosopis*, still used as fodder. Houses are still built of brick, but are now provided with stone foundations and have plastered and red-painted walls. Ground stone tools show great diversity, and many varieties of mortars have been found. The chipped stone industry, almost entirely blades, very fine cores, but few sickle blades, and microliths including crescents and arrowheads, is similar to that of the upper pottery-bearing levels of Jarmo, Tepe Sarāb and Tepe Gūrān. Noticeable is the first use of pottery, both monochrome and painted. Intramural burial habits continue and the dead are accompanied by turquoise ornaments, labrets, stone and shell beads strung into 'loincloths'. At the end of this period the site was deserted, but some continuity may be inferred from the presence of pottery of 'Muḥammad Jaʿfar' style in the lower levels of Tepe Sabz, which represents the Susiana sequence of Le Breton,[1] marking the first introduction of irrigation techniques into the alluvial lowlands c. 5500 B.C.

Before describing these important events which laid the basis for the rise of civilization in southern Mesopotamia in the later states of Sumer and Elam, parallel developments in the highlands of western Iran must be briefly reviewed, for it is here that pottery seems to have made its first appearance, and not in the plain.

[1] §VIII, 1, 79 ff.

Ganj-i-Dareh Tepe and Tepe Asyāb. Situated east of Kirmān-shāh and south of Bīsetūn respectively, at an altitude of 1300–1400 m., these two aceramic mounds are the earliest yet found on the Iranian plateau. They are comparable in date to Shanidar and Zawi Chemi and the former site has yielded a carbon 14 date of *c.* 8700 ± 150 B.C. (GaK-807).[1] Whereas Tepe Asyāb[2] shows only pits, possibly the base of reed huts or tents, indicative of seasonal occupation, Ganj-i-Dareh Tepe produced a 20 ft. deposit of solid 'architecture', indicating permanent settlement. There is no evidence yet for food production here, but animal bones are abundant and the ash deposits may produce cereal remains when analysed. At Tepe Asyāb coprolites contain remains of plants, and bones of lizards, frogs or toads, but their human provenance is disputed. The flint industry lacks geometric microliths, burins, sickle blades, obsidian and polished stone tools.

Tepe Sarāb.[3] The finds from this site, another small mound in the same plain, are considerably more advanced, even if its 'architecture', consisting of pit-like depressions probably again representing tents or reed huts, indicates a seasonal settlement of semi-nomadic villagers whose permanent village was in a lower valley, like Tepe Gūrān, 350 m. lower than the Kirmānshāh plain. The end of the Tepe Sarāb period has been dated to 6065 ± 150 (Gūrān H), and datings from Sarāb itself give 5883, 5932 and 6245 B.C., suggesting perhaps 6300–6000 as a possible date for this culture. Pistachios and snails seem to have been particularly common on this site, but cereal food is now known in the form of Emmer wheat (Sarāb), two-row hulled barley, and wild two-row barley (Gūrān).[4] Agriculture was therefore practised. The flint industry of Sarāb is said to resemble that of Jarmo, but as the site is unpublished, no further details are available. The other finds consist of fine stone bowls, some oval in shape, a monochrome red ware and a fine painted ware, all with parallels in Tepe Gūrān. Not paralleled there are some very fine clay figurines of seated women, evidently representing the Mother Goddess,[5] as well as some very naturalistically modelled figurines of wild animals, among which that of a charging wild boar is outstanding.

Tepe Gūrān.[6] Here, 60 km. further south, at the northern end of the fertile plain of Hulailan, 950 m. above sea level, P. Mortensen dug a trench which revealed eighteen successive

---

[1] *Science,* 153 (1966), 386 ff.   [2] §III, 1, 2008 ff.
[3] §III, 4, 111, n. 5.   [4] §III, 4, 112, and information from Dr H. Helbaek.
[5] §I, 1, fig. 28.   [6] §III, 4, 110 ff.

building levels in a deposit of 25 ft., roughly datable to the millennium between *c.* 6500 and 5500 B.C. The mound is oval, measuring about 110 × 80 m. The lowest 5 ft. of deposit on the site consisted of the remains of decayed wooden huts with rectangular or slightly curving walls, seasonal occupation of the type found at Tepe Sarāb but earlier in date. These people were goat herders living on the site only in winter time, and hunting gazelle and several species of birds.[1] The three lowest building levels are aceramic (V–T); the next three see the appearance of undecorated greyish-brown ware in coarsely made thick-walled bowls with vertical or slightly curved sides, wet-smoothed or burnished (level S), a finer plain buff ware (from R onwards) and an archaic painted ware (R–O), chaff-tempered like most Iranian pottery, and painted in red on orange-buff burnished slip. The patterns are widely spaced and extremely simple, mainly linear. Shapes are bowls and beakers with curved or vertical sides and flat bases. This early pottery has as yet no parallels.[2]

About 6300 B.C. permanent settlement takes the place of seasonal occupation. Agriculture is now practised (barley); querns, mortars and sickle blades appear. Mud-brick houses are introduced on stone foundations, but side by side with them wooden huts still survive (P–N). The latter disappear soon. Goat is still the only domestic animal, but other big animals are now hunted, such as wild cattle. Flint dominated the production of a blade industry with few microliths, but obsidian was also imported from the north. Sickle blades with a gloss along the edge were set in wooden handles; other types included end-of-blade scrapers, borers and numerous notched blades. Characteristic of this first phase of the mud-brick village was undecorated buff ware, already known before, and a standard painted ware, orange-buff or reddish-slipped, straw-tempered, sometimes burnished and decorated in red patterns of obliquely placed blobbed lines. Bowls with curved sides and flat bases are characteristic of this pottery of levels O–H, which is identical with the imported painted pottery in the upper (ceramic) levels of Jarmo in north Iraq.[3]

A development of this Jarmo-type pottery first found in level L, and continuing likewise to level H (*c.* 6065 B.C.), is the Tepe Sarāb ware.[4] Its bowls are slightly carinated, often with convex outcurved sides and flat or rounded bases. The decoration is still obliquely placed, but the blobs have given place to more regular

[1] Information from P. Mortensen.   [2] §III, 4, 113 ff., figs. 15 f.
[3] §III, 4, 114 ff, figs. 16 f.   [4] §III, 4, 116, figs. 16, 18

small square, rectangular or polyhedric spots. Another form of decoration is confined to horizontal bands of lozenges, triangles and chevrons on rim and carination again as at Tepe Sarāb.[1] The buildings of this period show little change, but white and red gypsum floors occur as well as a mosaic of flakes of felspar set in red ochre, and these continue during the last phases when further pottery developments take place. In the upper levels (J–D) the Sarāb type of ornamentation develops into a close-pattern style,[2] still obliquely placed on carinated bowls larger in shape than the Sarāb ones. These close-style bowls with negative design are reminiscent of the later Ḥajji Muḥammad ware of South Mesopotamia and related wares in Khūzistān and may well be ancestral to them. A red burnished ware is known from levels H–D (post-Sarāb): open bowls and cups with flat or rounded bases, also known from Iran and north Iraq; but a specific type of the latest two levels at Gūrān (E–D) has a dimple base[3] characteristic of Tepe Sialk I, c. 5600 B.C. Burials seem to be rare, but at least one contracted burial was found in an oval grave in the aceramic deposit. As at Sarāb white and pink marble bowls[4] and jars were made, and lightly baked clay figurines representing women, animals and a phallus. Ground stone tools included polishers, pounders, querns, a celt, numerous sling-stones, beads, etc. Bonework included spatulae, awls and pins. No metal has been reported. Tepe Gūrān is important for its many links with other cultures and its long stratigraphic succession, carefully dug and already adequately reported.

IV. SYRIA AND LEBANON IN THE SEVENTH AND SIXTH MILLENNIA

Far too little is known about the earliest cultures of Syria and Lebanon as distinct from Palestine to give a complete and coherent account of their development during the tenth to eighth millennia B.C. Though cultures like the Kebaran and the Natufian have left traces in the caves of the Nahr el-Kelb and those near Jabrud, subsequent developments await a thorough archaeological exploration which has not yet taken place. As obsidian from central Anatolia reached Jericho in the late Natufian, perhaps after c. 8300 B.C., and Red Sea cowries appear as imports in Çatal Hüyük VII c. 6200 B.C., trade routes through Syria

---

[1] §III, 4, figs. 11 f.   [2] §III, 4, fig. 15 f–g.
[3] §III, 4, fig. 16, 1.   [4] §III, 4, fig. 19.

were evidently open, but little is known about the cultures of the time or the people through whose hands these imports passed. Only in the last few years have remains of the seventh millennium been investigated in Syria, at Ras Shamra on the North Syrian coast, and at Tell Ramad, south-west of Damascus. Here early cultures were found which are closely connected with Palestine and Jordan. For the matter of this section it is not practicable to observe the general scheme of this *History*, which distinguishes between Palestine and Syria (with the Lebanon), for the Syrian developments of this period are closely related to the Pre-pottery Neolithic B, as it is called, of Jericho, Beidha, and the Jordan valley in general.[1] Carbon-14 dates from Jericho have established that this culture covered the seventh millennium B.C. and at this site more than twenty building levels are represented. Characteristic are well-built large houses of rectangular plan, each with a main room and one or two ante-rooms, arranged around courtyards. Walls and floors are covered with lime plaster which is stained red, buff, pink and burnished, but it is not known how far the red plaster was carried up the mud-brick walls. Hearths, when found, are sunk into the floor and not raised. Burial habits are peculiar and perhaps suggest secondary burials, which are often incomplete. The dead are buried intramurally. Plastered and painted skulls with cowries or shells set into the eye sockets are peculiar to Jericho and may be the heads of revered ancestors rather than head-hunting trophies. This culture arrives fully fledged in the Jordan valley and marks a distinct break with the previous Pre-pottery Neolithic A, and it is suspected that its origins are to be sought farther north, in Syria. Recent excavations at Ras Shamra on the North Syrian coast and at Tell Ramad near Qattana, south-west of Damascus, have thrown light on this vital problem. At both sites the earliest, but thin, deposits Ras Shamra VC[2] and Tell Ramad I A and I B[3] have yielded remains of plaster floor apparently not stained red. The architecture of the period is not yet known, but plastered hearths, rounded at Tell Ramad, were found. The basalt querns with double basins and pounders and the flint and obsidian industry with burins and un-retouched sickle blades (and silica sheen), notched arrowheads, tanged arrowheads and daggers show close resemblances to those of Jericho Pre-pottery Neolithic B. Animal figurines occur, but pottery is unknown at both sites. Limestone bowls are common; bone tools are frequent. At Tell Ramad,

---

[1] See below, pp. 499 ff.   [2] §IV, 10, 151, ff., 257 ff., 492 ff.
[3] §IV, 6, 114–15, 120, pls. I, IV.

animal bones show only wild animals, deer and gazelle, whereas at Jericho the goat was domesticated; Emmer wheat and lentils were grown. Whereas close resemblances are found between Tell Ramad and Jericho Pre-pottery Neolithic B, such are less obvious at Ras Shamra in the north. Radiocarbon dates are available for both sites: 6665 ± 101 for the earliest and 6436 ± 10 for the end of the last of three building levels of Ras Shamra V C, whereas 6250 ± 80 and 5950 ± 50[1] date the next period at Tell Ramad (II), so that Tell Ramad I must have ended before 6250 B.C.

Tell Ramad II, dated to the last quarter of the seventh millennium, is the most prosperous period on the site. Houses are built on a rectangular plan with mud-brick walls on stone foundations, and floors are either of stamped earth or plastered, as in the previous period.[2] Funeral habits are like those of Jericho Pre-pottery Neolithic B with red plastered skulls. The stone industry resembles that of the period before, but denticulated sickle blades now appear. Clay statuettes of Mother Goddess type and animals are abundant and the economy of the period continues as before with the cultivation of grain, lentils being supplemented by the collection of almond, plum, pistachio and *crataegus*. Pigs are now definitely domestic, and perhaps also sheep, goat and cattle, whereas gazelle was still hunted. This period of Tell Ramad II is probably still contemporary with the end of Jericho Pre-pottery Neolithic B, but some innovations from the north of Syria had now reached Tell Ramad in the form of a white moulded and heavy pozzolanic ware,[3] probably imitating the limestone bowls of the previous period, and associated with this white chalky ware is the first crumbly pottery. These wares do not seem to have reached Palestine, and are a specific feature of western Syria, where they occur at much earlier dates in the north, e.g. at Ras Shamra V B[4] soon after 6400 B.C., at Tell Sukas and Hama on the Orontes. The white ware is found at Byblos too, in the earliest neolithic deposits, together with a dark burnished pottery the ultimate origin of which lies in Anatolia. The earliest levels of Byblos produce, around 6000 B.C., a hybrid pottery, a dark burnished ware coated with a white chalky slip on interior and exterior, as well as normal dark burnished ware, plain or decorated with shell-combed impressions.[5]

[1] §iv, 6, 36 f. and information from H. de Contenson.
[2] §iv, 6, 115, 121, pl. ii.   [3] §iv, 6, 116, pl. ix; §iv, 5, 36; §iv, 12, pl. 2.
[4] §iv, 10, 160 ff., 259 ff., 311 ff., 506 ff.; §iv, 5, 36.
[5] §iv, 7, pls. iv, 4, and ix.

In Syria, in fact, we see a local development from a culture like Ras Shamra V C, without pottery, to one in which various forms of pottery come into use. In Ras Shamra V B the white pozzolanic wares probably represent a local imitation of limestone bowls in a more tractable material, side by side with (or perhaps a little earlier than) the manufacture of a dark burnished ware, red and brown, with grit temper, derived through Cilicia from similar wares of the Anatolian plateau, the earliest known centre of pottery production in the Near East. At Çatal Hüyük, the excavations of 1965 have yielded evidence for the production of a heavy straw and grit-tempered burnished cream ware from level XIII onwards, perhaps c. 6750 B.C., from which the pozzolanic white ware of Syria may have been copied. In level VII, c. 6200 B.C., the fine grit-tempered dark burnished wares come into their own as a refinement of the earlier wares—their first appearance in small quantity is in level VIII, in about the same century B.C.—and it is this brown, greyish-brown or even black ware which reaches north Syria via Mersin in Cilicia, being present in Ras Shamra V B and 'Amūq A, and from there reaching Byblos by about 6000 B.C. Undecorated on the Anatolian plateau, it picked up impressed shell decoration in Cilicia and in the north Syrian coastal regions, and at Byblos this form of decoration, confined to the rims of hole-mouthed vessels in the north, was spread all over the body of the pot. As this hard-fired ware developed, the white wares gradually gave way and disappeared altogether. White wares are widespread in the Biqā' valley.

Throughout the development here sketched in its barest details, the north of Syria was well ahead of the Lebanon and the Damascus region and these areas in turn were far more advanced than Palestine and Jordan. Considerable time-lags are involved, which show that the techniques of pottery production spread south very slowly indeed,[1] and were not carried by a wave of colonizing agriculturalists. The slow appreciation of the advantages that pottery offered to settled communities was shared by the island of Cyprus, where the first attempts to produce pottery were abandoned in Khirokitia I, around 6000 B.C., in favour of stone vessels of a magnificence unparalleled elsewhere in the Near East.

Ras Shamra V B (and 'Amūq A) with its rectangular houses and plaster floors came to an end c. 6000 B.C., according to radiocarbon dates, a little after the Early Neolithic of Byblos began. Characteristic of this large site were rectangular houses[2]

---

[1] §iv, 12, 128   [2] §iv, 8, pls. iib, iv.

built of mud-brick or light materials such as walls of reeds plastered on both sides. The plan consisted of a main room with perhaps a storage chamber added. Each room had a hearth and sometimes a bench or platform near it along the wall, and floors were made of lime plaster as in Tell Ramad and Jericho Pre-pottery Neolithic B. Red floors are not reported. The houses stood by themselves, as at Jeitun in South Turkestan or at Nea Nikomedeia and Karanovo in the Balkans. The pottery has already been described, but it should be noted that much of it was not dark burnished, but orange or cream in colour. Small clay figurines were made as well as clay stamp seals which, like much of the flint industry including fine tanged arrowheads, pressure-flaked or not, and bifacially pressure-flaked daggers,[1] show unmistakable resemblances to that of Çatal Hüyük VI, c. 6000 B.C., on the Anatolian plateau. Obsidian is rare or unknown but greenstone axes were imported. Denticulated sickle blades (a feature not paralleled in Anatolia) show close resemblances to those of Tell Ramad II, a culture possibly of similar origin. Emmer wheat is reported from Byblos, as from 'Amūq A; otherwise no details are available about the economy of the site. The Byblos Early Neolithic culture is known from numerous places extending in an almost unbroken belt from Ṭabbat el-Ḥammām near Tarsus to Beirut.[2] In the hills another aspect of the culture is characterized by large tools, including axes for deforestation from Mukhtara[3] and Qara'un and similar tools occur in the Antilebanon north of Tell Ramad.[4]

Approximately contemporary with the Early Neolithic of Byblos is the Ras Shamra VA[5] (and the 'Amūq B) period, c. 6000–5450 ± 80, according to carbon-14 dates. In this period rectangular house-plans continue, and characteristic also is the development of finer dark-burnished wares, with fine impressions and incisions. There is a second variety decorated with pattern burnish, in patterns which seem to imitate basketry. A coarse plain ware with incised patterns is also found, which has perhaps been too readily identified with Hassūnah incised ware. Towards the end of the period we find the beginning of painting in red on cream ground with very unsophisticated patterns compared with their more advanced neighbours in the north (Cilicia and Anatolia). 'Husking-trays' of coarse ware, characteristic of the Hassūnah culture, reached Ras Shamra. The stone industry

---

[1] §IV, 2, 489 f., figs. 1, 2; §IV, 3, 491 ff., fig. 2 f.
[2] §IV, 3, fig. 1.   [3] §IV, 3, 498, figs. 5 f.   [4] §IV, 11, 175 ff.
[5] §IV, 10, 164 ff., 257 ff., 310 f., 503 f.; §IV, 5, 36.

developed from that of the previous period; flint is predominant but Anatolian obsidian is still imported and many of the types such as the tanged arrowheads, plain or pressure-flaked, continue the local traditions, which seem ultimately based on the rich industry of Çatal Hüyük. Polished greenstone axes are common, the material for which was probably derived with obsidian from Anatolia in exchange for flint.

Farther north, the site of Sakçagözü[1] has produced similar wares, as well as a variant in which fine incision takes the place of pattern-burnishing. Bowls with oblique sides are common and it has been suggested that some of the earliest Halaf vessels of the following period are derived from such prototypes. The distribution of pattern-burnished ware was not confined to western Syria, but extended well east of the Euphrates, where it was found on virgin soil at Chagar Bazar[2] and a number of other sites. Fragments of this greyish-black ware occur as imports at Hassūnah as late as levels IV and V (5335 ± 200),[3] immediately before the Halaf impact which characterizes Hassūnah VI. Syrian and Mesopotamian dates are thus in agreement.

Whereas a continuous development can be traced in western Syria from the seventh millennium to the beginning of the Halaf period c. 5300 B.C. (and beyond), a period during which new inventions from Anatolia gradually penetrate and are absorbed, a sudden break in culture is apparent in regions farther south. In Palestine and Jordan the settlements of the Pre-pottery Neolithic B period are apparently deserted c. 6000 B.C. and the new developments of Syria and Lebanon are not adopted. It seems that after a promising start these southern regions returned to nomadism, which is marked by a profound hiatus in the archaeological record.

A similar pattern can be discerned in the development of Buqras,[4] an early village site on the Syrian Euphrates near the confluence of the Khabur. Here the earliest two levels (Buqras I) have yielded houses built of *pisé* (as in north Mesopotamia), with stamped-earth floors, sometimes covered with mats. A chalk plaster is used on walls and parts of the floor. Small figurines of humans were made, but pottery is unknown. Besides tools of bone there is an epi-palaeolithic stone industry in flint and imported Anatolian obsidian with end scrapers on blades, arrowheads and sickle blades. Pounders and querns of diorite,

[1] §IV, 9. 132 f., pl. XXIII, XXIV, 8–10.
[2] *Iraq*, III, pl. III.   [3] §V, 4, 265.
[4] H. de Contenson, in *Ann. Arch. de Syrie*, 1966.

sandstone and basalt are found, but, surprisingly enough, no remains of plants. Wild cattle, bezoar (goat) and sheep were hunted.

In Buqras II there are four superimposed villages, now built in mud-brick, with pillars and benches and plastered floors. There is still no pottery, but bowls are made of polished gypsum and alabaster. The stone industry is derived from Buqras I, with flint and obsidian scrapers and arrowheads, and more and more burins. Sickle blades, querns and pounders disappear. The fauna of wild animals is the same and there is no trace of agriculture.

In Buqras III, the seventh village is of the same type with the same industries, but now a few sherds of dark burnished pottery appear, as well as a polished axe. Besides wild animals there may be some domesticated specimens of sheep and cattle. After this pastoral phase the village is deserted.

Buqras looks like an attempt by early farmers at settling in the Euphrates valley which failed, just as the early settlements in Palestine seem to have failed ultimately, though after a much more prolonged effort. It may be that their crops were not yet accustomed to conditions so different from their natural mountain habitat. The pattern is reminiscent of what happened at Ali-Kush in the 'Muḥammad Jaʿfar phase', with similar lowland conditions in north Khūzistān, which likewise ended in pastoralism and the desertion of the site.

Before describing the impact of the Halaf culture on Syria and its repercussions on Lebanon and Palestine, we must now turn to the earliest cultures yet discovered in the plain of Mesopotamia.

V. THE MESOPOTAMIAN PLAIN

The three superimposed camp sites found at the bottom of the tell of Hassūnah I A,[1] south of Mosul, with their peculiar pottery, are still the first signs of settlement in the Mesopotamian plain.

The following phase in which villages with agriculture are established is represented by Hassūnah I B and Tell es-Sawwān I, south of Sāmarrā on the east bank of the Tigris, the southernmost site of the Hassūnah culture.

Recent Iraqi excavations[2] at this site have yielded important evidence for the beginning of the Hassūnah culture in the form of developed mud-brick architecture and a rich cemetery

[1] § v, 4, fig. 27.   [2] *Sumer*, 20 (1964), 1 f., and 21 (1965).

of over a hundred graves associated with Tell es-Sawwān I, showing a sophistication of building and traditions of stone carving hard to reconcile with the idea that these early settlers were nomads from the desert. These people practised agriculture, the main crops being Emmer wheat and six-row hulled barley with an admixture of six-row naked barley, and small proportions of Einkorn wheat and Bread wheat. Other plants were *Prosopis*,

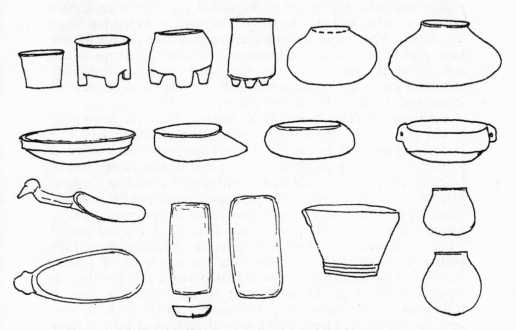

Fig. 20. Tell es-Sawwān I: alabaster vases from cemetery (Hassūnah I B period). After *Sumer*, 20 (1964), Arabic section, fig. 3.

caper, a thistle, and linseed, which required watering and hence irrigation.[1] Animal bones await investigation.

The architectural remains of Tell es-Sawwān I so far discovered show large buildings of plastered mud-brick with many rooms of rectangular plan, arranged around courtyards and streets. One of the buildings is interpreted as a temple and contained clay statuettes of Mother Goddess type as well as unfinished alabaster figures and stone vessels, of which over one hundred and fifty were found in the cemetery situated below these buildings. The dead were buried in a crouched position in graves cut into virgin soil and though most of the skeletons are those of children, some

[1] *Sumer*, 20 (1964), 45 ff.

belong to adults. An incomplete female burial was covered with red ochre and the body was richly adorned with beads of various stones, shell and dentalium.

Other gifts in the graves consist of pottery vessels (of Has-sūnah I B type), alabaster vessels of a great number of shapes, beads of copper, and alabaster statuettes (varying from 2 or 3 in. to 6 in. in height), one to three in each grave. Other graves have phallic symbols, which are never found together with female statuettes. Most of the latter are of the standing type,[1] but some are seated. Male figures, though rare, occur. Some of the figures have eyes of shell, inlaid in bitumen, and some have caps of the same material. The carving is accomplished and naturalistic. Clay statuettes also occur in the settlement of levels I and II, but not in the later levels with Sāmarrā pottery (III–V).

Radiocarbon dates from Tell es-Sawwān place the beginning of the Hassūnah culture in the early 6th millennium B.C. The pottery of Hassūnah I A consists of some fine burnished bowls and a great mass of very coarse straw-tempered light-coloured jars of hole-mouth type, tall or short, and with a sharp break in the pro-file, below which the vessel sharply tapers towards a flat base. It would appear that such vessels were made in two parts. Lugs, knobs and bars take the place of handles, which are unknown.[2] There is no painted pottery, nor as yet any incised design. This pottery is related to the pottery from the top levels of Jarmo, though not identical, and is now known to have a vast distribution from Tell Halaf in the north-west to the Susiana region of Khūzistān (in south-west Iran). This simple pottery seems to have been the substratum from which several variants of early pottery developed in the plains. In Cilicia and Syria this coarse ware element was accompanied by fine dark burnished wares of Anato-lian type, but in north Iraq and Khūzistān such dark burnished wares were not found, and the proximity of the Zagros zone soon led to the development of several variants of painted pottery. The stone industry of Hassūnah I A consisted of hoes of sandstone and quartzite, often with adhering traces of bitumen used for fixing them to wooden handles. These are probably agricultural tools, and rare in other parts of the Near East. This type[3] reappears together with polished celts as far north as Adler on the Black Sea coast at the foot of the Caucasus mountains. Celts with polished bits are common carpenters' tools. Flint and imported obsidian were used for blades, sickle blades, etc. and there are

[1] *Sumer*, 19 (1963), pl. IV.   [2] §v, 4, 276 ff., fig. 6, pls. XII, 2, XIII, I.
[3] §v, 4, figs. 19 f.

two projectile points[1] in obsidian of Anatolian/North Syrian type, showing evidence for contact with the north-west. Querns, pounders and other polished and ground stone tools are characteristic of the agricultural economy. Sling-stones are also found.

Painted pottery and incised pottery of Hassūnah Archaic type (Hassūnah I b–II)[2] also occur in the next building level of Tell es-Sawwān II, whereas at Matarrah only incised ware is found.[3] The architectural remains of Hassūnah I b and I c[4] are fairly simple, but only *pisé* was used. Rectangular small rooms are arranged around open spaces and there are remains of a round building. Hearths, querns and storage bins occur in the rooms. The latter are set into the floor and are coated with bitumen and gypsum. Their profiles are similar to Hassūnah I A pottery and possibly derived from it. Hassūnah II[5] shows more developed architecture, with rectangular rooms and internal buttresses, but still with many crooked walls. Infant burials are found in jars below the house floors, and occasionally there are adult burials, accompanied by funerary offerings such as pots, beads, etc. Among the plain pottery there appears in level II a new large oval vessel with heavily corrugated or slashed interior, the 'husking-tray',[6] which has a wide distribution from Hassūnah to Ras Shamra on the Syrian coast, to Eridu in south Mesopotamia, and perhaps also to Susiana. Characteristic of the pottery is an archaic painted ware, decorated in thick glossy or matt red paint on a burnished pink or buff surface with simple linear designs reminiscent of basketry. False chevrons and hatched patterns are common on simple bowls and collar-necked jars. There is a plain burnished ware, often decorated with incision on bowls and jars, the counterpart of the painted ware, and similarly decorated, with herringbone patterns, groups of lines or various arrangements of dots and lines, also known from Matarrah. The decoration of these archaic wares is unsophisticated in comparison with the earlier painted pottery of Tepe Gūrān and Tepe Sarāb in Iran and Hacılar in Anatolia, but more like that of north Syria and Cilicia in its rustic simplicity.

Hassūnah III–V marks the fullest development of this culture, paralleled at Matarrah and Tell es-Sawwān III–V, and Tell Shemshāra in the uplands near the Dokan dam.[7] At Hassūnah

---

[1] §v, 4, fig. 22: 9, 10.
[3] §v, 1, figs. 6–8, 16: 8–10.
[5] §v, 4, fig. 29.
[7] §v, 5, 79.
[2] §v, 4, 278, figs. 7 ff.
[4] §v, 9, fig. 28.
[6] §v, 4, pl. xviii, 1, fig. 3: 8–10.

architecture[1] has matured into fine rectangular plans of multiple-roomed houses with large and small rooms and gabled roofs. Interior features include buttresses, benches, screens, hearths, ovens and grain-bins sunk into the floor. Reed matting[2] covered the floors and weaving is indicated by spindle-whorls. The stone industry is impoverished, but copper is still unknown. A flint-

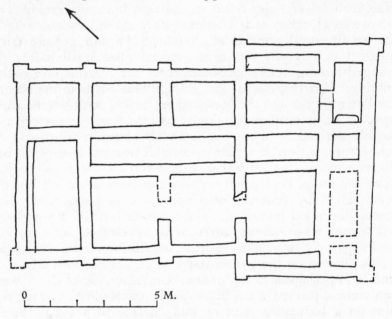

0   5 M.

Fig. 21. Tell es-Sawwān IV: temple (?) of Sāmarrā period.
After *Sumer*, 20 (1964), Arabic section, fig. 1.

bladed sickle was found in level III,[3] set in bitumen in a wooden handle no longer preserved. Obsidian and turquoise[4] show trade with the north and east. Red ochre, malachite and antimony are used as paints. Unbaked clay figurines attest the cult of the Mother Goddess.

The pottery consists of 'standard' wares,[5] showing a great improvement on the earlier 'archaic' wares. There are three varieties: standard incised, standard painted, and standard painted and incised, a combination of the other two. Coarse wares continue unchanged, including the use of 'husking-trays'. The shapes of the standard wares are more sophisticated: simple bowls, deeper bowls with straight rims, and globular jars of

---

[1] §v, 4, figs. 30–32, 36.   [2] §v, 4, fig. 38.   [3] §v, 4, fig. 37.
[4] §v, 4, 269.   [5] §v, 4, 279 ff.

varying dimensions and collar necks are typical and evidently developed locally from their archaic ancestors. Decoration, though, shows great improvement and much more elaborate patterning. The paints used, however, are now matt, and the surfaces unburnished. Handles and lugs are unknown; oval shapes occur, and most bases are flat.

Besides the local pots a new imported luxury ware is found, known as Samarrā ware.[1] It first occurs in level III, becomes more common in levels IV and V and continues in use side by side with Halaf in levels VI–VIII. At Tell es-Sawwān it appears again side by side with Hassūnah standard wares in level III, but in IV and V it is predominant. At Matarrah this is the only painted pottery found[2] and further north, at Tell Shemshāra,[3] Samarrā ware is the first pottery introduced, the earlier layers being aceramic but contemporary with the earlier Hassūnah development. At Samarrā itself, the pottery was found in a cemetery;[4] at Baghūz, on the Euphrates, in a badly explored settlement.[5]

The Iraqi excavations at Tell es-Sawwān may shed light on the Samarrā culture, which is otherwise known only from its painted pottery, decorated in red, brown or black on a cream ground. Painted and incised ware and plain ware have also been found. This pottery is quite distinct from Hassūnah ware and far more sophisticated; it combines rich geometric ornament with bold patterns,[6] often naturalistic, on the interior of large bowls, and many of the patterns imitate motion. Whirling dancers, running stags,[7] long-necked birds snatching fish,[8] and running maeander patterns introduce a dynamic tension unknown in the other Mesopotamian cultures of the period. Vegetation also figures in Samarrā pottery: there are palm trees, huts and trees,[9] animals gathered around a pool of water, long-necked animals in rows,[10] swimming waterbirds or flocks of birds in flight,[11] crawling scorpions, and rows of dancing girls[12] portrayed along the rims of bowls.

This temperamental naturalism in the Samarrā pottery, by its sheer contrast with the rustically sedate decoration of Hassūnah wares or the elaborate and refined dignity of contemporary Eridu ware of the south, has naturally been compared with the

[1] §v, 4, 281 ff. [2] §v, 1, pls. vii f.; fig. 16: 8–10, 22.
[3] §v, 5, 78. [4] §v, 3 passim.
[5] §v, 2 passim.
[6] §v, 3, pls. xxxi, 249, 165, and xxxviii, 250.
[7] §v, 3, pl. ix, 15; §v, 4, fig. 1: 8. [8] §v, 3, pl. vi, 4.
[9] §vi, 2, fig. 77, 10, 11, 17. [10] §vi, 2, fig. 77, 16.
[11] §vi, 2, fig. 77, 14. [12] §vi, 2, fig. 77, 19.

pottery of western Iran, and especially that of Sialk II, which also shows animal designs and pedestalled bowls, though not with cut-outs. A West Iranian influence can possibly be detected in the Sāmarrā ware, but the origin of this culture awaits investigation. Effigy vases, with representations of human faces,[1] were found both at Sāmarrā and in Hassūnah V, dated by carbon-14 to 5301 ± 206 B.C., and the *floruit* of the Sāmarrā culture may conveniently be placed in the second half of the sixth millennium B.C. It is possible but not certain that copper and lead were known in this culture, and irrigation probably began to be practised during this period, as a number of sites are situated well outside the region where the winter rains are sufficient for dry farming. The site of Tell es-Sawwān complicates the issue by suggesting the possiblity of irrigation even at an earlier period, that of Hassūnah IB. Alternatively, it is of course not excluded that at this period, the sixth millennium B.C., the annual rainfall was a little higher than it is now and less restricted to the hills. Sāmarrā influence spread wide and far and is noticeable in Syria at Yunus near Carchemish,[2] at Sakçagözü, in the 'Amūq, and in the Khabur at roughly the same time as the early Halaf period. Towards the south, its influence can be discerned in the Eridu and Susiana A or Ja'farābād culture of Khūzistān, to which we must now turn.

VI. THE HALAF CULTURE

The culture that succeeded Hassūnah in north Iraq is named after the mound of Tell Halaf near Ras el-'Ain, just south of the Turkish border in Syria, but the type site of the culture is Arpachiyah near Mosul. At Hassūnah the Halaf culture appears in level VI, soon after 5301 ± 206 (Hassūnah V) according to a radiocarbon date. Though there is no overlap with Hassūnah, there is one with Sāmarrā wares, which continued to be made during the early Halaf period and died out probably by 5000 or so. This overlap of Sāmarrā with Halaf is found not only in north Iraq, but also in Syria, from Chagar Bazar and Halaf itself to Carchemish and Tell Judaidah. The distribution of this interesting culture[3] is vast and it extends from the foothills of the Zagros to the Euphrates near Carchemish and Tell Turlu and even beyond to Gaziantep and the region of Adiyaman in the foothills of the Taurus. It did not extend as far south as the

---

[1] §v, 4, fig. 1, 2, pl. xvii, 2, 3.   [2] §vi, 1, pl. lxxvi, 2, 4.
[3] §i, 1, fig. 41.

Sāmarrā culture and sites with Halaf pottery increase in numbers northwards towards the Turkish frontier, especially in the Ṭūr ʿAbdīn area. A recent survey of south-eastern Turkey in the regions of Urfa, Diyārbakr and Siirt has yielded little additional evidence for the distribution of Halaf settlements which are known to exist in these regions.[1] Even on the Anatolian plateau true Halaf pottery has been found at Tilkitepe, east of Lake Vān,[2] and at Isaköy, Karahüyük and Arslan Tepe in the Malatya district. These settlements may indicate trading stations for the exploration of natural resources: obsidian in the case of Lake Vān, copper and gold around Malatya, and copper in the Diyārbakr (Ergani Maden) area. The spread of Halaf pottery towards the west, in Syria beyond the Euphrates and even into Cilicia, may also have followed in the wake of trading ventures.

The origin of this culture is obscure—it is not developed either from the Hassūnah or Sāmarrā cultures and it is certainly a new-comer in north Iraq. It has been suggested by Professor Mallo-wan that it developed out of the pattern-burnished wares by the rendering of basket-like patterns of these vessels in painting. This attractive theory finds support in the shapes of both the pattern-burnished and the earliest Halaf wares, which are simple, especially in the west. If this view is correct, the Halaf culture probably originated in the central area of its distribution, e.g. in the Khabur triangle, or the area between the Euphrates and the Jaghjagha rivers, which might account for a number of Anatolian resemblances.

The architecture of the Halaf period is peculiar: at Arpachiyah, three main phases can be distinguished stratigraphically:[3] Early Halaf (before TT 10), Middle Halaf (TT 10–7) and Late Halaf (TT 6). No buildings were found that can be ascribed to the Early Halaf period. In Late Halaf, however, there is a house with several rooms of rectangular plan, but still built in *pisé* as in the previous period.[4] Mud-brick is said not to make its appearance in Mesopotamia until the ʿUbaid period.[5] In the Middle Halaf period, however, we find buildings of cir-cular plan[6] on stone foundations (TT 10, 9), to which in the later building levels (TT 8, 7) a rectangular ante-room is added. The earlier tholos structures have diameters of 5·5–7 m.; they later increase in size to 9–10 m. in external diameter, and with ante-

---

[1] Information from Prof. R. J. Braidwood.
[2] Ankara Museum, unpublished.
[3] §vi, 2, 18 ff. [4] §vi, 2, 13, fig. 5.
[5] §vi, 2, 16, but see p. 25. [6] §vi, 2, 25 f., figs. 7–14.

rooms they reach dimensions of 16·5–19 m. The tholos part of the building was apparently domed, and the ante-room was either an open walled court or was provided with a flat or gabled roof. The walls were very solid, up to 2·5 m. thick. Approached by stone-paved roads, the concentration of the largest tholoi in the centre of the settlement suggested that these buildings were perhaps the shrines of the agricultural community at Arpachiyah. Recent excavations at Tell Turlu near Nizip in Turkey show that houses were constructed in exactly the same way. Hearths and bell-shaped grain-pits, sunk in the floor of the tholoi, which are again provided with rectangular ante-rooms (as also at nearby Carchemish),[1] show the secular nature of these buildings. At Carchemish kilns for baking pottery have also been found. The homogeneity of house plans and construction over this vast area is surprising for such an early period and contrasts sharply with the contemporary rectangular house plans of Ras Shamra IV in north Syria and Mersin XIX–XVI in Cilicia. Contracted burials[2] were found outside the tholoi at Arpachiyah, and the two graves against the outer wall of the tholos in TT 7 contained exceptionally fine pottery. Flint and obsidian knives are common grave goods. The stone industries of the Halaf period were well developed, obsidian being as common as flint, and used not only for cutting instruments, but for the manufacture of stone vases, beads, links for necklaces with perforations,[3] etc. Polished stone vases[4] are common at Arpachiyah, including beautifully made miniatures. The same interest in carving stone is shown in the seals, beads and amulets,[5] which are more varied than in any other early culture, including among them models of houses, bulls' heads and the phallus, of human finger-bones, of sickles and winnowing-fans, of birds and double-axe motifs. Black steatite was the favoured material and impressions on sun-dried clay[6] show that many of these objects were actually used as seals. Stone statues of Mother Goddess type are rather rare,[7] clay being more frequently used for their manufacture, as also for modelling attendant animals such as doves.[8] Crude figures in basalt and pumice-stone also occur. Besides the normal range of agricultural tools (querns, pounders, etc.), there are numerous polished celts, a limestone macehead, a perforated basalt axe, a painter's palette, etc. Both copper (pins, a chisel cast in a flat mould) and lead were

[1] §vi, 1, pl. 1.

[2] §vi, 2, 42.

[3] §vi, 2, 102, pl. xi, v c.

[4] §vi, 2, 76 f., fig. 44.

[5] §vi, 2, 90 ff., pls. vi ff., figs. 50 f.

[6] §vi, 2, pl. ixa.

[7] §vi, 2, pl. xa, 920, 921b.

[8] §vi, 2, figs. 45 ff.

found, and a peculiar vessel, the Arpachiyah cream-bowl, characteristic for the earliest Halaf deposits, probably imitates copper prototypes. The Halaf culture was the first to introduce metallurgy into Mesopotamia.[1]

Little is known about the economy of the period but mixed farming is indicated. Emmer wheat, barley and flax were grown and the latter crop suggests the possibility that linen was produced.[2] Sheep and goats were domesticated, and so apparently were cattle.[3] Bucrania and heads of sheep are among the most characteristic naturalistic motifs[4] on Halaf pottery. Not less typical are vast numbers of geometric patterns that seem to derive from textile origins[5] and, to judge by this elaborate profusion of motifs, spinning, weaving and also basketry must have been highly developed. Spindle-whorls are common. Full-time specialization is implied by the elaborate pottery, jewellery, metalworking, etc. The burnt building of TT 6 comprised potters' workshops,[6] stacked with pottery, and a stone-carver's shop; even the kilns lay in the centre of the site. Like Hacılar in western Anatolia, Arpachiyah may have been a centre for the production of luxury objects, a factory and trading centre, rather than an agricultural site.

This might also account for the brilliance of the pottery, especially the polychrome plates of TT 6,[7] matched only at Tepe Gawra,[8] but apparently unknown in the western Halaf centres of Syria. The development of Halaf pottery is of great interest and must be outlined briefly, but unfortunately there is no comparable stratigraphic sequence in the western part to match that at Arpachiyah. Technically, the only distinction of early pottery is poorer firing, but throughout the period the clays are pinkish or buff, the surface is smoothed or burnished, or treated with a burnished apricot slip on which the patterns are applied in a red or black lustrous paint. White stippling occurs first in TT 7, polychromy with patterns in both red and black in TT 6.

Characteristic of the early Halaf pottery are shallow bowls with flat bases and incurving sides, decorated with rough groups of parallel, wavy or zigzag lines, frequently enclosed in panels,[9] a form of decoration reminiscent of the pattern-burnished or incised wares of Sakçagözü and the 'Amūq as well as of the

---

[1] §vi, 2, 103 f.
[2] Information from Dr H. Helbaek.
[3] §i, 3, 31 ff.
[4] §vi, 2, 154, ff., figs. 73–76.
[5] §vi, 2, fig. 78.
[6] §vi, 2, 105 f.
[7] §vi, 2, frontispiece, pls. xiii ff., figs. 53–57.
[8] §vi, 4, pls. cx ff.
[9] §vi, 2, 151, figs. 69–72.

roughly contemporary pottery of Çatal Hüyük West (Early Chalcolithic II). Hatched lozenges are also common on this type of bowl and on simple bowls; they are found too on the Arpachiyah cream-bowls with bevelled base, which also are an Early and Middle Halaf type.[1] Circles surrounded with stippling, panels with stippling, and groups of straight and wavy vertical lines decorate these bowls.[2] Jars with squat, globular or biconical body and funnel neck show similar patterns, as well as the egg-and-dot pattern.[3] Also confined to early Halaf are naturalistic animals,[4] such as leopards, birds, deer, goats, snakes, hunters, and especially bucrania and rams' heads. Many of these naturalistic figures would seem more appropriate to wall-paintings than to the decoration of pottery, but no wall-paintings have yet been found in this culture.

Middle Halaf sees a prodigious development of sophisticated geometric design: chequer and 'double axe' patterns, fish-scale patterns, stippled squares, and schematization of bucranium design, both vertical and horizontal. Many of the shapes are extravagantly metallic; cream bowls continue to flourish; carinated bowls with bevelled rims and jars with huge funnel necks are common, as well as a larger form of simple bowl, heavily decorated on the exterior.[5]

In Late Halaf there is a profusion of splendid plates and vases with polychrome decoration, and of incised and painted vases,[6] resembling basketry, but no more cream-bowls. The great plates are among the finest Near Eastern ceramic products, with centre-pieces of stylized petalled flowers, Maltese and other crosses, bucrania, etc. These luxury products are so far confined to north Iraq; further west they are unknown.

From beginning to end, the Halaf pottery shows great homogeneity and, though there are some differences in a number of shapes between the western and eastern groups, the similarities far exceed the differences. White stipples, for example, occur at Boz Hüyük near Adiyaman, cream-bowls at Tilkitepe, bucrania as far west as Mersin, and as far south as Ras el-'Amiya, where they are copied in local wares. The impact of this pottery, probably exported, is notable in south Mesopotamia and especially north Syria, but whereas it penetrated into Cilicia, the highland cultures of south Anatolia, Hacılar I, Çatal Hüyük West II

---

[1] §VI, 2, fig. 71, 1, 7–9.   [2] §VI, 2, 131 ff., figs. 62 f.
[3] §VI, 2, figs. 64, 67.
[4] §VI, 2, fig. 77, 1–9; §VI, 3 (frontispiece); §I, 1, fig. 105.
[5] §VI, 2, fig. 66: 6, 7, fig. 76: 1, 3, 78.   [6] §VI, 2, pl. xx, fig. 60.

and Can Hasan, were not influenced by it, probably because they
already had their own well-established traditions by the time the
Halaf culture began. In the light of new Anatolian discoveries
in the last few years, one is struck by certain resemblances,
especially in Early Halaf, resemblances which in spite of the
originality of this culture seem to be stronger than Halaf links
with Sāmarrā or Hassūnah. There are many features that seem to
be Anatolian rather than Mesopotamian: the emphasis on bull,
ram, leopards, birds in association with a Mother Goddess, the
prominence of obsidian, metalworking and weaving, the naturalistic animal figures, the 'St Andrew's' crosses and the 'double-
axe' motifs in pottery and stone, the high quality and the burnishing, the use of lustrous paint, etc., are all features that we
have come to recognize as familiar from southern Anatolia
since the neolithic period in the seventh millennium. If this is a
coincidence it is a most striking one. Could it be that the Halaf
culture was founded in the second half of the sixth millennium
by the inhabitants, partly settled and partly perhaps still nomadic,
of the southern foothills of the Taurus mountains in the arc that
extends from north Syria to north Iraq? One might expect
these people to have been familiar with the higher cultures of their
western neighbours on the south Anatolian plateau. Semi-
nomadic beginnings may perhaps be inferred from the peculiar
architecture of this culture, which consisted of flimsy huts in the
bottom levels of Arpachiyah,[1] structurally perhaps not far
removed from nomad tents. As time went on, these were copied
as the round tholos-like buildings, to grow eventually into the
imposing tholoi of the Middle Halaf period. The sixth millennium in Palestine and south Syria saw a return towards nomadic
conditions, and when the first pottery-using cultures eventually
reached south Syria and Palestine, about a millennium after the
beginning of the Halaf culture (i.e. at the beginning of the 'Ubaid
culture), we again find a marked lack of architectural remains.
Circular pits, partly subterranean, seem to have served as substructures of round huts for people who were emerging from
nomad or semi-nomadic existence. The parallel is tempting, but
the answer to the question of Halaf origins can probably only be
given when more Early Halaf sites are excavated in western
Syria or south-eastern Turkey.

[1] §vi, 2, 165.

VII. THE HALAF PERIOD IN
SYRIA AND LEBANON

The Halaf impact on Syria west of the Euphrates is evident from the excavations in the 'Amūq Plain and at Ras Shamra IV. Whereas Yunus near Carchemish[1] and Tell Turlu near Nizip[2] represent the westernmost sites of the genuine Halaf culture, the areas further west show strong local traditions overlaid by a Halaf veneer which may be mainly confined to the import and copying of the superior Halaf fabrics—and that only up to a line drawn from Carchemish to Ras Shamra, south of which no Halaf pottery was found.[3] As in Cilicia, which also came under this influence, local traditions of pottery and architecture persisted, with fortifications and rectangular rooms of houses in mud-brick on stone foundations.[4] Pattern-burnished wares, red, grey and black, continue without any technical change, but Halaf shapes are adopted.[5] Imported Halaf wares stimulated local production of a matt-painted 'Syrian Halaf'[6] with a restricted range of shapes which excluded such typical Halaf vessels as cream-bowls or the more extravagantly metallic shapes. Motifs were keenly copied; but mixed with them were others derived from the Sāmarrā style—a mixture unknown in the Halaf culture itself. Bucrania and various animals occur, for evidently the religion of these people was not very different from that of their Anatolian or Halaf neighbours. Many patterns were adapted and transformed—'egg-and-dot' becomes an eye pattern at Ras Shamra; long triangles pendent from the rim are characteristic at this and other sites. A change in stone industry is found in the 'Amūq C, and the old projectile points, ultimately of Anatolian origin, go out of fashion. Too little is yet known about internal developments to specify when, during its development, Halaf influence made its debut in north Syria; in Cilicia it does not appear, apparently, until the Middle Phase, in Mersin XIX, c. 4900 B.C.

At Ras Shamra IVc Halaf influence first appears as in 'Amūq C, and during the next two phases, Ras Shamra IV b and A and 'Amūq D and E, local adaptations become more marked. These include the appearance of a new monochrome ware,[7]

---

[1] §vi, 1, 403 ff.   [2] Unpublished.   [3] §i, 1, fig. 41.
[4] §iv, 5, 36 ff.   [5] §iv, 5, 38; iv, 1, 137 ff., 505, 509.
[6] §iv, 10, 497 ff., pls. i, iii 9–22; §vi, 15, 16, 18.
[7] §iv, 5, 38 and fig. 17; §vi, 3, 71 ff; §iv, 1, 157 ff., 509 ff.

red-coated or red-washed, which takes the place of the earlier
pattern-burnished ware which had continued into 'Amūq
C and Ras Shamra V a. Among these vessels are jars with bow
rims, a shape that also occurs at Tell Halaf itself, but in these
western regions such vessels are provided with two loop handles,
placed on the body or on the junction of neck and body. This
innovation, the first appearance of proper handles, is probably
Anatolian and transmitted through Mersin XVII and XVI.
Other jars have necks which lean inward, and there are shallow
bowls with simple curving profile or flaring sides. Pedestals also
make their appearance. This red-wash ware is the plain ware of
the period, but some of the new shapes, such as the jars, are
painted, sometimes in bichrome, more often in red monochrome,
especially in the 'Amūq D period (Tell Kurdu), and in the Ghāb
section of the Orontes (Huwayiz and Idlib)[1] south of the plain
of Antioch. These North Syrian developments also made themselves felt in the Lebanon, where the middle levels of Byblos I
('Middle Neolithic') show an impoverished architecture, but still
with plaster floors. The red-ware shapes, including the bow-rim
jar (without handles), appear alongside much pottery that is clearly
a development of the earlier culture. Flat bases and more developed shapes appear, the red slip is burnished, and impressions
and herring-bone incision are common in reserved bands not
coated with a red slip.[2] Coarse, deeply incised wares also occur,
poorly executed. Pattern-burnished bowls are found. The poor
stone industry of the north has not yet penetrated Byblos, which
continues the old neolithic tradition.[3] Pebble figurines are still
being made. The contemporary dark-burnished pottery of Tell
Ramad III is similar,[4] but apparently lacks the red-wash component. It is closer to the impressed and incised wares of the so-
called Palestinian 'coastal Neolithic'. The stone industry is
poorer than that of the aceramic levels and the projectile points
have disappeared. No architectural remains have been found,
and the pottery comes from pits. Only part of the site was
occupied and prosperity has sharply declined, a pattern which
Tell Ramad shares with Byblos. From these two cultures the
first pottery-using cultures of Palestine are derived[5]—the
'coastal Neolithic', perhaps from Tell Ramad, and the Yarmukian,
from Middle Neolithic Byblos. The Palestinian pottery-Neolithic
has not yet yielded any evidence for architecture, and cannot yet

[1] §vii, 1.
[2] §iv, 7, pls. iv, 1–3, v, x; §iv, 8, pl. iii, 1.
[3] §iv, 2, 490, fig. 3.
[4] §iv, 6, 118 f., 122, pls. iii, iv c–d, v, vi.
[5] §iv, 4, 211.

be dated earlier than *c*. 4300 B.C., which marks the beginning of the 'Ubaid period in north Syria (Ras Shamra III B).[1] Preceding the spread of 'Ubaid influence was a further phase, dated to *c*. 4500 B.C.,[2] known from Ras Shamra III c, Tell Kurdu, in which only the red monochrome pottery survived. This phase may be contemporary with the Late Halaf of Arpachiyah (TT 6), but in the west it marks the break-up of settled conditions. Architectural remains are almost absent, both in the north at Byblos (Late Neolithic rectangular structures lack plastered floors)[3] and at Tell Ramad III c, and a hiatus in occupation follows at both of these sites. The pottery of this period at Byblos is extremely coarse and heavy; the stone industry changes,[4] and projectile points disappear. The period ends in a welter of barbarism and migrations.

VIII. SUSIANA AND SOUTHERN MESOPOTAMIA

In a previous section we have already described the establishment of early village sites on the edge of the alluvial plain in the Deh Luran district and we have seen how, soon after 6000 B.C., plain and painted pottery made its appearance in the 'Muḥammad Jaʿfar phase' at Ali-Kush, together with a decline in agriculture and a concomitant increase in pastoralism that led eventually to the abandonment of the site. After an interval of unknown length, which is due to excavation hazards and probably does not affect actual events, the thread of cultural development can be taken up at Tepe Sabz in the same area, the bottom layers of which show continuity with 'Muḥammad Jaʿfar'[5] in pottery and artefacts. This site, now being excavated, promises to give a reliable stratigraphical sequence of pottery which includes the four stages of pottery development in Susiana (A–D) devised by Le Breton[6] on the basis of soundings in various sites near Susa, the first two of which, Susiana A (Tepe Jaʿfarābād) and B (Tepe Jaui), being pre-ʿUbaid, interest us here.

Architecturally, the lower levels of Tepe Sabz[7] show continuity in the use of rectangular plans of rooms, constructed of large mud-bricks on stone foundations and wall-plaster. *Tauf* (*pisé*) now first appears for interior walls dividing rooms. Continuity

[1] §IV, 5, 38 f.   [2] §IV, 5, 38.
[3] §IV, 2, 489; §IV, 8, pls. I, i, and II.   [4] §VI, 2, 490.
[5] §III, 3, 106.   [6] §VIII, 1, 79 ff.   [7] §III, 3, 106.

is further shown by some pottery decorated in Muḥammad Jaʿfar style side by side with the new buff-ware pottery of Susiana. Agriculture is by now well established and includes Emmer and Einkorn wheat, a hybrid ('Bread'?) wheat, naked and hulled six-row barley, lentils, peas and flax, the latter showing the effective use of irrigation. Trade with the hills produced almonds and pistachios. Domestic cattle and perhaps dogs were now kept, besides goats and sheep. Coiled baskets and spindle-whorls show weaving, which is further emphasized by the elaborate patterning of the painted pottery, decorated in textile style. Tepe Sabz is but one of a number of sites, one of which promises to yield a series of temples, when it is excavated. The increase in village sites is matched in the Susa plain, where recently no fewer than thirty-four sites with Susiana A pottery were identified in a survey.[1] It is difficult to say when this intensive occupation of the lowlands of Khūzistān began, but the coarse wares of early Hassūnah type and the influence of Sāmarrā patterns suggest a date of about 5500 B.C. if not earlier. Generally speaking it would, however, appear that the main body of immigrants came from the south Iranian Zagros zone. Characteristic of the Susiana A and B periods[2] is a tradition of close patterns on pottery in which the ornament is often indicated in reserve, a tendency that gradually developed at Tepe Gūrān J–D[3] in the centuries on either side of 6000 B.C.

As the Tepe Sabz sequence is not yet published, pottery description is still based on the Susiana sequence and is therefore open to correction. The buff wares of Susiana A and B are painted in brown or black, less commonly in red. There are pedestalled vessels, sub-rectangular bowls with trough spout, simple shallow bowls, some with omphalos bases (as in Sialk I), collar-necked jars, and deep bowls painted inside and out. The first three types are paralleled in Hassūnah or Sāmarrā, but there are also west Iranian parallels, e.g. in the earliest Giyān V pottery[4] which seems to take the place of Tepe Gūrān in the southern Zagros zone. Naturalistic motifs are rare, but include dancing women,[5] holding hands, as in the Sāmarrā wares. Much of the ornament is in reserve; patterns are close, covering the greater part of the vessel with linear and spidery motifs among which zigzag lines, wavy lines and hatched lozenges are characteristic. Beakers and bowls with linear and restricted ornament are also

[1] §III, 139. [2] §I, 2, figs. 41, 42 (*Mém. D. P.* xxx).
[3] §III, 4, 117, fig. 17 *f–g*. [4] §IX, 3, pls. 40–42.
[5] §I, 2, fig. 41, 6 (*Mém. D.P.* xxx, fig. 12: 9).

found. Closely related to Susiana A is the earliest Giyan V A pottery and that of earliest Eridu. The Susiana B pottery seems to be a development. Among new shapes a flat carinated bowl with fine centre-piece is characteristic,[1] also a pedestalled, spouted beaker decorated in Sāmarrā style.[2] Many of the other shapes continue without appreciable change. Naturalistic ornament is rare, except at Kūzaragān, Tepe Khazīneh and Tepe Mussian, where there are human figures and bulls' heads.[3] Close-style patterning with reserve areas continues and new motifs include stylized petalled flowers, double-axes,[4] etc., which are also found in Halaf pottery. Close relations were maintained with Giyan V B and with the Ḥajji Muḥammad pottery of southern Mesopotamia, connections that soon gave birth to a distinctive style, known as 'Ubaid, throughout these southern plains.

To the west and south-west of the Khūzistān plain—the regions of Deh Luran and Susiana, and across the complex system of lakes and marshes fed by the sluggish waters of the Tigris and Euphrates—lies lower Mesopotamia, the ancient land of Sumer.[5] The area lies beyond the rain-belt which made dry farming possible along the foot of the Zagros and was apparently shunned by farmers until the development of early irrigation systems in the middle of the sixth millennium. The earliest occupation hitherto discovered was at Eridu XIX–XV and is now known as the Eridu culture. No building remains are known from the lowest level (XIX) and these may have been of a temporary nature. Four parallel walls of mud-brick mark level XVIII,[6] but above them a small rectangular shrine with two internal buttresses was erected in level XVII.[7] Outside there were two circular kilns. Shrine XVI[8] was a more elaborate affair in mud-brick with rectangular plan, and with an offering-table and altar set in a recessed niche at the back of the room. Internal buttresses were again present. The level XV temple was considerably larger, and again had numerous buttresses, but its interior features are not preserved.[9] It was built of long narrow bricks, having rows of thumb impressions on the upper side, like those of Sialk II. Again, there were kilns outside the structure. These superimposed shrines were supplanted by monumental

---

[1] §1, 2, fig. 42, 10 (*Mém. D.P.* xxx, fig. 23: 4)
[2] §1, 2, fig. 42: 1 (*Mém. D.P.* xxx, fig. 21: 7).
[3] §1, 2, figs. 27 f.   [4] §1, 2, fig. 42: 9, 10.
[5] See below, pp. 327 ff.   [6] §viii, 2, pl. vi, 122.
[7] §viii, 2, pl. vi, 122.   [8] §viii, 2, pl. vi, 121 f., pl. viii.
[9] §viii, 2, pl. vi, 121.

temples in the next period, of the Ḥajji Muḥammad culture, but the sanctity of the site was preserved throughout the following millennia, and these early and unsophisticated shrines lay below the towering zikkurrat of the Uruk period. Houses of the same period show small rectangular plans as in Khūzistān across the marshes, but the more spectacular finds are the pottery vessels made by the first settlers at Eridu.

The pottery is a well-tempered buff or sometimes reddish ware with a light slip, usually painted in a chocolate colour varying from black to dark brown which acquired a glossy colour in the firing. A thinner red paint is also found. Among the coarse-ware vessels are 'husking-trays', characteristic of Hassūnah. Typical shapes[1] include tall beakers, bowls with spouts, collar-necked jars, jars with everted rims, jars with internal ledges, shallow simple bowls, flat plates, carinated bowls, and deep bowls, also carinated. Most of these shapes have close parallels in Susiana, and the carinated bowls go back to Tepe Sarāb and Tepe Gūrān. Other shapes are reminiscent of Sāmarrā. The painting is elaborate, and reserve patterns are extremely common, giving many of the plates an appearance like basketry. The style of decoration is closest to that of Susiana A, where many of the patterns are also matched. As the Eridu culture arrived at the site fully fledged,[2] its origins must be sought elsewhere, probably in Khūzistān or the highlands above. The Eridu culture developed locally, it would seem, into that of Ḥajji Muḥammad,[3] perhaps with some further reinforcements from Susiana, for it is known to underlie a good number of Sumerian sites, such as Ur, Warka and Nippur. It spread north to the area of Kish, where the village site of Ras el-'Amiya marks its northernmost limit.[4] In short the Ḥajji Muḥammad culture is spread throughout the land of Sumer, is closely related to Susiana B, and is even known from Kūzaragān up the Saimarreh river in southern Luristān.

At the type site, Qal'at Ḥajji Muḥammad near Warka,[5] and at Ras el-'Amiya remains of buildings discovered are unimpressive, but at Eridu monumental temple architecture appears in levels IX–XI,[6] towards the middle of the period, but not in the earlier levels (XIV–XII). These mud-brick temples set on solid platforms with sloping faces approached by ramps are the prototypes for all later Mesopotamian temples placed on a zikkurrat. Their recessed façades derive evidently from the buttressed

---

[1] §VIII, 2, 124, pls. III, X.   [2] §VIII, 2, 125.
[3] §VIII, 2, pl. III.   [4] §VIII, 4 *passim.*
[5] §VIII, 5 *passim.*   [6] §VIII, 2, 119 f., pl. VI.

but thin walls of these early temples, which in turn go back to the simple shrines of the Eridu period. The Ḥajji Muḥammad temples of Eridu XI and IX consist of a long room with an altar at one end, surrounded by other rectangular rooms, one of which contains an offering-table. The main façades of the temples are deeply recessed, and there may have been several entrances, the main one lying perhaps in the narrow side, facing the altar. Towards the end of the period, the more solidly built and much larger temple VIII[1] shows the standard plan with the offering-table placed in line with the altar and directly behind the double entrance.

Considerable continuity between Eridu and Ḥajji Muḥammad phases is indicated by the shapes of the pottery and much of the patterned design, which continues a close style and reserve patterns. Glossy paint produced by firing is equally character-istic even if the tones change from the earlier chocolate to a green, dark mauve, or bright red colour. Carinated bowls, jars with internal rim ledge pierced by four holes, beakers, etc.[2] continue to be made.[3] Vertical zigzag patterns resemble basketry, petalled rosettes occupy the centre of bowls,[4] and geometric ornament[5] still prevails, though an occasional bucranium makes its appearance. Close contact is maintained with Susiana B, and even with regions farther afield in the Iranian foothills. Clay 'nails', or bulls' horns, and clay sickles make their first appearance, probably as votive offerings.[5]

Mixed farming formed the economic basis of this culture: bread-ovens are common at Ras el-'Amiya and bones of domes-tic cattle, sheep and goat were found there. At Eridu, the Ḥajji Muḥammad pottery occurs from level XIV–VIII, but in the latest layers a new style of pottery makes its first appearance in force,[6] that of 'Ubaid. Very small but elaborately decorated egg-shell bowls, painted in black on red in level IX, and in purple brown on a cream slip in VIII, still show close-style patterning or negative designs, unmistakably Iranian in character.[7] Tortoise-shaped vessels with reserve patterns first occur in level VIII,[8] together with other typical 'Ubaid wares, marking in many respects the beginning of a new period. The changes are gradual and it is evident that 'Ubaid developed out of Ḥajji Muḥammad

---

[1] §viii, 2, 119, pl. vi.
[2] §viii, 2, pl. iii; §i, 2, fig. 44; §i, 1, fig. 40 *k–m*.
[3] §viii, 5, pl. 22 *d*.   [4] §viii, 5, pl. 25 *e*.
[5] §i, 2, fig. 45; §viii, 2, pl. x top.   [6] §viii, 2, pl. iii.
[7] §viii, 2, 123, pls. iii, vii.   [8] §viii, 2, 123, pls. iii, vii.

just as the latter is derived from Eridu. This continuity of cultural evolution has led certain scholars[1] to simplify the sequence into 'Ubaid 1–4, Eridu being 'Ubaid 1, Ḥajji Muḥammad 'Ubaid 2, etc., against the better judgement of the excavators. As it tends to obscure the links of these two early cultures with Susiana and favours the theory of autochthonous development (which can no longer be maintained, in view of the recent discoveries at Ali-Kush and Tepe Sabz), the alternative system may have to be rejected.

There is a more important implication of the cultural continuity of southern Mesopotamia from the Eridu to the 'Ubaid period. In spite of the spread of a new pottery during the Uruk period, architectural traditions show the persistence of the old pattern of culture into the Uruk and Jamdat Naṣr periods, when the first glimpses of literacy identify the people of south Mesopotamia as the Sumerians. Although it was once believed that the Sumerians made their entry into Sumer from some highland area only in the Uruk period, scholars now tend to agree[2] that they were there before, at least during the 'Ubaid period; and, as 'Ubaid is the cultural culmination of two previous phases of development, Ḥajji Muḥammad and Eridu, it would be difficult to deny that the Sumerians were the first settlers of lower Mesopotamia. The discoveries of Seton Lloyd and Fuad Safar have thus traced the beginnings of Sumerian civilization back to the middle of the sixth millennium B.C. in the alluvial plain of ancient Sumer. For the next five millennia these people were able to dominate, at least culturally, the development of civilization in the land of the Twin Rivers and contribute substantially to the cultural heritage of the ancient Near East. But the alluvial plain of southern Mesopotamia was not the area where the first steps were taken towards the development of agriculture and stock-breeding, and only the development of efficient irrigation systems made agriculture possible. If the earliest inhabitants of Eridu were Sumerians, as we also believe, then it must be accepted that they made their homes in the plain only after having mastered irrigation techniques in their former abodes at the foot of the Zagros mountains, probably in Khūzistān. Heirs of nearly a thousand years in Iran of simple village life, of primitive agriculture, herding and hunting and the production of pottery, they were at last fully equipped to deal with a new and challenging environment. Sheltered from invasion by the lakes and marshes they were gradually able to develop a civilization that was to have

[1] §VIII, 3, 32 ff.　　　[2] §VII, 3, 32 ff.

few equals. Throughout their long history, connexions between the states of Sumer and Elam, even if hostile, remained as close as they had been in that early dawn of civilization when they shared the great flat lands beyond where shimmered the snow-caps of the Zagros mountains, their homeland.

IX. THE IRANIAN PLATEAU

Present evidence would suggest that pottery was first invented in Iran during the second half of the seventh millennium, perhaps soon after 6500 B.C., and was very soon decorated with painted designs. The centre of this development seems to have been the central Zagros (the region of Tepe Gūrān and Tepe Sarāb), and from there it spread both southward to Khūzistān (Muḥammad Ja'far phase) and north-westward to Jarmo. Recent discoveries in southern Turkmenia have revealed a culture that preceded Anau (I A), the Jeitun culture which also has both painted and unpainted pottery, perhaps soon after 6000 B.C.

On the Iranian plateau, east of the Zagros range, painted-pottery cultures have been found which were perhaps contemporary with those of Hassūnah and Sāmarrā in northern Iraq. These are situated in the Urmia basin (Ḥajji Fīrūz), in the regions of Kāshān, Sahveh and Shahriyār, west of Tihrān (Tepe Sialk, I and II), and perhaps as far east as Tepe Hisar, near Dāmghān. In Fars, the Tell Mishgī and Tepe Jarreh B cultures may conceivably date from the same period.[1]

Apart from pottery, very little indeed is known about these cultures. At Ḥajji Fīrūz,[2] south of Ḥasanlu, and at Yanik Tepe,[3] west of Tabrīz, remains of houses were found, built of packed mud, with rooms of rectangular plan set around open courtyards which contained open hearths and large storage vessels. At Ḥajji Fīrūz at least six superimposed building levels were found and carbon-14 dates were obtained from a burnt village, the second from the top, dated to 5152 B.C., and from the sixth level, dated to 5537 B.C. Earlier levels are present, but they lie below the water-table; at Yanik Tepe these levels contained only unpainted pottery. During the burning of Ḥajji Fīrūz II massacres had taken place and the victims were buried by the survivors in three mass graves containing twenty-eight individuals.[4] Red ochre was sprinkled over the dead, who were accompanied by

---

[1] §1, 1, 74; §1, 2, fig. 18.　　　[2] §ix, 6, 707, fig. 9.
[3] §ix, 2, 55 ff.　　　[4] §ix, 6, 707, fig. 11.

much pottery, both plain and painted, polished celts and flint blades. The pottery of this culture is simple, straw-tempered and poorly fired; the plain wares show few shapes and the painted wares are decorated in red or a fugitive pink paint on a cream surface. Designs are simple, unsophisticated and purely geometric. Plain bowls and deep biconical bowls or jars are characteristic.[1] The amount of painted pottery at Yanik Tepe farther north is much smaller and looks as if it were fading out northwards. With pottery, stone bowls still occur, as well as alabaster bracelets and figurines in the tradition of Tepe Sarāb, Tepe Gūrān, Jarmo and Tell Shemshāra.

Architecturally, the buildings of the following 'Dalme culture'[2] in Azarbāyjān show no marked advance, but the pottery is a very accomplished product. Known only from the Urmia region, its origin is obscure, but it still retains the biconical deep bowls or jars, which are now coated with a maroon slip on the inside, whereas the outside is decorated in a purplish black paint on a cream burnished surface. Patterns are elaborate and cover the entire pot. They may represent a development of the earlier Ḥajji Fīrūz ware: hatched triangles and lozenges are still common, but zigzag bands in reserve, rows of solid triangles and multiple chevrons are now also used.[3] All patterns are still geometric; and animal designs, so beloved in other parts of Iran, are conspicuous by their absence. Jars, bowls and beakers are the most common shapes, and monochrome plain wares also occur; heavy straw-tempering is characteristic, as in most Iranian wares. The other aspects of the culture are less well known; weaving and spinning are attested by whorls and loom-weights, and the patterns on the pottery may have been inspired by textiles. For tools local chert was more frequently used than imported obsidian. Metal is not yet reported. A carbon-14 date of 4216 B.C. was obtained for this period, which may be roughly contemporary with the Halaf culture further west.

Overlying the deposits with painted ware were others with a totally new type of unpainted pottery the surface of which is decorated by impressions made with tubes, combs, fingers and sticks; this is known as Dalme impressed ware.[4] This pottery has a much wider distribution, from Yanik Tepe and Dalme in Azarbāyjān to Tepe Syāhbīd in the plain of Kirmānshāh (with a carbon-14 date of 4039 B.C.) and the region of Khurramābād, where its relation to the Giyān V culture is still unknown. In

[1] §IX, 6, 707, figs. 6 and 2. [2] §IX, 6 707 f., fig. 10.
[3] §IX, 6, 707, figs. 3 ff.; §IX, 7; §I, 1, fig. 43. [4] §IX, 6, 708; 1, fig. 42.

Azarbāyjān this 'barbarous' pottery marks an interruption in the sequence of painted pottery and is in turn succeeded by Pisdeli painted ware of the fourth millennium, which, at least in its repertoire of patterns, is under the influence of northern 'Ubaid.

The Sialk culture. Tepe Sialk, the type site of this culture, lies near Kāshān and is a medium-sized mound covering six acres. The Sialk I deposits were 12 m. thick, those of Sialk II were 7 m., yet the excavators in the thirties of this century, unfamiliar with *pisé* (in Sialk I) and mud-brick (in II), failed to distinguish a single building level in this deposit of 60 ft. depth. This by itself suggests that buildings lacked stone foundations, which would be difficult to miss. Architectural remains were likewise not detected at Cheshme-i-Ali (Ray), Masreh, and Kara Tepe, 20 miles west of Tihrān (where only ovens and a sewer are mentioned),[1] yet these sites have produced very fine Sialk II pottery.[2] One might assume that the buildings of this culture, which urgently demands a modern excavation, did not differ much from those of the upper levels of Tepe Gūrān or of the Ḥajji Fīrūz culture farther north. Nothing certain is known about the economy except that mixed farming must have been practised; sheep and goats may have been domesticated, slingstones suggest hunting, and well-carved bone sickles[3] from Sialk suggest agriculture, but the nature of the crops is not known. New is the use of hammered copper in Sialk I, substrata 3 and 4, in the form of a round awl, two pins with biconical heads, a needle with a forged eye and a spiral.[4] The material was probably native copper from the Anarak (Talmessi mine) in the Kāshān district, not far from Sialk. Annealing is first attested in a pin from Sialk I or II, at which period tanged awls, buttons and bracelets were also made in copper. By period III, probably contemporary with Halaf and 'Ubaid, large copper pins, punches and cast axes were produced.[5] Like Anatolia, the metal-bearing highlands of Iran offer evidence for much earlier metallurgy than the Mesopotamian plain.

The only material which is relatively plentiful is pottery, both plain and painted, and it is this which has made this culture famous. The pottery of Sialk I[6] is a brownish ware, covered with a red or cream slip, decorated in matt black, with geometric ornament possibly imitating, like the shapes, sophisticated basketry. Deep bowls, pedestalled vessels and pot-stands are the

---

[1] §ix, 1, 30 f.   [2] §ix, 1, 27 ff.; §1, 2, pl. iv, 1, 2, 5.
[3] §ix, 3, pls. vii, viii, 1–3.   [4] §ix, 5, 4.
[5] §ix, 5 ff.   [6] §ix, 3, pls. iv ff., xxxviii f.

main shapes. Red and black monochrome wares are also found, the first having links with the upper layers of Tepe Gūrān, which produces a subsequent date for earliest Sialk. The pottery of Sialk I, it seems, reached the area east of the Kopet Dağ, the south-eastern extension of the Elburz mountains, giving birth, perhaps in the wake of a wave of immigrants, to the Anau I A culture.

The Sialk II pottery[1] is evidently a development of the previous fabrics and is decorated in matt black on red. The interiors of the vessels are covered likewise with a red slip and, as before, the ornament is applied either to the exterior or interior or to both. Geometric ornament still prevails, but naturalistic designs such as goats and long-necked animals (asses) make their first appearance. The quality of the pottery, frequently burnished, has made great advances. Sialk II is probably contemporary with Sāmarrā in the north Mesopotamian plain, and in Sāmarrā pottery many Iranian motifs appear, including naturalistically drawn goats, deer and other animals, unknown in the contemporary local Hassūnah pottery, and therefore probably derivative. Basketry designs are still there, in greater elegance, on deep-flaring bowls, carinated bowls or hole-mouthed jars similar to those of Ḥajji Fīrūz (and later Dalme). Pedestalled vessels develop into fruit-stands or stemmed goblets. Panelled decoration is now frequently applied instead of free-running design. An apparently unbroken development leads to Sialk III, roughly contemporary with Halaf (III, 1–3) and then 'Ubaid (III, 4–5) and Uruk (III, 6–7). Richly decorated goblets[2] and very deep bowls adorned with more naturalistic plant and animal motifs in black on cream, including birds and leopards, mark this period, paralleled further east in Tepe Hisar I A–C. In Sialk III, 4, contemporary with 'Ubaid, the potter's wheel appears.

Enough has been said to demonstrate the high potential of early cultures on the Iranian plateau, most of which are still inadequately known or published. Until much more is known about Iran, the measure of contact and the role of Iranian influence on early Mesopotamian developments can only be guessed, but even in the light of recent discoveries, however limited, it appears to have been great, if not decisive. The role of the highland zone in the development of early cultures in the Near East has been greatly underestimated, it would seem, and just as recent discoveries in Anatolia have shown that this country played a decisive part in the transmitting of culture to

[1] §IX, 1, 27 ff.; 1, fig. 46; §IX, 3, pls. IX, XLV f.   [2] §I, 1, fig. 45.

south-eastern Europe and probably also to north Syria, so Iran, its highland neighbour, similarly contributed to, if it did not initially stimulate, the development of culture in Iraq on its western flank and—a fact often forgotten or minimized—in the east as well. Soviet research into the origins and developments of the so-called Anau culture of southern Turkmenia has in the last decade made spectacular progress, and the modern methods employed have resulted in the reconstruction of a far more complete picture of cultural development in this important area, long regarded as a cultural backwater, than is available for any culture on the Iranian plateau. Nothing shows more clearly that the initial stimulus for this development on its eastern marches came from Iran itself, and it is hoped that in the near future excavations will be carried out in Khurāsān, which is virtually unexplored.

X. SOUTHERN TURKESTAN

A decade ago this remote region was usually treated as a poor orphan among the family of early Near Eastern cultures, but the recent discoveries are such that it would be invidious to omit it from this survey. The area is bordered by the Caspian Sea, the towering mountain ranges of Elburz, Kopet Dağ and Hindu Kush towards the west and south and forms a strip of fertile and cultivable soil edged by the sands of the Kara Kum desert. Geographically this is the beginning of central Asia, open to invasion from north and east and a boundary between the conflicting interests of cultivator and nomad. There is a tendency to overestimate the importance of time-lags where long distances are concerned, but it has recently been pointed out that the idea of agriculture could easily have spread: even a slow walker doing ten miles a day can travel from central Anatolia to central Afghanistan in about six months![1] Even if it took a century, the archaeologist would be unable to notice it with the means at his disposal. We must therefore be prepared for surprises and keep an open mind.

The prelude to settled life is similar to that in regions further west. At Ghār-i-Kamarband (Belt Cave)[2] and Ghār-i-Hūtū[3] on the Iranian part of the Caspian shore, at Damdam Cheshme and Jebel Cave[4] at the foot of the Balkan hills east of the Caspian in Turkmenia and at Ghār-i-Mār (Snake Cave) on the Balkh river near

---

[1] §x, 2, 640.   [2] §x, 1, 31 f., 49 ff.
[3] Unpublished.   [4] §x, 6, 203 f.; §x, 5, 12, figs. 1, 2.

Akkopruk in the northern foothills of the Hindu Kush,[1] a series
of 'mesolithic' and both 'aceramic' and 'ceramic neolithic' cultures has been found in recent years. This shows that the hill and
mountain zones bordering the fertile but narrow plains of South
Turkestan were inhabited by hunters of gazelle, ox, wild sheep
and goat, by fishermen and collectors of wild barley and wheat,
which, according to two radiocarbon dates (7140 ± 1400 from
Belt Cave and 6985 ± 100 from Snake Cave), was well established
by c. 7000 B.C. Sickle blades, though rare, are attested at the latter
site, together with long blades, burins and end scrapers, but no
geometric microliths, which are a characteristic feature[2] of the
east Caspian sites and the Jeitun culture of the Ashkhābād region
in the early sixth millennium.

Whereas the affinities of the neolithic wares (c. 6000 B.C.?),
both plain and painted, found in the Belt and Hotu caves are not
yet clear, developments in south Turkmenia seem to have been
twofold: in the Ashkhābād region, the earliest farmers of the
Jeitun culture had both plain and painted pottery, but further
east painted pottery was not made. At Ghār-i-Mār, the neolithic
development shows first a possibly aceramic phase with numerous sickle blades, blades, side scrapers on blades, points, burins
etc., dated to the middle of the sixth millennium (5510 ± 100),
followed by one in which both soft-baked plain ware and a fine
ware with zigzag incision is produced. Sickle blades are common; and carbonized plant remains, not yet analysed, may show
agriculture. Cattle, sheep and goat were domesticated by $5314 \pm$
100 B.C. This important evidence shows that far to the east of the
Jeitun culture mixed farming was probably in progress well
before the end of the sixth millennium. The incised pottery has
similarities to that found east and west of the Oxus up to the
Aral Sea, the Kelteminar complex of cultures which S. P.
Tolstov had tentatively dated to c. 5000 B.C. It has recently been
shown that the decoration of this pottery may have been influenced by the painted wares of Namazga II[3] (roughly contemporary with Hisar I A–B, Sialk III, 1–3, and Halaf, which
began c. 5300 B.C.). Incidentally, this is also the date for the
earliest penetration of pottery into south-eastern Europe
(Starčevo culture). This phenomenal spread of Near Eastern
culture extending from the plains of Hungary in the west to the
Aral Sea, Bokhara and the Hindu Kush in the east shows the
success of the neolithic economic evolution and goes far to
explain how exotic products such as turquoise from the Nīshāpūr

---

[1] §x, 2, 638 ff.   [2] §x, 6, 203 ff., fig. 2.   [3] §x, 4, pl. xix.

region of eastern Iran or lapis lazuli from Badakhshān near the
sources of the Oxus should appear in such early contexts as Ali-
Kush (turquoise before 6000 B.C.[1]) and Tepe Gawra (lapis lazuli
in 'Ubaid period), if correctly identified. Trade evidently preceded the introduction of the new economy from the Near East.

A considerable time-lag is involved between the establishment
of the first farming communities of the Jeitun culture and the
Kelteminar culture. The former is considerably older, and might
have begun in *c.* 6000 B.C.

The Jeitun culture. The site is a small mound covering 4000 sq. m.,
30 km. north-east of Ashkhābād. Three fifths of this open village,
with single detached houses of standard square plan, were
explored.[2] Nineteen such houses were excavated, usually 20–
35 m.[2] in size, and each with a small yard and adjoining farm and
storage rooms. The walls were built of *pisé* and were no doubt
plastered. The floors were covered with thick lime plaster, sometimes painted a reddish brown as in Tepe Gūrān, Ali-Kush,
Jericho, Çatal Hüyük, aceramic Hacılar and Menteşe. In the
centre of one of the walls was a large square hearth, with an
adjoining bin in one of the corners; opposite the hearth was a
small projection in the wall with a niche low down near the floor,
painted red-brown or black. The position of the doorway giving
entrance from courtyard or alley was most often placed near the
position of the bin.[3] The open planning of the villages of Jeitun
and Choban Tepe is reminiscent of the Early Neolithic villages of
Nea Nikomedeia and Karanovo I in Macedonia and Bulgaria,
and different from the Near Eastern agglutinative buildings of
aceramic Hacılar, Çatal Hüyük or Hassūnah. The economy of
Jeitun was mixed farming; barley and wheat impressions occur
in the *pisé*. About 300 bone sickles[4] with flint blades have
been found (similar to those of Sialk I). Hunting provided the
inhabitants with most of their meat, the quarry consisting of
bezoar, goat, *ovis orientalis* and *gazella subgutturosa*; only a small
percentage of sheep and goats shows signs of domestication.
The flint industry, besides producing numerous sickle blades, has
knife blades, borers, notched and trimmed blades, and still a
strong microlithic element comprising arrowheads, lunates,
triangles, trapezoids, micro-scrapers, etc., which are presumably
derived from the similar equipment of proto-neolithic hunters in
the area east of the Caspian (Jebel Cave, etc.). Other finds, such as
conical terracotta objects, have parallels in the Belt Cave and

---

[1] §III, 3, 106.   [2] §X, 6, 204 ff.; §X, 5, figs. 3, 4. See Fig. 22(*a*).
[3] §X, 6, fig. 2; §X, 5, fig. 5.   [4] §X, 5, fig. 18.

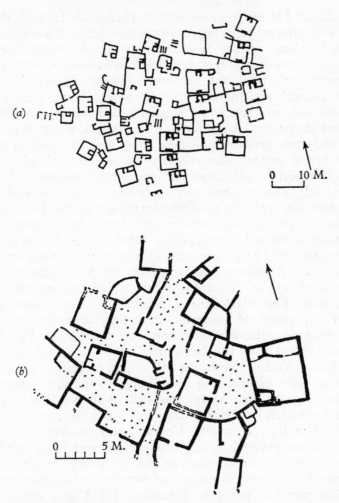

(a)

0   10 M.

(b)

0   5 M.

Fig. 22. (a) Jeitun: plan of the village; (b) Dashliji Tepe: plan of the village.
After V. M. Masson, *Srednaya Asiya i drevniye vostok*, figs. 3 and 21.

Sialk I.[1] The intermediate stages between these proto-neolithic
hunting cultures and the fully settled farming culture of Jeitun
have not yet been found, but attention should be drawn to a
number of parallels with cultures farther west. *Pisé* architecture,
rectangular plan, red plaster floors, straight sickles and also the
hand-made straw-tempered plain and red-painted pottery have
clear relations in the west. Clay-lined storage pits are comparable to those of Hassūnah, and storage vessels of Jeitun and

[1] §x, 5, figs. 5, 6.

later Anau IA[1] are reminiscent of Hassūnah IA with the same biconical shapes tapering towards the base. The patterns on painted Jeitun pottery are extremely simple; wavy lines, solid triangles, rows of brackets, parallel lines painted in reddish brown on cream perhaps imitate patterned baskets. Apart from cylindrical conical jars, there are simple bowls, bowls with S-shaped profiles and, in plain ware, square 'salad bowls' on flat bases. Incised decoration is unknown. Metal, too, was still unknown; polished axes, grooved polishers, awls, needles, points, beads of bone are common. Shovels are made from shoulder-blades. Spindle-whorls, indicative of weaving, amulets, including (imported?) cowries, and clay figurines of humans and animals complete the typically neolithic inventory of the Jeitun culture, which, in spite of numerous resemblances to western cultures, preserves a marked individuality. Of the burial habits nothing is known, the dead being presumably buried outside the settlement.

The Anau IA culture. The next phase of development is seen in the assemblage of Anau IA, about which, unfortunately, little is known. The black-on-red painted pottery shows a much richer repertory of patterns, including cross-hatched bands, solid triangles, chevrons and bordered wavy lines. Parallels can be established with the beginning of Sialk I, 1,[2] Sahveh and Cheshme-i-Ali IA. Shapes are still similar to Jeitun. Perhaps new elements from central Iran contributed to the foundation of this culture *c.* 5700 B.C. Metal was still unknown, but appears in Anau IB, which has been renamed as the following.

The Namazga I culture. Contact with central Iran (Sialk I, 3–4) was maintained during this period[3] and is reflected in the patterns of the dark-brown-on-red or white painted pottery, decorated with simple designs of ever increasing variety. Other indirect parallels point to Hassūnah III–V and contemporary Sāmarrā.[4] The pottery developed out of that of the earlier Anau IA and Jeitun phases and shapes remain related.[5] Of the two varieties, that on a white ground is now the more common. Patterns are still strongly geometric, but include linear ornament and the first appearance of naturalistically rendered goats (as in Sialk II).[6]

At Anau itself and especially at Yassa Tepe wall-paintings[7] have been discovered, probably in shrines, which imitate woven textiles, patterned in squares and triangles, plain or bordered in

---

[1] §I, 2, fig. 16, 1, 4; §x, 5, fig. 20.   [2] §x, 3, 26, fig. 6, pl. III, 1–12.
[3] §x, 3, 26, fig. 8.   [4] §x, 3, 26, fig. 9.   [5] §x, 3, figs. 2, 3.
[6] §x, 5, fig. 20.   [7] §x, 3, pls. II, IV, 1–3, XI.

red-brown, black, red, pink and white colours, often in several superimposed layers of paint. The patterns are closely related to those found on the pottery. A further feature of this culture are steatopygous clay figures of Mother Goddess type, frequently decorated with white paint,[1] as well as those of animals such as bulls and goats.

It is possible to trace an expansion of population[2] from the centre of this area around Ashkhābād to Artyk and Kashka, then to the eastern group around Sarakhs (occupied early in the period with 6–7 m. of occupation material), on to the Göksür oasis on the Tejen river towards the late phase of the period (2–2·5 m. of deposits). Here excavations on the site of Dashliji[3] have revealed three superimposed settlements, now fully excavated, that have yielded the best architectural remains of the period (see Fig. 22 (b)). The architecture is still very much like that of Jeitun and shows the same open plan with square houses, each with a small hearth and a raised platform on the opposite side of the room. Houses are still surrounded by various storage buildings and open courts. New, however, is the use of mud-brick which appears in two sizes (46–48 and 36–38 × 24 × 10 cm.).[4] Other innovations of the period are the use of copper knives and awls,[5] twisted beads and pins with semi-spherical heads, decorated spindle-whorls, paintings of textiles, and the increased production of two-row barley, which is thirty times as common as wheat (*Triticum vulgare*).[6] Though wild game was still hunted, cattle, goat, sheep and pig were now domesticated.[7] A carbon-14 date from Tilkintepe,[8] recalculated with the higher half-life, gives 4850 ± 110 for the second phase of Namazga I, which seems a little low in view of its typological comparisons with later Sialk I and II, late Hassūnah and Sāmarrā, which end *c.* 5300 B.C. according to recent carbon-14 dates.

The Namazga II culture. The next period in succession, Namazga II, was a long one, spanning the millennium between approximately 5300 and 4300 B.C. It is roughly contemporary with Sialk III, 1–3, Hisar I A–B in Iran, and Halaf in Mesopotamia. It can be divided into two periods: Early Namazga II (and Anau II, Kara Tepe 3, 4) and Late Namazga II (and Kara Tepe I B–II), each with its own characteristic pottery.[9] More-

---

[1] §x, 5, fig. 20.
[2] §x, 3, 26, fig. 5.
[3] §x, 3, pl. xvii; §x, 5, fig. 21.
[4] §x, 5, 131.
[5] §x, 5, fig. 20.
[6] §x, 3, 26.
[7] *Ibid.*
[8] §x, 3, 8.
[9] §x, 6, 207 f.; §x, 4, pls. 1 f.

over, marked differences now prevailed in the Göksür oasis, which produced a most interesting variant and, in Early Namazga II, unusual architecture. Early Namazga II saw a number of innovations; as at Sialk III, metallurgy made steady progress[1] and flat copper spearheads and axes now appear. Whereas barley is still the main crop sown, a new hybrid wheat, Bread wheat (*Triticum aestivum*),[2] appears in the Göksür oasis, and large and more naturalistically modelled figurines of Mother Goddess type[3] now prevail. Polychrome pottery,[4] decorated in black and red on an orange-cream base, with new shapes, such as cups, wide bowls and necked jars, replaces the simpler painted wares of the previous period. Besides geometric motifs, stylized human figures and goats are found.

In the Göksür oasis, however, the pottery is different; the elaborately decorated polychrome ware is rare and probably imported. Rare too is pottery decorated with oblique hatched lozenges (as in Sialk II). Most common is the Yalangach ware, less sophisticated in shape, derived from the Dashliji ware of the previous period and decorated with four parallel lines below the rim or with rows of triangles pendent from the rim of large pots.[5] Simple as the pottery may be, the architecture of the oasis in this early phase, locally known as the Yalangach phase, is remarkable. Yalangach Tepe[6] and Mullali Tepe[7] are fortified with a wall, 0·5–1 m. thick, provided with round tower-like houses, regularly spaced, and with diameters varying from 3·5 to 5 m. Hearths found in these rooms show that they were occupied as dwellings. Within the circuit of the walls are houses, roughly square in plan, with a rectangular hearth in one corner and irregularly adjoining store-rooms, a plan reminiscent of Dashliji. There are also a few round houses within the walls in the first settlement of Yalangach and at Mullali. In the second and later settlement of Yalangach the spacing of houses is different and some are built in rows with party walls[8]—the beginning of cellular planning which was to lead to the many-roomed houses of the Late Namazga II period. Also there are now differences in size, and larger, but still one-roomed, houses occur side by side with smaller ones.

Yalangach and Mullali with their round houses remind one of the round buildings of the contemporary Halaf culture, but they differ in lacking an ante-room and may here have served as towers

---

[1] §x, 5, fig. 24; §x, 4, pl. x.   [2] §x, 5, 143.
[3] §x, 5, fig. 24; §x, 6, fig. 3.   [4] §x, 4, pls. iii f.
[5] §x, 5, fig. 24; §x, 4, pl. ii.   [6] §x, 5, fig. 58.
[7] §x, 5, figs. 22, 60. See fig. 4 (a).   [8] §x, 5, fig. 59.

in the fortifications which were no doubt built as a defence against marauding bands of nomads. As we have already seen, the Namazga II culture influenced the design on pottery of the Kelteminar culture and it may have been against bands of these people, less sedentary than their neighbours, that the settlements in the Göksür oasis were fortified. However that may be, there is a clean break in the pottery tradition in the oasis between the early Namazga II (Yalangach) and the later (or Göksür) period, and a temporary intrusion of unpainted red-burnished, red-slipped and grey wares, the origins of which are unknown.[1]

This is followed by the gaily painted Göksür ware,[2] a bichrome ware in black and red decoration with crosses, half crosses, serrated lines, and geometrically drawn animals, patterns suggesting the influence of textile and kilim manufacture. The technique of decoration and the new repertoire of shapes first found in the west in Early Namazga II have now extended to the oasis. At the same time the polychrome ware disappears in the west and its place is taken by a brown-on-yellow painted ware, but it has inherited the same old patterns and shapes.[3] Both areas are united by a new development in building, that of rows of large many-roomed houses built on a unified plan along narrow streets.[4] Hearths are now placed in the centre of a room and no longer in the corner. The type site of this period is Göksür I, which, covering 22 acres, is the largest site in the oasis and a small town. On the edge of the settlement a cemetery of brick-built tombs was found.[5] These are of circular or rectangular plan, covered with a false vault of mud-brick. They were family graves and contained several burials. This, too, is an innovation of the period and a development of the burials in simple pits, sometimes lined with brick, that were found in the earlier cultures. Naturalistic clay figurines are finer and smaller than those made in the Yalangach period.[6]

The Late Namazga II period, then, saw the beginnings of urban development along lines familiar in other parts of the Near East, at a period which, it is estimated, is roughly contemporary with the end of the Halaf culture and the beginning of 'Ubaid in Mesopotamia. Its full realization, however, belongs to the Namazga III period, the equivalent of 'Ubaid and Uruk, of Hisar Ic and IIA and Sialk III, 4–7, as is indicated by numerous analogies and resemblances. New physical types

---

[1] §x, 6, 210.
[2] §x, 5, fig. 25; §x, 4, pl. ii.
[3] §x, 6, 208.
[4] §x, 5, fig. 61.
[5] §x, 5, fig. 25.
[6] §x, 5, fig. 25.

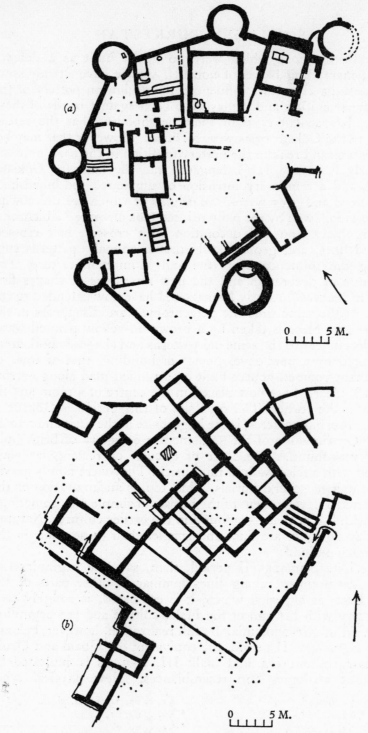

Fig. 23. (a) Mullali Tepe: portion of the settlement; (b) Kara Tepe: large house.
After V. M. Masson, *Srednaya Asiya i drevniye vostok*, figs. 60 and 62.

appear as at Sialk[1] and, although they are soon assimilated by the old population, leave their mark in a different orientation in the lay-out of the dead. Pottery and architecture show the persistence of local traditions. Influenced by the Göksür style, richly patterned deep bowls painted in dark brown on greenish white or red surface show geometric patterns of textile origin as well as mountain goats, solar circles, spotted leopards, cows and eagles, especially at Kara Tepe.[2] The architectural lay-out of Kara Tepe I B[3] shows a large square from which streets run out separating large houses with as many as fifteen to twenty rooms all arranged around a courtyard. Rooms are provided with central hearths made of pots without a base sunk in the floor; kitchens are situated in the courtyard and small narrow rooms serve as storage chambers. A new use is found for stone: there are stone seals, stone vessels, stone sculptures, including a statue of a bull.[4] Clay figurines, elaborately modelled show the figure of the Mother Goddess standing or holding a child,[5] exact counterparts to the well-known 'lizard-faced' 'Ubaid figures from Ur and Eridu.[6]

In view of the many resemblances between this period, that of 'Ubaid and Uruk, that of Namazga IV (and Hapus Tepe in the Göksür oasis) as compared with Sialk IV and Jamdat Naṣr, the single carbon-14 date[7] from Kara Tepe I B of 2900 ± 220 B.C., said to come from an early phase of Namazga III, is unacceptable, possibly because the sample was contaminated.

What these new excavations have established beyond doubt is that the Anau region, to use the long familiar term, did not represent a peripheral backwater compared with the rest of the Near East, but a centre of early and vigorous individuality, which developed a series of cultures by no means inferior to Syria and Palestine, or even Mesopotamia. Behind this development must lie the unknown potential of eastern Iran.

[1] §x, 6, 212.
[2] §x, 6, pls. xxvi f.; §x, 5, fig. 26.
[3] §x, 5, fig. 62. See Fig. 23 (*b*).
[4] §x, 5, fig. 29.
[5] §x, 5, figs. 27, 28.
[6] §x, 5, fig. 79.
[7] §x, 4, 7.

CHAPTER VII (*b*)

ANATOLIA BEFORE *c.* 4000 B.C.

XI. GEOGRAPHICAL INTRODUCTION

THE term Anatolia is used throughout this division to describe Turkey in Asia, including Cilicia, but excluding the regions east of the Amanus and south of the eastern Taurus, the cultures of which are evidently more related to those of Syria and northern Mesopotamia.[1] This crescent of mountains stretching without a break from the Mediterranean to the western borders of Persia neatly defines the southern edge of Anatolia, even though it never presented an impassable barrier. It often formed a cultural frontier, and there was sufficient traffic through the passes to make it act as a political frontier as well. Cilicia, or rather the plain of Cilicia, is often singled out as a more or less independent unit on account of a similar geographical position south of the Taurus, but recent research shows conclusively that, although it maintained contacts with both the Anatolian plateau and north Syria, it should both archaeologically and philologically be considered a part of Anatolia.

To understand the development of Anatolian cultures and civilization, a geographical knowledge of the country is a prerequisite. Three main factors must be emphasized: its size, its mountainous character, and its forests. Superimposed on a map of Europe Anatolia extends from Calais to the Russian frontier, from Denmark to Rome or from Amsterdam to Gibraltar. Anatolia is a highland country, most of it over 2000 ft. high and gradually rising to an altitude of 5000–6000 ft. in the east. Prehistoric Anatolia was mostly covered in forest and woodland and a great part of it still is so. Many of the now semi-arid and barren regions with a steppe climate are the result of man-made changes, over-grazing and deforestation, perhaps accelerated by a steady rise in winter temperatures since late Roman times.[2]

Completely enclosed by two parallel ranges of rugged mountains, the Taurus and the Pontic chains, all natural communications run from east to west. Both chains present precipitous cliffs

---

[1] Evidence of recent and unpublished surveys by Professor B. Alkim (Karasu valley), the author (Maraş region) and Mr C. A. Burney (Adiyaman-Besni region).
[2] §XI, 3.

along much of their course, and coastal plains are therefore few and far between, and of limited extent, with the single exception of the Cilician plain. Prehistoric occupation is found on the north coast only in the Samsun area and along the Rion valley in Colchis, where rivers running down from the high plateau have carved natural routes. Along the Mediterranean one finds the same situation. Neolithic remains are found in the Cilician plain and in the Calycadnus valley. Further west Neolithic and Early Bronze Age material occurs in cave sites north of Antalya, but Pamphylia, a forested piedmont area of the Taurus and not an alluvial plain, seems to have been shunned by prehistoric farmers. Nor is prehistoric occupation found along the Lycian or Carian coasts until the peninsula of Halicarnassus is reached.

The west coast, on the other hand, offers small and narrow plains favourable for early settlement and these communicate with the plateau behind through the river valleys of the Maeander, Hermus and Caicus. The Cayster, hemmed in between a wedge of Tmolus and Messogis can never have played a role in east–west communications, being accessible only from the west. In spite of recent exploration,[1] it is the only river valley of Western Anatolia where no prehistoric occupation is attested. Besides the Aegean coast road, only the natural route leading from Izmir through the plains of Manisa, Akhisar and Balıkesir to the Sea of Marmora was of any importance for north–south communication.

Numerous roads led from the high plateau to the west coast: of these the four principal must be mentioned. (a) The road leading from the plain of Eskişehir to the lowlands of İnegöl, continuing via Bursa and the Mysian Lakes along the north coast of the Troad to the Dardanelles, Thrace and Troy; (b) an alternative road leading from Afyon-Karahisar via Kütahya and Tavşanlı over the Domaniç Dağ to İnegöl; (c) a road leading down the Upper Maeander valley to the Lycus valley above Denizli and from there down the Maeander to the coast or through the Buldan gap into the Hermus valley, and finally (d) an alternative road from the Pisidian plateau around Burdur via Acipayam down to Denizli. That all these roads were in common use from the Neolithic period onward is shown by the presence of numerous prehistoric mounds along them and by the distribution of successive culture-provinces which do not stop at the plateau's edge. None of these roads would have presented any serious obstacles to movements or trade before the advent of wheeled traffic.[2]

---

[1] Mr D. H. French's survey, 1960.
[2] See §xi, 1, 32 ff., for a different, but unacceptable, view.

Communications on the high plateau are easy and greatly facilitated by many prominent mountains, visible a long way off. The great volcanoes of Erciyas, Hasan, Melendiz Dağ—active until the second millennium B.C.[1]—and the snow-covered peaks of the Taurus, Sultan Dağ, Murad Dağ, and Mount Olympus (Ulu Dağ) are prominent landmarks. Anatolia is well watered and the main obstacles to traffic and trade were mountains and forests, with their wild animals and at times robber bands.

The presence of a strong nomadic element in prehistoric times, especially in the non-agricultural areas, may be assumed on modern analogy.[2] By reason of their seasonal migrations nomads are most efficient agents for the transmission of culture. Although nearly every settlement of pre-Iron Age Anatolia is found in areas suitable for agriculture or pasturage—and most often on alluvial soil—this does not mean that the hills and mountains were not inhabited. The absence of sites—and especially mounds—in such areas is understandable enough. Construction in wood, natural in the forested hills, does not as easily lead to the formation of mounds as the mud-brick architecture of the plains. On distribution maps the mountain areas present a blank, but as this is exactly the region which produced wood, stone, and metal, it is fairly certain that the mountains harboured some settled inhabitants in addition to nomads.

XII. 'NEOLITHIC' ANATOLIA

Even if the processes of the economic evolution from food-gathering to food-production cannot yet be studied in Anatolia in sufficient detail, it is evident from recent finds that the South Anatolian plateau was one of the centres where such developments took place in the eighth and seventh millennia B.C.

Throughout Anatolia developments were far from uniform and though post-glacial and microlithic industries have been found, for example, at Macuncay, north of Ankara and at Tekkeköy near Samsun on the Black Sea coast[3] these are still isolated occurrences which demand further investigation, and more precise dating. More intensively explored is the south coast of Anatolia, especially the Antalya region and here a stratigraphic sequence can be established, apparently without a break, from

---

[1] According to Professor Necdet Egeran.
[2] §xi, 4, 186 ff. For a different opinion see §xi, 2, 30.
[3] §xii, 5, 344.

Upper Palaeolithic to the beginning of the Neolithic *c.* 7000 B.C. The Upper Palaeolithic of Kara'in cave (Level II)[1] and Beldibi rock-shelter[2] (Level D) show blade industries on flint and chert (accompanied by geometric microliths at the former site), as well as *art mobilier*[3] and rock engravings of bulls and stags.[4] The final Upper Palaeolithic is probably represented by the strongly microlithic industry of Belbaşi[5] which exhibits similarities to the Kebaran of Lebanon and Palestine. The third phase is represented by Beldibi (C and B),[6] again with a microlithic element of backed blades, lunates, sickle-blades, bone harpoons, and so on, which shows resemblances to the Natufian, but also has tanged scrapers and tanged arrowheads of local origin. In the very top level of Beldibi[7] a coarse burnished pottery makes its appearance, simple wall paintings may date from this period and at Kara'in obsidian blades are reported, both suggesting that contact was established with the settled Neolithic cultures of the Anatolian plateau, perhaps *c.* 7000 B.C. Apart from sporadic Neolithic sherds in most of the Pamphylian caves, there is no evidence for settled life in this area during the Neolithic, in strong contrast with the plain of Cilicia, where it is found at Mersin[8] and Tarsus,[9] Tirmil and no doubt numerous other sites. The reason for this difference is ecological; the alluvial plain has great agricultural potentialities, the rocky forest-covered piedmont zone of Antalya has not.

Evidence is steadily increasing to suggest that developments on the south Anatolian plateau followed a different course. The main reason is probably ecological; all the early sites on the plateau lie on alluvial ground in basins situated in intramontane valleys of the Taurus, such as Hacılar, Kızılkaya,[10] Suberde[11] in the south-west, or bordering the Taurus, such as Çatal Hüyük in the Konya plain, a new site near Aksaray, Pınarbaşı, Iğdeli Çeşme, or Kumtepe Incesu,[12] around the then active volcanic region south and east of Aksaray, which is the source of abundant obsidian, widely used for the manufacture of tools and weapons. Exported to Syria and Palestine since late Natufian times, perhaps *c.* 8300 B.C. (Jericho 'Protoneolithic'), the obsidian trade enriched Neolithic Anatolia, and ensured steady contact with regions south of the Taurus, rich in tabular flint. A good assemblage of

[1] §XII, 11, 41.
[2] §XII, 3, 151.   [3] §XII, 11, pls. xxxv–xxxvi.
[4] §XII, 11, pe. xxxvii; §XII, 3, pls. II, xv and §XII, 24, 78 f.
[5] §XII, 4, 253 ff.   [6] §XII, 3, 140 f., pls. I, xv.
[7] §XII, 3, pl. IV.   [8] §XII, 8. 11 ff.
[9] §XII, 9, 65 ff.   [10] §XII, 19, 166 f.
[11] §XII, 2, 30.   [12] §XII, 34, figs. 1–12; §XII, 31, 14.

Upper Palaeolithic has not yet been found in this region and the surface material from Avla Dağ,[1] which is mainly in obsidian, cannot yet by accurately dated, although it is probably post-glacial and definitely pre-Çatal Hüyük in date, in the absence of pottery and pressure-flaking. It may also precede in time the material of the new Aksaray site, which is typologically pre-Çatal Hüyük, and likewise aceramic. Microliths are unknown in any of these cultures, probably because obsidian was so abundant and could be found in large blocks, whereas on the south coast pebbles formed the raw material. In south-western Anatolia, Suberde and aceramic Hacılar[2] imported obsidian, but also made use of local chert nodules and small tools are therefore common, but regularly shaped geometric microliths are absent, in plateau tradition.

The earliest permanent settlements excavated are the villages of aceramic Suberde and Hacılar, both in south-western Anatolia, the first existing *c.* 6850 B.C. the second *c.* 7000 B.C. Whereas at Suberde the lower occupation layers have not yet revealed architectural remains, there is evidence for hut floors, a flint and obsidian blade industry without pressure-flaking,[3] but including arrowheads, and the use of copper in the form of an awl. In the later layers mudbrick buildings with plaster floors and platforms make their appearance. Hunting is predominant, pig possibly domesticated, agriculture probable, but not certain.[4] In a nearby cave (Kürtün Ini) small black paintings[5] show wild goat or ibex, and perhaps a bird. Aceramic Hacılar[6] is a settlement with seven building-levels, the fifth from the top dated to *c.* 7000 B.C. Architectural remains are simple and consist of mud-brick walls on stone foundations, grouped along an open court-yard containing numerous hearths and ovens, grain bins and postholes for awnings and sheds. The rooms are rectangular in plan, but have no doorways and were therefore probably entered from the roof. The main rooms have lime-plaster floors laid on a basis of pebbles, stained red and burnished, and the red plaster forms at least a dado along the base of the walls. Fragments with geometric patterns may suggest simple wall-paintings, and a small room, perhaps used in the cult, had a circular depression enclosed in a cream oblong left in reserve on the red-painted floor. The use of human skulls on floors may suggest ancestor-worship, but burials must have been extramural. Pottery or clay objects were

[1] §XII, 29, 95 f.
[2] §XII, 2, 30 ff.; §XII, 18, 70 ff.
[3] §XII, 26, 134 f., figs. 4–6.
[4] §XII, 2, 30 ff.
[5] §XII, 27, 87 f., fig. 1.
[6] §XII, 18, 70 ff.; §XII, 24, fig. 49.

unknown, but fragments of marble bowls were found. The stone industry consists of blades and flakes of chert and obsidian, but is too scanty to permit conclusions. Fully polished celts are known. Animal bones are rare, but show cattle, deer, sheep and goat. Only the dog is definitely domestic. Agriculture is attested: two-row hulled barley, emmer wheat, wild einkorn, lentil and several weeds were found. As not one of the seven building levels had been destroyed by fire, house floors were clean and the number of artefacts from aceramic Hacılar is minute and disappointing.

The next phase is well represented by the great mound of Çatal Hüyük,[1] a city site covering 32 acres, one of a score of sites of the period now known on the south Anatolian plateau, most of which are however villages. The period covered is that between c. 6700–5700 B.C., after which the city moved to a different position across the river. Fourteen successive building-levels dated by over a dozen carbon-14 dates provide a unique framework for this remarkable civilization, which developed uninterrupted over at least a millennium. The economy of this vast site, which may have housed a population of ten thousand souls, is based on hunting, advanced agriculture, stock-breeding and probably trade. Sheep, goat and dog were domestic, but the importance of hunting was not thereby diminished. Wild cattle, wild sheep, onager, half-ass, red, roe and fallow deer, ibex, wild boar, bear, hare, leopards,[2] and various birds, such as black crane, were hunted, but fishing in the river was less important. Agriculture had made tremendous strides forward during the seventh millennium and the rich deposits of level VI yield three forms of wheat (emmer, einkorn and bread wheat), two forms of barley (naked six-row barley and two-row barley), two sorts of peas, lentils, bitter vetch, crucifers grown for vegetable oil, as well as apple, almonds, hackberry, juniper berries, acorns, pistachio, imported from the hills.[3] This is the most varied diet known from any Near Eastern neolithic site.

A balanced diet is indicated by the well-preserved teeth of the skeletons, for at Çatal Hüyük the dead, Proto-Mediterranean dolichocephalic as well as brachycephalic,[4] were buried below the platforms in houses and shrines. Trade is indicated by the materials used in the settlement, for in the alluvial plain only clay and wood were to be found. Greenstone used for axes, adzes, chisels, and all carpenters' tools came from an outcrop in the plain;

---

[1] §XII, 20 ff., 25; §XII, 24, 81 ff.   [2] Information from Dr D. Perkins, Jr.
[3] §XII, 10, 121 ff.
[4] Information from Mlle D. Ferembach.

volcanic rocks (used for querns, pounders, mortars, agricultural tools) from Kara or Karaca Dağ and lava, used as pot-boilers, came from the same sources. Dolomitic limestone, used for polishers, came from the northern hills, white, blue and veined limestone from the Taurus, calcite and alabaster from the Kayseri region, and obsidian from around Aksaray. White marble must have come from the west, dentalium from the Mediterranean, flint from north Syria, large cowries from the Red Sea. Not only stones but metals were used; lead and copper, native or smelted, occur, from Level X, *c.* 6500 B.C.;[1] both are found in the Taurus and ground malachite and lazurite, haematite, limonite, vermilion and cinnabar are used as paints. Lead and copper are used for trinkets, tubes and beads, and perhaps for awls and drills, and silver and gold may have been known, but have not been found. Other imported materials include sulphur and pumice and it is evident that prospecting and trade played a significant role in Çatal Hüyük's economy.

The entire period, so far as the site is excavated, knew the use of pottery, though on a limited scale. From level XIII onwards a cream-burnished heavy grit or straw-tempered ware appears with simple bowl and hole-mouth shapes. From Level VIII we find a thinner dark burnished ware, an improvement, grit-tempered and used mainly as kitchen ware for cooking. It is not until Level V (*c.* 5900) that pottery becomes common and then we find the beginning of fine red and cream-burnished wares side by side with the dark cooking pots. By Level III (*c.* 5800), the first attempts are made to decorate the cream ware with smears of paint and in the final levels red, buff and cream wares prevail side by side with dark cooking pots. Throughout this pottery development the influence of basketry and wooden vessels is strong and from Levels VI *a* and *b*, *c.* 6000, B.C. we have a most well-developed set of wooden vessels carved from fir wood (*abies*)[2] and perhaps other woods. These show the preference for fine wooden vessels such as large dishes, bowls of various sorts, cups and boxes fitted with lids. Basketry and weaving are equally well developed; cereal straw and marsh grass were used for twilled mats and coiled baskets, fitted with lids. From the carbonized burials of Level VI there is evidence for fur, felt, and fine textiles,[3] probably of sheep and goats hair and perhaps bast fibre other than flax. Rope has survived and also red thread used for

---

[1] *Archaeologica Austriaca*, 35 (1964), 98 ff.
[2] Identified by Dr E. Tellerup of the National Museum, Copenhagen.
[3] H. Burnham in *A. St.* 15 (1965), 169 ff.

stringing beads. Cloth, skin, and fur garments were fixed at a woman's shoulder by pins, but male garments had antler toggles and bone belt-hooks and eyes. Leopard skins were probably ceremonial. Bone was further used for awls, needles, spatulae, spoons, scoops, polishers, handles of tools and weapons and sickles.

Obsidian and flint tools and weapons show a tool kit of over fifty types.[1] Flint, imported from north Syria is relatively rare and used for ceremonial daggers, scrapers, firestones, stout knives. Spearheads, arrowheads of several sizes, scrapers and blades of all sorts, including sickle blades, abound, but burins are rare and geometric microliths absent. Pressure flaking, unknown in the previous period, is widely practised, especially on the tanged projectile points. Other weapons are baked clay balls up to 4 in. in diameter, slingstones, and polished stone maceheads, whereas nets are depicted in wall-paintings. Obsidian mirrors are found in women's graves and may have been used for divination.

The architecture of Çatal Hüyük is fascinating; each house or shrine consists of a rectangular room with a narrow storeroom added along one side, built of proper mud-brick without stone foundations. Party walls are unknown. Buildings are grouped in extensive quarters next to each other and entered only from the roof. A few courtyards serve for sanitation and rubbish disposal. Streets are unknown and the outside of the settlement was formed by a blank wall without entry, behind which lay less important rooms, the prototype for the casemate wall. Wooden ladders fixed against the south wall of each main room led into the buildings, which were lit by small windows set below the eaves of the flat roofs in at least two of the walls, usually the south and the west. The light fell on the north and east walls, along which were set two main platforms, a square one in the corner for the men, a larger, flanked by two wooden posts, along the east wall for the women. A bench extended along this platform. Hearth and oven were placed along the south wall next to the ladder. Subsidiary platforms are sometimes present for other members of the family, such as children, and the dead were buried below these platforms which served as sofas for sitting and sleeping. Wooden posts and beams formed a timber framework for the plastered brick walls and these wooden elements divide the walls into a series of vertical and horizontal panels, some of which may be decorated with solid red panels (houses) or wall-paintings and reliefs (in the case of shrines). With minor variations this standard house plan prevails from Levels X to II, but earlier structures are less developed.

[1] From an unpublished manuscript by P. Mortensen.

Shrines or small temples are distinguished from houses by their religious decoration, the presence of cult statues in stone and clay and by richer burials with ceremonial weapons, obsidian mirrors, etc. The decoration takes several forms: one of these is plaster reliefs, in which the mother goddess is represented in anthropomorphic form. Her son or consort is in the form of a bull cut out in the plaster or more frequently as the head of a bull or ram, often incorporating the horn cores of the wild animal. Other cut out figures show deer and feline heads. Reliefs of leopards,[1] sacred animals of the goddess, are frequent and attractively painted. Symbolic representations are common; bucrania and benches with bull's horns in rows, modelled breasts containing skulls of vultures, lower jaws of wild boar, heads of weasel and fox, all scavengers and harbingers of death. Wall-paintings are common from Level X onwards and these frequently imitate red cloth(?) and gaily patterned textiles and kilims, hunting and fishing nets, rows of human hands, bulls, flowers and butterflies, or bees, etc. Less common and possibly commemorative are scenes of animal baiting and epic hunts in two shrines of Levels V and III with numerous human figures lively drawn, pulling tails and tongues of wild bulls,[2] red deer stags, wild boar, bear, and groups of onagers, donkeys, black cranes, and so on, scenes of running and dancing. Even more remarkable are pictures connected with death—scenes of enormous vultures pecking at headless corpses of men lying on their left side[3] or extended on their back (the normal position of the dead), a figure carrying human heads, or a scene of a man armed with a sling protecting a corpse from the attention of two black vultures. A representation of a mortuary building of reeds and matting shows numerous human skulls below and such scenes are evidently inspired by the funerary customs of the people at Çatal Hüyük. Upon death corpses were exposed, probably in a mortuary, until the soft parts had decayed. The skeleton, dry but still anatomically intact, was then wrapped up in textiles or basketry and interred with appropriate funerary gifts, jewellery for women and children, weapons for men, below the platforms in houses and shrines. Baskets and wooden vessels are common to all. A number of women was first painted with red ochre or cinnabar as in the Upper Palaeolithic and later at Ḥajji Fīrūz and Sialk. Blue and green paint were applied to certain skeletons, male and female in Levels VII and VI, but only to neck and eyebrows. Beads of the same colours (apatite and copper) take the place of paint in the later layers.

[1] See Plate 5 (*a*).   [2] See Plate 5 (*b*).   [3] See Plate 6 (*a*).

Statuettes are common; those of the lower levels are often made of marble, limestone, or alabaster, those of the later levels are mostly of clay, often painted. They depict the main deity, a goddess, both as mother and maiden and a male deity either as child, adolescent or bearded father figure. Whereas the bull, ram, stag as well as the leopard are associated with the male figure, leopard and vulture are the goddess's sacred animals. A large clay figure from the shrine in Level II shows the goddess supported by felines giving birth to a child.

The origin of this Neolithic civilization is still unknown and as excavations continue we may expect many more surprises. It is now evident that the Neolithic of Mersin and the 'Amūq plain of north Syria represent two offshoots of Çatal Hüyük, with a very similar but less sophisticated obsidian and flint industry, similar greenstone celts and similar dark burnished pottery which in these coastal regions, however, was sometimes decorated along the rim by impressions made with the edge of a shell or animal bone.[1] Such decorated pottery, unknown on the Anatolian plateau (or in Pamphylia, another offshoot) is characteristic for Cilicia, north Syria ('Amūq A, B), Early Neolithic Byblos and its affiliated cultures, Tell Ramad III A–B and the coastal Palestinian neolithic, but here we must reckon with earlier local traditions. Clay stamp-seals, and figurines are generally similar and Early Neolithic Byblos has a chipped stone industry that shows many parallels with Çatal Hüyük.

The end of Çatal Hüyük is still obscure. The site was moved across the river c. 5700 B.C. and as excavations have not yet reached the lowest levels of Çatal Hüyük west it is unknown whether a Late Neolithic is represented as at Hacılar IX–VI, some two hundred miles farther west, dated by the carbon-14 method to c. 5750/5700–5600 B.C. At this site,[2] the Late Neolithic arrivals were newcomers, but from where we do not know. They need not be descendants of the people of Çatal Hüyük and it is far more likely that they came from the Pisidian lake district, which during the previous period had shown some sort of western variant of the Çatal Hüyük culture, as yet untested by excavation. The changes are apparent; hunting has declined and with it the fine obsidian industry withers; mace and sling are now the main weapons. Wall-paintings disappear with the end of hunting, teeth decline as gritty cereal foods take the place of a balanced diet, steatopygy increases in the representations of female deities and the male, now that hunting is unimportant, is no longer represented in his

<hr />

[1] §xii, 19, fig. 4.   [2] §xii, 18, 42 ff.

own right. Elaborately decorated shrines give way to a domestic cult; statuettes appear in nearly every house. Painting, once confined to walls, finds a new vehicle on the improved cream coloured fabrics and though an occasional modelled bull's head is still found in Hacılar VI, they are now mainly found on pots, and in miniature. The textile patterns of Çatal Hüyük will reappear, but only after the late neolithic and then on pots of Hacılar V–II, together with a 'fantastic style', a schematized representation of animals, goddesses and symbols derived from the reliefs of Çatal Hüyük, and almost unrecognizable. Burial habits are unknown, as the dead are no longer interred in the houses, but it may be assumed that burial in cemeteries no longer necessitated the elaborate practices of excarnation.

In architecture new methods of planning make their appearance; houses are now arranged around open courtyards[1] and along narrow alleys and the settlement was probably protected by a defensive wall. In an area where stone was abundant the houses were provided with stone foundations, and even if a house still consists of a single main room, with the old storeroom now incorporated and only screened off, it now opens directly on to a courtyard by means of wide double doors. Moreover, the kitchen and additional service rooms are placed outside the building on either side of the entrance, lightly constructed of posts and wattle and daub. The main living room, rectangular in shape and up to 30 ft. long, still contains a hearth and oven facing the doorway, but posts now support a light upper storey with further rooms, accessible by a brick flight of steps or wooden ladders. In the main living-room on the ground floor, cupboards let into the wall, or built up in brick add to the amenities of living. Grain bins, rectangular plaster boxes placed along the wall, are common. The old system of sleeping platforms is abandoned, and so is a timber frame within the walls, which are here 3 ft. thick and consist of two rows of plano-convex bricks, plastered over in white.

The economy of the settlement is mainly agricultural and a continuation of that of Çatal Hüyük: emmer, einkorn, bread wheat, naked six-row barley, two sorts of peas, lentils, and now also chick-peas, as well as acorns, hackberries, etc. Chert blades are set in curved antler-sickles. Hunting had declined, sheep and goat are probably domesticated, cattle and pig appear, whether or not domesticated; the dog is known. Trade is as important as before and accounts for yellow and red ochre from Lake Eğridir, haematite (used for painting pots) and white marble from the

[1] §XII, 18, figs. 2–3.

hills, sulphur from the eastern end of Lake Burdur, sea-shells from the Mediterranean, obsidian and pumice from central Anatolia.[1]

Whereas the chipped stone industry has declined to a blade industry in local red, brown and yellow chert with some obsidian, some of it microlithic, the polished stone industry flourishes. Greenstone axes (rather than adzes) and chisels set in antler sleeves abound, polished maceheads are numerous and there is a flourishing industry of marble bowls, some up to 2 ft. in diameter, palettes, beads, etc. However, for statuettes clay is the usual material. The bone industry flourishes: apart from sickles there are finely made spatulae with terminals in the form of naturalistic heads of animals and even humans, awls, needles, spoons, belt hooks and scoops. Shell and especially mother of pearl is common for beads, pendants, etc., sometimes carved in the form of the mother-goddess. Weaving is indicated by mat and textile impressions and by abundant terracotta spindle whorls and loom-weights. Traces of copper occur in many buildings but no artefacts were recovered.

The Late Neolithic pottery is a development from that of Çatal Hüyük or its western equivalent, the Kızılkaya ware.[2] Brilliantly burnished monochrome red, grey, buff and mottled wares prevail, sometimes with black interiors. Vertically perforated tubular lugs are a characteristic feature. The hole-mouth shape still occurs together with basket handles, both typical of Çatal Hüyük, but is no longer common. Gracefully curving S-profiled bowls take the place of the straight-side bowls of Çatal Hüyük, and the influence of woodwork, predominant at the latter site, declines. Ovals are common, but square and rectangular vessels have gone. Very typical are great lentoid water jars, provided with four stout lug handles for carrying. Small jars now have marked lips, and many of the larger ones, cream coloured, bear simple painted decoration in the form of vertical stripes, hatching or chevrons in red, or more rarely in white. From these early painted wares, which were already appearing at the end of Çatal Hüyük (III–I), there was to develop the spectacular painted pottery of Hacılar V–I. Ritual vessels also make their first appearance in Hacılar VI; a drinking cup in the form of a woman's head and animal vessels showing a recumbent pregnant doe, a headless bird, a wild boar, some possible small cows or bulls, a double pig's head—animals already familiar from the earlier Neolithic of Çatal Hüyük. Small bulls' and bears' heads occur on the monochrome pottery, as well as fine bucrania, ibexes and

---

[1] Information from Dr H. Helbaek.   [2] §xii, 19, 166 f., fig. 6.

possibly even figures of the great goddess herself. It would appear that at Hacılar these figures previously painted or modelled in relief on the shrines of Çatal Hüyük were transferred to pottery decoration. In the Late Neolithic they still appear in miniature relief on monochrome wares, in the following 'Early Chalcolithic' they are painted on the pottery.

Evidence for religion is rich, not confined to specific shrines but distributed throughout the eight houses excavated. Typical of Hacılar VI are limestone slabs crudely incised with facial features or doll-like replicas in clay. The division between well-modelled cult statues and crude *ex-votos*, as found at Çatal Hüyük, also continues; and amorphous highly schematized clay figures, which once had wooden peg heads, occur side by side with magnificent baked clay figures up to 8 in. long. The latter are among the most remarkably naturalistic representations of the Anatolian goddess yet found.[1] She is shown as a young girl wearing her hair in a pigtail, with small breasts and a bikini-like garment, or as a mature naked woman with prominent stomach and buttocks, her hair tied up in a bun. Some wear tiaras and hold pet leopards, or are seated accompanied by children; others are dressed and shown resting. At least two are shown seated on one or two leopards, as at Çatal Hüyük, and one of them holds a baby leopard. A fine group shows a young goddess dressed in leopard skin playing with her son. These splendid figures, naturalistically rendered with loving detail are the evident development of the clay figures from the later levels of Çatal Hüyük, from which they differ only in detail of dress, hair-style and rendering of the eyes. They have parallels in the lake district, where at Çukurkent similar, but much smaller, figures have been found.[2]

Late Neolithic pottery had a remarkable distribution throughout western Anatolia. Northwards, wares related to the Late Neolithic of Hacılar reached the region of Lake Iznik via the Eskişehir plain. At Menteşe we find cream and light-grey coloured wares as well as fragments of red painted plaster;[3] at Üyücek, east of Iznik, oval vessels in similar pottery. The Fikirtepe culture[4] on the northern shore of the gulf of Izmit (still unpublished) presents a number of analogies with Hacılar of this period; such as ovals, disc bases, vertical tubular lugs, a number of bowl and jar shapes, bone spatulae, a degenerate blade industry, as well as a number of significant differences, such as dark burnished ware, incision, wooden shapes and intramural burial.

---

[1] §xii, 18, fig. 5–23.   [2] Ankara Museum, unpublished.
[3] §xii, 13, 54, 56.   [4] §xii, 1, 1 ff., figs 4–19 (pls. iii–ix).

Beyond the Anatolian plateau, monochrome pottery resembling that of Hacılar VI (and V) extends to the Aegean, and to some of the islands, such as Chios[1] and Skyros[2] where the fashion of vertical tubular lugs was also adopted. The inland sites of Morali, Nuriye and Ülücek[3] show some differences, such as the use of a straw temper and certain variations in shape. Painted wares are absent, both in the west and the north.

XIII. THE EARLY CHALCOLITHIC PERIOD

Although the transition from Late Neolithic to Early Chalcolithic was accompanied with destruction and upheaval at Hacılar, possibly also at Çatal Hüyük, but not apparently at Mersin, there is no evidence to suggest that the new culture was introduced from elsewhere. Quite to the contrary, all evidence points strongly to continuity of tradition. Certain changes do, however, appear and the most noticeable of these is the ascendancy gained by painted pottery at the expense of monochrome ware. The latter remained in use in its red, brown and buff and cream varieties, but its shapes were now those of the red-on-cream painted ware. Another feature of the period is the sharp decline in the chipped-stone industry, as the probable result of the first appearance of metal (copper) tools. It must be admitted that nowhere has metal yet been found in the earliest layers of the period, but by the end copper tools and pins occur at Mersin in Level XXI[4] and as fragments in Hacılar II*b* and I.[5]

Three geographically distinct Early Chalcolithic cultures are already known; the 'proto' and Early Chalcolithic of Mersin XXIV–XX in the Cilician plain;[6] the Çatal Hüyük West culture in the Konya plain[7] and Hacılar Early Chalcolithic (V–I*d*) in the south-west of Anatolia.[8] Contemporary cultures farther west and north are badly documented. Scattered sherds are found at Ayio Gala,[9] in the İzmir, Manisa and Akhisar plains, at Çukurhisar near Eskişehir,[10] Karadin near Iznik, etc. A series of carbon-14 dates from Hacılar allows one to date this culture at that site between *c.* 5600 B.C. and the first quarter of the fifth millennium B.C. In Mesopotamian terms it is roughly equivalent to the Hassūnah culture (with the later Sāmarrā phase) and Hacılar I,

---

[1] §xii, 7, 194 ff., figs. 12, 13: 1. [2] §xii, 28, 321 f., figs. 35–37.
[3] §xii, 6, 173 ff., figs. 3–5. [4] §xii, 7, 76, fig. 50.
[5] §xii, 18, 87. [6] §xii, 7, 45 ff. [7] §xiii, 1, 177 ff.
[8] §xii, 18, 86 and fig. 2 [9] §xii, 6, fig. 1: 3. [10] §xii, 14, 75, fig. 96.

beginning *c.* 5250 B.C. may overlap with the beginning of Halaf, if one puts its beginning at the same date.

Of the three south Anatolian cultures of this period, that of Hacılar is the best known. A selected 450 surface sherds are as yet the only evidence for the Çatal Hüyük West culture. That of Early Chalcolithic Mersin is based on sherds not more numerous,

Table 7. Chronological chart: Anatolia before 4000 B.C.

PERIOD	NORTH-WEST	SOUTH-WEST	KONYA PLAIN	CILICIAN PLAIN
LATE CHALCOLITHIC	Late Chalcolithic (of Beycesultan type?)	Beycesultan Late Chalcolithic 2 (XXXIV–XXIX) ------------ Beycesultan Late Chalcolithic 1 (XL–XXXV)	Mersin XVI-type culture with Painted pottery (Can Hasan)	Mersin XVI → Intrusive culture ------------ Mersin XIX–XVII 'Middle Chalcolithic'
EARLY CHALCOLITHIC	Hacılar I (?) ——— ↑ ———	Hacılar I–V (Painted Pottery culture)	Çatal Hüyük (West) (Painted Pottery culture)	Mersin XXIV–XX (Painted Pottery culture)
LATE NEOLITHIC	Extension of Hacılar Late Neolithic, Fikirtepe?	Hacılar VI–IX	Çatal Hüyük (West) ——— ↑ ———	Mersin XXV–XXVI (or XXVII?)
EARLY NEOLITHIC	Menteşe (?)	Kızılkaya	Çatal Hüyük (East)	Mersin XXVI/ XXVII– XXXIII ? Water
		[Base of Early Neolithic nowhere exposed]		
LATE MESOLITHIC		Beldibi (with pottery)		

but these came from some five stratified building levels. The relative size of these three sites is worth noting: Hacılar I measures *c.* 150 m. in diameter; Çatal Hüyük West *c.* 200–300 m. and Mersin a maximum of *c.* 200 m. Many contemporary sites are smaller. Of the architecture of Mersin little need be said. Level XXIV had a series of well-built domed grain silos with stone floors, but Levels XXIII–XX contained little more than rectangular rooms of badly denuded houses on the outskirts of an unfortified village. Çatal Hüyük awaits fuller excavation. At Hacılar, Level V is an ephemeral affair of squatters subsequent to the destruction of Level VI, and Levels IV and III are in no way different from the fortified village of Level II, which was almost completely excavated and thus provides a unique picture of an Early Chalcolithic settlement in the Near East.[1]

A rough rectangle, measuring 250 by 100 ft., was surrounded with a mud-brick fortification wall 5–10 ft. thick, provided with salients and small buttresses.[2] Three narrow doorways gave access to the settlement, but there may have been others in the destroyed east and south wall. Only one of these led directly into a building, the others opened on to a covered passage-way or an antechamber leading into open courts around which the houses were grouped. A normal house consisted of an antechamber and a main room having a square or rectangular hearth with raised kerb. Some of the richer houses had an additional room or a portico facing the court and had an oven in addition to the hearth in the main room. Each house was separate and all communication took place through courtyards of which there were three. Many of the houses had an upper story. The north-west corner of the settlement was occupied by a granary, with built or sunk grain bins. Two ovens for drying the corn stood in front of it in the courtyard. Three potters' workshops were found in the middle of the village. Newly finished pots, both painted and monochrome, were found together with querns for grinding red and white ochre, ochre cakes, painters' palettes, paint-cups and modelling-tools for fashioning clay statuettes. The eastern quarter of the settlement was allotted to domestic courtyards of small size,[3] set back to back with brushwood and plaster partitions, partly roofed. In each of these three were found a flat-topped or open bread-oven with a raised hearth in front, clay bins for the storage and querns for the grinding of cereals. Numerous pounders and pestles littered the floors together with masses of pottery.

In the north-east corner of the settlement was a stone-lined well, probably provided with a *shadūf* for raising the water. The village shrine—or so we interpret it—lay next to the well and north of the domestic quarter. It was slightly larger and more neatly built than the largest houses. A great hall could be divided into two parts by means of a sliding door or screen fitting into the slit of a partition wall. Each of these halves had a shallow recess in the back wall, which might have borne painted patterns or hangings. The western niche contained a standing stone and in

---

[1] §xii, 18, 97 ff., figs. 5–6.   [2] See Plate 7 (*a*).   [3] See Plate 6 (*b*).

front of it there were two oval hollows in the floor near one of which lay a spouted bowl. The niche was screened from the main room by a low screen. A flat-topped oven blocked an open door-way; in front of it was the hearth and a clay bin. In the larger eastern half there was a hearth on the floor in front of a raised alcove with the recess at the back. Along the south and east runs a colonnade of posts, which may suggest that the centre of the hall was open to the sky. Below the floor of this building were found several graves with double burials of mother and child, each provided with a single painted pot. These are the only burials found in the whole Level II settlement, but contracted burials in courtyards have been found in Levels III–V. The number of burials found is, however, so small that one suspects the normal habit was extramural burial in cemeteries, which have not been found. The Level II settlement was destroyed by fire, and prob-ably by enemy action.

Instead of building on the burnt ruins of the previous settlement, the newcomers at Hacılar built a huge fortress[1] around the ancient mound, but not without extensive cutting and levelling of the lower slopes. The external diameter of the fortress, constructed, according to carbon-14 dates, *c.* 5250 B.C., measured *c.* 150 m. which makes it a little bigger than Troy II. Only about one-fifth of this fortress has been excavated, but the contrast it presents with the earlier settlement could not be more pronounced. Surrounding an open space with a diameter of *c.* 100 metres radially arranged blocks of rooms were constructed separated from each other by walled courtyards, through which alone access to the blocks was gained. The fortress had a minimum of two stories, the lower forming a basement entered from above except in the case of what were evidently guardrooms. The walls were immensely thick (up to 12 ft.), often out of all proportion with the rooms they enclose. The rooms, often very large ($8 \cdot 5 \times 5 \cdot 5$ m.), have external buttresses as in Level II, but the hearths are now round or oval. The floors were covered with rush matting. Domed ovens are found in the courtyards. Materials of construc-tion are the same as before, but brick sizes vary in each building level. Stone foundations are no longer the rule as in the Late Neolithic. The upper story appears to have been of light con-struction and probably contained a number of loggias and veran-das looking out over the surrounding fields and orchards. To reach the upper story narrow corridors, which evidently once contained wooden steps, opened off the courtyards. The fortress

[1] §xii, 18, 92 ff., figs. 3–4. See Plate 7 (*a*).

was of considerable strength, but nevertheless burnt with many traces of massacre by some unknown enemy sometime in the early fifth millennium. The last traces of occupation on the site consist of an open village (I c) and some squatters' occupation (I d). Burial would appear to have been extramural.

The continuity in technical traditions is marked: there is no development in the stone industry and the same tools and weapons as were used in the Late Neolithic are found at the end of Early Chalcolithic. The beginnings of metallurgy are still badly documented. An innovation of Level II is the use of large flat stamp-seals of baked clay with incised maeander-like designs. Mother-of-pearl pendants are still very common, but clay statuettes of the Mother Goddess are, though technically competent, stereotyped and unimaginative when compared with their Late Neolithic counterparts. Only one standing type was in use from Levels V–II, but in Level I a seated type also appears. New is the use of obsidian inlay, used for eyes and in one case for the navel. Tendencies towards schematization are also evident in Level I. Theriomorphic vessels continue to be made, but the most interesting innovation is effigies in the form of a seated and dressed Mother Goddess, fully painted and with inlaid eyes, in Level I.[1] At the same time figurines of animals appear, hitherto rare if not unknown. Spindle-whorls of this period are flat discs of pottery, made from painted or monochrome sherds. A flourishing textile and kilim (woven rug) industry may be inferred from the numerous textile patterns seen on the painted pottery at Hacılar.

No changes in economy can be detected; from Hacılar II we have emmer and einkorn wheat, hulled and naked barley, lentils, field peas and bitter vetch—all already cultivated in the Late Neolithic period, if not before.[2] From Mersin XXII there is a little wheat (emmer?) and two-row barley.[3] The following animals are provisionally represented at Hacılar: sheep, goat, cattle, pig, dog, wild boar, deer, and tortoise.

By far the most spectacular contribution of the Early Chalcolithic period in Anatolia is its fine painted pottery. The three main cultures show considerable differences in shape, quality, painting, and patterns. By far the least accomplished group is found in Cilicia accompanied by a black burnished ware, decorated with *pointillé* incision filled with white chalk. The shapes of the painted ware are few and simple;[4] simple bowls and squat or globular jars with funnel or collar necks. Oval shapes are infrequent and lugs

[1] §xii, 18, 103 f., pl. xv.   [2] Identified by Dr H. Helbaek.
[3] §xii, 7, 73 f.   [4] §xii, 7, figs. 34, 52, 53.

and handles uncommon. Patterns are few and simple (bands, stripes, parallel lines, multiple chevrons) at the beginning. From Level XXIII onwards hatched bands between thicker lines gain in popularity, often in combination with chevrons.[1] The red paint at Mersin has a tendency to turn to brown and black at the end of the period and much of the painting is careless and the burnishing poor.

The painted pottery of the Çatal Hüyük West culture is more accomplished in every respect. Paint remains red, even though it is often somewhat washy. Burnishing is more careful, slips more common. Often the slip has a greenish tinge, either due to the marshy clay or to high firing. The dark burnished ware of Cilicia is not found in the Konya plain, where the monochrome wares are red, buff and brown; incision is likewise unknown. All the Cilician shapes are known in the Konya plain, but in addition there are three very typical local ones: a carinated bowl, a basket-handled jar and a jar with anti-splash rim. A fragment of the latter shape was found imported into Mersin XXI.[2] Oval vessels are not infrequent. Motifs are again predominantly linear, but reserve patterns occur. Vertical zigzags, multiple chevrons, interlocking inverted V's with or without fillings of dots, metope decoration in hatched blocks and concentric lozenges are common. Hatched bands in the Mersin manner are unknown. Large bowls are painted on both exterior and interior and may have borne great centre pieces as in Hacılar I. The painted pottery of the Konya plain looks like a superior and much enriched version of that of Cilicia, and one might perhaps suggest some plateau influence in the Cilician pottery, a theory that should be tested by excavation. Imports in Mersin XXIV–XXII firmly establish the date of the Çatal Hüyük West culture.[3]

The Early Chalcolithic pottery of Hacılar is of such technical perfection that a comparison with that of its neighbours (or successors) is bound to be detrimental to the latter. Only the finest products from Thessaly and the best Halaf ware reached such standards. Fine local clays and a long period of previous experience undoubtedly contributed greatly to this technical perfection, but the boldness in design of shape and the inventiveness of the decorative patterns, invariably taking full advantage of the space to be decorated, must be ascribed to the artistic sense of the Hacılar potters. Many of these early pots are not just fine examples of the potter's craft, but like many Greek vases they rank as works of art.[4]

[1] §xii, 7, fig. 54: 8, 12, 16.   [2] §xii, 7, fig. 56: 27.
[3] §xii, 7, fig. 34: 23 (xxiv); fig. 53: 7 (xxiii).   [4] See Plate 7 (b).

Shapes are numerous, varied, inventive and sophisticated, and often they would seem to betray metal prototypes. Chronologically the pottery falls into two periods, that of Levels V–II and that of Levels I a–I d. Shapes of the earlier period include carinated bowls: low ones with a single and high ones with a double zone of decoration. Oval cups, with one or two pinched spouts on the rim, are decorated with designs in panels, often with a different motif on either side. Jars have short or funnel necks and two 'Hacılar' handles, sometimes fashioned into the likeness of an animal head, with inlaid obsidian eyes. Patterns are linear only in the earliest Level V, representing the transition from the simple painted Late Neolithic ware. They gradually become more solid with patterns left in reserve. Apart from geometric solids, weird curvilinear designs culminate by the time of Level II in a variety and fantasy that is more reminiscent of Peruvian pottery than anything ever seen in the Near East.

In Level I a new set of shapes appears together with a pure linear style of decoration, which is not derived from the pottery of the previous level. Large carinated bowls prevail, decorated inside and out, often with great centre-pieces in the interior. Other bowls are square, oval or sub-rectangular. A great variety of cups, beakers and jars is found, many of the latter being ovoid or fashioned in the shape of a rugby football: these are possibly churns. Primitive loop handles replace the old 'Hacılar' handle. Spirals and maeanders, never quite absent in the earlier levels, become common in Level I. Stylized animals and human beings are exceedingly rare, but a human hand or arm, probably of apotropaic value, occurs from Levels VI to II. Motifs are too varied to be discussed here, but many seem to derive from textiles. White paint on red reappears abundantly in Level I.

The Early Chalcolithic settlements came to a violent end: both Hacılar and Mersin were burnt and Çatal Hüyük was, if not burnt, deserted for ever. The end of the period would appear to have fallen within the first quarter of the fifth millennium B.C.

XIV. THE LATE CHALCOLITHIC PERIOD

Whereas a 'Middle Chalcolithic' can be established in Cilicia (and less confidently in the Konya plain) as an equivalent for Tell Halaf in Mesopotamia and Syria, no such obvious division is practicable in Western Anatolia. Here, at Beycesultan, about twenty-five building levels (XX–XL) do not allow for sub-

divisions,[1] even though four successive stages can be recognized in
the pottery. The first two of these, Late Chalcolithic I (with six)
and II (with seven), building levels may correspond to Mersin
XIX–XVII (with four) and XVI z–XVI a (with five) building
levels. A recent carbon-14 date from Warka gives c. 4300 B.C.
for the beginning of southern 'Ubaid[2] and 4300 B.C. may therefore be taken as the end of Mersin XVI a and Beycesultan Late
Chalcolithic 2. We have already seen that Mersin XX was
destroyed by an enemy, and side by side with local painted wares
continuing the late Early Chalcolithic tradition there now appear
actual imports of Halaf pottery and local imitations of Halaf
vessels and techniques.[3] These start in Level XIX and continue
through XVIII and XVII. The architectural remains of these
phases are scanty and considerable unrest is suggested.[4]

In Level XVII[5] there begins to appear a new painted pottery—
the Mersin cream-slipped ware, painted in red, brown or black,
accompanied by a cream or red burnished ware with exaggerated
handles and a black burnished ware with white-filled *pointillé*
designs.[6] It has been suggested that the signs of disturbance
observed in these earlier levels (XIX–XVII) are associated with
the arrival of this new painted pottery which has no known
Cilician antecedents[7] and which would appear to be almost confined to Mersin. Unlike the Halaf vessels introduced in the former phase, these pots are quite non-Mesopotamian. But it is not
only the pottery that is foreign, but also the new architecture and
the sudden appearance of copper tools (chisels and axes) which
clearly shows the greatly increased demand and supply of this
material which was now available. Introduced in Level XVII,
this new culture gradually ousted the Halaf influence at Mersin
and in Level XVI a strong fortress crowns the mound.[8] This
remained in use for a considerable period and was in turn sacked
and burnt. Once more there are traces of a massacre. In the burnt
remains masses of pottery and objects allow one to reconstruct the
culture of Mersin at the end of Level XVI a, c. 4300 B.C.

The fortress is of extreme interest even though it is now no
longer an isolated example. A comparison with that of Hacılar I
reveals some similarities as well as important differences. The size
of the Mersin fortress is not known, but it would appear to have
been smaller than that of Hacılar I. Unlike the latter it stood on

---

[1] §xiv, 3, 38 ff.
[2] §xiv, 1, 8 (H 138/123).
[3] §xii, 7, 102 f.
[4] §xii, 7, 110 ff.
[5] §xii, 7, fig. 76: I, 3, 5–7, 12.
[6] §xii, 7, 141 ff., figs. 91–4.
[7] §xiv, 7, 13 f.
[8] §xii, 7, 131 ff., figs. 79–80a.

top of the steeply revetted slope of the mound which rose some 50 feet above the banks of the river, adding greatly to its defensive strength.

It appears to have been one-storied and its continuous roof provided a fine defensive platform for a garrison whose main armament was, as at Hacılar before, the sling. Directly behind the main defensive wall, some 5 ft. thick and provided with stout offsets, lay a series of barrack rooms, each lit by two slit windows set in the defensive wall. Each house consisted of a main room, equipped with grinding platform, grain-bin and other domestic arrangements, and a small walled courtyard in front. All living rooms once communicated with the next, but these doors were subsequently bricked up. The Water Gate, 6 ft. wide, was flanked by two projecting towers with guardrooms, a distinct advance on the Hacılar system. An important building, probably the ruler's residence, stood south of the gate and seems to have been a rectangular block divided down the middle by a long central courtyard containing a domed oven, with a range of rooms on either side.

Compared with the Hacılar I fortress, that of Mersin shows considerable advances in military architecture combined with older principles, such as one might expect to have developed during almost a millennium that separates these two earliest examples of Anatolian fortresses. It should be emphasized that this type of architecture appears to have originated in Anatolia and probably on the plateau. With Halaf or Mesopotamia in general it appears to have no connexion whatsoever.

It is not clear whether the culture of Mersin XIX–XVII should be ascribed to new settlers or to increased contact with its new Halaf neighbours. As there are strong signs of continuity in Level XIX, it might be argued that the second alternative is nearer the truth. Occasional Halaf sherds occur in the Konya plain and these are probably evidence of trade only, perhaps in metals, with an area which need not have been farther away than Mersin. On the other hand, the Mersin XVI culture is probably intrusive from the Anatolian plateau and it probably reached Mersin by the Calycadnus route from the plain of Karaman. Here, among others, the important mound of Can Hasan[1] produced not only the cream-slipped ware, with similar shapes, but also the red and brown monochrome and the polychrome painted pottery. Slingstones of baked clay are common, and only

[1] Now being excavated by D. H. French, see *A. St.* 12, 27 ff., 13, 29 ff., 14, 125 ff., 15, 87 ff.

the black burnished ware has not been found. It is possible that the latter is a local Mersin fabric, continuing an Early Chalcolithic tradition, but borrowing the new shapes. The same or a closely related culture appears throughout the Konya plain, of which that of Karaman forms the southernmost part. So, even before excavation, it would appear that this area, linked by a natural route to Cilicia since the Neolithic period, should almost certainly be considered as the original home of the Mersin XVI culture.

Whereas there is thus some continuity in the traditional use of painted pottery in the eastern half of Southern Anatolia, the picture presented by the south-west is quite different. Material of the Beycesultan Late Chalcolithic period overlies Hacılar I at a number of sites in south-west Anatolia,[1] virtually ruling out the theoretical possibility of an overlap. Between these two cultures there is the greatest possible break imaginable. Historically speaking the end of the Hacılar culture was probably produced by a movement of north(-west) Anatolian 'barbarians' with a much inferior culture. Dark burnished wares, full of straw admixture, with heavy and clumsy shapes and frequently ornamented in matt white paint now prevail. The number of patterns is strictly limited and the painting too fine for the heavy ware.[2] This form of decoration, dominant in Late Chalcolithic I, becomes less common in the next phase, when a number of new shapes betray contact with the higher culture of the Konya plain.[3]

Little is known of the architecture of these two earliest phases but the existence of mud-brick buildings without stone foundations and of rectangular rooms. Far more important is the discovery, in Level XXXIV at Beycesultan (the first of Late Chalcolithic 2), of a small hoard[4] of copper objects; bars, needles, drills, a fragment of a dagger, and a silver ring, showing the normal use of this once precious metal for ordinary household tools.

The distribution of the south-west Anatolian Late Chalcolithic 1–2 is fairly well known. Westward it reached Samos (Tigani),[5] Chios[6] and the Akhisar–Manisa region.[7] Some pattern-burnished sherds in Late Chalcolithic 2 may be linked to Tigani and to the still isolated site of Beşik Tepe in the Troad.[8]

[1] §xii, 18, 86.
[2] §xiv, 3, 44, fig. 5.
[3] §xiv, 3, 46.
[4] §xiv, 5, 47 ff., fig. 6: pl. iiiA.
[5] §xiv, 3, 47.
[6] §xii, 6, 198, figs. 14, 12–15.
[7] §xiv, 2, 99 ff., figs. 1, 2, 5.
[8] §xii, 6, 207, fig. 15.

CHAPTER VIII

THE DEVELOPMENT OF CITIES
FROM AL-'UBAID TO THE END OF URUK 5

I. BABYLONIA AND MESOPOTAMIA

TERMINOLOGY

AL-'UBAID is a small site which lies about 4 miles west of Ur
along the bank of an ancient canal.[1] There, H. R. Hall and
Leonard Woolley were the first to discover and record a prehistoric pottery, hand-turned and decorated with simple designs
painted in a dark pigment on a comparatively light ground; the
predominating colours were black, green, brown or chocolate on
pink or buff and the pots were sometimes slipped, sometimes un-
slipped. Characteristic of these so called 'Ubaid wares was a
carbonized, dark green, highly vitrified paint which had bitten
hard into the clay, the result of over-firing; in the later stages of
development this criterion makes 'Ubaid singularly easy to
distinguish. When the excavations revealed that this was a prehistoric pottery, the term 'Ubaid was applied to it and was also
used to define the period and the culture with which it appeared
to be distinctively associated.

After the excavations at the site of 'Ubaid had been concluded,
the same type of pottery was discovered in abundance at the
neighbouring, and much greater, site of Ur. It soon began to be
evident that this ware must have lasted for a long span of time,
which Woolley consequently sub-divided into three periods. Later,
however, when the Iraq Antiquities Department began to conduct
excavations on a wide scale at the great site of Eridu, an even longer
sequence, covering four successive periods, was established, and it
became possible to classify this pottery into a number of dominant
styles which had developed over a span of many centuries.

Deep down at the bottom of Eridu, the decorated pottery
was given the name of Eridu ware (or 'Ubaid 1), and this was
succeeded by another variety, Qal'at Ḥajji Muḥammad (or
'Ubaid 2), named after a type site which is situated near to Warka,
and this again was followed by two varieties of 'Ubaid ware
('Ubaid 3, 4), which in style came very close to that which had

---

[1] §1, 15, 7 f.

been found in abundance at Ur.[1] Whether we should call the entire series by the generic name of 'Ubaid is a matter for debate, but on the whole this distinctive and striking pottery does show a homogeneous development, and we may therefore accept the apparent continuity as indicative of a single consistent period of culture. We shall, therefore, apply the term 'Ubaid to the whole of that series of pottery which in the south, and to a large extent in the north, of Mesopotamia and even in Syria, appears in sequence after the earlier Sāmarrā and Halaf wares, and intervenes between them and the later pottery of the period which is often defined as Uruk. In order to appreciate the full significance of this stage in prehistoric development we must examine the site of Eridu where the most abundant discoveries both in pottery, architecture and small artefacts have illustrated this stage of development in man's prehistory.

Before considering Eridu in detail, however, it is necessary to define the terminology which we propose to use for the periods which intervene between the end of the 'Ubaid and the beginning of the Early Dynastic, that is to say, roughly speaking, for the period 3500–3000 B.C.

At a conference of the principal expeditions which were excavating in Iraq about 1929 it was decided to classify the pottery which had followed 'Ubaid under the names Uruk and Jamdat Naṣr after the type sites which had first produced these distinctive ceramics in abundance. Subsequently, however, it became the practice to use these terms to denote not only ceramics but culture periods, although there were obvious objections to this nomenclature. One of the principal reasons against the adoption of this terminology was that the polychrome pottery so distinctive of Jamdat Naṣr was found only at a few sites in Babylonia, and the term therefore corresponded with a highly specialized ware, not very widely distributed. Furthermore, the site of Jamdat Naṣr was only excavated on a small scale and the extent of the sequences within that mound was never fully examined.

Nevertheless, the term Jamdat Naṣr still appears to be a convenient label because we may associate it not only with a distinctive pottery, but also with an early stage in the history of writing, wherein tablets were written in the Sumerian language. This stage, well defined at Jamdat Naṣr, corresponds with what is known at the site of Warka as Uruk 3, and there it is preceded by an earlier stratum, Uruk 4, containing a yet older series of tablets, some of which are more nearly related to the pictographic beginnings of

[1] §1, 21; 28.

writing. Preceding Uruk 4, which was a flourishing architectural period, it is to be presumed that there must have been a stage or stages in which the invention of writing occurred. For that reason Delougaz,[1] in the course of the extensive work done by the University of Chicago in the Diyālā, introduced a new term, namely Protoliterate, which was intended to cover these earlier developments and to include Uruk 4–3 and Jamdat Naṣr.

The term Protoliterate is, however, inconsistently used. Delougaz intended it to cover Uruk 7–3, but A. L. Perkins sees no reason for not taking it back to Uruk 8. The two earliest of its subphases (a)–(b) have never been precisely defined, and until the deep levels at Warka have been more completely excavated, and the work on the Diyālā more fully published, we shall be unable to judge how far the Protoliterate scheme is valid for southern Mesopotamia as a whole. What has so far been proposed is: Protoliterate (a) includes either Uruk 8–6 (Perkins) or 7–6 (Delougaz); phase (b) includes the Uruk 4 tablets, Uruk-style glyptic, temple sequences E-anna V–IV (still not altogether satisfactorily stratified); (c) includes the earliest material from Khafājī Sin Temples I–III; (d) includes Khafājī Sin Temple IV and part of V—all underlying the Early Dynastic material.

Moreover at the site of Warka, for the stages preceding Uruk 4, the architecture, one of our most important criteria, is still defective; the ceramic development is often contaminated, and the lines of demarcation are therefore unsatisfactory.

It would, in fact, have allowed more room for manoeuvre had it been decided long ago to use the term Uruk to define the entire development of Mesopotamian culture which followed the end of 'Ubaid until the beginning of Early Dynastic I. None the less, it is, in our opinion, still convenient to use the term Jamdat Naṣr in defining the final stage of what we may call the Uruk period since, as we have already mentioned, Jamdat Naṣr corresponds with a pronounced phase in the development of writing, when the Sumerian element was linguistically and culturally dominant in the country. The term Uruk, therefore, we shall use to cover the stages in Mesopotamia corresponding with Uruk 12–4, and Jamdat Naṣr or Uruk–Jamdat Naṣr to correspond with Uruk 3. We have in any case to recognize that there can be no rigid lines of demarcation between one period and another. At least the old terminology is relatively simple and does not have recourse to a cumbersome compound of Latin and Greek.

Finally, a no less strong objection to the term Protoliterate

[1] §I, 10, 8, n. 10.

is that it leaves us without a label to cover the stages Uruk 11–8 which, in the present stage of our knowledge, are much better included within the Uruk period as a whole, for at these stages we are confronted with developments which are definitely post-'Ubaid, yet closely comparable with the assemblages which occur even as late as Uruk 4. The basic ceramic material which justifies this scheme was clearly illustrated and described in 1932.[1]

The nub of the matter is that the term Protoliterate is clumsy and ill-defined and has not yet justified itself. This term presupposes stages of writing anterior to Uruk 4, for which there is as yet no stratigraphic evidence in Babylonia, though it is indeed conceivable that a purely pictographic tablet such as the celebrated one found at Kish[2] may be older than Uruk 4. For these reasons we have decided to retain the old terminology, which should stand until such time as a much greater volume of architectural evidence is available for the periods succeeding 'Ubaid.

The remarkable series of developments embraced by the Uruk and Jamdat Naṣr periods in Babylonia affords many points of reference in defining the progress of civilization at centres far distant from the Tigris–Euphrates rivers. For this reason, our survey must begin with Babylonia which serves as a common denominator in assessing much of the technological progress that archaeology has revealed in prehistoric Assyria, Syria and Iran.

ERIDU

The Sumerians, who have left us the earliest literary traditions about the origins of civilization in Babylonia, thought of Eridu[3] as the first of the five cities that existed before the Flood;[4] they associated with it the god Enki, who was renowned for his wisdom and learning, his patronage of the arts and crafts, and his power over the sweet waters that flow beneath the earth. The city of Eridu, which is concealed beneath the mounds now known as Abu Shahrain, lies above 12 miles south-south-west of Ur; it has been partly dug, and its ancient remains have vindicated the accuracy of Sumerian tradition concerning its great antiquity.

Nothing earlier than the first settlements at Eridu has yet been discovered in Babylonia; the architecture of the prehistoric

---

[1] §1, 37, IV, compiled after the close of the deep soundings in E-anna, Taf.16–20. In §1, 37, U.V.B. VI, Taf. 2, there is a table of sequences for the periods VI–I but here the 'White Temple' was erroneously placed as early as VI: this building was correctly relegated to period III in U.V.B. VIII, 48 f.   [2] §1, 11, 4 and pl. 1.

[3] See Ill. Ldn News, 31 May 1947 and 11 September 1948.

[4] §1, 20, 59 ff.

temples is skilfully contrived, the pottery artistically adorned. From the beginning agriculture and fisheries must have prospered; but a number of grave natural handicaps had to be surmounted by all who lived there, for the city lay on the margin of a desert and was exposed to severe sand-storms which, in the end, made the place uninhabitable. But it is evident that in prehistoric times there must have been an abundance of fresh water—the gift of Enki who dwelt in the *apsū* below the city. Something of this legacy still exists, for in the low-lying ground at the foot of the mound the bedawin can still discover fresh water at a depth of about 6 ft. below the surface; this fresh water land is known by them as *usaila*.

Although a near neighbour of Ur, Eridu lay in a different geographical setting, for it was separated from that city by a steep cliff and stood at the southern end of a depression known as the *Khōr en-Nejeif* which becomes a quagmire during the winter and a furnace during the summer. The ruins are visible from afar in the unbroken steppe, both by day, and by night under the crystal-clear moonlight which illuminates the desert in these latitudes. At dawn the zikkurrat stands aloft like a fairy castle for the first half-hour after sunrise, and behind it the mile of camel-thorn, perhaps the source of the legendary Sumerian *kiškanū* trees,[1] takes on the aspect of a forest. It need not surprise us that this now desolate spot was once deemed to be a holy place and that the faithful journeyed there to leave offerings in the sand long after the city had ceased to be.

Although Eridu now lies nearly 150 miles distant from the Persian Gulf, at the time of its foundation, and for many centuries thereafter, it was probably directly connected with the seashore through a number of vast tidal lakes. Indeed the Sumerians themselves in their legends referred to the city in this way: 'all the lands were sea...then Eridu was made'.[2] Again, under the Third Dynasty of Ur, we read that Shulgi, the son of Ur-Nammu, cared greatly for the city of Eridu which was on the shore of the sea. Geophysical investigations have, however, proved that these ancient historic statements need not be interpreted as meaning that Eridu was a maritime site, but rather that it served as a port on a lagoon with direct communication to the Gulf. The evidence of stratification indicates that much of the ground in the neighbourhood was marshy. Sea, lakes, marsh, sand dunes and the river were the natural surround.

[1] R. C. Thompson, *The Devils and Evil Spirits of Babylonia*, I, 201.
[2] §I, 16, 62.

It is thus not surprising that the ancient settlers were a fisher-folk, who filled their painted kettles with fish and brought them into the temple as an offering which should tempt Enki to answer their prayers. We know also from their kitchen refuse that they ate molluscs, some kind of snail probably, and that there was much sand in their bread. Their teeth were ground down to the gums, and that probably implies a diet of coarse-grained and badly milled cereals.[1] We do not know to what extent the earliest settlers bred cattle, but we may be certain that this form of occupation increased in the Uruk and Jamdat Naṣr periods and became a prominent feature of Sumerian economic development. In the 'Ubaid cemetery there were the remains of three *saluki* hunting dogs[2] which could have been used for chasing the hares and gazelles that have always frequented the desert; the representation of the same animal on a seal at Arpachiyah[3] and Gawra[4] also suggests that this was another method of acquiring meat for the larder.

For a prehistoric site Eridu was an unusually large city: even today the ancient surface débris extends over a diameter of more than 500 yards in every direction. We may estimate that this ancient market-town had an area of approximately 20–25 acres and may in the 'Ubaid period have contained a population of not less than 4000 souls. It is also probable that at an early stage in its prehistory it was secured by a town wall, although this remains to be dug *in extenso*.

Traces of ancient canals have been observed in the neighbourhood of the site which must in prehistoric times have had direct contact with the main channel of the Euphrates itself although, unlike Ur, it does not seem to have been situated on the riverbank.

Pottery of the 'Ubaid and Uruk types lies in profusion over the slopes of the mound and many baked-clay sickles of a kind used only in the 'Ubaid period can still be picked up by the casual traveller. The centre of the site, in the vicinity of the zikkurrat, appears to have been reserved for temples, and beyond them lay a cemetery and many houses.

Architecture—private houses. The chief interest of the earliest dwellings is that they appear to have consisted partly of reed-huts and partly of mud-brick houses. In level 10 below the surface the sounding revealed the greater part of a hut built of reeds and plastered on both sides with clay;[5] the thickness of the walls was only 15 cm. The floor of the hut consisted of a mixture of

---

[1] §1, 29.   [2] §1, 22, 118.   [3] §1, 27, 99 and pl. IX, no. 612.
[4] §1, 36, pl. CLXIX, no. 167.   [5] §1, 32.

sand and clay; the hut itself was divided into a number of rooms in two of which there were low-lying oblong platforms or tables that appeared to have been used for cooking. A clay corn-bin, four clay stilts to support a cooking pot and a clay oven with a cooking pot inside it provided further evidence of the domestic arrangements. The contents of the hut consisted chiefly of clay net-sinkers and pottery; the rooms were filled with drift sand. Other houses at a higher level contained similar objects and, in addition, clay sickles, bent clay nails and large quantities of fresh-water molluscs. The huts in the lower levels appear to have been closely associated with mud-brick walls and one of them at least had served as the annexe to a brick-built house. The same combination of reed-hut and mud-brick house is found on reaches of the Euphrates in southern Iraq today.

In the upper levels the house plans were consistently simple. The normal lay-out was a long passage, no more than 2 ft. wide, with a pair of small rooms radiating off it on either side. The mud-bricks were unusually large and heavy; some of them measured no less than 49 × 26 × 8 cm.; but it is known that in northern Mesopotamia a large size of mud-brick was also favoured in the 'Ubaid period to which the majority of the houses in this sounding may be ascribed. The walls were as a rule no thicker than the longest brick and were often composed of alternating courses of headers and stretchers. The bricks contained little straw; there was a good plaster finish to the wall-faces. Some mud-brick houses which were excavated before the main expedition to Eridu took place, first by Taylor in the middle of the last century and then by H. R. Hall after the First World War,[1] bore traces of mural paintings on their walls—plain bands of red paint. It is not known for certain whether these houses belonged to the Uruk or Jamdat Naṣr periods but it is at least possible that they may be attributable to the preceding 'Ubaid period.

Architecture—temples. Most important of all the discoveries at Eridu was the remarkable series of prehistoric temples (see Figs. 24 and 25) underlying the zikkurrat which lay in the central and most hallowed part of the site. The zikkurrat itself was built by Amar-Sin (*c.* 2047–2039 B.C.), the third king of the Third Dynasty of Ur, who, according to an omen-text, died of 'the pinch of a shoe'.[2] It is tempting to suggest that his last illness was due to a septic foot contracted while walking through the sand to inspect the work at Eridu. The building was never finished and his successors gave up the task of competing with

[1] §I, 14, 187 f.   [2] See *J.C.S.* I, 261.

the sand dunes, which in places were battened down with mats against the prevailing wind. Similar climatic conditions had prevailed from the time of the very first prehistoric settlement, for the oldest building of all had been erected on the top of a sand dune, and between many of the successive temples, of which there were no less than 18 in all, beneath the zikkurrat, there were clearly marked strata of wind-blown sand. The sand dumps marked the lapse of time, often perhaps no more than a few months, between the abandonment of one temple and the re-building of another, and they provide additional proof of the continuity of life in the centre of the city from the earliest 'Ubaid until the Uruk period.

Of the eighteen building levels excavated, the top five, nos. 1–5, could be assigned to the Uruk and Jamdat Naṣr periods, and below them, nos. 6–18 spanned the whole of the 'Ubaid. It may be presumed that all of the mud-brick constructions, nos. 6–18, were religious buildings, for although the plans of some of them were defective, the probability is that all stood upon conse-crated, hallowed ground; they must have spanned many centuries, for the total depth of the sounding which embraced them amounted to no less than 12 m. in all. In describing these temples it is convenient to classify them into three main groups.[1] The first and earliest consists of temples 18–15, after which there is a gap, for the remains of 14–12 inclusive are fragmentary, and only wall stumps were accessible; it seems that at that period the site of the main temples was shifted to ground which subse-quently underlay the zikkurrat.

The next group in the main sequence consisted of temples 11–9 which differed in form from anything that had preceded them but were, however, genetically related to the third group that followed, namely temples 8–6, and with these we reach the end of the 'Ubaid period proper.

There is little to be said about the earliest walls of level 18, which were simply the remains of buildings standing upon a sand dune: we are by no means certain whether this was the original Eridu or if, beneath them again, by digging away the dune still earlier levels might have been discovered. That must remain a matter of doubt until further excavations can be conducted on the same spot. At level 17 (see Fig. 24 (a)) we are confronted with the bare plan of a building, a rectangular enclosure contain-ing internal projecting piers; the walls were very thin. This was followed by temple 16 where we have the first plan of a complete

[1] §1, 22, 115 f. and pl. VI.

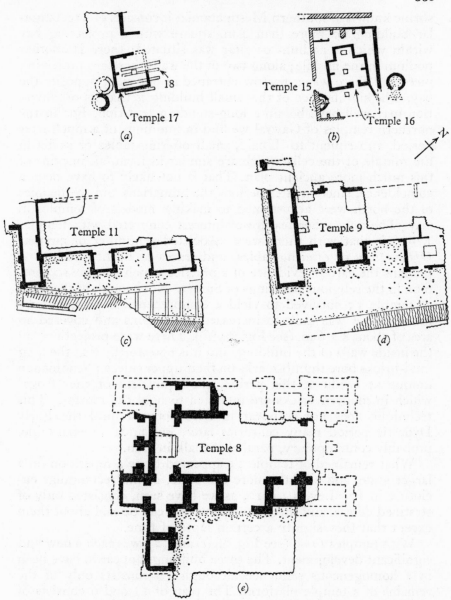

Fig. 24. Eridu. Plans of the early series of prehistoric temples showing development from the simplest form in level 17. Not to scale. (See pp. 334 ff.)

shrine known to southern Mesopotamia; it consists of a rectangular building no more than 4 m. square with a projecting bay within which a podium or altar was situated; there is another podium in the middle; along two of the walls there are projecting piers and there was a narrow entrance in one side, opposite the bay. The significance of this small building is that its organization may well have begun a long-standing tradition. For in the northern temples of Gawra[1] we find in buildings of a much later period, subsequent to 'Ubaid, small offering-tables or podia in the middle of the cella which are similar in form, an imprint of this much more ancient plan. That is not likely to have been a coincidence, since in later periods the Sumerians and the peoples of the north were accustomed to making models of temples in clay. The only other feature of interest connected with temples 17–16 is that with them were associated a number of circular *Opferstätten*, or offering-tables, and traces of burnt offerings— perhaps the earliest evidence of a practice which became so common in the religious buildings of Sumer. Not enough of the walls of temple 15 survived to yield a comprehensible plan, but we know that it was built to increased dimensions and covered an area of about 8 × 6 m. (see Fig. 24 (*b*)). There were projections on the inside walls of the building, and it is noteworthy that the long mud-bricks bore thumb-marks on their upper side, a phenomenon unique at Eridu at this period, the equivalent of the 'frogs' which in modern bricks are intended to hold the mortar. This technique does not reappear in Mesopotamia until the Early Dynastic period many centuries later, but finds a remarkable, probably contemporary, parallel at Sialk in Iran.[2]

What remained of temple 15 appeared to be a repetition on a larger scale, and slightly more elaborate, of the rectangular enclosure in 17. Levels 14–12, as we have seen, consisted only of stratified débris, and there is nothing that can be said about them except that they signify a certain lapse of time.

With temples 11–9 (see Fig. 24 (*c*) and (*d*)) we reach a new and significant development. The three buildings appear to have been in a homogeneous sequence although 10 consists only of the remains of a temple platform. The plan of 11 and 9 consists of an oblong building with central nave and rooms projecting from it. The altar or podium stood at the narrow end, and behind it there was a long passage with buttresses. Originally the projecting rooms in the long side of the building may have been more or less symmetrical on either side, and here we see foreshadowed

---

[1] §1, 33, pls. XII, XIV, XXV.   [2] See below, p. 448.

the tripartite temple ground-plan which became so characteristic a feature of Sumerian temples in the Uruk period.

Temple 11 was much larger than any building that had preceded it, and was 15 m. in length. The walls were thin, only one brick thick, and were strengthened by regularly spaced buttresses. A ramp 1 m. wide led up to the temple platform and there was evidence of a water-channel for drainage alongside it. This arrangement foreshadowed the sloping face of the presumed staircase in temple 9 and the elaborate stepped entrance to the shrine which became a feature of temple 7. But the interesting historical characteristic of this series 11–9 is that we appear to have a genetic connexion with a northern type of temple that appears in prehistoric Assyria at the site of Gawra in level 13, where the walls are similarly thin, and have projecting chambers and elaborate buttresses to strengthen them.

At temple 8 we are confronted with a formidable mud-brick building, larger than any that had been founded before, 21 × 12 m., approximately, in dimensions (see Fig. 24(e)).[1] The plan is now well and boldly articulated and the projecting rooms have been embraced within the whole and absorbed in the general plan, which is clearly tripartite in form. It is assumed that there was a staircase on the south-east side of what has now become an extended temple platform, and there was access to the nave both in the long and in the short sides. There was a podium or altar at the short south-west end of the building and an offering-table opposite it at the far end. A passageway behind the altar which had been a feature of temples 11–9 was now replaced by heavy cruciform buttresses against the south-west wall, forming two niches which gave an appearance of false doors and perhaps matched two real ones that may be restored by analogy on the opposite side of the building. Within one of these two niches was discovered a hole-mouthed, lenticular, painted vessel with a long tubular spout, a kind of fish-kettle; plentiful offerings of fish were also found here. Near the altar there was a large clay horn and a series of terracotta hooked objects with circular heads, their ends dipped in bitumen. Perhaps these offerings were parts of fishermen's equipment, for fishermen must have been closely associated with the temple, as is indicated by the number of fish-offerings.

Temple 7 (see Fig. 25(a)),[2] which measured 18·5 × 13 m., was an elaborate and more orderly version of temple 8. The main

[1] See also above, p. 335.
[2] See also *Ill. Ldn News*, 31 May 1947.

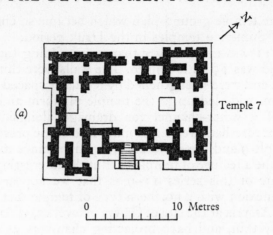

(a)   Temple 7

0   10 Metres

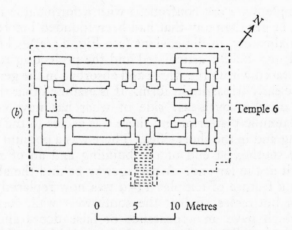

(b)   Temple 6

0   5   10 Metres

Fig. 25. Eridu. Plans of the two latest temples in the 'Ubaid series, 7 and 6.
(See pp. 337 ff.)

entrance was up a flight of steps which gave direct access through
a vestibule to the sanctuary and was situated on the long south-
east side of the building. The steps were flanked on either side
by small, smooth, and neatly rounded parapets. In addition to
the lateral entrances there were small entrances in the short side,
opposite the main altar. The altar at the far end of the room still
stood no less than 40 cm. in height, and the podium opposite it
near the two entrances at the end bore traces of fire. In this temple
there were two clay pavements separated by 40 cm. of débris
which contained ash and fish-bones; each pavement marked a
different phase of occupation, evidence that the building was by

no means short-lived. This tripartite temple with its elaborately buttressed façade is very similar in type to the standard form familiar to Uruk periods 4 and 3, and proves that those Sumerian temples are in direct line of descent from this older Al-'Ubaid series.

Temple 6 (see Fig. 25 (b)),[1] which measured 23 × 12 m., was narrower and more symmetrical; less prominence was given to the corner rooms. It is interesting that in this temple the two entrances in the short side had disappeared and there was access from the long side only. This and other evidence suggests that the position of the temple doors has no particular religious significance at Eridu. Various authorities, beginning with Walter Andrae, have suggested that the position of the entrances corresponded with differences in the cult. It is argued that we may detect a different form of worship, esoteric or exoteric, by observing whether the altar was directly visible to the entrant or concealed from him, that is to say, concealed from view through a bent axis entrance.[2] There is, however, some doubt about the validity of this theory, for it would have been very easy to conceal the altar, had this been desired, by a wooden partition, or a screen, or a curtain, as is the practice in some modern oriental churches today.

With temple 6 the remarkable series of Al-'Ubaid religious buildings at Eridu comes to an end: associated with them there was a rich succession of painted pottery which, after the architecture, is our most copious source of documentation for the period.

Pottery and terracotta objects: the 'Sumerian Problem'. In classifying the temples we observed that they could be conveniently arranged into three main groups: the earliest ranged from the bottom up to level 15; the middle groups from level 11 to 9; the latest from 8 to 6. We must now determine how far the main classes of pottery tended to correspond with the progressive architectural development; and it will not be surprising if the main technological and artistic changes in the ceramic do not take place *pari passu*. But we may anticipate our conclusion by saying that, broadly speaking, the architectural progression is reflected in that of the pottery, which, however, tends to more rapid change, as might be expected, for the process of creating a pot is quicker and simpler than that which is required to achieve a building.

A detailed account of the pottery is properly the domain of a history of ceramics and requires extensive illustration. It must

---

[1] *Ill. Ldn News*, 31 May 1947.
[2] §1, 31 (preface by W. Andrae, 2 ff.); §1, 3; §1, 2, 72.

therefore suffice here to consider the salient characteristics of the
'Ubaid development and to define the problems which concern it.
In the first place, as we saw at the beginning of this chapter, there
are some authorities who believe that the changes in the ceramic
through levels 18–6 at Eridu are sufficiently sharp to warrant a
different nomenclature for each of the four main periods of development.[1] We are therefore justified in using the terminology
first applied by the excavators to the more elaborate styles of two
classes of ceramic, which had preceded the 'Ubaid and had
been discovered at many sites, for example at Ur, Warka and
Nippur, before the excavation of Eridu. The broad divisions of
pottery on these lines are as follows: from the bottom up to level 15,
Eridu ware; from level 14 to 12 Ḥajji Muḥammad; level 12 to 8
'Ubaid; finally level 7 to 6 late 'Ubaid. Thus there are four main
periods in the development of ceramic corresponding with only
three for the architecture. But it is possible that this discrepancy
would be considerably lessened were it not for the fact that in
levels 14–12, where Ḥajji Muḥammad ware occurs, the architectural evidence is defective.[2]

The earliest levels, up to 15, characterized by the so-called
Eridu ware, contained *inter alia* a fine quality of monochrome
painted pottery, often with a buff or cream slip. The paint, which
was sometimes brown, black, or more rarely red, was more often
chocolate in colour; normally matt, it was glossy when thickly
applied. Such variations imply that both brush control and fire
control were irregular. Decoration was exclusively geometric in
character, as on all the primitive Mesopotamian ceramic at this
period and was principally based on rectilinear designs—
hatching, bands, zigzags, chequer patterns, while some designs
were left as a reserve. The shapes include deep goblets, vases,
bowls and occasionally large platters, and many, if not most, of
these vessels are, on the inside, and sometimes on the outside,
covered with designs—in sharp contrast with the late 'Ubaid
pots, on which, as we shall see, decoration becomes perfunctory
and is reduced to a minimum.

The significance of the highly decorated 'Eridu'[3] ware is that
some of it is undoubtedly derived from the more northerly school
of painting known as Sāmarrā and, in its most developed form,
Halaf, and may have been partly contemporary with the latter.
But these vessels were not imports; they were made locally, as can

---

[1] There may be as many as 19 pottery-levels, but not more than 18 building-
levels have been established.

[2] See Plate 8. [3] §1, 22, pl. x; §1, 28, 33 ff.

be determined from their sandy clay composition which bespeaks the district of Eridu itself. It is, however, important to recall that 'painted and unpainted coarser ware also occurs, as do sherds with the greenish colour often associated with the 'Ubaid ceramic'. At the bottom there was a 'relatively high percentage of coarse green pottery and a correspondingly smaller proportion of painted "Eridu Ware"'.[1] Such evidence tends to the conclusion that from the beginning we may detect the presence of a

5:27

Fig. 26. 'Eridu Ware' from Ḥajji Muḥammad, restored from fragments of two bowls; greenish-grey and brownish-violet paint on yellowish-buff clay: after §1, 40. (See pp. 341, 365.)

local fabric, such was commonly produced on other prehistoric sites in Babylonia, namely the true Al-'Ubaid ware, and that this was being produced side by side with a much more elaborate pottery, made locally but in the style of models that had long been familiar at Sāmarrā and much farther north, in prehistoric Assyria.

Following the Eridu ware, which begins to decline in output in level 15, we are confronted there, and especially in levels 14–12, with a distinctive type of pottery which becomes predominantly characteristic at this period. The fabric is known as

[1] §1, 28, 33.

Ḥajji Muḥammad ware after the prehistoric type site near Warka where it was first found in abundance (see Figs. 26 and 27). Characteristic of this pottery is a deep bowl with incurving sides which tend to form a sharp angle near the base (see Fig. 27). At the type site many other shapes also occur but this one is distinctive because it best displays the crowded and close-knit quality of the painted designs that are the characteristic imprint. The sides of the bowl are closely covered with a grid pattern that runs

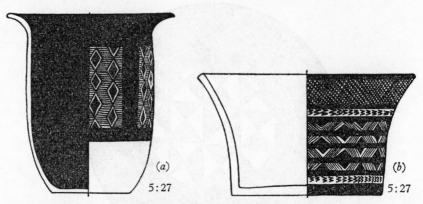

Fig. 27. Ḥajji Muḥammad pottery, restored from fragments: (*a*) olive green and brown paint on yellowish-buff clay; (*b*) brownish-violet paint on yellowish clay: after §1, 40. (See pp. 342, 365.)

obliquely to its vertical axis, leaving a reserve of minute squares as a background; on the outside there is often a broad band of paint in which there are reserves of triangular patterns. Many other combinations of simple geometric designs applied to bowls and vases occur (see Fig. 27): it is the miniature reserve and over-loading of pattern that obtrude themselves amongst many variations. Moreover, whilst the use of a slip is less common than hitherto, an innovation is the common application of a purplish-black paint, often slightly lustrous, although the older colours, brown, black, red and green, recur.

In these levels 14–12, the older types continue, but in lesser quantities, and while Ḥajji Muḥammad ware[1] marks a new technical development in ceramic, it is clear, especially at the type site, that both in design and in shape the fabric was influenced by the fashion of the northern wares which had also influenced the preceding 'Eridu' pottery.

[1] §1, 40.

We now come to the next period of ceramic development, which runs through levels 12–8 and is marked by the standard forms of the classical 'Ubaid ware which are ubiquitous on the prehistoric sites of southern Babylonia. It may well be significant that in level 12 we find for the first time evidence of the clay sickle so characteristic of the 'Ubaid period, an invention that must have been of practical importance to agriculture and probably answered an urgent need for an inexpensive and easily replaceable tool, an instrument obviously designed to coincide with the richer harvests which no doubt were the reward for a more extensive and efficient irrigation. We have already noticed that ceramic changes tend to anticipate architectural developments, and it is therefore no surprise that in level 11, the one after the first appearance of the clay sickle, we begin to find the first evidence of the new, tripartite temple ground-plan which was destined to become the standard form of building associated with the religion of the Sumerians. There may therefore be a case for seeing in about these levels the first traces of the peoples who subsequently, in the Uruk and Jamdat Naṣr periods, were to play so decisive a part in the destinies of Babylonia. It is also significant that for the first time in level 12 we find the classical 'Ubaid ware in abundance.

Nevertheless, however receptive the country may have been to the admission of peoples from abroad, we have to admit that at no prehistoric period in Babylonia can we discern any decisive break in archaeological continuity such as would give grounds for identifying any particular stage of development with the entry of a new people. Even in level 12 at Eridu where the architecture, an improved agriculture and an abundance of classical 'Ubaid pottery make a striking impact, we are but observing a process of technical evolution which follows naturally from what has preceded.

We are only entitled to talk of Sumerians, *sensu stricto*, when confronted with their writing, which appears for the first time in the period known as Uruk 4–3 (Jamdat Naṣr stage of Uruk). Some authorities have therefore argued that this was the time when the Sumerians entered the country, though none have been able to detect their antecedents elsewhere. Others have attempted to seek their presence at various earlier stages: the late Professor H. Frankfort, impressed by the archaeological continuity, was prepared to recognize the presence of Sumerians in the 'Ubaid period. He discounted the arguments that some of the older cities of Babylonia bore non-Sumerian names, both because the philological argument was uncertain, and because there was no proof that such names had been applied before the Uruk period.[1]

Nor can we accept the argument that an unbroken tradition of ecclesiastical architecture excludes the possibility of any major change in the character of the population. We have only to recall in much later times the seizure and use of Christian buildings by Muslim peoples in Damascus, Constantinople and elsewhere, although obviously the cult changed and there were modifications in the fixtures within the buildings.

However that may be, *tot homines, quot sententiae*: the presence or absence of Sumerians in Babylonia before Uruk 4 is a subject capable of endless debate. But we may agree in general with the statement of Joan Oates: 'Most authorities would argue the arrival of the Sumerians either at the beginning of the 'Ubaid or in the Uruk period, and most agree that the later Uruk period is too late.'[2]

Bearing in mind the tenuous nature of the evidence concerning the identification of any particular set of archaeological phenomena with a specific group of people, we may return to a consideration of levels 12–8 at Eridu where we were inclined to recognize the presence of Sumerians, and observe that within these strata we can witness a number of technical and artistic ceramic developments, which may be classified under two sub-divisions: first 12–10 and then 9–8. In the earlier of these two phases, older types of vessel such as slender bowls and coarse vases are still extensively used, but there are also some innovations, notably a long-spouted, hole-mouthed 'fish-kettle' (see Fig. 28 (*a*)) which, however, made a first appearance in level 13; other shapes such a spouted vase with a high ring-handle fixed to the rim, also found at Ur, appear for the first time. The next phase, whilst discarding one of the older types, a ring-based vase, introduced a number of new shapes and again illustrates the inventiveness of the 'Ubaid potter, his readiness to experiment whilst conserving some and rejecting other older fashions. But the most striking ceramic achievement of this latter phase 9–8 is the production of small and delicate hemispherical bowls, almost an egg-shell ware,[3] decorated with fanciful geometric designs including rosettes and stylized foliage covering the outer surface and making effective use of the background as counterchange.

[1] H. Frankfort, *Archaeology and the Sumerian Problem* (*S.A.O.C.* 4), 21 ff. and n. 4. Concerning non-Sumerian words see S. N. Kramer, 'Dilmun; quest for Paradise', in *Antiquity*, 37, no. 146 (1963), 111 ff., with reference to an article by B. Landsberger; see also above, pp. 148 ff.

[2] §1, 28, 46; *C.A.H.* 1³, ch. XIII, sect. I.   [3] §1, 22, pl. VII.

A delicately made painted clay 'horn' (level 9) and others un-painted, with mushroom heads, perhaps better described as bent nails (see Fig. 28 (*e*)), also now make their first appearance as well as coarser, unpainted specimens. No satisfactory explanation of the bent 'nails' has yet been given, but as they were associated with the temples it is not unlikely that some of them were *ex voto* deposits.

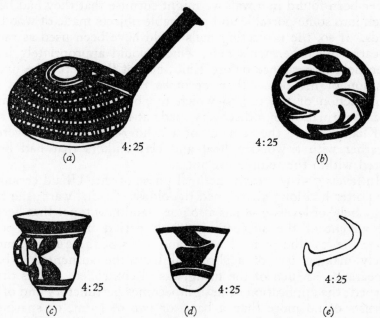

Fig. 28. Eridu, painted pottery and a clay nail or horn. (See pp. 344 ff.) (*a*) Fish-kettle, hole-mouth jar with long trumpet spout. Dark, purplish paint. The type first appears in level 13. (*b*) Bowl painted on the inside. (*c*), (*d*) Two goblets, one with handle, painted on the outside in dark paint on light clay; from the ceme-tery. (*e*) Bent clay nail. Associated with the later 'Ubaid temples at Eridu.

Whilst levels 12–8 witnessed some innovations, the older ceramic traditions were, however, by no means broken. As a whole, much of the pottery bears the authentic stamp of the developed 'Ubaid, and it is therefore of particular interest that the extraordinary painted 'fish-kettles', with their long trumpet-like and tubular spouts, now appear in every one of these levels, and are, as we shall see, equally at home in prehistoric Assyria, at the site of Tepe Gawra, where they appear in levels 19 and 17, not long after the end of the Halaf period. It is therefore possible that these archaic-looking vases were derived from the north, and we may accept them as proof of northern influence in the authentic 'Ubaid stage at Eridu. The justification for calling them 'fish-kettles' is that one of them, found intact in a niche behind the altar of temple 8, was full of fish-bones, and other fish offerings were adjacent, as well as a number of terracotta bent 'nails' with their ends dipped in bitumen. The bitumen indicates that the nails were fixed into some solid background, and since they have never been found in a wall we might surmise that they had been stuck into some portable and perishable objects made of wood or reeds. If so, the projecting nails could have been used as racks to carry the fishermen's nets, which would appropriately have been held in suspense before Enki, god of the deep. The juxtaposition of fish-bones then becomes understandable. This reconstruction of the use to which the bent nails was put may find confirmation in a discovery made at the Early Dynastic site of Khafājī where the remains of a fishing-net were discovered, together with a wooden float and clay sinkers that had been stored within the temple precincts.[1]

In levels 7–6 we reach the final phase of the 'Ubaid ceramic; the potter had long abandoned the oldest 'Eridu' ware; the fine 'egg-shell' of levels 9–8 has also gone, and new types that herald the advent of the succeeding Uruk period begin to appear. None the less the painted bowls and vases of these levels, more rarely making use of a slip, still have the authentic 'Ubaid appearance. Much of the firing was ill controlled, clay is often warped; the application of design becomes perfunctory and often consists of no more than a band or two of paint, or sparingly applied lozenges, triangles, zigzags, and curvilinear designs, occasionally stylized foliage. Many of these vessels, spouted drinking-vases, cups, goblets, bowls, and plates are not unattractive to look at. They begin to have the appearance of mechanical work, and although the bulk of the pottery appears to have been hand-made, a not inconsiderable number of vessels bear the striations that betray turning, and some of them may already have been thrown on a wheel—a practice that was to become common in the Uruk period.

The cemetery. The pottery discovered in temples 7–6 was illustrated in far greater abundance by a large number of vessels discovered within 200 graves of a cemetery (see Fig. 28), which originally numbered at least 1000 graves in all. The burials, as described by Seton Lloyd and Fuad Safar, were 'sunk into the clean, wind-drifted sand'[2] within mud-brick boxes, and after

---

[1] §1, 9, 55 f.   [2] §1, 22, 117.

interment filled with earth and sealed with mud-bricks. They were, like the temples, oriented towards the north-west, and a notable feature is that the skeletons were invariably extended, like some, but not all, of the bodies in the corresponding period at Ur. This practice of extended burial must have been tribal because at other sites it admits of some variation.

In the Eridu cemetery there were some family burials which necessitated the re-opening of the grave from time to time; and it was not unusual for the preceding bones to be roughly pushed aside—an irreverent clumsiness which remained a regular feature of later Babylonian burial practice. Pottery was deposited in every grave, and the collection recovered from this cemetery is invaluable for the study of this latest phase of 'Ubaid ware. For each individual a cup and a plate were indispensable and were no doubt intended to hold food and water for the departed dead, who may thus have been induced to refrain from haunting the living— if that deduction is justified from a study of the much later Babylonian magical texts. In addition to many other kinds of clay vessels there was occasionally a stone vase. Personal orna- ments were rare, but beads were found. 'In one case a deep band of such beads, of two colours arranged in a simple pattern, lay across the shin-bone, a little beneath the knee, as though they had been the fringe of some sort of skirt.'[1] In two of the graves the skeletons of dogs (*saluki*-like in appearance) accompanied their masters.

Within the cemetery two terracotta objects of outstanding importance were found. The first was a model of a sailing-boat with a prominent socket amidships, 'obviously intended for a mast'.[2] There were also hooks in the sides, for attaching stays, and others in the stern, apparently for a thwart.[3] These features and the 'hooked ornament at prow and stern' are reminiscent of the primitive sailing-boat, the *shakhtūr*, which still plies the lower reaches of the Euphrates today. We may picture these vessels as the regular type used by 'Ubaid fishermen. The second terra- cotta object of outstanding interest was a perfectly preserved figurine, found in a woman's grave (see Fig. 29). This figure is of exceptional interest, because most statuettes of the period are of the so called 'mother-goddess' type. Here, instead, we have a nude male with genitals clearly portrayed, and the slim, elegant, long-legged body characteristic of his more common female counterpart; that he is closely related to the female is certain

---

[1] §1, 22, 118.   [2] *Ibid.*

[3] See *Ill. Ldn News*, 11 September 1948, fig. 4.

because he has, like her, an animal, lizard-like or rat-like, head with high hat or *polos*. His arms are detached and he carries in the left hand a short staff or mace—his *bâton de commandement*. The shoulders are decorated with clay pellets which may have been intended to represent tattoo marks.[1]

A preliminary examination of nine skulls revealed that they had been much crushed by the weight of superincumbent earth, and measurement was difficult. Making allowance for these difficulties, one assessment was that 'one of the nine approaches brachycephaly, or broad-headedness; the rest are dolichocephalic or approaching mesocephaly'.[2] A later examination was less venturesome in its diagnosis,[3] but this one is consonant with conclusions on a limited amount of early skeletal material from Kish and from Ur. One important and definite piece of evidence was that 'in general, the mandible appears well-developed, with marked mental protuberance, and the jaw angle sharp, and in a few cases flaring, although of no great breadth. The teeth are remarkably worn, presumably owing to grit inclusions in flour'. We may at least be certain that the Eridu bread contained as liberal an admixture of sand as that of the workmen who excavated there nearly six thousand years later. Another impression which emerged from a first examination was that the Eridu skulls showed a marked prognathism, and this feature also was in agreement with the smaller amount of skeletal material which Arthur Keith examined at Al-'Ubaid itself: the Eridu men, however, appeared to have had less prominent noses.

Fig. 29. Eridu cemetery. Figurine, in buff clay, representing a male god (?) with lizard-like head. Decorated with appliqué pellets (representing tattoo marks?) and carrying a staff. Height, 5½ in. (See pp. 347 f.)

[1] See *Ill. Ldn News*, 11 Sept. 1948, figs. 1–2.   [2] §1, 29, 126.   [3] §1, 8.

No evidence of metal was recorded in the Eridu cemetery, and we may be certain that this was a very rare commodity throughout the 'Ubaid period. Personal ornaments were rare, but stone nose-studs(?) were used. Fragments of beautifully ground obsidian vases and smoky quartz occurred, as is not surprising, for these materials had long been known in the north. Other sites, in particular Ur, Warka and 'Uqair have helped to supplement our knowledge concerning objects of daily use.

Eridu: Summary of evidence—post-'Ubaid developments. The archaeological evidence derived from the thirteen 'Ubaid levels at ancient Eridu has made it clear that there was an unbroken line of continuity from beginning to end of the prehistoric periods which some might call 'neolithic' because of the absence of metal here and its rarity elsewhere at the time. The use of ground stone axes, and of simple, backed blades in chert and obsidian is another index of this period, and since copper occurs in the late stages of 'Ubaid at Ur,[1] there is justification for applying the term 'chalcolithic' to Eridu 8–6, though in fact neither this term nor neolithic has any precise content.

Considered in retrospect, the most remarkable feature in this long prehistoric process is the inverse measure of progression revealed by an analysis of the pottery and the architecture respectively. Whereas the painted wares found at the bottom of Eridu are artistically highly developed and elaborate in design, the first buildings are simplicity itself, and many centuries must have lapsed before they began to assume the basic form of ground plan which we associate with Sumerian civilization. Moreover, as the buildings became more elaborate and standardized in plan, the pottery lost its fullness of design, and tended towards repetition and a more mechanical output of relatively limited shapes.

The sum of the evidence makes it seem likely that the earliest inhabitants of southern Babylonia were in a simply organized tribal state when they first settled there, and that their main means of livelihood was fishing. Probably the majority lived in perishable reed-houses and their first mud-brick buildings were exiguous in size, their first shrine supervised by not more than one or two men. At this time it is clear from their pottery that they were strongly influenced by the artistic fashion which prevailed in prehistoric Assyria.

How long it took to emerge from this stage of development we do not know. Clearly there was extensive communication

[1] See below, pp. 352 f., 356.

with tribes living far outside their own area, for the second earliest period is represented by the Ḥajji Muḥammad pottery in Susiana, as well as at other sites in Babylonia. Travel abroad no doubt stimulated progress at home, and in the third stage of architectural development we find much bigger and more elaborate temples which must have corresponded with an increase in the size of the city and of its urban population. A token of this growth is to be found in the abundance of clay sickles which make their appearance from level 12 onwards, and we may suspect that the farmers of Eridu were then growing the primitive Emmer bread-wheat, barley, and flax of which Helbaek has detected traces in the 'Ubaid period at Ur.[1] The cultivation of wheat may well have corresponded with early attempts at irrigation, and it is hardly rash to suggest that traces of broad canals observed by Jacobsen and others at Eridu originated in this period.

We have already assented to the proposition, advocated by Joan Oates, that the whole of this period is sufficiently homogeneous to deserve the name 'Ubaid, although the excavators Seton Lloyd and Fuad Safar did well to call attention to peculiar differences in the two earliest stages of development by dubbing them with the names of Eridu and Ḥajji Muḥammad.

This period, as we have seen, came to a close with the temple of Eridu 6, a stage archaeologically enriched by the copious finds in a cemetery. Thereafter the foundations of a set of five temples have been traced, Eridu 5 to 1, culminating in a great mud-brick building set upon limestone or gypsum foundations—already a prehistoric cathedral. In this period we may observe the use, mostly in foundations, of cushion-like cement bricks with convex surface, shaped like long French bread-rolls, which may have been the ultimate ancestors of the Early Dynastic plano-convex bricks.

Evidence from the Eridu houses of this period has yielded monochrome red and grey pottery, wheel-turned, no longer handmade. We still appear to be in the truly prehistoric period which preceded writing, and the end phase of it probably corresponds with Uruk 5. These stages, most of which must have preceded the demonstrably Sumerian period of Uruk 4–3, are best illustrated elsewhere. Eridu, though still a great religious city, was perhaps no longer the most important in the land.

[1] §1, 17, 195.

UR–AL-'UBAID AND NEIGHBOURHOOD

A little over 12 miles distant from Eridu, on the bank of the main channel of the Euphrates, lay the city of Ur, which was probably not much inferior in size. The levels corresponding with the 'Ubaid period at Ur have been less extensively dug, for they are overlaid by an immense volume of later débris. But the excavations at Ur, which were begun long before those at Eridu, have provided important complementary evidence to illustrate the 'Ubaid way of life.

Since we have already described the early development of Eridu in some detail, we may be content with a more cursory examination of Ur and consider in what way it strengthens the more copious 'Ubaid evidence from that site.

No temples of this early period were discovered at Ur, although such buildings undoubtedly existed there. It is probable that they lie buried beneath the later zikkurrat and within its precincts, for in the forecourt of the great Larsa and Kassite enceinte, in front of the zikkurrat, thousands of 'Ubaid potsherds were found, thrown in dumps by later builders when levelling the ground.

In his analysis of the pottery, Woolley detected three main stages of development which he named 'Ubaid 1–3. The most extensive traces of 'Ubaid 1, the earliest settlement, were found in the great 'Flood Pit' F where, in addition to mud-bricks, which had been accidentally burned, the remains of wattle-and-daub houses, and reed huts, came to light in viscous clay; they had been built at a time when Ur was an island in a marsh.

This early settlement was succeeded at higher levels by evidence of two more stages, 'Ubaid 2–3, which included inhumation graves. Broadly speaking, Woolley's 'Ubaid 1 occupation was probably not much earlier than level 13 or thereabouts at Eridu; 'Ubaid 2 with its extended burials, painted pottery and mother-goddess figurines corresponded with Eridu 8–6; and 'Ubaid 3, which contained plain as well as the most perfunctorily painted ware, was probably transitional between the end of 'Ubaid and the beginning of the Uruk period. But an examination of the pot designs[1] indicates that in fact the earliest painted ceramics discovered in the bottom levels at Eridu were also present at Ur, and we may assert with confidence that Ur was first occupied not later than Eridu, although the bulk of the evidence obtained from the former city happens to represent the last two main periods of development in the 'Ubaid succession at Eridu.

[1] §1, 38, pls. 46–53.

In comparing the burial practices associated with these two cities it is significant that at Ur, in the period known as 'Ubaid 2, we find a series of extended skeletons, lying supine and, as a rule, laid out on a bed of potsherds, and that interred with them were votive deposits in the shape of simple painted pottery of the late 'Ubaid type. Moreover, there were also terracotta figurines representing the 'mother-goddess' with long svelte bodies;[1] some of them carried a child on one arm; their heads were lizard-like and crowned with a high '*polos*'—in fact they were the exact counterpart of the male warrior with mace that we observed in the cemetery at Eridu 6. Elsewhere at Ur many painted figurines of mother-goddesses in the 'Ubaid style occurred, and, as at Eridu, some male figures; at least two had long painted beards and hammer-shaped heads.

These figurines and the pottery therefore entitle us to correlate Woolley's Ur–'Ubaid 2 with the latest phases of 'Ubaid development at Eridu.

The next phase at Ur (Ur–'Ubaid 3), also revealed graves, but the skeletons were no longer fully extended; they were slightly flexed; the pottery associated with them was still of the 'Ubaid type, but some pots were not painted at all, others were per-functorily decorated with a single band of red or brown paint, and many vessels showed signs of mechanical turning. This transitional phase was obviously the next stage of development after Eridu 6. We have now reached the beginnings of the monochrome ceramic which is the index of the Uruk period.

Associated with a late Ur–'Ubaid grave there was one discovery of peculiar interest, a barbed copper fish-spear,[2] or harpoon, cold-hammered, which has provided us with proof that at the end of the 'Ubaid period metal was being worked, and that competently made weapons were already forged. However, it is clear that metal was still a great rarity; for very little copper of the 'Ubaid period has yet been found. It is possible that a few rare models of painted terracotta axes in the 'Ubaid style are copies of copper weapons, as was thought by the late Gordon Childe,[3] and, if so, socketed metal instruments were already in use. But it is equally possible that some of them reproduced originals in stone, of which more than one example—hammers, as well as axes—have been found.[4] However that may be, later Mesopotamian legend attributed the use of metal to their earliest known cities, for one of them, Bad-tibira, 'the fortress of the

[1] §1, 38, pls. 20–22. [2] *Ibid.* 88 and pl. 30, U. 14992, grave PFG/G.
[3] §1, 7. [4] §1, 38, pl. 16.

metal-smiths' is mentioned along with Eridu as one of the cities which were in existence before the Flood.[1] Nor should it be forgotten that in the deepest 'Ubaid levels at Ur a strip of worked gold has been found.[2]

The material evidence obtained from the discoveries in the 'Ubaid period at Ur is clear proof of the prosperous economy at the time. In this connexion, the observations of Hans Helbaek who has examined some of the plant remains are of particular importance.[3] It appears from the size of specimens of linseed discovered in the 'Ubaid levels that these plants could only have been the products of irrigation. We may draw the conclusion that the abundant remains of 'Ubaid settlements all over southern Babylonia must be due to the exploitation of the available water by improved methods and that this period marks a turning-point in the growth of cities through the development of irrigation.

Lastly, it may be recalled that the raising of livestock was an important avocation, for there are numerous models of painted cattle, and some birds.

Ur: Flood-pit and subsequent prehistoric sequences. In many different parts of Ur, Woolley revealed in the earliest levels banks of relatively clean water-laid sand which he alleged were fluviatile deposits—the result of a violent flooding of the river.[4] And in spite of some scepticism which has been expressed, occasionally in print, there is no reason to disbelieve the evidence given by Woolley on the basis of his observations at Ur, for it was supported by the microscopic analysis of specimens of clay and sandy particles which were submitted to the Petrographical Department of the Geological Survey in London.[5]

The principal evidence came from a deep sounding named Pit F, the surface of which measured no less than 25 by 16 m. At a height of about 4·50 m. above sea-level the diggers exposed a stratum of clean, water-laid sand, more than 3 m. deep. Although in general there were no signs of internal stratification, some darker bands in the upper levels and pockets of darker soil suggested to Woolley that the Flood deposit had been laid down in two sequent stages, possibly not separated by any considerable length of time. But this slight stratigraphic difference did in fact correspond with two different sets of inhumation burials (the earlier of which as we have already noted, were termed Ur 2, the later Ur 3) which marked the extreme end of the Ur–'Ubaid period and the transition to 'Uruk'.

[1] §1, 20, 65.   [2] §1, 38, 75.   [3] §1, 17, 192.
[4] §1, 39, 334 f.; §1, 38, 3 f.   [5] §1, 26.

To the historian the most important consequence of these observations is the conclusion that the alluvial débris in Flood Pit F and in the corresponding levels in other test-pits at Ur cannot possibly represent the authentic traces of the Biblical Flood so vividly described in the book of Genesis, which must ultimately derive from Flood legends related on Sumerian and Old Babylonian tablets. The Flood stories as told in the cuneiform scripts make it clear that the name given by the Sumerians to Noah was Ziusudra, who reigned as king in the south Babylonian city of Shuruppak, probably at the end of the period known as Early Dynastic I, perhaps in about 2900 B.C. or a century or so later. We have every reason to believe that Ziusudra was indeed a historical figure, for archaeology has substantiated the existence of mythological Hero-Kings, such as Gilgamesh and others, who followed him in the most ancient columns of the Sumerian king-list; and the fact of the matter is that the Flood, which we can now relate to a definite historical period in Babylonia, was far too late for identification with the great one observed by Woolley at Ur, which occurred towards the end of the 'Ubaid period, probably not very much later than 3500 B.C.

Most puzzling to the historian has been the failure to detect evidence at Eridu of the same fluviatile deposits at this time. But on reflexion this is not surprising, for the two sites are over 12 miles apart, and are separated by a limestone ridge. Moreover, whereas Eridu lay on the bank of a canal, Ur was situated near the main stream of the Euphrates. It must also be recalled that flood débris will only be left on a large scale when there is a barrier or obstacle to prevent it from being swept over the plains. Ur, as an island in a marsh, provided that obstacle—only thus can we account for the absence of similar evidence from the neighbouring sites of Eridu and elsewhere.

Many violent floods mentioned in Mesopotamian literature at other periods have passed by without leaving a trace. There is, however, some consolation for the disillusioned in the knowledge that at the site of Shuruppak itself, where Ziusudra reigned, and at Kish, cogent claims have been made for the identification of alluvial clay in a stratum which separates 'Ubaid from Jamdat Naṣr, and that here we can accept evidence which has eluded us at Ur of a phenomenon which may have been the authentic Flood faced by the Sumerian Noah.

Ur: Post-diluvial evidence, from 'Ubaid to Uruk 5. The evidence obtained from the Flood Pit F yields the clearest demonstration of post-'Ubaid sequences, and has been confirmed by many soundings at Ur. Above the clay Flood-bank there was a stratum no less than 5·5 m. thick, which consisted for the most part of potters' kilns and wasters. These kilns and their débris had been intruded into older building levels, for the most part destroyed, which, had they been preserved, would most probably have yielded well-stratified remains of the sequences between the end of the 'Ubaid period through to Uruk 5. This lacuna is unsatisfactory, and calls attention to one of the most pressing needs of Mesopotamian excavation—namely, to expose on an extended scale the archaeological sequences which intervene between the end of 'Ubaid and the extensive temple remains usually known under the name of Uruk 4–3, so well represented at the type site of Warka itself and elsewhere.

In the kiln stratum at Ur, however, there is débris which can legitimately be assigned to the immediate post-'Ubaid periods and marks the beginnings of the Uruk stage. White cement bricks belong here; they often have one convex face and may be the ancestors of the plano-convex brick which made its first appearance in Early Dynastic I: it is true, however, that a long gap has to be filled before this sequence can be proved. Another feature of architectural interest is the evidence that in the period which followed 'Ubaid we find for the first time traces of houses with mud-brick walls on stone foundations; the latter is a trait more frequently associated with the later stages of the Uruk period from 5 or 6 onwards.

In the kiln stratum, 'Ubaid-type potsherds preponderated at the bottom, but gradually gave way to the monochrome of the Uruk period which was characterized by some fine specimens of plum-red ware, of sealing-wax red, of polychrome Jamdat Naṣr, as well as of some monochrome grey ware. The discovery in the house-level above the kilns (stratum H) of a potter's wheel[1] was an indication of the change-over to mechanized pot-making which inaugurated the Uruk period.

It is doubtful if the Ur kilns themselves properly belong to the period which we are particularly considering,[2] for they were intrusive, and this potters' factory may not have been working before Uruk 4. Their main function was to produce a very roughly made type of bowl with bevelled rim, often known by the German name of *Glockentöpfe*, which seems to be common to the whole of the Uruk period. Be that as it may, in the same mixed stratum we find other débris which is appropriate to the immediately post-'Ubaid development—notably a copper chisel, a

[1] §1, 38, 62.   [2] From Al-'Ubaid to the end of Uruk 5.

copper spear-head, a copper fish-hook, and a copper needle—simple implements cold-hammered.[1] We are still at a stage earlier than that which produced metal in abundance.

There is some doubt whether we may assign to this early Uruk stage a white marble stamp-seal engraved with simple linear designs of a cervoid and horns,[2] reminiscent of some of the Uruk–Jamdat Nasr period seals found at Tell Brak in prehistoric Assyria. The evidence for seals of the early period is still scanty, and indeed only a few rare and isolated specimens of cylinder seals can be attributed to the period before Uruk 4. In the production of seals and stamps the north was probably in advance of the south. Consequently it is not possible to attribute the magnificent model of a soapstone boar[3] which was also found well down in the kiln stratum to a period much earlier than Uruk 4, for it is in effect a well-developed specimen of the stamp-seal common in the late Uruk period, nor again are we justified in assigning to any earlier period the fine Uruk-type cylinder seal, found near it, and illustrating a weavers' scene—that again properly belongs to the period of Uruk 4–3.

Other articles of interest which were survivals of the 'Ubaid into the early Uruk stages included clay sickles and bent nails, as well as decorative wall-cones which, although apparently found in 'Ubaid strata, have never yet been discovered *in situ* in an 'Ubaid wall. There were also stone querns and rubbers, and more than one chert hoe, a gardening implement well attested on many 'Ubaid sites, not only in Babylonia, but in prehistoric Assyria— they seem to have died out in the Uruk period. The presence of an amazonite ring bead[4] low down in this stratum is significant, for this must be an import from far afield—the Nilgiri hills in India have been suggested. Stone implements were not uncommon; there were some simple types of vases, and a quartzite arrow-head; ovoid clay sling-bolts were also found; glazed beads were already being produced.

Two strata of house-levels which also definitely belonged to the Uruk–Jamdat Nasr period occurred above the kiln-level: they are known as H and G, but we have now almost certainly reached a stage later than Uruk 5—we may note here the earliest known specimen of a glazed frit vase.[5] In these strata we have evidence of the prismatic *Riemchen* bricks, which only begin to appear after the close of the 'Ubaid period, and of reserved slip ware, and deep cups or goblets of a type which did not appear before the

[1] §1, 38, 65.   [2] *Ibid.* 65, pl. 44, U. 14476.   [3] *Ibid.* pl. 37.
[4] *Ibid.* 67.   [5] *Ibid.* 63.

Jamdat Naṣr phase and only became characteristic in the Early Dynastic period. In H a painted vase with roughly executed linear designs done in drips of paint is reminiscent of some curious vessels characteristic of Ninevite 3,[1] the period immediately subsequent to 'Ubaid in Assyria.

Ur: End phase of 'Ubaid, and Uruk sequences—problems. The absence of adequate architectural evidence leaves a gap which must be filled by future exploration. Pottery sequences, because ill stratified in these deeper levels, are also unsatisfactory. It is, however, clear that at Ur as elsewhere, immediately after the 'Ubaid period, pots tended to assume the more angular forms which we should expect at a time when metallurgy was becoming more common. The most difficult problem to decide is how early the plum-red wares and the polychrome pottery of Jamdat Naṣr began to appear. Usually associated with the end phase of the Uruk development, they occur amid the Ur débris so soon after 'Ubaid as to give grounds for the assumption that these celebrated and distinctive forms of wheel-turned and painted ceramics, together with some grey ware, began to become fashionable in the earliest phase of the Uruk period and coincided with the end of 'Ubaid.

Al-'Ubaid and district. The more extensive prehistoric excavations which have been undertaken since the conclusion of the dig at the comparatively small site of Al-'Ubaid, 4 miles west of Ur, have diminished its importance as a point of reference. But there are some misconceptions concerning it which need to be removed.

Although large quantities of painted potsherds were found, only a small number of more or less complete vases survived. Much of the pottery must originally have been deposited in a cemetery not far from the main mound in which an important temple was dedicated to the goddess Ninkhursag by the second king of the first dynasty of Ur. But this Early Dynastic temple is likely to have been the last of a much earlier series—there was certainly a predecessor in the Uruk–Jamdat Naṣr period.[2] It is a legitimate inference that there was in fact a temple of the 'Ubaid period also—probably of its late phase, Ur-'Ubaid 2–3. And if that hypothesis be accepted we may well adopt the suggestion made by C. J. Gadd[3] that the worship of Ninkhursag was practised at 'Ubaid from the time of its first foundation. This Sumerian divinity was presumably thought of as a mother-goddess who both nurtured the young and protected the dead, and it is possible that at the spring festival pilgrims from Ur travelled along a

[1] §1, 38, pl. 45, U. 14455.   [2] §1, 21, 27.   [3] §1, 15, 141 f.

canal, which can still be traced, to honour the goddess. The suggestion that the inhabitants were already devotees of the same mother-goddess is reinforced by the knowledge that at Ur they deposited in their graves figurines of a goddess suckling the young. The temptation to assume that already in the last two stages of the 'Ubaid period we are confronted by proto-Sumerians is therefore strong, as we have already seen in our examination of Eridu level 12.[1]

The bulk of the painted potsherds recovered from 'Ubaid were, as we have seen, of the standard, later type, decorated for the most part with simple rectilinear and curvilinear designs; but patterns based on plants, trees and foliage also occur. In addition to sherds of this type there are a few specimens which appear to be closely related to the older Ḥajji Muḥammad and the earlier Eridu ware. The inference to be drawn is that in the deeper levels there may still be traces of an earlier stage of settlement contemporary with the beginnings of Eridu, and that the late 'Ubaid mud dwellings overlie a series of older ones. At all events we are on safe ground in assuming that as early as the late 'Ubaid period there were humble dwelling-houses in the proximity of graves containing painted pottery, and that most probably the dead were under the protection of a mother-goddess whose temple lay within a stone's throw from their last resting-place.

It is, however, well to remember that no more than three burials containing painted pottery had survived, doubtless a very small percentage of the original graves which had been swept away by later burials of the Early Dynastic to Larsa periods. Of the seventeen skulls examined by Arthur Keith from the 'Ubaid cemetery,[2] none came from identifiable prehistoric graves—and it would appear that none was earlier than the First Dynasty of Ur, or the period known as Early Dynastic III. The statement no doubt correctly attributed to Leonard Woolley who 'assigns this group to a date about the beginning of the fourth millennium B.C.'[3] can therefore no longer be held valid, and indeed the assertion breaks down when we analyse the deposits in the graves. Keith's interesting conclusions—that the skulls of the ancient Sumerians were relatively narrow, that they were dolichocephalic, a large-headed, large-brained people, approaching or exceeding in these respects the longer-headed races of Europe, and that the men's noses were long and wide—is applicable to some of the 'Ubaid dead of the latter half of the third and the beginning of the second millennium B.C. It may well be that similar character-

---

[1] See above, p. 343. [2] §1, 15, 214 f. [3] *Ibid.* 214.

istics will eventually be discovered for their ancestors of the fourth millennium, but the evidence does not yet enable us to prove the point.

The small finds at 'Ubaid formed a typical ensemble of the period. There were polished, ground stone axes and adzes, heavy chert hoe-blades; flint saw-blades and sickles, made of both pottery and flint. In addition we have crystal, flint and obsidian arrow-heads, and numerous flakes and cores of obsidian and smoky quartz, also stone pegs and studs. Pottery cones and beads were common, but the former belonged to the post-'Ubaid period, while the bent nails, some of which, as we have suggested, may have been holders for fishermen's nets, were probably more ancient.

Perhaps the most interesting of the small objects recovered from 'Ubaid are a few painted terracotta objects which include part of a model boat with curved prow, as at Eridu, a lizard-headed mother-goddess fragment, and the lower half of a human figurine depicted as wearing close-fitting trousers laced up at the side.[1]

Two models of socketed axes are of peculiar interest—one is in greenish clay of 'Ubaid type, and the other has a design over the blade which appears to be a reproduction in paint of a sheath. While, as we have seen, some of these models may imitate stone originals, this one can hardly be anything other than a copy of metal and is one of the rare proofs of the existence of an efficient metal (probably copper) weapon at this early period. Lastly, a painted terracotta of the same period in the British Museum appears to illustrate a gabled house,[2] perhaps thatched, with a reed roof, and is comparable with a small steatite amulet of the Halaf period discovered at Arpachiyah.

Reijibeh X, Mereijeb. Two other marshy sites are of interest as demonstrating that in the 'Ubaid period there were subsidiary settlements within the district. A site called Reijibeh X,[3] which lies in a long and shallow depression 12 miles west of Ur, was represented by a low mound no less than 100 m. in diameter, covered with 'Ubaid pottery, flint hoes, flakes and typical 'Ubaid small remains. Woolley was of the opinion that this might have begun at a relatively early stage of the Ur–'Ubaid period. A second, similar site, also containing painted 'Ubaid sherds, was identified at Mereijeb, 10 miles south of Ur.[4] This again appeared originally to have been a small island and continued to be

[1] *Ibid.* pl. xlvii, xlviii.
[2] §1, 15, pls. xlviii, B.M. 117010; §1, 27, pl. vi*a*, no. 11.   [3] §1, 38, 10.
[4] *Ibid.* 24 but the map on p. 1 records it as more nearly west-south-west.

occupied in the post-'Ubaid period by villagers who made use of cement bricks. This later settlement could have belonged to the later stages of the Uruk–Jamdat Naṣr period. The plan of one of its cement-brick buildings could be construed as a temple with forecourt containing twin sanctuaries approached by antechambers,[1] but the pottery could be relatively late—some specimens were as late as Early Dynastic I.

URUK–WARKA

Warka is the modern name for the ancient site of Uruk (Erech of the Old Testament), which at the time of its foundation in the 'Ubaid period lay on the banks of the main stream of the Euphrates, about 40 miles north-west of Ur. It is probable that in the Uruk period the city covered an area of not less than 200 acres, of which perhaps a third consisted of official buildings, a third of houses, and a third of gardens and cemeteries. In the latter half of the fourth millennium B.C. there was much waste ground side by side with built-up areas, a phenomenon no doubt typical of ancient oriental cities.

There is every reason to believe that the city was prosperous and large in the 'Ubaid period, for, wherever the deeper levels have been penetrated, 'Ubaid-type painted pottery has appeared, and many sherds of this period are contained within the débris of much later occupations.

The two principal localities of the city within which traces of these early occupations have been detected are in the centre of the site and underlie the so called Anu and E-anna zikkurrats respectively.[2] The topmost building of the Anu zikkurrat is known as the White Temple, which belongs to the period known as Uruk 3, and cannot be earlier than the Jamdat Naṣr end phase of the Uruk period. Embedded within this same zikkurrat is a series of much earlier buildings of which we know comparatively little,[3] for they have only been probed by soundings and are as yet not closely tied by stratification to the better known sequences within E-anna. The lowest levels undoubtedly take us back to a very early period, as can be seen from counting the long succession of buildings embedded within the zikkurrat. At the top, level A, was a platform consisting of the filling of the White Temple B (Jamdat Naṣr). Level C was known as the Post-Hole Temple, perhaps a temporary erection while the White Temple was being built, and

---

[1] §1, 38, 83 and fig. 20. [2] §1, 30, 97–161.
[3] E. Heinrich in §1, 37, *U.V.B.* VIII, 27 ff.

if so was not much earlier than its successor. In the preceding levels D–E there were two temples apparently identical in plan, and D was virtually a duplicate of the White Temple. Since there was an abundance of copper in E, this too is hardly likely to be much earlier than Uruk 3, considerably later than the period which we are examining, and the underlying building in level F, the walls of which were painted with red and white stripes, is probably not much older; indeed a Jamdat Naṣr polychrome sherd was found in the débris here. Even in level G, which lay over 2·5 m. below the White Temple and included three main stages of building, we are not likely to be confronted with architectural remains earlier than Uruk 4. Nearly a metre below level G we come to level X, consisting chiefly of the remains of a ramp which led up to a temple that contained a gypsum pavement. Beneath this ramp was found a clay seal impression of an antlered stag,[1] made from a square stamp seal, which, on the analogy of seal impressions found, for example, at Nineveh and Arpachiyah and Gawra in prehistoric Assyria we may assign to a period either at the end of 'Ubaid or immediately succeeding it; similar designs also occur on early seals from Tell Brak[2] in prehistoric Syria. The great depth at which this building is embedded under the Anu zikkurrat in any case tends to suggest that it was founded at some early stage in the Uruk period, and since there is room for still earlier occupations below, H. Lenzen has no doubt rightly conjectured that the first buildings in the neighbourhood of the Anu zikkurrat were founded in the 'Ubaid period.

For detailed knowledge of the 'Ubaid period, however, we have to turn to the area of the E-anna zikkurrat, not far away from Anu's in the middle of Warka. There, on the south-east side of the zikkurrat, a German expedition conducted a deep sounding beneath the courtyard of a temple in level 5 down to virgin soil.[3] The succession of débris revealed no less than 18 separable strata, of which levels 5–18 were prehistoric; the total depth of the excavation was about 19 m., of which the bottom metre was virtually sterile. Within these strata the main stages of the 'Ubaid and Uruk periods were comprised—for the inhabitants of level 5 do not yet appear to have witnessed the invention of writing. The importance of this series is that it is the only one at Warka which displays a more or less uninterrupted prehistoric succession; but the evidence obtained from it is limited by the fact that it consists

[1] E. Heinrich in *U.V.B.* viii, Taf. 50 d.W. 16616; §1, 1, 31 and pl. 12, no. 216.
[2] §1, 25, pls. xviii–xx, pl. xxiii, no. 5.
[3] J. Jordan in *U.V.B.* iii, 5 ff. and Taf. 12, 13; *U.V.B.* iv, Taf. 2.

predominantly of potsherds, and that only at the top end of this long series is there any evidence of buildings which can be related to a determined sequence in the development of the prehistoric architecture.

Levels 18–14, which cover a depth of about ten metres, appear to correspond with the 'Ubaid period; 14–12 are transitional, and thereafter, in levels 12–5, we appear to have reached the Uruk period proper when red and grey ware become common and 'Ubaid sherds become rare. Only tentative conclusions may be drawn from the fragmentary nature of the evidence, and we have to allow for the fact that in a limited sounding of this kind stratification is not always satisfactory: successive strata were sometimes contaminated by earlier and by later débris. Nevertheless, a few facts of interest emerge. First, that the 'Ubaid pottery from these occupations at Uruk clearly represents a relatively late stage of its development and, in general, would seem to be not earlier than Eridu 8–6 and the corresponding Ur-'Ubaid 2–3. Secondly, the great depth of 'Ubaid débris, about 10 m. in all, must imply the lapse of a very considerable span of time, amounting at least to several centuries for the latter portion of the 'Ubaid period. On these grounds we are therefore entitled to infer that the entire 'Ubaid period must have been a very long one, and one might venture the proposition that five centuries would be a minimum estimate for it.

Another point of interest that emerges from an examination of the Uruk pit is that some monochrome red and grey carboniferous wares were present from the beginning, although these colours become truly characteristic only of the Uruk period proper, when they were manufactured by much improved technical processes.[1] It is also significant that a polychrome red and black sherd, apparently of the Jamdat Naṣr type, with simple geometric decoration occurs in the 18th or bottom level,[2] and gives rise to the suspicion already expressed, that this type of pottery has a very much longer history or prehistory than is usually believed. The first evidence of a *Glockentopf* appears to occur as early as level 12, from which time onwards these bevelled 'bell-bowls' become common; the same level is also notable for the first appearance of a plum-red ware and from then onwards the pot forms assume a more metallic appearance. In level 8 we meet the apogee of the red ware and nearly all the pottery begins to be wheel-turned; in level 6 we are already confronted by some types of spouted pottery closely related to Early Dynastic forms.

[1] A. von Haller in *U.V.B.* iv, 31 f. and Taf. 16–21.
[2] *Ibid.* Taf. 16 B, í W 10491 UM. 1.

When we examine the contents of the upper levels in the E-anna sounding it becomes difficult to correlate them with the architectural remains found elsewhere on the site.[1] Thus it is clear that from level 6 upwards there is a considerable quantity of pottery that could be classified as late Jamdat Naṣr (extreme end of Uruk period) and possibly Early Dynastic, especially the big, sometimes angular, vases with sharply defined necks, and the goblets.[2] For the present, therefore, we remain uncertain how to correlate these levels with the architectural remains of the great temples in E-anna, Uruk 4, which have been correctly assigned to the end phase of the Uruk–Jamdat Naṣr period and are contemporary with the beginnings of writing. Little in any case is known about the buildings of level 7 except that they used the habitual flat mud-bricks, and of level 6 we know only that there existed a big temple, the walls decorated with cone mosaic and constructed of small mud-bricks laid as headers in a method known as *Riemchenverband*. With the 'Limestone Temple' of level 5 we have reached the end of our period.[3] This building had assumed the tripartite plan of the standard Sumerian temple and had achieved the monumental character so magnificently displayed in the succeeding level 4, and indeed according to some authorities this building may have co-existed with 4 B—that is with the famous cone-decorated Mosaic Court, one of the glories of ancient Uruk. It does not seem necessary to assume, as some authorities do, that the use of limestone blocks implies the presence of a new and foreign governing body. The imported heavy and durable material is witness to the rising prosperity of a city which had grown so wealthy that it was becoming obliged to enumerate its possessions in writing.

Uruk—summary of evidence. The first settlements were founded, as at Ur, on marshy soil; the inhabitants lived in reed huts and before long made extensive use of flat mud-bricks. The evidence from E-anna indicated that the earliest settlers occupied the site in a late stage of the 'Ubaid period.

But according to Lenzen, elsewhere in Warka, beneath buildings of the Uruk 3–4 period, sherds have been recovered of the 'Ḥajji-Muḥammad–Eridu period' and it is therefore likely that in some parts of the site traces of the earliest stages of 'Ubaid still remain to be discovered. Our knowledge of the beginning of the

---

[1] E. Heinrich in *U.V.B.* vi, Taf. 2. The table of sequences needs correction. See the revised opinion expressed by him in *U.V.B.* viii, 48, relegating the White Temple to Uruk III.   [2] *U.V.B.* iv, Taf. 19, 20.

[3] E. Heinrich in *U.V.B.* iv, 8 f.; §1, 30, 120 f.

Uruk period here is similarly defective; but at this stage we may deduce from collateral evidence the presence of capable builders who had begun to develop metallurgy, though little evidence has been found of it so far at this site. It is clear that the stamp seal did not begin to be extensively used till a relatively advanced period, and only at the extreme end of the Uruk period in level 4 did the seal cylinder come into common use—it was then needed for the sealing of documents and of merchandise. There is no evidence of any monumental sculpture before period 4; but in the prehistoric 'Ubaid we find numerous examples of the delicately made mother-goddess figurine, as well as a bearded male counterpart.[1]

A remarkable feature of the discoveries at Uruk is the very large number of burnt offerings that have been identified on the site; the commonest form consists of troughs dug into the ground and plastered with clay, sometimes lined with bricks.[2] As one deposit succeeded another the earlier one was often swept away or partly dismantled. The offerings consisted of animal bones and included birds and fish; they were continuously deposited from the 'Ubaid period through to the end of the Jamdat Naṣr. These *Opferstätten* varied considerably in size; the culmination of this practice is to be seen in a big building named the *Riemchengebäude* to which numerous deposits of pottery, stone, and mosaic-work were devoted and finally ritually burned before being buried. It is not unlikely that this was a dedication, a burnt sacrifice made when a temple named the 'Cone-Mosaic Temple' was dismantled to make way for a newer one, and that a part of the older temple furniture was thus consecrated in perpetuity before being replaced by a new set. The discovery belongs to the end phase of the Uruk period and may possibly mark the disappearance of a temple of Uruk 4, but the type of pottery associated with the sacrificial deposit appears to be later,[3] and other composite objects decorated with incrustation are typical of the Jamdat Naṣr style of Uruk 3.

Qal'at Ḥajji Muḥammad and Raidau Sherqi. The immediate district of Uruk was doubtless well populated in 'Ubaid times. Raidau Sherqi,[4] 5 miles to the north-west, extends over a distance of 70 by 140 m. and contained traces of spacious mud-brick dwellings which, to judge by the pottery, belonged to the end of the 'Ubaid and the early Uruk period, for it included *Glockentöpfe*. A second and more important site, a little over 10 miles south-

---

[1] *U.V.B.* iii, Taf. 21, and *U.V.B.* viii, Taf. 47.
[2] §1, 6.   [3] H. Lenzen in *U.V.B.* xiv–xv.
[4] E. Heinrich and A. Falkenstein in *U.V.B.* ix, 33 f.

west of Warka, on the banks of the Euphrates, was named Qal'at Ḥajji Muḥammad.[1] There the eroded remains of mud-walls and reed houses, together with bread-ovens, were observed at a time of low water, for the site lay near the banks of the river and was liable to flooding. The pottery collected from the surface represents, as we have already seen in our examination of Eridu,[2] a very early stage in the development of the 'Ubaid peoples. Here we have a range of pottery which preceded the standard 'Ubaid types of Eridu 12 and can be related to older types of northern ware familiar in prehistoric Assyria. The pot forms included bowls, vases, dishes and plates often fully decorated, for the most part with simple geometric designs both within and without. The paint was intended to be monochrome, but varied considerably in tone on the same pot owing to irregular fire control—cream slips were common.

This ceramic is strongly influenced by the style of Halaf, both in shape and design; to a much lesser extent, by Sāmarrā: it is locally made and not imported. The significance of this pottery is that it constitutes decisive proof of strong northern influence at one of the earliest ascertained stages of prehistoric development in southern Babylonia. Similar pottery has also been found in Susiana,[3] where some of the most characteristic of the painted designs are overall geometric patterns which leave tiny squares and strips of the body clay standing out in contrast to the richly applied brushwork decoration.

The pigments vary considerably in colour—dark black, dark brown, purple and red. It is probable that the site itself lasted well into the 'Ubaid period, for some types of pot appear to be more developed than others. The finds include a clay sickle not known before Eridu 13, ground stone axes, and a chert hoe.

The soundings at Ḥajji Muḥammad have raised some interesting problems. We know that similar material does exist at Uruk, and after taking new measurements above sea-level at Warka it seems possible that virgin soil was not actually reached at the bottom of E-anna, although there can be no great depth of accumulated débris below what has been examined there.[4] It is also significant that the Ḥajji Muḥammad ceramic presents a much richer series than the corresponding ware discovered at Eridu, and comprises in addition Eridu ware from the bottom of that site, besides some specimens of the later 'Ubaid style into which it developed. Ḥajji Muḥammad ware and the Eridu ceramic, although fully developed, are not more advanced in tech-

[1] §1, 40.
[2] See above, pp. 340 ff., and Figs. 26–7.
[3] See below, p. 428.
[4] §1, 40, 57.

nique and decoration than the Halaf ware known from the bottom
of Gawra (below level 20 there),[1] and from Arpachiyah. Northern
ceramic styles must have influenced the southern potters at a time
when Halaf ware was widespread in prehistoric Assyria and in
Syria.[2] But in the north we have some scanty evidence of an earlier
stage still, and we are probably right in assuming, if only from the
evidence of the wet nature of the soil at the bottom of Babylonia,
that the beginnings of settled life in the south were motivated and
energized by an older stage of northern development which had
the advantage of *terra firma* against marsh for the expansion of its
activities.

RAS EL-'AMIYA

This site[3] lies midway between the Tigris and Euphrates, about
5 miles north of Kish, and is important because it has yielded
stratified remains of the Ḥajji Muḥammad and 'Ubaid periods, in
contrast with Kish itself which hitherto has not produced evidence
of anything earlier than Jamdat Naṣr. The discoveries at Ras el-
'Amiya, however, suggest that this earlier evidence may one day
come to light deep under the alluvium at the much more extensive
site of Kish also, and that the Ḥajji Muḥammad period may well
have been one of extensive village settlement in southern
Babylonia.

Pottery of these early periods (see Fig. 30) began to be exposed
here when bulldozers were cutting canals for the Mussayyib drainage project, otherwise no trace of ancient remains would have
been visible. Beneath about 2·5 m. of sterile humus, sand and
clay, the soundings directed by D. B. Stronach yielded a sequence
of five occupation levels which contained houses and bread ovens;
the walls were built both of *pisé* and of mud-brick.

Had it been possible to excavate this site on a larger scale we
might have been able to determine more precisely than elsewhere
the various stages of development in Ḥajji Muḥammad ceramic.
The excavator's conclusion is that here we may observe 'the
gradual disappearance of many of the close style patterns that
characterise the Eridu and Ḥajji Muḥammad phases, together
with certain phases in the quality of the paint and the shape of the
vessels'.[4] Thus what we may discern at Ras el-'Amiya is a period
of transition from Ḥajji Muḥammad into 'Ubaid, and a pottery
which alike in shape and in form betrays that strong northern
Halaf influence, also observed at Eridu, including the plain

[1] See below, p. 393.   [2] §1, 40, 57.
[3] 1, 35.   [4] §1, 35, 97

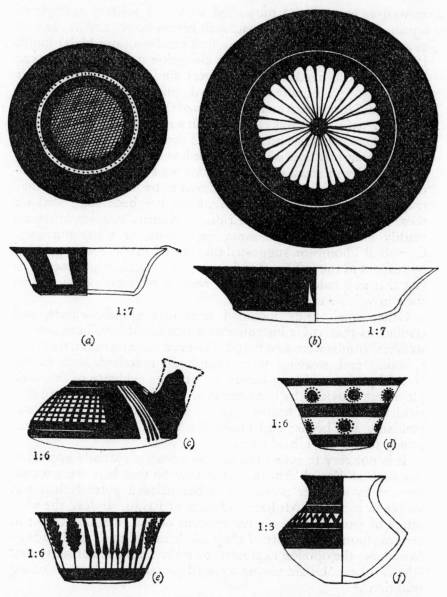

Fig. 30. Ras el-'Amiya, carinated bowls painted inside and out, and painted vases and bowls. (See pp. 366, 368.) (a) Pale grey clay and matt, greenish-black paint. (b) Grey to buff clay, purplish-black to greenish matt paint. (c) 'Tortoise vase' with spout; pinkish-buff clay, white slip, greenish-brown paint. (d) Bowl, greyish-buff clay, burnished, greenish to black paint. (e) Bowl, buff clay, creamy buff slip, black matt paint. (f) Vase, greyish clay, matt greenish-brown paint.

as well as painted and burnished wares. A solitary example of a pure Halaf type, 'the Arpachiyah cream-bowl', occurs, as well as a painted vase depicting a mouflon head—a pure Halaf motif. It is interesting to find this style alongside delicate 'Ubaid-type bowls depicting reeds and foliage very similar to vessels from Ur (see Fig. 30(e)). Finally we have the distinctive Ḥajji Muḥammad and 'Eridu' forms with a small portion of the pattern left as a reserve (see Fig. 30(a)). At Ras el-'Amiya, in a relatively restricted series of sequences, we thus find examples of three distinctive prehistoric styles, apparently flourishing more or less contemporarily.

The series of small objects includes bent clay nails with mushroom heads, which here are considered to be mullers, and so they may have been, though a different use has been suggested for those found in the temple at Eridu.[1] Primitive peoples, however, readily make use of the same implement for many purposes. Campbell Thompson suggested that these bent nails were gripped by reapers in the left hand and served as knuckle-protectors. The fact that as a rule the heads bear no sign of wear speaks against their invariable use as mullers.

Other small finds included terracotta spindle-whorls, and remind us that at Ur instruments which could have been used as weavers' combs were also found. We need have no doubt that both spinning and weaving were commonly practised both in the 'Ubaid period and long before it. Further evidence of domestic ploys was provided by bone needles. In addition there were flint sickles and obsidian knives; ground stone axes; clay pegs; stone pendants and beads; and finally the typical chert hoe so commonly found on 'Ubaid sites.

It is not easy to assess the evidence from a partially excavated site such as Ras el-'Amiya, but it may be that here we are confronted by a richer panorama of the painted pottery than was visible in the Ḥajji Muḥammad stage at Eridu. Indeed the wide range of painted wares is reminiscent of the rich assortment of ceramic found on the site of Ḥajji Muḥammad itself, and leads us to endorse the opinion expressed by more than one authority that 'the two later 'Ubaid phases were all part of a single, developing tradition'.[2]

TELL 'UQAIR

This site,[3] like Ras el-'Amiya lies approximately mid-way between the Tigris and Euphrates, farther north, and must once have been on the main channel of the Euphrates or on a subsidiary canal. It

[1] See above, p. 346.   [2] §1, 35, 97 and n. 4.   [3] §1, 23.

is within sight of the ancient city of Kutha (Tell Ibrāhīm) about
50 miles south of Baghdad, and in prehistoric times may have
borne a relationship to this larger religious city as close as that of
Al-'Ubaid to Ur.[1] At 'Ubaid sherds with bird-designs were also
found in a deep sounding at Tello (§1, 30, 81). *Ibid.* p. 105 for
evidence of Uruk period pottery at this site.

The first 'Ubaid settlement at 'Uqair was, like many other
early sites, founded on marshy soil and may have been a camping
place, for no traces of walls were discovered—a thick layer of reed
matting or rushes was the earliest sign of occupation. Thereafter,
in a succession of 'Ubaid levels, walls were found to have been
built, first of *pisé*, then of mud-brick. In the uppermost of these
settlements there was a house, irregularly built with courtyards
and rather flimsy walls, separated by a street from a formidable
mud-brick building the walls of which were nearly a metre thick
and composed of large rectangular bricks arranged in a succession
of irregular piles. There was, however, nothing primitive in the
planning of this building with its corridors over 10 m. long, but
relatively narrow, and designed to carry roof timbers with a short-
ish span; and we may infer that there was an internal staircase.
There is not enough evidence, however, to decide if this building
was a temple—if not, it must have been the headman's house.

With the domestic buildings, the usual 'Ubaid small finds were
associated in abundance—bent nails of terracotta; net-weights,
loom-weights, whorls; clay animals (models of cattle); chert hoes
and many bone implements, including awls set in bitumen
handles; in addition there were the clay sickles which, as we have
seen, first appear in Eridu 12.[2] Among the painted terracotta
objects there is a miniature socketed hammer-axe, presumably the
copy of an original in stone, and another, unpainted, which may
be a copy of a copper axe; there are also several painted figurines
including one of a female with steatopygous rump decorated with
markings that may depict trousers and are reminiscent of Kurdish
apparel.

A good series of 'Ubaid painted pottery, not over-decorated, is
in a style which belongs to the later stages of development—
Ur-'Ubaid 2–3 and Eridu 8–6. Its chief interest is that it exhibits
an unusual number of animal designs—comparatively rare in the
'Ubaid period—including birds, fish and stags.

A representative series of later prehistoric architectural remains
following 'Ubaid carried the history of the site through six more
main levels which probably began as early as Uruk and ended in

[1] See above, p. 357.   [2] See above, p. 343.

late Jamdat Naṣr—both *Riemchen* and large rectangular bricks were used.

By far the most important discovery at 'Uqair was a spacious building of *Riemchen* mud-bricks, known as the 'Painted Temple' (see Fig. 31), set on a high platform with buttressed façade, and

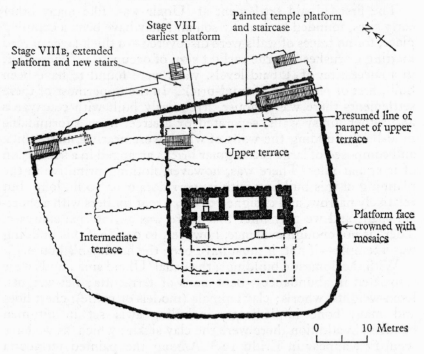

Fig. 31. 'Uqair, the Painted Temple, showing platform, stairs and terraces.
(See pp. 370 f.)

approached by three sets of elaborate staircases flanked by low parapets; the platform building had once been decorated with black-headed cone mosaics. The plan of the temple was on the lines of the normal lay-out familiar in southern Babylonia from the late 'Ubaid period onwards; it was tripartite and consisted of a central nave flanked by chambers on either side. The façade had shallow niches and broad buttresses which were a regular feature of ecclesiastical architecture. In one of the side chambers there were stairs up to the roof; at the far end of the nave, in the sanctuary, there was a stepped podium composed of miniature *Riemchen* bricks—an altar or table of offerings—and another one in the middle of the sanctuary near its opposite end.

The most remarkable features of the temple were its wall paintings which must once have covered most of the building and were
partly salvaged through the skill of Seton Lloyd and Fuad Safar.
The podium at the end of the sanctuary appeared to be decorated
with men bringing cattle to the god, and various geometric
designs depicted the buttressed façade of a temple—a mosaic of
colour in which red, black and white were dominant. A seated
and a couchant leopard, also included among the murals, were
figures appropriate to the god—for at Uruk skeletons of a lion
and a leopard were found in association with the later Jamdat
Naṣr period White Temple.

The Painted Temple at 'Uqair will be described subsequently,[1]
but it is appropriate that it should also enter the record here, for it
has a claim, though perhaps a doubtful one, to belong to a stage of
development preceding Uruk 4. None of the polychrome-painted
pottery of Jamdat Naṣr type was found with it, but there was a
sherd of grey burnished ware and another of the red polished,[2]
typical of Uruk: only a single sherd with a bent spout introduced
a measure of doubt, for this type is generally thought to occur
relatively late in this sequence. However that may be, the Painted
Temple was twice renovated after its foundation and followed by
five or more later buildings, either on the same site or off the edge
of the platform. The length of the time sequence involved and the
use of cement bricks, as in the early Uruk stages elsewhere, lead
us to agree with the excavators that the Painted Temple is relatively early, and indeed may be even more ancient than they had
supposed (possibly related to some stage not long after the close
of the 'Ubaid period), for the next earlier remains on the site are
those of the 'Ubaid settlements.

The description of the articles discovered with the buildings
subsequent to the Painted Temple belongs to a succeeding chapter. Here it may be recorded that no finer series of Jamdat Naṣr
pottery has been found and that, in association with this, we have
the first evidence of written documents, semi-pictographic tablets,
inscribed in Sumerian. The reference to a leader of the assem-
bly(?); to wages in kind including wool and fish; to a carpenter,
secretary or steward and overseer, messenger and servant, though
related to the Jamdat Naṣr period, are surely indicative of this
small township's administration at much earlier stages of its
existence, as is suggested by the well-organized layout of the
'Ubaid-period building which we noticed in the earlier levels.

[1] *C.A.H.* I³, ch. XII, sect. II.   [2] §I, 23, 148.

JAMDAT NAṢR

A small site[1] situated in the district of 'Uqair is now mainly of
interest as the type site which lent its name to the first discovery
of this now famous polychrome pottery in association with
'Sumerian' tablets. A mud-brick building, perhaps a temple, was
discovered. Moreover, since this mound was about 6 m. in height,
it must have contained within it some remains of earlier periods
preceding Jamdat Naṣr, as is suggested in particular by the chert
hoes found there, but not necessarily by the clay sickles, which
evidently survived for a long time after their popularity in the
'Ubaid period.

SOUTHERN DIYĀLĀ DISTRICT

As we move some miles northwards from the district of Kish,
there is a curious absence of evidence for any remains of the 'Ubaid
period and this may well be significant in the case of the big
Diyālā sites such as Ischali, Khafājī and Eshnunna (Tell Asmar)
which have been more or less extensively excavated. It is true
that when the excavators reached virgin soil the settlements
appeared invariably to have lain on marshy ground, and we must
allow for the possibility that something older may be concealed
under the ooze,[2] and that the water table has probably risen since
antiquity. Moreover, the files of the Iraq Antiquities Department
record no less than nine mounds along the southern reaches of
the Diyālā from which 'Ubaid sherds have been collected.[3] Furthermore, as we leave the Diyālā and continue eastwards to
Mandali, not far from the foothills of Iran, we come to large
mounds where 'Ubaid, Ḥajji Muḥammad and earlier wares appear.

We need more information about the distribution of the pottery
throughout Babylonia before we can draw any safe deductions or
appreciate the reason for the relative scarcity of 'Ubaid pottery
in the villages of the lower Diyālā and 'Adhaim rivers. Some established villages or townships there must have been at this early
period, for, as we shall see, the distant north from the district
of Kirkuk to Mosul bears abundant testimony of 'Ubaid period
remains, and intermediate links are needed to substantiate the
continuous contact between the northern and the southern ends
of the country.

Remains of the Uruk period have been observed in the lower

[1] §1, 24.   [2] O.I.C. 20 (1936), 16, 25.
[3] T. Abu Zabeb, T. Tamerkhan, T. Dujaka, T. el-Hadid, T. Abu Rasain,
T. Abu Yiwalak, T. Dibis, T. Kumaz, T. Abu Kabeir.

levels of some Diyālā mounds, for instance at Khafājī in the Temple Oval,[1] where sherds of grey and red pottery appeared, but there was nothing to add to the more ample picture which we have already obtained from the various sites already discussed.

No significant architectural remains of the Uruk period have yet been recorded from the best known Diyālā sites. The earliest series of Sin Temples at Khafājī, Sin I–III, are thought to belong to the stage Uruk 4–3.

GEOGRAPHY AND THE POLITICAL PATTERN

During the 'Ubaid and immediately succeeding prehistoric period it is clear that cities and small townships were concentrated along certain more or less definite lines—clearly canals which served as the lifelines for such communities. Jacobsen has well demonstrated that

these cities with their surrounding villages were limited essentially to points along two separate lines: on the one hand that of the Euphrates with Nippur, Shurrupak, Uruk, Ur and on the other that of the Iturungal-Sirara with Adab, Zabalam, Umma, Bad-tibira, and the Girsu and Lagash region. Between these two lines, effectively separating them, lay open desert, the Edin of the Sumerians, and also between the settlements on either line lay vast stretches of desert and swamp. This geographically imposed separateness of the settlements is noteworthy, for it set narrow limits for the developing political units and must have tended to act, once the immediate border of the individual settlements had been reached, as a powerful restraining factor encouraging separatism and hampering attempts at further effective unification of the country as a whole. We may see it as a constant background force in Sumerian political history responsible for the—compared to Egypt—very late unification of the country and for the always tenuous character of that unification; whenever opportunity presented itself Sumer would always fall apart again into the old city-states.[2]

The assumption is, therefore, that where desert and swamp interrupted settlements along the line of water-ways, natural or artificial, this made for a series of independent and mutually exclusive townships—at all events politically exclusive. But archaeology provides a necessary corrective to that theory; for in architecture and the arts, in the development of ceramics and in the interplay of graphic design we see from the earliest times continuous evidence of the most distant contact, which demonstrates that water-lines were also lifelines conveying ideas and products as on a conveyor belt—from one end of the factory to another.

[1] H. Frankfort in *O.I.C.* 20 (1936), 25.   [2] §I, 19, 98f.

On the basis of Sumerian mythology, which describes the conclaves and debating houses of the gods, we may obtain some idea of the pattern of government on earth. Jacobsen has therefore argued that, from Early Dynastic times at least, there was in Sumer a form of primitive democracy or government by consent obtained in an assembly.[1] Falkenstein, on the other hand, considers that the assembly composed of Sumerian free citizens or *unken* was no more than a consultative body summoned *ad hoc*.[2] Whatever the truth may be, the impressive pattern of craftsmanship in the city life of the Uruk and the 'Ubaid periods, the general appearance of orderliness and the handing down of traditional technology, whether in building, methods of agriculture or canalization, must imply some form of prescribed control, most probably based on autocratic government—often, no doubt, more or less broadly composed, depending on the character and quality of the momentary head of the state and his advisers no less than on a system of nepotism, which has always played a dominant, if not a predominant, part in tribal societies wherein the family unit was collectively engaged in the primary tasks of agriculture and fisheries.

DISTRICT OF KIRKUK: NUZI

This site[3] lies in the district of Kirkuk, about 20 miles south of Altın-Köprü on the lesser Zab river, and is thus geographically intermediate between the territories of Assyria in the north and Babylonia in the south. Scanty information gleaned from deep soundings proves that 'Ubaid ware was used in the early levels of this settlement following after Halaf, and the accumulation of débris warrants the belief that the 'Ubaid occupation was followed by other prehistoric sequences—about which virtually nothing is known—not only on the mound of Yorgan Tepe (Nuzi) but also at Kudish Saghir and probably elsewhere in the same district. Indeed in the *Liwa* of Kirkuk, 'Ubaid sherds have been recorded by the Iraq Antiquities Department at nine other mounds as follows: in the Kirkuk area itself, Qal'at Saifak, Ujagh Tepe, Tell 'Arafat; in the Kepri area, Tepe Derwiesh; in the Daquq area, Tell el-Mukhfiya, Merbat Abu Khanajer; in the Chamchamāl area, Qal'at Ka, Kurd Qal'at, Tepe Sirkerwan.

If we proceed eastwards beyond Kirkuk towards the frontiers of Iran we shall also find evidence of 'Ubaid sherds at several mounds in the Shahrazūr Plain, Qadha of Halabja. In the Rania plains, 'Ubaid ware has been picked up on the following seven mounds:

[1] §1, 19, 99.   [2] §1, 13, 801.   [3] §1, 34.

Qal'at Rania, Kurdi Buskin, Shemshāra, Basmusian, Qarashina, Kamarian, Ed-Deim. We may assume that a high proportion of these sites continued to be occupied in the Uruk period also. The list is of interest because it reveals the wide dispersal of these early families of ceramic from the plains of Babylonia and Assyria into the mountain lands that bordered them.

MATARRAH

The site[1] lies about 20 miles due south of Kirkuk and has been noted by R. J. Braidwood as 'just above the 200 metre contour... on the hilly flanks of the "Fertile Crescent"'. This ancient prehistoric hamlet revealed in its latest level some traces of 'Ubaid pottery. Braidwood has noted that 'the line of the 200-metre contour might be taken as more or less coincident with the isohyet delimiting the southwestward extent of winter rains sufficient to yield a grain crop without the aid of irrigation'. Some 10 miles south of Matarrah we appear to reach the limit of 'Ubaid settlement in this area, coincident with the drier steppe which appears to have been a barrier to these early prehistoric farmers who depended largely on natural supplies of water. In the dry country south of Kirkuk, and north of Babylonia, 'Ubaid remains are therefore understandably sparse. The conclusion to be drawn is that such simple communities had to be, and no doubt were, mobile and every one of them that lived in the fringe-rainfall margin of the plain probably had to face a drought or a failure of the harvest every four years. There are indeed good modern parallels. In 1949 the entire population of the district outside Makhmur for this reason moved lock, stock and barrel into the Kurdish hills, and most of them returned a twelvemonth later.

BETWEEN THE LOWER ZAB AND DIYĀLĀ RIVERS

The paucity of 'Ubaid and Uruk period material in this extensive tract of territory is remarkable by contrast with the abundance of it in prehistoric Assyria and Babylonia. We conclude that, agriculturally, this no-man's-land must have been less suitable for development in prehistoric times; and, in contrast with the south, much less extensively canalized. It is probable that the water supply was less amenable to control, and that some tracts of this territory enjoyed less rainfall. It may be that future investigation will provide us with a corrective to this view, but at present the

[1] §1, 4; 5.

ancient mounds which could be marked on the map of what we may term central Iraq would be far fewer than those of the north and the south. Perhaps there are missing links to be found along the banks of the Tigris, for Sāmarrā,[1] a pre-'Ubaid site some 90 miles north of Baghdad, is evidence that early prehistoric centres could exist in this zone. Indeed the most recently discovered evidence of yet another Sāmarrān site is Tell es-Sawwān[2] covering about 2½ hectares of ground, about 7½ miles to the south of Sāmarrā, a prehistoric village perched on a high cliff along the left bank of the Tigris. Here we have a settlement perhaps founded in the sixth millennium B.C., which may considerably antedate the earliest 'Ubaid remains at Eridu. Five successive periods of buildings constructed of moulded mud-brick display an un-expected competence in this form of building. Already in the earliest period there was a 3 m. deep defensive ditch for the protection of the houses, which contained some fine specimens of alabaster vases and of painted Sāmarrā ware as well as Hassunan. But the most remarkable discovery, one that has a peculiar relevance to the 'Ubaid culture, was a collection of some 50 alabaster statuettes carved to represent full-breasted, corpulent females. These un-gainly figures have rudimentarily fashioned heads, eyes incrusted with shell and bitumen, and a number of them wear on the top of the head a conical cap of black bitumen, which may represent hair, or possibly a *polos*. The bitumen head-dress looks as if it must be ancestral to that which is strikingly characteristic of the fifth millennium 'Ubaid period figurines discovered at Ur[3] and at Nineveh[4]—more elegant in form than the primitives of Sawwān.

Much also probably awaits discovery on the less investi-gated frontiers in the foothills between Iraq and Iran—territories which are not easy of access—as well as along the banks of the Euphrates and Tigris rivers. Most promising is the Mandali-Badrah area, east of Baghdad, along the Zagros foothills, where there was a conjunction of all the main prehistoric sequences.

II. ASSYRIA

The 'Ubaid and succeeding prehistoric periods are well repre-sented at certain sites east of Tigris between the Khusr and the Zab rivers, notably at Nineveh, Tepe Gawra, at Arpachiyah and in the Jebel Sinjār, which together yield an abundance of archi-

---

[1] §I, 18.   [2] §I, 12, 1–2 and pls. I–v.
[3] §I, 38, pls. 20–2.   [4] §II, 13, pl. LXXII.

tectural and archaeological material for comparison with that of southern Babylonia. But while the 'Ubaid ware is closely comparable, when we come to that of the succeeding periods we find considerable divergence between north and south, and for this reason some authorities have elected to refer to the prehistoric successor of northern 'Ubaid as the Gawra period,[1] during which, especially at Nineveh and the Jebel Sinjār, grey ware became dominant. But there seems to be no particular advantage in using this term for a prehistoric succession which shows great diversity, and it may eventually appear that Gawra was by no means a typical northern site. We shall therefore continue to use the term Uruk period to cover the whole development between the end of 'Ubaid and the beginning of the Early Dynastic. The term Jamdat Naṣr has no real application to the north, except in so far as it may be used to designate the end phase of the Uruk development and coincides with the beginnings of writing.

TEPE GAWRA

For some time to come, Tepe Gawra is likely to remain the type site, a primary source of reference for any discussion of the prehistoric sequences in Assyria from the 'Ubaid period onwards, because of the abundant discoveries of architecture and ceramics, as well as of small objects. But Gawra differed in the nature of its sequences from many other sites in Assyria because of its proximity to the mountains, which placed it in close contact with hillmen who did not always elect to settle in the plains. Hence in the 'Ubaid and Uruk periods Gawra diverges markedly from prehistoric Nineveh, which seems rather to have been linked with developments west of Tigris—for example, in the Jebel Sinjār.

Tepe Gawra is about 14 miles east-north-east of Nineveh under the lee of the snow-capped mountain which is now known as the Jebel Maqlub. In ancient times a *wādi* carried water to the foot of the settlement, which lay in rich agricultural and pastoral country watered by the river Khuṣr. This tributary of the Tigris ran through a valley which opened out from the mountains into the fertile Ninevite plains, and Gawra is one of the many prehistoric sites along that thoroughfare, but the setting of this small township was dominated by the hills, and the peoples in its neighbourhood are still hardy mountaineers.

The main sequences of occupation from top to bottom of the mound have been numbered from 1–20, of which number 1 is the

[1] §1, 30, 194 ff.

latest; number 20, the earliest, dates back to the beginnings of the
'Ubaid period in the south, for its ceramic can be closely related
to Eridu ware. In this chapter, which is concerned with the post-
Halaf development down to the end of the Uruk period proper,
before the Jamdat Naṣr phase of literary development, we shall
be most closely concerned with the long series of strata embraced
by Gawra 20–9, during which, the accumulation of débris rose
by about 15 m. and corresponded with a span of time which may
well have covered some 2000 years. We may expect, in the course of
the next decade or two, to recover further evidence for carbon-14
analysis and thereby to obtain a number of much needed fixed points
for a more precise chronology. Except for one disconcertingly
low figure which may require revision, the pattern of dates so far
available seems to indicate that the beginnings of the 'Ubaid
period at Gawra can hardly be later than about 5000 B.C. and may
well be earlier.[1]

Gawra: Architecture—temples. From the 'Ubaid period onwards there is a long and unbroken continuity of style, elaborate
at the end, but directly derived from simpler antecedents at the
beginning. Some types of building may disappear for a time, but
they emerge again subsequently.

One of the most interesting and characteristic forms of this
northern prehistoric architecture is the *tholos*, or domed building
on a circular ground plan, which had already been extensively
used on a large scale in the Halaf period at the neighbouring site
of Arpachiyah.[2] The earliest example of it at Gawra occurred in
level 20 and consisted of a small mud building which probably is
of the latest phase of the Halaf period; its diameter was a little
over 5 m. There were three internal buttresses, irregularly spaced,
which besides supporting the walls could also have served as end-
pieces for a bench. Traces of walls in the same stratum were composed of exceptionally small, miniature bricks measuring 13 × 9 ×
5 cm. The *tholos* is of exceptional interest because it is a form of
building which constantly recurs through the prehistoric north.
Two more *tholoi* were discovered in level 17, better and more
solidly constructed, with at least five internal piers and two entrances. Thereafter no more were found until the Uruk period
level 11 A when the most magnificent of all these structures which
enclosed no less than seventeen rooms came to light—the largest
of the kind yet discovered anywhere (see Fig. 32).[3] The external

[1] Gawra 18–17, 3446 ±325 B.C. (Libby 1955: 82–83), quoted in *Antiquity*, 34
(1960), 26. See also J. G. D. Clark in *Antiquity*, 39 (1965), 45 f., with table of
carbon-14 dates on 47. [2] §1, 36. [3] *Ibid.* pl. VII.

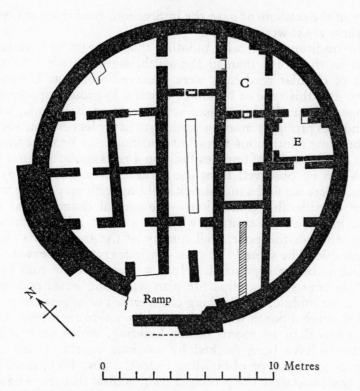

Fig. 32. Plan of the Round House at Tepe Gawra, stratum 11A. (See p. 378.)

diameter measured between 18 and 19 m. and the external walls, which were 1 m. thick, formed an almost perfect circle. The approach was up a steep ramp through a broad entrance, on either side of which there were exceptionally heavy piers increasing the wall to a thickness of 2 m. There can be no doubt that this was a very lofty building. The biggest room, in the middle, measured no less than 13 × 2·6 m., and a mud partition, free at either end, ran longitudinally across it. Two of the rooms, C and E,[1] contained internal stepped buttresses and a recess, respectively, and give rise to the suspicion that these were shrines: the building therefore served a religious purpose as well as being a dwelling-house and providing storage accommodation, for one of the rooms appears to have been a granary. At Arpachiyah some burials were clustered against the outside walls of the building, and their piously preserved stone foundations, the association of mother-goddess figurines with them, and their position in the

[1] §1, 36, pl. VII.

centre of the settlement gave the impression, confirmed at Gawra, that these *tholoi* were temples.

The tradition of circular building thus appears to have lasted longer in the north than in the south, where as we have seen, traces of circular reed huts were observed—both at Ur and at Eridu. But this type of building, wasteful in ground space,[1] soon disappeared in the big urban settlements of Babylonia, where ground was probably more valuable than in the less crowded north.

The same continuous thread of tradition may be traced in the much longer series of temples built on a rectangular ground plan which can be observed from the earliest 'Ubaid level (19) upwards. Here we find a mud-brick building with very flimsy walls, but of considerable dimensions—the central chamber was over 10 m. in length—a contrast with the earliest minute shrine at Eridu, though the poor, frail quality of the building is closely comparable. The same basic plan continues into the next stratum 18, but is better organized. Here we see that the nub of the building consists of a tripartite plan with long nave, podium or altar in the middle, and flanking chambers. The approach appears to be through a porch which has subsidiary side chambers. There are no less than 20 rooms in this building, which on two sides appears to have been flanked by spacious courts. There is no evidence for this type of building in level 17 in which, as we have seen, two *tholoi* were the principal architectural feature. The rambling series of buildings here consisted otherwise of an intricate complex of chambers insufficiently excavated to yield a coherent plan. It is, however, noticeable that there were courtyards with ample space for the unloading of merchandise; that access through doorways was zigzag and never direct, and that in addition to the flimsiest walls there were a few of very considerable thickness— up to a metre and a half—which may have been intended to support an upper storey.

Unfortunately, after level 17, in which the religious tradition is linked to the earliest foundations in 20 by the presence of *tholoi*, we lose trace of any rectangular building that we can positively identify as a temple for some time, although one building with nine chambers mainly concentrated around an oblong central nave in 15 A is big and regular enough to deserve a religious title. A new and spacious building marks an innovation in level 14, for the foundations consist exclusively of stone boulders—the first occasion on which stones rather than bricks or *pisé* were used architecturally in Gawra. This complex of seventeen rooms has

---

[1] See below, p. 385.

been described as 'secular in character'.[1] But the great central
hall, some 12 m. in length, and over 3½ m. wide, suggests an
ecclesiastical rather than a lay building—the matter is open to
debate. However, the preservation of the ancient stone foundations by the builders in the succeeding level suggests that these
old stones were regarded with some piety, as in an earlier period
at Arpachiyah where the ancient foundations of religious buildings were similarly respected.

It is in level 13 that we obtain a view of three magnificently
planned, spacious temples which radiated round a great central

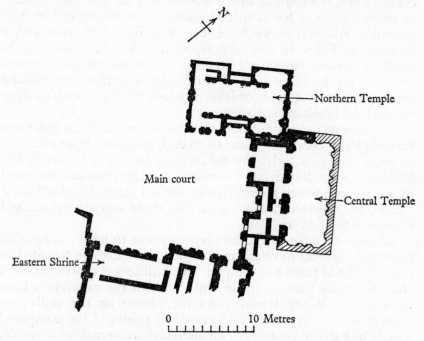

Main court

Northern Temple

Central Temple

Eastern Shrine

0   10 Metres

Fig. 33. The Painted Temples at Tepe Gawra, stratum 13. (See p. 381.)

court, of which the maximum dimensions were nearly 20 m. (see
Fig. 33); these edifices occupied a substantial portion of the
whole acropolis. Three sides of this court were flanked by buildings known as the Northern Temple, the Central Temple and the
Eastern Shrine respectively; the corners of each were orientated
by the cardinal points of the compass.[2] They were built of mud-
bricks and the walls were, as had long been the rule in Gawra,
astonishingly thin, no more than a brick and a half in thickness;

[1] §1, 36, 36 and pl. xiv.   [2] §1, 36, pl. xi.

but they were strengthened by an elaborate series of stepped buttresses, containing niches and recesses—a type of façade associated with religious buildings, both in the north and in the south,
from the 'Ubaid period onwards. These buildings appear to
have been brilliantly coloured; red, black, ochre and vermilion
washes once adorned the walls and the façade.

The plan of the Northern Temple[1] is undoubtedly reminiscent
of a temple of 'Ubaid period 3 at Eridu (Eridu 11–9);[2] its strange
and most unusual system of interior partition walls must have
been devised to support long and heavy beams for a roof over the
central nave, the span of which was about 4 m. The plan of each
of these buildings has a special character, northern rather than
southern, and yet, as we have seen, it is linked in style with a
building at Eridu in southern Babylonia. The intricate façades
must be derived from a tradition of timber construction appropriate to the northern hills of Kurdistān. The plans crystallized
eventually in the temples of level 9, where the links with modern
Kurdish architecture are apparent.

We have no indication about the manner in which the spectacular temples of Gawra 13 came to an end, and there is no evidence
to suggest a sack. In the succeeding level 12, however, the
buildings were destroyed in a violent conflagration accompanied
by a massacre, which appropriately marked the end of the 'Ubaid
period, for thereafter, as we shall see, there was a very marked
change in the pottery.

In level 12 most of the buildings appear to be secular rather
than ecclesiastical in character,[3] although we may be tempted to
identify one of them as a temple. This building is centred about a
chamber more than 11 m. in length which the excavators have
named 'The White Room' from the plaster on the walls—its
corners were orientated by the cardinal points of the compass.[4]
The White Room contained two niches, characteristic of a temple,
in one of the short end walls; many graves were found under the
floors, more indeed than were associated with the temple of level
13, where five child burials were found below the floors of the
Eastern Temple. There were approximately ten subsidiary chambers and the approach was from a great courtyard. The lay-out of
the building follows the ancient tradition of tripartite arrange-

[1] §1, 36, pl. XII, and Fig. 33 here.   [2] See above, p. 337.
[3] Disagreeing with A. J. Tobler in §1, 36, 25, who said that the excavated area
in stratum 12 contained 'no religious structures'. Tobler's objection that numerous
domestic utensils and ovens were associated with the building is no proof that it was
solely of a domestic character.   [4] §1, 36, pl. VIII, IX.

ment—in these early periods less orderly in the north than in the south. A second building, similar in plan, not quite so large in dimensions, was found at the same level and is likewise distinguished from all other buildings by having two niches in the central room; for this reason alone we may readily identify it as another temple.

Level 11, which, like many of the succeeding levels, contained two main phases of occupation, was notable, as we have already seen, for the presence of the great 'Round House', a *tholos* (in 11A), which reflects the culmination of a very ancient tradition. But, architecturally as well as ceramically, this level does mark a new period (still strongly influenced by older traditions). We may regard this as likely to be more or less contemporary with the beginnings of the Uruk period in the south, and it is therefore significant that we now meet a new type of temple, in rather a simple form, that inaugurated a series which at Gawra was to run uninterruptedly through until the Early Dynastic period.

The temple in Gawra 11[1] occupies an approximately square plot of ground measuring 9·75 m. in both length and breadth, and is the smallest of the series which follows. Essentially the plan consists of an oblong sanctuary, with niche in the end wall, opening out of a long, central chamber with podium. Access to the temple was through a porch with a wide doorway which confronted a spacious courtyard or piazza. There were flanking chambers on either side of the sanctuary; traces of red paint were found on the walls and there was white plaster on the niche in the sanctuary; the corners were orientated by the cardinal points of the compass.

We may be tempted to see in these Gawra buildings the origin of the Megaron which, at a considerably later period, was to become so characteristic a feature of Anatolia—at Troy and Beycesultan—and eventually of the Mycenaean world.[2] Many missing links need to be found before we can establish a direct connexion, but the suggestion is an attractive one. However that may be, here at Gawra we may again look for the origins of this type of plan to the Kurdish hills where we may happily still see

---

[1] *Ibid.* pl. xxiii, squares 4–3, K–J, 14 f. and pl. v.

[2] S. Lloyd in §11, 7, 163 f. takes a contrary view, that the Gawra porch temples originated in Anatolia. But the examples illustrated by him (fig. 6) are from Gawra 8 C and therefore relatively late. They derive from Gawra 11 and 11 A which belong to the early Uruk period and must be considerably older than the analogous buildings at Troy and Poliochni. See also K. Jaritz, 'Mesopotamische Megara als kassitischer Import' in *Z.E.* 83 (1958), 110 ff. H. Frankfort's view that 'the cultural stage' known as the Uruk period originated in Anatolia, has not been substantiated; see his 'Archaeology and the Sumerian Problem', *S.A.O.C.* 4 (1932), 33.

the headman of the village sitting in his sun-lit porch—two great wooden pillars on either side of him supporting a log and brush-wood roof. In studying the later architectural developments of this type of building at Gawra it is easy to imagine that such posts may once have existed in front of this type of building. In the temple of level 11A, which comprised rooms 74–78, twenty graves and a single tomb had been dug from beneath the sanctuary and surrounding areas.[1] The corners of the building were orientated by the cardinal points of the compass.

Level 11, which overlay 11A, was notable architecturally for another, better constructed temple with porch—similar to its predecessor. Here the nave has a white-plastered niche at the short end, and the inner sanctum is delimited from the nave by two heavy projecting walls not close enough to form a doorway, thus giving the end of the room the appearance of a chancel.[2] This temple was originally 9·75 m. square, a little larger than its predecessor. Near the entrance there was a podium made of clay and cement, raised a little above the level of the floor, as in the later temples of levels 9 and 8. Fifty-four burials were found in the vicinity of this building.

After a makeshift occupation in level 10A wherein the majority of the buildings appear to have been of a secular character, with flimsy walls, we come again in level 10 to the largest porch-type temple yet encountered. This one underlay the classical examples discovered in level 9, by which time we may reckon that we are coming towards the end phase of the Uruk or Jamdat Naṣr period, though there is no evidence of writing at Tepe Gawra. One other religious structure in level 10 is of interest, a big rect-angular room 1003[3] which was perhaps built to serve as a com-memorative chapel for an underlying tomb, and reminds us of the occasional evidence in prehistoric times that the dead were, both in Assyria and in Babylonia, remembered by the living for one generation or more, during the span of living memory.

The spacious porch-temple in level 9 measured 13·00 by 11·40 m. and was more substantial and heavily buttressed than any of the preceding ones, which, as we have seen, begin in level 11. This regular and beautifully planned building,[4] orientated like its predecessors, contained, close to the entrance, a clay and cement podium which, to judge from the ashes around it and the fire-scarred top, was a sacrificial hearth standing only just above the level of the floor—and there was a second one in a big hall on its north-east side, the only asymmetrical chamber in the building.

[1] §1, 36, pl. vi.   [2] *Ibid.* 14 and pl. v.   [3] *Ibid.* 60 and pl. iii.   [4] *Ibid.* pl. ii.

The tripartite porch-temple with its elaborate buttresses and hearths continued in use through level 8 in which there were no less than three such buildings on the acropolis; one of these (17·5 × 13 m.) was larger and more spacious than ever before.[1] At this stage, at the extreme end of the Uruk or Jamdat Naṣr period, this form of temple went out of fashion after a very long history. The porch-temple had first appeared at about the beginning of the Uruk period in 11, directly after the end of Al-'Ubaid: the form gives an architectural unity to Gawra 11–8 over a long span of time, for several sub-periods are embraced by these levels.

Gawra temples—summary. In the long succession of temples which span the beginning of the 'Ubaid to the extreme end of the Uruk period we may discover an unbroken architectural tradition which may well extend over a period of fifteen hundred years or more. There are two striking examples of the longevity. First we have the *tholoi* or circular buildings which are a take-over from the Halaf period, continue in the 'Ubaid through levels 19 and 17, and find their apogee in the great 'Round House' of 11 A. Thereafter we find no more round buildings. It is true that, as K. A. C. Creswell has shown, if a given area has to be enclosed the shape with the shortest boundary is a circle.[2] But where ground space is restricted, a greater saving in brickwork is made by building rectangular houses with common boundary walls. Consequently, as land became more valuable with the growth of urban population in the Uruk period, the *tholoi* disappeared from the acropolis. Rectangular buildings were substituted, though they suffered from a disadvantage in requiring more timber for roof construction. For this type of architecture the basic plan was a tripartite building with long, more or less central nave, which served as a sanctuary and contained a podium or altar. From the beginning of the 'Ubaid period at Gawra we find a relatively spacious temple, in marked contrast with the tiny shrine at the bottom of Eridu. This type of mud-brick building had a long history and appears in an elaborate form in Gawra 14—on stone foundations.

We may look on levels 19–14 as a steady architectural progression, the culmination of which witnesses the magnificent series of 'Ubaid temples in Gawra 13 when the larger part of the acropolis appears to have been given over to ecclesiastical purposes—the populace was presumably relegated to the plains. One of these elaborately buttressed temples is undoubtedly reminiscent of a building in Eridu 11 and must imply contact with the south, for some of the delicate pottery associated with this stage

[1] §1, 33, pls. ix–xi.   [2] §ii, 3, vol. ii, part 2, 18 ff.

is comparable. In the next level, 12, the White Room may have been the nave of a tripartite temple, and is in any case related to a form of architecture which goes back to the beginning of 'Ubaid.

Level 11 A inaugurates a new form of ecclesiastical architecture, the temple with porch, but this was essentially a development of the old tripartite plan. In the succeeding level 11 the ground plan was fully developed on a system which from level 10 onwards was characterized by elaborately buttressed façades, reminiscent of Gawra 12 and continued with variations into Gawra 8, which marked the end of the Uruk period. Broadly speaking, therefore, for the first part of the 'Ubaid levels, 19–14, the architecture was relatively simple in form and in 13 reached its climax. The latter achievement, towards the end of 'Ubaid, provided the impetus for a more solid form of architecture—the temple with porch which persisted through the whole of the Uruk period.

Gawra: Architecture—houses. A study of the secular architecture at Gawra is less profitable than of the ecclesiastical; generally speaking, ground plans are irregular and untidy, and it is difficult to discover any systematic development: of town-planning there is virtually none. It is significant that the biggest and most regular conglomeration of lay buildings appeared in level 19[1]—probably because at the beginning of the 'Ubaid a clean sweep had been made of the older Halaf occupations. Here, beyond the temple, we observe two compounds with over 50 rooms between them, radiating off two spacious courtyards, one of them rectangular, and measuring about 11 by 4 m. From then onwards the lay buildings assume a rather rambling makeshift character, though there are exceptions—such as the houses built round courtyards in 15, and long magazines in 15 A which included a building in the south-east end of the mound that has the appearance of a gatehouse to control pack-animals entering the citadel.[2] We must, however, admit that we cannot always claim certainty in our identification of temples and houses, and it may well be that the temple was often a replica of house plans. For example, in level 14, the big stone building with wings situated above a large oblong nave has claims to being called a private house rather than a temple.[3]

In general, however, throughout the 'Ubaid and Uruk periods those parts of the citadel which were not occupied by temples were clearly adapted, rather untidily, to dwellings which were primarily designed to serve farmers who required considerable areas of open space for their pack-animals, courtyards, bins, and

---

[1] §1, 36, pl. xx.   [2] §1, 36, pls. xv, xvi.   [3] See above, p. 381, n. 1.

storage magazines, as well as dwelling-rooms. In Gawra 12 we have a long street built on a curve following the lay-out of houses with large courtyards, whilst a narrow lane meets it to run out to the edge of the mound; cobbles were not infrequently used for streets and courtyards. In this settlement also the houses at the edge of the mound were planned in *échelon*, perhaps with an eye to defence. Defensive planning is even more evident in the first Uruk period settlements, 11 and 11 A, where we find the heavy, walled 'Round-House', probably a temple, on the *échelon* system again. No defensive walls ringing the settlement were discovered —but they may have existed, and the considerable height of the mound at this period was in itself a protection.

A remarkable illustration of the changing fortunes of Gawra was the contrast between level 13–12 when the acropolis appears to have been almost wholly given over to temples (end of 'Ubaid period), and the succeeding Uruk period when the ground given over to houses exceeded by far that of the temples. One has the impression that the populace, or the richer elements of it, had clambered up the mound for safety. This impression is confirmed by the very large number of graves with rich votive deposits buried under both houses and temples on the acropolis. In the Uruk period it would appear that even the dead needed the protection of the living.

Gawra: Graves. It is remarkable that out of nearly 500 persons whose remains were recovered from the earliest prehistoric settlements as late as Gawra 8, about 80 per cent were infants or children. This high proportion of infant mortality is not surprising when we remember conditions which still obtain in some parts of the Orient today. But no doubt there was also a large cemetery on the flat lands at the foot of the mound, and excavation there might well redress this balance. Indeed in level 17 ('Ubaid period), out of thirty-one burials nineteen were adults. These early burials were all simple inhumations including, in level 18, the urn burial of an infant.

Skeletons were as a rule contracted or flexed; but in level 16 there was a single extended burial, a solitary example of a practice which, as we have seen, predominated in the latest 'Ubaid period at Eridu and Ur. At the end of the 'Ubaid period in Gawra 12 there were 120 burials in all,[1] most densely concentrated under the building which may be named the 'White House'.[2] There

[1] §1, 36, 103.
[2] The complex which contained the 'White Room'; see A. J. Tobler, *ibid.* 42 and pl. VIII.

appears, however, to have been no specific rule which governed the location of graves, for some were buried in the proximity of houses, often under the floor, others in or near to temples. Votive deposits in the shape of painted pottery were common and other forms of deposit included marble bowls, a stone palette, terracotta gaming-pieces, a rattle, and a Vannic obsidian knife-blade. The pottery often contained traces both of wheat and of barley, and remains of animal bones were evidence of the meat offerings, no doubt chiefly mutton, which were provided as sustenance for the dead. The purpose of such offerings was, if we are to judge by the later literature, to satisfy the spirits' needs and thereby prevent the ghosts of the dead from haunting the living. Perhaps a similar concept lay behind the furnishing of terracotta figures, erotic in character, in certain graves of the 'Ubaid period at Ur and Eridu.

An urn burial of the last 'Ubaid period, level 12, contained the body of a child less than ten years old, perhaps a shepherd boy, for underneath his head there was a bone pipe. The playing-pipes or flutes found at Gawra are amongst the oldest yet discovered; they have two, four and six stops. These simple instruments evidently belonged to a musical, peasant folk and are of a kind still in use at the present time. From the Uruk period a number of mouth-pieces have been recovered; some of them may possibly have been used in connexion with a double-reed instrument known by the Arabs today as the *mizwij*.

The principal change in the burial practices of the Uruk period, in contradistinction to the 'Ubaid, was the remarkable series of built tombs of which no less than 80 were found in between levels 11 A and 8 B, that is, as late as Jamdat Naṣr. These tombs varied in construction: some were of mud-brick, others of mud-brick combined with stone walling; others again were cist-graves entirely constructed of stone—either dressed limestone slabs, or large boulders held in place with mortar. In level 9 there were two tombs with wooden floors, and in 10 one of them (no. 107)[1] contained post-holes in the floor, as well as in the walls. There was evidence of matted roofs; timber and plaster were frequently used; some of the tombs must have supported gabled roofs with a central ridge-pole held up by vertical struts. The construction of the tombs thus furnished corroborative evidence for the use of timber in the temples. In one instance only (no. 107),[2] a small building appears to have been erected directly over the top

---

[1] §1, 36, pl. III, Squares O, M, 5, 6, below room 1003; see *ibid.* 75 for an account of the post-holes.   [2] §1, 36, 60 and pl. III.

of the tomb, and may have been a commemorative chapel. It is interesting that the stone cists appear to have been reserved for children:[1] this alien form of building must have been introduced from the mountains, and we should look to Iran for its source of origin, although at present we are unable to identify it.

In eight of the tombs of the Uruk period, traces of pigment were found on the skeletons: the colours were blue, green and in one instance red. As only the more expensively equipped tombs contained traces of such colouring matter it seems most probable that the colours had penetrated to the bones from brightly dyed garments which had once covered the body. Red ochre was also found on the bones of certain burials at Sialk in Iran[2] from the earliest prehistoric periods onwards.

Another remarkable feature of the Uruk period tombs at Gawra was that several of them contained an astonishing number of beads. Tomb 102 in level 10 A possessed more than 25,000; a burial in 11 had 3000; one in 9 had 8500, and one in 8 C several thousand. A deposit of over 750 cowries must have come from the Indian Ocean through the Persian Gulf. Among the materials used for beads and amulets we may note lapis lazuli, ivory, turquoise, jadeite, carnelian, haematite, obsidian, quartz, diorite and faience. Many of the stones must have been imported from Persia, others must have come from Armenia. Lapis lazuli in the form of a seal may doubtfully be attributed to the end of the 'Ubaid period.[3] The 450 lapis lazuli beads in one of the graves, Tomb 109, in level 10 probably originated in distant Badakhshān and imply a trade route with Afghanistān at a period which may be contemporary with one of the later phases of the Uruk period. Indeed it appears that lapis lazuli, of which a number of choice examples occurred, began to become abundant in Gawra 10 and, if we are to relate this phenomenon to the evidence from southern Babylonia, we may reckon that Gawra 10 is approximately contemporary with Uruk 4 or the beginnings of writing. There is, however, evidence that lapis lazuli was traded to Iran and the frontier site of Gawra, which was nearer to its source, earlier than to Babylonia. It is possible that Gawra 10 was contemporary with the end of the Uruk period and preceded Jamdat Naṣr and, broadly speaking, it may be related in time to the sequence Uruk 6–4.

Other articles in the same Tomb 109, including turquoise beads, must have come from Iran; the limestone vases were also imports,

---

[1] *Ibid.* 78.   [2] §iv, 18, 76, 78.

[3] §1, 36, 88 and pl. clxix, no. 167, pl. lxxxviii c. Lapis beads are said to occur in level 13 ('Ubaid period), *ibid.* 192.

as were the beautifully made obsidian vases from other tombs in the same level.[1]

The prosperity of the city in the Uruk period is also attested by the abundance of gold objects found in the tombs—sumptuary articles of adornment including beads, rosettes with pendent ribbons or tabs, mostly head ornaments, probably fastened on to cloth; heavy gold buttons and studs.[2] Golden headgear is greatly favoured by the women of the neighbouring villages today, but they do not allow themselves the luxury of ivory combs, of which several curved examples shaped for wearing on the head were found in the tombs—indistinguishable from their modern, bone counterparts.

The finest specimen of the goldsmith's work is, however, a small electrum head of a wolf, made of a single piece of strip metal hammered over a bitumen core, but the ears were separately affixed and attached to it by means of copper pins.[3] The animal was represented with wide-open mouth; and the lower jaw was held in position by an electrum pin; the teeth were made of a fine-drawn electrum wire; the eye-sockets contained bitumen for the eyes which must have been incrusted with coloured stones, shell, or faience. This little masterpiece found in Tomb 114 of stratum 10, which also contained a gold rosette with lapis lazuli centre and a lapis lazuli seal, was probably made at an advanced stage of the Uruk period, either in or before the Jamdat Nasr stage, and well illustrates, together with other metal articles, the development and abundance of metallurgy which had taken place, probably some centuries after the close of the 'Ubaid period, and which was the most significant contribution of the stage we recognize under the general name of Uruk.

Gawra: Metallurgy. The progress of metallurgy at Gawra is perhaps more useful than any other criterion for appreciating the technological changes which occurred during the long span of time involved between the beginning of the 'Ubaid and the end of the Jamdat Nasr period.

In the 'Ubaid levels, less than half a dozen metal objects were found, and all those examined were apparently of pure copper without trace of tin, and mostly cold-hammered. There can be little doubt that at this early period metal was so valuable that it was re-melted, and little can have been discarded. In levels 12–11, the end stage of the 'Ubaid period, two copper axes were found with approximately 95 and 92 per cent of copper as the main component—the principal admixture in the latter was

[1] §1, 36, pl. LIII.   [2] §1, 36, pls. LVIII, LIX.   [3] §1, 36, pl. LIX(b).

nickel; these were solid, and look as if they had been cast in an open mould.[1] In the earlier stage of the same period, from level 17, we have a small ring and a chisel. When we come to the Uruk period, however, we find in levels 11 A–9 nearly two dozen implements, apart from copper buttons, including chisels, awls and pins but in level 8, where we have reached the Jamdat Naṣr period, the number of metal objects increases to twenty-two pieces; at its close in level 7 the number is forty-two, and in Gawra 6, the Early Dynastic period, there were no less than 334 specimens—a dramatic illustration of the metallurgical progression.

Rare as metal is in the 'Ubaid period, the specimens contributed by Gawra in the north, coupled with a few implements from the earliest levels at Sialk in Iran, suggest that owing to the easier access to the source of supply, metallurgy began rather earlier in the north than in the south; but once this progress had gained momentum, the south, at all events at the end of the Early Dynastic period, overtook the north both in output and in quality of production.

Gawra: General evidence from small finds. The varieties of chert and obsidian implements, flakes and cores, and ground stone axes, in so far as they have been examined, do not appear to differ in character from those found at other neolithic sites in Assyria and in Babylonia. These simple industries had enjoyed a long survival —a big flint core is illustrated from stratum 9.[2] Stone palettes and mace-heads were characteristic of the 'Ubaid period, grinding-stones and gaming-pieces are ubiquitous.

A notable improvement in the stone work is, however, to be detected in the Uruk period, where from 11 A onwards we find some fine examples, including a black marble hammer, and a grey slate mace-head[3] which has been compared by Gordon Childe with a type of later neolithic boat-axe from Scandinavia.[4] Bone implements, mainly awls and spatulae, were common, and the bone pipes have already been noticed.

We have mentioned the stone vases of which the finest examples were found in the tombs of level 10 (relatively late in the Uruk period); two of them have trough spouts. These specimens are of particular interest because they recall the discovery of fragments of obsidian dishes at Warka in Babylonia, sandwiched between levels C and D[5] in the Anu zikkurrat at

---

[1] §1, 36, pl. xcviii, nos. 1 and 2; described as adzes in the analysis on p. 212.
[2] §1, 36, pl. xciv(*b*).   [3] §1, 36, pl. xciv(*d*).   [4] §11, 2, 209.
[5] *U.V.B.* viii, 36, 51, Taf. 58–9 and section Taf. 21; *U.V.B.* iii, 28 and Taf. 20; §1, 30, 86 and 106.

Warka—which could be attributed either to the Jamdat Naṣr phase of the Uruk period or to the Uruk period itself. Nevertheless, the use of obsidian is well attested in the preceding 'Ubaid stage as well as in the Halaf period which at Arpachiyah yielded implements, a fine specimen of an obsidian vase, and a necklace and perforated links made of that material.[1]

One of the most informative categories of objects at Gawra is the seals and seal amulets which were found from the 'Ubaid period onwards. The 'Ubaid examples consist of simple discs, buttons and squares in a variety of stones and carry simple rectilinear, occasionally cruciform figures. There are contemporary examples in Iran, but here, in the north, they clearly anticipate their adoption in the south, for they were still very rare in the 'Ubaid period on Babylonian sites.

An early and important development in the output of seals appears to have occurred in Gawra 1 3 where many examples, particularly of clay impressions, were found in a well which, it is categorically stated by the excavators, was sealed by paving stones at that period and thereafter never reused. This interesting series illustrates a variety of scenes including ritual dances. On one of them we see a human figure wearing a horned mask, who may be a rainmaker, and is followed by an ibex. Many horned animals are depicted, and there are some examples of hunting dogs—a *saluki*'s head was found in the well itself. In the early period, level 1 1 A, there is the representation of a scene portraying a dance in front of a shrine or altar(?), and another from the same level shows two magicians(?) stirring a magical brew in a witches' cauldron.[2] Other scenes figure a row of dancers, a man with a bident, masked men and human beings engaged in the act of copulation—one pair on a stool, accompanied by a serpent. There are no scenes more evocative of village life in the 'Ubaid and Uruk periods; they illustrate in a vivid shorthand the simple fundamental beliefs and practices of the peasant in prehistoric Assyria—the close dependence on animals, especially horned beasts, is noticeable, and an artistic sense of arrangement in their display.

Many examples of figurines both in terracotta and in sun-dried clay were found in the 'Ubaid levels at Gawra. Most interesting are the painted models of a squatting mother-goddess, who in Syria has been found seated on a circular stool.[3] Some of these figures appear to be veiled, and only the eyes are visible; all of them have peg-shaped heads and it may be that there was a fear

[1] §I, 27, pl. v(c) and pl. x.   [2] §I, 36, pl. CLXII, no. 82.
[3] §II, 11, pl. I, nos. 1–3.

of allowing an anthropomorphic representation of the human face; garments appear to be depicted; crossed braces, trousers and elaborate belts are also shown. There is little doubt that some of the figurines found in the 'Ubaid levels are in the ancient tradition of earlier Halaf types, or older Halaf figurines carefully preserved: these northern forms are easily distinguishable from those familiar in prehistoric Babylonia: the fear of representing the head in human guise is common to both. Sometimes these figurines are reduced to mere stumps, and it is possible that some of them were gaming-pieces. In the 'Ubaid period, from level 12 there is a painted terracotta model of a leopard which no doubt was then a beast very common in the hills; there were also plain and painted bent nails, sometimes with mushroom heads, carding-combs(?) and spindle-whorls.

One of the most remarkable forms of figurine was that of the 'spectacle' idols, which have been misinterpreted as hut symbols and weights by various authorities: they cannot have been weights, for most of them are very roughly and irregularly made—indeed no two are alike, and there is no discernible standard.[1] Their relation to a hut or house is based on the supposed resemblance to the voluted reed-bundle symbol of the Sumerian goddess Inanna, but this theory is irrelevant in the north and far-fetched in the south.[2] On a Syrian amulet we have a representation of them as mounted on pedestals,[3] and at Brak[4] a big one may have stood in the sanctuary of the temple. The earliest examples appear already towards the end of the 'Ubaid period in level 12, and continue through the Uruk—gradually becoming more *soigné*;[5] there was a very fine example in stone, attributed to level 9,[6] and two models in level 8 C at the end of the Jamdat Naṣr period; at Brak in Syria we can see these spectacle idols turning into eye-idols.[7]

Gawra: The pottery. As at most prehistoric sites, the copious pottery is a sensitive indicator of change and development: a richly illustrated handbook would be needed to do justice to it. We must here be content with a brief summary of the evidence and stress the importance of a few outstanding types and some of the most striking technological developments.

The bottom settlement of the mound, Gawra 20, together with certain areas outside it, produced in some abundance specimens of the fine Halaf pottery which can be most richly illustrated at the

[1] §1, 36, pl. LXXXVI (*a*).
[2] §II, 1, 1–67 and Taf. I, III.
[3] §1, 25, pl. XXVI, no. I.
[4] See below, p. 408.
[5] §1, 36, pl. LII (*b*) from level 8 C and pl. LXXVI (*a*) from level 12.
[6] §1, 33, pl. XLIV (*c*).
[7] §1, 25, pls. XXVI, LI.

site of Arpachiyah.[1] In the next settlement, 19, a new style of pottery, that of 'Ubaid, appeared in some quantity, and perhaps the most interesting feature of the ceramic development at Gawra is that here, better than anywhere, we can follow the prehistoric sequence of development out of the older northern style and its succession. In some respects the new style marks an abrupt change, in others we see a very close relationship to the older wares, and occasionally a pure Halaf-style vessel appears in the 'Ubaid levels; but that there is a marked change cannot be denied.

Typical of the new, 'Ubaid style, are slender bowls with thin walls, decorated for the most part on the outside only, rather sparingly, with severely geometric designs. The most striking difference in the new pottery is that in the bowl shapes there is a preference for ogival curves; the insides of the bowls are no longer elaborately decorated, and the stipple so common in Halaf ware is rarely used; the paint is now more usually matt than lustrous. It is also characteristic that many bowls have a painted ring near the bottom just above a rounded base, and on one delicately made specimen from level 18 the arrangement of the painted design gives the impression of a ring to which cloth or leather had been attached:[2] the pattern betrays the skeuomorphic origin of the vessel. On the whole, however, there was in the 'Ubaid period a distinct falling off in the quality of the majority of vessels, but nevertheless the finest pots were delicately made and sometimes neatly painted.

It is, however, evident that contact with the older school left its mark on the newer. One example of this is a remarkable 'Ubaid bowl found in Gawra 17, which has a more or less rectilinear painted design of a running human figure, perhaps intended to represent a man, with coat tails flying, dancing round a pole which is in front of the figure. The painter turned this round-bottomed bowl upside down in order to portray a scene which would appear to be an adaptation of the older stylized *bucranium* design characteristic of Halaf.[3]

While many of the vessels found in Gawra 19–14 were perfunctorily decorated, sometimes not at all, a distinct change occurred in Gawra 13, the advanced stage of 'Ubaid, in fact its last period but one, where we find a rich series of bowls and vases the outsides of which are sometimes decorated all over—the patterns are nearly always geometrical, except for a few stylized plants. But this apparent richness is really a reflection of the usage to which the vessels were put, for, as we have seen above, the acro-

---

[1] See below, pp. 398 ff.
[2] §1, 36, pl. LXXIII (*d*). See also p. 400, Fig. 34(*a*).   [3] *Ibid.* pl. LXXV (*a, b*).

polis of Gawra was wholly devoted to temples, and these vases must have been used for ecclesiastical purposes. The vessels made effective use of counterchange, of the interplay of dark designs and the lighter body clay. One of these vessels bears a pattern which could be interpreted as the façade of a building with a triangular opening or window aloft—a representation of a kind that appears in later Uruk seals in Babylonia.[1] Two unpainted incense burners[2] from the same stratum also have triangular openings and may perhaps be related to a painted vessel from Eridu 6 of the later 'Ubaid period, a not improbable correlation, for on both sites we have in these respective levels reached the end of the 'Ubaid period.

With Gawra 12 we reach the last stage of 'Ubaid. In addition to the normal run of geometric designs we find the application of painted decorations usually referred to as 'sprig designs', a slovenly method of representing vegetation; there are a few quadrupeds and ducks, and one vessel named 'the landscape vase' depicts animals, vegetation and running water in a mannered, modernistic style: this one has been compared with a design that occurs in the Iranian pottery of Sialk III, 7.[3]

After the burning of the last 'Ubaid settlement in Gawra 12, with the exception of a few survivals, we are confronted with a new stage of unpainted ceramic lacking in distinction, but there are pronounced changes of form; painting becomes very rare and even the older shapes have largely disappeared. Some brown and a little grey or black ware occurs in levels 11–10, as in Nineveh 3.[4] A distinctive and rare form of pottery consists of incised, impressed and punctuated vases, as well as appliqué designs, mostly on beakers. A long delicately made trough-spouted vessel in 11 A[5] is reminiscent of a type which became common in the Jamdat Naṣr period in the south, but in general this is a northern ware which has little contact with Babylonian styles—the types are more easily matched in Syria, on sites such as Chagar Bazar. With levels 9–8 we have probably reached the later Jamdat Naṣr period, with which we may perhaps find traces of reciprocity in the seals, the figurines, and the stone vessels; but the pottery goes its own way.

It remains only to decide to what stages in the 'Ubaid period the Gawra pottery belongs, and here we may turn to a remarkable criterion. Between levels 19 and 17, in the earliest phases of

---

[1] *Ibid.* pl. cxxx, no. 204.   [2] §1, 36, pls. cxxxii, no. 228, and lxxviii(*d*).
[3] *Ibid.* pls. cxxxix, no. 309, and lxxviii(*a*); see below, p. 450.
[4] See below, p. 401.   [5] §1, 36, pl. cxli, no. 342.

'Ubaid at Gawra, we find a vessel type of exceptional interest. This is a squat, lenticular, hole-mouthed vessel with an unusually long trumpet-shaped spout.[1] A purplish red or a reddish brown paint on an even cream slip was applied to the greater part of the surface; there was a linear and zigzag pattern, and only a small part of the background was left as a reserve.

It is highly improbable that this elaborate type was invented independently at more than one centre, for outside the 'Ubaid period it has never recurred in the immensely long history of Mesopotamian ceramic. The fact that it has been found at Eridu is therefore of great importance, and we must conclude that the different manifestations of the type had a common origin, that is to say that they were invented at a single centre. Where that centre was we do not know, but it is perhaps more probable that this type of vase was invented in the south rather than in the north, for the colour and the overall design leaving small reserves of body clay are more akin to Ḥajji Muḥammad ware than to any other, and this hypothesis agrees with the fact that it appears in northern Gawra in the company of vessel types common in the south, and that in the north it persisted for a much shorter span of time. Thus, as we have seen, in Gawra it appears through levels 19–17 in the early stages of the 'Ubaid period, directly after the close of Halaf, whilst at Eridu the type first occurs in level 13 directly after the disappearance of Ḥajji Muḥammad ware in the earliest phase of 'Ubaid proper. We are therefore not likely to be far wrong in suggesting that Gawra 19–18 was approximately contemporary with Eridu 13, a suggestion which is confirmed by the resemblance of other northern and southern pot types at those levels.

At Eridu, however, this trumpet-spout pot enjoyed a long popularity and was clearly a vessel used in the temple ritual, for no less than 31 specimens survived through levels 13–8 and one specimen was found in a niche of the sanctuary of temple 8 and was full of fish-bones.

Broadly speaking, then, Gawra 19–17, still strongly under the influence of Halaf, represents the earliest phase of 'Ubaid, and may be related approximately to Eridu 13 in the south following Ḥajji Muḥammad. Minor and not very significant changes occur in Gawra 16–14, which witnesses some decline in the quality and towards the end bears comparison with Eridu 9–7, while, as we have seen, the subsequent level 13, which is the last 'Ubaid stage but one, is marked by wares specially made for the temples—

[1] §1, 36, pls. cxxiii, no. 113, and lxxv(d).

and with Gawra 12 we must have reached the last stage of 'Ubaid, Eridu 7–6, in the south.

Gawra: Summary. Once again we have seen, as at Eridu, that the pottery is a more sensitive indicator of change than the architecture, for its pace of development is naturally more rapid. Here the close relationship of the earliest 'Ubaid to the developed stage of Halaf is immediately apparent, just as in the south the earliest 'Ubaid proper is equally closely related to the preceding Eridu–Ḥajji Muḥammad series. But the most interesting conclusion to be drawn from comparing the two sites is that the pace of development at each was approximately the same, and that certain well-defined stages must have been more or less synchronous—Gawra 19–17 corresponding to Eridu 13–11 and Gawra 13–11 to Eridu 7–6 or thereabouts. We therefore cannot say, as once appeared to be possible, that the southern prehistoric developments were posterior to the north. It may be that in the north the antecedents will be found to go back further, for there is probably a long period of Halaf development anterior to the earliest corresponding phases at Eridu, and so far in Babylonia we have failed to discover what had preceded the rich ceramic that first appears in Eridu 18.

It is more difficult at Gawra to obtain a coherent picture of the architecture, though this would become clearer if more of the mound were excavated. Round houses on circular plans were, it seems, endemic in the north, but did not survive on the acropolis after the Uruk period. From the beginning we can trace the existence of a tripartite plan in some of the more important buildings, but the execution of these plans differs much from that in the southern sites. In Gawra 13, however, there is an unmistakable relationship with a temple plan in Eridu 11. But the most significant northern development of all is the elaborately buttressed and recessed tripartite temple with porch that appears for the first time in Gawra 11—the Uruk period, a development subsequent to 'Ubaid which ran through to the end of Jamdat Naṣr in Gawra 8.

One architectural phenomenon of the prehistoric architecture that needs stressing is the extraordinary flimsiness of many of the mud-brick walls; in Gawra 19 and 18, for example, in the most important buildings they are not more than a brick and a half thick, and in the rainy climate of the north could not have endured for any considerable length of time. Yet the long sequence of change in all the arts, and the increasing evidence for carbon-14 dating, indicates that the full span of the 'Ubaid and Uruk periods was a very long one—perhaps nearly a millennium. The conclusion must inevitably be that a great volume of the evidence is missing—particularly the architectural evidence—and that buildings were often renewed without leaving a trace. Some of the Gawra temples are the best proof of this hypothesis, and can only be isolated representations of an immensely longer series. There are of course occasional exceptions, such as the 'Round House' in 11 A, the walls of which were thick enough to have a long survival value. In metallurgy the gradual increase in the number of specimens is proof of a long-drawn tradition of manufacture, betraying an innate strain of conservative ideology, which is also manifested by the series of clay mother-goddesses with their stump-like heads and rich steatopygous endowment.

ARPACHIYAH

This site[1] lies about four miles east of the river Tigris and Nineveh and has yielded important evidence of the 'Ubaid period, mostly in the form of painted pots, which were found as votive deposits in a cemetery that had contained fifty graves in all. The cemetery was for the most part concentrated outside the main settlement, in open ground on the west side of the acropolis in the middle of which four levels of meanly built mud-houses of the 'Ubaid period were discovered. These poor dwellings could hardly represent a span of more than two centuries at the most, probably less, and we do not know how long an interval separated them from the underlying buildings of the Halaf period,[2] for the evidence from the fifth level below the surface, TT 5, which might have been intermediate between the two periods, was defective. However that may be, the theory that these 'Ubaid houses were short-lived is confirmed by the fact that in the cemetery not one grave overlapped another, and it therefore seems that all had been buried within the span of living memory—not more than five or six generations—coinciding with the limits of personal piety. It is possible that some kind of headstone or cairn, or perhaps a wooden post, had once marked the site of every grave.

The problem of deciding how long the late 'Ubaid occupation lasted at Arpachiyah cannot be resolved by an examination of the pottery, but we may reckon that the main cemetery, as we have seen, did not span more than two centuries. The rich series of pottery types appear to fit best with the ceramic styles that were

[1] §1, 27.   [2] See above, p. 276 ff.

fashionable towards the late end of the 'Ubaid period, that is to
say that there are several specimens which can be matched in Ur-
'Ubaid 2–3 and in Eridu 7–6, especially the vases with unimaginative, stereotyped geometric designs such as lozenges, chevrons and
zigzags, solid triangles and one with a lanceolate leaf pattern,
which cover only part of the outside of the vessel (see Fig. 34).[1]
Another indication that many of these vases came rather late in
the 'Ubaid period is the series of big bowls with broad curvilinear
bands painted on the inside, sweepingly applied, comparable with
pottery found in the temple stratum of Gawra 13 (see Fig. 34 (b)).[2]

It is, however, also to be recalled that one delicately made bowl
from Arpachiyah is painted with a design which appears to reproduce cloth tied to a ring at the base of the pot and closely resembles a vessel from a grave in Gawra 18 (see Fig. 34 (a)).[3] The two
vessels could easily have been made by the same potter; but the
one from Arpachiyah was found in a grave isolated from the main
cemetery and may well be of an earlier date. There are, however,
other delicate vases from Arpachiyah TT 1–4 which come close to
vessels from Gawra 20–11. The proper conclusion to be drawn
is that the bulk of the Arpachiyah cemetery falls late in the
'Ubaid period; that there are some pots in the traditional styles
of the earlier 'Ubaid period, and that at least one grave may be
contemporary with the early phase.

Nearly all the graves were simple inhumations; in one instance
G 14 and 15 a cairn appeared to mark the site of a grave which
contained two skeletons, and in one single grave G 21 there was
an extended burial—the body was supine as in the 'Ubaid period
at Ur and Eridu—this particular grave contained a rare polychrome vase decorated in a red and black paint.[4] Many burials
were recorded as fractional and were thought to have been
comparable with an allegedly ritual form of fractional burial in
Balūchistān, but in fact this similarity has no significance. The
incompleteness of the skeletons was almost certainly due to the
ravages of wild animals and to the presence of acids in the soil, as
subsequent experience has taught us.

Among the small objects of the period we may note a curious
form of terracotta and sun-dried clay double-conoid bead,
decorated with incised markings—a type that can be matched
both at Al-'Ubaid itself and at Lagash (Tello) in the 'Ubaid

[1] §1, 27, fig. 34. [2] *Ibid.* fig. 32 and §1, 36, pl. cxxvii, no. 179.
[3] §1, 27, fig. 38, no. 2; §1, 36, pl. lxxiii (d).
[4] §1, 27, fig. 37, no. 4. A similar type of knobbed vase was found in Eridu 11–
IM. 55024 in Baghdad.

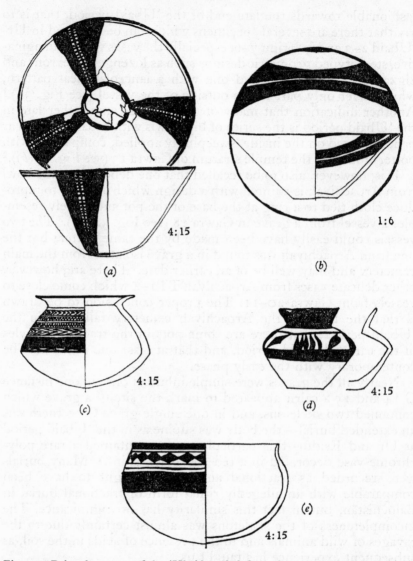

Fig. 34. Painted pottery of the 'Ubaid period from the cemetery at Arpachiyah. (See p. 398.) (a) Painted bowl, carbonized black paint on buff clay. The design may represent a stitched hide or stiff material suspended from a metal ring. From an 'Ubaid period grave. (b) Bowl decorated inside and out with broad, sweeping bands of black paint shading to brown on a cream clay. From an 'Ubaid period grave. (c) Vase decorated in black paint on a well-levigated light drab clay. From an 'Ubaid period grave. (d) Vase decorated with a lanceolate leaf pattern between bands; dark paint on light clay. From an 'Ubaid period grave. (e) Bowl decorated with a row of solid lozenges between bands; dark paint on light clay. From an 'Ubaid period grave.

period, another convincing proof of contemporaneity. Finally, a set of seal impressions is also of interest, because of the stamped designs of horned quadrupeds comparable with types found in the late 'Ubaid period at Gawra.[1]

Arpachiyah: Summary. This relatively small village settlement corresponds in the main with the later 'Ubaid phases at Gawra: the handicrafts at both sites were often closely comparable and could equally closely be matched on southern Babylonian sites. Only a little grey ware was found at Arpachiyah, which, in this respect, differs markedly from the neighbouring prehistoric site of Nineveh (Koyunçik), although there is one remarkable lustrous grey ware vase, without a handle, which looks as if it might be the earliest known specimen of a prehistoric *pot de chambre*.[2] There was no evidence on the acropolis of Arpachiyah of any occupation subsequent to the 'Ubaid period, although it is not improbable that at the foot of the mound later remains might one day be discovered.

NINEVEH (KOYUNÇIK)

The great mound of Koyunçik,[3] ancient Nineveh, which lies 4 miles west of Arpachiyah, probably dominated the district in the Uruk and Jamdat Naṣr periods; but we know little about its extent in the 'Ubaid phase. All the evidence concerning its pre-history has come from a deep sounding, and it may well be accidental that no 'Ubaid pottery was found therein.

After the end of the Halaf period it is probable that a part of the site was abandoned for a time, because in the deep sounding there was a series of wet levels of alternating mud and sand, with hardly any traces of human occupation.[4] The stratification seems to have indicated a pluvial phase which preceded a marked change in the ceramic. Immediately above it, in what is known as Ninevite 3, there was a number of seal impressions made from rectangular stamp seals—these were impressed with designs of gazelle, ibex and other quadrupeds, very similar to those of the 'Ubaid period discovered at Arpachiyah and Gawra.[5] In spite of the rarity of painted pottery and the absence of typical 'Ubaid ware in this stratum, it may therefore be assumed that the beginning of it overlapped with that period. In this connexion it is interesting that clay sickles were also found:[6] they are of a type known only in the 'Ubaid period at Eridu, Ur, and elsewhere in Babylonia.

The dominant pottery of Ninevite 3 was a burnished grey

---

[1] *Ibid.* pl. IX(*a*).   [2] §I, 27, 71 and fig. 40, no. 5.   [3] §II, 13.
[4] §II, 13, pl. LXXIII.   [5] *Ibid.* pl. LXIV.   [6] *Ibid.* pl. LXXI, nos. I, 2, 4.

ware. Some of these vessels were large urns which contained the
bodies of infants, together with a few glazed steatite beads, but
there were no other offerings. The child burials recall those of
the Uruk period at Gawra, but the urns are of a different type.
Some traces of stone walling were found, and a little of the plain
pottery resembled that of Gawra, but the material culture of these
two sites seems to have differed considerably at that period.

In the subsequent stratum, Ninevite 4, we have positive
evidence that this city was then a very large site and that it was
in close contact with Babylonia, as can be proved by the discovery
of hundreds of crudely made bowls with bevelled rims: the bell-
like *Glockentöpfe*, so common in Babylonia in both the Uruk and
the Jamdat Naṣr periods. These bowls were usually found bottom
upwards in the soil, and as a rule contained traces of vegetable
matter. It is not improbable that they were buried with food
offerings to scare away demons from the houses, like the incanta-
tion bowls with late Semitic inscriptions which were similarly
deposited more than three millennia later. These crude prehistoric
bowls have been scattered over an area more than a quarter of a
mile wide. Thus there is no doubt that Nineveh was then extensively occupied. At that time most of the pottery became markedly Babylonian in type and many parallels for the different kinds
of vessels may be observed at Ur, Uruk and elsewhere. A large
vessel with high neck and angular shoulders, clearly based on a
metal form, was common; some of these vases were covered with
a red slip; others were incised; and many had lug-handles which
resembled the beak of a bird and were perforated horizontally.[1]
There were also some cylinder seals and seal impressions which
were in the style of Jamdat Naṣr.[2] The indications both in ceramic
and glyptic of a close concordance with southern styles belongs,
however, to the period of transition from Jamdat Naṣr to Early
Dynastic I, and is in sharp contrast with the preceding Ninevite 3
which coincided with a late phase of 'Ubaid and the early stages
of the Uruk period, when the northern culture developed independently of the south.

Before leaving the country east of Tigris[3] it is well to remember
that much early neolithic and chalcolithic evidence remains to be
recovered in the mountainous territory of Kurdistān at the north-
eastern end of Iraq. Typical, no doubt, of many other ancient sites

[1] §II, 13, 165 and pl. LII, nos. 9, 10.   [2] *Ibid.* pls. LXV, LXVI.   [3] §II, 12.

are the Baradost caves, which are situated over the Ruwāndiz plain and canyon of Ali Beg, about 5000 ft. above sea-level, four hours climb from the village of Havdiyan. Here, for example at Diyan and Bīsetūn, hearths, potsherds and bones were thought to be evidence of occupation by nomads and hunters. Many of the sherds were of a coarse grey ware; there were also traces of Hassūnah, 'Ubaid, and grey and red wares of the Uruk period. Some hole-mouthed vases resembled pottery discovered in the 'Hut Sounding' at Eridu. These caves are still used intermittently by Kurds for a month or two each year as shelters during the season when they are collecting wild fruit, and also in the autumn, when they are hunting game: the nearest running stream is now at Havdiyan. It seems probable that the caves were used for similar purposes, and intermittently occupied in the 'Ubaid and Uruk periods, and it is clear that the urban ceramics of Babylonia and Assyria had found their way to the remote confines of the mountains and provided material improvements for semi-nomadic peoples who, in all other respects, were probably bound by an economy which had sufficed for a viable existence in the neolithic period.

THE MAKHMUR PLAIN

Near the centre of the plain which is bounded by the two Zab rivers, the Tigris, and the Irbil–Altın Köprü road, there is a typical prehistoric settlement just outside the small township of Makhmur,[1] on the high-lying mound of Ibrāhīm Bayis. Here prehistoric mud-brick houses have been found, together with painted pottery which belongs to the later phases of the 'Ubaid period. The plain is a dry one and therefore probably only contained the overflow of prehistoric peoples—those of them who were prepared to migrate in seasons of drought and had access to land and hunting grounds in the hills, to which they could migrate when necessary.[2]

THE JEBEL SINJĀR

Important evidence of the Uruk–Jamdat Naṣr sequence has come to light at a number of ancient mounds in the Jebel Sinjār,[3] together with some traces of 'Ubaid, in the form of potsherds. These settlements were situated on a prehistoric road which linked together the two geographical regions now known as northern Iraq and Syria. At Eski Mosul, about 20 miles north-

---

[1] §II, 5; 6, fig. 1, opp. p. 56, and pl. x.
[2] See above, p. 375.   [3] §II, 9; 8.

west of Nineveh, the river Tigris makes a sharp westerly bend, and from there a series of prehistoric mounds is aligned across the plain in the direction of the hills. There is an easy way across the south-eastern end of the Jebel to Tell A'far, and thence westwards many ancient settlements stud the fertile steppe along the southern flanks of the Sinjār to a distance of not more than 10 miles from it. These villages, which lay within range of the natural rainbelt precipitated by the hills, were so situated as to avoid the necessity of resorting to irrigation. Across this belt of agricultural and pasture land there was an easy thoroughfare via the district of lake Khatūniah (the Lacus Beberaci) to Tell Brak, which lay at a nodal point in the Khabur–Jaghjagha valley for the transmission of caravans between Syria and Mesopotamia.

Much of the prehistoric pottery found on these Sinjār sites was also common to Brak, and there can be no doubt that the two districts were closely linked at the period which we are considering. On more than a dozen mounds prehistoric potsherds have been recorded, and among them certain types of the later 'Ubaid pottery were identical with the Mesopotamian and Babylonian varieties. In the next sequence there was an abundance of bowls of a polished and burnished grey ware which belong to the same series as that discovered at Nineveh (level 3) and at Uruk. It is also claimed that one class of vessel occurred frequently at Mersin XIII in Cilicia.[1] In addition, there were on the Sinjār sites large numbers of the very roughly made *Glockentöpfe*, the bowls with bevelled rims which are common to the Uruk–Jamdat Naṣr sequence, both at Nineveh and at Uruk itself.

The most extensive prehistoric remains were found in a rapidly conducted excavation at a mound named Grai Resh, which lies across the modern road between Tell A'far and Beled Sinjār, about 4 miles east of the Beled. In the lower levels of this high mound there was 'Ubaid painted pottery, and above this two settlements which may be assigned to a transitional period. The early Uruk settlement in level 3 appears to have been defended by a heavy town wall of great thickness.

The principal excavations were conducted in the subsequent level 2, which yielded a well-planned building of the Uruk–Jamdat Naṣr sequence (see Fig. 35).[2] At the time of its discovery this mud-brick building was described as a private house, but it may well have been a temple. The plan conforms to the tripartite arrangement of prehistoric temples: there is a long central room which was probably the sanctuary, and at its short ends there are

[1] §II, 8, 19.   [2] §II, 8, fig. 2.

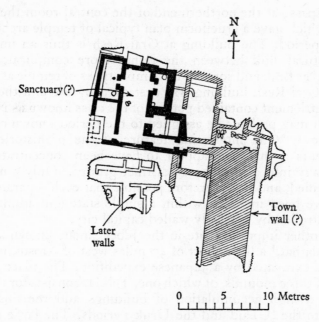

Fig. 35. Grai Resh, Jebel Sinjār, plan of sanctuary(?) and remains of
private houses. (See pp. 404 ff.)

the traditional niches so frequently associated with temple architecture. On either side of the central room there are flanking
chambers, and the association of a double-looped 'spectacle' idol
in terracotta is typical of the period.[1] The central room, which we
presume to have been the sanctuary, was painted over with white
plaster. The building contained a large storage jar filled with wheat
and barley, and other jars had held meat. There were also chert
knives and lance-heads side by side with one made of copper.
Bones and horns of sheep or goats as well as of water-buffalo were
also found. Clay models of animals, spindle-whorls, sling-bolts, a
pear-shaped stone mace-head of veined blue marble, a circular
stamp seal engraved with a human figure, beads, bone implements, a basalt mortar, querns, rubbing-stones and pounders were
typical of the Uruk *ensemble*, and appropriate to what must have
been primarily an agricultural settlement.

It is true that most of the objects found in the building seem to
have been of a domestic character, but we have already observed
that the god's needs were much the same as man's. Moreover, the
corners of the building were orientated by the cardinal points of

[1] *Ibid.* pl. III, fig. 7.

the compass; at the northern end of the central room there were
wings which gave a cruciform plan typical of temple architecture
at that period. The building at Grai Resh is thus an important
architectural link between the rather more complicated 'Eye
Temple' at Brak and some of the simple types of temple at Gawra.

The Grai Resh building was destroyed by fire and the subsequent settlement contained pottery of the class known as Ninevite
5, which may perhaps be assigned to the period known as Early
Dynastic I. One interesting feature of the prehistoric Sinjār
settlements is that they appear to have been concentrated geographically into a number of distinct groups. Only a minority
was fortified, and it is therefore possible that each separate group
may have been included within a single state and administered
and controlled by a heavily walled capital city.

One other important site in the Jebel Sinjār, known as Telūl
eth-Thalathat,[1] a little short of 40 miles west of Mosul, has been
partially excavated by a Japanese expedition. The place is composed of three mounds, of which one, Tell II, consists for the most
part of a high accumulation of buildings and remains which
belong to the 'Ubaid and the Uruk periods. The large number
of strata indicate the lapse of a considerable span of time and
confirm the impression that these two periods covered the greater
part of a millennium.

All buildings were of mud-brick and the architecture was
generally primitive and the walls roughly built, as a rule not more
than a brick or a brick and a half in thickness. There was, however, one outstanding building which was correctly identified as a
temple, for it was built on an unusually large scale and on the
tripartite plan currently adopted at this period. The internal
measurements of the large central chamber were about 7·2 by
3 m. and there appeared to be a podium or altar at the short end.
There were five chambers on one side of the nave and three on the
other. It is not improbable that the central chamber, which has
been dubbed courtyard by the excavators, was roofed. There were
layers of ash on the floor, apparently the remains of burnt sacrifice,
and the greenish-brown or buff potsherds were all typical northern
Uruk fabric.

Buildings of the 'Ubaid period yielded no regular plan, but
some of them consisted of houses composed of irregularly built
rooms having access from courtyards. Some large and heavy
mud-bricks used in the walls measured as much as 23 × 43 × 8 cm.
Pot burials and simple inhumations were associated with these

[1] §II, 4.

houses. Also associated with them were typical 'Ubaid paraphernalia consisting of flint and obsidian blades and scrapers,
and there was one sickle blade set in bitumen. In addition there
were pottery spindle-whorls, clay pegs and animal figurines.
Circular grain silos, or corn bins, and bread ovens bespoke the
agricultural activities pursued by the inhabitants. Exceptional
were the skeletal remains of a baby whose head was alleged to
have been artificially deformed, and an ivory head of a club.
Nearly all of the 'Ubaid pottery appeared to be of a relatively late
type which is not likely to have covered a longer span than the last
two stages of 'Ubaid at Eridu and at Ur. There was one painted
and ribbed goblet decorated with stripes, and with solid lozenges
containing a horizontal reserve; two projecting ledges or flanges
ringed the upper and lower portion of the pot: this unique piece
cannot at present be matched elsewhere.[1] A crinkled bowl painted
with solid triangles looks like a degenerate descendant of the more
delicate wares of Eridu 11–9.[2]

This mound and Grai Resh, the only two prehistoric sites
extensively excavated in the Sinjār, are no doubt typical of a series
of prehistoric agricultural small country towns whose inhabitants
were largely engaged in the pursuit of agriculture and stock-
breeding. But it is probable that their activities were considerably
limited by a rain zone which depended on precipitation from the
mountains, and the water supply must have been scanty. The fact
that the more distant steppe contains only rare traces of ancient
habitation suggests that the rainfall was as erratic then as it is now.

HASSŪNAH

This early prehistoric village[3] lies approximately 22 miles south
of Mosul and a lesser distance west of the river Tigris. Most of
the remains were considerably earlier than the 'Ubaid period,
but from the latest levels, high up in the mound, approximately
800 sherds were collected. They have the appearance of belonging
to the penultimate stage of the 'Ubaid period, that is to say, they
may be related to Eridu 13–9 or thereabouts, but may also include
a smattering of the latest phase.[4] Small finds were characteristic
of the 'Ubaid assemblage, and the bones indicated a typical
pastoral community, while agriculture was actively pursued. The
location of Hassūnah is therefore of interest, for it was sited on a
shoulder of arable land between two depressions formed by the

---

[1] §II, 4, pl. L, no. 2. [2] §II, 8, pl. L, no. 1.
[3] §II, 10. [4] *Ibid.* pl. xxi.

arms of two wādis which ensured a natural water supply. The
entire area could be enclosed in a rectangle of about 200 × 150 m.,
and this was therefore a very small prehistoric community which
may have amounted to twenty or thirty families in all. Prehistoric
remains appear to have been sparse in this area and the settlers
probably ventured rather far from the beaten track in order to
take advantage of the favourable water supply.

III. SYRIA

TELL BRAK

The Jebel Sinjār lies astride the frontier between Syria and Iraq,
and from the tip of its western end to Brak, one of the biggest of
the ancient settlements in eastern Syria, the distance is no more
than 20 miles as the crow flies. It is therefore not surprising that
there are strong archaeological links between these two areas.

At Brak[1] many 'Ubaid potsherds were found in the lowest
levels of the mound; most of them appeared to belong to the later
stages of the period. The 'Ubaid pottery appears to have been
succeeded by a hand-polished red ware, sometimes of a brilliant
sealing-wax red and decorated with plain bands and festoons. The
sherds belonged to what were once big jars with metallic-looking
rims and lugs; ring bases were common.[2] They illustrate advances
in technique and new shapes which occur on Babylonian sites of
the late Uruk–Jamdat Naṣr period, but here in the north the
design reflects also something of the much older Halaf tradition,
and there is one polychrome vase, red, black and cream.[3] There is
a possible connexion between some of these sealing-wax red wares
and pottery found in the prehistoric levels at the Iranian site of
Susa of the Jamdat Naṣr period.[4]

A landmark in the history of north Syrian architecture is provided by a series of temples of which one has been completely
excavated. This one, known as the 'Eye Temple', because of the
thousands of black-and-white alabaster eye-images associated with
its débris, was probably built in the last stage of the Uruk–Jamdat
Naṣr period. But it was preceded by at least two older temples
known as the Red 'Eye Temple' and the Grey 'Eye Temple'
respectively, from the colour of the brickwork. It may be presumed that these earlier edifices, which probably also date from
the late end of the Uruk period, perhaps not earlier than Uruk 4,
were built on the tripartite plan of the 'Eye Temple' itself, a variant

[1] §1, 25.   [2] *Ibid.* pl. xliv.   [3] *Ibid.* pl. xliv, no. 4.   [4] §iii, 9, 101.

of southern Babylonian buildings. This architecture and some hundreds of amulets in the form of animals and birds and some cylinder seals are often nearly identical with material found at the site of Uruk itself, 800 miles downstream on the river Euphrates.

The importance of Brak therefore consists in the fact that it provides the strongest possible evidence for a close connexion between the capital cities of the lower Euphrates and the district of the eastern Khabur valley, in the 'Ubaid and later Uruk periods. Indeed so strong is the connexion shortly before 3000 B.C. that one might infer a close political, and certainly a close commercial, relationship. The ubiquitous *Glockentöpfe* occur at Brak, and the 'spectacle' idol. The latter is in one instance represented as standing on a pedestal in the temple,[1] and thousands of little alabaster images, in naturalistic style, had been deposited as votive offerings.[2] This type of naturalistic 'eye' idol has never been found elsewhere, but close analogies have been observed in the Anatolian district of Maraş.[3] Thousands of glazed 'frit' beads puddled in with the mud-brick of the early temples provide interesting evidence of the antiquity of this industry, which evidently goes back to the Uruk period.

CHAGAR BAZAR

This site[4] lies about 20 miles north-north-west of Brak, on the Wādi Dara, and 25 miles south-west of Kamichlie and ancient Nisibis. Here there was a long series of prehistoric settlements which went back to the early neolithic period and good evidence of Sāmarrā ware which was followed by a considerable succession of Halaf. It is, however, significant that apart from a few sherds which might be deemed to be 'Ubaid there was no evidence of any quantity of that ceramic. This observation is also true of the site of Tell Halaf itself, on the upper Khabur. We are therefore entitled to conclude that the district was not attractive to the 'Ubaid peoples who, when they spread westwards, were more interested in western Syria than in the provincial backwaters of the Khabur. It is also not unlikely that Halaf pottery in these remote provinces may have endured longer than elsewhere and that the developed forms of it are contemporary with 'Ubaid.

It is indeed difficult to estimate to what extent change in ceramic reflects also new elements in population as well as new elements in technology. But it is safe to conclude that techno-

[1] §I, 25, pl. XXVI, no. 2.
[2] *Ibid* pl. XXV, LI.
[3] *Or.* n.s. 27 (1958), Fasc. 4, Taf. LVIII.
[4] §II, 11; §III, 12.

logical change nearly always implies some contact with the outside world, giving or receiving. We may therefore regard the
upper Khabur valley as one of the less receptive localities in the
Halaf period, for it seems either to have overlooked contemporary
change in Assyria and Babylonia, or to have resisted the impulse
of the peoples responsible for the 'Ubaid developments.

Another interesting form of negative evidence from Chagar
Bazar is, that after the close of the Halaf period there was a long
abandonment of the site, at all events of its central part, for not a
trace of Uruk and Jamdat Naṣr material was found. The next
traces of occupation could be assigned to Early Dynastic I.

A most primitive form of steatite cylinder seal was, however,
found in the last but one of the Halaf settlements: the scene
depicted a ritual dance of human beings with linear heads. This
object is either the earliest known cylinder seal, or else evidence
of a very late stage of Halaf.[1] The only known parallel is a rare
limestone seal, possibly of the Jamdat Naṣr period, from Kish,[2]
which, though not identical, illustrates the same kind of primitive
figures apparently engaged in dancing.

Upper Khabur valley: Conclusions. The district must have been
a rich and fertile pastoral and agricultural country in prehistoric
times, for from the top of the mound of Chagar Bazar alone we
could count over 200 settlements on the sky-line, many of them
of great antiquity, and in a survey conducted by the British
School of Archaeology in Iraq, in 1934, hundreds of ancient
settlements were noted within the three points of a triangle
formed by Ras el-'Ain (Tell Halaf–Guzana), Kamichlie (ancient
Nisibis) and Hasaka: each of these three sides measures about
60 miles.[3] The comparative rarity of 'Ubaid ware in this area was
therefore, as we have noted, significant, and further work is
needed either to correct this impression, or to indicate that there
was a gap after the main Halaf occupations, or to discover through
carbon-14 tests if, in this district, the Halaf ensemble continued longer than elsewhere.

BALĪKH VALLEY: TELL MEFESH; TELL JIDLEH

The marshy country of the Balīkh valley,[4] in central Syria, was
not naturally conducive to the establishment of important townships, for communications were always difficult and, since the river

[1] §II, II, pl. I, no. 5.
[2] §III, 10, pl. VI, no. 1; but similarity of subject need not imply contemporaneity.
[3] §III, 13, 12.   [4] §III, 14.

can never have been easily navigable, urban control, except at the extreme end of the valley, was neither practicable nor worth the exercise. Nevertheless, the overland route through this difficult territory was used from time immemorial, for there was a short cut from the north from Harran down the Balīkh to the Euphrates, and another, east–west, linking the coastal with eastern Syria. Moreover, this was good pastoral land, with a rich water supply. The district, however, suffered from one impediment to continuous settlement, for it must have been malarial. Cattle-breeding and fishing, with some agriculture, were doubtless the primary pursuits. Whilst there is evidence of ancient materials and objects typical of western Syria and the Orontes valley, it is clear that throughout its history the Balīkh fell on the whole within the orbit of Mesopotamia; the connexions were predominantly with the east, and to a lesser degree with the north.

The prehistoric settlement named Tell Mefesh is probably typical of many hamlets that were already in existence in the fifth and fourth millennia b.c. It lies 25 miles south of Tell el-Abyaḍ, about 7½ miles west of the river Balīkh, within a stone's throw of the modern track to Raqqah, and is situated on the banks of an ancient wādi which must once have supplied it with water. The mound is 15 m. high and the area of occupation about 8½ acres. Excavations revealed a mud-brick house of the 'Ubaid period, but only a small part of the plan was recoverable. The roofing material consisted of poplar, willows, and reeds. The rooms were small, not more than 8½ ft square, and attached to them was a courtyard which contained grain-bins in which large quantities of barley, *Hordeum vulgare* or *H. hexastichon*, were found. Animal remains included a large goat with a spiral horn, perhaps an early stage in the development of the Mamber goat, a large ox and a small *equus*.

Some good specimens of painted pottery were found in the house, unquestionably of the 'Ubaid period, but the designs on some of the bowls were strongly influenced by the Halaf style and applied to 'Ubaid shapes—a hybrid ware which thus exhibited an interesting blend of the older and newer styles. An attractive example of this pottery is a painted bowl on which we have empanelled designs of birds, perhaps storks, feeding.[1] A soapstone gable seal[2] engraved with the design of a goat is a rare example of an 'Ubaid seal-amulet: this was the period at which seals were beginning to be used for the first time. A primitive baked-clay figurine with an antlered head, characteristically

---

[1] §III, 14, fig. 7, no. 6.　　[2] *Ibid.* pl. xxiv, no. 1.

'Ubaid in its svelte modelling, was also found.[1] The 'Ubaid house was destroyed by fire and had no subsequent occupation above it. Traces of an earlier Halaf occupation were revealed below. An exceptionally large painted grain-jar of the 'Ubaid period is the best specimen of its kind yet discovered.

The conclusion to be drawn from an examination of the prehistoric pottery of Tell Mefesh is that the 'Ubaid ceramic was strongly influenced by that of earlier styles, most of all by Halaf, and to a lesser extent by Sāmarrā. As in the case of Chagar Bazar, we may be tempted to suppose that here also some manifestations of the Halaf ceramic were in fact contemporary with 'Ubaid.

No trace of Uruk ware was observed at Mefesh, but at Tell Jidleh, a small mound which lies 2½ miles south of 'Ain el-'Arūs (near Tell el-Abyaḍ) sheer over the west bank of the Balīkh, grey and red Uruk-type sherds were found, and this stage of development must certainly occur elsewhere in the valley.[2]

THE UPPER AND MIDDLE EUPHRATES

Negative evidence tends to indicate that the wave of 'Ubaid influence had more or less spent itself before reaching this particular tract of Syria. If the Manbij–Meskineh–Aleppo triangle is extended to include Lake Jabbul we may observe many mounds with traces of early prehistoric occupation.[3] A simple variety of painted pottery with dark designs on a light ground has some affinities to that of 'Ubaid, but there are no striking parallels to the classic examples of that ware. Some of the pot forms of Ninevite 3 (contemporary with 'Ubaid) are, however, known to occur, and it is also of interest that some miles upstream from Meskineh, at Tell Nas and Musharfa, the *Glockentöpfe* of the Uruk–Jamdat Naṣr sequence were discovered.

In concordance with the ceramic picture which we obtain from this district of Syria it therefore comes as no surprise to find that the circular, prehistoric mud-brick kilns founded on rubble and pebbles, at Yunus,[4] which produced the painted pottery for Carchemish, yielded, almost exclusively, types of Halaf ware. The concomitant flint and obsidian industry included simple stone implements, such as celts, pounders and grinders for working the clay and are of a type that persists unchanged into the 'Ubaid period.[5] Similar results were obtained in the acropolis, where

---

[1] § III, 14, pl. xxvi, no. 2.   [2] *Ibid.* 136.
[3] § III, 15.   [4] § III, 20.   [5] *Ibid.* 150, fig. 2.

Halaf sherds appeared, but no 'Ubaid, except for a bent clay horn or nail of a type familiar at this period in Babylonia.

Once again, at Carchemish, we meet clusters of the *Glocken-töpfe*[1] which presumably were being manufactured here in the Uruk–Jamdat Naṣr periods, as at so many other sites in western Asia; an incised, burnished ware with haematite wash may also belong to the same sequence.[2]

It is of interest that at Til-Barsib, some 12 miles downstream from Carchemish, on the opposite bank of the river, amid the early painted pottery there was a unique sherd of 'Ubaid ware, a fragment of a goblet, decorated with a curvilinear design, in a black vitrified paint on a greenish clay, highly characteristic of that ceramic.[3]

It is surprising that along the middle reaches of the Euphrates there is no conspicuous evidence either of 'Ubaid or of Uruk ceramic. Nothing important from these early periods has yet emerged from the unsounded depths of Mari; and a few miles below it, on the opposite bank of the river, the prehistoric site of Baghūz has produced an abundance of the earlier Sāmarrān ceramic, but nothing of the immediately succeeding periods.

The absence of 'Ubaid–Uruk over so long a stretch of territory is puzzling, and the ground requires further investigation, for it is hard to explain the close connexion between a site such as Brak and Warka in these periods without postulating a route along a part of the middle Euphrates. There is, however, enough evidence of a line of prehistoric mounds across the Jebel Sinjār through Irbil, Kirkuk and Kifrī, through the Ba'qūbā–Mandali district,[4] to indicate another method of contact with the south.

WESTERN SYRIA: THE ORONTES VALLEY AND THE 'AMŪQ PLAIN

We know from an archaeological survey of the 'Amūq plain that this fertile district, through which the Orontes river bends westwards to the sea, was well populated in prehistoric times. The plain, which is bordered by mountain ranges on three sides, is roughly triangular in shape: the three points of the triangle coincide approximately with Antioch, Rihaniyyah and Kirikhan. The area enclosed is about 500 sq. km., including the lake of Antioch, and, out of a total of 178 settlements which have been mapped,[5]

---

[1] §III, 21, pl. 52.   [2] *Ibid.* pl. 66.   [3] §III, 18, 122 and pl. xxxv, 18 *bis*.
[4] For example, 'Ubaid sherds have been observed at Telūl Abu Zabeb (Ba'qūbā), and at T. Tamerkhan and T. Dujaka (Mandali).   [5] §III, 1.

rather more than one third bore traces of pottery which belonged to the early prehistoric sequences down to the period of Jamdat Naṣr. It seems that the population was gradually increasing, and it is probably safe to reckon that before the Early Dynastic period there were not less than 100 small villages and some larger townships in the district. The sites of these early settlements do not appear to have been chosen with an eye to defence, indeed it seems that the early settlers occupied the country peacefully and did not anticipate attack. The villages were most thickly concentrated in the Orontes–Afrin valley along traffic routes that linked Aleppo, Alexandretta, and Hama, each of which must have been an important centre from the earliest times, though the prehistoric port of Alexandretta has yet to be discovered.

The prehistoric sequences in this area have been classified into a number of phases by R. J. Braidwood, as a result of the partial excavation of various mounds, particularly Judaidah, Çatal Hüyük, Dhahab and Kurdu, and through assessing comparative material at a large number of other sites.[1] The earliest phases A–D antedate the period which we are considering. It is in phase E that we may find for the first time evidence of southern Mesopotamian style ceramic; but the majority of it is correctly described as "Ubaid-like' rather than 'Ubaid. Some polychrome, as well as polytone, pottery appears; the latter is familiar in the south, but the former is a significant deviation from normal southern standards. In E there was a break in continuity, and in F we find Canaanean blades as well as some pottery previously well established. The significance of this phase is that from here onwards we begin to observe the gradual introduction of pottery thrown on the wheel and types related to Ninevite 3—but no grey ware. For connexions we look as far afield as Tarsus, Malatya, Carchemish, Hama K and Byblos B. Here, in the 'Amūq, we have evidence, at the close of the old 'Ubaid, of a long-drawn convulsion which seems to have followed on a general displacement and widespread migrations. Stage F was a long one: here we find evidence of metal-work, cast pin, dagger and chisel, and the first traces of the *Glockentöpfe*.[2] We have doubtless reached the very end of the Uruk period.

The bone and stone industries of the period in the 'Amūq plain do not show any significant deviations from the standards known elsewhere in this tract of Western Asia at the time. It is, however, of interest to note that arrow-heads seem to make their appearance for the first time in the 'Ubaid period and are likely to have

[1] §III, 2; 11.   [2] §III, 2, 246 and fig. 185.

served a useful purpose not only for human offence, but for fowling in the marshes—a method of securing game which would have supplemented the doubtless common practice of netting. Sling-bolts and javelins were in use, but there was no marked preponderance of lethal weapons. We may suspect that in this era the best method of uprooting a settlement was by burning—as the ashes of so many Western Asiatic small townships proclaim.

As regards diet, we learn from Helbaek that the 'Amūq Emmer and hulled barley had been cultivated long before the 'Ubaid period and that two common weeds, oat-grass and rye-grass, later supplied progenitors for the cultivated species.[1] Fishing, and most probably fowling, must have helped to supplement the available diet[2] of bread, meat (pork, mutton and beef) and vegetables, amongst which we may hazard the guess that the ubiquitous lentils, still an important element in the Syrian system of triennial crop rotation, must have been available.[3]

Reverting to the stone industries, it is significant that flint and chert were much more common than obsidian: the reverse was the case in the corresponding periods at Mersin, which was nearer to the Anatolian sources of obsidian. Nevertheless, the fact that obsidian was used implies that distant trade with the north was not uncommon, and a few stamp seals of a northern type may have been made as early as the 'Ubaid period. The cylinder seal did not come into use until the Uruk era.

The information obtained from Braidwood's survey of the plain of Antioch concerning the 'Ubaid and subsequent periods was supplemented by the small-scale excavations in the Orontes valley made by Ahmet Dönmez at Tell esh-Sheikh[4] and by Sinclair Hood at Tabara el-Akrād,[5] as well as by soundings conducted in the deeper levels of Hama by Harald Ingholt.

Tell esh-Sheikh, which lies 2 miles west of Açana-Alalakh near the river Orontes, was a prehistoric hamlet which contained a long succession of prehistoric occupation from neolithic times onwards. In the third settlement from the bottom, which succeeded the Halaf stage, there were a number of deep, thin-walled bowls typical of the shapes affected by 'Ubaid, and effective use was made of counterchanged design by balancing the dark pigment against the lighter ground as at Gawra and Arpachiyah. Although 'Ubaid influence is unmistakable, the Tell esh-Sheikh pottery is clearly a local adaptation of the familiar style. The rigidly symmetrical designs and the frequent use of a stipple suggest that

[1] §III, 2, 540–3. [2] *Ibid.* 67. [3] §III, 6, 89 and 96.
[4] §III, 19, 24–31 [5] §III, 7.

we have here a fusion of the two styles—a development which we observed at Tell Mefesh in the Balīkh valley.[1] We conclude that the 'Amūq-plain potters of this period were affected by developments of the 'Ubaid ceramic in earlier Syria, Assyria and Babylonia, but that, being relatively remote from the epicentre, and therefore more rarely in contact with it, they developed a degree of independence from the 'Ubaid world and derived much less from it than from the older Halaf traditions.

At Tabara el-Akrād, a mile and a half to the east of Tell esh-Sheikh, there was a succession of seven settlements of which the lowest (level 7) appeared to correspond with the upper levels at Tell esh-Sheikh whilst levels 5 and 6 above it betrayed some affinities with Mesopotamian Uruk. In the earliest level there were traces of a heavy mud-brick building, evidence enough to indicate how desirable it would be to obtain more information about the architecture of these early stages of man's development in this part of northern Syria. The pottery can only be indirectly related to the classical 'Ubaid style and is certainly a deviation from it: but one interesting steatite gable seal depicting an ibex and a branch fits well enough with the late 'Ubaid style of seals from Gawra.[2] In the two succeeding levels red-washed pottery with burnished surfaces appears and there are sherds with carinated rims, reminiscent of Uruk–Jamdat Naṣr ware and having some affiliation with the Early Bronze Age pottery of Palestine. Here we are in the regular line of descent after 'Ubaid, and while there are indications of fashions familiar in Mesopotamia it cannot be maintained that there are any direct relations with south Babylonian developments.

HAMA

Hama[3] has, for many millennia, been one of the dominant sites in the Orontes valley, for it lies on a main route through to the district of Aleppo. Moreover, 30 miles to the south lay the ancient site of Homs, where there was an east–west route which ran from Tripoli on the Mediterranean, through Palmyra, to the Euphrates.

Deep soundings through this great mound have exposed on a restricted scale a long series of prehistoric levels, of which the three lowest strata, K–M, account for a depth of approximately 14 m. of accumulated débris. The contents of each of these strata reveal a variety of disparate material, and we may assume considerable contamination, for several periods are often represented

---

[1] See above, pp. 410 ff.   [2] §III, 7, fig. 12, no. 5.   [3] §III, 8.

in any one stratum. There is, however, sufficient evidence to establish the accepted sequence from Halaf to 'Ubaid and then to Uruk–Jamdat Naṣr. But while it appears that in stratum L there are sherds of the lustrous Halaf ware, nothing that has so far been published can be related to the classical 'Ubaid, though doubtless some of the painted bowls with simple geometric designs might be called 'Ubaid-like; but a terracotta stamp resembles crude articles of a kind found elsewhere at the same period.[1] It is interesting that there were already traces of houses built on stone foundations, and of basalt hearths.

In the next higher stratum, K, there are traces of houses built on circular ground plans, as at the comparable period in Gawra, as well as of the normal rectangular houses. Also characteristic of this stratum were a number of pot burials. The mixed material in this level does show some resemblances to various articles of Uruk–Jamdat Naṣr type, as well as to others that are considerably later. We may note the roughly made flint-scraped *Glockentöpfe*,[2] as well as painted vases with geometric designs in a style abnormal to Babylonia and Assyria. We may also observe a rather roughly made form of black stone 'spectacle' idol, of a type familiar at Tell Brak and elsewhere, as well as an abnormal bell-shaped specimen pierced with three holes,[3] perhaps reminiscent of an object from Susa.[4] Some of the terracotta stamp seals are in the Jamdat Naṣr style. Finally we may perhaps attribute to this period two burnished votive(?) clay horns which are said to resemble specimens from Gawra. The fragments of four remarkable life-size limestone statues decorated with traces of painted plaster are most probably Early Dynastic and therefore subsequent to the period which we have been considering—they are perhaps contemporary with the Khirbet Karak ware found in the same stratum.

We may therefore conclude that, in so far as Hama was representative of the middle Orontes valley for the neolithic or chalcolithic periods, the pottery was apparently free of direct 'Ubaid influence, but that in the late stages of the Uruk–Jamdat Naṣr there were seals and at least one idol wholly in that style; but, except for the *Glockentöpfe*, pot forms were different. Once again we find that in the interior of Syria Mesopotamian influences decreased progressively according to the distance of the situation from the Jebel Sinjār.

[1] §III, 8, pl. III, no. 3.　　　　[2] *Ibid.* pl. IV, no. 3.
[3] *Ibid.* pl. V, no. 3; pl. VII, no. 3.　　　　[4] §III, 16, pl. XXXVI, no. 3.

COASTAL SYRIA: RAS SHAMRA (UGARIT)

When at last we come to the end of our long journey westwards from the Tigris–Euphrates valleys and reach the Mediterranean coast, a surprise awaits us, for at the famous site of Ras Shamra,[1] anciently known as Ugarit, we find, for the first time after leaving the western end of the Jebel Sinjār and the eastern Khabur valleys, unmistakable evidence of classical 'Ubaid pottery. We have observed that on the way the contemporary ceramic often assumes an 'Ubaid-like appearance,[2] but here, after the end of the Halaf period, some of the pot forms and many of the rather unimaginative geometric designs can be closely matched in Babylonia and Assyria, although it must be admitted that the fabric is often different; but a greenish clay and vitreous black paint, so characteristic of Babylonia, is by no means uncommon, as well as a grey-black on a greenish-cream slip.[3] Varying colours of the body clay produce polytone effects, and there are many painted wares with ribbing, as well as punctuated and incised decoration. The simple stone industries, use of chert, flint and obsidian, and occasional traces of native copper are also characteristic of the period. An abundance of obsidian implies frequent intercourse with Anatolia.

The evidence recovered by C. F. A. Schaeffer was obtained from no less than nine soundings, some of which penetrated 18 m. of débris, down to virgin rock. In the lowest level, 5, there was abundant evidence of three main stages of neolithic, 5 A–C, including the aceramic stages encountered at Çatal Hüyük in Anatolia, Beidha in Jordan, and elsewhere. Above these stages of neolithic came what Schaeffer has termed the chalcolithic stages: level 4, characterized by the accompaniment of painted pottery in three main phases—the earliest, 4 C, displayed connexions with Cyprus; 4 B, Halaf; 4 A, a tendency to degeneration of Halaf, and locally produced ceramic. Remarkable was the discovery that traces of fortification existed in these Halaf levels: a solid, curved and sloped rampart with a revetment of heavy stones which appeared to have enclosed the north-east sector of the mound at that early period.[4] It seems possible that these heavy defences may date back to the first Halaf stage 4 B and that they were initiated by the invaders who had succeeded peoples connected in three phases C, E, F with Cyprus. However that may be, the effort made to erect and maintain these Halafian defences was justified in the event, for at the end of that phase a violent invasion

---

[1] §III, 17.
[2] *Ibid.* pl. III, 4 on p. 248.
[3] *Ibid.* 4 79 and fig. 5, also pl. IV, 1 on p. 250.
[4] *Ibid.* 187 f.

occurred. There was a sack, and much evidence of burning, in Halaf and subsequent levels.[1] The Halafians were then succeeded, in level 3 C, by a people who habitually used a pottery made of a whitish fabric or grey biscuit covered with a uniform red slip or smear;[2] simply made bowls and flint sickles accompanied this pottery, which may perhaps be interpreted as evidence of an invasion from the south—that is to say from the Lebanon and Palestine. This period was apparently only of short duration and it was followed by a profound change in 3 B which represents a complete take-over by the 'Ubaid assemblage.[3]

In harmony with this 'Ubaid occupation was a burial consisting of a skeleton laid out on a bed of potsherds—a practice familiar in Babylonia during that period, for example at Ur; polished stone axes were common, together with the regular blade industry; the bones of pig, boar, ox, sheep *inter alia* were also identified. The 'Ubaid accumulation amounted in places to a depth of not less than 3–4 m.[4] (IIIB–G) and again represented a considerable period of time. A carbon-14 date of 4184 ± 173 has been assigned the basal 'Ubaid overlying Halaf at Ras Shamra[5] and agrees well with a carbon-14 date obtained for early 'Ubaid at Warka.[6] In these restricted soundings no complete house-plans were recovered, but there was sufficient evidence of rough, undressed stone walls as well as mud-brick. It seems that the rather lightly baked, greenish-cream clay increased proportionately in the later levels as against a predominant chamois colour for the earlier 'Ubaid, which Schaeffer believes to be local—the earlier phase representing imports.[7]

In the resolution of this problem at Ras Shamra we are faced with our principal and most intriguing task. Are we justified in assuming an 'Ubaid invasion or not? Admittedly the evidence for this hypothesis is much stronger here than at any other site immediately to the east—for example in the Orontes valley. The change-over to 'Ubaid from the preceding Halaf is at Ras Shamra sharply defined by an intervening stratum, and we must agree with Schaeffer that we are confronted by an actual invasion— presumably of dispossessed 'Ubaid peoples driven westwards in a search for *Lebensraum*. It would be more difficult to believe

---

[1] *Ibid.* 188; 362, 366, 369 and fig. 49, p. 391.   [2] *Ibid.* 189.
[3] §III, 17, 191.   [4] *Ibid.* 196.
[5] P. 389 in *Radiocarbon*, 5 (1963), 83; see also H. de Contenson in *Bull. A.S.O.R.* 175 (1964), 47 f.
[6] 4115 ±160 B.C. for basal 'Ubaid at Warka, where the earliest phases were not represented; see §III, 5, 32.   [7] §III, 17, 600.

that these violent transformations were the result of following changes of fashion elsewhere. How then did these 'Ubaid invaders—if we are right in believing in them—arrive on the coast? For the present, it looks as if we must posit some northern route which by-passed the middle and southern reaches of the Orontes, where, as we have seen, the changes seem to have been due to fashion rather than to invasion. If so, the answer must still lie hidden in some of the mounds of northern Syria and south-east Asia Minor, a convenient transit route for migrants who had left the endemic 'Ubaid *habitat* in the Euphrates valley. The solution should come from the next generation of diggers, and perhaps more extended work on one or two mounds in the Orontes valley itself may yield unsuspected evidence of a more direct 'Ubaid contact rather than, as at present, of 'Ubaid imitation.

The 'Ubaid peoples' exit from Ras Shamra is as mysterious as their entry. They left without a trace after a long period of occupation, which may well have exceeded five centuries. A long gap must lie between their departure and the newcomers in level 3 A, for these peoples, with their Khirbet Karak pottery and piriform jars, belong to a period contemporary with the Early Dynastic of Mesopotamia. At Ras Shamra (Ugarit), therefore, the Uruk–Jamdat Naṣr period is, so far as the evidence goes at present, unrepresented. A puzzling phenomenon that needs explanation, and another challenge to the coming generation of diggers.

BYBLOS

The early sequences revealed at the great site of Byblos[1] differ remarkably from those which we have discovered at Ugarit, and there is no evidence whatever of any direct contact with 'Ubaid. There is, however, a stage in the prehistoric development at which there are significant parallels, particularly metal-work, seals and impressions, with Babylonian materials of the Jamdat Naṣr period. It is probable that most of the other prehistoric Phoenician sites, with their strong maritime outlook, were similarly independent of Mesopotamian developments and had far stronger connexions with the culture of Palestine. An account of these sequences therefore properly belongs to a discussion of Syro-Palestinian prehistory, and for the present the developments revealed at Ras Shamra (Ugarit) must be regarded as exceptional, reflecting as they do the violent turns of fortune which were suffered by its inhabitants, who lived at a nodal point of contact

[1] §III, 3; 4.

with the Mediterranean, with Anatolia, with Palestine and with overland traffic from the Tigris–Euphrates valleys.

At Byblos it is level 2, second from the bottom, also known as Énéolithique B, which Dunand believes to be contemporary with Uruk 4–5, but in fact certain similarities between Byblos B and 'Amūq F suggest that this stage is also partly contemporary with the Jamdat Naṣr period. The settlement appears to have covered most of the superficies of the mound. The inhabitants lived mainly in circular huts 3–4 m. in diameter but all that remained of them was a beaten earth or pebble-covered floor with a low enclosing wall consisting of two or three courses of small untrimmed boulders; there was no trace of a superstructure, which must have been a flimsy covering of skins or matting. At this period the potter did not use a wheel, nor did he bake his wares in a kiln. There was no burnished or painted decoration except for an occasional brownish slip and some simple linear incisions as well as circles stamped with a reed or applied blobs of clay. The first copper appears in this level 2 but it is rare, for out of 851 tombs only 5 yielded copper daggers.[1] A relative abundance of silver rings and beads suggests contact with Anatolia. Most of the tools were still made of flint: choppers, knives, saws, scrapers. Stamp seals were in use. The dead were buried in large jars which were placed in grottos or buried in the ground. Only in the succeeding level were the wheel and kiln used by the potter. If the remains of Byblos B are in fact contemporary with the Uruk period, we must assume that Byblos developed very late, for other neolithic sites in Western Asia were technologically much in advance. In sum, the restricted evidence of possible Mesopotamian influence at this early period indicates that the relations of Byblos with the Tigris–Euphrates valleys were indirect and not the result of any Mesopotamian occupation.

IV. IRAN

The land of Iran embraces the same varieties of desert and sown, of mountain and plain, and of climatic contrasts as Mesopotamia, but there is one fundamental difference between the two, for Iran has no trunk rivers to unite one end of the country with the other. Streams which run down from the mountains die a quick death in the desiccated salt-plains; the distribution of the larger rivers has tended to concentrate homogeneous developments within restricted areas. Moreover, wherever the mountains and the foot-

[1] §III, 4, 583 ff.

hills are intersected by fertile valleys, an adequate supply of water from the melting of the snows, from springs, and from streams has sufficed for the sustenance of small communities with few mouths to feed. In addition, the mountains of Iran are rich in minerals, in stone and in metals. Iranian smiths and stonemasons have not been obliged to travel far abroad.

In consequence, when we come to survey prehistoric Iran in the periods contemporary with those of Uruk, we shall find a much greater variety of regional characteristics: relatively small pockets of prehistoric settlement of a marked individuality and exhibiting many differences in the pattern of handicrafts, pottery, buildings and burial customs. The varieties of patterns are comparable with the varieties of modern Persian carpets, unified none the less by a character which we can often discern to be Iranian. The general level of development is inevitably influenced by contemporary achievement abroad, even though in the remoter districts there are the inevitable time lags. But Iran was in constant touch with Mesopotamia through the many mountain-passes that provided the thoroughfares between the two countries, and where the mountains receded, as in the south, the cultural connexions were stronger. Thus in Elam and Susiana, where the tribes moved unhindered by physical barriers, development was at many periods indistinguishable from that of Babylonia. None the less, the number of great urban centres in Southern Iran was very much smaller than that of its western neighbour, and whereas in the former it was the tribes, in the latter it was the cities that were dominant.

KHŪZISTĀN

The province of Khūzistān is a natural projection of southern Iraq, both geophysically and climatically, and it is therefore not surprising that the prehistoric patterns of both these areas are closely comparable; indeed we may suspect that in ancient, as in modern times, the tribes wandered freely, unhampered by geographical barriers; intercourse can only have been limited by established monopolies of grazing-grounds and of wells. These human barriers, however, must have been powerful, for there are marked differences of cultural development even between the western and eastern ends of Khūzistān itself as we shall see from a comparison of prehistoric remains, first in the Deh Luran–Mussian district watered by the rivers Ṭib (Mehmeh) and Duwairij, and then in Susiana at sites in the basins of the Karkhah, Sha'ur and Diz.

Deh Luran district. The Deh Luran district has been described as a natural winter grassland; but as the annual rainfall is
confined to the period from November to May and the rivers
become a trickle during the summer, it seems likely that the tribes
migrated to higher mountain pastures for a part of the year—as
is still the practice today. The two small rivers, Ṭīb and Duwairij,
normally not more than ankle-deep in water, intersect the Jebel
Ḥamrīn, the mountainous drop-curtain between Assyria and
Babylonia, and through its passes the tribes of Amara in Iraq have
long been joined to those of Khūzistān. The latter country, like
much of southern Iraq, is desolate and parched in the summer but
the number of dried up river-beds in the Deh Luran district perhaps indicates that a little more water may have been available in
prehistoric times and that, like the inhabitants of the modern
towns, the ancients may have constructed canals to channel the
rain-water for the irrigation of their fields. The ox-bow remnants
of a silted-up stream-bed near Ali Kush are still visible, and this
and other beds may have been canalized in prehistoric times.

The 'Ubaid–Uruk sequence occurs on several sites in the
Deh Luran, and the beginning of it may be seen in a better perspective than in Babylonia, for recently American and Danish
expeditions have been unearthing abundant evidence of the
much earlier neolithic stages of settlement. Moreover, a series of
carbon-14 dates have begun to establish a chronological chart for
these transitions.

The best evidence for the pre-'Ubaid periods has come from
the site of Ali Kush[1] ($2\frac{1}{4}$ km. west of Mussian), at which the
following phases *c.* 7000–5700 B.C. have been recognized.[2] First
in time comes the Bus Mordeh phase, the earliest stage of sedentary life in Deh Luran. This is an aceramic pre-pottery neolithic;
the houses were built of unfired slabs of clay; there were hearths
of compost with carbonized seeds, sun-dried clay figurines, and
large quantities of chipped stone tools. Wild legume seeds were
extensively collected, but there is evidence of incipient cultivation
in the form of Emmer wheat and two-row barley. Goats were
probably herded, but perhaps not yet domesticated; a vegetable
diet was amply supplemented by the flesh of gazelle, onager, wild
ox, and boar; and fishermen caught carp, catfish, clams and water-
turtles—the kind of diet that could for the most part have been
equally well obtained on the lower reaches of the Euphrates.

The next, known as the Ali Kush phase (*c.* 6500–6000 B.C.)
witnesses an improvement in house-building, with mud-bricks and

[1] §IV, 22.   [2] §IV, 23, 105 f., with references.

mud-plaster. More grinding-stones were found and there were
flint and obsidian tools resembling those at Jarmo.[1] Hammered
native copper makes its appearance. Other improvements also
occurred in the arts and crafts: most important is the evidence of
two varieties each of wheat and barley, which signifies progress in
agriculture. Goats and sheep may now have been domesticated;
better butchering tools were made to carve the meat of the more
intensively hunted wild ox and onager. A delicious diet of marrow
was one of the best and most invigorating items on the pre-
'Ubaid menu.

The third phase at Ali Kush (known as the Muḥammad Ja'far
phase), c. 6000–5700 B.C., witnessed brick houses on stone foundations; walls were painted as well as plastered; and painted and
unpainted pottery appeared for the first time. Flexed burials were
discovered below house floors; there were turquoise ornaments and
loin-cloths of shell and stone beads—forerunners of the bead
skirt found at Eridu.[2] Whether this phase represents a recession
in agriculture remains to be seen, for an increase of sheep and
goats was accompanied by a decline in the quantity of cultivated
cereals and an increase in wild vegetables. Goats appear to have
been domesticated. The nearest parallels for this stage appear at
Jarmo in Iraqi Kurdistān, at Sarab and Tepe Gūrān in Iran.

A gap of some five centuries separates the next known developments in Khūzistān, which have been detected at Tepe Sabz[3]
(close to Ali Kush), where we now find an overlap with the Susiana
sequences. The top of Ali Kush is, in spite of the stratigraphic gap
and chronological gap, ancestral to the bottom of Sabz, which
includes a series of developments that may span the period 5200–
4000 B.C. House-building methods show little change except for
the adoption of pisé or tauf for party walls.

Buff-ware pottery as in Susiana makes its appearance; coiled
basketry, domestic cattle, dogs (possibly domesticated) also occur.
We now pass from incipient to efficient agriculture which in the
previous phase had shown a propensity to 'réculer pour mieux
sauter', as cultivated plants now included naked and hulled six-
row barley, Einkorn, Emmer, and hybrid wheat, lentils, grass
peas, flax. Almonds and pistachios must have been gathered by
migratory shepherds. According to Helbaek, the size and range
of cultivated flax at Sabz[4] is evidence for the beginnings of irrigation. In the upper levels of Tepe Sabz we find stamp seals, bent
clay nails and copper, and have now clearly reached what would

[1] See above, pp. 120–21.   [2] See above, p. 347.
[3] §IV, 36, 125.   [4] §IV, 23, 106.

be known on Mesopotamian sites as the end phase of 'Ubaid and transition to Uruk. Nearly a dozen villages illustrating this phase are known in Deh Luran—three of them at a junction of an ancient irrigation canal with the river Ṭīb.

Tepe Mussian–Khazineh and neighbourhood. Tepe Mussian,[1] situated 12 km. east of the river Ṭīb and 3 km. west of the Duwairij, was partially excavated by the Mission de Morgan in 1902–3; it was the biggest mound in the district, for it had a superficies of about 450 × 300 m. and its topmost point stood just under 19 m. above the level of the plain. In the immediate neighbourhood the French Mission conducted soundings at a series of other mounds which also revealed prehistoric remains of the chalcolithic and Early Dynastic periods, including Tepe Khazineh, Aliābād, Fakhrābād, Tepe Mohr, Tepe Murād-ābād, and Tepe Muḥammad Ja'far (probably to be identified with Ali Kush).

It is clear that at the great mound of Mussian we have a long series of occupations subsequent to the latest at Ali Kush and in part contemporary with those of Tepe Sabz. At Mussian and at Khazineh there was pottery of the 'Ubaid period, including the variety with a greenish paste, and 'Ubaid shapes and 'Ubaid style of decoration were in evidence. Moreover, at Mussian there is one potsherd covered with a dark paint, with undulating parallel bands left as a reserve of the body clay, in the unmistakable style of Qal'at Ḥajji Muḥammad or early Eridu–'Ubaid.[2] Probably also we are justified in comparing some of the painted geometric pottery gathered from Mussian both with Eridu–'Ubaid 2 and with the earliest Eridu–'Ubaid 1, that is to say, with the very beginnings of the known south Babylonian occupations. If this important equation be accepted, it is reasonable to conclude that here in Khūzistān we may observe an unbroken sequence of painted pottery through the mounds of Ali Kush and Tepe Sabz into the very beginnings of the 'Ubaid style: an interesting bowl from Khazineh decorated with linked bukrania may be contemporary with early Eridu ware.[3] Although the evidence has not yet been published in full detail, it would appear that the rich and fully decorated pottery found at the bottom of Eridu was an outburst of lavishly applied geometric design that developed without any intermediary stages out of the simple linear styles which we find in the beginnings of painted ceramic.[4] The evolution of the painted 'Ubaid was therefore probably in a linear develop-

[1] §IV, 17.
[2] §IV, 17, fig. 140 on p. 96.
[3] *Ibid.* fig. 264 on p. 135.
[4] See p. 341 and Fig. 26.

ment similar to that of the Halaf and Sāmarrā styles, which likewise appear to have been a sudden efflorescence from very simple origins.

A variety of small finds at these sites also provided evidence of the 'Ubaid, Uruk and Jamdat Naṣr sequences, the latter well illustrated by many examples of seals at Mussian. There were two baked-clay 'horns' of the type that we have frequently observed in Babylonia.[1] Flint and obsidian implements, polished stone axes and a stone hoe from Mussian,[2] as well as painted spindle-whorls, are also in the 'Ubaid tradition. It is incidentally of interest that the same close links with Babylonia persisted in this part of Khūzistān through to the Early Dynastic period—for example in the painted scarlet ware of Aliābād.

Deh Luran district: Conclusions. The beginnings of neolithic occupation in this district may be discerned in a series of settlements at an early stage of agricultural cultivation. Their inhabitants were developing on lines comparable with those observed at Jarmo in 'Iraq, at Sarāb and Tepe Gūrān in Luristān, and at Çatal Hüyük in Anatolia, but the Iranian sites seem to have been comparatively poor, less well endowed than, for example, Çatal Hüyük.

Perhaps the most interesting conclusion to be drawn is that, in what has been termed the incipient stage of cultivation, the inhabitants of these sites were at least partially nomad and not settled for more than half of the year. Only when a more efficient cultivation began to yield surplus stocks can it have become possible for the majority to remain sedentary. The turning-point in this progress is revealed by the pottery, for in the earliest stages, when man was mobile, there was no incentive to the baking of pots, which were easily smashed in transit. As soon as it became worth while making kilns, in relatively permanent establishments, the householders took to using pottery and were thus enabled to boil as well as to roast their food—the latter a form of cooking more practical for the nomad.

With a sedentary way of life came luxury, and the widespread practice of painting pottery in the 'Ubaid period is indicative of prosperity due to a surplus of food. Man, however, has been perpetually restless and mobile, and from the early stages of the neolithic onwards there is abundant evidence of trade in obsidian, copper, sea-shells, bitumen, and probably also in grain and livestock. It was this mobility which kept far-distant tracts of territory in touch with one another. The exploitation of local mineral resources and the supply of raw materials, such as flint and obsi-

[1] See p. 345 and Fig. 28 (*e*).   [2] §IV, 17, fig. 114 on p. 86.

dian, must have been prominent in the diffusion of ideas and of technology. Much of this progress is well illustrated in the rather poor territory of Khūzistān, because there we happen to be possessed of a particularly long sequence of archaeological information. And inevitably we draw the conclusion that the multiplication of man forced him to settle wherever he could, often on comparatively poor natural feeding-grounds. From the early period of the neolithic he was already confronted with the problem of *Lebensraum*.

KHŪZISTĀN–SUSIANA

About 50 miles eastwards of the Mussian district we come to another river system in Khūzistān, consisting of the Karkhah, the Sha'ur and the Diz, which carry a greater volume of water down from the mountains than the more westerly Mehmeh and Duwairij rivers. Otherwise, it is doubtful whether these plains of eastern Khūzistān differed climatically from those farther to the west, for the summers are torrid and the ground parched. The fact remains, however, that in western Khūzistān there was no ancient city comparable in size to Susa, from which French archaeologists have unearthed a prehistoric legacy of no mean order. We are fortunate, moreover, that, from the dependent mounds of Bandibāl, Jaui and Ja'farābād within a radius of about 10 miles, it has been possible to recover a sufficient volume of evidence which can be classified within an acceptable series of prehistoric sequences.

The basis of the system of determined sequences for the beginnings of settled life in Susiana depends chiefly on an analysis of the painted pottery styles which eventually have been found in a reasonably dependable stratification, to a lesser extent on seals and metallurgy. The skilled work of Le Breton has resulted in a classification which resolves itself into five sequent cultures of early painted pottery which he has determined as Susiana *a*, *b*, *c*, *d*, *e*.[1] The latest of this series, Susiana *e*, is equivalent to Susa A, which embraces the beautiful and artistically designed and sophisticated painted pottery formerly known by J. de Morgan, its first discoverer, as Susa I.[2] It took more than 50 years to decide whether this remarkable ceramic was the oldest known painted pottery or a relatively late development. H. Frankfort[3] argued that the abstract style of design characteristic of Susa A stood at the very beginning of a development which was moving from abstraction to realism or naturalism: Leonard Woolley[4] on the

[1] §III, 9.   [2] §III, 16, 1 ff.   [3] §IV, 16.   [4] §IV, 38.

contrary asserted that because it was a funerary ware and, as he alleged, buried below houses, it must have been contemporary with, and could not have been earlier than, the ceramic which de Morgan had denominated as Susa II. Both of these opinions have been proved to be wrong.

The fact is that at the sites in the neighbourhood of Susa, as previously mentioned, five styles of pottery succeeded one another. At Ja'farābād within the lowest horizon of the mound the design on the pottery consisted of 'basket-work' patterns, cross-hatching, negative treatment and, occasionally, incisions. These designs reflect the style of Susiana *a* and analogies may be drawn with Sāmarrā, Halaf and Ḥajji Muḥammad. Le Breton's conclusion was that these painted wares, though distinct from the pre-'Ubaid styles, are comparable especially with Sāmarrā, and look older than Halaf: Susiana *a* may belong wholly to the Hassūnah Period.[1] Some analogies, less precise, could also be drawn with Eridu and even with Ḥajji Muḥammad. The most important conclusion to be drawn is that these ceramic developments, which precede the classical 'Ubaid, may be related to those familiar in prehistoric Assyria and that they are subsequent to the simple styles of Ali Kush (see above), overlapping with Tepe Sabz. Susiana *a* thus provides evidence of a lineal ancestry to 'Ubaid, in agreement with the evidence from Mesopotamia proper.

The next stage, Susiana *b*, suggests contact both with Halaf and with Ḥajji Muḥammad and according to Le Breton implies movements of peoples rather than mere contact. In the light of recent evidence from Western Khūzistān we may agree with a hypothesis that Susiana *a* is approximately contemporary with Eridu 18–15 and that *b* may be contemporary with Eridu 14. It has, however, been objected that Susiana *b* represents a stylistic, but not necessarily a stratigraphic, division in the series and this has complicated the task of relating it in time to developments at Eridu. However that may be, Susiana *c* is analogous with early 'Ubaid, and its successor *d* has, *inter alia*, analogies with Gawra 13 and with Tell esh-Sheikh in western Syria.

It follows that Susiana *e* or Susa A coincides with the end of 'Ubaid and the early Uruk period. The brilliant pottery of Susa A, although mainly Iranian in inspiration, owes something to Babylonia (see Figs. 36 and 37). Le Breton has put the matter well. 'None of its distinctive features comes from Late 'Ubaid. But both in painted pottery and in red ware (which we regard as an indigenous production) a few unusual, unprecedented features

[1] §III, 9, 84.

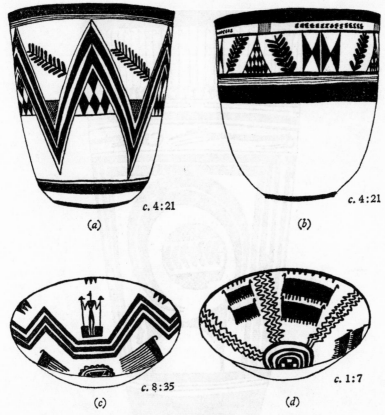

Fig. 36. Susa A painted beakers and bowls depicting water, plants, a demon grasping two spears set up on pedestals, 'oiseaux-peignes' and various geometric designs; mostly dark brown paint on whitish clay. (See p. 428 ff.)

cannot well be explained unless at the time they began to occur in Susa the 'Ubaid culture was still alive under the form known to us through Eridu 6, 'Uqair and Gawra 13.'[1] The penchant for producing red ware must inevitably reflect the concurrent technological processes of Uruk.

Whenever it was invented, this famous ceramic must have spanned several centuries in the life of the great city of Susa. It was found for the most part over a depth of some three metres in a cemetery which had accumulated outside the town wall and contained over 2000 burials. The baking of this pottery, some of which consisted of exceptionally high beakers or goblets (see Fig. 37), was a remarkable technical feat and demanded skilled

[1] §III, 9, 91.

c. 8:21

Fig. 37. Susa A tall goblet depicting long-necked birds, running dogs and empanelled caprid; dark brown paint on whitish clay. (See p. 429 ff.)

control of the kiln temperatures to avoid collapse of the thin walls of the pottery in the initial stages of firing, and its makers were therefore clever technicians as well as gifted artisans, for their designs have a perpetually modern appearance, an aura of time-less geometricity. On the many hundreds of vases that have sur-vived, plucked from the votive deposits in inhumation graves, we have an abbreviated cinematographic record which gives a vivid picture of the Susians. Tall sedge-reeds were growing in the marshes (see Fig. 36 (a) and (b)), there was an abundance of water which teemed with fish and water-fowl and with tortoises; hunting dogs like *salukis* were used in the chase (see Fig. 37), long-necked water-fowl, frequently represented on the wing, were

probably snared, netted, and brought down with bow and arrow; tall spears like the spade of the Babylonian god Marduk were set up on pedestals, confronting a demon (see Fig. 36(c)); snakes were important enough to be represented, together with goats and ibex. Some designs can be interpreted as irrigated plots of land. So much can be gathered from the pictorial record and supplemented by the catalogue of small finds.

Finally, a tribute is due to the artistry of the potters.[1] The elegance of Susa A is due to a sensitive feeling for the adaptation of design to the shape of the pot, to a largesse in the drawing of sweeping curves and rectilinear patterns which were never overcrowded and swept over the surface in a brilliant extravagance of freehand drawing. In the development of the potter's art, these designs command our admiration as a prehistoric climax of ceramic achievement.

Contemporary with the pottery was a considerable output of stone stamp seals, some of them unusually large, many of them hemispheroid.[2] Some button seals are distinctive of 'Ubaid; the hemispheroids distinctive of Susa A are also identical with Jamdat Naṣr types. The designs consist either of purely rectilinear and curvilinear patterns or of geometric, crudely drawn animals— mostly cervoids. The glyptic development of Susa A corresponds approximately with the late 'Ubaid of Gawra 13 and the prognostications of Uruk in Gawra 12. Hemispheroids can be matched in Giyān VC;[3] buttons are characteristic elsewhere, for example, at Tello and at Gawra.

One of the most important criteria for assessing the development of Susa A or Susiana e in relation to progress outside Iran is the metal-work, which consists of a number of implements, all of copper, including flat axes, large and small chisels, pins and disc mirrors, the latter resembling post-'Ubaid mirrors from Tello.[4] In general, the quantity and variety of these instruments suggest that metal was then more abundant than it was in Babylonia, where, as we have seen,[5] metal was still exceedingly rare—only stray finds providing evidence of a simple metallurgy in the 'Ubaid and Uruk periods. But in this respect Iran seems to have priority, for there was evidence of metal-working in Sialk I, which is probably not later than Hassūnah–Sāmarrā. The types found with Susa A are more characteristic of Sialk III.

A most interesting discovery at Susa was an implement wrapped in a linen cloth, which proves that the flax known to have been

---

[1] See Figs. 36, 37.　　　　　　　　[2] §III, 9, fig. 8 on p. 92.
[3] See below, p. 438.　　[4] §III, 9, fig. 9 on p. 93.　　[5] See above, p. 352.

grown much earlier by the inhabitants of Ali Kush was now put
to a purpose that has proved of untold value to mankind. Expert
examination has made it appear that the finer samples attested
extraordinary dexterity in the handling of the threads and twists,
and that such fine linen could only have been achieved after many
centuries of experience.[1]

We may also attribute to Susa A the paraphernalia characteristic of the 'Ubaid and early Uruk stages in Babylonia. Most of
the material is ill stratified, but includes flint and obsidian cores
and blades, flat stone axes and socketed hammers, flint arrow-
heads. As yet no carbon-14 date has been obtained for Susa A, but
by reference to analogous material at Bakūn and to an 'Ubaid date
at Warka[2] we may hazard a guess that some of Susa A is not later
than the first quarter of the fourth millennium B.C., and perhaps
flourished around 3500 B.C., bearing in mind the probability that
this stage of development was a long one.

Susa A was, as we have seen, probably co-terminous with the
end of the 'Ubaid and the beginning of the Uruk period; thereafter we come to a great diversity of material which in de Morgan's
time was generally classified as Susa 2 (our Susa A was his Susa
I). But as Susa 2 merely acted as a cover for anything subsequent
to Susa 1 Le Breton adopted a series of further divisions, namely
Susa B, C, D, each of which was subdivided Ba–Bd; Ca–Cc,
Da–De. Only the categories B–C concern us here, for Bd carries
us down as late as Uruk VI; with Ca there are traits which appear
similar to Uruk V–IV. The assemblage of material which has
come out of the excavations at Susa to represent the stages subsequent to Susa A is as considerable as it is diverse, and here can
only be briefly touched on in general terms in order to indicate the
close connexion with Babylonia; nor would it be profitable to do
more, for, as we have seen,[3] precise demarcations in the early
stages of the Uruk period are still unfixed. However that may be,
an imperfect stratification has yielded some clues.

After Susa A there was an intermediate period within which
traces of at least six levels of occupation, doubtless including
mud-brick buildings, were traced. The old painted pottery did
not die out all of a sudden, but it may well be that a change in
burial customs came at a time when the dead were no longer concentrated within a single cemetery, and the incentive to a large-
scale production of fine wares may therefore have been less strong.
The most striking characteristic of Susa B was a pronounced
change in the shapes of the pottery, much of which suddenly

[1] §III, 16, 163.   [2] See above, p. 419.   [3] See above, p. 357.

conformed to Babylonian types, and without doubt reflected a close and direct relationship with southern Babylonia in the Uruk–Jamdat Naṣr periods.[1] This was a time when the prosperity of Babylonia was making itself felt far afield, even to some extent at Tepe Sialk and, for example, at Tell-i-Ghazīr.[2] Unpainted pottery predominated, and through its angularity reflected an output of the more expensive metal vessels. A glance at the repertoire of shapes from Susa B enables us to establish con-nexions with a variety of types that can be paralleled from Uruk 17–6.[3] Included among the types are many kinds of spouted and lugged vessels, vessels with twisted cord handles, and the inevitable *Glockentöpfe*. Unfortunately some of the vessels could also be attributed to the late Uruk–Jamdat Naṣr stage of develop-ment and the typology in general, while providing proof of Mesopotamian links, fails to yield definite synchronisms.

With the stamp seals we may be on more solid ground; they reveal that there was no complete break with the past and provide evidence of a native tradition independent of Mesopotamia, although in step with the general trend of stylistic development. But, as Le Breton has indicated, the poverty of Warka 5 contrasts with the vitality of glyptic in Susa B. The fact is that at this period Babylonia lagged behind Iran in this respect: it is the northern sites in Mesopotamia that have yielded the majority of the stamp seals. The advance in style at Susa can be judged from the designs of animals on hemispheroid stamps; they are more freely drawn and give the impression of being in motion. Human figures, or demons with human bodies and animal heads, recall the figures on seals from archaic Giyān and the magical figures of the early Uruk stage in Gawra 12–11.[4]

At the end of Susa B, in the stage now known as Susa C, we come to an abundance of glyptic, namely stamp seals, hemispheroids and cylinders which are clearly contemporary with the extreme end of the Uruk period: Uruk 4–3 and Jamdat Naṣr. This is the time at which writing is about to begin—and belongs to the stages known as Ca and Cb.

Khūzistān: Conclusions. The eastern district of Khūzistān (or Susiana) was, it seems, more fertile than the district to the west of it, and the difference between the two is perhaps reflected by the relative size of its largest sites, Mussian in the west and the greater extent of Susa in the east. But perhaps, when the time comes for extensive excavations at the former site, the balance

---

[1] §III, 9, figs. 10–11 on pp. 96, 98.   [2] §IV, 27, 54.
[3] §III, 9, fig. 10 on p. 96.   [4] *Ibid.* figs. 15–17 on p. 102.

between the two will be redressed. However that may be, in our study of the regional developments it is clear that in the 'Ubaid stage there was more evidence of settled as opposed to semi-nomad sites, and an expansion of urban development must have been due in the main to irrigation and a more efficient agriculture.[1]

As more food became available, more mouths survived to consume it. Already we may discern the beginnings of the terrible population problems that confront us today: the perfect equilibrium between production and consumption is a notion of the golden age which, so far, has existed only within man's imagination, but has never been realized beyond it, however wide the open spaces may have been at the beginnings of prehistory.

NORTHERN LURISTĀN: TEPE GŪRĀN

The evidence available from this part of Iran for the most part precedes the 'Ubaid period, but the pattern of early development helps us to understand the later sequence, and in this respect it is instructive to examine briefly the results obtained by a Danish expedition to Tepe Gūrān,[2] a site that lies in the Saimarreh valley (Karkhah river), 950 m. above sea-level. Between this part of Luristān and the higher uplands of Harsīn, Delfan, and Alīshtar (1600, 1800 and 1650 m. above sea-level respectively) the tribes move freely from the lush pasture of winter to the higher pasture of summer, and thus repeat migrations which must have been a regular feature in the prehistoric periods, when the primitive architecture bespoke dwellings of a semi-permanent character. In this respect we have seen a comparable setting in the plains of Khūzistān.[3] Here in Luristān, before the desiccation of summer, one may ride through a plain with some thirty villages set amid cornfields which are watered by 'numerous irrigation canals nourished from many brooks in the side valleys'.[4] The earliest agricultural landscape may well have provided much the same picture.

The mound of Gūrān itself consists of about 8 m. of deposit which perhaps spans a millennium, c. 6500–5500 B.C., and soundings revealed a transition from hut to house during the earliest ceramic levels. This transitional stage probably preceded the establishment of permanent houses at Tepe Sarāb, which was an up-country temporary seasonal settlement of shepherds situated 60 km. to the north, in the plain, 7 km. east-north-east of

---

[1] Excavations in progress at Choga Mish near Ahwāz are revealing extensive traces of late Uruk ceramic.

[2] §IV, 29.   [3] See above, p. 426.   [4] §IV, 29, 104.

Kirmānshāh.[1] The implication is that the earliest settlers were primarily herdsmen, and that agriculture began developing in the later stages. In Gūrān the earliest levels were aceramic and there followed an extremely coarse type of pottery to be succeeded by the kind of ware that can be paralleled at Jarmo and then at Sarāb.[2] Some primitive figurines were also manufactured.

The succession of prehistoric layers follows the pattern that may be observed at many neolithic sites elsewhere. In the twenty-one strata (comprised under the letters A–V: A being the topmost) the bottom 1·5 m. contained the remains of wooden huts and hearths with traces of open fire-places; these levels T–V were aceramic. In P we have the first mud-house, on stone foundations, and a wooden hut; in N and O, both types of dwelling were in use, and in M, mud-houses were regularly built on stone foundations; white and red gypsum coated the floors; domed ovens were in use as at Jarmo and contained carbonized grain, consisting of hulled barley (*Hordeum distichum*) and a few grains of wild two-row barley (*Hordeum spontaneum*).

The pottery sequences, like the architectural, conformed with the general pace of development elsewhere in western Asia. Above the three lowest aceramic levels, we find in R–O crude sherds of greyish-brown ware together with primitive figurines representing women and animals. At this same period, in addition to some buff wares, we have the first evidence of archaic painted sherds, sometimes slipped and burnished, decorated with simple forms of widely spaced rectilinear designs, sometimes no doubt imitating basketry and net-work. These first steps in painted ceramic conform closely with those taken by the earliest potters in Assyria, for example, at Nineveh. A little higher up in levels O–H, we have sherds of what is termed standard painted ware, apparently decorated all over with an arrangement of blobbed lines, again as at Jarmo; and in L the shapes of the ware become more elaborate and the designs more assured, for the blobs are replaced by small rectangular or polyhedric spots; sometimes these designs are restricted to horizontal bands below the rim and above the carination of bowls, a type of decoration also found at Sarāb.

The development of painted ceramic in J–D, the latest of the neolithic levels, seems particularly relevant to our understanding of the early sequences in southern Babylonia, for here we are confronted with sherds in a 'close-pattern style'[3] with obliquely

---

[1] §IV, 2.   [2] See *Ill. Ldn News*, 22 September 1960, pp. 695 f.
[3] §IV, 29, 116 and fig. 17.

arranged geometric decoration, and in addition a negative-design technique which appears to be very similar to the painted pottery of Ḥajji Muḥammad,[1] that is to say, it conforms with the second earliest stage at Eridu. It is thus logical to conclude that at Eridu itself, and elsewhere in Babylonia, we may yet discover simpler painted wares of the types which at Gūrān preceded the 'close-pattern' style. Otherwise we must adopt the alternative hypothesis that the Ḥajji Muḥammad and probably also 'Eridu' ware at Eridu was intrusive from Iran, or more specifically from the western borders. Both flanks of the mountains which separate Iraq from Iran may in the future provide the fullest evidence of an unbroken ceramic continuity throughout the Neolithic period.

In H–D, red burnished and slipped wares occurred and these could be matched by some types from Sialk I. The conclusion drawn by Mortensen is that 'Sialk I belongs to the same period as Hassūnah–Sāmarrā in N. Iraq, and that in Iraq the Hassūnah phase followed the Jarmo phase, probably with a modest gap of time between the two'.[2] It follows, if we accept this statement, that, broadly speaking, the latest neolithic levels at Gūrān may overlap with the bottom of Eridu, that is, with the beginnings of a cultural continuum in Babylonia.

Other industries observed at Gūrān again conformed with the prehistoric pattern, for example, the flake and blade industry, with a few microliths (lancets and trapezes). As only a small percentage of the pieces had been retouched, it seems that the raw material, all of which had to be imported, was readily available: not more than 10 per cent of these tools were obsidian. Other lapidary material comprised flint, stone bowls, a celt, sling-balls, polishers and rubbers as well as standard utensils such as palettes, mortar-pestles, mullers, and querns of ground stone. Awls, pins and spatulae were of bone. Shell, mother-of-pearl, and baked clay were used for making ornaments and figurines; there was a ground-stone rendering of a human phallus, but otherwise no very realistic models were found. In general, agricultural tools became common only in the upper levels, and the conclusions drawn by the excavators was 'that the first people who settled at Gūrān were primarily herdsmen, living in wooden huts, and that agriculture developed little by little together with a village of solid mud-walled houses'.[3]

Up to the beginning of 1965, only one carbon-14 date is available for the neolithic of Gūrān, 5810 ± 150 B.C. for level H,[4] which

[1] See above, pp. 341 f.　　　[2] §IV, 29, 118.　　　[3] §IV, 29, 120.
[4] Personal information from P. Mortensen in a letter dated 8 April 1965.

would appear to be unexpectedly high if the close-pattern-style sherds in levels J–D are to be related to Ḥajji Muḥammad.

Gūrān compared with Sarāb. The sequences established at Gūrān may be compared with others which have been revealed by the work of R. J. Braidwood in the plain of Kirmānshāh, 60 km. to the north, where many different stages of prehistory have been exposed. For example, at Tepe Sarāb, 7 km. east-north-east of Kirmānshāh, there was an up-country seasonal settlement of permanent houses which was a stage later than the transitional hut-to-house occupation at Gūrān. But the buff and red burnished wares and the painted pottery style from Sarāb are, according to Mortensen, identical with 'the middle one of the three decorative styles on standard-painted ware from Gūrān levels M–D'.[1] Sarāb thus appears to be at least in part contemporary with the later levels of neolithic Gūrān, and no doubt other settlements in the Kirmānshāh plain will be found to belong to similar sequences. C.-14 dates from the two sites indicate an overlap. Thus three samples for Sarāb have been dated 5655 ± 96 B.C.; 5694 ± 89 B.C. and 6006 ± 98 B.C., covering a span of about four centuries.[2] That site is thought by some authorities to be typologically later than Jarmo.

The early chronology indicated by these carbon-14 sequences leaves open to doubt the relationship of the close-pattern styles of Iranian painters as exhibited in Gūrān to those found at Eridu, which, if connected, would demand an unexpectedly high date for the earliest settlement at Eridu. However that may be, Mortensen believes that there is a typological correlation to be established between Shemshāra 13–9[3] and Ḥassūnah 4–6, which, in turn, would have been preceded by Jarmo, Gūrān and Sarāb.

An examination of the developments mentioned above falls outside the scope of this chapter, which begins with 'Ubaid. But these discoveries are nevertheless relevant to an understanding of 'Ubaid, and the evidence from Iran must invite us to consider the possibility, indeed the probability, that remains earlier than any yet known may still be found in the neighbourhood of Eridu itself as well as on either side of the mountains which divide Iraq from Iran. Proof of this hypothesis may be expected from surveys which are now being conducted in the Mandali-Badrah district.

---

[1] Preview of an article prepared by P. Mortensen for *Sumer*, 20, 20 ff.
[2] *Radiocarbon*, 5 (1963), 91 f. [3] §IV, 29, 121.

TEPE GIYĀN

The mound of Giyān[1] is situated at a height of about 1800 m. above sea level, in the last of the valleys that flank the north scarp of the mountains of Luristān. Like Tepe Gūrān[2] it is on a tribal migration route which pivots about Harsīn, Delfan and Alīshtar. Only 25 miles or so to the north-west lies the Hamadān–Tihrān thoroughfare, and there was easy access to Mesopotamia via Qaṣr-i-Shīrīn, as well as to Susa via the valleys of Luristān. It is therefore not surprising that in the long course of its prehistory Giyān reflects not only a strong native tradition of its own, but also contact with prehistoric Assyria on the one hand and Susiana on the other.

Only the bottom 10 m. out of a total accumulation of 19·5 m. are of concern to the periods which we are examining—the remainder is later. McCown has conveniently classified the early accumulation as follows: Giyān VA, 18–19 m; VB, 18–14 m.; VC, 14–10 m.; VD, 10–8 m.[3] The architectural remains were unfortunately defective, though traces of *pisé* walling on rough stone foundations were observed. The significant evidence consists of painted potsherds and of a few stamps and button seals— the latter mostly from VC; a few only from VB. One example from VC illustrates a pair of human beings with linked arms, and another a pair of creatures part human, part animal, wearing a horned mask[4] and engaged in the sexual act; they compare with seals from Gawra 12 and Gawra 11 of the late 'Ubaid and Uruk periods respectively.

As regards the pottery, VA will bear comparison with Halaf, VB with the red ware of Sialk II; in VC there may be parallels with the later stages of 'Ubaid 3–4 and some with Susa A, and in VD with Sialk III, 6–7.

Giyān is thus comparable with other sites, for example in Susiana, in that it illustrates the full cycle of prehistoric progress through the 'Ubaid period, but the early evidence is fragmentary, and only becomes substantial in Giyān IV, at least a millennium later.

AZARBĀYJĀN

Evidence of early prehistoric occupation in this province of north-west Iran comes from a number of scattered sites, none of which has as yet been excavated extensively. But we can at least

---

[1] §IV, 7. [2] See above, p. 434.
[3] §IV, 26, 13. [4] §IV, 7, pl. 38, nos. 22, 24.

discern traces of walls in solidly built mud-brick, and of a painted ceramic, basically simple in character, running through the neolithic into the chalcolithic stages, undoubtedly covering a long span of time. In this area of Iran the handicrafts of the earliest peasant communities give the impression of being relatively primitive in comparison with those of Luristān, Khūzistān and Fars—perhaps because they were in less direct touch with Mesopotamia.

Yanik Tepe,[1] 20 miles south-west of Tabrīz, has provided some typical evidence of this kind. It contained, in a period which probably falls about the middle of the fourth millennium B.C., a pottery predominantly red-slipped, very simply decorated with elementary geometric designs which can be matched within a ceramic province all along the east side of Lake Urmia. For the same period we have some remarkable evidence for the application of a translucent obsidian which was set into the eyes of a primitive relief design of a human face below the rim of a bowl.[2] The most obvious source for this obsidian would have been Mt Sahend, not far to the east, which, together with the Araxes valley and the country south of Tabrīz, was destined to become a source of copper, tin, silver and gold.

Further evidence of a chalcolithic stage of development characterized by a very simply decorated pottery, possibly corresponding with a late stage of ʿUbaid, comes from Geöy Tepe,[3] 5 miles south-east of the town of Riẓā'īyeh—again close to Lake Urmia. In level M,[4] the last main stratum but one in this high mound, we find traces of mud-brick walling on rough stone foundations with remains of a dado of stones set vertically against the face. Some fragments of copper were found, together with a simple chert blade industry and a small quantity of obsidian. The animal bones included an incisor tooth of *Equus* sp.—the crown of it artificially rubbed down. Much of the pottery was a buff-coloured slip ware with simple brown and black geometric designs; its character appears to be Anatolian rather than Mesopotamian in so far as it may be brought into any direct foreign relationship. This simple ware may possibly be contemporary with some late stage of ʿUbaid, but no exact comparisons can be drawn.

In the district of the Solduz valley, a few miles south of Urmia, whilst Ḥasanlu was being excavated, a survey was made under the auspices of the Pennsylvania Museum of a number of prehistoric sites, and soundings were made at several of them. These

[1] §IV, 3; 134.   [2] §IV, 3, 138 and pl. XLIII, no. 12.
[3] §IV, 5.   [4] *Ibid.* 17 ff.

mounds lay on or near transcontinental cross roads linking Anatolia, Iran and Mesopotamia via the Kel-i-Shin pass; there was also a direct route towards the lesser Zab along the Ruwāndiz Gorge. Of the seventeen mounds examined in this valley, watered by the Gadar river, a number have produced sherds of pre-Bronze Age type preceding the standard grey wares which are found in connexion with larger urban settlements such as Ḥasanlu and Nagadeh. The inference drawn by Dyson and Young is that an initial period of decentralized village settlement prior to the end of the Bronze Age (when Ḥasanlu was fortified) preceded 'the consolidation of the population into several major centres'.[1]

The painted pottery from one of these mounds, named Pisdeli ware, forms part of a simple assemblage such as we have many times observed on early sites elsewhere: it includes obsidian and chert blades, bone awls from splintered long bones of animals; a bone axe-like tool; a clay animal figurine, perhaps a sheep; bones of *Canis* sp., *Capra* or *Ovis* sp., and *Bos* sp; clay spindle-whorls. This background lends some justification to the correlation of the rather simply painted geometric designs on the pots with some stage of 'Ubaid, probably rather earlier than the even more simple pots of Geöy M which we have noted above. Unlike Geöy, Pisdeli has no ring bases, which occur relatively late in the 'Ubaid stage, and some comparisons have justifiably been made with Gawra 19.

Assuming that the products of Pisdeli can be related to those of 'Ubaid—more particularly of prehistoric Assyria—the excavators have pertinently asked who the people were and where they originated. We have no reason to call them anything but Iranian, and who can say whether or not they had some tribal affinity with certain farmers in Assyria. Are not Kurds scattered precisely over these areas today?

Dyson and Young remark that agriculture without irrigation would seem to have been impossible in this valley unless the climate has changed since antiquity, and we have no reason for thinking that it has. Surely this may be regarded as a confirmation of the inference that irrigation with large canals was extensively practised in Babylonia at the time, and that the practice of it, though probably on a much smaller scale relying on simpler methods, such as spill and storage, had also reached the north. Other sites, namely Ḥajji Fīrūz and Dalme Tepe,[2] contain even earlier sequences, of the sixth and fifth millennium B.C. respec-

[1] §IV, 11, 19 f.
[2] T. Cuyler Young in *Ill. Ldn News*, 3 November 1962, 707 f.

tively, according to some carbon-14 tests. These ancient ceramics, like those that we have examined in Luristān and elsewhere, may have been ancestral to the 'Ubaid development, though no direct line of descent can at present be traced. It remains only to note that a single carbon-14 date from Pisdeli gives 3500 ± 160 B.C.[1] which, so far as the evidence goes at present, would seem to mark a relatively late stage in the long-protracted 'Ubaid period.

South of the Caspian, in the district of Māzanderān and west of Gurgan, very little significant material has so far emerged that may be satisfactorily related to the 'Ubaid and Uruk stages of development. We may, however, expect that in addition to the *tepes*, of which many have probably disappeared from this region (dug away for fertilizers), exploration of the caves will in time to come yield interesting results, for in this way we may discover links connecting the 'Ubaid with very much earlier stages. Hints of these long connexions have already been discerned in the Hūtū Cave excavated by Carleton Coon,[2] where red ware similar to Cheshme Ali and Sialk II has been excavated, and grey ware also displaces a much earlier stage of painted ceramic. The work of Coon in the Hūtū and Belt caves has more recently been followed by that of C. B. M. McBurney,[3] who has examined cave deposits in north-eastern Iran. These relatively recent activities will no doubt in the future have an important bearing on the whole range of prehistoric development in northern Iran.

Tell-i-Bakūn. Adjoining Khūzistān to the south-east lies the province of Fars, and here our most important information for the prehistoric period comes from the site of Bakūn,[4] which consists of two small mounds, A and B, 2½ km. south of Persepolis, in the plain of Merv Dasht. These mounds were first excavated by an American, and subsequently by a Japanese, expedition which extracted some additional information, especially from the osteological remains. Little is known about Bakūn B which is the older of the two and may go back, at the time of its foundation, to a neolithic period preceding the use of painted pottery, which is found only in its upper levels and throughout Bakūn A.

The settlement lay in good pasture land, and although agri-

[1] §IV, 11, 26.   [2] §IV, 8, 128 ff.   [3] §IV, 25.   [4] §IV, 24.

culture was practised this must have been a more precarious occupation on account of the lack of running water for irrigation; farmers were here largely dependent on rainfall.

The principal remains were compressed within an accumulation of about 3 m. of débris which contained a series of houses classified into a main succession of 4 levels, Bakūn A 1–4, of which level 1 was the earliest and deepest. Within this accumulation there was a series of houses; the walls were of mud, mostly *pisé*, and it is probable that some mud-brick was used as on other comparable sites. The maximum dimensions of the chambers did not generally amount to more than about 5 × 4 m; they were intended to be rectangular but were very roughly and inaccurately built. The plan gives the impression of an irregular agglomeration of remains built for the convenience of peasants who could, if need be, shelter within them a few animals and store their cereals. Kilns, hearths, and bread ovens were discovered. There is no warrant for drawing any definite conclusion about the social structure of the society occupying these houses beyond the fact that they were a simple peasant folk, and Herzfeld's theories are unjustified.[1] No traces of metal appear to have been found, but there were flint- and obsidian-backed blades. Button seals and stamps made of various kinds of stone, including steatite, were not uncommon; they bore geometric designs, were oval, triangular and rectangular, in the style of those found at Giyān V C.[2] There was a number of stone vases including one elegant cornet-shaped vessel.[3] The usual primitive stone agricultural implements were found: pounders, hammers, rubbing-stones and the like. There were also clay firedogs, scrapers and polishers, sickle-blades and many spindle-whorls. By far the most informative of all the discoveries was the painted pottery, which was often artistically decorated (see Figs. 38 and 39). The paintings on the Bakūn pottery consist of ornamental designs abstracted from nature and placed in zones, in a simple rhythm of repetition. The most delicately shaped vessels are thin-walled beakers. As in Susa A, we have a sensitive feeling for the arrangement and display of pattern, a fine sense of spacing and of the striking effects to be obtained by counterchange, by the contrast of the dark paint against a light ground, so that the design can often be read as both positive and negative (see Fig. 38). The drawings were all geometric in character, both rectilinear and curvilinear, and well adapted to the contours of the vessels. In the animal drawings realism is only lightly joined with naturalism. Parts of both

[1] §IV, 21, 10.   [2] §IV, 24, pls. 81–2.   [3] §IV, 24, pl. 18, no. 13.

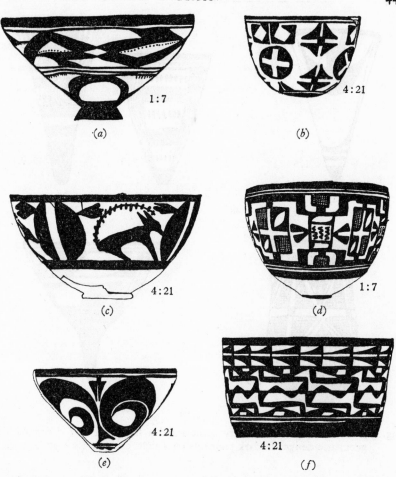

Fig. 38. Bakūn A painted pottery decorated with stylized animals, an anthropo-morphic figure (*d*), and geometric designs in dark paint on a light ground. The colours are predominantly browns on a buff or cream clay. (See pp. 442 ff.)

human beings and animals are used to express the whole. Bold and sweeping curves decorate the surface of the pottery which is often thin-walled and delicate. In addition to floral patterns we have designs of demons with grotesque hands, of snakes, turtles, birds, mouflon, ibex, boars, does, lizards, fish and several kinds of horned beasts, including some which may be matched with Sialk III, 6–7.[1] There seems to be little doubt that the ornamentation reflects the standard decoration of textiles. Some cornet-shaped vessels are in keeping with ceramic developments that occurred

[1] §IV, 24, pls. 66 f.

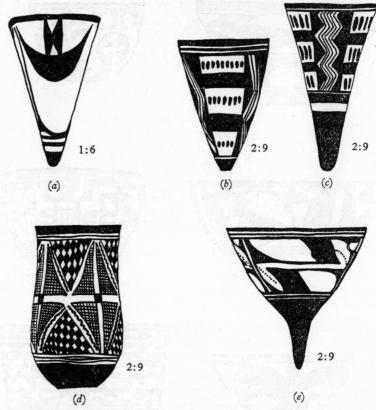

Fig. 39. Bakūn A painted pottery cornets and a flat-based vase decorated with geometric designs in dark pigments on a light ground. (See pp. 442 ff.)

during the Uruk period in Mesopotamia (see Fig. 39).[1] There are a number of clay figurines representing the mother goddess and decorated with swastikas, the sign of life, painted on the shoulders.[2] The bodies are either fiddle-shaped or cylindrical and the heads peg-shaped. At the end of the period the painted wares on a buff ground appear to give way to some red wares which, as the evidence from Nukhūdī[3] shows, is probably considerably later.

Stylistically the pottery designs and the decoration of the vessels are in keeping with the ceramic developments known as Susa A and it is clear that some designs have much earlier antecedents in Mesopotamia. On the present evidence this ware is likely to

[1] §iv, 24, pl. 4, no. 6, pl. 12, nos. 1–2, pl. 16, nos. 9 and 11.
[2] *Ibid.* pl. 7, nos. 1, 4.   [3] See below, p. 446.

date not later than 3500 B.C. and must have lasted for several centuries with little change. We seem here to be in the early phases
of the Uruk period.

Tell-i-Gap and related sites. The soundings conducted by the
Tokyo University expedition at Bakūn[1] added to the range of
material previously found but did not significantly alter our knowledge of this site. Much more rewarding were its excavations at
another site in the Merv Dasht plain named Tell-i-Gap,[2] 12 km.
south-east of Bakūn. Here we are confronted by a similar culture
with a much longer duration, within which we may observe a
long series of Bakūn ceramic with a continuous line of descent
from a painted pottery which has something in common with the
'Ubaid style.

The material from this mound was classified as coming
from eighteen levels which could be subdivided into two periods.
Gap 1, the earlier, comprised levels 13–18, and Gap 2, the later,
levels 1–12.

Dwellings consisted of rooms with *pisé* walls enclosing fire-
places and hearths; floors were sometimes paved with potsherds,
which were also used as foundations for the walls. Sickle-blades,
stone querns and pestles were found in the houses. The occupants
were engaged both in hunting and in agriculture, for of the many
animal bones, 70 per cent belonged to wild forms which included
dama, deer, wild boar and gazelle. There was also evidence of
Bos taurus, Ovis, Canis familiaris, Vulpes. No adequate varieties
of hunting implements were found, with the exception of a few
stone balls.

The rich series of painted pottery was particularly significant
in that the designs and shapes of Gap 2 (later period) had much in
common with Bakūn A, with which it must have been at least
partly contemporary. There appears, however, to have been no
break between Gap 2 and the earlier Gap 1, which also displayed
some correspondence with Susa, notably in the 'comb-teeth'
patterns. Negative designs are said to be commoner in Gap 1, in
which some of the beakers were obviously comparable with the
'Ubaid style of ceramic.[3] In general, the evolution of the painted
styles appears to conform with that observed in Susiana, and the
excavators compare the early pottery with examples from Jaui
and Bandibāl on the one hand,[4] and with prehistoric material said
to have been gathered from Tell-i-Iblīs,[5] near Kirmān, and from
sites in Sīstān on the other.

[1] §IV, 12.   [2] §IV, 13.   [3] *Ibid.* figs. 22–4.
[4] *Ibid.* 21.   [5] §IV, 37, 18.

Two carbon-14 dates were determined at Gakushūin University: for Gap 1, 5870 BP = 3912 ± 170 B.C.; for Gap 2, 5440 BP = 3482 ± 120 B.C.[1] Since Gap 2 is predominantly comparable with Bakun A we have here a satisfactory equation, for it is to be suspected that this period was subsequent to 'Ubaid, approximately contemporary with early Uruk. This last date is higher than one determined by the British Museum laboratories for nearly contemporary material discovered at Tell-i-Nukhūdī.[2]

The Japanese excavators noted that other mounds in the same district bore traces of similar pottery, including Tell-i-Jarreh, Tell-i-Shoga, Tell-i-Kadima and Tell Mishgī; all of them belong within the same cultural cycle and prove that this was a prosperous period of primitive agricultural and pastoral activity in this part of Iran. In the same province of Fars, Aurel Stein also investigated a number of mounds which bore traces of the Bakūn A type of painted pottery, seals, chert, bone and stone implements, part of an assemblage which betokened a widespread prosperity throughout this region at the time.[3]

Tell-i-Nukhūdī. This[4] was a small prehistoric settlement near the river Pulvār, comprised within the later and better known Achaemenian settlement named Pasargadae. The remains consisted of an accumulation of about 3 m. of débris—a series of house-levels, with walls composed of rather large mud-bricks and of *pisé*; some stone was used in the foundations; there was some evidence of red plaster on the walls; hearths and bread-ovens were also found.

The top three levels, I*a, b* and II, contained red pottery, usually plain, sometimes slipped, occasionally with sparse traces of paint. In these levels, in contradistinction to what lies below, we have the first evidence of copper implements, pins and a hammer which typologically can hardly be earlier than the latter part of the third millennium B.C. The material from these later levels corresponds with some that was gathered from Bakūn A 5. Most important, therefore, was the stratigraphic evidence recovered by the excavator, Miss Clare Goff, that there was most probably a break in continuity with Bakūn A and indeed it seems likely that there was a considerable interval of time between the two cultures. None the less, it is possible that elsewhere these intrusive red-ware fabrics may prove to have a longer history. However that may be, this red ware is too late to be included within the scope of this chapter

[1] §IV, 13, 23.
[2] B.M. 171, 3100 B.C. ± 150, based on Libby half-life of 5570; see below, p. 447.
[3] §IV, 33.   [4] §IV, 19; 20.

which is concerned only with the periods preceding Jamdat Naṣr.

The contents of the two lower levels of Tell-i-Nukhūdī corresponded very closely with those of Bakun A, although of course the pottery had its local variations. The links with Giyān VC, both as regards painted designs and the stone button seals, are obvious, and are the same as those already known from Bakūn, while again some designs are comparable with those of Susa A. There is no evidence of pottery made on the fast wheel, though, as on many pots of Bakūn A, there are indications of turning. Nukhūdī also yielded some fine examples of delicately painted beakers, and an artistically made ring-based bowl decorated with a procession of painted does(?).[1] Weirdly designed animals, including horned beasts, were not uncommon.

It is interesting that one carbon-14 date[2] gives a determination of *c.* 3100 B.C. ± 150 for level IV, the earliest in this mound, some indication that a part of Bakūn A is subsequent to 'Ubaid and coincident with a part of the Uruk period. But many more determinations are yet required before we can obtain a reliable pattern of dates for these early stages of Iranian prehistory.

TEPE SIALK

The site[3] lies approximately 2½ miles south-west of Kāshān, in a high valley about 1000 m. above sea-level, and is situated on the western margin of the central Iranian desert, in close proximity to a chain of mountains which is the source of water for the district. Geographically it was appropriately sited to become an important station on a trade route which fringed the desert and had connexions with prosperous centres in the Elburz mountains, as well as with others in western and south-western Iran. The archaeological sequences reveal tendencies to trade with both west and east: first west, Sialk I–II, then east, Sialk III, and finally again a close relationship with the west, Sialk IV.

The main occupation was confined to two mounds. The earlier of the two, the northern one, consisted of a total accumulation of not less than 13 m. of habitation deposit, over a superficies of approximately 320 × 110 m. Sialk I contained five sub-levels,

---

[1] §iv, 19, fig. 9, no. 1 and pl. 1 and p. 62.

[2] See above, p. 446, n. 2, but a half-life of 5700 is probably more accurate, and gives a correspondingly higher date. As third-millennium dates are in several cases apparently five centuries too low, on carbon-14 computations, we might accept a date of at least 3400 B.C. for the earliest part of Nukhūdī.   [3] §iv, 18.

I, 1–5, beginning at the bottom with reed and brushwood huts, a type of primitive occupation which must also have been characteristic of Khūzistān. There was, however, a rapid progression in the architecture, for after I *pisé* and some mud-brick were used in wall construction. Painted pottery as well as unpainted was in common use from the very beginning, buff and red ware, as well as some black and grey. The geometric designs applied to simple bowl shapes are undoubtedly in keeping with the earliest painted styles of prehistoric Assyria and may possibly mark a stage preceding Halaf.[1] It is therefore all the more remarkable that at Sialk we also have evidence from the beginning of hammered copper.[2] Simple types of awls and pins have a claim to be the oldest known metal work in Iran and are at a stage reminiscent of the early neolithic of Çatal Hüyük in Anatolia, which, however, may have been considerably earlier in time: unfortunately no carbon-14 dates are available for Sialk. A bone holder for a flint knife from Sialk I represents a male figure with hands and arms reverently folded across the front of the body in an attitude of obeisance which is already astonishingly Persian![3]

In Sialk II we meet for the first time with a period of occupation which may possibly be related to a very early stage of ʿUbaid, for in II, 1, 2, we find walls composed of long, straw-tempered, sun-dried mud-bricks, hand-moulded, which have frog-marks, or thumb-prints, in pairs on the surface, no doubt intended as additional lodgement for mud-mortar. Very similar bricks were found at Eridu in the walls of a temple in level 15, and this near identity suggests a possible correlation with the early stage of Eridu–ʿUbaid I.[4]

The pottery, however, does not betray close links with any stage of ʿUbaid: on the contrary, some of the simple designs, mostly in the inside of the pots, are reminiscent in character of Halaf ceramic; this similarity of fashion could be expected if they were more or less contemporary with early Eridu.[5] A strong element of red ware probably agrees with ceramic fashion in northern Iran, at a site such as Cheshme-i-Ali.[6] All the pottery is hand-turned. Stone bowls occur, and there is some evidence of turquoise and carnelian beads. Copper implements are still primitive, but become more abundant. There is a progressive improvement in the quality of the stone awls and hoes, and of the brickwork.

---

[1] *Ibid.* pl. xxxix, S. 1274 and S. 1647 for comparison with §1, 27, fig. 72.
[2] §iv, 18, pl. lii.　　　　　　　　　　[3] §iv, 18, pl. vii.
[4] *Ibid.* 26, pl. xi, no. 4 and §1, 22, 121. See above, p. 336.
[5] See above, p. 340.　　　　　　　　[6] §iv, 26, 3 and 3–4.

Red ochre was used in the wall plaster; the dead were buried under the house-floors.

Sialk II must have lasted for some considerable time, for it includes an accumulation of débris amounting to not less than seven metres in depth. Although marked by continuous technological improvements, Sialk II is in a direct line of descent from Sialk I, and it would be surprising if the two stages had lasted less than half a millennium—they may even have spanned a whole one.

With Sialk III we begin an important new stage of development in the prehistory of the place. The inhabitants abandoned the old north mound, which no doubt had become inconveniently high, and after some interval of time, which may not have been a long one, shifted their abodes to a new part of the site which is now known as the southern mound; this covered a superficies of about 260 × 190 m., a plot of ground large enough to house several thousand souls.

Again there was no break in the continuity of civilization, but in every branch of technology there is evidence that considerable strides were made, and we may affirm with confidence that at least a part of Sialk III with its seven sub-levels, III, 1–7, coincided with some phase of the 'Ubaid period, in spite of the tenuous nature of the evidence, which does, however, give us some cross-relations with Gawra and prehistoric Assyria. Towards the end of Sialk III we may reckon that we have reached the Uruk–Jamdat Naṣr period. Perhaps the most significant developments of Sialk III are the introduction of pottery turned on the wheel, an innovation that first became common in the Uruk period in Mesopotamia and is attested in III, 4, and of a more spacious expansive architecture. Copper is now cast instead of hammered; there is a series of daggers, well-made chisels and pins, and a single example of a socketed axe cast in an open mould.[1] The simple variations of stone button seals are characteristically Iranian and some of them can also be matched in prehistoric Assyria.

In Sialk III we have for the first time a series of plans,[2] unfortunately fragmentary, of buildings erected on no mean scale. Walls were carelessly and irregularly constructed, of both moulded mud-bricks and pisé, and red paint was occasionally applied to the plaster as in III, 6, 7. The most coherent plan begins to appear in III, 7, where we have a series of oblong chambers up to 4 m. in length giving access to larger squarish rooms which look like covered courts. From III, 2, onwards, and

---

[1] §IV, 18, pl. LXXXIV.   [2] *Ibid*. pl. LXI.

especially in III, 4, the façades of some walls are relieved with a series of projecting panels which, in the manner of the façades on religious buildings of the 'Ubaid period in Mesopotamia, broke up the monotony of long stretches of wall and cast a series of attractive shadows so long as the sun was not at its meridian.

There is, however, no need to assume that these buildings at Sialk were temples, for there is in them no obvious shrine, and occasional hearths imply rather a domestic character. These architectural features, the coloured plaster on the walls, and a big mud column in a passage-way of III, 6, perhaps indicate buildings intended for the local prince or chieftain and his family. Pebbles were used in the foundations of III, 4 and 7, and from the latter period onwards walls become progressively thicker. Curved walls in III, 3, and III, 6, appear to correspond with bends in the public thoroughfares. The whole series from III, 2, onwards represents building on no mean scale, and the thickness of some walls may already imply the use of vaults. These formidable buildings provide the first evidence for considerable public architecture in the 'Ubaid period of Iran.

One dramatic discovery was made in a well-planned building of this period. In a big corner room of III, 5 there was the skeleton of a woman lying near a window and protecting two small children with her arms. Here three members of one family had been crushed by the fall of the walls and roof—possibly the result of an earthquake—and the mother was found where she died, perhaps in the act of calling for the help that never came.

Sialk III was lavishly endowed with a gaily painted pottery which bears more intricate and elaborate designs than those of II, but is in the natural line of descent from it (see Fig. 40). There are here, as we have already seen, a few comparisons to be made with pottery of the 'Ubaid period in Mesopotamia. A painted bowl from III, 1 is similar in shape and design to vases from the Eridu cemetery (end of the 'Ubaid period);[1] the design known as the 'concave whorl'[2] appears in Gawra 13, and there are other parallels. A sherd depicting dancing men closely matches the subject and design on a seal of Gawra 13, and some of the snake designs are also related. True ring-bases do not occur till III, 7, and were not commonly used before Gawra 12, that is to say, in the latest 'Ubaid (4) period. A sherd with a landscape design provides yet another analogy for the same stage of ceramic at Gawra.[3] A painted beaker from III, 6, a

---

[1] §iv, 18, pl. LXII, S. 394.   [2] *Ibid.* pl. LXII, S. 1693.
[3] *Ibid.* pl. LXXXIII, C. 3.

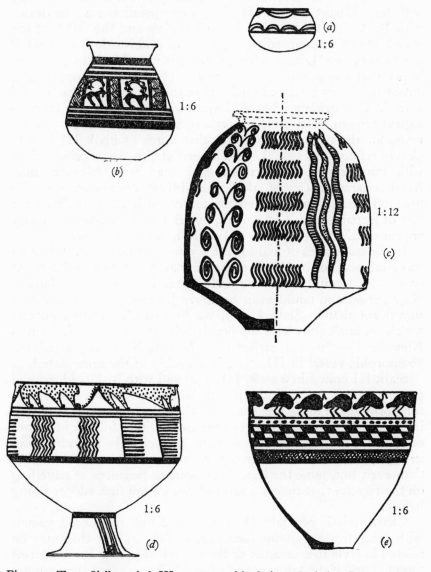

Fig. 40. Tepe Sialk period III, pottery with designs depicting ibex, serpents, leopards, birds, plants terminating in volutes, and geometric motifs. The colours are black and blackish-brown on red and chamois slips, or on a light grey clay. (See p. 450.)

greyish ware with greenish cast, again provides a close analogy with late 'Ubaid, and in III, 6–7, some parallels may be drawn with Bakūn A and Susa A. These parallels and the fact that the wheel, which undoubtedly originated in prehistoric Babylonia at the turn of the 'Ubaid–Uruk period, is introduced in III, 4–5, imply that the greater part of Sialk III, certainly from III, 4 onwards, cannot be dated earlier than the last stage of the 'Ubaid period. This evidence has an important bearing on the chronological sequences at certain northern sites in the Elburz mountains, for there can be no doubt that much of Sialk III is very closely related to Hisar I,[1] and indeed at this period connexions with north-east Iran were stronger than with Mesopotamia. Most characteristic of the Sialk–Hisar connexion are the pedestal vases, some of them decorated with attractively drawn files of leopards, III, 6–7.[2] Ibex, mouflon and the like frequently appear on sherds—again very similar in style to Hisar.

In the last stages of Sialk III it is possible that the stratification was confused, for in III, 6, there were at least two unpainted pot types which could hardly be earlier than the end of the Jamdat Naṣr period and could even be Early Dynastic.[3] It is therefore significant that in Sialk III, 7, we find painted chalice-goblets which are analogous with the prehistoric Assyrian ware known as Ninevite V—also not earlier than Jamdat Naṣr, and a painted zoomorphic vessel in III, 7(b), is probably of the same date.[4]

Sialk III ended in a sack, III, 7(b) and with it the old painted pottery comes to an end, though some vessels were still perfunctorily decorated. The sharp break in ceramic styles may well imply some gap in time between the two periods, but the influence of Sialk III may still be occasionally detected. The main building in IV, 1, however, is novel in conception, and the walls are thicker than ever, but, none the less, there seem to be traces of panelling on the façades that reflect a form of decoration first adopted long before.

Characteristic of Sialk IV are painted and unpainted vessels with long trough spouts (see Fig. 41 (a), (b), (c)) that may be related in style to a ceramic of the period which Le Breton terms Susa C,[5] and if the temporal relationship be accepted they are not likely to be earlier than the end phase of the Jamdat Naṣr period, as is also suggested by bowls with bevelled rims, while some types

---

[1] See below, pp. 456 ff.   [2] §iv, 18, pl. lxvii, S. 152, 137.
[3] §iv, 18, pl. lxix, S. 55, S. 135.
[4] Ibid. pl. lxxi, S. 111 and pl. lxxiii, S. 1697.
[5] §iii, 9, 99, fig. 13; see above, p. 432.

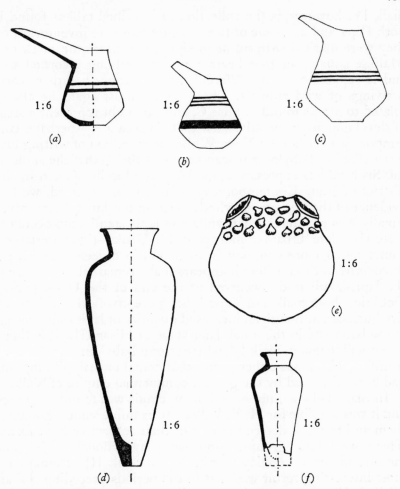

Fig. 41. Tepe Sialk period IV pottery. (See p. 452.) (*a*), (*b*), (*c*) Painted vases with trough spouts. (*e*) Double-hole-mouth vase, decorated with appliqué pellets. (*d*), (*f*) Two vases of grey-black clay.

of long-bodied vases with splayed necks could conceivably belong either to that period or to Early Dynastic I (see Fig. 41 (*d*) and (*f*)).[1] The double hole-mouthed vase decorated *à pastillage*[2] also belongs to the same horizon and has a long history in Babylonia and in Syria (see Fig. 41 (*e*)).[3]

Much the most important and significant discovery made in

[1] §iv, 18 pl. lxxxix, S. 483 and S. 1608; compare these forms with §iv, 10, pl. 179, C. 517.273 (E.D.I.).
[2] §iv, 18, pl. xc, S. 77.   [3] §i, 25, pl. lxviii, no. 2 and p. 225.

Sialk IV, however, is the collection of inscribed tablets found in both IV, 1 and 2. Some of these documents were inventories, for they were marked with numeral signs; one bears the mark of a Maltese square, another bears a sign resembling a corded sack and is capable of many different interpretations.[1] Others carry drawings of wild animals. These tablets must again be closely related to others found in Susa C, and no doubt represent a stage of development more advanced than Warka 4 A—perhaps contemporary with Jamdat Naṣr. While the invention of writing may be ascribed to Babylonia it seems most probable that the signs on the Sialk tablets expressed some language locally spoken in this district of Iran. Contemporarily, as might be expected, we find evidence of the first use of cylinder seals in the Jamdat Naṣr style. Finally it is of interest that while one lapis lazuli bead occurs in Sialk III—late 'Ubaid or more probably Uruk—this material[2] becomes much more common in Sialk IV, in agreement with the discoveries at Susa, where it appears that a remarkable increase in the lapis-lazuli trade occurred at the end of the Uruk period. Doubtless both Sialk and Tepe Hisar were involved in this lucrative business, although an increased quantity of lapis only appears at the latter site in the much later stage of Hisar III. It is therefore possible that in Sialk IV, where strong Babylonian influence is manifest, Hisar was either partly abandoned or insignificant, and had been displaced by the greater commercial empire of Sialk.

In Sialk I–IV a number of human crania was found in graves, and it was possible for H. V. Vallois[3] to examine some eighteen of them and to make determinations of their respective head forms. There were four groups, comprising hyperdolicho-, dolicho-, meso- and brachycephaly (beginning in Sialk II). Perhaps the most interesting result was that in the periods preceding 'Ubaid (Sialk I–II) five out of eleven skulls were hyperdolichocephalic, whereas only one out of four displayed this extreme long-headedness in the early 'Ubaid period, Sialk III, 3, and thereafter there was no more evidence of this type. Brachycephaly appeared as early as Sialk II and continued through IV, perhaps a foretaste of a characteristic which became pronounced in the much later Iron Age Sialk.

Another significant trait was a progressive deterioration of the teeth: 3·5 per cent were affected in Sialk I and 8·8 per cent in Sialk II, and this decline became considerably more marked in the much later Iron Age periods. Decay was noticeable in the molar

---

[1] §IV, 18, pls. XCII–XCIV.　　　　[2] § IV, 18, 69, 70 and pl. XXX.
[3] §IV, 18, vol. 2, 116 f.

teeth, never in the canine and incisors. The conclusion is inevitable that this progressive dental trouble was due to a change of
diet, and one suspects that it was related to an increased supply of
cereals, perhaps accompanied by a proportionate decrease in the
quantity of meat available for the larder. There is scope for further
research on this point.

Nothing exceptional was noted in the examination of the Fauna
by R. Vaufrey[1] except the discovery in Sialk II of *Equus caballus
Pumpellii* Duerst. Otherwise, osteological remains were traced of
Canis familiaris (Sialk II), *Sus* sp. (Sialk II), *Gazella* sp. (Sialk I,
II), *Capra aegagrus* (Sialk I), *Ovis vignei* (Sialk I, II), *Bos taurus*
(Sialk I).

Sialk: Conclusion. The rich material discovered at Sialk demonstrates a long and steady internal development of native styles
which were never altogether out of touch with technological
advances in the Elburz, in Susiana, in Assyria, and, to a lesser
extent perhaps, in Babylonia. As a rule, where we find evidence
of the influence of Babylonian styles, this is likely to have been
transmitted through intermediaries, except perhaps in Sialk IV,
when the widespread Babylonian trade of the Jamdat Naṣr period
began to find the most distant outlets.

We have observed in the preceding pages the principal Mesopotamian sites at which connexions with western and central Iran
(Sialk) may be established. In eastern Iran, however, the evidence
concerning both the process of internal development and of relations abroad in the earliest periods is more tenuous. It has, however, become apparent that the hypothesis alleging a concentration of buff-ware cultures in southern Balūchistān and in Sind, in
contrast with red-ware cultures in the north (such as Tepe Hisar),
is no longer valid. Field work has now demonstrated that red
wares extend southwards through central Kalat; that buff wares
are characteristic of the Quetta region and that 'identical designs
adorn both red and buff wares on a number of sites'.[2] As regards
foreign connexions there are at present hardly any eastern Iranian
sites which can be related satisfactorily to the early 'Ubaid–Uruk
period which we are considering in this chapter. Only at Rana
Ghundai in the Zhob valley, as we shall see when we come to
examine Hisar, can we pin down a prehistoric series of painted
pottery which must be contemporary with Sialk III. Otherwise
the bulk of the material from both Sīstān and Balūchistān is
subsequent to the beginning of the third millennium B.C. In
Afghanistān, however, as we shall see below, there are early

[1] *Ibid.* 195 ff.   [2] §IV, 9.

sequences in the province of Kalat. At one other site, Mundigak near Qandahār, it is alleged that in its earliest settlements connexions may be discerned with Hisar I C and with Sialk III, 7, but the evidence is defective; almost all of the pottery was made on the wheel.[1]

TEPE HISAR

The prehistoric part of the site[2] consists of a series of mounds some 600 m. in diameter, situated 3 km. south-east of the modern town of Dāmghān, about 4000 ft. above sea-level, on the south side of the Elburz mountains which flank the Caspian Sea. At all times it must have been an important entrepôt for trans-Caspian trade, a link in a long chain of connected settlements of which only a very few have so far been excavated. The accumulated débris of Hisar has been classified into three main periods, I A–C, II A–B, III A–C, each with sub-phases: Hisar I A is the earliest of the series. Although a rich variety of material was discovered we need not examine it in detail, for Hisar I and the earliest phase of Hisar II follow the general pattern of Sialk III so closely that the two sites can be taken as contemporary at this period; they must have been in close touch, and were probably connected by a route which passed through the gap in the Elburz mountains known as the Caspian Gates.

In examining the material from Hisar, however, we must take the precaution of admitting that much of it was not securely stratified, and the excavator himself gave a warning that occasionally the assignment of evidence to a specific sub-level could be erroneous. But broadly speaking we may accept the conclusion that Hisar I was characterized by a painted pottery; that in Hisar II, while grey ware predominated, painted pottery declined both numerically and in the quality of its designs. Some of the material assigned to Hisar II A is, however, suspect—the monochrome grey ware vases, elegantly shaped on high pedestals— and could more appropriately be related to Hisar II B, which may possibly have initiated a new period of occupation following a partial abandonment of the site. None the less, there is evidence that some grey wares were found in graves of Hisar II A.[3]

The architecture of Hisar I and II consisted of poorly built mud-brick and *pisé* houses, and in the first two periods the dead were buried under the floors. The total area of the settlement in Hisar I seems to have occupied about 10 acres of ground, and

[1] §IV, 6, 126 f. and folding table at end of book.　　[2] §IV, 32.
[3] §IV, 32, figs. 67–9 (Hisar II A) and fig. 70 (Hisar II B).

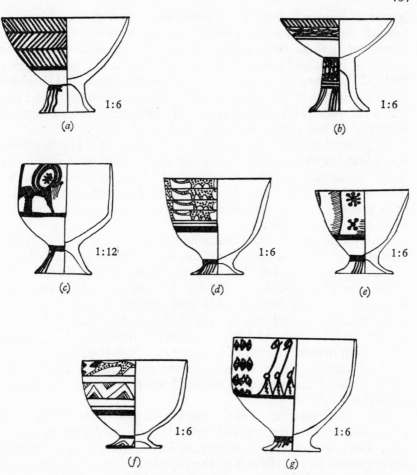

Fig. 42. Tepe Hisar, painted chalices and pedestal vases depicting caprids, leopards, long-necked animals, branches, sun symbols and various geometric designs. Paint is frequently brown on reddish-brown or grey-brown ground; (a) from Hisar I B, (b)–(f) from Hisar I C, (g) from Hisar II A. (See p. 456.)

the depth of débris on an average amounted to about 4–5 m. We may estimate a population of approximately 1500–2000 persons during this early period, which must have spanned several centuries.

Hisar I contained a painted pottery, made by hand in I A and afterwards wheel-turned (see Fig. 42). It included red and brown wares, and the pigment itself was sometimes grey in colour. The pots were decorated with the usual simple geometric patterns; the animal designs included files of water-fowl, birds, ibex, gazelles, leopards, human beings, snakes and trees often disposed in zones around pedestal vases. Similarity of decoration and technique implies that these vases belong to a ceramic province also represented at Sialk and confirms our conclusion for the later stages of Sialk II that these products belong to the end phase of 'Ubaid and the early stages of the Uruk period. They are abundant in Hisar I and II. After II A, new shapes and motifs appear, and these are posterior to the period which we are considering.

In general we may admit that Hisar I A–C and II A represent a single cultural period probably not earlier than the end phase of 'Ubaid, coinciding with some stages of Uruk, as is borne out not only by the pottery, wheel-turned after I A, but also by beads, seals and the metallurgy, all of which can be closely related with developments at Sialk.

Enormous quantities of beads had already occurred in Hisar I, including clay, shell and carnelian, as well as some lapis lazuli[1] in II A, turquoise and gold. This devotion to beads is characteristic of the later phases of the Uruk–Jamdat Naṣr period. There is also a variety of stone button seals and ornaments; the types find many parallels elsewhere, in Susa A, Giyān V c, Sialk III, 4, and Gawra 11 A.[2] M. L. and H. Erlenmeyer have recently given an interesting demonstration of the way in which the simple designs on the Hisar I seals are reflected in the pot-styles of Susa A, just as the seals of the preceding Sialk II are reflected in the designs of Giyān V c.[3]

Even more instructive is the metal-work, with its rich series of cast pins, needles, tracers and awls, daggers, and a heavy copper celt. Copper implements were rare in I A but showed a notable development in I C. Much of the copper had an admixture of up to 3 per cent of tin, apparently a natural alloy which cannot lay claim to being purposeful bronze. Flint blades were also used, and it is interesting that there was no evidence of obsidian, which was present, though only rarely, at Sialk.

In Hisar I, 144 burials were discovered in all; they were inhumations, skull and body usually on the right side in the contracted position, but without any regular orientation. The percentage of females was surprisingly small, rather less than one third of the total, but the evidence is insufficient to enable us to affirm that polyandry was practised. Infant mortality was fairly heavy. Few persons lived to be over the age of 50, most died adult between the ages of 21–45. Traces of garments and of matting

---

[1] §iv; 32, 133, H. 3003.
[2] Compare *ibid*. pl. xv, H. 4601 with §1, 36, pl. clx, no. 3.   [3] §iv, 14.

were found with the inhumations which had votive offerings
deposited with them. No special cemetery appears to have been
reserved for the dead at this time; indeed burials were ubiquitous:
in lanes, in rooms, in abandoned areas and in open places.

After Hisar II A there appears to be a considerable gap in the
sequence and we then reach a period subsequent to Jamdat Naṣr.

As we have seen above, some of the elegant grey wares which
have been assigned to II A fit better in II B, for they agree well
with pot types from Shāh Tepe which appear to be in a relatively
late sequence; an even later stage was manifest at Türeng Tepe.

The chronological correlations which we appear to be justified
in establishing with Mesopotamia are as follows:

Hisar I A = early Uruk and perhaps late 'Ubaid;

    I B = Uruk period, and Sialk III, 4–6;

    I C = Uruk period and Gawra 11 A.

We have also seen that this last stage of development probably
coincides approximately with Giyān V.

In Hisar II A the designs on the painted pottery, for example
the leopards, show a tendency to deformation, away from the
greater realism of an earlier stage in Iranian painting which was
most clearly demonstrated in Sialk III, 5, 6.[1] Representations of
these animals became truncated and in II B the geometric patterns
were perfunctorily applied and mark the decline of the older
painted styles.[2] Until further work is undertaken at Hisar it
is unsafe to attempt to determine the date of the sequences
Hisar II B–C, but it is possible that they may be contemporary
with some stage of the Early Dynastic period in Mesopotamia.
The strong Mesopotamian influence which during the Jamdat
Naṣr period was apparent in Sialk IV is altogether missing in
Hisar.

Hisar: Foreign relations. The importance of Hisar I–II is that
it provides us with a remarkable synchronism with Sialk III in
central Iran on the one hand, and with a known period of development in the prehistory of northern Balūchistān on the other. This
is proved by the discovery in the Zhob valley at the site of Rana
Ghundai of a painted pottery decorated with black buck on
pedestal vases, closely related in style to typical ware of Hisar I.
The equation is with Rana Ghundai II,[3] the second earliest stage
of development at that site, and it seems probable that the established route linking these two parts of Iran was through Nīshāpūr,
where, it is alleged, painted sherds that may be related to Hisar I

---

[1] §IV, 18, pls. LXVI, LXXX; §IV, 32, pl. XXI, H. 4460.
[2] §IV, 32, pl. XXIV.   [3] §IV, 30, 119 f. and fig. 13.

have been found. Here, therefore, at Hisar we have an important key to the prehistoric sequences, which indicates that already in the Uruk period there was a peripheral movement of traffic round the central desert of Iran which kept far-distant tracts of territory in touch with one another. It should also be noted that on the opposite north side of the Elburz mountains, at sites such as Türeng Tepe[1] and Shāh Tepe, the later Hisar sequences have been found, and it is not unlikely that in the deeper levels at the former site connexions would be found at least as far back as Hisar I, as they have been in the deepest levels of the latter.

The lowest strata at Shāh Tepe appear to be for the most part much later than the 'Ubaid and Uruk–Jamdat Naṣr periods, since grey ware was dominant from the first, and painted pottery rare. There were, however, red-ware vases with designs in black paint, as in Hisar I C.[2] Nevertheless, we have ample proof that most of the Shāh Tepe material is not earlier than Hisar II B, and many of the grey and black ware pot types can be assigned to the third rather than the fourth millennium B.C., for example, the knobbed ware also found in Hisar II B.[3]

In spite of the fact that the earliest Shāh Tepe occupations are post-Uruk, the osteological faunal material is relevant, for it must reflect some older, as well as some more recently introduced types. Thus J. W. Amschler[4] considers the skull of an ox of the *brachyceros* type to be a representation of the wild species from which the early domestic cattle of western Europe were descended. The domestic stock included, besides, short-horned cattle, sheep, and swine; allegedly also the horse, the ass, and the camel. We cannot omit a reference to these identifications even though they are based on a paucity of evidence—one bone each from III and very few from II. The diagnosis of domestication or variety is therefore provisional, but as far as the horse and camel are concerned, it recalls the evidence long ago adduced from remains in the early levels at Anau.

Standing as it does near the north-east entrance to Iran, Hisar is one of our earliest witnesses to the immemorial flow of prehistoric traffic which kept western, central and eastern Asia in touch with one another. The ramifications of that contact lie beyond the scope of this chapter, and we are still only in the initial stages of exploration. But a preview of these wide vistas

[1] §iv, 39; 40. [2] §iv, 1, pls. xli–lxii, xc–xci and p. 251.
[3] §iv, 1, pl. xxi, figs. 167, 168.
[4] *Ibid.* 345 for reference to his report on the animal remains.

of knowledge has in the last decade or so been provided by the
intensive excavations conducted under the auspices of the Turk-
menian Academy of Sciences at Namazga Tepe and at related
sites south-east of Anau, west of Merv.[1] This more recent work
has given direction to the findings in the great mound of Anau
where Pumpelly excavated at the beginning of this century. At
Jeitun (30 km. north-north-east of Ashkhābād), and in the
Namazga district, we may discern most of the early stages of
development which we have already discussed in this chapter—
stages which go back to the very beginnings of agriculture and
are succeeded by increasing urbanization, geometrically decorated
pottery and progressive efficiency in metallurgy.

In Anau I[2] we may detect links with Sialk I, and V. M. Masson has convincingly demonstrated the links between Anau II–
III, Sialk III and Hisar IB through IIA. Further correlations
can be established with prehistoric Quetta and with the cultures
of northern Balūchistān.[3] The most ancient sequences were observed at a site named Kile Gul Muḥammad, where a painted
ceramic was noted with a possible relationship in decoration and
in form to types found at Geöy Tepe in Azarbāyjān.[4] Typologically related to Kile Gul Muḥammad pottery is the Togau ware
of northern Kalat noted by Beatrice de Cardi, who also examined
a number of sites in central Balūchistān. Here in the Surāb
district, material from Anjiran is comparable with discoveries
made in the neolithic levels of the Belt cave[5] and Sialk I–III,
as well as with the earliest levels of Hisar from which the Baluchi
painted Togau ware was derived. Relationships farther east with
Indus Valley sites are more tenuous for this period, but will
doubtless become more firmly established when the water-
logged levels of Mohenjo Daro have been excavated with hydrau-
lic equipment. In southern Balūchistān in the Kej valley, and in
the Makrān, the evidence so far available for these early periods
is defective and for the most part does not antedate the third
millennium b.c. We have the impression that the earliest farmers
did not attempt to cultivate the more difficult and inhospitable
tracts of south-east Iran, and that these districts only became inhabited when shortage of irrigated land had resulted in tribal
movements away from the more naturally rich fields of habitation
elsewhere in western Asia.

We noted at the beginning of this section the inclination of pre-

[1] §ɪᴠ, 28.   [2] §ɪᴠ, 31.
[3] §ɪᴠ, 15; 24; 9.   [4] Compare §ɪᴠ, 9, 18, fig. 2 with §ɪᴠ, 5, pl. 1.
[5] See above, p. 441.

history in Iran to follow a compartmented development, district by district, in accordance with its own natural mountain barriers. Communities tended to be isolated because of the absence of great trunk rivers; and irrigation on a big scale under unified control as in southern Babylonia was not possible, though much was achieved in smaller areas. Yet in spite of these handicaps we have seen that every part of Iran was in due course affected by the pace of technological development in other parts of Asia. The results of archaeological investigation, wherever conducted, in the far corners of Iran and in its centre, have enabled us to establish certain sequences, chronological as well as typological, and there is little doubt that in the course of the next half century, aided by the powerful chronological weapon which the carbon-14 method provides, every important development in Iranian technology—agriculture, stock-breeding and the arts of civilization—will be intelligibly linked with corresponding advances that were taking place with the growth of cities from the Mediterranean in the west to China in the east.

CHAPTER IX (*a*)

PREDYNASTIC EGYPT

I. INTRODUCTION

T H E Predynastic Period is the name given to the time before the first historical dynasty of Egypt as far back as we can trace an unbroken line of civilizations. It is separated from the last stages of the Palaeolithic Period by a hiatus, a period during which no permanent occupation can be traced either in the Nile Valley or in the hills that bound it. It develops into the brilliant period of the archaic dynasties, which mark its end and which in their turn were the foundation of the Pyramid Age.

The length of time needed for this development must have been considerable, but we cannot yet measure it in terms of years before the beginning of the Christian Era. When the carbon-14 method of dating, based on the measurement of the remaining radio-activity of the radioactive isotope of carbon (carbon-14) has passed the experimental stage, some of our difficulties may disappear.

To overcome the dating difficulties Sir W. M. Flinders Petrie devised a system which was intended to establish the historical sequence of the predynastic periods, not in absolute dates but in relation to each other. When he first evolved it in 1901 he had excavated the large predynastic cemeteries of Naqāda and El-Ballās and those which he published under the title of *Diospolis Parva*. His system[1] was an attempt to bring some order into the material from the thousands of tombs which he had excavated, by establishing 'relative ages' or 'sequence dates' (S.D.). This system was based on the comparison of groups of pottery found in a series of graves containing certain characteristic pots. Petrie assigned fifty stages to the whole Predynastic Period, as it was then known, and numbered them S.D. 30–80, leaving S.D. 1–29 for earlier cultures should they be discovered. These stages were further grouped into two main divisions; an earlier division from S.D. 30–37; and a later from S.D. 38–80, eventually altered to S.D. 76 when Petrie came to the conclusion that the Dynastic

[1] §II, 38, 4–12.

[463]

Period began at S.D. 76.[1] Even this lower date has had to be revised, and it is now considered that the beginning of the First Dynasty corresponds with S.D. 63.[2] These stages, it must be emphasized, do not correspond with any calendar or absolute dates, nor is there any guarantee that they were all of equal length; they merely indicate a series of consecutive steps so that an object dated S.D. 32 is earlier than others dated S.D. 33 and S.D. 34, but the period of time separating those three stages may vary to a greater or a lesser degree.

Petrie's division of the material into two main sections still holds good, but the system of sequence dates is in need of complete revision and can be used only after checking each individual case. The reason for this is that the two main classes of pottery which were used as the foundation of the system are now known to have ranges different from those originally assigned to them. The white cross-lined pottery, to which Petrie gave a very short life from S.D. 31–34, in fact continued until S.D. 38, and may even have continued into the later stage, as Brunton maintained.[3] In consequence, some of the tombs which Petrie dated to S.D. 31–34 on the strength of the discovery in them of white cross-lined pottery may have to be dated considerably later.

For the later period Petrie took the wavy-handled pottery as his characteristic type, and assumed for it a development, or rather deterioration, in form on which he based his dating. This assumption also has proved to be mistaken and the sequence dates assigned to graves on the strength of this argument have to be altered.

Moreover, the system of sequence dating is at present based entirely on the results of the excavation of cemeteries and the study of tomb equipment. It needs to be supplemented by the evidence of excavations in stratified settlements.

Petrie's interest in sequence dates did not cease when he had devised and published his system. In his first modification he divided the known predynastic cultures into three, instead of two, groups[4] and subsequently named them Amratian (S.D. 30–37), Gerzean (S.D. 38–63), and Semainian (S.D. 64–76). These names were derived not from Naqāda where these cultures were first discovered, but from excavations of lesser importance near villages whose names he adopted for his revised grouping.

This revised system did not find the same ready acceptance as its predecessor, for Semainian covers mainly, if not wholly, the

[1] G, 16, 55.
[2] §I, 3; §II, 14; §II, 25.
[3] §II, 11; §II, 13.
[4] G, 14, 46–50.

Protodynastic Period. Most scholars retained the division into two periods, which they called Amratian and Gerzean, and these names are still used by some writers. Others, however, taking into account the fact that both civilizations were first found by Petrie at Naqāda and that the cemeteries there are the largest and most important of their age so far known, have preferred to adopt the terms Naqāda I for the earlier, and Naqāda II for the later period. As will be shown, there is no total break between the civilizations, as the unconnected names Amratian and Gerzean might suggest, but rather a grafting of something new on to an old stem. Accordingly, the terms Naqāda I and Naqāda II will be used here.

To these two predynastic periods a third period has been added, the Badārian, as a result of the excavations of Brunton and Miss Caton-Thompson near El-Badāri. In a stratified excavation at El-Hammāmīya Miss Caton-Thompson was able to demonstrate that the Badārian Period preceded Naqāda I.[1] It is at present the oldest known civilization of predynastic Egypt.

Tombs dating from these consecutive periods have been found in excavations at numerous sites in Upper Egypt, Badārian only in the neighbourhood of El-Qāw, Naqāda I only south of Asyūt and in the Faiyūm, and Naqāda II in Lower Egypt also. The only predynastic Egyptian site claimed to be older than all the others was found by Junker, Scharff and Menghin at Merimda Beni Salāma on the edges of the western Delta.[2] This, it is claimed, is a 'neolithic' culture related to that found in the Faiyūm by Miss Caton-Thompson who gave it the name of 'Faiyūm Neolithic'.[3]

THE COUNTRY

The people who first ventured into the Nile Valley must have found a countryside very different from that of modern Egypt. To-day a majestic but controlled Nile runs in the midst of well-tended fields which reach as far as the fertilizing waters can be brought, at which point the desert begins abruptly. Each town and village lies on its own artificial mound which keeps it above the yearly inundation. At the beginning of the periods with which we are concerned here the Nile must have flowed through thickets of papyrus and rushes, similar to those that can now be found only much farther upstream, and these must have abounded with animals harmful to man. For a third of the year life on the

[1] §II, 13, 69–79 (see below, p. 467). [2] §II, 4; §II, 23.
[3] §II, 47.

floor of the valley was impossible for men and herds because of the inundation. It is not surprising, therefore, that the earliest settlements are found on the low spurs of the desert out of reach of the inundation and swamps. These low terraces of the Nile Valley were not then the desert they are now; they could still support trees and other vegetation, as has been shown by the excavation of the roots and trunks of trees in places where none could exist today.

It is not known when these early settlers first began to cultivate fields on the floor of the valley. It must have been hard work even to clear a plot sufficient for their small needs, but once this had been done the fields would repay the cultivator for all his efforts, for here was inexhaustible soil. Each year the inundation would fertilize the earth and grain could be sown year after year in the same place. This must have been an inducement for early man to become sedentary.

There is no way of telling where the precise borders of this predynastic Egypt lay. The southern frontier may well have been relatively vague and undefined, for though the bulk of the known early cemeteries lie north of Luxor, a few graves of Naqāda I date have been found a few miles south of Aswān at Khōr Bahan in Nubia. In the extreme north the Mediterranean formed the natural frontier of the land.

This long, but not very wide, stretch of land was divided, as excavation has shown, into three distinct parts. The earliest settlers, including those of Naqāda I times, are not found farther north than Asyūt, and it is here that the frontier with Lower Egypt must have been. This was pointed out long ago by von Bissing,[1] by Schneider[2] and most convincingly by Sethe[3] who said: 'Siut and its nome always, even in later times, played a special part as a kind of frontier town or boundary. There ended the "Head of Upper Egypt" (*tp šmʿw*), i.e. the southernmost part of the country beginning at the cataract of Elephantine, the Thebaid of Greek times,[4] and there began the *Heptanomoi* which as early as the New Kingdom was ascribed to Lower Egypt. Perhaps the name of the town, which may mean nothing more than "guardian", refers to this role as frontier post.' Wainwright pointed out that this frontier corresponded with the geographical

---

[1] Bissing-Kees, *Untersuchungen zu den Reliefs aus dem Re-Heiligtum des Rathures* I, 32.

[2] Schneider, *Kultur und Denken*, 38.   [3] Sethe, *Urgeschichte*, 48, 74.

[4] See *C.A.H.* I³, ch. xx, sect. III. On the reading *tp-šmʿw* (more probably *tp-rs*) see Gardiner, *J.E.A.* 43 (1957), 6–9.

character of the Nile Valley, and that there was a 'natural' frontier between Asyūt and Cusae.[1] These arguments have not, however, prevented many modern scholars from identifying the Lower Egypt of the ancients with the Delta. The absence of settlements of the Badārian and Naqāda I civilizations north of Asyūt clearly suggests that in predynastic times, Asyūt marked the northern limit of Upper Egypt and its cultures.

Cemeteries and settlements of the later part of the Naqāda II Period have been found as far north as the region of modern Cairo. The neighbourhood of Cairo, therefore, seems to have been the northern frontier of Lower Egypt.

To the north of this is the Nile Delta, the third division of predynastic Egypt, at whose western edge, to the north-west of Cairo, is the settlement of Merimda.

II. THE PREDYNASTIC CIVILIZATIONS

BADĀRIAN

The first stratified excavation in a predynastic village was undertaken by Miss Caton-Thompson near the modern village of El-Hammāmīya when she found a midden formed of the debris of predynastic settlements.[2] It was more than six feet deep, overlaid by a wash of clean white limestone scree about eleven inches thick and resting on a deposit of breccia of great hardness some twelve inches thick. Below this unbroken layer of breccia was a relatively clean stratum of limestone rubble and dust, undisturbed and certainly not affected by later infiltrations, in which were found some Badārian sherds and flint implements. Immediately above the breccia, forming the lowest part of the midden, were more Badārian flints and sherds in what the excavator calls 'a temporary camping-ground'. Over this Badārian layer was a disturbed layer, and above that were two more strata, of which the lower contained objects of the Naqāda I Period, and the upper objects of Naqāda II.

Remains, generally not more than a few inches deep, of what Brunton called either villages or towns were found on many spurs at the foot of the cliffs, especially in the area numbered El-Badāri 5500. Here, said Brunton, 'seems to have been the centre of the Badārian town'. No details of these settlements are given, apart from the inventory of the finds, which include cooking pots, some of which still stood in what may have been hearths (holes in

---

[1] *Ann. Serv.* 27 (1927), 93 ff.   [2] §II, 13, 69–79.

the ground surrounded by 'ashy' earth), samples of the finer, rippled pottery, bone piercers, the remains of baskets, and rough flint flakes.

More of these domestic remains and also cemeteries were discovered by Brunton in later excavations at El-Mustagidda[1] and El-Matmar,[2] both in the El-Badāri district. At El-Mustagidda, in the neighbourhood of Deir Tāsa, he considered that he had found a civilization, which he called 'Tāsian', even older than the Badārian. He based his identification of this culture very largely on a particular type of pottery consisting of deep bowls with a small flattish base and angular sides narrowing towards the mouth. These vessels, divided by Brunton into two classes according to their colour—brown, or grey-black—seem to be cooking pots. All the other objects tentatively assigned to the Tāsian culture (limestone axes, palettes of hard stones, and black-incised beakers) could not be proved to be specifically Tāsian by the original excavations at El-Mustagidda or the subsequent work at El-Matmar.

A single type of pottery seems to be a rather slender foundation on which to base the claim for the existence of a new culture, particularly as there is no stratigraphical evidence by which to separate Tāsian from Badārian. In the cemeteries, moreover, 'Tāsian' graves are mixed with those of the Badārian Period and do not appear to occupy separate parts in the cemeteries. It may be suggested, therefore, that it is too early to speak of a 'Tāsian civilization' as distinct from the Badārian; our knowledge of the Badārian is still far too scanty to enable us to exclude with any degree of certainty the possibility that the so-called typical Tāsian bowls will be found in a site that may with certainty be ascribed to the Badārian Period.

Information concerning the Badārian settlements has been increased by the discovery at El-Matmar of the remains of a number of granaries, irregular in shape and lined with basket-work. Only Badārian pottery was found near them. It consisted mainly of cooking pots, of which some of the undamaged examples were still standing *in situ* upside down in thin layers of ashes, indications of hearths. These, and the querns which were not infrequently found in the same places, show that the grain was not only stored in the granaries, but that it was also ground and eaten on the spot. Brunton was undoubtedly right in calling these areas villages more permanent than the hunting-camp of the lowest stratum above the layer of breccia at El-Hammāmīya. The

[1] §II, 11.   [2] §II, 12.

grain found in these granaries was starch-wheat or emmer (*Triticum dicoccum*), and barley.

None of the villages preserved any traces of houses. Whether the Badārians lived in tents or constructed huts of perishable materials is for the present an open question. They must have occupied the region of El-Badāri fairly densely, for many of the spurs showed traces of their presence. All this speaks in favour of their having been more than casual visitors to the Nile Valley; they seem to have settled permanently on the low spurs. With this conclusion the number and size of their cemeteries agree. The cemeteries at El-Badāri and El-Mustagidda each contained more than three hundred graves, but at El-Matmar the Badārian cemetery was small.

Most of the Badārian graves are oval; only some of the larger and more important are rectangular, often with rounded corners. Graves of women were in general larger than those of men. Some had niches large enough to accommodate one or more pots. Remains of coarse matting found together with sticks suggest some sort of roofing. Each grave, as a rule, contained a single contracted burial, though occasionally there were two or more burials. Most of the bodies faced west, the head being generally to the south. The bodies were either put into hampers, or wrapped in matting, more rarely in skins of goats or gazelles, or perhaps in shrouds, though it is difficult to ascertain whether the remnants of linen material found belonged to shrouds or to garments worn by the dead. Both skins and linen were worn, sometimes as kilts or short skirts, but large shirts or robes were also favoured. As bone needles, in some cases still with the threads, were found only in the graves of males, tailoring must have been a prerogative of the men. The position of the linen in some graves indicates that turbans were in fashion. In one case (El-Mustagidda grave 302)[1] the cloth had fringes.

Some of the men wore girdles or belts of blue cylindrical beads —in one case interspersed with white, arranged in many strings around their waists. Investigation proved most of the blue beads to be steatite glazed blue in imitation of turquoise, though some beads of real turquoise were among them. Beads of soft stones, and only rarely of hard stones or of copper, shells, and the pink tubes of organ coral, singly or in strings, adorned necks, wrists and ankles. In three instances small amulets were found with beads: two represent hippopotami; the third is an exquisite little carving in bone of the head of a gazelle and was 'apparently' worn at

[1] §ɪɪ, 11, 34.

the ankle.[1] These amulets may have been hunting charms. Bracelets, of ivory, bone or horn, were worn on the forearm; broad and narrow types have been found, all normally having a sharp ridge round the circumference. A characteristic feature was the decoration of some of these bracelets, either with a chevron pattern of inlaid blue beads, or with a succession of rounded knobs. Bone and ivory were also used for ornamental combs and were sometimes crowned with carved animals or birds. Whether the studs of smooth black pottery were worn in the ears, as Brunton suggested, or served some other purpose is difficult to decide. A small stud of pale green stone was found *in situ* in the right nostril of a man (El-Badāri, grave 5359).[2]

Cosmetics were used by both men and women. They were kept in small ivory vases which the Badārian craftsmen carved with great skill. Everyone had to grind his own cosmetics on palettes of slate or other stone. The Badārians preferred rectangular palettes, the shorter sides curved or notched, perhaps in order to fix them between sticks to prevent their slipping when used. The material ground on these palettes was green malachite, which, after grinding, was mixed with some fat or resin, perhaps with oil of the castor plant of which seeds were found, and made into a smooth paste which could be applied to the face or body.

Animals and humans were buried in the same cemeteries. The bodies of the animals were wrapped in matting and linen, and their graves did not differ from those of humans except in their lack of tomb furniture. The remains found were those of small carnivores, either dog or jackal, cows and sheep.[3]

Ivory or bone was the material used for spoons and ladles, some of which have elaborate handles surmounted by the figures and heads of animals.

The most common, and the most characteristic, part of the tomb furniture is the pottery. Potsherds also made up the bulk of the finds in the 'temporary camp' at El-Hammāmīya.[4] Broadly speaking, Badārian pottery can be divided into two main groups: the coarse ware, and the fine ware.

The coarse ware is either smooth brown or rough brown and the shapes are simple. Bowls and deep cooking pots are common; they do not have lips or necks, and nearly all have rounded bases. Bottles occur occasionally, and among the smooth brown is a deep-keeled bowl which is found infrequently.

---

[1] §11, 13, 27. [2] §11, 13, 10.
[3] Dr D. M. S. Watson, who identified the specimens, speaks of a 'cow-buffalo'.
[4] See above, p. 467.

The best specimens of the fine ware have thinner walls than any other predynastic Egyptian pottery, the rims being so thin and brittle that many have crumbled away. Such vessels can be of great beauty. Three types of fine ware are known: polished red (which means that it has a red slip which was polished or burnished with a pebble before baking), polished black, and red or brown polished with a black top. The shapes do not differ much from those of the coarse ware, but the deep-set keel occurs very frequently. The most characteristic feature is the rippled surface which decorates many of the finest pots, and is even found, though somewhat sketchily, on some of the coarse pots. This rippling was produced by combing the surface of the still soft clay with an implement having closely set teeth and then burnishing with a pebble.[1]

The black top is another decorative feature of Badārian pottery, a feature that is also characteristic of some later predynastic wares. Black-topped pottery is found in Nubia and the Sudan from very early times; it remained in fashion there long after the Egyptians had abandoned it. Until the New Kingdom it was repeatedly brought into Egypt by intruders from the south. It is likely, therefore, that the Badārians came originally from the south, for there this technique and rippling seem to have their home.

Some Badārian pots have interior patterns made with a burnishing pebble which makes them appear shiny on a matt background. Plant- and branch-designs occur, crossed lines, and lines round the edges.

Among the mass of pottery found at El-Badāri a few specimens stand out by reason of their unusual form and texture, or their decoration. There are the black beakers, heavy and thick-walled, and incised with geometrical patterns into which a white substance has been rubbed to make them more conspicuous. These vessels have long been a problem, for no specimen which can be dated with certainty has yet been found in an excavation, although a number of well-preserved examples, known to have come from Egypt, have reached museums. One was discovered by Brunton in grave 569 at El-Badāri,[2] but the grave was disturbed. Near the feet of the body was a group consisting of the beaker in question, a slab of selenite, and a large flint knife. The selenite slab had traces of wood around it and Brunton suggested that it might have been a mirror, an object that would be unique among predynastic antiquities. The flint knife, pressure flaked from both

[1] See Plate 9 (a).   [2] §II, 13, 3 and pl. xxvi.

sides, resembles early dynastic types but has no Badārian parallel. It is impossible not to question whether this group was really part of a Badārian grave. Scattered along the west side of the grave and near the arm were a rough brown pot, a beautifully rippled bowl, which was undoubtedly Brunton's reason for dating the grave to the Badārian Period, and a pot of pinkish buff ware 'resembling that of predynastic wavy-handled jars', having a narrow neck and four vertical handles round the middle. The type of the last-mentioned pot is not Egyptian; it belongs to the group found in the Royal Tombs at Abydos and called 'Aegean' by Petrie.[1] In no circumstances can it be dated to Badārian times; it may be late predynastic or protodynastic. The explanation of this heterogeneous collection seems to be that at the same level as grave 569, and so close to it that it was numbered 569a, was another grave in which was a mud coffin of 'late predynastic, or, more probably, protodynastic date', and a slate palette, which Brunton considered to be Badārian and to have been part of the original equipment of grave 569. It seems more likely that both graves are protodynastic and that the Badārian pots are intrusive. This is the more probable since Brunton stated that the plot in which the graves were found had served as a rubbish dump in modern times and had been constantly used as a burial ground from Badārian until Roman times. From the evidence at present available, it does not seem possible to ascribe the black beakers to Badārian times; more probably they belong to the protodynastic period which, as we know, produced some late and peculiar offshoots of Petrie's black-incised ware of Naqāda II.

Our knowledge of Badārian flint industry is largely drawn from El-Hammāmīya which preserved a wider range of types than the graves. Rather unexpectedly, and in contrast with the achievements of the potters, the flint industry is rough and poor. It is predominantly a core industry made from nodules found on the surface of the desert and not from the much better flint in the limestone cliffs. This indicates that the original home of the Badārians must be sought in a region which lacked flint and forced them to use inferior stone. Since the flint-bearing tertiary limestones extend northwards from near Esna to the Mediterranean, such a region can only be sought to the south.

The most common Badārian tools are small push-planes with steep ends, bifacial sickle-stones with serrated cutting edges, and saws made in the same technique but rather more rare. The types of their axes and adzes are not known.

[1] Petrie, *Abydos*, i, pl. VIII, 6–8.

The Badārians possessed some copper, of which some beads and a single small tool, perhaps a pin, were made.

Very few weapons have been found, and these only winged or leaf-shaped arrow heads, which suggests the use of bows, though none of the latter have come to light. Some wooden sticks which Brunton called throw sticks, were recovered. They generally occurred in pairs and, being flat, it is perhaps more likely that they were castanets. They are curved in a way similar to the castanets which are seen in the hands of some men represented on pots of the Naqāda II decorated ware.

Nothing is known of the political organization of the Badārians. Their settlements were of some size, and in them they conducted mixed farming: agriculture and the breeding of livestock. Hunting and fishing must have played an important part in their economy, especially fishing to judge from the number of fish-bones found at El-Hammāmīya and in the graves. Their industries were probably still practised by both men and women when the need arose, and not by professional craftsmen; yet they must have produced a surplus of finished articles or of raw material with which to barter for those things which they could not make themselves. Brunton considered that the glazed beads found in such large numbers were imported, and also the copper, and perhaps even the manufactured copper objects. Many of the shells used for personal ornaments came from the Red Sea or the Persian Gulf. Most important is the fact that the grain, wheat and barley, which the Badārians cultivated, and their domesticated animals, especially sheep and goats, were of Asiatic origin and must originally have been acquired through some contact with Asia. The first contact must have been prior to their arrival in the Nile Valley, for they already practised agriculture when first we meet them there.

The study of the human skeletons from El-Badāri and El-Mustagidda has shown that already at that early age the population was of mixed origin, some having a fine, and some a heavily built skull. Their skulls were closely related to those of the people of Naqāda I and II.

NAQĀDA I

The civilization of Naqāda I was discovered in 1895 by Sir Flinders Petrie in the large cemeteries which he excavated near the modern village of Naqāda.[1] Petrie also discovered the town sites connected with these cemeteries, but in those early days no

[1] §II, 39 (see above, pp. 463–5).

stratified excavation was undertaken. De Morgan's excavations in the same region, in what he calls the 'kjœkkenmœdings de Toukh', were no more helpful, for nothing is known of his excavations apart from a quantity of material without reference to the circumstances of its discovery.[1] The only reliable work in a settlement is that of Miss Caton-Thompson at El-Hammāmīya,[2] supplemented by the excavations of O. H. Myers at Armant.[3] Both these places were settlements of little importance in antiquity, and were relatively late Naqāda I, beginning at about S.D. 35. We lack, therefore, stratigraphical evidence on which to base a typology of pottery or flints with which to date the graves, and we are compelled to rely on Petrie's sequence dating.

Since Petrie mistakenly assigned to the white cross-lined pottery[4] a duration of S.D. 31–34, a fatal misunderstanding has arisen. In a few graves Petrie found the decorated ware of Naqāda II in a Naqāda I context and concluded that the decorated ware must have been produced in a nearby country at a time when Upper Egypt used the white cross-lined. This fallacy has haunted our studies ever since. As Brunton showed[5] not only did the white cross-lined pottery exist through Naqāda I, but it also continued into early Naqāda II. It follows, therefore, that the graves of Naqāda I that contain either true decorated pots or imitations of them, far from belonging to the beginning of the period, must be assigned to the end of Naqāda I, or to the period of transition.

Our most important source of information for the Naqāda I civilization is still the cemeteries of Naqāda where it was first discovered. Brunton was of the opinion that a break of some kind must have intervened between the end of Badārian and the beginning of Naqāda I. This he inferred from the fact that Badārian and later predynastic cemeteries were always on separate sites. Miss Caton-Thompson, however, suggests a considerable overlap of cultures at the end of the Badārian period which she thinks may have lasted until well into the S.D. 30's, and this in spite of a disturbed layer at El-Hammāmīya between the Badārian and Naqāda I strata. O. H. Myers, on the evidence of his material from Armant, supports Miss Caton-Thompson, for he found Badārian pottery, especially the black-topped brown and the smooth brown ware, in his Naqāda I stratum.

In the midden at El-Hammāmīya, above the disturbed post-Badārian stratum, were the ruins of a number of small huts or

---

[1] G, 12. [2] §II, 13, 69 ff. [3] §II, 35, vol. I, 163 ff.
[4] See Plate 9 (f). [5] §II, 13, pl. xxxviii, type C 16 m.

storehouses[1] which, as the potsherds in and around them showed, belonged to the later part of Naqāda I and the earliest part of Naqāda II (S.D. 35–45). The huts were roughly circular and varied in diameter from three to seven feet. The enclosing walls were made of mud mixed with limestone chips and blocks and were about one foot thick. The external surfaces often bore imprints of bundles of reeds or straw that had been pressed against them; the inner face was of smooth, grey mud which merged without break into the beaten mud of the slightly concave floor. These walls formed continuous circles and must have acted as skirting or support for a superstructure or roofing of perishable materials of which no trace had survived. There were no doors or openings in the walls, and entry into the interior must have been effected through openings presumably at the junction of the wall and superstructure, a circumstance which would have necessitated an awkward drop of between 18 and 33 inches according to the height of the wall above the floor. In similar huts found in the top stratum at Merimda on the fringes of the western Delta the tibia of a hippopotamus was used as a step;[2] we may imagine a similar device here. Whereas one of the circles had a hearth on its north-west side and was clearly a habitation, one of the smallest was filled with desiccated sheep or goat dung and was evidently a fuel store: the circles must therefore have served more than one purpose.

Enough sherds of both wares were found in the huts to confirm Petrie's assumption that the white cross-lined pottery began earlier than the decorated ware.

Wooden posts and postholes discovered in one corner of the El-Hammāmīya settlement, and explained as the remains of windscreens, were similar to those found by Garstang at El-Mahāsna.[3]

The only other settlement excavated with due attention to the levels is that worked by O. H. Myers at Armant.[4] This site was shallow and had no visible stratification nor any remains of huts; some cooking pots, however, were found upright *in situ*. The settlement is reminiscent of those mentioned by Brunton in the neighbourhood of El-Badāri. Its life is dated from S.D. 35 to the end of the Predynastic Period.

On the evidence of the pottery, the settlement at El-Mahāsna must have dated back to Naqāda I, but only a very sketchy plan and description exist. Of the two settlements which Petrie found

[1] §II, 13, 82–8.
[2] §II, 23: 1932, 47 and Abb. 1 and 2.
[3] §II, 19, 5–8; pl. 4.
[4] §II, 35, vol. I, 163–258.

near Naqāda, that which he called the South Town is the more important. It lies on the bank of a wādi opposite the historical temple of Seth Nubti, and was the predynastic town of Nubt (*nbt*). Petrie speaks of fortifications and quasi-rectangular houses built of the same small bricks as were used in some tombs of Naqāda II. The small published map shows part of a settlement very different from all those mentioned above; this was indeed a fortified town. The area excavated by Petrie measured about 100 metres square. This was not the original extent of the city, which must have been larger, and part of it was built over in the New Kingdom. The material brought back from Nubt is considerable, and includes sherds, stone vases, spindle whorls, ivories, flints, slate palettes and a solid copper pin. The white cross-lined pottery suggests that the town existed in Naqāda I times, but neither the material nor any of the buildings can be dated by stratigraphical evidence. It would have been interesting to know whether the fortifications were already in existence in Naqāda I. That settlements had walls we know from the unique fragment published in *Diospolis Parva*, from Abādīya, grave B 83;[1] it is a portion of a clay model of a battlemented wall behind which stand two men on the look-out. Grave B 83 is rather loosely dated to S.D. 33–48, which corresponds in age with the settlements of El-Hammāmīya and Armant.[2]

The shapes of the graves are not different from those of the Badārians. Whether the largest and rectangular tombs were again mostly those of women is difficult to ascertain on account of the lack of observation. The largest and fullest grave at Abādīya (B 101, *Diospolis Parva*) was that of a woman. Other big graves contained up to seven bodies of both sexes including children. The custom of wrapping the bodies in mats or shrouds, or putting them into wicker baskets still persisted.

Bodies were buried in the contracted position, as in the Badārian Period, usually with the head south and the face west. They were decked in all their finery, but of their dress we know even less than of that of the Badārians. Remains of linen and of skins sewn together have been found, but there is no indication of the types of garments to which they belonged. A pair of model sandals in ivory (S.D. 32) was recovered.[3] The green face paint was still ground on green slate palettes. Palettes in geometrical forms prevail, though some in animal form are also found. The most common are the rhombic palettes, some of these were made

---

[1] §II, 38, 32, pl. VI; §I, 4, fig. 160 (see Plate 12(*b*)).
[2] §II, 38, pl. X, 19.   [3] §II, 38, pl. X, 19.

in enormous sizes up to 42 centimetres and more in length, whilst others are not longer than about five centimetres. These are too small to have had any practical use, and must have been amulets. Some of the larger rhombic slates have decorations at one or both of their tips. The horns and ears of the cow goddess occur several times. Other palettes are in the shape of Nile turtles, hippopotami, hartebeests or birds. The curious double bird appears here for the first time.

Haircombs were smaller than in Badārian times; the top was usually plain or was sometimes carved with the figure of a bird or quadruped. Among the latter is the remarkable figure from El-Mahāsna which is generally taken to be the earliest representation of the strange animal of the god Seth, though lacking one of its characteristics, its tail.[1] The double bird occurs, though some of the carvings thus described by Petrie are the ears and horns of the cow-goddess. New are the long ivory pins worn in the hair, either plain or with an incised pattern, and with a knob or bird at the top. An elegant piece is flat and ends in a serpent.

Armlets of shell, bone or ivory remain in favour, and also rings of ivory, some of them decorated with a knob. Beads are still mostly of soft stones; long strings of pottery beads also occur. The handsome belts of blue beads worn by the Badārians are now out of fashion.

The commonest grave equipment, the pottery, can be divided into the fine and the coarse ware; the latter is rare in graves of this period. The fine ware includes red polished, black polished, black topped on red, and, for the first time, a painted ware of definite type—the white cross-lined. The shapes are still mostly simple: bowls or beakers, some with lips, slender vases and bottles. Occasionally an odd shape is found: vases with four feet, chalices with cylindrical base, and a pot made of two communicating tubes. The texture is no longer so thin or so fine as in Badārian days, and the beautiful Badārian vases are now replaced by stone vessels cylindrical in form. Probably towards the end of the period, basalt vases with small feet were introduced, forerunners of a type more common in Naqāda II.

The white cross-lined pottery is by far the most interesting product of Naqāda I.[2] White or cream colour is used on the polished red ware or, occasionally, on the black topped. The patterns are mostly geometrical; only rarely are scenes including men and animals depicted.

Many of the motifs are known from the painted vase civilizations of western Asia, but it is not yet possible to trace how the

[1] §II, 6, pl. XII, 2. [2] See Plate 9(f).

connexions between these distant countries were effected. Since the civilization of Naqāda I seems to have had its roots to the south of Egypt, whence peoples with kindred cultures entered Egypt again and again far into historical times, it seems likely that these influences came by way of the Persian Gulf, where painted vase civilizations have been found at Bandar-Bushire and Old Hurmuz, and along the south coast of Arabia; but this is mere hypothesis.

Together with the patterns and the art of painting, some of the shapes of pottery were taken from these foreign sources; the footed chalice, the beaker with a wide, flat bottom, the carinated pot with narrow mouth and straight neck, all these are common in Iran but unusual in Egypt where they disappear with the cross-lined painting.

Our knowledge of the Naqāda I flint industry is greatly hampered by the lack of dated material from settlements. It is evident, however, that the flint industry had developed greatly since Badārian times. Gone are the days when crude surface nodules were used. Only the best quality of mined flint could serve to produce the large double-edged knives, up to 35 centimetres long and only a few millimetres thick, with finely serrated edges, the fish-tails, and the curved knives.[1] All these objects were made by the same technique: the flint was first thinned down to the required shape and then pressure flaked from both sides. This is not the product of casual workers, but of highly skilled craftsmen. Here for the first time we are confronted with an industry, the mining and flaking of flint. This, in turn, implies that the community was now able to support some of its members who were not engaged in the production of food, and this would not have been possible unless the community had accumulated a certain amount of wealth.

In the graves flints are rare and are restricted, in the main, to the show-pieces just mentioned; these could hardly have been of any practical use and may have been regarded as possessing some magical potency. The South Town of Naqāda furnished the best collection of household flints at present known, but it is difficult to separate those of Naqāda I from those of Naqāda II. The only help is provided by the material from Miss Caton-Thompson's excavations in the Faiyūm,[2] but here, once again, we are confronted by difficulties in dating.

In the Faiyūm, Miss Caton-Thompson excavated two *kōms* in which she found, together with pottery and other domestic re-

[1] See Plate 10 (*b*).   [2] §II, 47.

mains, the flint industry, which had long been known in this area, for the first time *in situ*. She called this culture 'Fayum Neolithic A', and attempted to show that the settlements she had excavated were in all probability earlier than Naqāda I and II, because twisted flint blades characteristic of Naqāda II were found on the top of the *kōms*, and no Neolithic A was found in the Naqāda II settlement inside the Faiyūm. No more definite conclusion could be drawn from the ancient shore lines, for the Naqāda II remains lay well within the range of the neolithic lake levels.[1] This tends to show that Naqāda II cannot be much later than Faiyūm A, even though it may not be contemporaneous. This does not support the dating of Faiyūm A to Badārian times.

Among the flints from the South Town at Naqāda are nearly all of the types of Faiyūm A: the small axes, flaked and with ground cutting edges, triangular and winged arrow-heads, leaf-shaped points, planes, hoe-shaped tools, and sickle-stones, all worked bifacially from cores and with the shallow retouch like those of the Faiyūm.[2]

Petrie was very thorough in his collecting at Naqāda and he appears to have brought home every artefact. Examination has shown that while some Naqāda II graves contained dozens of small unworked blades, there were none in those of Naqāda I. In the Faiyūm, also, the small blades are found after Faiyūm A in what is called Faiyūm B. These facts lead to the conclusion that the Faiyūm A flint industry is closely related, if not identical with, that of Naqāda I, and not earlier in date. With this conclusion also agrees the fact that the disc-shaped mace head found in Faiyūm A is also the characteristic mace head of Naqāda I; no mace heads are known at El-Badāri. The pottery of Faiyūm A is much coarser than anything known from Naqāda I; however, it has such forms as the chalice with cylindrical base, and the vase with four feet,[3] though reduced to mere knobs (like Naqāda F 24 b).

There is not much to be said about the weapons of the Naqāda I people. The new weapon, if it is a weapon, is the disc-shaped mace head, of which some that have been found in tombs may have had only a symbolic use. The small hole provided for hafting is insufficient for a strong handle, and any handle, particularly one of horn or ivory, like those found in a tomb at Diospolis Parva,[4] would snap if used with any violence. Also the long flint knives do not seem very efficient weapons, for they would not stand any rough handling.

[1] §II, 47, vol. I, 69.
[2] G, 3, vol. II, 24 ff.
[3] See above, p. 477.
[4] §II, 38, 24, 33, pl. v.

Copper is still very scarce in the graves. It may be mere chance that the only finds were some copper foil, and small pins whose heads were made by curving over one end to form a loop.[1]

The complete absence of gold from graves of the period is probably to be explained by the accident of preservation. Gold would naturally be the first object sought by the tomb-robber. It seems highly unlikely that the people of Naqāda, who used copper, should have been ignorant of gold, which, unlike copper, need not be smelted from the ore, and which could be found in their very neighbourhood, between the Nile and the Red Sea, in mines which are rich enough to be worked again to-day. In this context the ancient name of Naqāda is significant. It is *Nbt*, the feminine form of the Egyptian word for gold. Towns are feminine in Egyptian; the name of the town would mean gold. While it cannot be proved that this name goes back to Naqāda I, there is no reason to suspect that the name of the town changed during the transition from predynastic to historic times. If Naqāda was indeed the town 'Gold' it might indicate that the town obtained its name because possession of gold, working it and trading in it, were its outstanding characteristics, just as in historic times Egypt was the land of gold. If gold was the source of the wealth of the Naqāda I people, it would explain how they paid for their imports of turquoise, glazed beads, lapis lazuli and other luxuries; and it may also explain the cause of its downfall, when the lure of gold attracted foreigners, first as traders, but eventually to invade Upper Egypt, there to develop the Naqāda II civilization.

Only a guess can be hazarded regarding the political and social organization of the Naqāda I people. They were town dwellers who fortified their settlements. They buried magical implements in some of their largest tombs, an indication that magicians or witch doctors were important members of the community, perhaps even their leaders. It was in these tombs that some rare objects were found: the female figurines, and the vases with the symbols of the fertility goddess.[2]

Farming, supplemented by fishing and hunting, was the main source of livelihood. In addition, the first industry known in Egypt, that of flint mining and flaking, was developed, and perhaps gold mining should also be included.

[1] See Plate 10 (*c*).
[2] G, 3, vol. I, 36, pl. III; see Plate 9 (*d–e*).

NAQĀDA II

With the civilization of Naqāda II a new and strong impulse seized the people of Upper Egypt. A foreign people, more advanced and with an urge to develop and spread, may first have arrived as peaceful traders in the Nile Valley and then have been tempted by its riches and the possibilities of development which it offered to make it their home. We do not know what was the country of their origin. Some have suggested they came from the Delta, but recent excavations have not confirmed this conjecture. Others think they came from some part of western Asia, for it is generally assumed that the strong Semitic element in the Egyptian language is due to them and that the Hamitic element is due to the older population: the archaeological evidence would agree with this theory.

The Naqāda II people must have been of a type that could merge, physically and mentally, with the older inhabitants, and must have possessed those qualities that were required to turn a gifted and interesting prehistoric people into the nation that took a leading position among the civilizations of its time.

The route by which those foreigners, under whose influence and inspiration the Naqāda II civilization was developed, came from their country of origin to Upper Egypt is not known. The only place outside the strict limits of the Nile Valley in which has been found the typical style of drawing ships that we find on the painted pottery characteristic of Naqāda II[1] is the Wādi Hammāmāt. This agrees with Petrie's assumption that it was by this route that they entered Egypt and accords well with the fact that the oldest signs of their presence in the Nile Valley have been found at Koptos on the east bank and, across the river, at Naqāda and Diospolis Parva, all these being places near the mouth of the Wādi Hammāmāt.

Another suggestion is that these foreigners came by land from Palestine, and, after first settling in the Delta where they developed their superior civilization, conquered Upper Egypt. This theory is based on the fact that the wavy-handled pottery, one of the new types which they introduced, is also found in Bronze Age Palestine and it is suggested either that Palestine was the centre from which this type of pottery was introduced into the Delta, or that there was a centre of distribution in the eastern Delta. No wavy-handled pots have been discovered in any excavation in the Delta; moreover, the wavy-handled pots are known only towards the

[1] See Plate 9 (*b–c*).

end, and not from the beginning, of the Naqāda II period.[1] There is no proof that there was an early link between Egypt and Palestine through Sinai.

Egyptian tradition has always maintained that the north was first civilized by Menes from the south, and it would be rash to dismiss that tradition without very strong reasons.

The newcomers exerted a profound influence on every aspect of life in the Nile Valley. It seems that at this time the increasing desiccation of the valley proper, brought about by agriculture encroaching on swamps and thickets, and perhaps also by decreasing rainfall, coupled with a growing population due to advances in civilization and prosperity, may have compelled more intensive utilization of the floor of the valley. At the same time life in the valley probably became more attractive so that people began to settle there. It has been suggested, therefore, that it was in Naqāda II that artificial irrigation was introduced.[2] An irrigation system based on the digging of canals, with their attendant drains, and the endless problems connected with the regulation and utilization of water, cannot have been the work of an isolated individual or community, or even of a district or province; it demanded the concerted action of a whole populace and a sense of discipline and responsibility and restraint; it implies centralized control or direction, and a highly developed communal and social sense. An irrigation system of canals can hardly have been developed in Upper Egypt until there was a very large degree of unity and, probably, unified leadership. Though this must have existed towards the end of Naqāda II, we do not know whether the requisite political and social conditions obtained during the whole of Naqāda II.

Assuming that there was some degree of irrigation, nothing is known of the system of agriculture or land tenure. It is not known, for instance, if the land was owned by individuals, if it was divided out afresh after every inundation, or if it was worked communally. The later fiction that all land belonged to the king who, therefore, had to provide the funerary offerings, may well go back to predynastic times and show that the arable land was not divided and that the fruit of the soil was distributed by the leaders of the communities. We know that a proportion of the grain was parched in large kilns, composed of dozens of pots, each more than 50 centimetres high, grouped within an enclosure wall.[3] This supports the theory that some sort of communal economy existed. At the beginning of the dynastic period we find

[1] G, 3, vol. I, pp. 40–1.   [2] G, 3, vol. II, p. 142.   [3] §II, 37, 1–7, pl. I.

that the king owned large estates from which he gave bounty to his subordinates. Thus it seems as if the land, which originally the leader had to administer for the community, had by then become his private property. Junker has shown in his study on Pehernefer, a nobleman of the early Fourth Dynasty, that it was probably from these large estates that the Egyptian nomes developed.[1]

There is no archaeological evidence so far that predynastic Egypt consisted of a number of small states which were eventually united under one ruler. Certain it is that at the end of Naqāda II a king who had power over Upper Egypt began the conquest of Lower Egypt and thus laid the foundation of the kingdom of Upper and Lower Egypt.[2] This event was one of the great achievements of Naqāda II, as Egyptian tradition emphasizes.

After the Naqāda II people had entered Upper Egypt and settled there they spread northward from Asyūt into Lower Egypt. That this invasion was not carried out by foreigners, but was an advance of the people of Upper Egypt, is shown by the archaeological finds. In the tombs of the Lower Egyptian cemeteries, so far the only source of our knowledge, the later wares of Naqāda II were found together with the black-top pottery characteristic of the earlier culture which could only have been acquired in Upper Egypt. The large, but incompletely excavated settlement of Ma'ādi must be mentioned in this context, for it has been claimed to be of the Naqāda II Period.[3] Studies on the spot certainly revealed no evidence to support this dating. As far as could be ascertained the settlement was wholly dynastic.

The Faiyūm must have held a special attraction for these Naqāda II people, for three cemeteries belonging to different communities have been excavated where the route to the Faiyūm leaves the Nile Valley, and a surface station has been found in the Faiyūm itself.

North of the Faiyūm on the south-western edge of the Delta lies Merimda where part of a rural settlement was excavated.[4] It had three strata. Of the lowest, little was left. No houses were found. The middle layer had oval or horseshoe-shaped huts and the top layer oval huts partly sunk into the soil and constructed of *pisée* or lumps of mud. Besides the polished red ware, the black, the black top and the rough, a very distinctive pottery was found. It is polished red in parts, and on the parts left unpolished

[1] Z.Ä.S. 75 (1939), 63–84. [2] See C.A.H. I³, ch. XI, sect. I.
[3] G, 20, vol. I, pp. 529 ff. A, 2, 122–34, 144–46.
[4] A, 2, 103–16, 141–43.

a pattern is incised. This is either a herringbone motif or a series of parallel strokes. The nearest analogy to this technique is found in certain pots of the Nubian A-group pottery. Merimda also yielded some black-topped and black-mouthed pottery. The excavators themselves mentioned the resemblance of the Merimda material to the Nubian group.[1] The flint work, a mixture of bifacial and blade work, the many axes of stone other than flint, the abundance of bone tools and the palettes not made of slate are all features which are common to Merimda and Nubia. Like the A group, the Merimda people possessed a number of pieces imported from Upper Egypt, such as a fine spearhead[2] and headrests.[3] Like the A group also they should be dated from the Naqāda II Period to the Early Dynastic Period. Thus it will be necessary to consider whether the people of Merimda, like those of the A group, were some desert tribe which was in process of settling down and, finding the more attractive parts of the Nile Valley already occupied by the Egyptians, had to be content with some out-of-the-way place.[4]

Reliably dated evidence of the Naqāda II Period from Upper Egypt is far from plentiful. El-Hammāmīya is a small place, the occupation of which began in Badārian times and lasted into Naqāda II. Armant, only partially excavated, covers the time from the end of Naqāda I to Naqāda II. Of the settlement of El-Mahāsna we know as little as of the villages and towns which Brunton found on the spurs of the low desert in the neighbourhood of Qāw. Petrie excavated part of the town of Naqāda, which was walled and had rectangular houses. The predynastic town of Hierakonpolis has never been excavated.

To the south, a series of Naqāda II cemeteries extends as far as Sayāla in Lower Nubia, with a distant and isolated outpost in a cemetery near Gammai.[5]

Slender though they must be reckoned as evidence, the ruins of Naqāda and a house found under the temple of El-Badāri[6] show that the Naqāda II people lived in roughly rectangular houses probably consisting of one roofed room and a forecourt. The pottery model of a house discovered at El-Amra and now in the British Museum, 46 centimetres long, must be explained in this way.[7] It is rectangular, with walls showing a pronounced batter; in one of the short walls is a door, and high up in the opposite wall are set two small windows; the roof, represented like the lid

---

[1] §II, 23, I, 176 f.　　[2] §II, 23, 3, pl. VI *b*.　　[3] §II, 22, p. 51, pl. 19.
[4] 4A, I.　　　　　　　[5] §II, 8, 12.　　　　　[6] G, 3, vol. II, pp. 128 ff.
[7] §II, 42, pl. 10, 1–2; G, 3, vol. II, pl. XII (see Plate 12(*a*)).

of the box, suggests the low vault familiar from the archaic seals. It covers only half of the structure, and, as it is intact and not a fragment, it seems likely that the part next to the door in the wall is intended to be an open court, and that only the house itself in the back was roofed.

The more elaborate graves of the Naqāda II people were rectangular, but round graves were still used by the poor and in them the bodies lay in a loosely contracted position with face west and head south. Some of the better graves were lined with matting or with wooden planks, which were the ancestors both of wooden coffins and the internal wood panelling of First Dynasty tombs. Towards the end of the period, what Brunton called 'chambered tombs' came into use for the more important members of the community. The chamber was little more than a recess hollowed out of the side and floor of the pit, usually on the east side, and in this narrow space the body was laid, the remainder of the pit serving for the storage of the tomb equipment. The graves were roofed with tree trunks, planks or matting, which were sometimes plastered. The custom of wrapping the bodies in matting slowly died out as wooden coffins became more frequent. Linen has been found in several graves; examination of this linen has shown that the continuous weft and a selvedge were in use. In Naqāda tomb T. 26 (S.D. 69) Petrie found the first known piece of knitted woollen fabric, in white and brown. He particularly emphasized that the knitted material, which must have been of some size, was contemporaneous with other contents of the grave.[1]

Beads and amulets now increase greatly in number and are more often made of hard stones, among them lapis lazuli. Beads of silver, gold and obsidian also occur. Most of the stones are found in the Nile Valley, but lapis and obsidian must have come from a distance. As far as is known, silver does not occur in Egypt. A silver adze was found at El-Ballās,[2] and a silver figure of a hawk at Naqāda.[3] The adze is a substantial object of the type with square neck which is characteristic of the period. A silver dagger and knife, and an object of uncertain significance, an oblong piece of gold, seven centimetres long, wrapped in a piece of silver foil, are now in the Cairo Museum.[4] They were found together with a stone axe and other stone tools in a tomb at Hamra Dōm, Gebel et-Tārif, whence came other Naqāda II material in the Cairo Museum. The dagger resembles another from El-Amra tomb B 230 now in Cairo, which after cleaning also proved to be

[1] §II, 39, 24. [2] §II, 39, pl. LXV, 6.
[3] §II, 39, pl. LX, 14. [4] G, 17, pl. 58 (14516).

of silver.[1] It is remarkable that so much silver has survived and that apparently so much was used. Gold is much rarer than silver in graves of this period, and is mostly used as thin foil. It is not known whether this is merely due to the chances of discovery, or whether, for reasons unknown to us, gold was really rarer than silver in Naqāda II times.

At El-Girza Wainwright found some gold beads threaded into a necklace together with iron beads which are of meteoric origin; no other predynastic iron beads are known. Two pendants of gold foil were found at El-Ballās and El-Mahāsna.

Copper objects became much more common in Naqāda II; it was used for harpoons, daggers, knives, needles, finger rings, beads and many other small articles.[2] The pin with the simple loop head is still the most common type. Another pin has one end drawn out to a fine wire which is coiled several times around the stem to form the head; this type is also known from western Asia. Some of the small tools found together in graves seem to have formed sets and may have been used for toilet purposes; similar sets are known from early Iran and Mesopotamia. Daggers, which are very rare, are of two main types. The more primitive type was found twice at El-Amra, one example—that made of silver—still having its ivory handle;[3] at the broad end of its triangular blade is a triangular tang which was inserted into the handle and fixed by a single rivet; the handle has a flat, semi-circular knob and has two curved wings which fit over the blade so as to give a somewhat firmer hold than the single rivet could provide. Both daggers have midribs.[4] The Hamra Dōm silver dagger also belongs to the type with midrib.[5] The second type, found by Petrie at Naqāda (tomb 836, S.D. 63),[6] is long and slender, with a trapezoidal tang which has two rivet holes at its outer extremity; each side of the blade has a midrib and hollowed face.

Copper adzes have thin, straight necks and cutting edges bevelled from below. They have either parallel sides and straight cutting edges, or concave sides and splayed cutting edges.[7] The silver adze from El-Ballās belongs to this second type.[8]

The earliest predynastic copper axe discovered in Egypt was found by Brunton in tomb 3131 at El-Matmar. It is nearly six-

---

[1] G, 3, vol. II, pl. II, 1; §II, 42, pl. VI, 1, 2 (see Plate 10 (g)).
[2] See Plate 10 (d–f).   [3] See Plate 10 (g).   [4] G, 3, vol. II, pl. II, 1 and 9.
[5] G, 17, pl. 58 (14514) = G, 3, vol. II, pl. II, 4.
[6] §II, 39, pl. LXV, 3 = G, 3, vol. II, pl. II, 5 (see Plate 10 (h)).
[7] See Plate 10 (e).   [8] §II, 39 (the broken specimen), p. 14.

teen centimetres long and weighs 3½ pounds; in shape it is trapezoidal, with bulging sides, a square neck, and deeply rounded
corners to the cutting edge.[1] Chemical analysis revealed a composition of 97·35 per cent copper, 1·28 per cent nickel, and small
amounts of arsenic, iron and manganese.[2] Because of the nickel
content, which is not found in Egyptian copper, Brunton thought
that the axe might be an import from Mesopotamia; it certainly
does not look like a first attempt by the Egyptian smith. The
rounded corners which will cut wood smoothly suggest a carpenter's tool. This axe is dated S.D. 38–46 and is of a much more
sophisticated type than those found at the end of this period;
this, however, may be due to the fortunes of excavation. The later
axes are rectangular, with square necks and slightly curved cutting
edges.

The use of stone vessels increased very considerably during this
period, and even more during the early dynasties. Beautiful vases,
bowls, cylinders, squat, barrel-shaped, and double vessels, or vases
made in the shapes of birds and animals, were made from colour-
ful stones, such as serpentine, red and white breccia, basalt, por-
phyry, alabaster, schist, and others, but above all of limestone
(36 per cent as Lucas has shown, against 21·5 per cent basalt, and
16 per cent of alabaster). The quantity of the vases produced, and
the technical skill needed for their production, no longer made
by hand but with the help of still another new invention—the
stone borer—make it likely that the manufacture of stone vases
had now become specialized as an industry, employing skilled
workers.

The development of the two industries of copper and limestone stimulated as they must have been by the availability of
most of the necessary raw materials in the Memphite neighbourhood, must have led to an increase in the importance of that
region at the expense of Upper Egypt. It is not surprising, therefore, that tradition should ascribe the foundation of Memphis to
the founder of the First Dynasty, particularly in view of its geographical position.[3]

The changes that affected all the other products of Egypt did
not leave untouched the pottery; it too underwent profound
modifications. The black-topped pottery became increasingly rare.
The polished black and red wares remained, but the red changed
from a dark plum colour to a brick red. This change of colour

[1] §II, 12, pl. XVI, 47.
[2] H. C. H. Carpenter, Letter in *Nature*, 130, no. 3286, 22 Oct. 1932, pp. 625–6.
[3] See *C.A.H.* I³, ch. XI, sect. II.

was due to the difference in the clay from which the pots were made; instead of the Nile mud used for the earlier pottery, a cleaner and better clay was preferred to produce what O. H. Myers has called the 'desert ware'. Myers considers that this clay was drawn from the lower desert at a few localities only, and that it is likely that specialized, wholesale production of pottery in one or two centres began with the introduction of this ware.[1] At the same time the slow wheel was introduced, at least for throwing the necks of some narrow-mouthed vessels.[2]

The new clay was of a light colour after baking, either buff or pink according to the temperature of the firing. The polished red ware was produced by covering the clay with a slip and polishing. Towards the end of the period, and overlapping into dynastic times, the technique which Menghin calls 'Besenstrich' (broom-stroke) was also introduced; it was probably produced with the help of a broom or brush.

On this better clay as a background the Naqāda II people painted directly with a dark red colour; this is Petrie's 'Decorated Ware'. The fact that the Decorated Ware uses motifs of earlier Asiatic cultures not found on the Naqāda I painted ware shows that it derived its inspiration from an area different from that which influenced the white cross-lined pottery. Thus, although an Asiatic source must be sought for both of the Naqāda styles of painted pottery, the source of each must have been different. Whereas the influence of Naqāda I seems to have come from the region of Iran, the influence of Jamdat Naṣr in Mesopotamia is indicated for Naqāda II.

The changes in decoration were accompanied by changes in the shapes of the vessels themselves. Instead of the open bowls with patterns on the inside regularly found in the white cross-lined ware, shouldered or bellied, narrow-mouthed vases decorated on the outside became usual. The narrow mouth could be closed by a pottery lid, another innovation of the period. Many of the pots have lug-handles, either tubular or triangular, which are pierced horizontally. The shouldered vases with three or four lug-handles are of a type closely related to Jamdat Naṣr painted vessels.

In Egypt, as in the countries of western Asia, two painted vase civilizations followed each other, but, though related, the one did not descend from the other. In Mesopotamia, they were separated by a culture that used plain pottery, sometimes with engraved designs. In Egypt, also, at the beginning of Naqāda II, there

---

[1] §ii, 35, vol. i, 50.   [2] §ii, 35, vol. i, 167, 177 ff.

was a ware with incised decoration. A herringbone pattern occurs, and impressions around the neck of some vases, as if made by a cord pressed into the wet clay, look like necklaces. There is no indication that this incised pottery is the sign of a separate period in the development of Egyptian civilization dividing the two Naqāda cultures; Naqāda I and Naqāda II are closely linked together and the incised pottery must have been introduced together with the new style of Naqāda II painting.

Life in Egypt, as shown by the pictures on the decorated ware, seems to have been markedly different from that of the earlier period. For the people of Naqāda II it must have been quite a common spectacle to see boats with the shrines of their gods, each identified by his or her emblem on the pole, being rowed in procession on the Nile, which was, at all times, the normal means of travel for men and gods; nothing similar is known from Naqāda I. One, two or three boats may be drawn on a single vase, each boat having two small cabins, one of which, as shown by the standard fixed to it, is the shrine. Some of the standards bear symbols known from later times, but others cannot be identified.

The emblems on the boat standards are the same whether they occur on pots found in excavations in Lower Egypt near the entrance to the Faiyūm or in Upper Egypt, and so are the symbols of the gods whose images were used for slate palettes. There is no indication that some of these symbols and gods belong to the north rather than to the south. The other scenes and objects depicted on the decorated ware are mostly religious ceremonies or sacred objects such as trees; scenes of hunting are very rare.

Two more types of pottery, both unknown to Naqāda I, have to be mentioned. The first is the pottery Petrie called 'wavy-handled'. It comes rather late in the period, at about S.D. 60.[1] In form, it is like the shouldered, narrow-mouthed vase of the Decorated Ware, and some of the wavy-handled pots are indeed painted. The pottery is made of a good clay, greenish buff or pink in colour. The handles, from which this class derives its name, are ledges with 'wavy' scalloped outline to afford the fingers a better grip when the pots were being carried on the head. In Egypt this feature does not seem to have been found practical and it soon degenerated into mere ornament. The origin of these pots was in Palestine, where they are dated to the Early Bronze Age.

The other type is an incised pottery of which two varieties exist, each originating probably from a different source. The first variety, Petrie's 'black-incised' ware, was mostly used for

[1] G, 3, vol. I, pp. 40–1.

open bowls with the pattern incised on the outside and on the rim; sometimes pendent triangles are engraved inside, just below the rim. The pots are of a coarse, black clay, the incised patterns filled with a white substance. The patterns differ completely from those of the painted ware. The most common resemble a series of door-frames placed one within another on the sides of the pot; a somewhat amorphous design may be on the base, though the latter is flat and the pot would stand on it. Some of these pots are influenced in shape by the squat stone vessels of Naqāda II. This type of pottery, though rare, remains in use until the Pyramid Age, when it assumes more complicated shapes.

The second variety of incised pottery is of much simpler style. It has already been mentioned above (p. 489) as a companion to the Decorated Ware. Finger or nail impressions at regular intervals were used as decoration. This type of pottery seems to be more frequent in settlements.

Of the 'Rough Ware' as Petrie calls it, with which must be reckoned part of his Late Ware, dozens of examples are found in a single tomb. Large storage jars and small saucers are made of a clay to which a considerable amount of chaff has been added. The pots are smoothed, but are without slip, and are often very coarse. Some served as cooking and other domestic vessels. Some pots with low walls have thick, flat bases from which the body rises at a sharp angle on the outside, but is rounded inside. The pots tend to be very uneven owing to their having been cut untidily from the clay from which they were made. The shapes are few, and include simple, oval dishes. This type of pottery has the appearance of a cheap, mass-produced ware, made with the minimum of effort, but by an experienced hand.

The flint industry of Naqāda II is the most accomplished and beautiful hitherto found anywhere. To an already well-developed craft a new technique was added: the detaching from prepared flint nodules of long blades which were converted into knives with carefully blunted backs. The twisted blade which looks as if somebody had twisted its lower part in a different direction from that of the top, is a 'leit-fossil' of the time. It would be expected that this new method of manufacture, which could be produced so much more quickly and was more efficient, should soon have ousted the older and more difficult technique. Indeed, for tools of everyday use it seems to have done so; sickle-blades are now used instead of the bifacially retouched sickle-stones, and in some graves dozens of sharp little blades are found, mostly not retouched, though some have blunted backs. For larger tools, however, and especially for the choice pieces, the bifacial technique was never abandoned. The flint axes are stout, either oval or rectangular, and are worked on both sides; the cutting edge was made, or resharpened, by a transverse blow against one side, which neatly detached a flake across the width of the tool. These axes, though very rare in the graves, occur in quantities in the settlements such as Naqāda and Armant.

Other techniques were used for making knives, for which the best flint was chosen. Grinding before flaking was common; flaking became an ornament. The ripple-flaked knives,[1] from which flakes were detached so regularly that the surface seems to be fluted, were already highly prized at the time when they were made and they were set in precious gold and ivory handles. The ripple-flaked knives (the technique occurs on knives only) form a closely related group, dated between S.D. 55 and 65; the highly developed skill needed for their manufacture may well have been the secret of a single workshop. Spearheads and daggers were ground and finely trimmed too, but, rather surprisingly, blades were treated in the same way; not only backs and cutting edges were retouched, but also great parts of the surface.

The chisel-headed arrowheads and lunates were another novelty of the blade technique, and could be produced more quickly than the bifacially worked tips. Together with these was introduced that efficient weapon, the pear-shaped mace head, which was made of various hard stones. This weapon, which was known in Mesopotamia from the earliest times, remained in use in Egypt at least until the New Kingdom. The Naqāda II people, equipped with better weapons than their predecessors in the Nile Valley, must also have possessed a more warlike spirit, not only to enable them to make themselves masters in Upper Egypt, but to inspire their various expeditions to the north.

We do not know whether the Naqāda II people had only one king who ruled over all Upper Egypt from the time of their conquest of that part of the land, or whether the formation of a unified kingdom of Upper Egypt was only accomplished at or somewhat before the 'Union of the Two Lands', which Egyptian tradition ascribes to Menes, and which marks the foundation of the First Dynasty and the beginning of dynastic times. The fact that on the Narmer Palette and similar monuments the king stands alone, with no other chieftain with him, indicates that at that time, at least, he was an absolute monarch who suffered or had no rival. Even less is known about the political system of

[1] See Plate 10(a).

Lower Egypt. On the Palermo Stone, the register above those concerned with the First Dynasty preserves a few kings wearing the Red Crown, whose names are otherwise unknown. The compiler of the annals was unable to add any historical events to these names, and presumably no written records had survived to his day; perhaps none had ever existed.[1]

A notable innovation of the Naqāda II Period was the introduction of the cylinder seal; it can only have come from Mesopotamia, where it was known so much earlier. Two original seals of the Jamdat Naṣr period and imported into Egypt were found at Naqāda itself in tombs of Naqāda II date[2] and one, possibly an Egyptian imitation, at Naga ed-Deir.[3]

III. RELIGION

It must always be a precarious undertaking to deduce the religious beliefs of a people before the age of writing from the scanty material remains that have come down to us. The Badārians have left no temple or sacred image; all we have are their cemeteries and the refuse heaps of villages or towns.

The cemeteries themselves with their well-built graves in which the dead were buried with all their finery and provided with food, testify to the belief of the Badārians in a life after death, a life not much different from what they knew on earth. In the same cemeteries, and wrapped in shrouds just as the humans, some animals were buried: cows, jackals and sheep. The cow, 'the First of the Cows' as she is called later on, represents the great mother, and we may assume that the statuettes of naked women found in a few graves were dedicated to her, perhaps by women who desired a child.[4] The jackal was in later days the lord of the necropolis and the god of the dead; he may have had this function already with the Badārians.

We may assume that the Badārians practised some magical rites, though there is not much evidence for it. When a man fastened the little bone head of a gazelle to his ankle (pp. 469–70) he may have hoped for the speed of the gazelle, or when he painted his face green, which is the colour of life and vegetation as contrasted with the yellow of the desert, he may have believed that some life-giving power would be transferred to him. More pains were taken with the preparation of the green cosmetic material

---

[1] See *C.A.H.* 1³, ch. xi, sect 1 and Plate 25.   [2] G, 3, vol. i, p. 48.
[3] §ii, 26 (see *C.A.H.* 1³, ch. xi, sect. vi).   [4] §ii, 10; see Plate 11 (*a*).

and all the objects used for its production than for the red, or the black, which suggests that the green colour was the most important.

We know somewhat more about the peoples of Naqāda I and II, because more of their cemeteries have been excavated. The great care lavished on tombs and cemeteries remains an outstanding characteristic, which may testify to ancestor worship and certainly to a belief in an after-life. Chance has preserved for us the image or fetish of the fertility goddess in tomb 1449 at Naqāda. Dating from the end of Naqāda I, it is in the shape of a vase on the exterior of which are represented in relief a human head flanked by two cow's horns and a pair of arms holding the breasts which descend from the rim of the vase behind the head. Similar arms holding the breasts, symbolizing the fertility goddess, are shown on other vases.[1] Together with the cow horns mounted concentrically on sticks they represent her standard and they are the most common of the various standards painted on the boats of the decorated pottery of Naqāda II. To the fertility goddess belongs a young male god—her son and lover—the *ka-mutef* (Bull of his Mother) of historic Egypt. We find him wearing twigs or feathers in his hair performing a ritual dance among a party of women, or in a wildly agitated dance with a single partner painted in white on the cross-lined pottery of Naqāda I. Dancing as part of a ritual belonging to the cow goddess is shown on some of the decorated vases of Naqāda II. Women dance the 'cow-dance' (still nowadays performed in the Sudan), their arms raised and curved inwards towards their heads, simulating cow horns. On one of the decorated vases the sacred marriage of goddess and god is shown.[2] It takes place under the awning of one of the shrines in a boat, and on the same vase the first example of a divine triad is painted, the goddess, her lover and, presumably, her daughter. The figure of the goddess is the largest by far, and has an enormous round head.

Other deities known from dynastic times are represented by their emblems for the first time on decorated vases: the crossed arrows of the goddess Neith,[3] the still unexplained object symbolizing the god Min,[4] and, towards the end of the period, or, perhaps already early dynastic, the falcon of Horus,[5] all on standards in front of the shrines. None, however, can rival in popularity with the symbol of the fertility goddess.[6] As the little

---

[1] §II, 38, pl. 5; see Plate 9 (*d–e*). [2] G, 3, vol. II, pl. XIII, 1–3 see Plate 9 (*b–c*).
[3] G, 3, vol. II, p. 150, fig. 24. [4] G, 3, vol. II, p. 149, fig. 20.
[5] G, 3, vol. II, p. 150. [6] G, 3, vol. II, p. 151.

shrine generally pictured in the boats also occurs under a special species of trees, we have to assume that these were holy trees.

Amulets and objects used in magical rites greatly increased in number during the Naqāda periods.[1] Slate palettes too small for practical use, and called 'magic' by Petrie,[2] ivory tusks in pairs, one hollow and one solid which may symbolize male and female, small receptacles either with grooves or with holes around their tops which may have contained 'medicine', and tags of ivory or slate; block figures of men and women found in pairs or in series some-times together with the magical slates may have belonged to the outfit of magicians and have served in some divination rite.[3] The two graves of Naqāda II in which such outfits were found belonged to women. We may suspect sympathetic magic in the scenes of hunting hippopotami and crocodiles which occur in both styles of predynastic Egyptian vase painting.

The custom of placing statuettes in some graves persisted, and from Naqāda I onwards not only figures of women, as in Badārian times, but also of men, certain animals, and, at the end of the period, the falcon. Among the animals represented are lions, also only towards the end of the period, hippopotami, cattle, pigs and, perhaps, the Seth animal. The cattle occur in groups on trays and may be *ex-votos* to ensure the fertility of the herds, and the same holds good for the pigs. The falcon and the lion are of special interest, because they are the gods with whom the king is identi-fied in dynastic times. The falcon, or perhaps one of the falcons, represents Horus, but no name can be attached to the lion, though the king as a lion with a human head—the sphinx—is one of the most impressive and characteristic creations of Egypt.

IV. ART

Just as the basic religious beliefs of the Egyptians began to take shape in Badārian times, so did their sense of style and form, their acute observation of nature and their way of condensing what they had seen to the bare essentials. A small ivory hippo-potamus[4] figurine and two of the female figurines[5] from El-Mustagidda and El-Badāri are exquisite products of a fresh and naïve naturalism. A statuette of a woman, also from El-Badāri,[6] shows that an abstract style existed as well. She is reduced to a

---

[1] See Plate 11 (*e*).   [2] G, 14, p. 38, 96.
[3] G, 3, vol. II, p. 62.   [4] §II, 11, pl. XXIII, 3 (see Plate 11 (*d*)).
[5] §II, 13, pl. XXV, 3, 4, 6, 7 (see Plate 11 (*a*)).   [6] §II, 13, pl. XXIV, 3.

lump of clay on which the female parts only are detailed; the small head has no features; she has no arms, no separation of the legs—she has become a symbol familiar to her contemporaries.

From the very beginning Egyptian applied art at its best preferred simple, smooth forms. Pottery, flint and bone were worked to perfection, nothing rugged was allowed to stay.

With Naqāda I and the beginning of vase painting a new field of art was opened up. The style of the early painted vases is strictly geometrical in imitation of their Asiatic models, a style for which the Egyptians had very little use. Soon they began to disturb the symmetry of the patterns with little extras. Since they did not feel that the pattern on a vase need be in harmony with its structure, they took the different elements out of their context, and displayed them at random all over the vase. The patterns were painted as if on a sheet of papyrus, a flat strip transferred to the curve of the vase. This happened with the painted pottery of Naqāda I, as well as with that of Naqāda II, showing how strong a tradition existed.

Many more representations of landscape and domestic scenes, of men, women and animals occur on the Egyptian vases than on those of their counterparts in western Asia. Ritual dances,[1] hunting scenes,[2] men working on looms[3] are shown on vases of the earlier style, all taken from the daily life of the Naqāda I people. With the new style of painting of Naqāda II a new wave of geometric patterns came in, and fared no better than did that of Naqāda I. The outstanding subject of the decorated vases is the procession of boats[4] each carrying a shrine to which the standard of a divinity is attached. A conventional style of representation was evolved showing already some of the characteristics of later Egyptian painting: the lower part of the human body is shown in profile, the upper part in front view, the importance of a person is shown by his large size, water is shown by parallel zigzag lines. As also in later periods, the more lively and naturalistic representations are reserved for minor features.

That, towards the end of Naqāda II, painting was employed on a more ambitious scale than merely for decorating vases is shown by the wall paintings of the famous Hierakonpolis tomb, the only example preserved that can possibly be ascribed to Naqāda II.[5] It contains a most interesting combination of motifs. The men dancing with outstretched arms and the gazelles caught in a trap

---

[1] G, 3, vol. II, 64, fig. 14.   [2] §II, 6, pl. XXVII, 13.
[3] §II, 13, pl. XXXVIII, 70K.   [4] G, 3, vol. II, pl. XIII.
[5] §II, 14.

occur even on vases of Naqāda I.[1] The boats with their shrines and the awning on top (p. 493) are found on the decorated ware, but the king or chieftain grasping the kneeling enemy by the hair and slaying him with his mace is not known before the First Dynasty. This strong sense of tradition, accepting the new without relinquishing the old, is a most characteristic feature of the Egyptians.

No piece of predynastic Egyptian sculpture has yet come to light. Small figurines are all that have hitherto been found. Human figurines of ivory are very rare. A single example exists from Naqāda I.[2] It is the figure of a man found at El-Mahāsna in the same tomb as the small ivory often taken to be the first representation of the god Seth (p. 477). It is a schematic piece of work, slender with an ovoid head and over-long arms. No complete ivory figure of a woman has survived from Naqāda I, only the leg of one in a Naqāda grave.[3] From Naqāda II two kinds of figurine are known: the coarse ivory peg-figures of women of the armless type carrying water jars on their heads, and the so-called block figures, thin pieces of ivory or slate in which the human form is reduced to a rectangular block with a triangular head.[4]

Clay figurines of men, women and animals give a better idea of the art of the time. Two statuettes of women from the large tomb B 101 at Abādīya are outstanding, though they have lost their heads and part of the legs.[5] Both have narrow waists and full hips, one seems to be dancing, the other is of the armless type. The same grave contained two stone and two clay hippopotami, and a slate palette also of a hippopotamus, a most amusing piece of applied art.[6] Two statuettes of dancing women were found in a tomb at Mohamerīya.[7]

Towards the end of the Predynastic Period the falcon in the archaic crouching position occurs in several tombs; it was also found in the South Town of Naqāda.[8] It, as well as the amulet formerly called the bull's head but in fact the symbol of the fertility goddess,[9] amulets in the shape of fish, birds, crocodiles and other animals made of ivory, slate, carnelian and other stones, was manufactured with the same mastery of the material and perfection in form that has distinguished Egyptian applied art all through its long history. All these amulets had a long life and still existed in dynastic times. This continuity strongly

---

[1] §II, 19, pl. III; §II, 42, pl. xv.   [2] G, 3, vol. II, pl. IV (see Plate 11(c)).
[3] Naqāda, t. 273 (unpublished).   [4] §II, 39, pl. LIX, 1–5, 7, 11.
[5] G, 3, vol. II, pl. V, 3. See Plate 11 (b).   [6] G, 3, vol. II, pl. V, 5.
[7] G, 3, vol. II, p. 69, pl. V, 4.   [8] §II, 39, pl. LX, 20.
[9] G, 3, vol. II, pl. VI, 2. See Plate 11(e).

suggests that there was no break in civilization between the pre-
and proto-dynastic periods, and the similarity of the tomb furniture of the common people in both periods points to the same
conclusion. In many instances it is difficult, if not impossible, to
deduce whether a grave is predynastic or early dynastic. Nothing
suggests that there was a period of transition. The beginning of
the First Dynasty was really a political, not a cultural, event.
There were princes before the First Dynasty, as the Palermo
Stone shows, and they may have been buried near the so-called
Royal Tomb at Naqāda. On the Palermo Stone, however, they
are represented wearing the Red Crown which, in historical
times, was the emblem of Lower Egypt.[1] At what period it
acquired that significance is not known; nor indeed has any early
representation of the crown been found in Lower Egypt. The
earliest representation at present known occurs on a sherd of
Naqāda I found in a tomb at Naqāda in Upper Egypt.[2]

[1] See Plate 25.   [2] §II, 48.

CHAPTER IX (b)

PALESTINE DURING THE NEOLITHIC
AND CHALCOLITHIC PERIODS

THIS title conforms with the conventional nomenclature of the archaeological periods, but it has become obvious how far such terms are inadequate—at least in relation to the Near East. In Palestine there was an initial phase of the Neolithic period in which pottery was not known, a fact which it is hard for European pre-historians to credit; in the 'Chalcolithic' period metal was scarcely used and in the 'Early Bronze' age which followed only copper was yet known. It seems preferable to demarcate the different periods according to the successive stages of human development: (1) the first settlements (Neolithic without pottery) in which there was a transition from an economy of food-gathering (hunting and collecting) to an economy of production (breeding of livestock and agriculture), villages of hunters who were beginning to be shepherds and farmers; (2) villages of farmers and potters, who drew their main source of livelihood from the breeding of domestic animals and/or the cultivation of grain crops and who had a knowledge of pottery (Neolithic with pottery); (3) villages of farmers, potters and metalworkers, who were beginning to work in, and make use of, copper (Chalcolithic). A new era was to open with urban life and the first fortified cities (Early Bronze). These divisions are in themselves somewhat arbitrary: the adherence of groups of people to the soil had begun with the Mesolithic period; the advent of pottery is a convenient point for marking the transition to the second phase, but it does not of itself signify a change in the village economy, nor did the beginnings of metalworking have a very profound effect upon living conditions. On the other hand, development did not proceed at the same tempo in different areas: plains and valleys were more advanced than hill country; primitive ways of life continued for a long time in the semi-desert regions of the periphery.

V. THE FIRST SETTLEMENTS: HUNTERS AND FARMERS

The first relatively permanent dwellings apart from caves go back to the Mesolithic period in Palestine, the Natufian.[1] The most advanced development is apparent at 'Ain Mallaha ('Eynān);[2] at this exceptional site on the bank of Lake Ḥūleh three levels of round houses grouped over an area of 1000 sq.m. provide evidence of occupation, which was probably continuous, by a relatively populous group which supported itself predominantly by fishing, but also by hunting and intensified collecting, though there is no proof either that the cereals were cultivated or that animals were yet domesticated.

An enclosure, followed by an oval house, which were constructed in front of the cave of Wādi Fallāḥ (Naḥal Ōren), in the Carmel range,[3] belong to the same period. The succeeding level contained fourteen round houses built on a series of terraces. They were in the tradition of the 'Ain Mallaha houses, but smaller, and had stone walls, preserved at a height of up to a metre, floors of rammed earth, occasionally of pebbles (often two floors, one superimposed on the other), with a stone-paved hearth. The flint and stone implements are in the Natufian tradition, but include new elements, especially some large bifacial tools, picks, axes and adzes, sharpened to an edge by the removal of a transverse flake; there are few arrows and only a small quantity of obsidian, some pestles and a hollow quern. This collection is Neolithic. The axes and adzes show that there was work on timber, the picks may indicate work on the land and, together with the quern and numerous sickle-blades, may provide evidence of the beginnings of agriculture.

The most important site, however, for the study of this stage of development and its successors is Jericho, in the Jordan valley. As early as 1935–36 J. Garstang[4] distinguished, above a dense layer containing microliths, eight levels (XVII–X) which were characterized by the absence of both metal and pottery, by a stone and flint industry which was certainly Neolithic, and by buildings; pottery made its appearance at level IX, without any change being apparent in the stone industry; level VIII marked the development of flint tools and also of pottery. At level VII the Early Bronze Age levels began. These results were considerably augmented, and also modified, by the excavations of K. M.

[1] See above, p. 121.   [2] §v, 26; 27.
[3] §v, 35.   [4] G, 3; 4.

Kenyon from 1952 to 1958.[1] Towards the northern limit of the *tell* a rectangular area, which had been prepared on the rock and surrounded by a stone wall, was dated to the Lower Natufian period (Natufian I according to the usual classification) by microliths and a bone harpoon which were discovered there. This structure is interpreted as a place of pilgrimage, probably a sanctuary, visited by Mesolithic huntsmen who, like their quarry, came to the spring. In the middle of the *tell* a small area of the rock is covered by a deposit 13 ft. deep, formed by innumerable layers of earth, which are all that remains of the flimsy huts which were built one on top of another in succession over a very long period. But it is not possible to say whether they represent an established settlement or seasonal encampments. This 'nucleus *tell*' has yielded flint tools which are in the Lower Natufian tradition; obsidian is quite plentiful and there are numerous bone objects; the whole collection is regarded as 'proto-neolithic'.[2]

The succeeding phase is called at Jericho 'Pre-pottery Neolithic A'. Above the 'nucleus *tell*' there appear suddenly round houses built of mud-bricks, plano-convex in shape. Their floors are a little below ground level and they are reached by steps or a descending slope. This new agglomeration extends far beyond the limits of the 'nucleus *tell*' and has been developed over an area of about 10 acres. It may have been surrounded a little later by an enclosure. At one point, to the west, the built-up area is bounded by a wall 1·50 m. wide, preserved to a height of 3·90 m. Against the wall, on the inside, a solid tower was built, 8·50 m. high; a covered staircase contrived within the body of the tower made it possible to ascend from the bottom to the top.[3] Two later phases can be distinguished in the history of the wall and of the tower. In the second phase, the wall was rebuilt along a parallel line, slightly further to the west, and a ditch was dug in the rock in front of the wall. Rounded constructions, store-rooms or water-tanks, were built against the tower, and the lower entrance to the staircase ceased to be accessible except through a trap-door. In the third phase the tower was enlarged by the addition of a casing 1 m. thick, against which store-rooms similar to those of the preceding phase were soon to be built; the staircase was no longer used. The wall was increased in height and the lower part of it contained the rubble from the preceding phase.[4] Similar walls, of which only the bases were preserved, were found at the northern and southern limits of the *tell*; hence it seems probable

---

[1] G, 6, 39 ff., 60 ff.; §v, 13, 51 ff.   [2] §v, 17, 116 f.
[3] See Plate 13(*a*).   [4] G, 5, 87 (111 f.); 88 (70 ff.); 89 (102 ff.); 92 (93 ff.).

that the whole agglomeration was surrounded by a defence-wall. The defensive purpose of the tower is less apparent, since it was situated inside the enclosure and leaned against the 'rampart' without actually being embodied in it; it was masked by adjoining structures, and the staircase, which would have enabled the defenders to reach the top, was very soon blocked.

There was an abundant but not very typical flint industry, which included sickle-blades, a few arrows, numerous graving-tools and piercers, bifacial implements such as chisels, adzes and picks. Obsidian tools were plentiful, but small; bone was widely used. All this material represented a continuation of the Natufian tradition of the 'nucleus *tell*'.[1] In contrast with this continuity of industries, however, the sudden advent of properly built houses in place of the huts of the 'nucleus *tell*' can scarcely be explained as simply a local development. It is more probable[2] that this innovation was imported from outside. The houses at Jericho are related to the round houses of Wādi Fallāḥ, where the flint implements were also in the Natufian tradition and resembled those of Jericho; the change at Jericho may be attributed to an influence coming from the Mediterranean coastal region.

The introduction of architecture, however, is not the most important feature. At Wādi Fallāḥ the first attempts at agri-culture had been made; the application of the new methods at Jericho, where natural conditions were most favourable, may ex-plain its exceptionally rapid development. The extent and density of the site suggests a settled and numerous population, which has been estimated at 2,000 and which could scarcely have subsisted as the periodic inhabitants of the 'nucleus *tell*' had done, on the natural resources of the oasis. Although the grains from these levels have not yet been identified, it may be inferred that the systematic cultivation of cereals was by this time an accomplished fact; confirmation would seem to be afforded by the querns, the pestles and the store-rooms built against the tower, one of which, at least, contained grain.

There is no evidence of domestic animals, with the possible exception of the goat.[3] The meat eaten was game, especially gazelle, which was either hunted by the settlers themselves or obtained by barter from the nomads of the surrounding country; arrows in fact are not numerous. The abundance of gazelle bones suggests that these animals may have been rounded up and kept in captivity, as was done later by the Egyptians.[4]

[1] §v, 17, 116 ff.
[2] G, 7, 152 f.
[3] G, 9, 132 f., correcting §v, 38.
[4] G, 9, 434; §v, 38, 70.

Another explanation has been suggested for the prosperity of Jericho at this period: that it was due not so much to agriculture as to trade.[1] Tools made of obsidian, which came from Anatolia, are evidence of economic relations with the outside world; in return, Jericho could export minerals from the region of the Dead Sea, chiefly salt, but also bitumen and sulphur. It is certainly possible that these resources had been exploited from the outset, but it is doubtful whether they created a trade of any real importance, since so far human porters were the only known means of transport.

The construction of the tower and of the enclosure wall, the system of irrigation required by an expanding agriculture, the installation of salt-pans (if any) and the subsequent maintenance of these undertakings, the water supply, the distribution of produce, the conduct of business with the outside world, all these matters would necessitate an organized community, obedient to its leaders, and following accepted rules. Is it possible to speak of a city yet? Jericho would then be by far the earliest city in the world, not the earliest which can have existed, but the earliest now known. It is a question which has provoked lively discussion.[2] While it is undeniable that Jericho had at that time progressed very much further than the sites along the Mediterranean coast of Palestine and, even more, than the sites of the semi-desert region which are about to be considered, it seems unlikely that all the elements of an urban civilization had as yet been mustered. Houses and a rampart do not themselves constitute a city; an irrigation system may be installed and maintained in what is still a village. Moreover, urban life requires at least some degree of specialisation in different branches of activity by the inhabitants, as well as a surplus of manufactured products and the barter of this surplus by means of trade. It does not seem as though Jericho adequately satisfied these conditions.

Whatever terminology be used, Jericho at that time was in the same class as the first villages known in Western Asia, such as Jarmo,[3] in the foothills of Iraqi Kurdistān, which was smaller; Çatal Hüyük,[4] in the plain of Konya in Anatolia, which was three times the size of Jericho and which exemplified an even more advanced economy; in South-West Anatolia pre-pottery Hacilar;[5] on the Syrian coast, the lowest level of Ras Shamra;[6] in Cyprus the earliest Khirokitia.[7] The distribution of these early

---

[1] G, 2, 246 ff.; §v, 1. [2] Cf. esp. §v, 2; 3; 6; 14; 15.
[3] §v, 4, 38 ff. [4] §v, 21; 22. [5] §v, 20, 70 ff.
[6] §v, 7. [7] §v, 10; 11.

villages and the diversity of their tools demonstrate that the transition to a productive economy was not confined to the foothills of the 'Fertile Crescent'. The cultivation of cereal crops and the domestication of animals must have taken place independently at about the same time in various sites or regions among the hills and plateaux of Western Asia, where wheat and barley grow wild and where the forbears of our domestic animals were living free. Even in Palestine the Jericho oasis was neither the first nor the only starting-point for such progress, since the first attempts at agriculture were probably made on the coast (Wādi Fallāḥ); it may only be said that at Jericho the natural conditions of the oasis aided such development and gave it a particular character.

The existence of a Palestinian 'province' in this first phase of the Neolithic period is attested also by the site of Abu Suwān, near Jerash,[1] where the stone implements are similar to those of Jericho[2] and Wādi Fallāḥ.[3]

The semi-arid region of the Judaean desert followed a different course of development. On the terraced slopes of El-Khiām[4] there is no evidence of the Lower Natufian phase (represented at Jericho), but above the epi-palaeolithic industries are those designated Natufian III–IV (not represented at Jericho) which in fact constitute a new industry, characterized by a preponderance of piercers made from blades, the development of arrows from piercers in increasing numbers[5] and the rarity of sickle-blades. This 'Khiamian' culture represents a local development which was derived directly from the Upper Palaeolithic. In its turn it was to give rise to Taḥunian, which will be discussed later. There is no proof of the sedentary character of these settlements. The large number of arrows and the almost complete absence of agricultural implements (sickle-blades, picks) presuppose a population which supported itself primarily by hunting, cultivated the soil very little or not at all and had probably not yet reached the pastoral stage. The domestication of the goat and the ox has been conjectured,[6] but is by no means certain.[7]

For the best documentation of the ensuing phase, called at Jericho 'Pre-pottery Neolithic B', it is necessary to return to Jericho. After an undefined period of desertion and decay, the site was reoccupied by a new population.[8] It appears from a study of the bones that the anthropological type was more

---

[1] §v, 16.   [2] §v, 17, 119.   [3] G, 7, 151.
[4] §v, 12; 23.   [5] §v, 24.   [6] §v, 23, 214 f.
[7] G, 7, 131; §v, 4, 130 f. and 142.   [8] G, 6, 47 ff.

advanced that that of the preceding phase, which was purely Natufian. The flint tools were different[1] and were characterized particularly by long thin blades which were used to make different types of arrows, sickle-blades and graving-tools; the great scarcity of axes, adzes and picks is noteworthy, the soil being prepared for sowing with 'digging sticks', pointed sticks pushed through heavy, perforated stones. The querns were of a different shape: they had a double saddle and were without a rim at one end. The most striking change is apparent in the architecture, which suggests the arrival from elsewhere of a tradition already well established. The houses had rectangular rooms, with corners more or less rounded; bricks were in the shape of flattened cigars and had their surfaces marked with thumb-prints in a herring-bone pattern. Floors and walls were washed with lime which was polished and often coloured; tanks and containers constructed against the walls were used for storing water and provisions. The existence of a defensive enclosure-wall is much less probable than in the preceding phase. There was certainly not one at the outset; after quite a long interval a megalithic wall makes its appearance, but only at two separate points in the west which may or may not have been connected. It was erected against the remains of the first levels of the same phase and may be regarded as intended for defence purposes or simply for the support of a terrace on which new houses had been built. The wall in any case lasted for only a short time: it gave way under the pressure of the accumulated earth. Another wall, built further out, was in turn overlapped by the extension of the inhabited area.[2]

It is to this phase that the first conclusive evidence of domestic animals belongs: goats,[3] at least two breeds of dogs,[4] and perhaps cats[5]. Numerous bones of pigs, sheep and oxen indicate at least the presence of species capable of being domesticated; small figurines in animal shapes were modelled in clay. The economy was still based on hunting and agriculture. Relations with other countries were extended: in addition to obsidian from Anatolia, Jericho imported a small quantity of turquoise, which must have come from Sinai, and cowrie-shells from the Mediterranean coast.

A little light has been thrown on the religious ideas of this group. A large rectangular room has annexes with curving walls

[1] §v, 17, 117.
[2] G, 5, 85 (83 f.); 86 (47 f.).
[3] G, 9, 131 ff.; §v, 4, 131; §v, 38, 70 ff.
[4] G, 9, 93 f.; §v, 4, 128; §v, 39.   [5] G, 9, 390; §v, 39, 54.

and a fine plastered floor, in the middle of which a basin has been hollowed out; this building has been identified as a temple.[1] It is possible that a small room in a house may have been a private sanctuary: there was a niche containing a flat stone which could have supported a cylindrical stone found among the ruins of the house; it may have been the precursor of the *maṣṣēbōt* of the Canaanite era.[2] Fragments of two groups of statues modelled in unbaked clay were found in 1935.[3] Each group consisted, apparently, of a man, a woman and a child; the best preserved fragment is a male head of almost life size, flat as a disc but curiously expressive, with modelled face, hair and beard indicated by strokes of paint and the eyes represented by two sea-shells. These statues were first related to the pottery levels, but the most recent excavations have restored them to the previous period by revealing, in the last pre-pottery level, fragments of human images of almost life size and even more stylized.[4] These statues certainly had a religious significance and were probably divine effigies, the two groups at Jericho, each of which contained a god, a goddess and a child-god, constituting the first appearance of the divine triad, which had such a long and important history in the Near East.

Evidence of another cult, ancestor-worship, was provided by the extraordinary discovery of ten skulls, separated from the skeleton and deprived, with one exception, of the lower jaw. On these skulls the facial muscles had been modelled in plaster, and the eyes replaced by sea-shells; the skull-cap remained bare, except for one which was painted with black bands; another skull had a moustache painted on it. Such details and the differences of expression between the faces show that an attempt was being made to reproduce a likeness of the dead.[5] Seven of the skulls were found heaped in the ruins of a house, two came from another room in the same house, the last was by itself in the northern part of the *tell*. Under the floor of the house where the main group was preserved forty persons had been buried; the skeletons were for the most part in disorder and the skull was missing from many of them, though the lower jaw remained.[6] The plastered skulls which were found must certainly have come from the same place. From an examination of the burials and the bones[7] it appears that the bodies were generally buried intact and that the removal

[1] G, 5, 86 (51).   [2] G, 5, 84 (72).
[3] G, 4, 22 (166 f.).   [4] G, 5, 92 (91 f.).
[5] G, 6, 51 ff.; G, 5, 85 (86 f.); 88 (74 f.). See Plate 13 (c).
[6] G, 5, 86 (48 f.).   [7] §v, 9,

of the skulls took place after interment, when the decomposition of the flesh had begun but was not yet far advanced, since some of the bones had remained articulated in the skeletons disturbed for this purpose. The whole process took place before the laying of the floor above the skeletons, and this floor was contemporary with the house where the plastered skulls were preserved.

The custom of interment under the floors of houses was general during this phase and has been encountered in different parts of the *tell*. Burial of the body in a huddled position, as in the preceding phase, was subsequently succeeded, without being entirely discarded, by burial at full length. Skulls were often removed, but not all were given a lifelike appearance in the manner just described; they were buried separately, often in pairs. This practice, which further attests a veneration of the dead, originated much earlier, since groups of skulls separated from the skeletons and laid in order were found in the first phase of the Neolithic period.[1]

So far Jericho has been the most instructive site for this phase, but its importance may be outweighed by very recent discoveries. In Transjordan, at Seyl 'Aqlat (Beidha), near Petra,[2] a village was discovered in which architectural evolution can be followed through six periods. Using exclusively local sandstone, it begins with polygonal houses (VI), continues with round houses (V) and sub-rectangular houses with slightly curving walls (IV); floors and walls were plastered and steps led down to the ground floor. Then comes a major change: the two succeeding villages (III–II) contained buildings apparently composed of corridors on to which opened narrow separate cells. These cells were separated from one another by platforms which were sometimes wider than the cells themselves. From the plan, which would have been unsuitable for dwellings, and also from the materials found in the rooms, it seems likely that these were workshops, and it has been possible to distinguish a slaughterhouse and the shop of a manufacturer of bone implements. The platforms may perhaps have been buttresses providing support for the erection of a light upper storey for habitation. There was also, in the second and third villages, a large house which had a cream-painted floor with a wide red band running parallel with the walls and around the hearth and a low platform (table or seat); this painting was continued on the walls. The final village returned to the earlier architectural plan; houses were rectangular with walls painted in one or two colours.

[1] G, 5, 88 (75). [2] §v, 18; §v, 19. See Plate 13 (b).

The connexion with Jericho is demonstrated not only by plastered floors, but by the same flint implements, the same double-saddled querns and the same custom of burying skulls separately (this did not apply to children and not always to adults). A small quantity of obsidian has been found. There is some evidence of the presence of the domestic goat, and hunting was widely practised. The number of querns and pestles seems to show that cereals were cultivated, and such an economy implies that the region was less arid than it is today—it is now a walk of an hour and a half to the nearest spring.

West of Jerusalem, Abu Ghōsh[1] had rectangular houses with stone walls and limestone floors. The flint industry was similar to that at Jericho, comprising chiefly arrows and sickle-blades, but in different proportions: there were many more arrows; axes and chisels were also more numerous and were often polished over a greater or less extent of their surfaces. There were no picks or hoes, but a round stone with a hole in it may have been part of a 'digging-stick'. There were elongated querns and pestles. From abroad came various obsidian tools and axes of a stone and a shape suggesting Syrian origin. Objects made of bone were relatively scarce. Bones of cattle and of goats were plentiful but have not been examined sufficiently for it to be established whether they came from domestic animals; at all events, there were figures of animals modelled in clay. The abundance both of arrows and of the bones of gazelle and wild boar shows that hunting provided at least part of the subsistence, the remainder being supplied by the cultivation of cereals.

At Wādi Fallāḥ[2] the upper level belongs to the same category. There are rectangular buildings with paved floors, axes with a polished edge, adzes, arrows, sickle-blades and knives, querns with double saddle, small quantities of obsidian and jade. The interest of this site lies in the fact that it displays the same sequence of phases as has been found at Jericho from the Natufian period onwards. Some of the same features occur in the two lower levels of Munḥāṭa,[3] south of Lake Tiberias, in the Jordan valley. A flint industry which is very closely akin to those at Jericho and at Abu Ghōsh, and querns with a double depression, provide further confirmation of this relationship. Farther north, near the southern tip of Lake Tiberias, by a ford over the Jordan, the lowest layer of Shaikh 'Ali (Tell 'Eli)[4] contained round buildings and industries which are related to the first phase at Jericho.

[1] §v, 25.
[2] §v, 35, 2 f.
[3] §v, 28; 29.
[4] §v, 30; 31; 32.

Above was a rectangular house, beneath the floor of which bodies had been buried in a contracted position, with the skulls missing, so that there may have been some connexion with the second phase at Jericho. A flint industry, similar to that of Jericho, and lime-washed floors were found at the base of Tell el-Fār'ah, near Nablus.[1] It is probable that some of the small settlements often restricted to a single house, which are ranged along the little valleys descending towards the Jordan or at the foot of the Carmel range in the plain of Esdraelon,[2] should also be attributed to this phase.

All these settlements, which may be grouped around Jericho as the typical site, constitute a relatively homogeneous collection, though local divergencies are by no means excluded. There are signs of the development of settled occupation and increases in population, both of which were due to a more productive culti-vation of the soil and to the domestication of animals. At Jericho, which is the best documented site, it is clear that this new group came from abroad and it now seems likely that its origin should be sought in Syria.[3] It has already been shown that there were traces of Syrian influence at Abu Ghōsh. At Tell Ramad, south-west of Damascus,[4] the lowest layer reveals a definite connexion with Pre-pottery B at Jericho: there are the same flint implements, the same querns, limewashed surfaces and a section of brick wall, and finally plastered skulls. Farther north the evidence becomes uncertain; the suggested comparisons with the non-pottery layers at Ras Shamra are not convincing.[5] However, it is tempting to connect this new phase in Palestine with Anatolia, the source of obsidian, with the extraordinary development of Çatal Hüyük and particularly with non-pottery Hacılar, where there was evi-dence of plastered floors and walls, painted and polished, of ancestor-worship attested by skulls preserved separately and of the same economy in the early stages of agriculture and stock-breeding.[6] It is the intermediaries, however, which are lacking. Moreover, there is no relationship to be noted or investigated with Mesopotamia which, from Jarmo onwards, pursued an independent course.

In Palestine itself development in the less favoured region of the Judaean desert was also either independent or retarded. At El-Khiām,[7] above the 'Khiamian' level, successor to the epi-palaeolithic industries, there were found a proto-Taḥunian and a

[1] G, 8, 68 (559 f.).   [2] G, 2, 229 ff.; §v, 30.
[3] G, 7, 153 ff.   [4] §v, 8.   [5] §v, 34, 153 ff.; §v, 7, 35.
[6] §v, 20, 73.   [7] §v, 12; §v, 23, 166 ff.

Taḥunian level, with a great stone wall. The name 'Taḥunian', which is derived from the Wādi Taḥūneh south of Bethlehem, where numerous implements were picked up on the surface,[1] has been used to designate the whole Pre-pottery Neolithic period in Palestine. It is preferable, however, to restrict its use to the industries of the Judaean hills, of southern Palestine and of the Transjordan desert during the second phase of the Neolithic Pre-pottery period. Indeed, at El-Khiām, Taḥunian evolved naturally from Khiamian and bore little resemblance to Neolithic Pre-pottery B at Jericho. It comprised an abundant microlithic industry, many arrows and scrapers and very fine graving-tools, few sickle-blades, very few of the axes, chisels and picks which were numerous and typical in the settlements of Wādi Taḥūneh. This discrepancy may perhaps be explained by a different econ-omy, but more probably by the haphazard nature of surface exploration, which overlooked the small pieces.

In Transjordan, 200 km. east of the 'Arabah, at site B of Wādi Dhubay,[2] the stone foundations of circular huts were pre-served, and a supply of Taḥunian arrows and graving tools. Sickle-blades and large implements were absent; in these semi-desert conditions the group still subsisted by means of hunting. Still further east at the site of Kilwa[3] there was evidence of a similar industry and also numerous picks. These tools were found near some rocks, on which drawings of animals, especially wild goats, were incised, and it is possible that some of them belonged to this period. Similar engravings were found in the Negeb and in Sinai; in the absence of tools with which they could be associated, it seems dangerous to seek to date them by shades of patina or by considerations of style.[4]

It is not yet possible to put forward with any confidence absolute dates for the two phases of the Neolithic Pre-pottery period. Such dating can be based only on carbon-14 tests and it is dis-turbing to note that the numerous dates for Jericho obtained by this means vary appreciably from one laboratory to another and that the most recent tests give the earliest dates. In 1960[5] the following dates were given: for phase A, 6850 B.C. ± 210; for phase B, 6250 B.C. ± 200 and 5850 B.C. ± 160. The dates pub-lished in 1963[6] were: for phase A, 6935 B.C. (GL-43); for phase B, 6840 B.C. (Gro-942) or 6710 B.C. (GL-41). More recent tests[7] give: for phase A, dates at intervals between 7825 ± 110

[1] §v, 5.   [2] §v, 37.   [3] §v, 33.
[4] G, 2, 181 ff.   [5] G, 6, 44 and 56.   [6] G, 9, 31.
[7] Radiocarbon (Suppl. to American Journal of Science), 5 (1963).

(P-378) and 7705 ± 84 (P-379) or between 8350 ± 200 (BM-106) and 8230 ± 200 (BM-110); for phase B beginning, 6660 ± 75 (P-380) and 6708 ± 101 (P-381), for phase B middle (!) 7006 ± 103 (P-382) and 7220 ± 200 (BM-115). The choice between these dates is quite arbitrary; the latest dates seem the most probable. So far only one date has been published for another site of phase B, that of Seyl 'Aqlat: 6830 ± 200 (BM-111).[1] It may be conjectured only that these first villages of huntsmen and incipient farmers in Palestine date from about 7000 B.C.

VI. FARMERS AND POTTERS

The invention of pottery, with the consequent addition of baked earthenware vessels to the domestic utensils available, did not of itself indicate a change in living-conditions and in village economy. At Çatal Hüyük in Anatolia[2] pottery, introduced at a date which carbon-14 fixes very early (before 7000 B.C., which is indeed too remote), remained for a long time very rare and did not take the place of wooden vessels; at Tell Ramad in Syria[3] the non-pottery level was separated from the pottery level by a level in which white plates and dishes of moulded lime were found; nevertheless the economy remained the same throughout the three levels. If a new phase in Palestinian history is regarded as beginning with the introduction of pottery, it is because its appearance on the sites or as a result of excavation is a convenient landmark for archaeologists, and particularly because in Palestine the introduction of pottery followed a long interval after the end of the Pre-pottery Neolithic period and because it actually did coincide with important changes.

Some of the sites of the second phase of the Pre-pottery Neolithic period were abandoned completely: Seyl 'Aqlat, Wādi Fallāḥ, the terrace of El-Khiām. At others, such as Jericho and Shaikh 'Ali, the stratification clearly indicates an interruption in occupation; at Abu Ghōsh and at Munḥāta the position has so far been less clear. New settlements were founded in increasing numbers all over the country. The settlers who took up their abode there and those who came to reoccupy ancient sites arrived in Palestine with a pottery industry already established and they brought with them a new type of habitation: they lived in huts which were generally partly below ground level, in pit-dwellings.

[1] §v, 19, 23.   [2] See above, pp. 306 ff.; §v, 22, 232.
[3] §v, 8.

There was an almost complete lack of solid buildings throughout practically the whole period. Those pits which had been dug in the previous levels and were cut into by the pits of subsequent levels upset the stratigraphy; moreover, strata of this period have generally been reached only by *sondages*; finally, the publication of results of recent excavations still remains very incomplete. The situation seems very complex and too many elements are lacking to enable the confusion to be resolved, so that both the grouping of the sites in relation to one another and their chronological classification must remain hypothetical.

A first group is constituted by certain sites of the Mediterranean coast and of North Palestine,[1] where a 'dark-faced burnished ware' was found, with or without incisions. Incised patterns also occurred without the burnishing and assumed various forms: deep incisions in parallel lines or in a herring-bone design, rectangular or wavy painted patterns, imprints made by shells ('cardial ware') or with the finger-nail, dotted patterns ('point incision'). The southernmost sites are Teluliot Batashi[2] and Wādi Rabaḥ[3] near Tel Aviv; the most northerly are Kfar Gilʿādi[4] and Tell Turmus[5] near the sources of the Jordan. The same pottery was encountered in the lesser sites of the plain of Esdraelon, at the foot of the Carmel range, particularly at Hazorea (Tell Abu Zureiq and Tell Kiri),[6] and penetrated as far into the Jordan valley as Shaikh ʿAli, south of Lake Tiberias.[7]

Two other classes of pottery may be designated according to the sites at which they were found in the purest form: Jericho and Shaʿar ha-Gōlān (Yarmuk). At Jericho, in the excavations of 1935 and 1936,[8] J. Garstang distinguished, above the non-pottery strata, a level IX containing pottery. The clay had been mixed with straw and the vases were modelled by hand in simple shapes; outer surfaces were covered with a red slip, unevenly burnished except on large vases. The summit of the level yielded a finer class of pottery, painted brown and burnished except for decorative horizontal bands or chevrons. The stone industry was the same as in the previous non-pottery levels. The following level, VIII, was characterized by a more highly developed stone industry; tools were made of a different kind of flint, were smaller and showed signs of more touching-up. The pottery was distinguished by the intentional admixture of mineral particles with the clay, the use of the potter's wheel for necks and for small

[1] G, 2, 269 ff. [2] §vi, 8. [3] §vi, 7.

[4] §vi, 9, 21. [5] §vi, 13. [6] §vi, 13.

[7] §v, 32. [8] G, 3; G, 4, 22 (163 ff.), 23 (70 ff., 77 ff.).

vases, the finishing of surfaces, better firing, a richer variety of shapes. Special characteristics were inverted rims, the 'bow-rim' neck, the loop-handle with widened attachments, the replacement of the painted decoration of level IX by incisions, especially in herring-bone pattern, the absence of burnishing except on small vases. Buildings attributed to both levels continued the tradition of the non-pottery phases.

The above description must be considerably amended in view of the recent excavations of K. M. Kenyon.[1] Above the ruins of the last settlement of the Pre-pottery Neolithic period and after a long interval there came immigrant settlers who brought pottery with them. The stratigraphy of the layers of the Pottery Neolithic period is very uncertain and it is with some hesitation that Miss Kenyon has identified two phases: Pottery Neolithic A and Pottery Neolithic B. This distinction is based much more on the typology of the pottery than on stratigraphical evidence. In fact, the description of the two groups of pottery thus distinguished is generally consistent with that given to the pottery of 'levels' IX and VIII of Garstang's excavations, with this difference, that the decorated pottery of level IX is no longer regarded as more recent than the rest of the pottery of this same level, but is distinguished from it as fine pottery contrasted with coarse pottery. In preference to two successive phases, A and B, it would perhaps be better to recognize at Jericho a single Pottery Neolithic period, in the course of which a development would become apparent resulting from the introduction of pottery B and the influence of another group, the Yarmukian, which will be discussed later.[2] Apart from pottery, which was a complete innovation, the other utensils were no longer the same as in the Pre-pottery Neolithic period: the fine querns had disappeared; stone vases were much more crudely made. The flint industry was also different, the most notable change being the appearance of the deeply serrated sickle-blade.[3] But the most striking contrast with the previous phases is to be found in the style of the dwellings. There was still no sign of any solid architecture, but circular earth-floors indicated the position of huts and there were many more round holes from pit-dwellings, around which walls of mud and pebbles were built. It was only towards the end of the period that remains of buildings appeared, with straight or curved walls in plano-convex brick on stone foundations; a wall 2·25 m. broad was traced for a distance of 19 m., but

---

[1] G, 5, 85 (84 ff.), 86 (54 f.), 92 (105 f.); G, 6, 60 ff.
[2] G, 2, 273 ff.; G, 7, 157.   [3] G, 6, 62 f.

is was not possible to determine whether it represented an enclo-sure or a defensive wall.[1] Pit-dwellings were found in all the excavated parts of the *tell* and their density suggests a relatively numerous population. In spite of the changes which have just been mentioned, the way of life was not very different from that of preceding periods: the economy continued to be based on breed-ing of livestock and agriculture; details are still lacking with regard to the crops which were cultivated and the animals which were domesticated, but they at least belonged to species known in the Pre-pottery Neolithic period. Jericho was therefore a large village of farmers and, it may now be added, of potters.

The site which is representative of a third group is Sha‘ar ha-Gōlān, at the mouth of the Yarmuk in the Jordan valley. This site, which is known only as a result of utility works and by several archaeological *sondages*, was investigated by M. Stekelis, who established it as the typical site of a special class, the Yarmukian.[2] The single level which yielded all the finds was described as being formed of grey earth and broken pebbles, and no building was found. It seemed not unlikely that this grey earth and these broken pebbles were all that remained of walls similar to those which, at Jericho, were erected above the pit-dwellings and it is probable that an observer familiar with this type of dwelling could have traced the pits which had been surrounded by these walls. There was abundant evidence of the flint industry—many picks, hoes, chisels and axes, some of them with a polished edge, many piercers, many deeply-serrated sickle-blades (which Stekelis called 'saws'), fewer finely serrated sickle-blades, relatively few arrows. Stone tools included, in addition to querns, pestles and mortars. The pottery was coarse, the clay being mixed with straw and with large particles of quartz and basalt; the shapes were heavy, with flat bases, sometimes showing the imprint of the rush mat on which the pot had been modelled. Surfaces were smoothed and sometimes had a slip. Only incised decoration was used—especially bands defined by two incised lines and filled with herring-bone incisions; these bands en-circled the necks of pots or outlined triangles or zigzags on the belly. Art is represented by a female form carved in limestone, by a head modelled in clay, by numerous pebbles incised with conventional representations of a female body, a human face or sexual organ. These images apparently had a religious significance and were perhaps connected with a fertility cult. Such an outlook would have been in accordance with the mode of existence of the

[1] G, 6, 65.   [2] G, 2, 263 ff.; §vi, 15; 16; 17.

population. They lived partly by hunting (arrows, bones of game broken for the extraction of the marrow) and by fishing in the lake and the rivers (large stones used for holding the nets in place). But above all they were herdsmen (bones of domestic animals) and tillers of the soil (picks, hoes, sickle-blades, querns). Weaving was attested by basalt spindle-whorls and by perforated stones which could have been weights for looms.

At the present stage of investigation and publication, it is very difficult to bring into line with these two typical sites the other discoveries made in Palestine. The pottery of 'Jericho A' has been noted at the following sites: at Teluliot Batashi, in con-nexion with a pit-dwelling;[1] at Wādi Rabah three sherds not clearly stratified;[2] at Lydda a collection which is important but mixed with later pieces;[3] at Abu Ghosh a handful of sherds,[4] at Megiddo, level XX (badly stratified);[5] at Tell ed-Duweir one sherd in a cave.[6] 'Jericho B' pottery is more widely represented. It appears—usually associated with Yarmukian influence—at the bottom of the great *tells* of north Palestine: Megiddo level XX,[7] Beth-shan in the pit-dwellings and level XVIII,[8] Balata-Shechem also in pit-dwellings,[9] the northern Tell el-Fār'ah in 'Middle Chalcolithic';[10] it is at this last site that pit-dwellings have been best observed and described. 'Jericho B' pottery is also found in secondary sites of the Jordan valley: at Shaikh 'Ali level II, mixed with the 'dark-faced burnished ware',[11] at Tell esh-Shūneh level I with a pit,[12] at Tell Abu Habil level I with pits.[13] This type, mixed with others, has penetrated as far as the caves of Murabba'āt in the desert of Judah.[14]

With this Jericho group may be linked another site which has features in common with it but which presents a rather individual aspect. At Ghrubba in the Jordan valley, opposite Jericho and a little to the north of it,[15] a pit-dwelling, several times reoccupied during this period, has yielded pottery which includes certain forms similar to those of Jericho (B rather than A), but which is

[1] §vi, 8.
[2] §vi, 7, 159.
[3] §vi, 9, 18.
[4] §v, 25, 140 f.
[5] §vi, 14, pl. 18 (1–4, 12, 13), 20 (7–10).
[6] §vi, 19, fig. 1 and p. 300 (cave 6019).
[7] §vi, 14, pls. 18 (5–11), 20 (1–6).
[8] §vi, 5, 124, pl. 1; §vi, 6, 6 f., pls. 11, 20–27, 111, 17–19.
[9] §vi, 18, 36 f.
[10] G, 8, 54 (397 ff., fig. 1), 55 (545, fig. 1), 62 (552, fig. 1), 68 (560 ff., fig. 1, pls. 36–9).
[11] §v, 32.
[12] §vi, 3; §vi, 4, 12 ff.
[13] §vi, 4, 31 ff.
[14] §vi, 1, 14 ff.
[15] §vi, 12.

distinguished by the abundance of decoration painted in thin lines and by the absence of any incised pattern—a fact which differentiates Ghrubba clearly from the Yarmukian type.

The Yarmukian type seems to have been more limited in extent than the Jericho type and it is possible that it may have been diffused chiefly through the agency of Jericho B, in which the herring-bone incisions must have been due to Yarmukian influence. Some of the sites in question have been mentioned earlier in connexion with the Jericho group. The Yarmukian type also appears, this time in conjunction with that of the coastal group, on the sites of the plain of Esdraelon, near Tell Kiri and Yoqne'ām.[1] It reveals itself in a purer form, apparently, not far from Sha'ar ha-Gōlān in the Jordan valley at Munḥāta above the pre-pottery levels[2] and, further south, at Khirbet es-Sōda.[3] Yarmukian sherds have been noted as far south as Murabba'āt, where the same basalt whetstones as at Sha'ar ha-Gōlān[4] have also been found.

The absence of stratigraphy or at least of an adequate stratigraphy makes it impossible to put forward with any assurance a chronological classification for these three groups. The general impression is that they are to some extent contemporaneous and it is very difficult to say exactly when the use of pottery began in Palestine. Yarmukian is not the earliest group, as Stekelis believed,[5] nor is that of Ghrubba, as was asserted by J. Mellaart.[6] It seems that the pure Yarmukian and Ghrubba types are earlier than Jericho B, but there is nothing to suggest that they are earlier than Jericho A and they cannot be placed between Jericho A and Jericho B since the demarcation line between these two phases is uncertain and in any case they are not separated by an interval.

Classification may be assisted, to some extent, by a study of the relations between Palestine and neighbouring regions. From this aspect it would be tempting to give priority to the coastal group, in which the 'dark-faced burnished ware' and incised decoration established a connexion with North Syria and Cilicia ('Amūq A-B-C); intermediaries would be provided by Ras Shamra VA-B and IVC, by the bottom of Ṭabbat el-Ḥammām, by Byblos Early Neolithic, by the first pottery level of Tell Ramad; Palestine is more closely linked with these last two sites, which are also the nearest geographically. The coastal group

[1] G, 2, 264.   [2] §v, 28; 29; 36. See Plate 13 (d).   [3] §v, 36.
[4] §vi, 1, 21, fig. 2, 28–31, 37–9, 44, pl. 5, 27–8.
[5] §vi, 15, 19.   [6] §vi, 12, 32 f.

would thus take its place in the interval which, at Jericho, follows the end of the Pre-Pottery Neolithic period.[1] The dates obtained by carbon-14 for Byblos are 5043 ± 80 B.C. for the middle strata, 4592 ± 200 for the summit; the dates given more recently for Ras Shamra are 5528 ± 89 B.C. for level VA, 6052 ± 113 B.C. for level VB, which agrees with the carbon-14 dating of the lowest level of Mersin ('Amūq A) as 5995 ± 250 B.C. The lower limit of the dates provided for Pre-pottery Neolithic at Jericho would thus be attained. It is still necessary, however, to insist on the uncertainty of these dates, and it must also be emphasized that this same type of pottery continued for a long time in Syro-Cilicia, that Palestine is at the extreme limit of its area of distribution and probably received it later.

In fact, it is with the last phase of the Syro-Cilician group ('Amūq C) that the material from the coastal region of Palestine may best be compared, especially the more typical pottery of Wādi Rabaḥ, and that is probably also true of the Early Neolithic at Byblos. The links between Palestine and the north are more clearly apparent, however, in the succeeding phase, that of 'Amūq D, the pottery of which displays 'bow-rims', red slip, vases on a pedestal, small handles triangular in section which are typical of Jericho B.[2] The intermediaries are provided by Ras Shamra and Byblos, probably with chronological inconsistencies and local variations. At Ras Shamra,[3] red slip, then the 'bow-rim', the loop-handle with widened attachments, and vases on a pedestal are typical of levels IVA-B and IIIC; for this last carbon-14 gave the date 4582 ± 81 B.C. At Byblos[4] the 'bow-rim' and many varieties of incised decoration appear in the Middle Neolithic period, the handle with widened attachments in the Late Neolithic; material from Wādi Rabaḥ corresponds with the middle phase, that of Jericho B with the middle and late phases. At Byblos these two phases seem to occupy the second half of the fifth millennium and to overlap into the fourth.

The interest of Byblos lies in the fact that it presents, at the same time, a link with the third Palestinian group, the Yarmukian.[5] Deeply serrated sickle-blades, arrows and incised pebbles appear at Byblos from the early Neolithic period, and also the incised herring-bone pattern, but this last is an inadequate criterion, for it persists throughout the Neolithic period. It is, however, with Middle Neolithic at Byblos that Yarmukian has

[1] §vi, 2, 498 f. [2] §vi, 20. [3] §v, 7.
[4] §vi, 3, 72. [5] G, 6, 66 f.; §vi, 2, 497.

most points of contact, both in stone objects and in pottery shapes. The same flint tools are plentiful in numerous deposits of the Lebanese coast and it was probably from the Lebanon that this culture penetrated, after some delay, into Palestine.[1] It is important to note, on the other hand, that the same period at Byblos provides simultaneously parallels with the Yarmukian at Sha'ar ha-Gōlān and with the Pottery Neolithic at Jericho, thus indicating that these two groups were at least to some extent contemporaneous.

In addition to this close connexion with Byblos and to the more distant relationship with Syro-Cilicia, it has been suggested that there was also Mesopotamian influence, of the epochs of both Tell Halaf and Hassūnah. But comparisons made with the pottery of Tell Halaf[2] are not very convincing and are more relevant to material from Ghassūl, which is later than Jericho, as will be seen, and is also later than Tell Halaf; only the 'bow-rim' could connect Jericho B with Tell Halaf, but the intermediate link must have been North Syria, where this form is attested. The influence of Tell Halaf is apparent in this region, moreover, both in imports and later in imitations, from phase C of 'Amūq onwards, and it reached Ras Shamra at level IV C. Other comparisons have been suggested between the pottery of Wādi Rabaḥ and certain 'Halafian' pieces from Mersin, but this merely leads back to the Syro-Cilician group. It was through the same group that the influence of Hassūnah could have reached Palestine; it has been assumed at Ghrubba.[3] It is true that the painted decoration from this site strongly resembles that of Mersin 'Early Chalcolithic', which itself has connexions with Hassūnah; Ghrubba would thus have been appreciably earlier than Jericho B. But Ghrubba did not possess this decoration except in a bastardized form and also included later characteristics, such as red slip, the 'bow-rim', and the 'hole-mouth' jar, which lead back once more to the Syrian tradition of 'Amūq D. If Ghrubba was earlier than Jericho B, it was only by a very small margin.

The value of these comparisons is not simply that they allow of some chronological classification of Palestinian material. They reveal the links which at that time united Palestine with the outside world. These connexions were all with the north (like those already observed in Pre-pottery Neolithic) and they were unilateral: Palestine was solely a recipient. It was also the farthest point to be affected by these influences and it did not yet play the

[1] §vi, 2, 499 f.   [2] §vi, 10.   [3] §vi, 12, 31 f.

part, assigned to it by its geographical position, of a cultural bridge between Asia and Africa—a part which it did not play until later and even then to a lesser degree than has sometimes been suggested. The first known villages of Egypt, the Faiyūm A, are contemporaneous with the end of this period (mean date given by carbon-14: 4250 B.C.), but do not appear to share any points in common with the Palestine sites.

The pottery industry therefore must have been introduced into Palestine by different groups who penetrated there probably in different epochs and from different directions. The wide diversity both of types of pottery and of areas of distribution would thus be explained. The group from the coast came down by way of the coastal plain and thrust spearheads into the interior (Wādi Rabaḥ, plain of Esdraelon); certain elements may perhaps have made their way through southern Syria to Kfar Gil'ādi and to Tell Turmus. The Yarmukian group, if its Lebanese connexions can be confirmed, may have taken the road leading from Sidon to the Jordan valley through the pass of Merj 'Ayūn. The Jericho group, whose links with the far north are the most clearly defined, could have arrived by way of the Orontes valley and the Syrian Biqā'; from the Jordan valley they must have swarmed to the west through the Beth-shan pass in the plain of Esdraelon as far as Megiddo, by Wādi Fār'ah as far as Tell el-Fār'ah. In several regions the streams met and intermingled.

It is probable that these immigrants brought with them other innovations apart from pottery. Bones of calves, goats, sheep and dogs found at Sha'ar ha-Gōlān have been adduced as evidence of stock-breeding;[1] a domestic ox was noted in the lowest level at Megiddo.[2] While surer and more general confirmation must be awaited, it is open to conjecture that the Palestinian peasants of that time were breeding cattle, sheep and possibly pigs, in addition to goats which had been domesticated since the Pre-pottery Neolithic period. It has been established, with a greater or lesser degree of probability, that these animals were domesticated in north Syria from 'Amūq A-B,[3] at Ras Shamra from level VB onwards.[4]

These immigrants were in any case farmers, which explains the wide dispersal of the population: they settled everywhere where there was water and a little cultivable soil at the outlets of the small valleys running down into the coastal plain, the plain of Esdraelon or the Jordan valley; with the exception of certain favoured regions, these settlements were very small, some of them

[1] G, 9, 175; §vi, 15, 16. [2] §vi, 11, 139.
[3] §v, 4, 120. [4] §v, 7, 35, n. 5, and 36.

being occupied by no more than one large family, and they were not settled for long periods.[1]

Such individualism and such relative mobility may perhaps explain the insubstantial nature of the dwellings which, where they can be discerned, are huts or pit-dwellings. The brick houses at Jericho, if indeed they belong to this period, date from the end of it. The rectangular house at Wādi Rabaḥ and the 'architecture' noted at Tell Turmus are exceptions and may be explained by the closer relations maintained by the coastal group with Byblos and Ras Shamra, which contained rectangular houses at the corresponding period. But this primitive form of dwelling and this very impermanence may be explained also by the social type of the new population of Palestine. The two explanations are not mutually exclusive, since the people may have been nomads who were in the course of becoming settled. Later, in the Intermediate Early–Middle Bronze Age Period,[2] the penetration of the cultivated lands by other groups from pastoral areas gave rise to the same phenomena—the juxtaposition of various different elements and the absence of solid architecture (at this later period, the eclipse of urban life). It is no paradox to attribute to nomads the introduction of pottery and certain other developments; before the establishment of trading on a larger scale, nomads played an important part in the transmission of new ideas and the diffusion of influences.[3]

One problem remains: this phase occurred at the beginning of the fourth millennium; if the latest date, about 6000 B.C., be retained for the end of the preceding phase, Pre-pottery Neolithic, Pottery Neolithic must have lasted two millennia, a period which is far too long for a process of becoming sedentary which, in such a long stretch of time, never culminated in the construction of solid dwelling-houses. It is also too long in view of the scanty developments of material products and the relatively meagre layers left by this phase in stratified sites. It follows therefore that the hiatus between Pre-pottery Neolithic and Pottery Neolithic, which is particularly apparent in the stratigraphy of Jericho, must have occupied the greater part of these two millennia and that the 'coastal Neolithic', if it really belonged to this hiatus at Jericho, did not itself follow the Pre-pottery phase until after an interval. This interpretation would agree reasonably well with the carbon-14 dates mentioned above for the corresponding strata at Byblos, less well with the dates so far published for Ras Shamra. If

---

[1] G, 2, 230 ff.; §v, 30.   [2] *C.A.H.* I³, ch. XXI, sects. v–vi.
[3] G, 7, 157.

human occupation in Palestine was interrupted for a long time after the Pre-pottery Neolithic period, this would also explain why many settlements of this era were finally abandoned at that time and why its inventions, especially architecture, were forgotten. But it will then be necessary to explain how the Pre-pottery Neolithic population came to disappear and why Palestine remained unoccupied for more than a millennium; so far it has not been possible to answer these questions.

The farmers and potters who resettled Palestine did not, save in exceptional cases, penetrate into the mountainous region (Abu Ghōsh) or the Judah desert (Murabba'āt), which did not offer conditions favourable to their way of life. It is not known what happened at that time in the semi-arid regions of southern Palestine and Transjordan. It seems likely that the Taḥunian period continued there without profiting from innovations introduced into the north; in settlements of these regions which belong to the succeeding period a proportion of the stone tools still followed the Taḥunian tradition.

VII. FARMERS, POTTERS AND
METALWORKERS

The term 'Chalcolithic' indicates, in contrast with Neolithic, a period during which tools were made of metal (copper) concurrently with stone. Great confusion in fact prevails in the application of the terms 'Neolithic' and 'Chalcolithic' by Palestinian archaeologists. Material from Jericho VIII, called by J. Garstang Chalcolithic in 1935 and Late Neolithic in 1936, became Pottery Neolithic B with K. M. Kenyon.[1] The corresponding material from Tell el-Fār'ah was called first Middle Eneolithic then Middle Chalcolithic by R. de Vaux.[2] G. E. Wright classified Jericho VIII as Middle Chalcolithic in 1938, as Early Chalcolithic, together with Yarmukian, in 1961.[3] According to J. Kaplan in 1959, Jericho VIII and the related groups were Chalcolithic, but Jericho IX and Yarmukian were Neolithic,[4] which agrees with the views of W. F. Albright in 1954 and in 1960.[5] In 1963 R. Amiran described Yarmukian, Jericho and related groups as Neolithic.[6] The latest synthesis, by E. Anati,[7] accepts

[1] G, 4, 22 (143), 23 (68 f.); G, 6, 63.
[2] G, 8, 68 (589 f.).
[3] §VII, 72, 26; §VII, 74, 79.
[4] §VI, 9, 21 f.
[5] §VII, 4, 29; G, 1.
[6] §VII, 7, 33 ff.
[7] G, 2.

the attributions made by the excavators of each site, with the results that Yarmukian and Jericho A-B are classified as Neolithic, but the lowest levels of Tell el-Fār'ah, Megiddo, Beth-shan, which were contemporary with them, as Chalcolithic.

Actually all these sites and strata belong to the same stage of human development, described in the preceding section, and not a single copper object has been found in them. It may well be said that for a long time metal continued to be a rare material and was consequently re-used; that its absence is due to that rarity, to the hazards of excavation and to the deterioration of objects. It may also be said that metalwork was known even earlier in other regions of the Near East (Tell Halaf) and of Anatolia (Beyce-sultan, Mersin). These arguments are not very convincing, how-ever: a sufficient number of Palestinian sites has now been investigated for some traces of metal to have been found if it had been in such common use as to have had an influence on living conditions; moreover, the evidence is equally negative or slender in the centres believed to have had cultural and material relations with these Palestinian groups; no metal occurs in the correspond-ing levels of Byblos or of Ras Shamra; in the 'Amūq the first traces of metal date from the 'First Mixed Range' and could be contemporary with these Palestinian strata, but good metal tools do not appear until phase F, which is clearly later.

It seems preferable, therefore, not to look for the beginning of a new period in Palestine until archaeology provides proof of the use, and even the manufacture, of metal tools there. This development was progressive and did not become apparent everywhere at the same time. The living conditions of the early farmers and potters gradually became changed, not so much by the new tools, which for a long time remained infinitesimal in proportion to the stone implements, as by the requirements of the new industry, including the establishment of centres in areas where metal was found and/or fuel for forging it, communica-tions with these mining or smelting centres which were sometimes distant, the growth of a class of artisans who depended on the farmers for their subsistence and, consequently, the formation of more highly organized and populous communities.

The new elements appeared first and most clearly in the marginal areas, some of which had never before had a settled population, such as the region of the Dead Sea, the northern Negeb and the Mediterranean coast. Local and temporal dif-ferences between the sites of these three groups did not seriously affect the uniformity of this culture, which is called Ghassulian.

It was in fact first identified at Teleilat Ghassūl, which consists of three small *tells*, low hillocks close to one another in the plain which extends north of the Dead Sea and east of the Jordan.[1] Four levels have been distinguished, but only the uppermost level, IV, has been widely explored. On each hillock there was an agglomeration of rectangular or trapezoidal houses, of irregular plan, huddled one against another or separated by lanes, without any attempt to form a town and without an enclosure wall. The walls were sometimes of stone, generally of brick which was often set on a stone foundation. There were abundant flint tools, characterized by scarcity of arrows, numerous sickle-blades, fan-shaped scrapers made from tabular flint whose cortex was preserved on one face of the implement, and, especially, adzes and a particular type of chisel. The remaining tools comprised, apart from querns of simple shape, pestles and mortars, bowls, vases with pierced pedestal. The pottery was made of a clay which was generally coarse but quite well fired. It was distinguished by a variety of shapes: large wide-mouthed jars, with or without necks, bowls or goblets, sometimes with a small handle near the base, horn-shaped vessels, spoons and a vessel once called a 'bird-vase', which has now been explained as an imitation of a leather receptacle, the water-skin used for carrying liquids or the similar skin designed to be hung up by both ends and rocked for making butter, a churn.[2] The bases of pots often retained the imprint of the rush-mat on which they had been modelled.[3] Decoration was of two kinds: a plastic decoration of incisions or of raised bands generally ornamented with impressions, or painted decoration with simple geometric designs in a dark colour on a cream or pink ground. In some of the houses there were remarkable wall paintings,[4] but the significance of the remaining fragments is uncertain; they comprise a cult-scene, heads, animals mythical or real including a bird in a very naturalistic style, geometric patterns. From level IV several metal objects were obtained: two axes, the blade of a third and fragments of eight points. One of these fragments has been analysed and its copper found to contain 7 per cent of tin,[5] but it is difficult to imagine that, at such an early date, 'bronze' was produced by alloyage. In the same layer there was evidence of weaving, provided by possible spindle-whorls, bone implements explained as shuttles, and a shred of fabric composed of vegetable fibres.[6] Level III, which was less

[1] §vii, 41; 47. [2] §vii, 5; 33; 36.
[3] §vii, 18. [4] See Plate 14 (*b*).
[5] §vii, 47, 75 ff. [6] §vi, 11, 140.

widely explored, presented the same general features; a copper hook was also found.[1] The deep levels II–I, were scarcely touched by the first excavations, but more information has been gained by a recent season.[2] A critical examination of the results[3] indicates that the four 'levels' are difficult to distinguish; they sometimes run into one another and at some points they do not all exist, which certainly suggests that occupation was continuous, while the 4 m. of deposits indicate that this occupation must have lasted for several centuries. The culture is remarkably homogeneous and wall-paintings are encountered at all levels, but it would be extraordinary if there were no signs of development over so long a period. In fact, walls on a stone base do not appear before level II, horn-shaped vessels are absent from the lower levels and a more detailed study of the pottery should reveal further changes.

Ghassūl was a village of farmers and the small quantity of arrows found suggests that there was little hunting. There were silos containing cereal grains, and also date and olive stones.[4] Since it has adequate irrigation, the region is suitable for the cultivation of date-palms, but olives grown there do not bear fruit. Unless a change in climate is to be imagined,[5] it must be assumed that the olives were brought from the mountains and that the economy of Ghassūl was not entirely self-sufficient. There is no evidence on the site of funerary customs, apart from some burials under the floors of houses and burials of young children in funerary jars. Some kilometres farther east, however, at 'Adeimeh, a vast cemetery was found where fleshless bones had been deposited in cists or micro-dolmens; this cemetery has been regarded as belonging to Ghassūl[6] and the hypothesis remains probable, in spite of certain objections.[7]

Subsequent discoveries have brought Ghassūl out of the isolation in which it first appeared, and the name 'Ghassulian' has sometimes been applied to everything which is regarded as 'Chalcolithic' in Palestine. This usage is inaccurate, but there exist certain sites, especially in the southern half of the country, which were related to Ghassūl and were almost contemporary with it.

The group which is both the most interesting and best known belongs to the neighbourhood of Beersheba, where man was then settling for the first time. The settlement was established

[1] §VII, 41, 12 n. 1, pl. 66, 2.   [2] §VII, 52.   [3] §VII, 62.
[4] §VII, 47, 40.   [5] G, 2, 312 ff.
[6] §VII, 66; §VII, 72, 30 and 36, n. 40.   [7] G, 2, 310; §VII, 55, 403 ff.

above an underground water-level extending over several kilometres which can be reached today—and should have been accessible then—by means of several wells. Investigation has revealed half a dozen agglomerations, which are about 1 km. apart but connected by isolated dwellings. The principal sites explored are Tell Abu Māṭār,[1] Bir eṣ-Ṣafadi,[2] Khirbet el-Bitar (Ḥorvat Beter).[3] They have a common history. The first dwellings were subterranean or semi-subterranean chambers, hollowed out of the loess and loam, reached by shafts, interconnected by passages and equipped with hearths and silos. These dwellings are piled on two or three levels, separated by desertions which were probably due to periods of exceptional drought. Such a way of life is not necessarily indicative of the origin of this group of people; the subterranean dwellings were dictated by the natural conditions of the region: they were easily dug out of the silt of Beersheba and they gave protection against heat and dust. Similar caves in the same region were inhabited in Byzantine or Arab times and until very recently.[4] In the upper level the type of dwelling changes; here are rectangular houses built of brick on a stone foundation. At Ṣafadi the houses were constructed around a central hall, an arrangement which already existed in the subterranean dwellings.

The total number of these habitations could have housed up to a thousand persons; they lasted over a period of two hundred to three hundred years, and shared a homogeneous culture. Flint implements[5] were akin to those at Ghassūl (fan-shaped scrapers, chisels, etc.) but were less carefully made. The relative numbers of the various kinds of tools were different, and there were no arrows. The stone industry also produced some fine basalt pots, bowls, almost all of which were decorated with triangular hatching on the rim, and cups with pierced pedestal. Pottery[6] included features which are indisputably Ghassulian and certain typical shapes recur (the horn, the 'bird-vase' or 'churn'), but there were some notable differences: the wide-mouthed jar without a neck (hole-mouth) was much more in evidence and its rim was often decorated with finger-prints; there were numerous small shallow bowls. Bases were often cut off by a thread, and the bowls were shaped on a wheel as were some of the necks of large vases. There was no imprint of rush-matting on the bases of pots. Decoration usually consisted of bands of red painted on the rim or round the belly; incised decoration was very rare. There was

[1] §vii, 56.   [2] §vii, 57.   [3] §vii, 23.
[4] §vii, 8.   [5] §vii, 75.   [6] §vii, 16; 23; 56.

a special class of fine pottery: the clay was smooth, white, beige or buff in colour; the usual shape was a short-necked vase with a rounded belly and a series of lug-handles, alternately vertical and horizontal. Painted decoration was rare and confined to spots of red on the lug-handles with occasionally a band of the same colour on the rim.

The inhabitants were essentially farmers. They cultivated wheat, barley and lentils.[1] They reared mainly sheep but also goats and a few cattle and they kept dogs to guard their flocks.[2] The absence of pigs can be explained by the unfavourable conditions of this semi-desert region. Several industries flourished, with some specialization within each group. Ṣafadi devoted itself to work in ivory and bone, and three statuettes were found there, as well as figurines, pins and pendants.[3] A figurine and a bone pin were also found at Abu Māṭar,[4] but this site was primarily a centre for metalwork: not only have copper objects been found, such as pear-shaped mace-heads, a hollow stick with an ornamental tip, an awl, a cylinder, rings, but also the workshops where they were made, the positions of the open fires where the ore was melted down, the furnaces constructed for its refining, the crucibles in which it was melted and possibly fragments of the moulds in which the objects were cast. Nuggets of ore, dross and scraps of metal have been discovered at all levels. The copper was practically pure and came from an exceptionally rich ore; ore and dross were likewise found at Khirbet el-Bitar. This ore came from Wādi Feinan, on the eastern slope of the 'Arabah, more than 100 km. away.

Hard stones, basalt and haematite, were brought from the same region. The Beersheba groups were in contact with even more distant countries: a small quantity of turquoise came from Sinai, sea-shells found in the course of excavation belonged to the fauna of the Mediterranean or the Red Sea and to one kind of freshwater shellfish which exists only in the Nile valley. Ivory may have come from Syria or Palestine, for up to the first millennium B.C. the elephant was hunted in north Syria and hippopotamus on the Palestinian coast.

The Beersheba civilization extended over the whole of the northern Negeb, where there is an annual rainfall of less than 30 cm.,[5] to the east as far as Tell 'Arad and to the west as far as the sites of the Wādi Shallaleh–Wādi Ghazzeh (Naḥal Besōr). Some of those which had been known for a long time[6] were studied afresh

---

[1] §VII, 50; 76. [2] §VII, 9; 30. [3] §VII, 58.
[4] See Plate 15 (a.) [5] Cf. the map in §VII, 56, 176. [6] §VII, 45.

and additional ones were explored.[1] There has been much discussion of the chronological classification of these sites,[2] and it must now be revised. All of them belong to the Beersheba-Ghassul civilization, probably to an advanced phase of it, and they did not survive for more than a century or two. Dwellings there were only semi-subterranean, since the nature of the terrain made it impossible for them to be hollowed out entirely underground; in some cases they were surface-huts; there is one instance of a house with rounded corners. The pottery types are those of Ghassul-Beersheba, with variations: decoration in relief occurs more frequently than painted decoration, the horizontal handle is not much in evidence and the Beersheba class of fine pottery is lacking. Flint implements included axes, beautifully made fan-shaped scrapers and also arrows. Basalt pots with flat bases or pierced pedestals were found. The metal industry is attested by fragments of malachite and by several copper objects. Animal-bones show that there had been sheep and goats, cattle, pigs and dogs. In relation to the communities of Ghassul and of the Beersheba region, this civilization appears to have been marginal: the populations were less attached to the soil; they looked to agriculture for subsistence, but were essentially pastoral and were still occupied with hunting.

Another group which comes within the same category but is peripheral inhabited the caves of the Judaean desert. Even before the discoveries at Ghassul, discoveries of 'Ghassulian' flint, pottery and stone vases had been made in the caves of the Wādi Khareitun, south-east of Bethlehem, Umm Qaṭafah, Umm Qalaʻa, ʻIrq el-Aḥmar.[3] Some atypical Chalcolithic sherds were found in caves of the cliff of Qumrān.[4] A more important collection came from caves at Murabbaʻāt, including flint and pottery which showed an affinity with Ghassul and Beersheba.[5] Further south, above the spring of ʻEn-Gedī, an enclosure with a mound in the centre of it has been regarded as a sanctuary and dated to the Chalcolithic epoch by its pottery, which is related to that of Ghassul–Beersheba.[6] Almost all the caves which have recently been explored between ʻEn-Gedī and Masada were occupied at this period; of particular importance are those of Naḥal David (Wādi Seder),[7] Naḥal Ḥever (Wādi Ḥabra),[8]

[1] G, 2, 296 ff.   [2] §VII, 72, 23 ff.   [3] §VII, 51.
[4] §VII, 12, 12–13 (caves 36 and B); Rev. bibl. 63 (1956), 574 (cave 11).
[5] §VI, 1, 14 ff. and 34.   [6] §VII, 49.
[7] §VII, 11, 173 ff.
[8] §VII, 2, fig. 7, 1–15; 10, 1–7; §VII, 3, 188 ff.

Naḥal Seelim (Wādi Seyal) which has a structure similar to that of 'En-Gedī and mace-heads in copper and haematite of the Beer-sheba type,[1] and Naḥal Mishmār (Wādi Maḥras).[2] In one of the caves of this last valley[3] there were found, in addition to Ghas-sulian pottery, remains of leather, basket-work, cloth, perhaps the wooden framework of a loom for horizontal weaving and, above all, a deposit of more than four hundred copper objects,[4] including more than two hundred mace-heads and also wands or hollow rods with ornamental heads, axes and chisels, and kinds of decorated 'crowns'. The metal was copper with a high arsenic content. In addition to this hoard of metal objects there were mace-heads made of haematite or other stone and small perforated plaques of hippopotamus ivory. It is astounding to find such a collection belonging to the Chalcolithic period, but this date seems to be indicated not only by the archaeological context, but also by similar metal and ivory objects found in other Chalcolithic caves of the region (Naḥal Seelim) and at Beersheba.

The desert of Judah was never again to be so densely populated, even when a Jewish religious community settled at Qumrān shortly before the Christian era or when the rebels from the Second Jewish War in the second century A.D. sought refuge in the caves of Murabba'āt and of the 'En-Gedī region. On the analogy of these events it has been conjectured that the Chalcolithic settlement must have resulted from political or social disturbances in the more propitious regions of Ghassūl or the Negeb.[5] How-ever, it is by no means certain that this settlement occurred later than that of Ghassūl and Beersheba, and the populations of these two centres were not expelled from them by invaders.

An even closer relationship with Beersheba is apparent in the sites of the coastal region. The most northerly—and the first to be discovered—is Hedērah, in the plain of Sharon.[6] Several other sites are grouped around Jaffa and Tel-Aviv: Benei Bārāq,[7] Givā-tayim, Yabneh, 'Azor.[8] A further site is situated at the foot of the hills at Ben Shemen, near Lydda.[9] At all these sites pottery which is identical with that of the uppermost level at Ṣafadi and at Abu Māṭār appears in conjunction with second degree burials. Chambers were hollowed out of sand-hills or soft rock and fleshless bones were laid there in bundles or, more frequently, enclosed in ossuaries. These ossuaries were sometimes made of

---

[1] §vii, 1, 13 f.; §vii, 10, 6 f.
[2] §vii, 13, 30 ff.
[3] §vii, 14, 215 ff.
[4] See Plate 14 (a).
[5] G, 2, 303; §vii, 11, 180.
[6] §vii, 68.
[7] §vii, 37; 53.
[8] §vii, 59.
[9] §vi, 13.

stone, but more frequently of *terra cotta*. The most numerous collection came from 'Azor, where the fragments of some hundred ossuaries were recovered, some twenty of which could be reconstituted.[1] Two ossuaries were in the shape of an animal, some fifteen resembled oval jars; all the others were in the shape of a house and show what was the appearance of houses of this period. They were rectangular, with the roof arched, pointed or flat; the doorway was in one of the shorter sides; it was wide enough for the insertion of a skull and was often closed by a movable door. The façade had a pediment which rose above the roof and was ornamented with a projecting ledge, sometimes with a painted decoration suggesting the form of a man, animal or bird. Dormer-windows were often cut in the rear wall and sometimes in the sides. Roofs were generally painted with geometric or plant patterns; side-walls with horizontal bands. Some ossuaries were mounted on four feet. Beyond the coastal plain fragments of ossuaries were also found in the cave of Umm Qaṭafah[2] and possibly in the cave of Abu-Uṣbuʿ.[3]

These funerary houses deposited in caves were almost like villages of the dead, but it is not known where the villages of the living were situated; in the rare instances where a surface settlement, with its related objects, has been found near ossuary caves, it has been of later date; thus, at 'Azor[4] such a settlement was established after the roof of the cave had collapsed. When it is remembered that ossuaries are accompanied by pottery of the type found on the Negeb sites and that no cemetery has been discovered on these sites, it may be conjectured that the ossuary-caves served as cemeteries for inhabitants of the Negeb who, taking their flocks, left their villages in the dry season and brought with them the bones of their dead; bedawin cemeteries are sometimes very far from their regular camping-places.[5] According to this hypothesis, the shape of the ossuaries would suggest a connexion with the last period of Beersheba culture, when the dwellings were rectangular houses, properly built.

As in the surface settlement at 'Azor, the last phase of this civilization is represented at Gat-Govrīn,[6] on the borders of Shephēlah and the Negeb; this was a seasonal settlement of pit-dwellings, which had been used for only a very short time. In the north there is evidence of this same last phase in the lower level of Meṣer,[7] not far from Ḥedērah.

---

[1] See Plate 15 (*c*).   [2] §vii, 59, fig. 13.   [3] §vi, 9, 18.
[4] §vii, 24; §vii, 59, 19 ff.   [5] §vii, 59, 27.
[6] §vii, 60.   [7] §vii, 21, 7 and 9.

This culture penetrated sporadically into the mountain-region; 'cream ware', the earliest pottery of Gezer, was related to Beersheba.[1] The connexion is even more clearly apparent in a group at the northern Tell el-Fār'ah, that of cave U;[2] the coarse pottery is best paralleled at Beersheba and the fine pottery is practically identical with the pottery of this region; the similarity is further reinforced by four second-degree burials contained in this cave. This material is also related to the pottery of the lower strata of the *tell*, where in addition may be observed Ghassulian elements,[3] of a kind also encountered in levels XX–XIX (mixed) at Megiddo.[4] But the proportion remains minimal, and the northern sites have a tradition of their own to which reference will be made later.

The course of development of this Ghassūl–Beersheba culture appears in fact to be as follows: it began with the subterranean dwellings of the Beersheba region, some of which may have been contemporary with levels I–II at Ghassūl. Level IV (and III?) at Ghassūl corresponded with the upper level (with buildings) of the Negeb sites, with which the ossuary caves of the coastal region were contemporary. After the abandonment of the Negeb villages, the culture continued in certain sites of the Wādi Ghazzeh and in the surface settlements of the coastal plain ('Azor, Gat-Govrīn, Meser). This was perhaps the only period when the caves of the Judaean desert were occupied. This reconstruction, which is based on stratigraphy and on a comparative study of archaeological material, agrees only in part with the dates so far obtained by carbon-14, as follows: Safadi, middle level, 3640 ± 350 B.C. and 3310 ± 300 B.C.; Horvat Beter 3325 ± 150 B.C.; Nahal Hever 3499 ± 125 B.C.

This culture which took root in regions which had not hitherto been inhabited and under which new styles and new techniques (metalwork) were introduced, was certainly intrusive in Palestine, but its origin is obscure. Such anthropological investigations as have been made[5] suggest that the beginning of this culture coincided with the arrival in Palestine of a brachycephalic people belonging to the Armenoid or Anatolian race. The evidence of metalwork also points in the direction of the copper-producing regions and the discoveries of Mersin and of Beycesultan in

---

[1] §vii, 6.
[2] G, 8, 64 (553 ff.).
[3] G, 8, 54 (407, nos. 20, 21: fragm. of a churn) and 55 (546, no. 4).
[4] §vi, 14, 45 f.; cf. §vii, 22.
[5] §vii, 26, 222; §vii, 57, 141; §vii, 59, 27.

particular show that it had been practised there for a long time; the high arsenic content of the objects of Naḥal Mishmār could indicate that the metal was of Anatolian origin. The second-degree burials and the ossuaries of the coastal sites bring to mind the funerary usages of central and eastern Europe; the extensive use of wood in building, as attested by the architecture of the ossuary houses, and the ossuaries mounted on feet reminiscent of houses on piles, are suggestive of a tradition which had originated in a country both damp and well-wooded. The funerary urns of Europe which are most similar to the Palestinian ossuaries and are also closest in time (beginning of the third millennium) come from sites near the shores of the Black Sea,[1] thus pointing to the far north. This whole interpretation remains hypothetical, but other analogies which have been put forward are at least as much uncertain. The comparisons which have been made with the 'bandkeramische Kultur' of the Danube Basin[2] are limited to the very simple forms which can be found in all primitive pottery and this culture is later than that of Ghassūl–Beersheba by about a millennium. No more is it possible to relate the painted pottery of Palestine with that of Tell Halaf;[3] there can be only recognized in it a remote influence deriving from the styles of Mesopotamia and north Syria in the 'Ubaid epoch. There is clearly no question of the Ghassul–Beersheba culture having come from Egypt, but there are several parallels which may indicate contact or ephemeral influences.[4] Moreover, the statuettes of Ṣafadi and Abu Māṭār have features in common with the earliest Egyptian ivories[5] and it has already been mentioned that certain freshwater shells were brought from the Nile valley to the region to Beersheba.

The end of the period is shrouded in the same obscurity. Ghassūl, the sites of the Beersheba region and of the Negeb, the caves of the desert of Judah and the settlements of the coastal plain were abandoned—perhaps in that order—without there being any indication of destruction by violence or of foreign invasion, and these areas were to remain for a very long time, some of them for ever, without settled occupation. The Ghassūl–Beersheba culture, which made its appearance without any preliminaries, disappeared without any sequel.

It has already been said that this culture scarcely reached as far as the mountains and the north of the country. In these regions the culture which remained predominant was that of the farmers and potters discussed in the preceding section; it was

---

[1] §vii, 59, 34 ff. [2] §vii, 29. [3] §vi, 10.
[4] §vii, 31; 35; 40. [5] §vii, 58, 16 ff.

followed by a new culture which in turn made little progress towards the south.

This new culture was first observed at Megiddo in stages VII–V and levels XX–XIX (mixed) and in several tombs,[1] at Beth-shan XVII–XVI,[2] and at 'Affuleh[3] and was designated 'culture of the plain of Esdraelon'.[4] It was then found not only in the same region, for example at Tell Abu Zureiq, near Megiddo,[5] but at the following sites outside the plain of Esdraelon: Tell el-Asawir[6] at the mouth of the pass leading from Megiddo to the coastal plain, and, nearby, at Meṣer, levels II–I,[7] Khirbet Karak at the southern tip of Lake Tiberias,[8] then, further down the Jordan valley, at Shaikh 'Ali[9] and Munḥāṭa[10] on the right bank; Shūneh[11] on the left bank and even 'Arqūb edh-Dhahr[12] on the Transjordanian plateau. This culture is also encountered lower down the Jordan valley at Tell Umm Ḥamad esh-Sharqi,[13] at Jericho[14] and at the neighbouring site of Tulūl el-'Alayiq;[15] it is well represented in the mountains at Tell el-Fār'ah near Nablus at the 'Upper Chalcolithic' level;[16] there is evidence of it at 'Ai,[17] at Tell en-Naṣbeh,[18] at Gezer in the 'crematorium'[19] and at Jerusalem in tomb 3 at Ophel.[20] It thus covers the Jordan valley between Lake Tiberias and the Dead Sea and also the mountainous region within the same latitudes, with advance-posts farther north at Kabri[21] and at Kfar Gil'ādi.[22] In the south certain elements found their way as far as the caves of the Judaean desert, as at Murabba'āt[23] and as far as the Wādi Ghazzeh sites, particularly site H,[24] in the Negeb. It overflowed into the Shephēlah and into the coastal plain, where it mingled with the Ghassūl–Beersheba culture at Tell ed-Duweir,[25] at Gat-Govrīn[26] and at 'Azor (surface settlement).[27]

---

[1] §vii, 25; §vi, 14; §vii, 28, tombs or part of tombs, 9, 903, 1103, 1106, 1126, 1127.

[2] §vi, 6.   [3] §vii, 69.

[4] §vii, 72, 42 ff.   [5] G, 2, 232 and pl. facing 290.

[6] §vii, 19.   [7] §vii, 21.

[8] §vii, 46.   [9] §vii, 63.

[10] §v, 28, 561; §vii, 29.   [11] §vii, 17.   [12] §vii, 54.

[13] §vii, 27, 318 ff., 505 ff., pls. 98–104, 156–62.

[14] §vii, 39, 4 ff.   [15] §vii, 65, 14 ff.

[16] G, 8, 54 (400 ff.), 55 (546 ff.), 56 (102 ff.), 58 (566 ff.), 59 (573 ff.), 62 (548 ff.), 68 (560 ff.).

[17] §vii, 48, tombs B, C, G.   [18] §vii, 44, tombs 5, 6, 32, 52, 67.

[19] §vii, 15.   [20] §vii, 70, pls. viii–xii.

[21] §vii, 64.   [22] §vii, 34.

[23] §vi, 1, 14 ff.   [24] §vii, 45, pls. xxxvi–xxxvii.

[25] §vi, 19, pls. 11–13.   [26] §vii, 60.

[27] §vii, 59, figs. 40–2.

This culture is known particularly by the objects composing its tomb furniture. The tombs themselves were large; they were dug horizontally in the rocky hillsides, with well-carved rectangular entrances. The basins which in some cases were connected with the tombs provide evidence of a funerary cult. Some of these tombs contained several hundred interments which, very probably at Jericho[1] and perhaps also elsewhere, were second-degree burials. In one instance at Jericho and perhaps also at Gezer the skulls were disposed separately and the bones had been partly burnt.[2] The most numerous types of pottery which have now been published came from the tombs at Tell el-Fār'ah, near Nablus.[3] It was pottery of good quality, with a wide range of shapes and variations suggesting that the potters had considerable dexterity, resource and aesthetic sense. Painted decoration was very rare. Two main classes were usually found together in these tombs: (1) a red pottery, generally burnished, which comprised wide-mouthed pots without handles, jugs and juglets with rising handles, bowls and cups; (2) grey burnished pottery with large basins, bowls, cups on high perforated feet; the edges were generally carinated and ornamented with a series of knobs.

These two kinds of pottery were not much in evidence outside the tombs in the corresponding levels of occupation, where coarse pottery was more common, especially jars on a flat base with horizontal handles smooth or notched, wide-mouthed and without a neck, with a thickened rim often ornamented with notches. Moulded bands were applied around the belly, on the shoulder or near the base.

The bone industry was well developed and included piercers of different thicknesses and blades with one end pointed, the other being pierced with a hole; they could have been used as weaving-shuttles. Characteristic products of the flint industry were the fan-shaped scraper, which it had in common with the Ghassūl-Beersheba group, and blades of triangular or trapezoidal section, of the type called 'Canaanite', which first made its appearance at that time. Small quantities of obsidian were found; a large core of obsidian, of Armenian origin, which was found at Kabri may perhaps date from this period.[4]

Metal was in use; apart from points and rings discovered in tombs, the principal finds were: at Meṣer[5] a clay spoon for metal-

[1] G, 6, 86; §vii, 39, 4.   [2] §vii, 39, 21 ff.; §vii, 15, 106 f.
[3] See Plate 15 (b).   [4] §vii, 67.
[5] §vii, 21, 7 (220) and 9 (28).

casting and five axes in almost pure copper of the same pattern as those at Ghassūl; at Beth-shan, level XVI,[1] two axes of a more advanced type, with an awl and a dagger(?).

In contrast with these tombs, which were well formed and rich in offerings, the occupation levels were conspicuous for their poverty and an almost complete lack of architecture. At Jericho, no level of the *tell* could be related to the tombs of this period; at Tulūl el-'Alayiq no building at all was found; at Tell el-Fār'ah the only habitations were pit-dwellings, as in the preceding period;[2] the same was true of 'Affūleh,[3] of Khirbet Karak[4] and perhaps also of Munḥāṭa.[5] At Shūneh a rectilineal wall had been erected in the course of this period.[6] At Meṣer there were apsed houses at level II, a rectangular house at level I.[7] At Beth-shan level XVII contained only doubtful remains of walls and level XVI one isolated house.[8] At Megiddo the first buildings, apsed houses, did not appear until stages V–IV, that is to say at the transition to the Early Bronze Age;[9] levels XX–XIX of the *tell* contain buildings, even a sanctuary, but the stratification is uncertain.[10]

Conclusions which have so far been reached on anthropological grounds are not entirely in agreement. At Megiddo, all the skulls which were measured were 'Mediterranean', without a single 'negroid' exception.[11] At Jericho there were two groups: dolichocephalic proto-mediterranean and dolichocephalic eurafrican respectively;[12] out of four skulls at Tell el-Asāwir two were proto-mediterranean, two resembled the Alpine race;[13] two races were likewise distinguished at Gezer,[14] but it is difficult to accept this distinction.[15] In any case, it is noticeable that the brachycephalics of the Ghassūl–Beersheba culture are not described anywhere.

A typological analysis of the grey burnished pottery of the tombs of Tell el-Fār'ah and comparison with other sites have led G. E. Wright to distinguish three types and to formulate a relative chronology for the tombs.[16] But this division is not confirmed by the stratigraphy of the occupation levels at Tell el-Fār'ah, at Beth-shan or at Meṣer,[17] and it is not yet possible to

[1] §vi, 5, pl. ii, 2. [2] G, 8, 68 (563f.).
[3] §vii, 20. [4] §vii, 46, 167.
[5] §v, 28, 561 f. [6] §vi, 4, fig. 18A.
[7] §vii, 21, 9; figs. 2, 3, 4. [8] §vi, 5, 124 f.
[9] §vii, 25, fig. 2. [10] G, 8, 68 (564); §vii, 22; §vii, 38, 52* f.
[11] A. Hrdlička, in §vii, 28, 192. [12] §vii, 42.
[13] §vii, 26, 222 [14] §vii, 43, 353 ff. [15] §vii, 15.
[16] §vii, 73, [17] G, 8, 68 (575).

define the different phases within this period. Another problem is that of distinguishing between the grey burnished pottery and the red pottery, whether burnished or not. The tombs at Jericho contained only red pottery, but grey burnished pottery was found at the neighbouring site of Tulūl el-ʻAlayiq. Miss K. M. Kenyon deduced that there were two groups (her A and C groups) almost contemporary but of different origins, which became intermingled at Tell el-Fārʻah.[1] The problem requires wider consideration. Red pottery, without grey burnished pottery, was found outside Jericho at ʻAi, Tell en-Naṣbeh, Gezer and in tomb 3 of Ophel at Jerusalem, that is to say in the southern zone of the culture now being studied, but it appeared in conjunction with grey burnished pottery in the northern sites of Tell el-Fārʻah, Meṣer, Beth-shan, Megiddo, Shūneh, ʻArqūb edh-Dhahr, ʻAffūleh, Khirbet Karak; certain tombs at Tell el-Fārʻah, however, contained only red pottery.

A possible explanation of such a distribution is that these two types of pottery represent two population-groups, one of which, the bringer of red pottery, may have arrived first and penetrated farther to the South. The origin of these groups is still obscure and it is possible only to note that there was some contact with other countries. For the first time a definite relationship was established with pre-dynastic Egypt (Naqāda II):[2] small pots with a single handle, bowls ornamented with a row of conical knobs and, above all, the ledge-handle; this form entered Egypt from Palestine, probably in conjunction with deliveries of oil; it then followed a different course of development in each of the two countries. There is a certain resemblance between the red and grey burnished pottery and that of the Uruk period in Mesopotamia; they share the same dislike of painted decoration and the same preference for red and grey burnishing; one of the types from Tell el-Fārʻah has an exact counterpart in a type from Uruk VII–VI.[3] On the other hand the grey burnished pottery bears a likeness to the products of 'neolithic' Crete, of Rhodes and of Malta;[4] moreover the red and grey burnishing and the raised handles inevitably recall certain traditions of Anatolia. Although it is not possible to trace the intermediate stages or to establish any direct affiliation, it seems likely that this culture may have owed much more to the Eastern Mediterranean basin than to Mesopotamia and that it owed even less to Egypt; it was in fact Palestine which contributed to Egypt rather than the reverse.

[1] §VII, 39, 4 ff.
[2] §VII, 31; §VII, 32, 3 ff.
[3] G, 8, 56 (138), 58 (585).
[4] §VII, 25, 61.

The situation is further complicated by the existence of a third group (group B of K. M. Kenyon); this group consists of pottery decorated with red lines, joined in clusters or crossing one another, which formed a geometric design sometimes covering the whole surface of the vases, inside and outside. Other vases have a burnished decoration, continuous or chequered. The shapes are also distinctive: deep bowls, small globular jugs with two lug-handles close to the neck, small dippers with loop-handles, wide-mouthed pots with a vertical false spout serving as a support for the dipper; it was this group which was formerly put at the head of the Early Bronze Age pottery, as Early Bronze I a.[1] At Jericho it appeared in the uppermost stratum of tomb A 13 while the lower strata contained only red pottery (K. M. Kenyon's A group);[2] hence it seems likely that, first, the two groups were distinct and, secondly, this painted pottery was introduced somewhat later than the red pottery. The difference in time must in any case have been small, for the two types occurred intermingled in the deposits of 'Ai, Tell en-Naṣbeh, Gezer and in tomb 3 of Ophel. This painted pottery also made its appearance, in small quantities, in the most northerly sites, where red pottery and grey burnished pottery were intermingled with it, at Tell el-Fār'ah, Tell el-Asāwir, and as far as 'Arqūb edh-Dhahr in Transjordan. The three groups are thus at least partly contemporaneous.[3]

The simultaneous occurrence of these three groups, when recognized, brought great confusion into the nomenclature. The last group, of the painted pottery, is considered as being a forerunner of the Early Bronze Age.[4] G. E. Wright[5] and R. Amiran[6] therefore decided to attribute the groups of red and grey burnished pottery also to the Early Bronze Age, leaving only the Ghassūl–Beersheba culture within the Chalcolithic period. K. M. Kenyon,[7] followed by E. Anati,[8] also allowed Ghassūl–Beersheba ware within the Chalcolithic period, but assembled the three groups of red pottery (A), painted pottery (B), and grey burnished pottery (C) under the heading of 'Proto-Urban' culture, regarding it as the formative period of the urban culture which was to be characteristic of the Early Bronze Age.

There are two reasons for rejecting these new classifications. The first is that the culture of the red and grey burnished pottery in the north and centre of Palestine is very different from the

[1] §vii, 72, 58 ff.   [2] §vii, 39, 47 ff.
[3] G, 8, 55 (548), 56 (137 f.); §vii, 39, 4 ff.; §vii, 54, 61 ff.
[4] C.A.H. I³, ch. xv, sect. i.   [5] §vii, 73.
[6] §vii, 7, 61 ff.   [7] G, 6, 84 ff.   [8] G, 2, 343 ff.

Early Bronze Age culture and could not have been a preface to it. The Early Bronze Age pottery was to be characterized by new clays, new shapes, new decoration. Villages of huts, sometimes containing a few buildings, were suddenly to be replaced by fortified cities; apart from the major sites which had in fact been already occupied at earlier periods and were to continue so for a long time, such as Beth-shan, Megiddo, Tell el-Fār'ah, Jericho, there were other sites which were to be abandoned completely, such as Munḥāṭa, Meser, or only to be reoccupied much later, such as Tell en-Naṣbeh. The only valid link with the Early Bronze Age is the group of painted pottery which might indeed be regarded as leading up to the Early Bronze Age, but this group is the least important and the latest to appear and should not be considered as characteristic of them all. The other reason which militates against these classifications is that they divide two categories which represent the same stage of human development: the sites with red and grey burnished pottery are the villages of farmers, potters and metalworkers, like the sites of Ghassūl–Beersheba culture; to which may be added the fact—and this argument appears conclusive—that the two categories are partly contemporaneous.

It is true that the position of Ghassulian in the sequence of events in Palestine has for a long time remained uncertain, and also its connexion with the other cultures. Now, however, the situation has been somewhat clarified and can be summarized as follows: Ghassūl was later than Jericho VIII and Pottery Neolithic, and the site of Jericho appears to have been abandoned during the occupation of Ghassūl. However, the culture of Jericho VIII persisted at other sites (Megiddo, 'Affūleh, Tell el-Fār'ah) where, as has been shown, there penetrated elements of the Ghassūl–Beersheba culture which had been established and remained concentrated in the south. The bringers of red or grey burnished pottery settled in the north while the Ghassūl–Beersheba culture was still flourishing; it is possible that the newcomers borrowed from it a typical implement, the fan-shaped scraper, and that the grey burnished pottery vases with pierced pedestal were an imitation of similar basalt vases found in the Ghassulian culture. This explains why 'Proto-Urban' elements are encountered in the sites of belated Ghassūl–Beersheba culture, such as Gat-Govrīn,[1] and, conversely, why Ghassulian elements appeared side by side with red and grey burnished pottery in level II at Meser.[2] The distinction between the two cultures is much less chrono-

[1] §VII, 60.   [2] §VII, 21, 9 (23–6).

logical than geographical. Ghassulian culture was probably the first to be extinguished, without leaving any heirs. It is also probable that the bringers of painted pottery settled originally in the central region between Jericho and Gezer and did not penetrate further south, but spread, at first hesitantly, towards the north.

This outline agrees with the only carbon-14 date which is available for the northern culture. The latest occupation of tomb A 94 at Jericho is dated 3260 ± 110 B.C.[1] The dates which have been quoted above for the Beersheba sites are not much earlier. The duration of the culture around this date is difficult to estimate. It could have begun about 3400; it continued until the definitive Early Bronze Age (Early Bronze I*b*), about 3100 B.C.

VIII. THE 'MEGALITHIC CULTURE'

There remains one aspect of culture which it is difficult to place in the course of development which has just been described, but which requires a brief mention. Over the entire edge of the Transjordanian plateau numerous dolmens are to be found, often assembled over wide areas. These megalithic monuments occur less frequently in Palestine, but are nevertheless distributed over the whole of the mountainous region, from Hebron to Galilee.[2] Some have been excavated and have yielded nothing from which it would be possible to date their erection.[3] Elsewhere, objects belonging to the Bronze or the Iron Ages, or even the Roman epoch, which have been found in the dolmens[4] indicate only that they were re-used at these periods either for shelter or for some other purpose. One fact remains certain: dolmens in Palestine, as in Europe, were originally constructed to serve as tombs.

Their date has sometimes been set too low, but the tendency is at present to regard them as perhaps being older than they are by attributing them to the Pre-Pottery Neolithic Age[5] or a little later.[6] The truth is that nothing can be proved, for not one of these dolmens, which are devoid of any object belonging to the period of their erection, can be related to the datable remains of any human settlement. The earliest European dolmens belong to the end of the Stone Age, but those of Talyche and the Caucasus date from an advanced period of the Bronze Age. No conclusion can be drawn from this comparison of elements which are neither

[1] §vii, 39, 8.　　　　[2] G, 2; §vii, 66; §viii, 2.　　　　[3] §viii, 4.
[4] §viii, 5.　　　　　　[5] G, 1.　　　　　　　　　　　　[6] §viii, 1.

identical nor attributable to the same race and which are geographically very far apart.

It may be stated only that the construction of these dolmens and their grouping in extensive cemeteries implies the existence of a population which had progressed beyond the primitive stages; moreover the hewn doors and grooves which are to be seen in some Transjordan dolmens suggest that metal tools were used. If the burial-ground at 'Adeimeh was actually the cemetery of Ghassūl, it should be added that its cists were in fact micro-dolmens and that some large dolmens at this site may have belonged to the same cemetery. The example of Ghassūl and 'Adeimeh and, even more, the Negeb sites and the ossuary caves of the coastal plain (if they were interdependent, as has been suggested) indicate that the cemeteries could have been far from the dwellings, so that the areas covered by dolmens bordering the Transjordanian plateau could have belonged to certain sites in the Jordan valley which were studied in the preceding section.

Another explanation is also possible: these dolmens could have belonged to a non-sedentary population. It is indeed noteworthy that, in Palestine as in Transjordan, they are distributed about the mountainous region which would be more suitable for stock-raising than for agriculture. They could perhaps have been erected by semi-nomad shepherds, who wished to give their dead a more permanent dwelling than was available to the living. At all events, the great interest which was taken in life beyond the tomb is the sole information so far provided by these problematical monuments.

CHAPTER IX (c)

CYPRUS IN THE NEOLITHIC AND CHALCOLITHIC PERIODS

IX. GEOGRAPHY

I t is commonplace that Cyprus forms a stepping-stone between Europe and Asia, and that her history holds a mirror to the sequence of great powers, now Asiatic, now European, who have dominated the lands of the Near East and the waters of the east Mediterranean. Such dominance has not always been in the same hands at the same time; a maritime power and a land power have more than once contended with each other to win control of an island whose strategic and mercantile importance has been quite out of proportion to its size. During the fifth century B.C., Athens strove unsuccessfully to wrest Cyprus from the control of Persia; in the sixteenth century A.D., Venice fought a losing battle against the Osmanli Turks to maintain ownership of the island and the key to the rich trade-routes of the Levant and beyond which it provided. This succession of foreign masters is conspicuous in the cultural history of Cyprus. That history is of some seven and a half thousand years duration, only for a part of which has the island occupied her neighbours' attention. Before the development of comparatively reliable ships, Cyprus was left in unmolested isolation for centuries at a time. For a period of more than three thousand years, from early in the sixth millennium B.C. onwards, her relations with surrounding regions amounted to no more than three or four ethnic changes, each of which must represent an incursion of people from overseas. During all this long period there are the most meagre indications of foreign trading contacts. It is, therefore, during the Neolithic and Chalcolithic periods in Cyprus, between c. 5800 and 2300 B.C., and to a lesser extent during the Early Bronze Age, between c. 2300 and 1800 B.C., that it is possible to observe a series of cultural developments that are essentially Cypriot. From the Middle Bronze Age onwards, Cyprus became more and more involved in the ambitions and quarrels of her powerful continental neighbours; by the middle of the second millennium B.C., in the Late Bronze Age, this involvement was complete and the island had become one of the main clearing houses for the seaborne trade of the Levant and Egypt with the mainland of Greece and the islands of the Aegean.

With its area of 3584 square miles Cyprus is the third Mediterranean island.[1] Her north coast lies under the eye of Anatolia, only 43 miles away at the nearest point; the Taurus is clearly visible from the Kyrenia hills. The Karpass peninsula looks to the Gulf of Alexandretta and the mouth of the Orontes; Cape Andreas is only 76 miles from Latakia, in north Syria; there are days when the Amanus can be seen from the same cape. Salamis bay lies open to traffic from the ports of the Levantine coast; the passage is an easy one, for hardly have the heights of Lebanon been lost astern when the peaks of Troödos are raised ahead. Egypt and the mouths of the Nile lie to the south and south-east, considerably further off; it is a journey of 264 miles from Larnaka to Port Said. Rhodes, the nearest point in the Greek world, is over 250 miles to the west; the Peiraeus is at least as far again.

The island is of comparatively recent geological origin.[2] Traces of its inundations beneath the sea are still clearly visible in the eroded flat-topped hills in the vicinity of Nicosia, and the record of Cypriot fauna is appropriate to a region once an integral part of Asia. The mountain ranges are extensions of Amanus and Casius.[3]

The mountain ranges are the island's most prominent features. The Kyrenia hills form a narrow but lofty limestone ridge (3357 ft. at its highest) along the north coast, from Panagra in the west to Ephtakomi. Between these hills and the sea is a narrow but fertile and well-watered plain, whose rich perennial springs and readily cultivable soils attracted relatively dense settlement from the earliest times. The lower slopes of the range on the landward side also have fine springs; *Kephalovrysis*,[4] which feeds the modern village of Kythrea, in the Roman period sent some of its waters by aqueduct to supply the needs of Salamis.[5] Three passes (Vasilia, Kyrenia and Lefkoniko) connect the north coast with the hinterland. The Troödos mountains and the foothills that form their flanks occupy the greater part of western and central Cyprus. They form the watersheds for the major rivers whose valleys have cut deep into the massif, providing communications between the coast and its remoter areas. The foothills, especially to the north and north-east, have been of great economic

[1] G, 15; G, 16; G, 20.   [2] G, 10, 2–4.   [3] G, 10, 4.
[4] Italic distinguishes locality from village names.   [5] G, 10, 253.

importance from the Bronze Age onwards, for they include copper-bearing rocks, which occur where igneous deposits (pillow lavas) are overlapped by sediments, chiefly the Idalian marls. Between the two mountain ranges the central plain stretches from coast to coast, from Morphou bay on the west to Salamis bay. This plain, much of which is alluvial, is roughly divisible into two sections hinging on Nicosia, the modern capital. The eastern section, the Mesaoria, now has the best cornlands in the island. Through it run the courses of the Pediaios and Yalias rivers. They formerly reached the sea in Salamis bay in a long inlet which formed the harbour for the Late Bronze Age city at Enkomi.[2] This inlet is now a salt-marsh; even in the rainy season intensive utilization of the water prevents the flow of these rivers reaching the sea. Much of the Mesaoria may have been heavily forested until comparatively late antiquity; certainly there is scant evidence for its early occupation.[3] The west half of the plain, narrow at Nicosia, widens out as it reaches Morphou bay; the existing coastline is of modern origin, for the shore is constantly being built up by the alluvium of the Serakhis and Ovgos rivers. This half of the plain, particularly in the vicinity of these rivers, found favour with the Neolithic farmers and their Early Bronze Age successors.[4] There is no lack of light and easily worked soils, while building stone and stone for making vessels and tools abound in the gravels of the river-beds. Both the marshland at the coast and the courses of the rivers themselves harboured wild fowl, while larger game—red deer, Persian fallow deer, ibex, moufflon, pig and perhaps wild cattle[5]—must have frequented the forest lands to the north, now the *maquis* of the Karpasha forest and the Ayios Georghios Rigatos plateau.

Much of the south coast, particularly between Cape Pyla and Pissouri, consists of a discontinuous series of small plains where the coastline is repeatedly broken by the mouths of the numerous water-courses which drain the highlands to this side of the island. Many of the earliest settlements were located a little way inland near the banks of one or other of these rivers.[6] The Paphos district, which comprises much of west and south-west Cyprus, is somewhat divorced from the rest of the island by outliers of Troödos which, both north and south, reach the sea in places. The valleys of several rivers—Khapotami, Dhiarrizos, Xeropo-

[1] G, 7.   [2] G, 10, 12; G, 15, 124.
[3] G, 3, 139.   [4] G, 3, 133–9.
[5] §x, 2, 431–7; §xii, 1, 235–6; *C.A.H.* i³, ch. xxvi(*b*), §viii, 15, 286 and 292.
[6] §x, 3, 3.

tamos and Ezuza—reach far back into the massif. Their banks attracted Chalcolithic settlers, like the valleys further east.[1] The Paphos region is especially rich in Chalcolithic settlements. Surface exploration[2] in what is now almost entirely a *maquis* in the Akamas peninsula has found a surprising number of sites of this period, after which the region seems to have been abandoned until much more recent times. It may well have been the methods of the Chalcolithic farmers which brought the *maquis* into being.

Modern shipping, needing deep-water berths, finds Cyprus notoriously ill-equipped with harbours. By ancient standards, however, the innumerable coves and beaches of the north coast, the beaches and river-mouths of the south must have satisfied most local needs. In addition, a few good natural harbours existed which have since disappeared, including the inlet of the sea on which ancient Citium (now Larnaka) was built[3] and the much greater inlet a few miles away, the site of the present day Larnaka salt-lakes, beside which grew up a mercantile city of great importance in the Late Bronze Age.[4]

The island enjoys a tolerable climate. The extreme heat of summer is alleviated by the changing breeze induced by the sea. Frost is virtually unknown in the plain but, in a good season, the winter's snows melting on Troödos provide water in the main rivers until the early summer. Agricultural productivity is at the mercy of a meagre and uncertain annual rainfall, and there is no reason to suppose that the prolonged and disastrous droughts which have been recorded in historical times were unknown in remote antiquity.[5] The coming of rain can at times be even more destructive than its lack, for it may fall with cataclysmic violence to destroy growing crops and sweep the soil from cultivated slopes. From time immemorial industrious Cypriot farmers have built thousands of miles of terrace walls to avert the worst effects of such storms.

X. THE EARLIEST SETTLERS IN CYPRUS

Remains of the Palaeolithic Period have not yet been found in Cyprus.[6] Mesolithic deposits are also unknown. Though the future may alter this situation it is with a settled community of food producers that the history of Cyprus at present begins. The

[1] §XIII, 2, 75–6.   [2] G, 3, 134, n. 1.
[3] *Kypriakai Spoudai* (1961), pp. 21–39.   [4] G, 3, 136.
[5] G, 10, 246.   [6] G, 19, 1–4.

Neolithic Period was only recognized well after the main framework of the island's archaeology had been constructed; it was unknown to Myres, for example, when he wrote his general introduction to Cypriot archaeology in 1914.[1] Neolithic and Chalcolithic settlements were first identified by Gjerstad and his Swedish colleagues in the 1920's when the sites at Phrenaros,[2] Petra tou Limniti,[3] Lapithos[4] and Kythrea[5] were excavated and published. Dikaios then made the period his own and, by the publication and interpretation of his work in survey and excavation,[6] has both laid the foundations and built the structure of what is known of the pre-Bronze Age cultures of Cyprus.

The application of radiocarbon methods of dating to Cypriot archaeology has had a profound effect.[7] In what follows it will be assumed that such carbon-14 dates merit respect, though not necessarily unquestioning adherence. Previous estimates[8] had established the first settlers by c. 4000 B.C.; the end of the Chalcolithic Period and the consequent transition to the Early Bronze Age was placed c. 2500 B.C. The combined duration of the Neolithic and Chalcolithic periods thus amounted to some 1500 years. But carbon-14 tests suggest that the upper limit should be raised to c. 5800 B.C. At the same time, the onset of the Early Bronze Age has been lowered to c. 2300 B.C., giving a total length of 3500 years to the stone-using cultures. While it may be gratifying to discover that human settlement in Cyprus shares the high antiquity attributed to comparable cultures in Mesopotamia, Palestine and Anatolia, it is difficult to make the known Cypriot sequence cover this enormous span of time. While the future may bring to light stages at present unrecognized in the sequence, it is also possible that there were substantial periods during this 3500 years when Cyprus was uninhabited.

Dikaios[9] has defined two principal Neolithic cultures, which he has categorized as Neolithic I and II respectively, with an intermediary phase, Neolithic I b.[10] A period that was originally designated Neolithic III, typified by the site at Erimi,[11] is now classified as Chalcolithic I. A second Chalcolithic phase has also been isolated, helping to bridge the gap between the Stone Age cultures and the Bronze Age immigrants who supplanted them.

Comparatively few Neolithic I sites have been located. In addition to the type-site of Khirokitia, small stations are known at

[1] G, 14. [2] §x, 4. [3] G, 9(i), 1–12. [4] G, 9(i), 13–33.
[5] G, 9(i), 277–99. [6] G, 8, 1–5; §x, 2 and 3; §xii, 1; §xiii, 2.
[7] §x, 3, 192–204. [8] §x, 2, 326–36. [9] §x, 3.
[10] §x, 3, 180–1. [11] §xii, 2.

widely spaced points along the north coast at Petra tou Limniti,[1] Troulli[2] and Cape Andreas.[3] Recent identifications include a site at Cape Greco[4] in the extreme south-east, and a large settlement far inland at Kataliondas.[5] Of these sites, Khirokitia and Petra tou Limniti have been excavated.

The settlement of Khirokitia is built on the steep slopes of a hill, *Vounoi*, on the west bank of the Maroni river, some 4 miles inland from the south coast.[6] Only a part of the hill has been excavated, but it seems likely that almost the whole of it was occupied during the Neolithic I period. Since the site was unencumbered by remains of later periods, and the Neolithic structures lay close beneath the cultivated soil, a much larger area could be cleared than is normally possible for so early a period. The Khirokitia culture, or Neolithic I, remains obstinately *sui generis*, and the source from which it reached Cyprus has not been traced.[7] It is characterized by the use of round houses (or 'tholoi'),[8] their lower courses built of stone. Mud-brick or *pisé* was used for the upper walls and the domed roofs. A progression could be observed from relatively flimsy construction in the earlier phases of the settlement to a masonry at once massive and more competent in the later stages. The life of these houses was often protracted; many contained a long succession of renewed floors and hearths, and their fabric often showed abundant signs of repair. Not surprisingly, the layout of the village was relatively haphazard;[9] the houses were packed in close to one another. A substantial stone-built causeway[10] traversed the site, running obliquely through the settlement from the level of the river up to the hilltop. This structure was of sufficient importance to the village to be kept in being throughout its history. As the surrounding levels rose when new huts were erected on the partly levelled remains of their outworn predecessors, the level of the causeway was correspondingly increased. It must imply not only a communal effort in its original establishment but also the persistence of a public conscience in ensuring its maintenance over the years. Little else was recovered that suggested organized communal activities. None of the fifty or more excavated houses is elaborate enough in size, construction or appointments to have served a family or individual set apart from their fellows in a dominant social or religious role. The largest house, tholos I *a*, had an internal diameter

[1] G, 9(i), 1–12.   [2] §x, 3, 63–72.   [3] G, 11 (1962), 372–3.
[4] G, 11 (1963), 348.   [5] §x, 1.   [6] §x, 2.
[7] §x, 3, 192–4.   [8] §x, 2, 14–231.   [9] §x, 2, pl. 1.
[10] §x, 2, 186–95.

of 6 m.; internal features suggest it had a semi-loft as well as a ground floor. Traces were also found of a covered passage extending round the east, west and north sides of this house, associated with which were two smaller tholoi, apparently used for various domestic purposes, and a fourth building (tholos XII a) which appeared to have been added to this complex in the later stages of its history, possibly to absorb an exceptional growth in the numbers of an unusually flourishing family group.[1]

The Khirokitians seem certainly to have raised grain crops. Stone corn grinders figure amongst the domestic tools found,[2] and the flint industry included sickle blades. In the absence of carbonized grain, the types of cereal plants cultivated remain unknown. It is less certain that any animals had been domesticated for food during Neolithic I;[3] some animal remains belong to wild species, which must have been hunted or trapped. Pig, goat and sheep bones may represent domesticated species, but the evidence is equivocal.

A rich series of material objects, found abandoned on the house floors or buried with the dead, illustrates the technical ability of the population and the degree to which their competence in food production left time and energy for other pursuits. With an enigmatic exception early in the life of the settlement,[4] the manufacture or use of pottery was unknown. Vessels and containers were doubtless made of such perishable materials as wood, basketry and leather; they were also made of stone. There was a plentiful production of stone vessels in many forms, sometimes with the refinement of relief ornament or integrally made handles.[5] The material chosen was usually andesite or some closely related hard stone, inexhaustible supplies of which were ready to hand in the bed of the river nearby. The commonest vessel type was a bowl made in a great variety of shapes and sizes; dishes, trays, ladles and mortars also occur.[6] The forms of some of these vessels may have been derived from wooden originals.[7] The stone workers made much else besides, including ground and polished axes and chisels and such rougher tools as mauls, hammers, pounders, grinders and pestles.[8] The flint industry was not of high quality;[9] its raw material was nearly all of local origin, though the few blades and flakes of obsidian must have come from a foreign source.[10] Flint tools include tanged flakes, gravers,

[1] §x, 2, 14–39.   [2] §x, 2, 292.   [3] §x, 2, 430–7.
[4] §x, 2, 264–6.   [5] §x, 2, 232–53. See Plate 16 (a).
[6] §x, 2, 253–60.   [7] §x, 3, 15.   [8] §x, 2, 277–86.
[9] §x, 2, 409–15.   [10] §x, 2, 316 and 412.

scrapers, sickle blades and a straight axe. The absence of projectiles is noteworthy. Other tools—awls, borers, gouges and
needles—were made of bone,[1] and suggest both leather and
textile work, for the latter of which there is further evidence in the
presence of spindle whorls, mostly made of limestone.[2] The purpose of a number of small stone cones, their bases and often their
surfaces engraved with patterns of intersecting lines, and a
number of unshaped pebbles treated in much the same manner,[3]
remains enigmatic, though some which were pierced for suspen-
sion may have been used as amulets.

Extremely stylized human statuettes were made of hard stone;[4]
these are not of the so-called mother-goddess types frequently
encountered in contemporary assemblages in neighbouring
regions. They have no indication of sex; their function is quite
uncertain. With them should be mentioned a unique head,
possibly of a woman, modelled in unbaked clay.[5]

The disposal of the dead points to the importance of the family
as a social unit. At the end of his life, a Khirokitian's tightly
contracted body would be laid in a small pit dug in the floor of his
house. Burial took place fairly soon after death; and there is no
sign of the two-stage burial rite which seems to have been normal
at Çatal Hüyük, or of reverential treatment of skulls as at
Jericho. Gifts were left with the dead; stone vessels were found
in many graves and more than one body had been decked with a
necklace of cornelian (or steatite) and dentalium beads.[6] Not
infrequently precautions seem to have been taken to make sure
that the dead did not stir forth from their graves; heavy stones
(querns were sometimes used) were laid over the top of the
bodies.[7] The burial rite described was the same for men, women
and children. In the later history of the site, double burials (often
a woman with a child) became more frequent.

Conclusions about the Khirokitians based on studies of their
skeletal remains are somewhat contradictory. While one authority[8]
finds them sufficiently specialized to be unable to point to any
population pool in the adjoining regions from which they could
reasonably be derived, another[9] has isolated physical characteristics that suggest that the original settlers came chiefly from
a stock that had moved eastwards from the Balkans, most probably from the region of Thessaly–Macedonia; a smaller element
is supposed to have derived from Cilicia or Lower Armenia. It

[1] §x, 2, 293–6. [2] §x, 2, 284–5. [3] §x, 2, 286–91.
[4] §x, 2, 296–8. [5] §x, 2, 299–300. [6] §x, 2, 304.
[7] §x, 2, 218; §x, 3, 12–13. [8] §x, 2, 416–30. [9] G, 6.

is at least clear that their most distinctive feature was their short-headedness, which was probably exaggerated in many cases by artificial cranial deformation—though this, too, has been denied.[1] The skull types were sufficiently homogeneous over a considerable period to suggest that the population 'was inbred to the degree found in fairly isolated human breeding groups'. Mortality was high among infants; of 120 skeletons, 28 per cent belonged to children under a year old. Prospects were better for those who survived the first year of life; only 10 per cent of the dead belonged to the age groups between 1 and 24 years old. Seventy per cent of adult deaths fell between the ages of 25 and 40. Men had a greater life expectancy than women; a few did not succumb until they were between 55 and 60.

XI. THE END OF NEOLITHIC I
AND ITS SEQUEL

The topmost deposits at Khirokitia contain traces of an occupation no longer typified by the use of stone vessels but by pottery vessels made in a fabric known as 'Combed Ware'.[2] Whatever structures had been associated with this phase seem to have been completely destroyed by erosion and recent cultivation. Before the application of carbon-14 dating methods to the Cypriot Neolithic sequence, it had been assumed[3] on the Khirokitia evidence that the Neolithic II period, of which this Combed Ware is diagnostic, closely followed the end of Neolithic I. But the laboratory dates suggest a gap of some 1500 years between the site's abandonment by the Neolithic I community and its reoccupation in Neolithic II. Neither at Khirokitia nor at Petra tou Limniti was there any clue to the identity of the disaster which brought the Neolithic I period to its close; there was certainly no sign of a violent end to Khirokitia. Possibly a natural calamity, widespread in its effects, overwhelmed the frail grasp of the Neolithic I communities, followed by a substantial period when Cyprus was uninhabited. Certainly, it is not until c. 3500 B.C. that the next fixed point is reached with the founding of the Neolithic II settlement at Sotira by the Combed Ware people, of which more will be said below.

At Troulli, a coastal headland ten miles east of Kyrenia, is a Neolithic settlement with two distinct phases of occupation.[4] The earlier appears to be of Neolithic I date; it was marked by an

[1] G, 6, 52. [2] §x, 2, 267; §x, 3, 39–40. See Plate 16(b)
[3] §x, 2, 307–13. [4] §x, 3, 63–72.

absence of pottery, the use of stone vessels and other features familiar from Khirokitia. In the later phase, painted pottery was used with a distinctive type of ornament, of which rings left reserved in the ground colour of the clay are characteristic.[1] This Troulli culture (the Neolithic Ib of Dikaios' classification) may partly fill the gap between Neolithic I and II; it certainly has no relationship with Neolithic II material culture. So far, the only other Neolithic Ib site identified is at Dhenia,[2] in the western part of the central plain. Little is known of it.

In the absence of a carbon-14 date for Troulli, and without a full and stratified sequence in which the true relationship between the reserved ware of Neolithic Ib and the combed wares of Neolithic II could be observed, it is impossible to decide the merits of this proposal. Troulli may prove to be a contemporary of Neolithic II; it may even be later.

XII. CYPRUS IN THE NEOLITHIC II PERIOD

There is at present nothing in south Cyprus to interpose between the end of Neolithic I, which apparently took place c. 5000 B.C. and the arrival of the people who used Combed Ware 1500 years later. The origin of these people is unknown, though it has been suggested[3] that they may have affinities with the Beersheba culture of south Palestine. They arrived not long before the middle of the fourth millennium B.C., establishing themselves at a small number of sites on or near the south coast; there are traces of them in central Cyprus,[4] but they have left virtually no mark on the north coast.

Three of their sites have been investigated; mention has already been made of Khirokitia. At *Kokkinoyi* in the village lands of Kalavassos Dikaios excavated[5] a number of somewhat primitive Neolithic II structures, whose lower parts consisted of round or irregular pits sunk in the soft bedrock. Some of these preserved traces of a central post, which seemed to have supported a very light superstructure of wattle and daub. A succession of occupied floors[6] was found in several huts to prove that these were more than ephemeral shelters. Their simple character is in marked contrast to the excellence of the pottery found in and on the floors, a small proportion of which was Combed Ware; the majority was the monochrome Red Lustrous ware. There was

[1] G, 8, pl. II, 4. [2] G, 11 (1962), 374–5. [3] §x, 3, 198–9.
[4] §x, 3, 184. [5] §x, 3, 106–12. [6] §x, 3, 107.

also a small quantity of a fabric whose white surface is decorated with linear ornaments in red paint, a manner of decoration which was to have a long history in the succeeding Chalcolithic period.

The character of Neolithic II is best known from the excavation of the *Teppes* hill at Sotira,[1] near the south coast four miles north-west of the later city of Curium. An area of 2000 square m. on the level summit of the hill was cleared. The slopes were too eroded to justify excavation, but they had probably also been built on. A small cemetery was located at the foot of the south-east slope.[2]

The earliest of the four phases of occupation at Sotira came to an abrupt close when its houses were destroyed by fire. It was from a sample taken from this phase that a carbon-14 test gave a date of 3500 ± 150 B.C. The degree of continuity between periods I and II suggests domestic mischance rather than hostile act as the occasion for the disaster. There was no sharp division between periods II and III, though there was a marked increase in the size of the site in III, when nearly the whole plateau top was occupied by buildings. Period III ended abruptly $c.$ 3150 ± 150 B.C., when all the houses of the settlement were overthrown in a severe earthquake. Period IV was in the nature of an epilogue. An effort was made to clear the earthquake debris from the hill-top by stacking the bulk of it in the form of a 'retaining wall' on the north edge of the plateau. The remains of the period III houses were levelled and temporary dwellings of no architectural pretensions were hastily erected in their place. After an interval of uncertain but brief duration the site was abandoned and never reoccupied.

Not the least interesting feature of Sotira is its architecture. Six different types of house-plan can be recognized,[3] ranging from those which are almost circular, through oval houses and rectangular buildings with rounded corners to horseshoe-shaped huts and those which in effect defy classification and can only be termed 'irregular'. The Sotirans, indeed, were remarkably empirical in their attitude to building, and quite uninhibited by tradition. There is striking contrast here with Neolithic I when, at Khirokitia at least, architectural tradition was adhered to strictly. This lack of architectural uniformity within the limits of a single settlement makes less remarkable the very obvious differences between the types of Neolithic II dwellings found at Kalavassos and those of Sotira. Were it not for the Combed Ware which is common to both sites, their relationship might not have been suspected. Dikaios, indeed, sees in these divergencies[4] the

---

[1] §XII, I.   [2] §XII, I, 142–7.   [3] §XII, I, 148–58.   [4] §X, 3, 198.

arrival in Cyprus of a people with an ill-formulated architectural tradition, possibly to be connected with the Beersheba culture of southern Palestine, where a not dissimilar use of half-sunk dwellings is approximately contemporary with Sotira. Kalavassos, then, represents their earliest settlement in Cyprus, when they still followed an architectural practice which experience was to prove unsuitable. By the time Sotira came to be founded, the half-sunk dwelling had been abandoned in favour of free-standing houses with a variety of ground-plans.

The Sotira houses were more lightly built than the Khirokitia tholoi. On roughly constructed stone foundations up to $\frac{1}{2}$ m. wide, seldom more than three courses high, the upper walls were built of mud-brick or *pisé*. The light roofs seem to have been of brushwood and *pisé* carried on more solid rafters resting on the walltops. Most houses have either post-holes or cup-stones in their floors to show that posts must have been used to take some of the thrust of the roof from the walls.

Sotira's plan[1] suggests that much domestic work was performed within the individual houses. These have no courtyards, and few domestic installations were built outdoors. Cooking was done in the houses; for, while there were no hearths or ovens outside, at least one hearth was standard equipment in every house. Parts of some houses were partitioned off by flimsy walls to form small subsidiary rooms, some of them used as working areas; there is evidence of flint-knapping and the preparation of ground stone tools in such contexts.[2] Others contained troughs, or pits in the floor, for the preparation or storage of foodstuffs. On every house-floor querns and corn-grinders were found, evidence both for crop husbandry and food preparation. The picture of the house as the main working unit is given further emphasis by the presence in every one of vessels of pottery and stone, flint blades, stone grinders, pestles, hammers and polishers, and bone tools.

Arrangements for the comfort of the owners of the houses were few, apart from occasional masonry benches rendered with mud-plaster, which doubtless served as sitting or sleeping places, recalling earlier practice in Neolithic Anatolia.

The Sotirans did not bury their dead inside their houses. A small cemetery was found at the foot of the hill, with a dozen graves.[3] The dead were buried singly, their bodies tightly contracted, in shallow oblong pits. Several graves were not cut into the bedrock, but merely sunk into superficial layers of soil and occupation debris. There were no grave offerings, but several

[1] §XII, I, pls. 8 and 10.   [2] §XII, I, 162.   [3] §XII, I, 142–7.

bodies had been covered either by a single large stone or several smaller ones before the grave pit was refilled; this recalls a custom at Khirokitia; querns were not used at Sotira, however.

Study of the Sotira skeletal remains[1] suggests a physical type that had little in common with the Khirokitians. Cranial deformation was not practised. Though the sample was very small, it suggests a slightly higher average age at death than at Khirokitia. The evidence is insufficient, however, to suggest a significant improvement in living conditions.

The brief post-earthquake phase at Sotira marks the end of Neolithic II. The limited distribution of the sites of this period implies that the users of Combed Ware never achieved a very strong grasp on Cyprus. If the earthquake which destroyed Sotira III was at all widespread in its effects, it may well have been the lever which dislodged them, and the pattern of events at Sotira, with its brief reoccupation, may be proved typical of the whole region. The debilitating effects of the aftermath of such a calamity may have rendered the survivors susceptible to disease, and they could well have been swept away by the effects of an unwonted epidemic.

XIII. CHALCOLITHIC CYPRUS

There is a hint of continuity between the end of Neolithic II and the start of Chalcolithic I, for small quantities of Combed Ware have been found in the earliest deposits on at least two Chalcolithic sites.[2] A date c. 3000 B.C. seems a reasonable estimate for this transition, in view of the carbon-14 date for the destruction of Sotira III, and the evident brevity of the interval between the abandonment of the Neolithic II sites and the development of Chalcolithic I.

Chalcolithic settlement was far more widespread than that of the earlier cultures. Except for the Karpass peninsula and the Mesaoria, there are no considerable areas without evidence of occupation.[3] Some regions, indeed, particularly the environs of the perennial springs on the lower slopes on both sides of the Kyrenia mountains, were densely settled. Besides the normal open settlements, limestone caves and rock clefts were now occupied, particularly in the vicinity of Aghirda and Krini, south-west of the Kyrenia pass.[4] Several areas which had apparently been unoccupied in Neolithic I and II attracted intensive settlement.

---

[1] §XII, 1, 223–9.   [2] §X, 3, 198–9.
[3] §X, 3, 3.   [4] §XIII, 1; §XIII, 2, 72–9; *Arch. Reports*, 1958, 25.

The Cape Krommyon peninsula is a case in point, with a succession of coastal sites extending eastwards from Liveras to Vasilia, matched by inland settlements in the vicinity of Myrtou, Dhiorios and Kormakiti.[1] A comparable settlement pattern has been recorded in the far west, in the Akamas peninsula.[2]

The character of Chalcolithic I material culture has most clearly been defined by the classic site of Erimi, in south Cyprus, a few miles south-east of Sotira.[3] Contemporary sites were examined by the Swedes at Lapithos[4] and Kythrea[5] (both in north Cyprus), and by Dikaios at Kalavassos site B[6] and at Ayios Epiktitos,[7] a settlement near the coast five miles east of Kyrenia.

Erimi is a deeply stratified site close to the modern village, on the east bank of the Kouris river. While only a small area was explored, a succession of houses was uncovered which, taken in conjunction with the architectural evidence from Kalavassos site B, provides a fair illustration of Chalcolithic domestic buildings. Note must be taken both at Erimi and at Kalavassos site B of a slightly disconcerting link with the Neolithic II architecture of Kalavassos A, but not with the Neolithic II architecture of Sotira. The first Erimi houses were partly cut into bed-rock, and only after the accumulation of successive occupation levels had brought the floors above the original surface of the bed-rock did the houses become free-standing.[8] At Kalavassos B this change only took place at the very end of the life of the settlement. The floors of the earliest buildings were sunk deep into the bed-rock; within their compass light timber-framed huts were built.[9] By contrast, the houses investigated at the settlements on the north coast seem without exception to have been free-standing.[10]

Chalcolithic I houses were of simple design. They were usually round, and might be up to 6 m. in diameter. The upper structure was a light wattle-and-daub frame. Certain differences occur in the substructures, so that the more advanced dwellings were built with one or two courses of masonry into which the posts of the timber frames were set.[11] The superstructure seems to have been carried on a heavy central post, for whose base a circular platform of clay and small stones was often prepared on the beaten earth floor. Hearths appear both inside and outside the huts. The latter might be in the open air, but sometimes were placed in small semi-circular constructions attached to the main dwellings.

[1] §x, 3, 3. [2] G, 3, 137. [3] §xiii, 2.
[4] G, 9(i), 13–33. [5] G, 9(i), 277–99. [6] §x, 3, 133–40.
[7] §xiii, 2, 73–4. [8] §x, 3, 128. [9] §x, 3, 133.
[10] G, 9(i), 13–33; G, 9(i), 277–99; §xiii, 2, 74. [11] §x, 3, 113–15.

Relatively few Chalcolithic burials have been found. At Erimi[1] a small number of pit-graves occurred, either inside or immediately adjoining the dwellings. In one case the body was found beneath a pile of heavy stones, recalling custom both at Khirokitia and Sotira. At least one Erimi burial[2] included the antlers of a stag and animal bones; the same gifts were found with a contemporary burial at Karavas on the north coast.[3] Pottery vessels and personal ornaments have also been recorded as grave gifts, most recently at Kouklia.

A Chalcolithic I settlement has not yet been examined in sufficient detail for any clear picture to emerge of village economy in the late fourth millennium. Nevertheless, some inferences can be drawn from the general pattern of Chalcolithic settlement.[4] The Cape Krommyon region in north-west Cyprus offers a particularly clear illustration. Here, between Liveras and Vasilia on the coast, and in the hinterland to the south, is a remarkable proliferation of settlements, some of which, notably *Kornos* by the shore near Kormakiti, and its neighbour *Galales*, must have been of substantial size. The area of these settlements is now very largely a *maquis* with at best a shallow soil cover yielding a mediocre grain crop even in good years. The Chalcolithic farmers no doubt found the area covered by light forest, which they were able without serious difficulty to clear for their crop husbandry. Much of it will have been of a park-like quality favourable to the harbouring of game, and to the pasturing of their own flocks. In addition, immediately adjoining the coastal settlements is a succession of coves and inlets of the sea, where shellfish were to be had for the gathering and the inshore fishing had not yet been devastated by the dynamiters.

Combed-Ware had been the hallmark of Neolithic II. Apart from vestigial amounts in the earliest levels at Erimi and Kalavassos site B it played no part in Chalcolithic I. The Red Lustrous pottery that was widespread in Chalcolithic I, however, seems probably to have had its origins in Neolithic II.[5] But the most characteristic pottery of the period was the so-called Red-on-White ware.[6] This attractive fabric made use of geometric and stylized ornaments in red to brown pigment painted on a white-slipped ground colour. The range of shapes was small, and consisted chiefly of deep basins, some with handles, bowls and bottles.[7] None of these shapes can be matched in Neolithic II. Axes and

---

[1] §x, 3, 117.   [2] §xiii, 2, 11.   [3] §xiii, 2, 74.
[4] §x, 3, 3; G, 3, 137.   [5] §xii, 1, 184–6.
[6] §x, 3, 118–21; §xiii, 2, 28–36. See Plate 16(*d*).   [7] §x, 3, fig. 58.

chisels continued to be made of ground and polished fine-grained stone. In addition, there was a poor school of lapidaries producing rough stone vessels, chiefly mortars in andesite or limestone.[1] At Erimi at least, the flint industry was not impressive;[2] based chiefly on the manufacture of blades and scrapers, it is notable for the absence of projectiles. The artistry of Chalcolithic I is seen at its best in the minor stone and terracotta sculpture. The stone figures, for which picrolite is the normal material, provide highly stylized representations of nude female figures.[3] Their degree of schematization is more reminiscent of Early Cycladic marble sculpture than of the obese mother-goddess figures that have been found so widespread in Neolithic and Chalcolithic contexts in the lands that surround the east Mediterranean. Even so, the Cycladic echo is a trifle faint, and the characteristically cruciform posture of the Cypriot figures[4] seems peculiar to the island. Minute copies of these figures were made as amulets,[5] and there is a noteworthy statuette from the region of Pomos[6] depicting the usual woman wearing just such an amulet suspended from her neck. Finally, mention should be made of the earliest appearance of a metal artefact in Cyprus, in the form of a fragment of a copper chisel-like tool from a deep layer at Erimi.[7]

Chalcolithic I chronology rests on carbon 14 dates. A sample from the earliest deposits at Kalavassos site B[8] has been attributed to 3180 ± 130 B.C.; this coincides satisfactorily with the carbon-14 date of 3190 ± 130 B.C. for phase III at Sotira. Carbon-14 dates for charcoal samples in the upper levels at Erimi suggest that a terminal date of c. 2500 B.C. cannot be far wrong.[9]

The foreign associations of Chalcolithic I are no easier to find than those of Neolithic I and II. It has been suggested that the superficial resemblances between the painted pottery of Chalcolithic I and the Dhimini wares of the Thessalian Neolithic sequence[10] is of historical significance. But even before carbon-14 dates made such an association chronologically improbable, it had become obvious that the resemblances were more apparent than real. In other aspects of material culture, particularly in architecture, the two regions have virtually nothing in common.

Some patterned pottery found in Level IVC at Ras Shamra[11] has been thought to be of Cypriot manufacture and, more specifi-

---

[1] §XIII, 2, 46–7. [2] §XIII, 2, 51–3. [3] §XIII, 2, pl. 29.

[4] G, 12, pl. 3: 1. [5] §X, 3, fig. 62. [6] G, 12, pl. III: 2. See Plate 16(e).

[7] §XIII, 2, 50. [8] §X, 3, 198. [9] §X, 3, 198–9.

[10] G, 19, 22–4. [11] §XIII, 4, 170–1.

cally, of Chalcolithic I type. It has even been suggested that Cyprus acted as an intermediary between south-east Europe and the Near East in the Chalcolithic period.[1] This view is beset by insurmountable chronological difficulties, for the date of Level IV C at Ras Shamra must be substantially earlier than the earliest possible date for Chalcolithic I in Cyprus. On the other hand, the suggestion that some painted sherds found in an E.B. II level at Tarsus[2] might have come from some Cypriot Chalcolithic site is chronologically possible.

It seems clear, indeed, that in the Neolithic and Chalcolithic periods Cyprus had very little contact with any of her continental neighbours. This is not altogether surprising at a period when mastery of the sea still lay far in the future, as also did those technological advances which increasingly were to drive the self-contained food-raisers of an earlier day into a position of dependence upon their neighbours for certain rare and precious commodities.

XIV. CHALCOLITHIC II: CYPRUS IN TRANSITION TO THE BRONZE AGE

By c. 2500 B.C. the settlement at Erimi had been abandoned.[3] Though this date has not received independent confirmation at any other Chalcolithic I site, it is generally assumed that the end of Erimi is typical of events all over the island. We have to infer a serious calamity in Cyprus in the middle of the third millennium B.C. Though the identity of this calamity is quite uncertain, it was probably of natural rather than human agency. It was accompanied by the wholesale desertion of settlements throughout the island and the almost total disappearance of the distinctive features of Chalcolithic I material culture from the centuries that follow.

According to current estimates,[4] the Early Bronze Age did not begin until c. 2300 B.C., two centuries after the disappearance of the Erimi culture. Our understanding of what took place in Cyprus during those two centuries is very limited, but some progress has been made in defining a rather shadowy material culture, now called Chalcolithic II, which has been identified and described by Dikaios[5] from test excavations carried out at a handful of sites on the west side of the central plain. It is here in

---

[1] §XIII, 4, 170–3.   [2] §XIII, 3, 112.   [3] §x, 3, 199.
[4] §x, 3, 204; cf. C.A.H. I³, ch. xxvi(b), §VIII, 15, 285.   [5] §x, 3, 188–9.

particular that the short-lived nature of early sites in Cyprus is of particular disadvantage; for there is no settlement at which an unbroken sequence from Chalcolithic I into the full Bronze Age has been preserved.

The most important of these transitional Chalcolithic II sites is at Ambelikou, four miles south of Soli.[1] The area excavated was of small extent, and little architectural evidence was recovered except traces of a round hut, which seems to have resembled Chalcolithic I types.[2] The distinction between Chalcolithic I and II is best seen in the pottery; the decorated Red-on-White wares so typical of Chalcolithic I had almost entirely disappeared at Ambelikou, where the dominant fabrics were Red Lustrous and Red and Black Lustrous wares.[3] Near the village of Philia in the Ovgos valley[4] a similar ceramic situation was found by Dikaios at a settlement site (site B) not far from another of normal Chalcolithic I type. Here, at Philia site B, was found a fabric called 'Black-Slip-and-Combed-Ware' by Dikaios[5] which otherwise occurs, albeit sparsely, in the first Early Bronze Age contexts, as in the *Alonia* settlement of Kyra,[6] and the tombs nearby.[7] The same fabric has been identified in E.B. II contexts at Tarsus,[8] hinting, perhaps, at the direction from which the subsequent settlement of Cyprus came in the Early Bronze Age. In any event, it provides a useful chronological check on the date of the beginning of the Early Cypriot period.

[1] *Ill. Ldn. News*, 2.3.46, 244–5; §x, 3, 141–9.
[2] §x, 3, fig. 66.
[3] §x, 3, 147.
[4] §x, 3, 150–1.
[5] §x, 3, 150.
[6] §x, 3, 152–5.
[7] §x, 3, 172.
[8] §xiii, 3, fig. 263.

CHAPTER X

THE STONE AGE IN THE AEGEAN

THE existence of a Neolithic culture in the Aegean area was first recognized during the opening years of this century—at Dhimini and Sesklo in Thessaly by Staïs and Tsountas,[1] in the regions of Elatea and Chaeronea (in Phocis and Boeotia respectively) by Soteriades,[2] at Boeotian Orchomenus by a Bavarian expedition,[3] at Cnossus in Crete by Evans.[4] Within the first decade the picture of that culture was already filled in in considerable detail and subsequent excavations supplied it with both breadth and depth. But while stone artefacts of pre-Neolithic types were thought to have been found at times on the Greek mainland, no stratified remains surely of Palaeolithic or Mesolithic types were found until 1941, when Stampfuss cut a trench into the fill of the Seidi Cave,[5] located at the south-east corner of the Copaïc Basin, about two miles east of Haliartus. Only then was it fairly certain that men in the food-gathering, rather than the food-producing, stage had lived in Greece, but the exact date of these finds remained in question. It was the work of Milojčić and the German expedition to Thessaly which first lengthened enormously the record of human occupation in Greece, with the discovery in 1956 of an Aceramic Neolithic culture at Argissa[6] and then, in 1958, with the location of numerous sites of Middle and Late Palaeolithic occupation along the Peneus River west of Larissa.[7] These have been followed by similar discoveries in other parts of the Aegean as well as in Thessaly, and by a re-appraisal of earlier reports, so that a somewhat continuous sequence covering perhaps as much as 100,000 years now begins to take shape.

I. PALAEOLITHIC AND MESOLITHIC

As part of the German expedition to Thessaly, a study of the steep sides and gravel banks of the Peneus River was undertaken in September 1958 by the geologist Dr Dieter Jung. On the first day of his survey Palaeolithic stone artefacts and fossilized

---

[1] §II, 21.   [2] §III, 9; §III, 8.   [3] §III, 1.
[4] §VII, 3, vol. I, 34 f.   [5] §III, 10.   [6] §II, 12.
[7] §II, 8.

bones were found and in rapid succession at least fifteen sites were located along the river in a ten-mile stretch to the west of Larissa;[1] this number grew to well over twenty the following year. While the majority of these finds were made in gravel banks which had fallen from the sides due to erosion by the river, in three places found in 1958 the bones and tools were still in place in the deposit with which they were originally associated; one of these is at the site of Argissa, where the relation to Neolithic remains can be ascertained. The remains of human occupation lay in a horizontal layer of gravel conglomerate almost eight metres below the level at which the remains of the Aceramic Neolithic occurred. Most of this accumulation is the sediment from the bottom of a great lake that covered much of Thessaly; its division by three dark layers represents periods in which the lake dried up and vegetation grew, until the next inundation.

Further stratigraphic observations along the Peneus River in 1959[2] showed three distinct layers in which the Palaeolithic remains occurred. The lowest of these contained coarse flake tools of Levalloiso-Mousterian type and was rich in fossil remains of large fauna. The intermediate layer produced abundant small flake tools but few fossil remains and these of small animals; the tools are of a Lower Aurignacian type. The third and uppermost level, just under the thick sediment of the lake, produced a developed small blade industry. Geological studies of the Middle Thessalian basin in 1959 yielded further finds of Palaeolithic tools. In 1960 Theochares found Middle Palaeolithic remains in the banks of the Peneus River around Larissa.[3]

Only the finds of 1958 have been reported in any detail.[4] Of these, a considerable number out of about 250 stone artefacts found belong in the Levalloiso-Mousterian tradition of Western Europe, though they are atypical as compared with these western industries. They are, however, clearly Middle Palaeolithic and must be dated somewhere between 50,000 and 30,000 years ago. It is possible that a few pieces may be related to much earlier Abbevillian-Acheulian types, but this is not yet certain. Aurignacian-like types of the Upper Palaeolithic era are also present. All are made from flakes of dark red-brown carnelian, the source of which has been located in the Pindus Mountains north-west of Kalabaka, some fifty miles to the west of the find spot. The absence of cores indicates that at least the original working was done farther to the west and only flakes or finished

[1] §II, 8.   [2] §II, 7, 153–6.
[3] §II, 15, 171.   [4] §II, 8.

tools were brought to the Larissa Plain. Blade tools are rare; the flake tools vary greatly in size and some are quite small. They were struck from a core prepared in a Levalloisian technique and through scant retouching were then fashioned into various tools; these include a variety of scrapers, points and borers, as well as some blade scrapers.

Of the large number of bones found with the tools, most were extremities, indicating that only parts of the slain animals were brought back to camp. Some leg bones seem to have been split and worked to make awls or points. Bone tools may also have been used in the making of stone implements. The animals represented by the fossilized bones include rhinoceros, hippopotamus, elephant, horse and various ruminants, generally characteristic of a warm climate.

The picture that emerges as a result of these discoveries is one of considerable human occupation of the Thessalian Plain certainly by Middle Palaeolithic times, possibly even earlier, and its continuous habitation into at least the early Upper Palaeolithic period. Only open camp sites are known in Thessaly thus far, but if the small stretch of the Peneus River banks that has been searched is any indication, they were in fairly heavy concentration.

Men of Neanderthal type apparently roamed not only the Thessalian Plain but other parts of Greece as well; this is indicated by the finding in 1960 of a fossilized skull of Neanderthal type in a cave near Petralona in Chalcidice.[1] In the same year chance finds of four Middle Palaeolithic or perhaps Upper Palaeolithic (Lower Aurignacian) tools were made in Elis.[2] This discovery was followed up by a French team, led by A. Leroi-Gourhan, which in 1962 confirmed the Palaeolithic occupation of the region by finding three quaternary horizons in the regions of Amalias and Katakolo.[3] These produced hundreds of tools and flakes of flint, the oldest of which are again of Levalloiso-Mousterian type, Middle Palaeolithic in date, the next a series of flints in Levalloisian tradition which are transitional from Middle to Upper Palaeolithic, the latest a microlithic industry which is Late Palaeolithic–Mesolithic in date.[4] In 1963 this same expedition found numerous Middle Palaeolithic implements at many sites in Elis and also found many Palaeolithic tools in the region of Megalopolis. The greatest concentration found that year was near the village of Vasilaki,[5] on the border between the provinces of Elis and Arkadia, some twenty-two kilometres from

[1] §I, 3.   [2] §V, 15.   [3] §V, 12.
[4] A, 28; A, 29.   [5] A, 10.

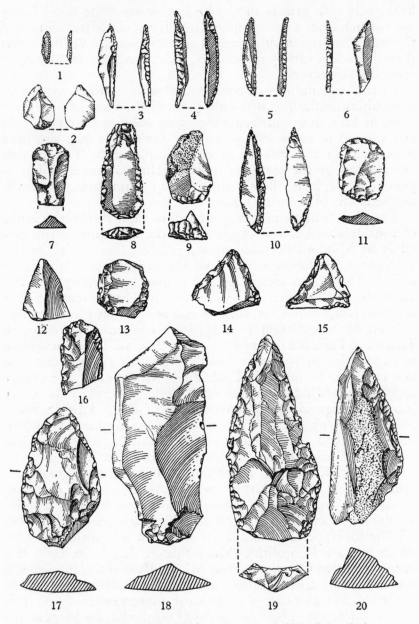

Fig. 43. Advanced Palaeolithic tools, 1–11; Middle Palaeolithic
tools, 12–20; from Asprochaliko, Epirus. Scale 1:1.

the coast. Here were found both implements of well-developed Mousterian type, made from river cobbles and thus of unusually large size, and a blade industry of more recent date. A flake point of Levalloiso–Mousterian type found on the surface in the Riniza Valley in the Argolid[1] remains an isolated find.

A British expedition, led by E. S. Higgs, began in 1962 a reconnaissance of Western Macedonia and Epirus and soon established that Palaeolithic flint industries were not uncommon in these areas.[2] More material, including many chipping floors, appeared in Epirus than in Macedonia, but a very rare Acheulian hand-axe was found near Kozani.[3] Excavations were begun in 1963 and have continued since. The first were in the Kokkinopolis area of Epirus, originally referred to as Pantanassa,[4] but it is the excavations in 1964 and 1965 at the rock shelter called Asprochaliko, on the right bank of the Louros River a little north of Kokkinopolis, that have yielded the most important results.[5] The somewhat limited excavations have produced over 75,000 artefacts in the two seasons and, most important, these are from well-stratified deposits. The earliest industry is similar to the Levalloiso–Mousterian of North Africa and the Levant and includes heavy scrapers, Mousterian points, D-scrapers and flat cores, such as are also found in the Red Beds at Kokkinopolis. Associated with these are bones of bear, deer and a now-extinct rhinoceros, all of which were hunted.[6] A carbon-14 date from the base of this deposit is about 40,000 B.C.[7] This series is closely associated with that found by Milojčić and Theochares along the Peneus River, as well as with the earliest series from Elis. In the stratum above there was a crude, but prolific, industry comprising small implements of Mousterian type—side scrapers and small tortoise cores. Still higher up, in a separate stratum, is an industry made up primarily of backed blades; it dates to about 24,000 B.C.[8] The latest industry, in still another stratum of deposit, is microlithic, comprising minute flint triangles, crescent artefacts, burins or gravers, many scrapers, shouldered points and a series of blade-like artefacts blunted down on one side.[9] The last is very like the industry from Romanelli Cave in Italy, for which a date of around 10,000 B.C. has been obtained.[10] A most promising cave discovered in 1965 was scheduled for excavation in 1966. Most recently Levalloiso–Mousterian

[1] §v, 1.   [2] A, 11, 202.   [3] §1, 2.
[4] §iv, 3.   [5] A, 21, 10–21. See Fig. 43.   [6] A, 20, 24–5.
[7] Reported in *Archaeological Reports for 1965–66*, p. 13.
[8] A, 21, 24.   [9] A, 20, 24.   [10] A, 20, 23–4.

industries have been reported from the island of Corfu.[1] That
the Middle Palaeolithic industries are to be dated to the time of
the first Würm phase has been suggested on the basis of comparisons with similar finds from Level XII of the Crvena Stijena
cave in Yugoslavia.[2] In Bulgaria, too, Mousterian-like industries
begin the Palaeolithic series.

It is thus clear by now that before the end of the Middle
Palaeolithic period, say roughly 50,000 to 30,000 years ago,
the Greek peninsula was occupied from Macedonia to Elis, and
possibly in the Argolid as well; the single skull from Chalcidice
suggests that the inhabitants were of Neanderthal type. Evidence
for earlier occupation, in the Lower Palaeolithic, though still
scant, seems to be forthcoming. Upper Palaeolithic industries
of Lower Aurignacian type followed the Middle Palaeolithic
almost everywhere.

When the Thessalian Plain, and most likely other parts of
Greece as well, became inundated, possibly between 30,000 and
20,000 years ago, man must have taken to the higher ground of
the periphery, perhaps descending again in the several periods of
desiccation. Remains of such peripheral occupation of Thessaly
in the latter part of the Upper Palaeolithic have not yet appeared,
nor indeed have they been sought systematically, but it is possible that the occupation of the Seidi Cave in Boeotia was the
result of a parallel situation.

Whether or not the formation of Lake Copaïs in central
Greece was in any way connected geologically with the inundation
of Thessaly has not been established, but it remained a lake after
Thessaly was drained except for such vestigial lakes as Boebeis
and Nessonis at the eastern rim of the Thessalian Basin. Shallow
caves, or rock shelters, at the south-east corner of the Copaïc
Basin were occupied by Palaeolithic man, according to the evidence of a sounding in the Seidi Cave and observations in a
trench cut for a water channel just in front of the nearby Pyrgos
Cave.[3] The first cave, in which a trench was excavated in October
1941, is only a little above the basin and is easily accessible from
it. It had been occupied from Geometric to Hellenistic times,
but immediately below was a layer 1·20–1·40 metres thick in
which Palaeolithic implements and fossilized bones occurred in
some quantity. Here the majority of the stone tools were of chert,
some of flint and quartzite; one blade was of rock crystal. Unlike
the earlier industries of Thessaly, that represented in the Seidi
Cave is largely a blade industry, with flakes and cores used much

[1] A, 45.   [2] §VIII, 3, 62 f.   [3] §III, 10.

less often and for curved scrapers and keel scrapers respectively. Knives, saws, borers, gravers and a variety of other points, including notched points, predominate, but there is also a considerable variety of scrapers. It is interesting that among the scrapers are fifteen keel scrapers made from cores in a manner that harks back to Aurignacian techniques. On the other hand, there are small round scrapers that are typically Mesolithic. A wide selection of microliths includes forms that go back to Gravettian prototypes. This combination of Aurignacian, Magdalenian and Gravettian features suggested to the excavator that the Seidi Cave assemblage belongs to the blade cultures of the late Upper Palaeolithic and the Mesolithic periods, but again these industries were sufficiently atypical to make exact co-ordination with western European cultures difficult. The Seidi Cave industry is now shown to resemble closely that from the uppermost stratum of the Asprochaliko Shelter in Epirus.[1]

For some years the Seidi Cave material remained an isolated phenomenon and, since the material was removed from Greece, it was not possible for others to examine it. However, a control excavation at the same site in 1956 yielded similar remains, while at the same time the first stratified Palaeolithic sequence was found to the north in Yugoslavia, in the rock shelter of Crvena Stijena in Montenegro.[2] Here, in a depth of almost twelve metres, were eighteen strata, the earliest of which contained stone implements of Mousterian type. The excavators have noted specifically the similarity between the material from their Levels VII–V and that from the Seidi Cave; they would term both Late Palaeolithic–Mesolithic. They have been able to suggest, further, that these levels mark the end of the Würm II glacial phase, while Level IV, an Aceramic phase, marks the beginning of the post-glacial age. Thus a date around 10,000 B.C. ± 1000 years cannot be very far off for the occupation of the Seidi Cave and possibly the Pyrgos Cave as well.

That Thessaly too was re-occupied after it had reverted to dry land is indicated by a couple of Mesolithic microliths found in the Argissa area. But there are indications that by this time the human occupants of Greece were capable of travel by sea, for on the island of Scyrus in the Sporades, only some twenty-two miles from Cyme on the east side of Euboea, Theochares[3] has recently found remains of microliths, largely of flint but some of obsidian, which he believes to be certainly Mesolithic; some stone artefacts from the island may be even older, Late Palaeolithic, types. Several shallow caves and shelters located north-west of the town of Scyrus are possible occupation sites that await investigation. The probable occupancy by Mesolithic times at least of this island in the north Aegean has suggested the likelihood that the island of Zante (Zacynthus), the southernmost of the Ionian Islands, only half as far from the Peloponnese as is Scyrus from Euboea, may also have been inhabited at this time. In 1936 masses of worked chert were found in an area about fifty metres square on the Kastello hill at the southern end of the island.[1] Both flake and blade tools are represented—scrapers, borers, points—as well as microliths. While published as a Neolithic assemblage, the material from Zacynthus is so like that from the Seidi Cave and from Scyrus as to suggest that here too early man had settled before the first appearance of food-producers in Greece. Just to the north of Zacynthus lies Cephallenia, on the south-eastern shores of which flint-working was clearly a major occupation.[2] While the tools found here have recently been dated much later, and the age of the surface finds from both Elis and the Argolid has similarly been lowered drastically,[3] there is a distinct possibility that they go back to Mesolithic or Late Palaeolithic times; the subsequent corroboration of the early dating for the Elean finds has already been mentioned.

With Greece now known to have been inhabited from Mousterian times and possibly earlier, how continuously we do not yet know, it is time to reconsider the reports by Markovits of the finding of Upper Palaeolithic and Mesolithic remains in the Megarid and the Argolid. The work in the former area was concentrated on the rocky cliffs known as the Kaki Skala, and after investigating many caves one, called the Zaïmis Cave, was tested by a trench, which has been described preliminarily and a section of which has been published.[4] In an average depth of two metres there are ten strata of which IV, the main Neolithic level, has seven sub-levels. Level V seems also to be early Neolithic with pottery, but VI is devoid of either pottery or worked stone, the latter of which then appears in abundance in Levels VII–IX. Markovits characterized the microlithic industry of Levels VII–IX as Azilio-Tardenoisian and compared it especially with North German finds. In another cave, named the Ulbrich Cave,[5] somewhere between Nemea and Nauplia but not more closely located in any of the reports I have seen, Markovits also made a trial cut,

---

[1] §IV, 6.   [2] §IV, 5.   [3] §IV, 4.
[4] §III, 6; §III, 7.   [5] §III, 7.

which showed seven strata in a depth of some 0·60–0·70 metres. Mesolithic tools occurred as early as in the second level; Levels III and IV contained Azilio-Tardenoisian type flints and numerous bone tools. The bone tools in Level V are made from bones of larger animals and the flints are of Late Magdalenian types. Level VI showed no traces of human culture and animal bones were very rare; the lowest level, VII, produced many flint tools of Aurignacian type, some bone tools and abundant shells.

Markovits began his work in 1928 and continued for the next four or five years, during which he issued numerous fragmentary reports in anthropological and speleological journals, largely in his native Austria and in Greece. Many reports noted as 'in press' for 1933 never appeared, and no more complete publication of the material from either cave was ever made. Perhaps because of the time when the discoveries were made, possibly because of the audience to which the reports were addressed, little or no credence was given to Markovits's discoveries, but on reading the reports now with the benefit of recent finds, it does seem likely that thirteen years before the excavation of the Seidi Cave and thirty years prior to the Thessalian discoveries, similar material had been found along the Kaki Skala and in the Argolid. That these discoveries now be confirmed by further excavation in both caves, as well as in others in both areas, is imperative. It is clear that we are only at the beginning of the discovery of Palaeolithic and Mesolithic remains in Greece; it is also clear that while scepticism is healthy, negativism is anti-progressive.

II. ACERAMIC NEOLITHIC

The revolution that changed man from a food-gatherer to a food-producer, from a migratory hunter and collector of wild fruits to a settled agriculturist and tender of domesticated animals, has been one of the chief preoccupations of prehistorians, especially those working in the Near or Middle East, since the end of the Second World War. That these early farmers lived in settled communities and had all the perquisites of Neolithic society, except that for a long first phase they did not know the use of pottery, was becoming known already several years before the beginning of the last war, especially at Jericho.[1] But it was the work of Braidwood and the Oriental Institute expedition at Jarmo and in the surrounding area in Iraqi Kurdistān,[2] from

[1] §x, 9.   [2] §x, 3.

1948 to 1955, that shed the greatest light on this transitional phase from Mesolithic to a Neolithic with pottery. Kathleen Kenyon's work at Jericho revealed the surprising heights to which the Aceramic Neolithic culture had risen.[1] It has been generally accepted that this revolution was carried out in the Near East, but that the results very quickly affected south-east Europe was made apparent by the discovery in October 1956 by the German expedition at Argissa of the first remains of a Pre-ceramic Neolithic culture in the Aegean.[2] Soon afterwards a section of the acropolis of Sesklo fell away, owing to an earth-quake, and revealed much deeper Neolithic strata than had been known there. At the bottom of these was an accumulation from the Aceramic Neolithic period.[3] This was investigated at once by Theochares, again the following year[4] and most recently from 1962 on.[5] Wider areas were dug at Argissa in 1957 and 1958 while in the latter year a Preceramic Neolithic level was found by Theochares at Souphli Magula, on the right bank of the Peneus River just north-east of Larissa, and investigated in a limited area.[6] Surface finds indicate other possible Preceramic Neolithic remains at Nessonis in north-eastern Thessaly,[7] at a site on the Titaresius River near Tirnavo,[8] at Pharsalus in south-central Thessaly[9] and at Ayios Theodhoros near Karditsa in south-west Thessaly.[10] One indication of possible Aceramic Neolithic remains outside of Thessaly has come from a mention by Milojčić[11] of microliths in the Historical Museum of Berne, deposited there in the mid-nineteenth century. Some of these are said to come from Anavryta, near Athens, others from various places in Greece, including the tumulus at Marathon and the area around Athens; the stone industry is said to resemble that of the Thessalian Aceramic Neolithic. Another indication comes from Corfu, where Sordinas has possibly found an Aceramic level at Sidari,[12] for which there is a carbon-14 date of about 6000 B.C.

We have, then, only three excavated sites with Aceramic Neolithic strata, and all in a fairly limited area in eastern Thessaly. The material from Argissa, where an area of over fifty square metres was dug and the settlement can be traced for a total

[1] §x, 8. [2] §ii, 12. Map i, 5. [3] §ii, 14. Map i, 7.
[4] §ii, 16, 74–8. [5] §ii, 19; §ii, 20.
[6] §ii, 16, 78–85. Map i, 3. [7] §viii, 13, 328. Map i, 2.
[8] Reported by Theochares in a lecture given in Athens in March 1964.
[9] §ii, 15, 171. [10] §ii, 16, 73.
[11] §viii, 13, 331f [12] A, 45.

length of at least eighty metres, has been definitively published; for Sesklo there are preliminary reports which do not mention the area excavated for this earliest phase; at Souphli the area is about half that at Argissa (according to the preliminary report). The depth of deposit for the Aceramic phase averaged 0·30–0·40 metres at Argissa, but attained a maximum of 1·00 metre; at Sesklo the average was 0·30–0·45 metres, the maximum *c.* 1·13 metres, falling into three strata, while at Souphli the deposit was *c.* 0·80–1·00 metres thick and was divided into three strata averaging 0·30 metres each.

From all three sites it seems clear that from the start these villages were rather thickly settled, the earliest inhabitants living in small huts, the floor of which was cut into virgin soil to a depth of from 0·30–0·60 metres. The largest pit hut yet dug, at Argissa, is *c.* 4·00 × 2·20 metres. Hearths and pebble floors occur in some cuttings. The superstructure was apparently of reeds and branches, possibly with mud daub; the large amount of ash and carbonized matter in these earliest strata is due to the nature of the structures. Some small pits lined with clay may have served for storage. As occupation debris accumulated, houses seem to have been built at ground level with stamped earth floors and to have had hearths; the walls may have been supported by posts, for which post holes bear evidence. One such hut floor at Argissa, at the − 7·88 metre level, has a width of *c.* 5·00 metres and about 4·00 metres of its length is preserved. A house apparently of larger dimensions is being excavated at Sesklo.[1]

Possibly because of the limited scope of excavations in Preceramic levels in Greece thus far, no burials of the period have been found. That they might be expected within the settlements is indicated by the presence of intramural burial in Preceramic levels at Khirokitia in Cyprus[2] and at Jericho[3] and Naḥal Ōren[4] in Palestine.

The equipment of these earliest farmers and herdsmen consisted largely of bone and stone tools, implements and weapons; bone tools may outnumber those of stone at Sesklo and Souphli. The stone implements comprise both chipped and polished types. Obsidian seems to have been used for one-third to two-thirds of the chipped stone tools, carnelian and flint or chert for the rest. The industry was essentially one of blades, often with retouche, or of fragments of blades in trapeziform or triangular shape, the

[1] A, 48, 5–6.
[2] §x, 5, 214 f.
[3] §x, 8, 53, 85.
[4] §x, 13, 11.

well-known microliths.[1] Besides the blades, there are points, borers and scrapers, possibly also arrowheads. Most of these small blades and fragments must have been mounted in bone or wooden hafts for use as knives, sickles, awls, etc. Larger stone pounders or grinders and green schist or red sandstone 'palettes', sometimes with a hole bored near the centre, must have served for the grinding of grain, but may also have been used in treating skins. Heavier stone tools are lacking, as perhaps are axes, and Milojčić suggests that heavy agricultural implements were made of wood.[2] Argissa produced large quantities of river pebbles which had been subjected to repeated heat and are believed to have been heating stones used in cooking. There is no evidence that stone was hollowed out and shaped into vessels; such are so common in many other centres of Aceramic Neolithic civilization as to give the name 'Stone Bowl Phase' to the period. Stone was used, however, for small objects which have been named 'ear-plugs'; there are four in greenstone from Souphli, at least seven in stone from Sesklo and one from Argissa. Their use is unknown; both decorative and religious purposes have been suggested.

The hundreds of bone tools are largely points or awls made from fragments of small or medium-sized hollow extremity bones which usually retain the articulation at one end while the other is cut or chipped much in the manner of stone tools, frequently in an asymmetrical fashion, with most or all of the cutting from one side.[3] Ribs were used for blades, spatulae, scrapers or polishers, more rarely for needles. Since only a small percentage of the bone tools were polished, unlike the subsequent period when polishing became the general rule, it is difficult at times to distinguish made tools from unworked splintered bones. Souphli has produced two bone objects called fishhooks, large and well formed, but one of these is remarkably like the hook of a buckle from Çatal Hüyük[4]. Bone was also used frequently for hafting stone tools, and large bones probably served as hammers as well, particularly for striking blades from cores.

That clay was already being used to make various objects is possibly indicated both at Argissa and at Souphli, each of which produced a clay sling bullet of biconical shape; while that from Souphli is from the uppermost Aceramic level and may therefore belong to the following period, that from Argissa was found in Pit *a*, at the very bottom of the Preceramic stratum. However,

---

[1] See Plate 17.   [2] §II, 12, 25.   [3] See Plate 17.

[4] §IX, 14, pl. xxvII, *c–d*. Originally called two bone pendants, they are now recognized as hook and eye belonging together.

Pit α also produced four sherds from Early Neolithic vessels, believed to have been brought down to this level in post holes, and the same might be true for the sling bullet. Pit γ at Argissa yielded a burnt clay 'anchor'; no pottery had contaminated this pit. An 'ear-plug' of clay and what may be a piece of a clay figurine came from the −8·20 to −8·10 metre level at Argissa. What is perhaps most interesting is the mention by both Milojčić and Theochares of what seem to be first attempts at making vessels of clay. In the −8·10 to −8·00 metre level at Argissa were found two thick-walled vessels of unbaked clay,[1] but Milojčić is not sure whether these are first attempts at making pottery or are just unfinished pieces from the level above. At Souphli,[2] however, there occurred in the middle one of the three Preceramic strata two fragments made of badly fired, or perhaps sun-dried, pottery, on one of which were traces of red paint. The third stratum separates these from the pottery-bearing levels and Theochares notes that the fragments were totally different from the earliest pottery at the site. In 1963 Theochares found very primitive pottery in the upper part of the Aceramic level at Sesklo; he assumes that this represents a local beginning of pottery making which then continued in the first full pottery phase.[3] Except for these, there are no vessels of any kind at the Preceramic sites, though a sea-shell found at Souphli has the lip so cut as to suggest that it may have served as a vessel. Baskets, gourds, skins, etc., must have served these people as containers. A clay-lined pit at Argissa (Pit α) may have served for storage. Pieces of clay mixed with straw and hardened by accidental firing are probably daub from huts; some may be from hearths.

If the so-called 'ear-plugs' are for ornament, they are almost all we have, though a piece of pierced sea-shell from Sesklo may also have been decorative and there may be a bead or two. This contrasts sharply with the number of stone bracelets, beads and pendants known especially from Jarmo, where the 'ear-plugs' also occur.[4] Clearly the grinding and polishing of stone that is so common in the Near East was largely outside the competence of the first Aegean farmers.

That these people were farmers, however, is shown by the amount of wheat, barley, millet, lentils and other legumes, possibly olives as well, found in charred remains in all three settlements. Their herding activities are witnessed by the thousands of bones of domesticated animals, largely sheep but also goats,

[1] §II, 12, 20 f. [2] §II, 16, 82.
[3] §II, 20, 31. f.; A, 48, 7. [4] §X, 2, fig. 20.

swine and cattle. Their food supply was further augmented by some hunting, especially of deer, hare, game birds and small birds, and by collecting of shellfish, as well as fishing; the collecting of wild nuts and fruits must also have continued.

This still very fragmentary picture of the earliest village-farming communities in Greece is enough to associate the Aegean manifestation with that known more fully from Jarmo, Jericho, Khirokitia and other Near Eastern sites. They share the microlithic industries, the stone 'palettes', the 'ear-plugs', the abundance of bone tools, the primitive agriculture and the first domesticated animals. Yet architecturally the Near Eastern sites are far more sophisticated than are those of Greece; the material assemblage of the former is richer and shows greater technical competence than does that of the Thessalian villages, which seem clearly to be provincial by comparison. This need not imply that the Aceramic Neolithic phase of Greece is later in date than that of the Near East, which is now placed in the eighth and seventh millennia B.C. We have carbon-14 determinations for the earliest pottery-bearing levels in the Aegean which indicate a beginning of pottery-making there at about 6000 B.C.; the Aceramic Neolithic thus belongs in the seventh millennium. It was most probably a long phase, perhaps going back into the eighth millennium as well. Not unlike the Aceramic Neolithic of Greece are the manifestations of that phase in Yugoslavia, Hungary and Romania,[1] and these too must be dated similarly.

One question that must be considered is whether or not the Aegean area played any part in the revolution that changed man from a food-gatherer to a food-producer. Braidwood considers the revolution as a phenomenon which occurred in the hill country of northern Iraq, north-western Iran and perhaps southeastern Turkey, and spread from there,[2] but Miss Kenyon has argued that Jericho, and perhaps other such isolated areas where great fertility was conducive to long settlement, may have been the scene of independent change.[3] The startling discoveries of the last few years at Çatal Hüyük in the Konya plain of Anatolia[4] suggest that here is another possible focus for the Neolithic revolution. Nothing yet found in Greece, or in the European countries to the north, suggests that a similar process of change took place in Europe independently. It is more likely that the inhabitants of Greece received from Anatolia or farther east the benefits of a revolution already accomplished, in this case chiefly

---

[1] §VIII, 13, 332–5.   [2] §X, 1.
[3] §X, 10, 192 f.   [4] §IX, 13; §IX, 14; §IX, 12, 6.

a knowledge of agriculture and the raising of domesticated animals, permitting permanent settlement. In no sense can the material assemblage known thus far from the Greek Aceramic Neolithic sites compare with that known from the East. Greek settlements lack the developed architecture, the crafts of stone-working for vessels and ornaments, the human and animal figurines, the rather elaborate cult practices that characterize the Near Eastern settlements. If, as seems likely, the Aegean received its settlers of the Aceramic Neolithic period from the Near East, then this was perhaps the first of a long series of westward move-ments into the Aegean, possibly already by boat. That this was completely possible is shown by the widespread use in Thessaly of obsidian that most likely came from the island of Melos—the best evidence we have of an already developed commerce at this time. In turn, the Preceramic culture of Yugoslavia may be a northward extension from Greece, again foreshadowing a pattern often to be repeated.

Lastly, what was the relationship of the Aceramic Neolithic of Greece to the cultures which preceded and succeeded it? Of the three excavated sites (Argissa, Sesklo, Souphli), only the first has yielded evidence of earlier occupation, but the deep accumulation of silt from the lake which covered Thessaly separates the two periods. We are thus left at present without any indication of relationship between the Mesolithic and the Aceramic Neolithic cultures. Only excavation at sites yet to be discovered can show whether there was a gap or if the one directly followed the other. On the other hand, all three sites have Early Neolithic pottery phases immediately above the Aceramic stratum. Such contiguity does not necessarily imply continuity. Both Milojčić and Theo-chares have noted the total difference between the stone and bone industries of the Aceramic phase and those of the Ceramic phase. If a kind of pottery was attempted at either Argissa or Souphli, it bears no relation to the fully formed and competent pottery-making technique that appears from the very beginning at all Early Neolithic sites, but that found at Sesklo Theochares would consider to be the direct and immediate antecedent of the pottery of his E.N. I phase.[1] The figurines and the seals of the earliest pottery Neolithic assemblage in Greece had no ante-cedents in the Aceramic phase. The way of life was much the same; the rectangular houses built with frames of posts sunk into the ground are of the same order of competence in both periods. On this basis Theochares has recently suggested that life at

[1] §II, 20, 31 f.; A, 48, 7.

Sesklo was continuous and uninterrupted from the first inhabitation of the site in the Preceramic phase; clay sling bullets and
'ear-plugs' are also possible links between the Preceramic and
the Ceramic phases. From present evidence, however, the discontinuity is so much greater than the continuity in the material
assemblage as to suggest a break between the two phases. The
Ceramic Neolithic appears full blown, apparently an import, and
the new inhabitants occupy many new sites all over Greece, as
well as the few sites known to have been occupied in the Aceramic
phase. At the latter it is even possible that the new occupants
indulged in some levelling and ordering of the sites. This may
have deprived us of some evidence for the latter part of the Preceramic phase. What seems most probable is that the makers of
pottery took over these sites directly from their former occupants,
so that there was a continuity of occupation, though very likely
without a cultural continuity. At present, the first Ceramic
Neolithic phase cannot be shown to have developed locally out
of the Aceramic Neolithic culture.

III. THE CERAMIC NEOLITHIC PERIOD
AND ITS SUBDIVISIONS

With the appearance in the Aegean of the first Neolithic farmers
who also knew how to make pottery, we are suddenly confronted
with a multiplicity of settlements spread widely through the
mainland of Greece from Macedonia to Messenia, as well as in
Crete, in sharp contrast with the Aceramic Neolithic settlement
pattern as we now know it. We have already suggested a date of
at least 6,000 B.C. for the beginning of the new pottery phase; this
is supported by a carbon-14 date for the oldest pottery-bearing
level at Sidari on Corfu of 5720 ± 120 B.C. based on a half-life of
5570 years (about 5900 B.C. with the higher half-life of 5730
years).[1] The only other carbon-14 determination we have for the
first phase of the Early Neolithic is that for the next to the lowest
floor at Elatea in Phocis, for which the date is 5754 B.C. ± 70
years.[2] Many other determinations are awaited and these may
alter the present estimate, though probably not significantly.
From then on for some three thousand years, Greece, Corfu and
possibly Crete, and in the later phases other Aegean and Ionian

[1] Reported in *Antiquity*, 41, no. 161 (March, 1967), 64.
[2] A, 50, 310. Reasons for not applying the earlier dates from Nea Nikomedeia
and Cnossus are given on pp. 310 and 301 respectively.

islands as well, were occupied by Neolithic farmers whose material culture developed and changed in local and regional patterns. At times the entire Aegean area underwent more drastic change, the causes of which varied considerably from time to time. It is these major changes that form the basis for subdividing the Neolithic period.

While in the late nineteenth century all the remains of the Neolithic and Early and Middle Bronze Ages were lumped together and labelled 'pre-Mycenaean', by the turn of the century the Neolithic was clearly established as a separate period. Within the first few years after 1900, the Cnossian Neolithic deposit was divided into Early, Middle and Late phases;[1] at about the same time Tsountas divided the Neolithic of Thessaly into two phases, Early and Late or A and B,[2] and this became almost universal for the mainland for the next thirty years or so. That there was, however, something earlier than Tsountas's Thessaly A period became apparent in Kunze's study and publication of the Neolithic pottery from Orchomenus in Boeotia.[3] But it was at Corinth in 1937 that the existence of a period earlier than Thessaly A was first clearly established.[4] It was called Early Neolithic, but no distinction was yet made between the later wares that were the equivalents of Thessaly A and B, all of which were lumped together as Late Neolithic. Not until ten years later, owing largely to the interruptions of war, was a tripartite scheme for the Aegean Neolithic period fully propounded,[5] though it had been suggested as early as 1941.[6] Essentially the same division was made by Mrs Kosmopoulos for Corinth in her Periods I to III.[7] Further justification for the scheme was presented in 1952 (published in 1954).[8]

It has become increasingly clear that the tripartite scheme is most pertinent to the Peloponnese. For Central Greece we were almost completely lacking in stratigraphic information for the whole Neolithic period which could serve as a basis for a scheme of division, but this was provided in 1959 by the test excavations at Elatea.[9] Here in Phocis it is clear that the division between Middle and Late Neolithic is the same as in the Peloponnese, but from what is called Early Neolithic in the Peloponnese to Middle Neolithic there is a more gradual transition, and the whole could be considered as one long Early Neolithic period, which towards its end was altered by outside contact, most likely with

[1] §VII, 12, 158–64.　　[2] §II, 21, 73.　　[3] §III, 4, 47.
[4] §V, 20, 493.　　[5] G, 22.　　[6] G, 24.
[7] §V, 11.　　[8] G, 27.　　[9] §III, 14.

the well established Middle Neolithic of the Peloponnese. In Boeotia, to judge from Orchomenus, and even more from the surface material at Thespiae,[1] the situation seems to be the same as in the Peloponnese. In Thessaly, too, the main break is between the old periods A and B, the latter again being the equivalent of the Late Neolithic in central and southern Greece. All of the previous Ceramic Neolithic period Theochares considers as a very long Early Neolithic period, which he then divides into four phases, the last of which corresponds to the old Thessaly A period.[2] Milojčić has named the old Thessaly A period the Sesklo period and has divided the phases preceding it into a 'Vorsesklozeit', a still earlier 'Protosesklo' phase and, as the earliest, a 'Frühkeramik' period.[3] Still, I believe we shall see that in Thessaly more than in Phocis, though perhaps not to the same extent as in the Peloponnese and Boeotia, there are reasons for speaking of an Early Neolithic period, comprising largely what is earlier than the Sesklo period, and for using the term Middle Neolithic for the old Thessaly A, or Sesklo period.

In Macedonia, the discovery of remains of the Early Neolithic period came only in 1961 at Nea Nikomedeia.[4] Thrace has not yet produced anything so early, to my knowledge. In both areas there have been reported some material like that of the Thessaly A period, but the main body of Neolithic remains known thus far is of Late Neolithic date.

In the Aegean islands, other than Crete, what Neolithic remains we have are largely of the latest phase, and the same is true of the Ionian islands except Corfu. In Crete, only Cnossus offers enough depth of Neolithic deposit to suggest either the length of the period or its division into subperiods. In preliminary reports of the recent excavations, from 1957 to 1960, Evans's tripartite scheme has been retained, though two-thirds of the Neolithic deposit beneath the level of the central court is now shown to belong to the Early Neolithic phase, and it is suggested that some of the Late Neolithic deposit may have been cut away by Early and/or Middle Minoan settlers.[5] Whether or not this Cretan tripartite scheme runs parallel with that of the mainland is not now apparent; should some suggestions of the excavator prove to be correct, the Cretan sequence would not begin until the mid-fifth millennium at the earliest, thus at about the middle of the Middle Neolithic period on the mainland.

If, then, for the sake of uniformity and simplicity in presenta-

[1] §III, 2.   [2] §II, 19, 39–42.   [3] §II, 9, 19, chart.
[4] §I, 7.   [5] §VII, 5, ?.

tion, we use a tripartite scheme and devote separate sections to Early, Middle and Late Neolithic for the Greek mainland in general, it must be understood that the applicability of such a division varies from region to region and we shall attempt to point out such continuities as diminish the rigidity of the line of demarcation between periods. Actually, rigid boundaries are, on the whole, non-existent within the Neolithic period, but significant cultural changes are sufficient to make valid the tripartite scheme, and its use, in turn, makes easier the handling of the large body of material now at hand.

IV. THE EARLY NEOLITHIC PERIOD ON THE GREEK MAINLAND

That the Ceramic Neolithic period began with a very long first phase of slow development is becoming increasingly evident as more sites are tested in depth and as determinations from carbon-14 samples give us some idea of the age of the earliest deposits. The first phase at Lerna in the Argolid (Lerna I) comprised many floor levels in a depth of almost two metres.[1] At Elatea in Phocis a similar depth of deposit belonging to the Early Neolithic phase has an average of eight successive floors.[2] The depth of deposit at Sesklo, below the Thessaly A stratum and not including the Preceramic level, is about 1·50 metres, within which some ten floors have been distinguished.[3]

In contrast with our very limited knowledge of the preceding period, the first pottery Neolithic phase is known over a large part of Greece. Remains of this phase have been excavated at some thirty sites, though often in very limited areas, and surface finds indicate the existence of Early Neolithic deposits at some ten more sites; only three of these—Argissa, Sesklo and Souphli —have had Aceramic Neolithic strata excavated while a fourth— Nessonis—has yielded surface remains of the earlier phase. Sidari on Corfu also provides Early Neolithic above an Aceramic stratum.[4] Although not all the new settlements were founded simultaneously, it would be difficult to establish an order of priority. What is of interest is that most lie in the eastern part of the mainland, and all are either on or close to the coast or up valleys easily accessible from the coast. This suggests both an eastward and a seaward orientation for the Early Neolithic

[1] §v, 6, 138 f. [2] §iii, 14, 160–7.
[3] §ii, 19, 40 f. [4] A, 45.

culture, a pattern which continues throughout the Neolithic period. Proper reconnaissance of western Greece would probably change this picture to a small degree.

The new settlers chose sites close to a water supply, usually low knolls but sometimes rocky ridges such as at Sesklo and Corinth. Their earlier constructions were on, or in, hardpan and comprised both pit houses with their floors somewhat below surface level and others with beaten earth floors on the surface. In either case the superstructure was of wattle and daub on a frame of posts, the holes for which give evidence for them, or perhaps at times of a type of *pisé* or even mud brick, though the latter may not occur from the beginning of the period. At first these houses differed little from those of the Aceramic Neolithic period. Freestanding hearths were common, and it is usually only the beaten earth floors and the hearths, hardened by fire, which, besides the cuttings for pit huts and the post holes, give testimony of these early dwellings. We have mentioned the floor at the − 7·88 metre level at Argissa which most probably belongs to the beginning of the Early Neolithic period;[1] the hearth, the pits, the post holes give a good picture of one of these early houses. Mud brick appears at Argissa in the Proto-Sesklo level (middle Early Neolithic), but post houses and pit houses continued; in the upper, Pre-Sesklo, phase of the Early Neolithic period at Argissa, mud brick was more common, pit dwellings are no longer found, but there are smaller pits probably used for storage, and the post houses continue.[2] Sesklo offers much the same sequence, as does Otzaki for the latter phases. Pyrasus, which was probably founded somewhat later than Sesklo, has mud brick already in the lowest stratum, together with post houses.[3] At Elatea post houses prevail; earth floors and hearths are general, and in one house two large pivot stones were found. At Nea Makri, on the east coast of Attica, pit huts with cuttings 0·35– 0·40 metres in depth occur at the bottom; one is 5 metres long and more than 4 metres wide, roughly rectangular, and has a hearth at the centre. In the upper Early Neolithic level at Nea Makri there occur stone foundations, from 0·35 to 0·50 metres wide, for rectangular houses of mud brick; floors are of earth or pebbles and one semicircular hearth has a border of vertical stone slabs.[4] Lerna may have had pit houses at the start and also post houses, but here there are also stone foundations for rectangular houses; one such socle survives to a height of five courses.[5]

[1] §II, 12, 6 f.   [2] §II, 9, 9.   [3] §II, 18, 38.
[4] §III, 12, 4.   [5] §V, 6, 139.

By far the most advanced architecture of the Early Neolithic period is that found recently at Nea Nikomedeia in Macedonia;[1] while little is yet published of the material from the site, indications are that its Early Neolithic occupation was fairly short and probably falls towards the end of the period, this despite the very early carbon-14 date of about 6200 B.C. for the earlier of the two

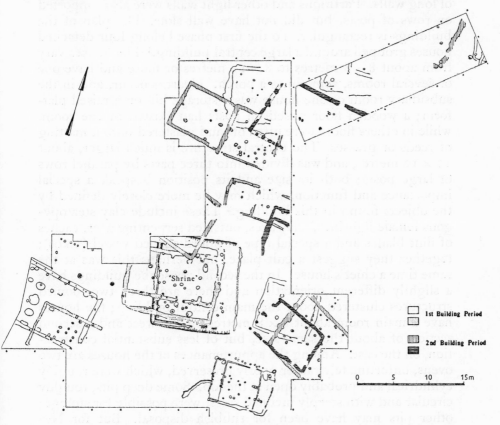

'Shrine'

☐ 1st Building Period

▦ 2nd Building Period

0   5   10   15m

Fig. 44. Nea Nikomedeia: plan of Early Neolithic structures.

main levels. Because a large section had been removed from the mound during the course of road building, exposing the Early Neolithic levels, it was possible to excavate a much larger area of the Early Neolithic stratum than is usual, and the area dug is 32 × 50 metres plus a trench 40 × 8 metres extending to the east, which did not reach the eastern edge of the settlement. Since the settlement was on the edge of a marshy lake or inlet of the sea,

[1] §1, 7, 269–71; §1, 8, 564–7. See Plate 18 (a).

special constructional features prevailed. Wall slots, often
U-shaped in section and about 0·60 metres wide, were cut down
0·35–0·50 metres into virgin soil for the main walls. Posts were
then driven farther into the ground along the centre of the slot,
at intervals of 1·00–1·50 metres, and these formed the framework
for the mud walls. Buttress posts were placed along the interior
of long walls. Partitions and other light walls were also supported
on rows of posts, but did not have wall slots. The plan of the
buildings is rectangular. To the first phase belong four detached
houses grouped around a large central building.[1] The houses vary
from about 8 × 8 metres to 8 × 11 metres or more and have one
or several rooms, sometimes a porch. Hearths occur, and in the
subsidiary room of one house was a storage bin on a raised platform; a wooden floor raised on posts had existed in one room,
while in others floors were often of mud plastered onto a matting
of reeds or grasses. The central structure is much larger, about
12 × 12 metres, and was divided into three parts by parallel rows
of large posts; both its size and its position bespeak a special
importance and function, which may be more closely defined by
the objects found in this building.[2] These include clay steatopygous female figurines,[3] clay axes, outsized serpentine axes, caches
of flint blades and a special type of gourd-shaped vessel (askos);
together they suggest a cult place, but perhaps this was at the
same time a chief's house. In the second phase the buildings have
a slightly different orientation and there are three two-roomed
structures clustered about the main central building; the houses
have a main room about 8 × 8 metres on the west and a second
section of about the same size, but of less substantial construction, on the east. Among the appurtenances of the houses are two
ovens, unfortunately rather poorly preserved, which were roughly
cylindrical and probably open at the top. Some deep pits, roughly
circular and with steeply inclined sides, were possibly for storage;
other pits may have been for rubbish disposal. But for Nea
Nikomedeia we should have little idea of the architectural capa-
bilities of the Early Neolithic settlers, for only here has sufficient
area been opened to give a picture of both the size and relationship of buildings. By chance we do have from Souphli the one
indication of the use of fortifications in the Early Neolithic period;
here a trench over 2 metres deep was dug into hardpan along the
southern edge of the settlement down to the level of the Peneus
River.[4]

[1] See Fig. 44.   [2] §1, 9, 604–7.
[3] See Plate 18 (b).   [4] §11, 16, 80.

The burial practices of the Early Neolithic inhabitants of the mainland have only recently become known to us and we do not yet seem to have any burials from the earliest phase of the period. A grave found at Argissa[1] is of the Proto-Sesklo phase; it is a burial in a pit of a child of about ten, in a strongly flexed position but lying prone. There were no grave goods, but the presence of animal bones suggests that pieces of meat had been placed in the grave. The pit was covered over with a paving of mud brick. At Lerna were found five burials of the latter part of Lerna I.[2] All are simple inhumations in roughly cut pits; all the skeletons were in the contracted position. While four had no offerings, in the fifth there was a black burnished bowl near the skull of a child of about five; in this instance the head was to the north-east, but in other graves it was to the west. Nea Nikomedeia has produced the largest number of burials. In 1961 was found in the lower level the burial of an adult (female) and two children, all placed in a storage pit;[3] the adult skeleton was tightly flexed and lay on its left side while the children, also in flexed position, faced the adult and were probably held in her arms. The heads were to the south, but there seems to have been no special preparation for the burial and there were no grave goods. In the same year, and also in the lower level, was found the burial of a child, tightly flexed, lying on its back, with head to the south. Twenty-one graves were found in 1963,[4] mostly with flexed skeletons placed in irregular pits; one lay on its back with legs upward and strongly contracted; a stone had been thrust between the jaws. None had any grave goods but pieces of meat may have been placed in the graves of three children. The skeleton of an adult found on the floor of a collapsed cave at Nemea[5] cannot be considered as a proper burial, but rather the result of an accident. There is, then, a striking uniformity of burial practices as known from Macedonia to the Argolid, to the extent that one can safely conclude that the first pottery users who inhabited Greece customarily buried their dead in a strongly flexed position in roughly cut pits within the area of the settlement; grave offerings other than meat were unusual.

Uniformly, too, these Early Neolithic settlers made steatopygous female figurines of clay, all most probably in standing position. They have not been found in graves; the many examples we have are, rather, from settlements, and five of the best preserved are from the large central structure at Nea Nikomedeia,[6]

[1] §II, 6, 164 f.   [2] §v, 5, 159; §v, 6, 138.   [3] §I, 7, 286.
[4] §I, 9, 605–7.   [5] §v, 3, 439.   [6] §I, 9, 604 f.

forming one of a number of groups of objects which all together give the impression that this was a shrine. These female figurines, with arms bent and hands usually either held on the breasts or cupped under them, have generally been considered as fertility figures, the so-called 'Mother Goddesses', and the finds at Nea Nikomedeia go far towards confirming and even strengthening this belief. The slit 'coffee-bean' eyes that are commonly found on figurines of this period would seem to be an imitation in clay of the cowrie shells used for eyes in the Near East, as early as in the plastered skulls of the pre-pottery Neolithic period at Jericho.[1] One such figure found on hardpan at Pyrasus[2] has four small clay pellets in a row along the shoulder, probably indicating buttons, and thus clothing, in a manner known at Tell Halaf.[3] Also found on hardpan at Pyrasus was one of two male figures surely datable to the Early Neolithic period;[4] the other is from Magulitsa[5] and both are seated and probably meant to be nude. In the now fairly large series of human figures from Thessaly there is a marked increase in the degree of stylization of figures in the last phase of the Early Neolithic period, but both Milojčić and Theochares note a return to more 'naturalistic' portrayal with the return of painted pottery at the beginning of the Sesklo phase;[6] this change has not been noted elsewhere. Clay figures of animals come from several sites, but they are often unidentifiable as to species; sometimes they clearly represent bulls, goats, a boar; birds are also represented. There are no human figures of stone in this period, but from Nea Nikomedeia come two frogs and part of a third beautifully modelled in greenstone,[7] while from Nea Makri there is a small stone figure of a bird. Certainly related to the human figures are anthropomorphic vessels, pieces of five of which were found at Nea Nikomedeia, all having faces modelled just beneath the rim; there is also a female figure in relief on a vessel.[8] Female and animal figurines of clay thus seem to have been part of the original repertory of the new settlers; only later in the Early Neolithic period do male figures appear, and figures of stone are also a later addition to the repertory. These later additions, together with the anthropomorphic vessels, may either be local inventions or be due to outside influences.

The working and fine polishing of stone seems to have been known to the first Early Neolithic settlers in Greece, though the craft was not possessed by their predecessors in the Aceramic

[1] §x, 8, 52. [2] §ii, 18, 65. [3] §x, 12, 99, pl. 105, 8.
[4] §ii, 18, 64 f. [5] §ii, 13, 45. [6] §ii, 5, 226–8.
[7] §i, 9, 604. See Plate 19 (a). [8] §i, 8, 566.

Neolithic period; the figures of frogs from Nea Nikomedeia are but one manifestation of this. Fully polished celts form the largest class of such stone-work and they occur in some quantity and variety in all Early Neolithic settlements. Axes, adzes and chisels are the common types, made largely of greenstone and other fairly hard stones. There are about a hundred from Nea Nikomedeia alone, and among them are a few very large axes, up to 0·20 metres in length, from the main central structure.[1] Almost as large are some of the heavy conical pestles from Elatea,[2] though these are never so smoothly polished as are the axes. To the same category of stone-working belong the millstones, hammer-stones, rubbing-stones, mortars, polishing slabs, and even pivot stones, that are found in Early Neolithic context. Here, too, belong numerous fragments of stone vases, many of them beautifully finished. We may have to do here with a survival of a class of containers much used in the Near East, but not in Greece, before the discovery of pottery. Early Neolithic strata at many sites have produced fragments of such vases, but none so many as Nea Makri,[3] where some of the finest pieces were found. Most of the stone vases are of marble or fairly hard stones; the shapes are largely hemispherical bowls on low ring bases, but low rectangular vessels also occur and some have incised decoration. Very likely also a survival from stone work of the Aceramic Neolithic phase are the stone studs, so-called 'nose-plugs', of marble and serpentine found at Nea Nikomedeia.[4] Those of the Early Neolithic period are more slender and more finely shaped and polished than are the so-called 'ear-plugs' of the earlier period. Rodden suggests, on the basis of a head of a figurine from Pyrasus, that these may have been used in head-dress decoration.[5] One more object illustrating the abilities of the Early Neolithic settlers in stone-cutting and -polishing is the steatite seal found in the middle level of the Early Neolithic accumulation at Pyrasus;[6] it and its double found at Philia, some 65 kilometres to the west in Thessaly, are the earliest stone seals we have (some clay seals are probably earlier). The pattern on these two stone seals, and on very similar clay seals from Tsangli and Nea Nikomedeia,[7] is maeandroid.

By contrast, the chipped stone industry of the Early Neolithic period is lacking in both variety and invention. It is very largely a blade industry which used flint (including chert and quartz)

[1] §I, 9, 606 f., figs. 11, 18.   [2] §III, 14, 205.   [3] §III, 12, 24 f.
[4] §I, 9, 604, fig. 17.   [5] §I, 7, 285.
[6] §II, 18, 66 f.   [7] §I, 9, 604 f., fig. 20. See Plate 19(b).

and obsidian in almost equal measure, though with considerable variation in the proportion from one region to another. The Early Neolithic strata at Nea Nikomedeia, for instance, produced no obsidian,[1] whereas farther south, as at Nea Makri,[2] almost no flint was used; the distance from the source of supply of obsidian, Melos, seems to have made the difference. At both Nea Makri and Lerna rather large and broad blades occur; elsewhere small and fairly narrow blades predominate. Flint rather than obsidian seems to have been used for scrapers in the Early Neolithic period, though obsidian scrapers do occur. Nea Nikomedeia again has the largest collection of Early Neolithic chipped stone tools reported thus far; about one-fifth are flake tools. From the large central building came two caches, each of about four hundred flint blades;[3] these had merely been struck from the core, probably at the source of the material, but not worked further. When needed, they were probably worked locally into finished implements and then mounted in wood or bone handles for use as knives, sickles, saws, etc. A limited repertory of bone tools, largely awls, supplemented the stone implements; some needles and spatulae occur and there are a few fishhooks. One very heavy bone hook from Souphli[4] may, on the analogy of one from Çatal Hüyük in the Konya plain of Anatolia,[5] be part of a buckle. The bone industry of the Early Neolithic period is different from that of the previous period in that the implements are now fully polished and the eccentric cutting characteristic of the Aceramic Neolithic phase no longer occurs.

What differentiates the Early Neolithic phase from its predecessor, however, is the widespread use of clay, chiefly for pottery but for a variety of other objects as well. We have already mentioned the baked clay stamp seal so like the steatite ones from Pyrasus and Philia. From Nea Nikomedeia have come ten clay seals with geometric motives such as chevrons.[6] One from the Proto-Sesklo level at Argissa, however, seems rather to have a leaf-shaped design.[7] Potsherds rounded off and pierced at the centre evidently served as spindle whorls, while from Corinth comes a real whorl in the fabric of the Early Neolithic variegated ware.[8] From Nea Nikomedeia there are objects which may be loomweights or bobbins and this site has also produced impressions on pottery of fine textiles, possibly woollen.[9] At Elatea

---

[1] §I, 7, 277.   [2] §III, 12, 26.   [3] §I, 9, 604.
[4] §II, 16, 83, fig. 14.   [5] §IX, 14, pl. xxvii, d.
[6] §I, 9, 604 f., fig. 20. See Plate 19(b).   [7] §II, 6, 164, fig. 4, 2.
[8] §V, 11, 41, fig. 15.   [9] §I, 9, 605.

have been found many unbaked clay objects which look like spools;[1] they were made by rolling a piece of clay, then holding it in the hand and flattening the ends; apparently they were dried by laying them around the hearths but received no further baking. Whether or not they were used as spools we cannot say. Made in much the same way were the more numerous clay sling bullets, unbaked or only poorly fired, which seem to have been the only weapon of the period.[2] While at a few sites some are found in later levels, and among these are better baked examples, the large majority are of Early Neolithic date. One baked clay object which might almost be classed as pottery is a rectangular dish from Elatea with low vertical sides; the two preserved sides curve to form a kind of spout, and we have suggested that this was a lamp.[3]

In mass, however, the pottery exceeds the combined total of all other finds, though its importance as a diagnostic element of the material culture is possibly not so great as its quantity. Clearly the first pottery made in Greece was in a tradition already long established and was the product of experienced potters; there are no experimental stages in the development of the first pottery evident in Early Neolithic Greece.[4] On the other hand, though competent, the first pottery is still simple, both in shape and in firing techniques. All of the Neolithic pottery is hand made. Hemispherical and globular shapes prevail for bowls and jars respectively; bottoms may be round or flat, but a primitive ring base may have been part of the original repertory. Small pierced lugs, set either horizontally or vertically, are the only form of handle. While a simple thinned lip was usual, slightly everted or thickened lips occur from the start, and the former may be offset by a shallow groove. Jars usually have vertical or lightly splaying collars, though the hole-mouthed jar without a collar was also known. There seem to have been no large vessels and few very coarse ones at the start of the period. Rather, the quality of workmanship was generally high and the vessels are often quite thin-walled, usually well burnished and frequently highly polished as well. The clay was usually well cleaned, and whatever grit or grog was used was fairly fine-grained; vegetable tempering seems not to have been used in Greece. Firing may have been done without a kiln, merely in a pit or on a hearth; high temperatures were not attained but the pottery was sufficiently fired for normal household uses. Usually the core is dark,

---

[1] §III, 14, 203 f.   [2] §III, 14, 202 f.   [3] §III, 14, 204.
[4] The earliest pottery at Sesklo may be an exception, but this is not yet certain.

as is the interior surface, and only the exterior is oxidized, as a rule only partially. Commonly there is a wide range of colour in the finished product, not only from vase to vase but often on parts of the same vase, giving a variegated effect which is frequently decorative and may at times have been intentional. While the nature of the clay in each area affected the colour of the finished vases, all over the mainland the earliest vases tend to the darker colours—grey-black, dark brown, red-brown to red or brown—and it was only towards the end of this first phase of the Early Neolithic period that light brown or red and buff were obtained with any regularity. A slip, especially red but sometimes white, was used already within this earliest phase to obtain a uniform exterior colour, but how early in the period this was done is not yet certain; Elatea finds indicate that both red and white slips occurred in rare instances from the very beginning of the period.[1]

It is now clear from several sites—Elatea, Sesklo and Argissa in particular—that there was a long first phase (the carbon-14 dates from Elatea indicate that it was as much as four hundred years)[2] during which only the kind of pottery just described was made and none had painted decoration. There was, however, considerable technical development during this period, perhaps the most noticeable being the more thorough firing that produced vases which generally had a lighter tone of the surface colour; there was also more controlled variegation, such as dark lip bands. Shapes became somewhat more articulated and pronounced, and higher ring bases developed; slight carinations at the belly of bowls and jars appeared, as did heavier and more widely everted rims. There developed a whole class of somewhat coarser wares of a spongy fabric, including some fairly large cooking pots. This fabric apparently resulted from using crushed limestone for grit, which burned out on the surface and left it pocked or spongy. An occasional applied pellet or strip of clay and the even less frequent use of incision seem to be the only forms of decoration used on pottery at the beginning of the period. There is a remarkable uniformity in the earliest pottery from Thessaly to the Peloponnese, a kind of *koine* which hardly outlasted this first phase of the Early Neolithic period.

A second phase of the Early Neolithic period began with the use of painted decoration on pottery; since the paint was at first applied directly to the body of the vase, such decoration was not practicable until the potters could consistently produce surfaces

[1] §III, 14, 167–72.   [2] §III, 14, 207.

sufficiently light in colour to give the desired contrast with the painted decoration. The paint used was much the same as the red slip of the first phase, perhaps thicker at times. Often the vase was burnished and polished before painting, sometimes after; in the latter case the paint at times spread as a result of the burnishing. Patterns were most often either simple linear ones such as zig-zags and chevrons or were comprised of triangles or lozenges, hatched, cross-hatched or solidly filled.[1] Very quickly local variations began to appear and in Thessaly during the Proto-Sesklo phase painted decoration developed more rapidly than elsewhere and achieved greater variety and fantasy; one bowl from Argissa[2] seems to have a band with a portrayal of human figures, probably women, just below the lip. Here a white slip is used as background for the painted ornament, and this practice was followed all over Greece after only brief experimentation with painting directly on the fabric of the vase. However, painting on the surface of the vase continued in both Thessaly and central Greece long after the use of white slip was general, while in the Peloponnese, especially in areas like Corinth which had a white clay generally producing a light fabric, the use of white slip was much less common throughout the Early Neolithic period. Painted decoration was usually concentrated on the shoulders of jars, both inside and outside on their collars, as well as just below the lips of bowls, less often on or just above the bases of jars. The shapes of the painted vases differed little from the unpainted ones; bowls and globular collared jars were common, but higher feet, sharper carinations, more wide-open bowls, sometimes with straight rather than curving sides, all developed as a continuation of the process of differentiation which had begun in the first phase. Occasionally a completely new shape, such as the askoi from Nemea and Nea Nikomedeia,[3] appeared. Most of the pottery, however, was still unpainted, but was generally of lighter surface colour than before. Plastic ornaments, especially rows of small clay pellets arranged in simple geometric patterns, became more common and there was possibly a little more incised decoration.

In the third, and last, phase of the Early Neolithic period, the Pre-Sesklo period in Thessaly, the development of the Thessalian painted pottery was interrupted by the arrival in quantity, especially in the northern half of Thessaly, of monochrome wares decorated first in the so-called 'Barbotine' technique and then

[1] See Plate 20 (*a–b*).   [2] § II, 9, 9, fig. 6, 5.
[3] G, 29, fig. 286; §1, 8, 566, fig. 9.

in the 'Cardium' style, both of which can be traced northward through Macedonia into Yugoslavia, whence they most likely came.[1] The ware is generally brown in colour and in the 'Barbotine' style is decorated by impressions made obliquely so as to raise some clay above the surface of the vase at the same time as the impression is made; finger-nails and small bones seem to have been used most frequently to make the impressions. The somewhat later 'Cardium' style is so named because of a belief that the cardium shell was used to make rows of small dot impressions; it is just as likely that a comb-like instrument was used. Bowls and small jars, on ring bases or with flat bottoms, are the common shapes. Although these wares are fairly coarse in fabric, the surface is usually well smoothed and at times polished as well. Similar wares are mentioned from both Epirus and the island of Leucas;[2] they would be the earliest record of inhabitation of west-central Greece. Together with these go the red or brown slipped wares, but no painted ware. While the impressed wares are not nearly so common in southern Thessaly, there too monochrome ware prevailed and painted ware was in eclipse.[3] All over Thessaly a drastic decline in the quality of steatopygous female figurines is noted in this phase, but a return to better quality came with the return of painted pottery at the beginning of the Middle Neolithic period.

Such an interruption of the painted pottery tradition is not noted in central or southern Greece. In the former the Chaeronea ware prevails, its fabric often the spongy type, which is hidden by a thick white slip on which the designs, still very simple, are painted in red or red-brown paint. Exceptional conservatism is displayed not only in the painted patterns but also in the shapes, for there are hardly any others than the hemispherical bowls and the globular collared jars.[4] In the Peloponnese we await the publication of the pottery from Lerna I to learn of the development there, but from what we know already it would seem to be at least as conservative as that of central Greece.

It is possible that only in this latest phase of the Early Neolithic period do we first have any record of habitation in Macedonia, for the earlier level at Nea Nikomedeia yielded both painted wares of the Proto-Sesklo type and finger-nail impressed wares of the following phase.[5] In the first case we may have to do with a northward extension out of Thessaly towards the end of the Proto-

---

[1] §II, 9, 10.
[3] §II, 19, 41.
[5] §I, 7, 281–5.

[2] §IV, 2, 335, Beil. 83, b.
[4] §III, 14, 176–9. See Plate 20 (a, b).

Sesklo phase, just at the time when the impressed wares, possibly with their makers, were coming down from the north. At any rate, it does not seem possible to date the foundation of the settlement at Nea Nikomedeia much before the middle of the Early Neolithic period of Thessaly, that is, some time during the Proto-Sesklo phase; this despite the fact that the lower level yielded a single sample for carbon-14 determination from which a date of about 6200 B.C. ± 150 years was obtained. One must wait for the results from numerous other determinations now being made, but it would be preferable to have some from samples taken from below the full depth of the mound rather than from the large area now so long open to ground water and various kinds of contamination.

One exceptional type of Early Neolithic pottery was found only at Nea Makri,[1] from the very beginning of the settlement. It comprises largely open bowls with vertical or lightly convex sides and flattened bottoms but no feet, which bear simple recti-linear patterns incised on the sides of the bowls and usually having a white filling in the incisions. The excavator, Theochares, has drawn a most plausible comparison with pottery that occurred in Levels XXV–XXIV at Mersin in Cilicia; the position of Nea Makri on the east coast of Attica makes this not at all unlikely.

Our picture of the material assemblage of the Early Neolithic settlers of Greece, while spotty, is sufficient to give us an idea of the villages in which they lived, the tools with which they worked, the way they buried their dead and even, perhaps, an inkling of some of their religious beliefs. We have, too, some idea of their economy in general and of their sea-borne commerce, especially as it supplied the demand for obsidian from Melos and perhaps also emery from Thera, to be used in the making of bowls and other finely cut and polished objects of stone. But agriculture and the raising of domesticated animals was the real basis of their economy, and from charred remains of vegetable matter and copious remains of bones we can get a fairly good idea both of the crops they raised and the animals they tended. Wheat and barley, lentils and peas seem to have been the principal crops, but there is evidence for pistachio nuts as well. Sheep and goats predominated among the domesticated animals, with pigs and cattle occurring in lesser numbers. The villagers supplemented their supply of meat by some hunting of deer, hare and birds and by fishing; some shellfish were collected and most probably eaten as were tortoises. There are few signs other than the fortification

[1] §III, 12, 10–14.

ditch at Souphli to indicate that their life was not peaceful throughout almost a millennium during which their culture prevailed in Greece.

This long and slowly developing Early Neolithic period in Greece must have begun early in the sixth millennium B.C. at least. We have already mentioned the carbon-14 date of about 6200 B.C. ± 150 years obtained from a single sample from Nea Nikomedeia for which there are reasons for reservation at the moment. From Elatea, on the other hand, we have three dates for samples from successively higher floors of the first phase of the Early Neolithic period and a fourth for a sample from the first level which produced painted pottery. They are: 5754 ± 70 B.C., 5630 ± 90 B.C., 5455 ± 100 B.C. and 5301 ± 130 B.C.[1] It would seem safe to assume, then, that the Early Neolithic period had begun by 5750 B.C. and that the second phase, with painted pottery, began about 5300 B.C. in Phocis; these seem to be conservative dates to judge from the comparisons with the earliest Greek ceramic culture that can now be noted in Anatolia and the Near East. We have mentioned the connexions of the white-filled incised ware of Nea Makri with that of Mersin Levels XXV–XXIV, which are Upper Neolithic and Proto-Chalcolithic respectively and are equated by Garstang with pre-Hassūnah and Early Hassūnah phases in the Near East.[2] For the parallel Late Neolithic of Hacılar there are carbon-14 determinations that suggest dates of 5600–5400 B.C.[3] But on the whole the earliest Greek Neolithic pottery is closer in its general characteristics to that of the end of the Early Neolithic period at Çatal Hüyük[4] than it is to the beginning Late Neolithic pottery at Hacılar (there may be a gap between the two), and so a date more towards the beginning of the sixth millennium is suggested for it. So too the figurines, the clay stamp seals and the chipped stone industry predominantly of blade tools all find close analogies with the latest Early Neolithic assemblage at Çatal Hüyük, so much as to suggest that it was from this region of Anatolia that the first pottery users came to Greece early in the sixth millennium B.C. That these first settlers were at times reinforced by new arrivals, either from the same region or from Cilicia, as suggested by the pottery from Nea Makri, seems logical, and with these arrivals new settlements were founded. Pyrasus,[5] for instance, does not appear to have been founded as early as Sesklo. Some new settle-

[1] A, 50, 310; G, 21, 182 f.   [2] §x, 6, 2.
[3] §IX, 16, 74.   [4] §IX, 13, 52–5.
[5] §II, 18, 41.

ments may, on the other hand, have been founded from old ones as the population grew; an extension into Macedonia after the middle of the period is suggested by Nea Nikomedeia. Finally, perhaps in the last third of the sixth millennium, people bearing a completely different kind of culture, as witnessed by their monochrome impressed pottery, arrived in Macedonia and northern Thessaly. The effects of their arrival were felt in southern Thessaly as well, though very likely not farther south; the development of the Early Neolithic material culture in central and southern Greece seems to have been uninterrupted throughout the sixth millennium.

V. THE MIDDLE NEOLITHIC PERIOD ON THE GREEK MAINLAND

There are clear indications that a change in material culture, very likely accompanied by the advent of some new population, took place in Thessaly in the latter part of the sixth millennium. Painted pottery, in eclipse for a few centuries, again became prominent, but it was a new kind of painted pottery that introduced the Sesklo phase (what Tsountas termed the Thessaly A period), and with it at Otzaki came new types of rectangular mud-brick houses and a return of the 'naturalistic' type of steatopygous figurines.[1] This was the beginning of another long period, represented at Otzaki by almost 4 metres of stratified deposit that again shows a tripartite developmental series in pottery and that contains eight building periods, with some structures rebuilt as many as five times. Thessaly now seems to have been much more thickly inhabited than before, though it is possible that many sites which we know from old excavations to have been inhabited in the Thessaly A period may have been founded earlier, for it is only since the last war that what we call the Early Neolithic period has been recognized in Thessaly. Together with newly founded settlements, the abandonment of sites is often an indication of population change, and Nea Nikomedeia is one site that ceased to exist at the end of the Early Neolithic period; it was refounded only in the Late Neolithic period. Everywhere in Thessaly at the beginning of the Sesklo phase we may have to do only with the expulsion or absorption of an intrusive element, but there is reason to believe that a new element was also added to the population.

[1] §II, 9, 12–14.

For the first time in Thessaly, stone foundations were built for the rectangular mud-brick houses. Pending final publication of the architecture from Otzaki, it would seem that a new type of house, almost square and with internal buttresses, usually two on each wall, came into use at the beginning of the Thessaly A period.[1] The type has long been known as the 'Tsangli' type, after houses P, Q and R, built one above the other at that site, and the separate house T.[2] Several are now known from Otzaki, interspersed at first among simpler one-room rectangular houses that have no buttresses. Nowhere else in Greece is the type known, though we shall see that in many rooms at Lerna there

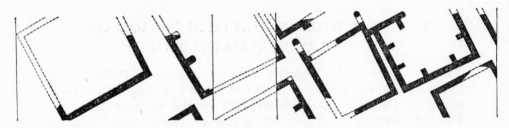

Fig. 45. Otzaki: schematic plans of houses of levels C and D.
Middle Neolithic period.

were short internal buttresses, and the final publication may indicate the existence of the type there as well. Most striking has been the very recent discovery of groups of the same type of house in Level 2 b at Can Hasan in the Konya plain of Anatolia;[3] the date of the buildings there is just pre-Halaf. In both Thessaly and Turkey interior partitions or subsidiary structures supported on posts are shown by post holes to have existed; built platforms, possibly used as beds, were fitted between and around buttresses. In both places it is possible that the entrance to at least some of the houses was by ladder from the roof. One-room rectangular houses, mostly broad-fronted, were standard at Sesklo, as at many other Thessalian sites. At Zerelia the precaution was taken of facing the exterior of the mud-brick walls of one house with upright slabs for protection from injury and damp.[4] Such an early use of orthostats can be paralleled in Level VIII at Jericho, probably of late Halaf date; and Level M at Geöy Tepe in Azarbāyjān,[5] of the same or slightly later date. Contemporary with and alongside the later reconstructions of the buttressed houses

[1] §II, 10, 164–8; §II, 9, 12. See Fig. 45.   [2] §II, 23, 115–21.
[3] §IX, 4, 35.   [4] §II, 23, 161.   [5] §X, 4, 153.

at Otzaki, but still well before the end of the Sesklo phase, occur
a couple of houses with typical megaron plan:[1] a main room,
square or somewhat longer than wide, with side walls extending
as antae beyond the cross-wall with the doorway, and posts in
front of the antae, thus forming a porch for the main room. Such
megaron houses may occur as early as the middle phase of the
Sesklo period and continue to its end. Sesklo too may have had
megara in the Thessaly A period.[2] Milojčić has very rightly
stated that there can no longer be any question of introduction
of the megaron into Greece from the north during the Late Neolithic period; he points to Jericho, but I would note that in the
last decade the megaron has been shown to have had a very long
history in Anatolia, at least from the Late Chalcolithic phase at
Beycesultan[3] and then into the Early Bronze Age, at which time
we have the best examples from Troy, starting in the lowest level
of Troy I.[4] Very likely it was from Anatolia that the form was
introduced into Greece; the date must have been during the
Halaf period of the Near East. At both Sesklo[5] and Magula
Hadzimissiotiki,[6] the latter in Lake Boebeis, there are remains
of walls considerably more substantial than those of houses, and
while these may be only terrace walls it seems more likely that
they served as fortifications, for which they are well located.

Unfortunately we still have no burials of the Thessaly A
period. We do, however, have multitudinous material remains.
We have already mentioned the reappearance of standing female
steatopygous figurines of the 'naturalistic' type known in the first
two phases of the Early Neolithic period in Thessaly. The stone
and bone industries remained much as in the earlier period. Besides the new types of architecture, it is in the pottery that one
can see the greatest development and change, and the new style
of painted pottery starts out the same all over Thessaly; this has
been known as the Tsani 'solid' style. In the deep accumulations
of the Thessaly A phase at Otzaki three phases in the development of the Sesklo culture can be differentiated.[7] In all stages
the chief pottery shapes seem to have been steep-walled bowls,
usually with flat bottoms, the walls straight until the last phase
when they develop an S-curve, and one-handled mugs on a flat
bottom or a high ring foot. Large jars, sometimes with a large
band handle, also occur throughout. In the early phase there are
large bowls with widely splaying rims; in the final phase shallow

---

[1] §II, 10, 164–7; §II, 9, 12. See Fig. 45.
[2] §II, 21, 86.   [3] §IX, 10, 25.   [4] §IX, 2, 47 f.
[5] §II, 21, 75 f.   [6] §II, 3, 62.   [7] §II, 9, 12 f.

open bowls on high ring bases, as much as 0·14 metres in height, occur. A fine white slip is common on the early painted ware, but its quality often deteriorates towards the end of the period; so too does the polishing of the surface. There is always some ware with the paint applied directly to the vase rather than over a white slip. The paint is dark red at the beginning, more nearly brown towards the end of the Sesklo period. The simple designs of the 'solid' style—rectangles, lozenges, triangles—are often arranged in overall zig-zag patterns, but there are also wide bands in zig-zags or chevrons; some of the latter are bordered with fine 'flame' patterns in the first phase and these remain common throughout, developing into very large 'flames' or saw-tooth edges in the final phase. However, the most interesting and significant of the painted designs are the whirl patterns which occur on the interior of bowls,[1] certainly by the middle phase and perhaps earlier; they are paralleled by the similar patterns on Samarran pottery,[2] of which they are the most characteristic feature. Alongside the painted ware the monochrome pottery continues, but the fine red-brown ware (A 1) disappears during the second phase; the brown household wares continue into the last phase. So too the scraped ware, in which a white slip is applied first and over it a heavy red slip, part of which is then scraped away exposing the white below and giving in effect a dark-on-light pattern, is in use in both the second and last phase. Clearly there are local differences within Thessaly itself after the common beginning with the 'solid' style; for at Tsani the late Thessaly A ware[3] is decorated in a fine-line style which resembles more the decoration on Neolithic Urfirnis ware, which we shall soon consider, than that of other Thessalian dark-on-light painted wares. Towards the end of the Sesklo phase appear new types of pottery like grey-on-grey ware, black burnished wares with plastic and white painted decoration, and even a kind of polychrome ware with patterns in red and brown on a matt white surface, which is different from the polychrome ware of the following period.[4]

The settlement at Servia in the Haliacmon Valley of western Macedonia would seem, to judge from the pottery, to be merely an offshoot from Thessaly in the latter part of the Sesklo period.[5] What little architecture was found at the site consists of remains of rectangular houses either of mud brick on stone foundations or of wattle-and-daub on a frame of posts. Circular hearths and

[1] §II, 9, fig. 12, 6.   [2] §x, 7.   [3] §II, 23, 136-41.
[4] §II, 9, 13.   [5] §I, 1, 63.

cobble and pebble pavements occur. Of special interest is a fortification trench 2·35 metres deep with one sheer face and one sharply sloping face.[1] The only other settlement probably of the period in Macedonia is at Polystylo in the plain of Philippi;[2] the major occupation here seems to be of the following period.

Reviewing the Thessaly A period, we see that the most striking new features are found in the architecture; first the houses with the internal buttresses and somewhat later the megaron. While the painted pottery could be a revival of that of the Early Neolithic period, the vases with whirl patterns definitely suggest a foreign origin in the Near East of the Sāmarrā period, and it is of particular interest that the buttressed houses of Can Hasan can be dated to this very same period. Together they suggest some reinforcement of the population of Thessaly by elements from Anatolia or northern Mesopotamia, or both, during the Sāmarrā period, which is now dated in the latter part of the sixth millennium B.C. The megaron arrived later, but probably by the mid-fifth millennium it had been introduced into Greece from Anatolia.

In much of central Greece—Attica, Boeotia and Euboea—and in the Peloponnese, the Early Neolithic period probably lasted somewhat longer than in Thessaly and was then put to an end by the arrival of elements different from those found in Thessaly. The change is much more marked in these regions. At Lerna in the Argolid there is actually a physical division, in the form of a layer of pebbles found widespread over the site, that marks the separation of the Early Neolithic strata from those of the Middle Neolithic period.[3] There are fully 2 metres of deposit and eight building levels at Lerna,[4] suggesting a fairly long period. As in Thessaly, stone foundations are now the rule for the rectangular mud-brick houses; the few from Lerna of the earlier period were exceptional. The houses at Lerna are composed of small rooms clustered together, with extra rooms added as needed. Many rooms have internal buttresses,[5] suggesting a possible relationship with those of Thessaly. The early floors are often coated with red or yellow clay, as are some storage pits. One-room rectangular houses are known from Hageorgitika to the south in Arcadia, rectangular stone foundations from Nea Makri to the north in Attica.

Burials of the Middle Neolithic period have been found at three places in the Peloponnese. At Hageorgitika was found a small oval cist grave, 0·60 × 0·36 × 0·20 metres deep, in which

---

[1] §1, 1, 43–53.   [2] §1, 6, 109–11.   [3] §v, 5, 160.
[4] §v, 5, 156.   [5] §v, 5, 157.

were laid the heaped bones of an adult; this was clearly a secondary burial.[1] At Prosymna in the Argolid there are also small pits with assembled bones, but in this case the bodies seem to have been cremated first.[2] In a level in the upper half of the Lerna II accumulation was found a beaker of Neolithic Urfirnis painted ware in which were the bones of an infant.[3] Whereas only two or three sherds were found in the grave at Hageorgitika, a good deal of pottery was found in the pits at Prosymna and most likely served as grave goods. Since this is all the evidence for burial practices in the Middle Neolithic period, it cannot be conclusive; nevertheless it is uniform in suggesting that secondary burial was now practised, at times after cremation, thus showing burial customs completely different from those of the Early Neolithic period.

The pottery of the Middle Neolithic period in central Greece and the Peloponnese is strikingly different from what preceded it. Because this pottery has a slip or wash which when fired shows an inherent lustre, it has been named Neolithic Urfirnis ware.[4] The name also distinguishes it from the Urfirnis ware of the Early Bronze Age which, while using a similar technique, seems in no way connected with the Neolithic variety. The Neolithic Urfirnis ware is thoroughly fired, having an orange-red to red-brown fabric that is hard and often very thin. The surfaces were apparently scraped with a broad implement, probably of bone or wood, and in the process pieces of grit or grog were dragged along, making grooves; while these have usually been smoothed away on exposed surfaces, the interiors of small-mouthed vessels bear these marks which make the ware easily recognizable.

The shapes are now much more sharply differentiated into their component parts, and even though the globular jug is used, its short cylindrical neck and cylindrical foot of about the same diameter and height[5] give it a very different appearance from those of the Early Neolithic period. The carinated shapes are especially characteristic:[6] cups or bowls with high concave rims and a ring base that may be of various heights; bowls or jars with an S-curve profile, sometimes interrupted by a carination and usually with a rounded or flat bottom; bowls with heavy incurved rims, often with a sharp carination and usually with a flat bottom; shallow bowls with a simple lip and a ring foot which is sometimes quite high. Tubular pierced lugs occur on the shoulder or body of

---

[1] §v, 9, 3.   [2] §v, 4, 25–8.   [3] §v, 5, 159.
[4] §III, 4, 31–5; §v, 20, 500–3. See Plate 20 (c–d).
[5] §v, 6, pl. 37, d–e. See Plate 20 (c).   [6] See Plate 20 (d).

jars and small pierced lugs of the ledge type occur occasionally, but large handles are much less common; the latter are usually circular in section and sometimes they are double. A very special kind of vessel in this ware is a large open bowl or pan, usually with flat bottom and straight or lightly curved sides (at times almost vertical), the interior of which is cut by deep grooves made so that some of the clay is raised above the surface. These vessels are usually covered with a rather coarse kind of Neolithic Urfirnis glaze and the interior may be flecked with glaze. Many of the vessels show use, which has resulted in smoothing off the bottom of the interior so that the grooving has almost disappeared.[1] It is impossible to know just what this use was, but the vessels are clearly the Greek counterpart of the so-called Hassūnah 'husking-trays', which appear early in the Hassūnah phase and continue in use through the Sāmarrā period and into the Halaf period.[2] Such vessels were also made in the typical Early Neolithic fabric and they may already have been used in that period.

A large part of the Neolithic Urfirnis ware has all exposed surfaces (that is, all but the interior of the body of jars and jugs and the under side of bases) covered with a slip or wash which is lustrous when fired; in most instances this is streaky and seems to have been applied with a brush.[3] When the traces of burnishing strokes were left on the surface, the slip collected in the shallow grooves and darker lines resulted. The colour of the slip varies from a light orange-red through various shades of red-brown and brown to a very dark brown which is almost black; in quality of lustre it also varies from a high glaze to quite dull surfaces, and this seems to depend on the quality of the clay and the finish of the surface to which it is applied. Often parts of vases were left in reserve and then decorated with patterns painted with the same kind of glaze-like paint. Such decoration is common on the high concave rims of cups and bowls, on the shoulder and collar of jars and on the interior of open bowls, much less frequently on the ring feet; in any carinated shape the decoration was usually limited to the part above the carination, while that below was covered solidly. By varying the thickness of the paint the colour was varied and it was possible to obtain a polychromatic effect by controlling the thickness of the paint; much variegation resulted, however, merely from the concentration of paint at the beginning, or end, of a brush stroke and its thinning out along the stroke. Decorative patterns are largely rectilinear, though wavy lines,

[1] §v, 5, pl. 48, e; §v, 6, pl. 38, b.   [2] §x, 11, 277 f.
[3] See Plate 20 (d).

braids and simple curved hooks do occur. In the deep accumulations at Lerna it was possible for the excavator to distinguish an earlier and a later style:[1] the former with simple parallel lines, zig-zags and chevrons, hatched or cross-hatched bands, lozenges or triangles, the later style with somewhat more complicated large patterns composed of the same simple elements, plus an occasional solid filled triangle or branch and 'rain-drop' motives in an open field. A 'triglyph-and-metope' arrangement occurs on the exterior of one bowl from Lerna.[2] There is a small amount of pottery on which the simple patterns are painted in black over the brown glaze, which usually is of fairly light tone to afford contrast. Even rarer is a type with pattern-burnishing over the glaze-paint. There was restricted use of applied pellets, discs or bands of clay, but a similar effect was obtained rather often on high ring bases by pressing a pointed instrument from the inside almost but not quite through the fabric, thus raising a knob of clay on the surface; the knobs form simple linear patterns.

The close relationship of Neolithic Urfirnis ware in fabric, shape, glaze-paint and decoration with the early type of Halaf ware of the Near East, perhaps most particularly in its rather provincial Syro-Cilician manifestation, has been thoroughly documented by Dr Ann Perkins.[3] Its abundant and abrupt appearance in the eastern regions of central and southern Greece must probably be attributed to the arrival of new population from the Near East, just about or not long after 5000 B.C. New elements in architecture and the new burial practices were probably also due to these new arrivals. They brought a new type of standing female figurine, much more slender than earlier ones, non-steatopygous, small-breasted. An excellent example from Lerna II is covered with a highly burnished red slip;[4] its hands are placed, finger-tips touching, over the abdomen. But more common are small female figures with pellet breasts, hands open on thighs alongside the pubic triangle, all decorated with linear patterns and wavy lines in the typical Neolithic Urfirnis glaze-paint; they have been found thus far at Asea,[5] Corinth[6] and Lerna.[7]

In a third area, Phocis, the culture of the fifth millennium ran still a different course from that of Thessaly to the north or

[1] §v, 6, 137, pl. 36, f–g.   [2] G, 29, fig. 324. See Plate 20 (e).
[3] G, 16; G, 25.   [4] §v, 8. See Plate 21 (a).
[5] §v, 10, 115, fig. 111, 7–9, pl. 11, j–k.   [6] §v, 19, 199 f., pl. 70, 1–2.
[7] §v, 6, 136, pl. 36, d–e; see Plate 21 (b–e) for a composite view of the upper parts of such figurines from Corinth and lower parts from both Corinth and Lerna.

Boeotia and other regions to the south; the type site for the region thus far is Elatea.[1] Here the dark-on-light painted ware (Chaeronea ware) developed with little change over a long period of time. Somewhat more complicated patterns, particularly the saw-tooth border or 'flame' patterns, seem to be due to influence from Thessaly. Shapes hardly changed, but the fabric improved steadily. In time the white slip as a background for painted patterns became very thick, white and chalky. Steatopygous female figurines continued to be made, and some were painted in the same way as the pottery. Neolithic Urfirnis ware eventually found its way into this area, probably as an import from Boeotia or beyond, but not until the second half of the Middle Neolithic period. Possibly at the same time some Neolithic Urfirnis ware reached Thessaly as well, for at Pyrasus it was found in the final phase of the Sesklo period.[2] At this time there occurred both in Phocis and Boeotia, and to a lesser extent farther south, what is called black-on-red ware. This was most likely a local development out of the type of Neolithic Urfirnis ware in which black painted patterns were applied over the Urfirnis glaze; now a red slip, lighter in colour than the Urfirnis glaze, was substituted for the latter, thus giving stronger contrast. There are pieces of pottery with Urfirnis paint on one side, slip on the other, but ultimately the slip prevails. The shapes are those of Neolithic Urfirnis ware, especially wide-open bowls on high stands, with cut-out triangular or circular holes (sometimes in groups) in the base, but also bowls with heavy incurved rims. The painted designs are very simple: parallel lines and hatched triangles, solid filled triangles and crescents. An exceptionally fine group of the high-footed bowls was found in a large pit in Trench 3 at Elatea, and it was observed that many of the bowls showed evidence of burning and scraping inside, suggesting use as incense burners; though the holes in the bases suggested that fire was placed under them, there is no trace of burning on the underside of any of the bases, and the holes, if not merely decorative, may well have served to guarantee even firing of the large stands.

Together with the black-on-red wares found in the pit at Elatea, deposits of Neolithic Urfirnis ware at Corinth, and the latest pottery of the Thessaly A period,[3] appears a whole new class of grey-black burnished wares which have almost the same repertory of shapes as does the Neolithic Urfirnis ware; the high-

footed bowls ('fruitstands') have a somewhat different tall base
which is rather narrow at the top and often flares widely towards
the bottom. Often a black slip is used to intensify the surface
colour, but burnishing alone frequently suffices for this and it is
common to have zones reserved in the overall burnishing and
then filled with simple pattern-burnished decoration. Much less
often fugitive white paint was used for decorative patterns; there
is also shallow grooving to produce a rippled surface, as well as
fine plastic decoration. The group from the pit at Elatea is one
of the best both as to quality and preservation of the pottery, but
although there are very large pieces of bowls, from a quarter to a
half of the vessel, no other pieces of any of the bowls were found.
It is possible, therefore, that we have here a case of ritual breaking
of vessels, in which the fragments were deliberately separated.[1]

One piece of black burnished ware is of special significance.
It comprises three of the four legs of the lower part of an unusual
vessel[2] and it finally gave the clue to the reconstruction of the
form; legs from such vessels had been known for over fifty years
from Phocis and from Corinth in particular, but the type of vessel
to which they belonged remained an enigma. These four-legged
vases can now be shown to have a large round or oval mouth with
the lip rising at a steep angle from between the front legs; the
back legs are higher than the front ones and the body rises in an
almost hemispherical form from the legs to the mouth; the whole
is then surmounted by a large round basket handle which rises
straight upward from just back of the lip.[3] The legs are usually
decorated with incised designs and the incisions filled with white
matter; in some later examples which must belong to the subsequent period the designs are curvilinear, even spiraliform, but in
these the fabric is more often brown than black, a change noted
in other types of black burnished wares as well. Besides the white-
filled incisions, the grooves outlining the tops of the legs are filled
with red paint and a thick red paint was applied to the 'feet' and
to the whole underside of the vessel among the legs. The interior
has a thin white paint overall, and in the cupped depression over
each leg there is a broad stroke of red paint from front to back.
The similar use of paint can still be seen on many of the legs
found earlier. Vases of exactly the same form and with similar use
of incised and painted decoration were found during the 1950's
in Yugoslavia, where they belong to the Kakanj and Danilo cultures of west-central and western Bosnia respectively. Here,
where more complete examples were found from the start, they

[1] G, 23.   [2] §III, 14, 190–5. See Plate 22(a).   [3] See Plate 22(b).

were at once called cult vessels; there is good reason to believe that the Greek examples were also used for cult purposes. Korošec[1] has suggested that the Yugoslav vessels belonged to a 'water cult', which would be supported by their occurrence at Elatea and Corinth, both places with exceptionally copious water supply, but it may also be possible that they form the female element in a fertility cult in which large clay phalloi, such as were found at Danilo and were similarly decorated with red paint, were the male element.

The black-burnished wares, long called 'Danubian' wares, are much more likely to be related to and derived from the Late Chalcolithic black wares of Anatolia, for which we now have a very long series from Beycesultan which begins during Halaf times and continues to the end of the fourth millennium.[2] Their arrival in Greece probably occurred only shortly before the end of the Middle Neolithic period and they then continued to be made in Greece, and probably to be imported as well, through the Late Neolithic period. Whether or not the grey wares which have been noted in similar context (at Corinth in particular)[3] were related to or were possibly a variety of the black burnished ware, it is not yet possible to say. The shapes are almost identical with those of the black ware, though the rims of the carinated bowls are often lower and thicker. Decoration is by white paint, rippling, grooving or shallow incision. Found first together with the black wares in the latest deposits of Neolithic Urfirnis ware, the grey pottery continued in use through the Late Neolithic period. Though it is known in quantity only at Corinth, where it was first recognized in 1937, it has subsequently been found at many Peloponnesian sites and at Astakos in Acarnania; pieces from central Greece and Thessaly have also been recognized. Though the grey ware has certain characteristics of its own, especially the fabric which is grey throughout and much resembles later Minyan ware, it is sufficiently like the grey-black burnished wares to suggest that it is a local development from the latter. On the other hand, the widespread occurrence of grey wares in western Anatolia may argue for a common source rather than an independent development in the two areas, and the grey ware, like the black, may also have come to Greece from Anatolia.

One other addition to the Greek material assemblage during the latter part of the Middle Neolithic period that is deserving of special mention is the stone arrowhead, apparently the first weapons other than clay sling bullets to be used on the mainland.

[1] §VIII, 12, 70.   [2] §IX, 10, 71–103.   [3] §V, 20, 503–11.

From both Elatea[1] and Corinth[2] there are tanged arrowheads of both obsidian and flint that are most probably of this date; they continue in use and become more numerous in the Late Neolithic period. We cannot yet say whether their appearance in Greece is connected with the arrival of the grey-black burnished wares, but the association of the bow and arrow with dark-faced burnished wares and of the sling with painted pottery, as suggested by Childe,[3] may in time be shown to have validity for Greece.

It is apparent that the fifth millennium witnessed a steady increase in the population of the Greek mainland as well as a spread into new areas and the thicker settlement of those already inhabited.[4] Some of this is to be accounted for by the natural growth of the population and even the founding of new settlements from old ones, and in many parts of the mainland there is sufficient continuity from the Early to the Middle Neolithic periods to indicate such internal development. However, there are also numerous and vivid indications of the arrival of new cultural elements, and in many instances it is clear that these were brought by newly arriving peoples. That this was largely a peaceful infiltration is suggested by the lack of evidence of large-scale destruction during the Middle Neolithic period. The abandonment of Nea Nikomedeia may speak to the contrary, but only for the very beginning of the period and in a northern outpost. The existence of fortifications in a few places in Thessaly probably indicates some apprehension, possibly on the part of newcomers who felt it necessary to consolidate their position. Whence they came can be determined with considerable certainty. The Thessaly A culture comprises house types and pottery which are associated with the Sāmarrān culture of the Near East, indicating that this phase must have begun in pre-Halaf times. The Middle Neolithic culture of the Peloponnese and of much of central Greece, on the other hand, is closely connected with early Halaf, for which a beginning date about 5000 B.C. is indicated by a carbon-14 determination from Level V at Hassūnah. Whether we have to do with a single migration of some scale or a slow infiltration over a long period, we cannot say. But it was not until the second half of the millennium, i.e. the latter half of the Middle Neolithic period, that new elements began to arrive from a different region, Anatolia, first in the form of the megaron house, later the black burnished wares and possibly the grey wares and the stone arrowheads as well. In all these instances,

[1] §III, 14, 206.   [2] §V, 14, 251.
[3] G, 4.   [4] Map 16.

one region of Greece was affected first, and only with time did the new cultural elements spread to other regions. It would seem that internal communications, though constant, were slow, whereas communication by sea was still rapid and most frequent, both coastwise in Greece and eastward with Anatolia and Syro-Cilicia in particular.

VI. THE LATE NEOLITHIC PERIOD IN THE AEGEAN (EXCEPT CRETE)

At the beginning of the Late Neolithic period there prevailed over most of the mainland a cultural uniformity such as had not existed since the break-up of the Early Neolithic *koine*. While it does not seem to have lasted very long, it gives a basis for tying together the whole of the mainland both culturally and chronologically, at least at the start of the Late Neolithic period. The most obvious single common element in the overall material culture is the pottery, matt-painted and polychrome wares,[1] which rapidly replaced the Thessaly A painted wares, Chaeronea ware and Neolithic Urfirnis ware. This discontinuity in painted wares, on the one hand, is balanced by the continued use of the grey-black and grey wares throughout the Late Neolithic period, but also by the use of the megaron form of house, at least in Thessaly, during this period.

The new pottery types are copiously represented in the Corinthia, all over central Greece and Thessaly, in the west at Ayios Nikolaos near Astakos and in the cave called Choirospilia on Leucas. Only a small amount seems to have reached Macedonia and there are also limited amounts of the matt-painted ware at Prosymna and Malthi in the Peloponnese. The fabric is always light, though it varies in shade from buff, sometimes pinkish, to very light greenish buff or grey, according to the clays in the various regions; the greenish tints are especially characteristic and were most often obtained from the light Corinthian clay. While the fabric was well fired, it is not so hard as that of the Neolithic Urfirnis ware and the ware is generally not so fine as the latter. A dull paint, varying from red-brown to black, was used for designs on the light surface, but not for covering large solid areas. High 'fruitstand' bases are common, both for open bowls and for globular collared jars. Such jars without a base are common; they have a large band handle from neck to shoulder.

[1] §III, 14, 197 f. See Plates 22 (*c*) and 23(*c–d*).

Cups or bowls with concave rims offset from the body by a sharp carination also have wide band handles from lip to carination; they generally have flat bottoms. Bowls with heavy incurved rims also occur in this ware. The shapes resemble closely those of the black and grey wares and also the Neolithic Urfirnis ware, though they have handles much more frequently and hardly ever have the ring foot. The decorative system and the repertory of designs of the matt-painted ware is very different from that of Neolithic Urfirnis ware, largely in that there are no solidly painted dark areas and thus there is much less tendency to restrict the decoration to horizontal bands or zones. The decorative motives are simple, largely rectilinear, though swags or festoons and wavy lines are common. Parallel lines and chevrons, hatched and cross-hatched areas, solid-filled triangles, checkerboards, hour-glass or butterfly motives, bands bordered by small triangles or running half-loops, are all found. Rims and jar collars are decorated both inside and out, and so frequently are open bowls; high stands often have bands of ornament running vertically for their full height and so, too, do some globular jars. In addition, there are numerous free-field patterns on both the body of jars and the interior of bowls: zig-zag lines, singly or in groups, placed horizontally or vertically; groups of wavy lines apparently made with a multiple brush, possibly marking its first appearance in Greece; butterfly motives, solidly filled or cross-hatched; a leaf or dart motive. Most interesting of all are the two faces, one of which occurs on the neck of a jar from Drakhmani (Elatea)[1] and the other on the full height of the side of a tumbler from Tsangli.[2] While a propensity for painting faces on or about handles or lugs existed in the Dhimini culture, and a similar kind of treatment is effected by incision in many areas of the Aegean towards the end of the Late Neolithic period, the two large painted faces are reminiscent rather of those on Sāmarrā,[3] Halaf[4] and Hacılar[5] pottery of an earlier period.

Like the Neolithic Urfirnis ware, the matt-painted pottery has been shown by Dr Perkins to have a close relative in the Near East, in this case the 'Ubaid ware, which in fabric, paint, designs and some shapes is strikingly like the Late Neolithic matt-painted ware.[6] Syro-Cilicia again offers some of the closest parallels, while Corinth has the most varied repertory of designs and its fabric most often has the greenish tinge so characteristic of 'Ubaid

[1] G, 29, fig. 499. See Plate 22 (c).   [2] §II, 23, fig. 54, a.
[3] §x, 11, pl. xvii, 2.   [4] §x, 12, 83, fig. 95, pl. xcvi, 2.
[5] §ix, 15, 103, pl. xv.   [6] G, 16; G, 25.

ware; one wonders if perhaps the Corinthian clay was chosen because it reproduced so well the colour of the 'Ubaid fabric.

The beginning of the Late Neolithic period is also marked by the appearance of polychrome ware in which the designs are painted in two colours, usually red and black, either on the buff ground of the vase or on a light slip.[1] The red paint, varying from orange to deep purple, is most often made lustrous by polishing; the black paint, sometimes blue-black or dark grey, is generally matt. This polychrome ware is closely associated with the matt-painted ware, to the extent that one side of a vase may be decorated with the one, the other side with the other; it occurs everywhere that matt-painted ware is found and shares with it many shapes and decorative patterns. All of this early polychrome ware is of the type in which separate elements of the decoration are painted in red or black; only later in the period does there appear a second type of polychrome ware in which the designs in red are bordered by black. Like the matt-painted ware, this early type of polychrome ware is also to be connected with the 'Ubaid period in Syro-Cilicia, where there occurs pottery with polished red and matt black patterns; while its patterns are at times derived from late Halaf ware, the use of matt black paint and its association with 'Ubaid pottery clearly places it in the later period.

In Thessaly, both at Arapi-Magula near Larissa[2] and at Kouphovouno in Volo,[3] it has been shown stratigraphically that the matt-painted and early polychrome wares antedate the appearance of the first Dhimini ware. Whereas the Dhimini culture soon became dominant in eastern Thessaly, elsewhere the matt-painted and polychrome wares, together with black and grey pottery, continue uninterruptedly through the Late Neolithic period. With them belong rectangular houses of mud brick on stone foundations; in Thessaly, however, the megaron continued in use and is in evidence at both Sesklo and Dhimini, together with fortification walls,[4] both very likely hold-overs from the previous period. The settlement at Servia in Macedonia continued to follow the Thessalian pattern in its Late Neolithic phase; here, belonging to the early part of the Late Neolithic period, was a burial of a male youth in a roughly circular pit, the body in the contracted position, a layer of grey ash containing fragments of grey-on-grey and black wares over the skeleton.[5] All the other Late Neolithic burials known are from the last phase of the period and will be considered later.

[1] §III, 14, 198.   [2] §II, 10, 188–91.   [3] §II, 17, 6–8.
[4] §II, 21, 75–9, 88–106.   [5] §I, 1, 54 f.

It is now clear that the importance of the Dhimini culture has long been overemphasized. It is incorrect to make it synonymous with Thessaly B, for it occupies neither the entire period chronologically nor all of Thessaly geographically. We have already cited the stratigraphic evidence that places its beginning somewhat after that of the Thessaly B period. As early as the first decade of this century, it was obvious that the Dhimini culture belonged in eastern Thessaly and had had little effect even on western Thessaly;[1] subsequently it became clear that its influence on the rest of Greece was small and was largely transmitted coastwise somewhat to the north and to the south. However, even though it was a highly localized manifestation, it flourished brilliantly for a while. This accounts in part for the importance so long given it in studies of Aegean prehistory, though more probably the fact that it was discovered early, revealed completely and published rapidly[2] accounts for its magnified importance. One factor alone, the use of spiraliform designs on both its impressed and painted pottery, has given rise to a vast literature, largely having to do with the relation between Dhimini and the various cultures of Europe which also have pottery decorated with spiraliform designs. Even to the present day there are those who would derive the Dhimini culture from south-east Europe;[3] for long the supposed simultaneous arrival of the megaron from the north was a cogent supporting argument, but we now know that the megaron arrived considerably earlier and from another direction. Wace steadfastly denied a connexion between Dhimini pottery and its supposed relatives in south-east Europe;[4] Childe reversed himself in 1947[5] and also spoke against such connexions, but in 1954[6] he seems to have returned to the older idea that the Dhimini culture was a southward extension of European cultures.

It was Miss Sylvia Benton who, on the basis of an analysis of Thessalian vase shapes and decoration, first concluded that Dhimini pottery was the result of considerable continuity from the Thessaly A period plus a generous borrowing from the Cyclades; she pointed out, too, that the new types of marble figurines that belong to the Dhimini culture are of Cycladic origin.[7] While she still accepted the possibility that the spiral was borrowed from the Danube, I have preferred to assume that the spiral came to Thessaly from the Cyclades,[8] perhaps first in the stamped or impressed form, which was then translated into

[1] §II, 23, 243.   [2] §II, 21; §II, 23.   [3] G, 18, 111–25.
[4] §II, 22.   [5] G, 2, 50 f.   [6] G, 3, 310.
[7] §IV, 1, 165–70.   [8] G, 27, 97; A, 50, 299.

very similar painted decoration. In both, the spiral is used in most instances in a thoroughly inorganic way, interspersed singly among linear geometric patterns,[1] sometimes even trimmed to make it fit into a panel; continuous or running spirals are rare. Among the shapes, flat bottoms and 'fruitstands' prevail, just as in Late Neolithic wares elsewhere in Greece, but angular shapes are rare and there are instead largely globular jars, incurved rim bowls, wide open bowls, sometimes with scalloped edges. As noted above, lugs often become the noses for painted faces, and on large flat lugs faces were also painted.[2] One scoop-like vessel with a wide band handle, the whole decorated with incised maeandroid patterns, was thought by Tsountas to be an import,[3] but it long remained without parallel; now several similar vessels have been found in graves on the island of Ceos[4] and the shape is known in Athens as well. Very likely such imports, some with maeandroid patterns but possibly others with stamped spirals, became the prototypes for both maeandroid and spiraliform decoration on Dhimini painted ware. The reasons for believing that the 'Syros' culture of the Cyclades, with its spiraliform ornament, was already fully developed before the beginning of the Early Helladic period on the mainland have been given by me elsewhere;[5] the first Early Cycladic phase would then be contemporaneous with at least the last part of the Late Neolithic period, while any Late Neolithic culture that preceded it on the islands would be co-existent with an earlier phase of the Dhimini culture.

The architectural complex at Dhimini with its multiple circuit walls, between some of which are megaron houses, and its great central court with an axial entrance on the south-west side directly opposite the megaron, is unique in Neolithic Greece. Here for the first time appears the arrangement which was standard by the time of Troy II c,[6] when a colonnade was added in the court. But both the megaron and the fortification walls occur in the earliest levels at Troy, and we have seen that both were present in levels of the Thessaly A period. If the beginning of Troy I was contemporaneous with that of the Early Bronze I period at Beycesultan, as suggested by French,[7] or the early part of that period according to Mellaart,[8] its date must fall back two or three centuries before 3000 B.C. In this case a parallel development of

---

[1] See Plate 22 (*d*).   [2] §II, 21, pl. 23.   [3] §II, 21, pl. 16, 3. See Plate 23 (*a*).
[4] §VI, 1, 265, pl. 92,*f*; §VI, 2, 316, pl. 46, *e.f.* See Plate 23 (*b*).
[5] G, 27, 94; A, 50, 302.   [6] §IX, 3, 261–3, fig. 455.
[7] §IX, 5, 118, fig. 3.   [8] §IX, 10, 112 f.

the highly integrated architectural complex, including enclosed court, propylon and megaron, would be demonstrable, this despite the fact that the Dhimini culture shares few if any other aspects of its material culture with early Troy.

Towards the end of the Late Neolithic period one can sense an increase in the movement of peoples into and about the Aegean, possibly a preliminary phase of maritime commercial enterprise such as characterizes the subsequent Early Bronze Age. Many cultural elements are associated with and possibly derive from western Asia Minor. These include new varieties of the grey-black burnished wares, particularly those decorated with pattern burnishing, which is sometimes neatly arranged in zones or panels but often is of a careless scribble variety covering large areas of bowls. White paint and plastic ornament also occur on these late black wares.[1] A red-brown variety of pattern-burnished ware appears at the same time in the Troad at Beşik Tepe,[2] on the Greek mainland at Prosymna[3] and Corinth,[4] on Aegina[5] and now also in the tombs on the Kephala promontory on the island of Ceos.[6] A cemetery of cremation burials in urns of black polished ware was discovered in 1958 just south of the site of Souphli-Magula in Thessaly;[7] the burials were in medium-sized vessels, while smaller vases of the same ware were left as offerings. Rippling, grooving and incision all appear on the carinated vases with high concave rims, often with one handle just above the keel, and several of the vases bear white incrusted paint as well. Of quite different nature, but of similar date, are the three inhumation burials found in the uppermost Neolithic levels at Lerna[8] and apparently belonging to a phase which has otherwise been cut away by levelling operations of Early Helladic times. These are contracted burials in pits, and with them were found vases placed as offerings in the graves; a few of the vases bear pink incrusted paint, while one is well burnished brown-black ware. Different again are the thirty-five graves recently found in a cemetery on the Kephala promontory on Ceos;[9] the graves are cists usually built of medium-sized stones and in plan are oval or rectangular with rounded corners. Sometimes slabs set upright are used for the sides and the graves are covered with slabs; on the cover slabs was often built a solid rectangular platform of stone, two or

---

[1] See, for instance, §II, 2, Beil. XXVI.
[2] §IX, 9, 126–8.
[3] §V, 4, 375 f.
[4] §V, 14, 250.
[5] §III, 15, 20–3.
[6] §VI, 2, 316, pl. 47 *h*, *i*.
[7] §II, 1, 70–2.
[8] §V, 6, 136 f.; §V, 7, 205.
[9] §VI, 1, 263 f.; VI, 2, 314–17; A, 9, 364.

three courses high, the purpose of which is unknown. We have already mentioned both the scoop-like vessels with incised decoration and the pattern-burnished wares found in these graves. In general the pottery appears to be Late Neolithic in type and is related to that from both Athens[1] and Aegina. But in many ways the grave types and some of the objects from them are precursors of those of the Early Cycladic period, which probably followed closely upon and were related to these very late Neolithic graves. There are some jar burials on the Kephala as well. The cemetery lay below a settlement that climbed up the side of the ridge. The cemetery at Souphli seems also to have lain outside the settlement, but the graves at Lerna may very possibly have been intramural, following a tradition which we have seen in an earlier grave of the Late Neolithic period at Servia in Macedonia, and which applies to the contracted burial of a child in the uppermost Neolithic level at Elatea.[2]

The black wares of the Souphli cemetery are part of a cultural assemblage which is believed by Milojčić to have formed a separate chronological phase, at least in some parts of Thessaly, immediately after the Dhimini phase.[3] He indicates that there followed an ultimate phase of the Late Neolithic period which he calls the Rakhmani Culture,[4] characterized by crusted ware. It cannot be shown that these are chronologically distinct phases elsewhere in Greece, or even everywhere in Thessaly, and it would appear that in many parts of Greece they are co-existent. With them in the Peloponnese are to be associated the late variety of polychrome ware on which the patterns in orange-red paint are bordered by lines of dark blue-grey.[5] To the north of Thessaly, in Macedonia and Thrace, the grey-black burnished wares predominate in the Late Neolithic period,[6] but there are several varieties of incised and painted wares as well. Black-on-red wares and incised wares with curvilinear and spiraliform ornament abound at Olynthus in Chalcidice[7] and at many other sites, and their decoration has often been associated with and even derived from that of Dhimini ware. While general similarities exist and the cultures are roughly contemporaneous, a direct derivation of the Olynthian pottery style from Dhimini seems out of the question; the closest relations are with the rest of Macedonia and Thrace and, for the painted pottery especially, with regions to the north. So, too, the so-called graphite painted wares that appear at the end of the Late Neolithic period in Thrace and

---

[1] See Plate 23(c–d). [2] §III, 14, 163. [3] §II, 9, 24 f. [4] §II, 9, 25 f.
[5] §V, 4, 373 f. [6] §I, 1, 66–77. [7] §I, 4, 39–49.

Macedonia,[1] and sometimes spread to the south, are of European derivation, just as are the crusted wares.

The varieties of cultures present in different parts of Greece in the latter half of the fourth millennium B.C., together with the move into and first permanent settlement of many of the Aegean islands—Aegina, Ceos, Myconos,[2] Antiparos[3] and Naxos[4]—are indications both of the arrival of new peoples from east and north and of the beginning of a new way of life. More than ever, the end phase of the Late Neolithic period takes on the appearance of a prelude to the initial phase of the Bronze Age, when a strong influx of people from Anatolia again placed the Aegean firmly in the Near Eastern cultural area, with only its northern fringes open to influence from the Balkans and continental Europe. Through these contacts with its hinterland, however, Greece continued to transmit the more advanced culture of the East to the still Neolithic Europe of the third millennium B.C.

VII. THE NEOLITHIC PERIOD IN CRETE

The discussion of Neolithic Crete quite separately from the rest of the Aegean is justified by the very different nature of its material culture, except perhaps in its latest phase. The record of the greatest part of the Neolithic period is obtained almost exclusively from one large site, Cnossus, for which we now very fortunately have a recent excavation of sufficient scale to give a fairly complete picture of the Neolithic culture.[5] The mound formed by the deep accumulation of Neolithic habitation debris, in some places as much as 10 metres, was used as the site for the Minoan palace, in preparation for which the knoll was levelled so that the paving stones of the central court of the palace rested directly on Neolithic fill; and some Neolithic accumulation, how much we do not know, was certainly removed from the top of the mound. The greatest expanse of the Neolithic settlement is about the same as that of the later palace, including its exterior courts— an area of not less than 11 acres. Sir Arthur Evans tested this deposit with pits at various points[6] and Mackenzie, in the first study of the Neolithic pottery from Cnossus, recognized three stages in its development;[7] these were later called by Evans the

---

[1] G, 18, 124 f.
[2] §VI, 5, 395–8.
[3] Preliminary reports appear in *Archaeological Reports for 1965–66*, 16–7 and *B.C.H.* 90 (1966), 912–17.
[4] §VI, 5, 398–9.
[5] §VII, 5.
[6] §VII, 3, vol. I, 32–55.
[7] §VII, 12, 158–64.

Lower, Middle and Upper Neolithic phases. Early and Late were at times used instead of Lower and Upper by Evans and later by Pendlebury.[1] A re-study of the material from the early test pits resulted in the division of the early period into two sub-phases.[2] It was the initiative of Sinclair Hood, then Director of the British School at Athens, that led to the new excavations, which were begun by him in 1957 and then continued under the direction of John D. Evans from 1958 to 1960.[3] For these, four areas each 5 metres square and with 1 metre baulks between were laid out in an area 11 metres square in the northern half of the central court of the palace. The four areas were dug for about 2·50 metres, when substantial structures were encountered in the northern half, square *BD*, and work was stopped here; in area *AC* the baulk was removed and the area (11 × 5 metres) was dug to bedrock. A test trench (*XY*) one metre wide was dug at the northern edge of the site, where the depth was only *c*. 2·50 metres, and contained remains of the Early Neolithic II and Middle Neolithic periods.

In area *AC* bedrock was cut by pits of all sizes, up to 1·20 metres in diameter, many of which contained ash, charcoal, carbonized grain and animal bones, and most of which showed signs of fire. Smaller holes were for posts or stakes. A thin deposit of habitation debris over the whole area, averaging 0·20 metres, also showed frequent traces of fire. In one area was a mass of carbonized grain (hexaploid wheat, emmer and barley) bordered along one edge by four stake holes in a straight line; in one of the holes was still part of a carbonized stake, made of oak. Seven skeletons of children, from newborn to about seven years old, were found, six in a group merely laid in the earth in the contracted position, the seventh placed in flexed position in a small oval pit cut in bedrock and covered with a stone; no grave goods were found with any of the burials. There were no permanent structures in this level and it is considered to have been a camp site set up by the first arrivals. These people had brought no pottery with them and made none during the time of this earliest settlement; this is not considered to indicate that their culture was aceramic, but rather that they had not yet set up the means for producing pottery. The material remains are scant and show little variety: two stone axes, a number of pieces of obsidian and only a few of flint, with only one of the latter showing any retouch; three long bone spatulae, thought to have been used in scraping flour from querns after grinding (though querns were

[1] §VII, 17, 35–45.   [2] §VII, 6.   [3] §VII, 4; VII, 5.

not found in this level); a good number of bone points and one bone chisel; some beads of shell or stone and one of clay; a stone toggle and a circlet or small bracelet of stone.

For the next two strata (IX and VIII) the nature of the fill is very different both from the stratum below and from all those above, this due largely to the fact that it was composed mostly of the remains of fired bricks with a wide variation in their colour, giving a polychrome effect streaked with black ash and charcoal. The earliest solid structures on the site were built of these bricks, together with a certain amount of stone, often discarded querns or mortars; the bricks varied considerably in size, but averaged 0·50 × 0·20 × 0·05 metres in House E of Stratum IX. This house had a roughly square room, the foundations for which were of brick and stone construction, though *pisé* may have been used in the upper part of the walls; the roof was of clay over brushwood. Higher up, in Stratum VIII, was part of another rectangular house built with fired brick, the floor of beaten earth and on it the remains of two small domed ovens; daub with the imprint of branches gave evidence of the roof construction. In the floor was a large circular pit, about 1 metre in diameter, full of ash. Two large pits at the east end of the area were filled with ash, earth and much pottery, and in one were two stone figurines, the exceptionally fine standing male figure already well known[1] and a very small amuletic figure. Pottery was not present in great quantities in either of these strata, but the pits yielded a half-dozen fairly complete vessels.[2] Throughout the Neolithic accumulation house floors were remarkably free of debris; pits were more productive of finds. From both levels there are querns, mortars, axes, much obsidian, a little flint, many bone points and a few chisels, beads, bracelets, pendants and toggles; from IX came part of a clay figurine, the earliest from the site, while from VIII there are three stone figurines, two of which have already been mentioned. In IX were a small lump of malachite and two lumps of azurite, apparently prized as colouring matter; they are the only metal found in the Neolithic levels at Cnossus during the latest excavations.

A change in building materials, the use of *pisé* rather than fired brick, began with Stratum VII, and the new type of construction continued for the remainder of the duration of the Neolithic settlement; it results in a very different appearance of the strata, now no longer brightly varicoloured but instead showing large patches of light-coloured clay from decomposed walls

[1] See Plate 23 (*e–f*).   [2] See Plate 24.

alternating with dark habitation debris. It is suggested that the abandonment of the use of fired brick came with the realization that it was unnecessary in the relatively dry conditions that prevailed at Cnossus. A house of at least two rooms, each about 4 × 3 metres, took up most of the area, but a cobbled court to the north of them was noted. The rectangular foundations were of stone and lumps of very soft limestone (*kouskouras*), often but a single row that gives an appearance of flimsiness to the construction which is probably incorrect as the mud walls were thicker than the foundations. In the clay floor of each room were two circular depressions, and many more were found in the floors below; all showed traces of fire and all had frequently been plastered over. It is suggested that they, and a larger circular hollow in the cobbled area, were cooking holes, and that these rather than vessels were used for cooking; none of the large or coarser vessels showed any traces of fire and they were probably used only for storage. Again many querns were among the stones used in construction, and clay daub from the roof was found. This was the last substantial structure in area *AC*, for in the strata above this area seems to have been a space between buildings and therefore there were cobble and pebble pavements, hearths, pits, traces of flimsy sheds or enclosures—all the signs of outdoor activities such as are common to this day in villages.

Strata VI and V are still within the Early Neolithic I phase. The objects found in them include much the same repertory of stone and bone tools and implements as found in the earlier levels, except that stone mace-heads are noted first in VI and continue to appear in all strata above it. From V come a number of highly schematized representations of standing human figures made of stone and shell; at this level appeared the first squatting figures in clay. Except for these innovations and the usual developmental changes, there is a high degree of uniformity in the material culture from Stratum IX through V, with some 4 metres of accumulation, a greater depth than that for all the subsequent Neolithic occupation. The pottery of the Early Neolithic I phase is very homogeneous, competent from the start, adequately fired, though more brittle than later wares. At first there is little distinction between fine and coarse wares, though the former were always burnished and largely black, whereas the coarser wares show a greater variety in colouring and often were not so carefully burnished. With the improvement in firing methods, burnishing of coarse ware ultimately became unnecessary and the vessels were merely smoothed. Bowls and jars are the common shapes;

20-2

there is considerable variety in the former, which may be carinated or have offset or incurved rims. There is great variety, too, in handles: ring handles, tubular lugs, flap and wishbone handles, trumpet lugs and triangular ears, some perforated. The most characteristic decoration on Early Neolithic I pottery is either plastic—strips of clay, large knobs or rows of small pellets—or incised in the pointillé technique with bands, triangles, zig-zags, step patterns, etc., outlined with incised lines and covered with dots, all then normally filled with a white paste or occasionally a red paste. Simple incised designs without dots also occur, sometimes alongside the punctate designs.

The Early Neolithic II phase is represented by the one thick Stratum IV, 1·00–1·50 metres deep, in area AC and by three building levels in trench XY, indications of a fairly long period. Since the Early Neolithic II walls in trench XY have exactly the same orientation as the Middle Neolithic and Late Neolithic walls from area BD in the central court some distance away, it would seem that as early as the Early Neolithic II phase began a standard orientation for buildings that was maintained thereafter and implies town planning over a large area. The fill in area AC is composed of many thin levels of refuse which slope down to the east. As in Strata VI and V, there are hearths, some of them fairly large built ones, small clay structures, pebble pavements, shallow pits. In the pottery there is much continuity, especially in shapes and certain features, with that of the Early Neolithic I phase. The fabric, too, changes little, though the coarser ware is better fired and shows less variegation; much of it is no longer burnished. The fine ware is more often black than red or brown. It is the decoration which shows more change: plastic and pointillé decoration continues, though less frequently than before and diminishing in quantity with the Early Neolithic II deposit. The incised decoration without dots becomes vastly more popular on fine wares and now reaches its height. There is a distinct Early Neolithic II style in incised ware, using a greater variety of patterns but showing a marked carelessness and irregularity in execution, in contrast to the very careful execution of the Middle Neolithic period. The incisions are deep, the patterns few and simple, all linear and usually arranged horizontally. Stratum IV yielded an exceptionally large number of figurines, fragments of thirty in all, one made from a rib bone and the rest of terracotta.

Strata III and II are of the Middle Neolithic period; these strata were excavated in all four of the 5 metre squares. In area BD were found two structures belonging to Stratum III: house A, a roughly square room about 4 metres on a side, the stone and *kouskouras* foundations of which were nearly 1 metre high in places and had slight internal buttresses, and house *B*, which was trapezoidal and had solidly built walls of stone and clay also up to 1 metre in height. Floors and walls were smoothly coated with clay; a clay platform in one corner of house *A* was bordered by stones; a cupboard on the north wall may have had a window behind it. In house *B* there was a cobbled shelf or bench. There were only scrappy architectural remains from Stratum II. Of great interest is the appearance in these Middle Neolithic levels of numbers of clay loomweights, clay and occasionally stone spindle whorls and clay 'shuttles'. All three seem to appear at the same time, giving clear evidence of their association as equipment for spinning and weaving. This does not preclude the existence of spinning and weaving earlier (a number of pierced discs made from potsherds may have been an earlier form of spindle whorl) but they show the use of new types of equipment for these purposes, which continued in use in the Late Neolithic period. The Middle Neolithic pottery prevails largely in level II B, for in the upper level II A the beginnings of the development to Late Neolithic pottery is already evident. While the fine Middle Neolithic wares are still burnished and the colour is predominantly black, but with some brown and red pieces, the walls often thinner than before, the coarse ware is now largely smoothed and pale colours predominate. The shapes have not changed greatly, though the profiled carinated bowls become very popular and are the chief recipients of the new type of rippled decoration. The flap and wishbone handles have largely disappeared, but a new type of pronged handle, often quite long, is in vogue for certain shapes, particularly ladles. There is much incised decoration, but very little pointillé and no real plastic applications. Patterns in incised decoration change, with large hatched triangles now being staple. But it is the rippled decoration, almost always applied vertically, which is especially characteristic of the period. Very little obsidian, and less flint, was found in these strata, but in both, as well as in Stratum I, much rock crystal occurs.

Stratum I was found along the north and south sides and chiefly at the east end of the large area in the central court, but at the west and over much of the central part of the area it had been removed in the levelling for the palace. Remains are thus not numerous, but it is important that by joining this area with that dug by Sir Arthur Evans in 1923–4,[1] it was established that the

---

[1] §vii, 3, vol. ii, 1–21.

large building complex which he then discovered surely belongs to Stratum I. Since the area dug earlier was at a considerable distance to the south of the one recently dug, the building was farther down the slope and so escaped removal in the Middle Minoan levelling operations. It was, in fact, possible to recognize two building levels, though the walls of the upper level were much disturbed; these latter have a slightly different orientation from those below. The multi-roomed building complex of the lower level, disclosed in an area about 13 metres square, was thought to comprise at least two large houses and their dependencies, though with common walls, so that the whole has the appearance of a continuous agglomeration of rooms interspersed with courts that have pebble pavements; the house floors were of earth carefully covered with clay. A large built hearth was found in each house, one against the wall, the other slightly away from it. The Late Neolithic pottery from both old and new excavations shows a drastic reduction in rippled ware, lighter surface colours in the fine wares—brown, red, or even lighter tones, a characteristic 'wiped' surface on coarse ware, the rough finishing of which had been limited to wiping with a cloth or a bunch of grass. Trough-and-bridge type spouts become fairly common in fine ware; Sir Arthur found in the houses the prototypes of the later chalices, here with lower bases, some decorated by incision but others already showing pattern burnishing. Incision is the main form of decoration, now often accompanied by strings of dots and other patterns that show a revival of the pointillé technique. Incised patterns are smaller than before, the incision less deep, the execution often careless. There are two important additions to the material assemblage which, like the proto-chalices, are harbingers of a new age: the first is a copper axe from the floor of one of the pebbled courts and the other is the number of fragments of stone bowls, which Sir Arthur thought related to pre-dynastic and proto-dynastic stone vessels in Egypt.

As a result of the recent excavations, our knowledge of Neolithic Crete has been greatly augmented and the position of Cnossus as the key Neolithic site on the island is more firmly established than ever. The excavator, J. D. Evans, thinks of it as more like a township than a village because of its great size.[1] He remarks, however, that the material equipment was at a low level of specialization and technological achievement. The pottery was from the start in an established tradition and the craft was clearly brought from elsewhere; he believes that some of the

[1] §VII, 4, 53.

pottery may have been the work of at least part-time specialists. The inhabitants, however, had no strong tradition for the manufacture of chipped stone tools, and bone tools often outnumber those of stone. Stone axes, usually fully polished when small but often only roughly picked except for the cutting edge when large, were found in all levels. A peculiar fact is the almost total lack of stone adzes and chisels, only one of each being recorded; it would appear that there was no strong woodworking craft. On the other hand, from Stratum VI on up stone mace-heads occur with considerable frequency; to my knowledge they are unknown elsewhere in the Aegean in the Neolithic period. The clay spindle whorls, loomweights and 'shuttles' are also different from anything we know in the Neolithic Aegean; elsewhere only the pierced discs cut from potsherds are common. The anthropomorphic figurines are largely in a different tradition from those of mainland Greece. The use of fired brick in the building of Strata IX and VIII finds no parallel in the Aegean. Lastly, the pottery, too, is in a different tradition from that of the Greek mainland in most of the Neolithic period, and in looking for its possible source, J. D. Evans finds the greatest affinities with pottery traditions of north-west Anatolia—Kumtepe, Troy, Poliochni and Chios, though he believes this Anatolian tradition to be of a much later date than the earliest pottery of Cnossus. In this he is basing his date on the carbon-14 analysis of a piece of carbonized wood found in a stake hole in bedrock; this yielded a date of 6100 B.C. ± 180 years.[1] Another sample, from the very top of the Early Neolithic II deposit, gave a date of 5050 B.C. ± 180 years,[2] suggesting a duration of just about a millennium for the Early Neolithic period. This would make some of his pottery almost three thousand years earlier than that of north-west Anatolia to which it is most similar, and Evans suggests, therefore, that this north-west Anatolian tradition had a much longer history than has been suspected and that in an earlier, and simpler, form it may have been the parent of the Cnossus Neolithic culture. He realizes that the gap is great, but believes that this is due to our lack of knowledge of the Neolithic culture of western Asia Minor.[3]

The fallacy in J. D. Evans's argument is revealed by the fact that we now have a good picture of pottery production of about 6000 B.C. not only in Greece, but in Anatolia and the Near East as well. Throughout this large eastern Mediterranean area there is a general uniformity in these early ceramic products, none of which are in any degree as advanced as is the earliest pottery

[1] §VII, 4, 57.   [2] §VII, 4, 57.   [3] §VII, 4, 59–60.

found at Cnossus. This earliest Cnossian Neolithic pottery is already in a stage of advancement, especially as to shape, which does not begin to be achieved in the eastern Mediterranean until the middle of the fifth millennium at the earliest; it seems to me incredible that the potters of Cnossus were so much out of step and so far in advance of all the rest of the potters of the eastern Mediterranean. It is easier to believe, if necessary, that the carbon-14 dates, based thus far only on single samples, are too high. There is, however, another possibility which Evans seems not to have considered. As far as I can see, there is no continuity between Stratum X and that above it; the real continuity begins with IX and goes throughout the remainder of the settlement's history. In fact, there are some clear discontinuities, such as the existence of very well-formed bone spatulae in X which are never seen again and the lack of figurines, which appear first in IX and are then present in all subsequent levels. The reason for the lack of pottery as given by Evans is unsatisfactory. If the occupants of Stratum X knew how to make pottery, it is inconceivable that they brought none with them and made none even for so short a time as he believes Stratum X to represent. Yet the kind of material culture represented in Stratum X would fit very well with the date of 6100 B.C. It seems to me much easier to believe in an original settlement of this date, possibly then abandoned, and a resettlement some 1500 years or more later, when the very different material culture represented in Stratum IX began. This would still leave in question the carbon-14 date of 5050 B.C. obtained for the end of the Early Neolithic period, but Evans is already unhappy about its relation to the earlier date, a difference of just about a thousand years represented by some four metres of accumulation, while the next 2·50 metres of fill, which would have been expected to accumulate at about the same rate, represents about two thousand years.[1] One can conceive of a western Anatolian culture of about 4500 B.C. at the earliest which could have been parent to that of Stratum IX at Cnossus; at 6100 B.C. this seems quite impossible at the moment. A beginning date for the first Cretan pottery of about 4500 B.C. or later would also go far to explain why Crete never was part of the painted pottery area that covered Greece at least from the late sixth millennium on. In the latter part of the fifth millennium Greece, too, received a black-ware culture from Anatolia. To be sure, the latter is different in details from that which reached Crete, and the parent cultures probably occupied different parts of Anatolia, but they

[1] §vii, 4, 58.

are in the same stage of development and present no such in-
congruities as would the dating of Stratum IX at Cnossus around
6000 B.C.

With regard to internal connexions, J. D. Evans concludes
that the Early Neolithic pottery of Cnossus is unique in Crete,
some sherds from Katsambas, just to the north-east of Cnossus,
being the only possible exception. There is a Middle Neolithic
occupation at Katsambas, which is discussed below, and Evans
saw some Middle Neolithic pottery found at Metropolis near
Gortyna.[1] He feels that the Neolithic material found at Phaestus
is almost certainly later than anything found at Cnossus and that
the same is true for all the other Late Neolithic or sub-Neolithic
sites on Crete. Cnossus may have had such remains, which were
removed in the levelling for the palace, but he does not believe
that many levels were cut away and suggests that there may have
been a gap in the Cnossus sequence.

The other Neolithic sites on Crete are many, at least thirty,
a dozen of which are known only from surface finds, while a large
number of the others have merely been tested in small areas. The
rather large Middle Neolithic building complex found at
Katsambas[2] (it is roughly 7 metres square) comprises a small
house of two, or possibly three, rooms with a small forecourt and
large enclosed courts with stables and other such shed-like structures on two sides; it gives the impression of a farm-house as
compared with the urban arrangements at Cnossus, but the
dwelling itself has the so-called 'but and ben' plan observed in
Late Neolithic buildings and later ones as well, in which the
scheme of communications is U-shaped. At Katsambas the
foundations were of stones and clay, the walls of mud brick. The
material assemblage is very much like that from nearby Cnossus;
it included one exceptionally fine black stone mace-head. A small
structure with the 'but and ben' plan was found at Magasa in
east Crete,[3] near it a rock shelter; both have been dated to the
Late Neolithic period, for the pottery shows some of the characteristics of the latest Neolithic wares from Cnossus. Very similar
is the Neolithic pottery from the Trapeza cave in the Lasithi
plain,[4] where again it is thought to be very late Neolithic. A local
variation, called Trapeza ware, is comprised largely of cooking
pots, on the rims of many of which faces are modelled around
tubular lugs, which become the noses; this is but another manifestation of the anthropomorphizing tendency in the decoration

[1] §vii, 4, 57.   [2] §vii, 1, 369–74.
[3] §vii, 2, 260–8.   [4] §vii, 18.

of Late Neolithic pottery. Beneath the palace of Phaestus, particularly under the south-west quadrant and downhill from it, there are abundant Neolithic remains.[1] These have had to be investigated mainly in tests in depth within the confines of the structure of the palace, so that there has been little opportunity to observe architecture, but successive floors, hearths and even wall fragments appeared. The pottery presents a rich variety of highly burnished fine wares, as well as coarser wares. Decoration by incision, white or red filled, punctate and plastic ornament all occur, but there is also a class of wares on which simple designs are painted over the lustrous dark surface with red ochre, sometimes with both red and white colours. In the latest levels there occurs the first pattern-burnished decoration. J. D. Evans believes[2] that the Neolithic period at Phaestus is almost certainly later than anything found at Cnossus and the excavator of Phaestus, Doro Levi, has also indicated most recently that what has been called Neolithic at Phaestus might better be termed sub-Neolithic or Chalcolithic.[3] This is probably also true of the type of pottery found in the Koumarospilio in western Crete[4] and in the Eileithyia Cave near Amnisus,[5] at Elenes in the Amari district,[6] and at numerous other places. In this latest phase of the Cretan Neolithic period there are many more resemblances to the material culture of the rest of Greece than were evident in the Cnossian Neolithic. Only at the very end of the Neolithic period did Crete become culturally a part of Greece, from which it had apparently remained isolated throughout the long development whose record lies in the mound at Cnossus.

[1] §vii, 9, 337–45; §vii, 10, 458–62.   [2] §vii, 4, 58.
[3] §vii, 11, 134.   [4] §vii, 15, 1–12.
[5] §vii, 13.   [6] §vii, 14, 295 f.

BIBLIOGRAPHY

ABBREVIATIONS

A.A.W.Wien. *Anzeiger der Österreichischen Akademie der Wissenschaften (Phil.-hist. Klasse)*

Abh. Berlin (München, etc.). *Abhandlungen der Preussischen (Bayerischen, etc.) Akademie der Wissenschaften, Phil.-hist. Klasse*

Abh. Mainz. *Abhandlungen der Preussischen Akademie der Wissenschaften, Math-naturwiss. Klasse*

Acta Arch. *Acta Archaeologica*

Acta Or. *Acta Orientalia*

Aeg. Inschrt. Berlin. *Aegyptische Inschriften aus den .... Museen zu Berlin*

Ägyptol. Forsch. *Ägyptologische Forschungen*

A.I.R.R.S. *Acta Instituti Romani Regni Sueciae*

A.J. *Antiquaries Journal*

A.J.A. *American Journal of Archaeology*

A.J.S.L. *American Journal of Semitic Languages and Literatures*

Alte Or. *Der Alte Orient*

An. Biblica. *Analecta Biblica*

An. Or. *Analecta Orientalia*

Anc. Egypt. *Ancient Egypt* (continued as *Ancient Egypt and the East*)

Ann. Arch. Anthr. *Annals of Archaeology and Anthropology* (Liverpool)

Ann. Arch. de Syrie. *Annales Archéologique de Syrie*

Ann. A.S.O.R. *Annual of the American Schools of Oriental Research*

Ann. Assoc. Amer. Geog. *Annals of the Association of American Geographers*

Ann. D.A.J. *Annual of the Department of Antiquities of Jordan*

Ann. N.Y. Acad. Sci. *Annual of the New York Academy of Sciences*

Ann. Serv. *Annales du Service des Antiquités de l'Égypte*

Antiq. *Antiquity*

A.O.S. *American Oriental Series, American Oriental Society*

Arch. Anz. *Archaeologischer Anzeiger.* Beiblatt zum *Jahrbuch des deutschen archäologischen Instituts*

Arch. Delt. ʼΑρχαιολογικὸν Δελτίον

Arch. de l'Inst. de Paléont. hum. *Archives de l'Institut de Paléontologie humaine*

Arch. Eph. (ʼΑρχ. ʼΕφ.) ʼΑραΧιολογικὴ ʼΕφημερίς

Arch. f. Or. *Archiv für Orientforschung*

Arch Orient. *Archiv Orientální*

A.R.M. *Archives royales de Mari*

A. St. *Anatolian Studies*

Ath. Mitt. *Athenische Mitteilungen, Mitteilungen des deutschen archäologischen Instituts, Athenische Abteilung*

B.A. *Beiträge zur Assyriologie und semitischen Sprachwissenschaft*

B.C.H. *Bulletin de Correspondance hellénique*

B.E. *Babylonian Expedition of the University of Pennsylvania*

Bibl. Aeg. *Bibliotheca Aegyptiaca*

Bibl. Arch. et Hist. *Bibliothèque archéologique et historique*

B.I.N. *Babylonian inscriptions in the collection of J. B. Nies, Yale University*

Bi. Or. *Bibliotheca Orientalis*

B.M. Quart.   *British Museum Quarterly*

Boll. Soc. Geol. Ital.   *Bollettino della Società Geologica Italiana*

B.R.G.K.   *Bericht der römisch-germanischen Kommission*

B.S.A.   *Annual of the British School at Athens*

Bull. A.S.O.R.   *Bulletin of the American Schools of Oriental Research*

Bull. A.S.P.R.   *Bulletin of the American School of Prehistoric Research*

Bull. Inst. Arch. London   *Bulletin of the Institute of Archaeology, University of London*

Bull. Inst. d'Ég.   *Bulletin de l'Institut d'Égypte*

Bull. I.E.S.   *Bulletin of the Israel Exploration Society*

Bull. M.B.   *Bulletin du Musée de Beyrouth*

Bull. M.M.A.   *Bulletin of the Metropolitan Museum of Art (New York)*

Bull. Soc. fr. d'ég.   *Bulletin de la Société française d'Égyptologie*

Bull. Soc. Geogr. d'Égypte.   *Bulletin de la Société de géographie (d'Égypte)*

Bull. Soc. préh. fr.   *Bulletin de la Société préhistorique française*

C.A.H.   *Cambridge Ancient History*

Cah. H.M.   *Cahiers d'histoire mondiale*

C.C.G.   *Cairo Museum, Catalogue Général*

Chron. d'Ég.   *Chronique d'Égypte*

C.-R. Ac. Inscr. B.-L.   *Comptes-Rendus de l'Académie des Inscriptions et Belles-Lettres*

C.-R. du congr. géol. int. (Belgique).   *Comptes-Rendus du congrès géologique international*

C.T.   *Cuneiform Texts from Babylonian Tablets etc. in the British Museum*

E.S.A.   *Eurasia septentrionalis Antiqua*

Geogr. Rev.   *Geographical Review*

Geol. Mag.   *Geological Magazine*

Gesch. Alt.   E. Meyer, *Geschichte des Altertums*

G.J.   *Geographical Journal*

Hierat. Pap. Berlin.   *Hieratische Papyrus aus den königlichen Museen zu Berlin*

Hist. Z.   *Historische Zeitschrift*

H.U.C.A.   *Hebrew Union College Annual*

I.E.J.   *Israel Exploration Journal*

Ill. Ldn News.   *Illustrated London News*

Jahrb. des d. arch. Inst.   *Jahrbuch des deutschen archäologischen Instituts*

J.A.O.S.   *Journal of the American Oriental Society*

J. Bibl. Lit.   *Journal of Biblical Literature and Exegesis*

J.C.S.   *Journal of Cuneiform Studies*

J.E.A.   *Journal of Egyptian Archaeology*

J.E.O.L.   *Jaarbericht van het Vooraziatisch-Egyptisch Genootschap, 'Ex Oriente Lux'*

J.H.S.   *Journal of Hellenic Studies*

J.N.E.S.   *Journal of Near Eastern Studies*

J.P.O.S.   *Journal of the Palestine Oriental Society*

J.R.A.I.   *Journal of the Royal Anthropological Institute*

J.R.A.S.   *Journal of the Royal Asiatic Society*

J.R.S.A. Ireland   *Journal of the Royal Society of Antiquaries of Ireland*

J.W.H.   *Journal of World History*

K.A.V.   *Keilschrifttexte aus Assur verschiedenen Inhalts*

K.F.   *Kleinasiatische Forschungen*

K.U.B.   *Keilschrifturkunden aus Boghazköi*

M.D.O.G.   *Mitteilungen der Deutschen Orient-Gesellschaft*

Mém. Ac. Inscr. B.-L.   *Mémoires de l'Académie des Inscriptions et Belles-Lettres*

Mém. D.P.   *Mémoires de la Délégation en Perse*

Mém. Miss. fr. Caire.   *Mémoires publiés par les membres de la Mission archéologique française au Caire*

Mitt. deutsch Inst. Kairo.   *Mitteilungen des deutschen Instituts für ägyptische Altertumskunde, Kairo*

Mitt. Inst. Or.   *Mitteilungen des Instituts für Orientforschung, Berlin*

M.J.   *Museum Journal, University of Pennsylvania*

Mon. Ant.   *Monumenti Antichi (Milan)*

M.U.S.J.   *Mélanges de l'Université St.-Joseph*

M.V.A.G.   *Mitteilungen der vorderasiatisch-ägyptischen Gesellschaft*

O.I.C.   *Oriental Institute Communications*

O.I.P.   *Oriental Institute Publications*

O.L.Z.   *Orientalistische Literaturzeitung*

Or.   *Orientalia*

Or. Suecana.   *Orientalia Suecana*

P.B.S.   *University of Pennsylvania. The University Museum. Publications of the Babylonian Section*

P.E.F.Q.S.   *Palestine Exploration Fund, Quarterly Statement*

P.E.Q.   *Palestine Exploration Quarterly*

P.P.S.   *Proceedings of the Prehistoric Society*

Praehist. Zeitschr.   *Praehistorische Zeitschrift*

Praktika   Πρακτικὰ τῆς 'Αρχαιολογικῆς 'Εταιρείας

Proc. Amer. Philosoph. Soc.   *Proceedings of the American Philosophical Society*

Proc. Brit. Acad.   *Proceedings of the British Academy*

Proc. R.I.A.   *Proceedings of the Royal Irish Academy*

Proc. Roy. Soc. A (B)   *Proceedings of the Royal Society of London,* A (B)

Proc. Roy. Soc. Tasmania.   *Proceedings of the Royal Society of Tasmania*

P.S.B.A.   *Proceedings of the Society of Biblical Archaeology*

P.W.   Pauly-Wissowa-Kroll-Mittelhaus, *Real-encyclopädie der classischen Altertumswissenschaft*

Q.D.A.P.   *Quarterly of the Department of Antiquities of Palestine*

Quart. Journ. Geol. Soc. Lond.   *Quarterly Journal of the Geological Society of London*

Quart. Journ. Roy. Met. Soc.   *Quarterly Journal of the Royal Meteorological Society*

R.A.   *Revue d'Assyriologie et d'Archéologie orientale*

R.D.A.C.   *Report of the Department of Antiquities, Cyprus*

Rec. Champ.   *Recueil d'études égyptologiques dédiées à la mémoire de Jean-François Champollion*

Rec. trav.   *Recueil de travaux relatifs à la philologie et à l'archéologie égyptiennes et assyriennes*

R.E.G.   *Revue des études grecques*

Rev. Anth.   *Revue Anthropologique*

Rev. bibl.   *Revue biblique internationale*

Rev. d'égyptol.   *Revue d'égyptologie*

Rev. géogr. physique et géol. dynamique.   *Revue de géographie physique et de géologie dynamique*

Rev. sci.   *Revue scientifique*

R.H.A.   *Revue Hittite et Asianique*

Riv. di Antropol.   *Rivista di Antropologia*

Riv. di Sci. Preist.   *Rivista di Scienze Preistoriche*

Riv. stud. or.   *Rivista degli studi orientali*

R.L.A. *Reallexikon der Assyriologie*
S.A.O.C. *Oriental Institute of the University of Chicago, Series in Ancient Oriental Civilization*
Sitzungsb. Berlin (München, etc.) *Sitzungsberichte der Preussischen (Bayerischen, etc.) Akademie der Wissenschaften*
Sov. Arkh. *Sovetskaya Arkhitektura*
Top. Bibl. B. Porter and R. L. B. Moss, *Topographical Bibliography of Ancient Egyptian Hieroglyphic Texts, Reliefs, and Paintings*
Trans. N.Y. Acad. Sci. *Transactions of the New York Academy of Sciences*
T. u. M. *Texte und Materialen der Hilprecht Sammlung*, Jena
U.E. *Ur Excavations*
U.E.T. *Ur Excavations: Texts*
Unters. *Untersuchungen zur Geschichte und Altertumskunde Ägyptens* (ed. K. Sethe, later H. Kees)
Urk. *Urkunden des ägyptischen Altertums*, ed. G. Steindorff, later H. Grapow
U.V.B. *Uruk: vorläufiger Bericht*
V.A.S. *Vorderasiatische Schriftdenkmäler*
We. Or. *Die Welt des Orients*
Wiad. Arch. *Wiadomości Archaeologiczne (Bulletin archéologique polonais)*
W.P.Z. *Wiener prähistorische Zeitschrift*
W.Z.K.M. *Wiener Zeitschrift für die Kunde des Morgenlandes*
Z.A. *Zeitschrift für Assyriologie und vorderasiatische Archäologie*
Z.Ä.S. *Zeitschrift fur ägyptische Sprache und Altertumskunde*
Z.D.M.G. *Zeitschrift der Deutschen Morgenländischen Gesellschaft*
Z.D.P.V. *Zeitschrift des Deutschen Palästina-Vereins*
Z.E. *Zeitschrift für Ethnologie*
Z. f. schweiz. Archäol u. Kunstgeschichte. *Zeitschrift für schweizerische Archaeologie und Kunstgeschichte*
Z.V. *Zeitschrift für Vorgeschichte*

BIBLIOGRAPHY

CHAPTER I

I. INTRODUCTION

1. Stille, H. *Grundfragen der Vergleichenden Tektonik.* Berlin, 1924.
2. Suess, E. *The Face of the Earth (Das Antlitz der Erde)*, 5 vols. (translated by H. B. C. Sollas). Oxford, 1904–24.

II. THE AFRASIAN PLATFORM

1. Blackett, P. M. S. 'Comparisons of ancient climates with the ancient latitudes deduced from rock magnetism measurements.' In *Proc. Roy. Soc.* A, 263 (1961), 1 ff.
2. King, L. C. *The Morphology of the Earth.* Edinburgh, 1962.
3. Runcorn, S. K. 'Climatic change through geological time in the light of the palaeomagnetic evidence of polar wandering and continental drift.' In *Quart. Journ Roy. Met. Soc.* 87 (1961), 282 ff.
4. du Toit, A. *Our Wandering Continents.* Edinburgh, 1937.
5. Wegener, A. *Die Entstehung der Kontinente und Ozeane.* Ed. 3 (English translation by J. G. A. Skerl, *The Origin of Continents and Oceans*). London, 1924.

III. THE EURASIAN PLATFORM

1. Bailey, E B. 'The Desert Shores of the Chalk Seas.' In *Geol. Mag.* 61 (1924), 102 ff.
2. Wager, L. R. 'Geological Investigations in East Greenland. Part IV. The Stratigraphy and Tectonics of Knud Rasmussens Land and the Kangerdlugssnaq Region.' In *Meddelelser om Grønland*, 134, Nr. 5, 1 ff. Copenhagen, 1947.

IV. THE TETHYS AND THE MID-WORLD FOLD BELT

1. Argand, E. 'La Tectonique de l'Asie.' In *C.-R. du congr. géol. int. (XIIIᵉ session, Belgique, 1922)*, 1, 171 ff. Liége, 1924.
2. Aubouin, J., 'A propos d'un centenaire: les aventures de la notion géosynclinale.' In *Rev. géogr. physique et géol. dynamique*, 2 (1958–9), 135 ff.
3. de Böckh, H., Lees, G. M. and Richardson, F. D. S. 'Contribution to the Stratigraphy and Tectonics of the Iranian Ranges.' In *The Structure of Asia*, ed. J. W. Gregory, 58 ff. London, 1929.
4. Carey, S. W. 'The orocline concept in tectonics.' In *Proc. Roy. Soc. Tasmania*, 89 (1955), 255 ff.
5. Glangeaud, L. 'Essai de classification géodynamique des chaînes et des phénomènes orogéniques.' In *Rev. géogr. physique et géol. dynamique*, 1 (1957), 200 ff.
6. Kober, L. *Der Bau der Erde.* Ed. 1. Berlin, 1921; Ed. 2, 1928.
7. de Sitter, L. U. *Structural Geology.* London, 1956.

V. ORIGINS OF THE MODERN SEAS, RIVERS AND MOUNTAINS

1. Cloos, H. 'Hebung, Spaltung und Vulkanismus.' In *Geologische Rundschau*, Stuttgart, 30 (4*a*), (1939).
2. Harrison, J. V. and Falcon, N. L. 'Gravity Collapse Structures and Mountain Ranges as exemplified in South-Western Iran.' In *Quart. Journ. Geol. Soc. Lond.* 92 (1936), 91 ff.
3. Holmes, A. *Principles of Physical Geology.* Ed. 2. London, 1965.
4. Lutaud, L. 'La tectogénèse et l'évolution structurale de la Provence.' In *Rev. géogr. physique et géol. dynamique*, 1 (1957), 103 ff.
5. de Martonne, E. *Géographie Universelle, IV, Europe Centrale.* Paris, 1931.
6. Merla, G. 'Geologia dell' Appennino Settentrionale.' In *Boll. Soc. Geol. Ital.* 70 (1951), 95 ff.
7. Ogilvie, A. G. 'Physiography and Settlements in Southern Macedonia.' In *Geogr. Rev.* 11 (1921), 172 ff.
8. Wager, L. R. 'The Arun River Drainage Pattern and the Rise of the Himalaya.' In *G.J.* 89 (1937), 239 ff.

CHAPTER II

I. THE NATURAL, EARLY POSTGLACIAL ENVIRONMENT

1. Hammond, E. H. 'Small-scale continental landform maps.' In *Ann. Assoc. Amer. Geog.* 44 (1954), 32–42.
2. Helbaek, H. 'Domestication of food plants in the Old World.' In *Science*, 130 (1959), 365–72.
3. Movius, H. L. 'Radiocarbon dates and Upper Palaeolithic archaeology in central and western Europe.' In *Current Anthropol.* 1 (1960), 355–91.

II. PHYSICAL CONDITIONS IN SOUTH-EASTERN EUROPE DURING THE LAST GLACIAL PERIOD

1. Butzer, K. W. *Environment and archaeology: an introduction to Pleistocene geography*. London, 1964.
2. Frenzel, B. *Die Vegetations- und Landschaftszonen Nord-Eurasians während der letzten Eiszeit und während der postglazialen Wärmezeit.* 2 vols. In *Abh. Mainz, Math.-Naturwiss. Kl.* 1959, No. 13; 1960, No. 6. Wiesbaden, 1959–60.
3. Poser, H. 'Boden- und Klimaverhältnisse in Mittel- und Westeuropa.' In *Erdkunde*, 2 (1948), 53–68.
4. Woldstedt, P. *Das Eiszeitalter*. Vol. II. Stuttgart, 1958.

III. PREHISTORIC GEOGRAPHY OF SOUTH-WESTERN ASIA

1. Bate, D. M. A. 'The fossil antelopes of Palestine in Natufian Times.' In *Geol. Mag.* 77 (1940), 418–33.
2. Braidwood, R. J., Howe, B. *et al.* 'Prehistoric investigations in Iraqi Kurdistan'. In *S.A.O.C.* No. 31 (1960).
3. Buringh, P. 'Living conditions in the lower Mesopotamian Plain in Ancient times.' In *Sumer*, 13 (1957), 30–46.
4. Butzer, K. W. *Quaternary Stratigraphy and Climate in the Near East. Bonner Geographische Abh.* 24. Bonn, 1859.
5. Butzer, K. W. 'Russian climate and the hydrological budget of the Caspian Sea.' In *Revue canadienne de Géographie*, 12 (1958), 129–39.
6. Garrod, D. A. E. and Bate, D. M. A. *The Stone Age of Mt Carmel.* Vol. I. Oxford, 1937.
7. Holm, D. A. 'Desert geomorphology in the Arabian Peninsula.' In *Science*, 132 (1960), 1369–79.
8. Howell, F. C. 'Upper Pleistocene stratigraphy and early Man in the Levant.' In *Proc. Am. Phil. Soc.* 103 (1959), 1–65.
9. Jacobsen, T. and Adams, R. M. 'Salt and silt in ancient Mesopotamian agriculture.' In *Science*, 128 (1958), 1251–57.
10. Lees, G. M. and Falcon, N. L. 'The geographical history of the Mesopotamian plains.' In *G.J.* 118 (1952), 24–39.
11. Neuville, R. *Le Paléolithique et le Mésolithique du Désert de Judée. Arch. de l'Inst. de Paléont. hum.* Mém. 24. Paris, 1951.
12. Nioradze, G. K. 'Das Paläolithikum Georgiens.' *Trans. II I.N.Q. etc. Congress*, Moscow–Leningrad (1935), 5, 225–36.
13. Reed, C. A. and Braidwood, R. J. 'Toward the reconstruction of the environmental sequence of northeastern Iraq.' In *S.A.O.C.* No. 31 (1960), 163–74.
14. Stier, H. E., Kirsten, E. *et al. Westermanns Atlas zur Weltgeschichte.* I. *Vorzeit und Altertum.* Brunswick, 1956.
15. Wright, H. E. 'Pleistocene glaciation in Kurdistan.' *Eiszeitalter und Gegenwart*, 12 (1962), 131–164.

IV. PREHISTORIC GEOGRAPHY OF EGYPT AND THE NILE VALLEY

1. Butzer, K. W. *Das ökologische Problem der neolithischen Felsbilder der östlichen Sahara.* In *Abh. Mainz, Math.-Naturwiss. Kl.* 1958, 20–49. Wiesbaden, 1958.
2. Butzer, K. W. 'Some recent geological deposits in the Egyptian Nile Valley.' In *G.J.* 125 (1959), 75–9.
3. Butzer, K. W. 'Contributions to the Pleistocene geology of the Nile Valley.' In *Erdkunde*, 11 (1959), 46–67.
4. Butzer, K. W. *Die Naturlandschaft Ägyptens während der Vorgeschichte und der Dynastischen Zeit.* In *Abh. Mainz, Math.-Naturwiss. Kl.* 1959, No. 2. Wiesbaden, 1959.
5. Butzer, K. W. 'Environment and human ecology in Egypt during Predynastic and early Dynastic times.' In *Bull. Soc. Géogr. d'Égypte*, 32 (1959), 36–87.
6. Butzer, K. W. 'Remarks on the geography of settlement in the Nile Valley during Hellenistic times.' In *Bull. Société de Géogr. d'Égypte*, 33 (1960), 5–36.
7. Butzer, K. W. 'Archaeology and geology in Ancient Egypt: Geomorphological analysis permits reconstruction of the geography of prehistoric settlement.' In *Science*, 132 (1960), 1617–24.
8. Butzer, K. W. 'Pleistocene palaeoclimates of the Kurkur Oasis, Egypt.' In *Canadian Geographer*, 8 (1964), 125–141.
9. Butzer, K. W. and Hansen, C. L. 'On Pleistocene evolution of the Nile Valley in southern Egypt.' In *Canadian Geographer*, 9 (1965), 74–83.
10. Caton-Thompson, G. 'The Levalloisian industries of Egypt.' In *P.P.S.* 12 (1946), 57–120.
11. Caton-Thompson, G. and Gardner, E. W. *The Desert Fayum.* 2 vols. London, 1934.
12. Passarge, S. 'Die Urlandschaft Ägyptens.' *Nova Acta Leopoldina*, 9 (1940), 77–152.
13. Sandford, K. S. *Paleolithic Man and the Nile Valley in Upper and Middle Egypt.* O.I.P. 18. Chicago, 1934.
14. Sandford, K. S. 'Problems of the Nile Valley.' In *Geogr. Rev.* 26 (1936), 67–76.
15. Sandford, K. S. and Arkell, W. J. *Paleolithic Man and the Nile Fayum Divide.* O.I.P. 10. Chicago, 1929.
16. Sandford, K. S. and Arkell, W. J. *Paleolithic Man and the Nile Valley in Nubia and Upper Egypt.* O.I.P. 17. Chicago, 1933.
17. Sandford, K. S. and Arkell, W. J. *Paleolithic Man and the Nile Valley in Lower Egypt.* O.I.P. 46. Chicago, 1939.

CHAPTER III

PALAEOLITHIC TIMES

I. EGYPT

1. Ball, J. *Contributions to the Geography of Egypt.* Survey and Mines Department, Cairo, 1939.
2. Bovier-Lapierre, P. 'Le Paléolithique stratifié des environs du Caire.' In *L'Anthropologie*, 35 (1925), 37 ff.

3. Bovier-Lapierre, P. 'Les gisements paléolithiques de la plaine de l'Abbasieh.' In *Bull. Inst. d'Ég.* 8 (1925–6), 257 ff.

4. Butzer, K. W. 'Contributions to the Pleistocene Geology of the Nile Valley.' In *Erdkunde, Archiv für wissenschaftliche Geographie*, 13 (1959), 46 ff.

5. Caton-Thompson, G. 'The Levalloisian Industries of Egypt.' In *P.P.S.* 12 (1946), 57 ff.

6. Caton-Thompson, G. *The Aterian Industry: its Place and Significance in the Palaeolithic World* (Huxley Memorial Lecture, Royal Anthropological Institute). London, 1947.

7. Caton-Thompson, G. and Gardner, E. W. *The Desert Faiyum.* 2 vols. London, 1934.

8. Caton-Thompson, G. and Gardner, E. W. *Kharga Oasis in Prehistory.* London, 1952.

9. Huzayyin, S. A. *The Place of Egypt in Prehistory.* Cairo, 1941.

10. Little, O. H. 'Recent Geological Work in the Faiyum and in the Adjoining Portion of the Nile Valley.' In *Bull. Inst. d'Ég.* 18 (1935–6), 201 ff.

11. Sandford, K. S. *Palaeolithic Man and the Nile Valley in Upper and Middle Egypt (O.I.P.* 18). Chicago, 1934.

12. Sandford, K. S. and Arkell, W. J. *Palaeolithic Man and the Nile-Faiyum Divide (O.I.P.* 10). Chicago, 1929.

13. Sandford, K. S. and Arkell, W. J. *Palaeolithic Man and the Nile Valley in Nubia and Upper Egypt (O.I.P.* 17). Chicago, 1933.

14. Sandford, K.S. and Arkell, W. J. *Palaeolithic Man and the Nile Valley in Lower Egypt (O.I.P.* 46). Chicago, 1939.

15. Vignard, E. 'Une nouvelle industrie lithique : le Sébilien.' In *Bull. Soc. préh. fr.* 25 (1928), 200 ff.

16. Zeuner, F. E. *Dating the Past.* Ed. 4. London, 1958.

II. WESTERN ASIA IN GENERAL

1. Garrod, D. A. E. 'The Relations between Southwest Asia and Europe in the Later Palaeolithic Age.' In *Journal of World Hist.* 1 (1953), 13 ff.

2. Howell, F. C. 'Upper Pleistocene Men of the Southwest Asian Mousterian.' In *Hundert Jahre Neandertaler*, ed. G. R. von Koenigswald (Utrecht, 1958), 185 ff.

3. Howell, F. C. 'Upper Pleistocene Stratigraphy and Early Man in the Levant.' In *Proc. Am. Philosoph. Soc.* 103 (1959), 1 ff.

III. SYRIA–LEBANON–PALESTINE

1. Ewing, F. J. 'Preliminary Note on the Excavations at the Palaeolithic Site of Ksâr Akil.' In *Antiq.* 21 (1947), 186 ff.

2. Ewing, F. J. 'The Treasures of Ksâr Akil.' In *Thought (Fordham University Quarterly)*, 24 (1949), 255 ff.

3. Fleisch, H. 'Dépôts préhistoriques de la côte libanaise et leur place dans la chronologie basée sur le Quaternaire marin.' In *Quaternaria*, 3 (1956), 101 ff.

4. Garrod, D. A. E. 'Excavations at the Cave of Shukba, Palestine, 1928.' In *P.P.S.* 8 (1942), 1 ff.

5. Garrod, D. A. E. 'A Transitional Industry from the Base of the Upper Palaeolithic in Palestine and Syria.' In *J.R.A.I.* 81 (1952), 121 ff.

6. Garrod, D. A. E. 'Excavations at the Mugharet Kebara, Mount Carmel, 1931 : the Aurignacian Industries.' In *P.P.S.* 20 (1954), 155 ff.

7. Garrod, D. A. E. 'The Mugharet el-Emireh in Lower Galilee : Type Station of the Emireh Industry.' In *J.R.A.I.* 85 (1955), 1 ff.
8. Garrod, D. A. E. 'Acheuléo-Jabroudien et "Pré-Aurignacien" de la grotte du Taboun (Mont Carmel) : étude stratigraphique et chronologique.' In *Quaternaria*, 3 (1956), 39 ff.
9. Garrod, D. A. E. and Bate, D. M. A. *The Stone-Age of Mount Carmel*, I. Oxford, 1937.
10. Garrod, D. A. E. and Gardner, E. W. 'Pleistocene Coastal Deposits in Palestine.' In *Nature*, 135 (1935), 908.
11. Garrod, D. A. E. and Henri-Martin, G. *Fouilles au Ras el-Kelb, Liban, 1959*. 16e Congrès Préhistorique de France, Monaco, 1959.
12. Garrod, D. A. E. and Kirkbride, D. *Excavation of a Palaeolithic Rock-shelter at Adlun, Lebanon, 1958*. 5th International Congress of Prehistoric and Protohistoric Studies. Hamburg, 1958.
13. Haller, J. 'Notes de préhistoire phénicienne : l'Abri de Abou-Halka (Tripoli).' In *Bull. M.B.* 6 (1942-3), 1 ff.
14. Kenyon, K. 'Earliest Jericho.' In *Antiq.* 33 (1959), 5 ff.
15. McCown, T. D. and Keith, A. *The Stone-Age of Mount Carmel*, II. Oxford, 1939
16. Neuville, R. *Le Paléolithique et le Mésolithique du désert de Judée. Arch. de l'Inst. de Paléont. hum.*, no. 24. Paris, 1951.
17. Neuville, R., and Vaufrey, R. 'L'Acheuléen Supérieur de la grotte d'Oumm Qatafa.' In *L'Anthropologie*, 41 (1931), 13 ff., 249 ff.
18. Picard, L. 'Inferences on the Problem of the Pleistocene Climate of Palestine and Syria Drawn from the Flora, Fauna, and Stratigraphy.' In *P.P.S.* 3 (1937), 58 ff.
19. Picard, L. *Structure and Evolution of Palestine*. Hebrew University, Jerusalem, 1943.
20. Rust, A. *Die Höhlenfunde von Jabrud (Syrien)*. Neumünster, 1950.
21. Stekelis, M. 'Rephaim-Baqa'a, a Palaeolithic Station in the Vicinity of Jerusalem.' In *J.P.O.S.* 21 (1947), 80 ff.
22. Stekelis, M. *The Implementiferous Beds of the Jordan Valley*. 4th International Congress of Prehistoric and Protohistoric Studies, Madrid, 1954, 391 ff. Zaragoza, 1956.
23. Turville-Petre, F. 'Excavations in the Mugharet el-Kebarah.' In *J.R.A.I.* 62 (1932), 270 ff.
24. Turville-Petre, F. and Keith, A. *Researches in Prehistoric Galilee, 1925-1926, and a Report on the Galilee Skull*. London, 1927.
25. Vaufrey, R. 'Paléolithique et Mésolithique palestiniens.' In *Rev. sci.* 77 (1939), 390 ff.
26. Wetzel, R. and Haller, J. 'Le Quaternaire côtier de la région de Tripoli (Liban).' In *Notes et Mémoires de la Délégation de France au Liban*, 4 (1945), 1 ff.
27. Zumoffen, G. *La Phénicie avant les Phéniciens*. Beirut, 1900.
28. Zumoffen, G. 'L'âge de la pierre en Phénicie.' In *Anthropos*, 3 (1908), 431 ff.

IV. ANATOLIA

1. Kansu, S. A. *Nouvelles découvertes préhistoriques dans les environs d'Ankara*. Ikinci Türk Tarih Kongresi. Istanbul, 1937.
2. Kansu, S. A. 'Stone-age Cultures in Turkey.' In *A.J.A.* 51 (1947), 227 ff.
3. Kiliç Kökten, I. 'Ein allgemeiner Überblick über die prähistorischen Forschungen in Karaïn-Höhle bei Antalya.' In *Belleten*, 19 (1955), 284 ff.

4. Pfannenstiel, M. *Die altsteinzeitlichen Kulturen Anatoliens.* Istanbul, 1941.
5. Pittard, E. 'Découverte de la civilisation paléolithique en Asie Mineure.' In *Archives suisses d'Anthropologie générale*, 5 (1928), 135 ff.
6. Pittard, E. 'Silex taillés levalloisiens recueillis dans les alluvions des plateaux d'Anatolie.' In *Rev. Anth.* 68 (1939), 69 ff.

V. THE NORTH ARABIAN DESERT

1. Buxton, L. H. D. 'Worked Flints from the N. Arabian Desert.' In *A.J.* 6 (1926), 432 ff.
2. Coon, C. S. *Seven Caves: Archaeological Excavations in the Middle East.* New York, 1957.
3. Field, H. 'Early Man in North Arabia.' In *Natural History*, 29 (1929).
4. Harding, G. L. 'Recent Discoveries in Jordan.' In *P.E.Q.* 90 (1958), 7 ff.
5. Kirkbride, D. V. W. 'A Kebaran Rock-shelter in Wadi Madamagh, near Petra, Jordan.' In *Man*, 58 (1958), 55 ff.
6. Rhotert, H. *Transjordanien.* Stuttgart, 1938.
7. Waechter, J. *et al.* 'The Excavations at Wadi Dhobai, 1937–1938, and the Dhobaian Industry.' In *J.P.O.S.* 18 (1938), 1 ff.

VI. SOUTHERN KURDISTĀN

1. Braidwood, R. J. 'From Cave to Village in Prehistoric Iraq.' In *Bull. A.S.O.R.* 124 (1951), 12 ff.
2. Braidwood, R. J. 'The Iraq-Jarmo Project of the Oriental Institute of the University of Chicago. Season 1954–1955.' In *Sumer*, 10 (1954), 120 ff.
3. Coon, C. S. *Cave Explorations in Iran, 1949.* University Museum, Philadelphia, 1951.
4. Garrod, D. A. E. 'The Palaeolithic of Southern Kurdistan.' In *Bull. A.S.P.R.* 6 (1930), 13 ff.
5. Solecki, R. S. 'Shanidar Cave, a Palaeolithic Site.' In *Sumer*, 8 (1952), 127 ff.
6. Solecki, R. S. 'Shanidar Cave, a Palaeolithic Site in Northern Iraq, and its Relationship to the Stone-Age Sequences of Iraq.' In *Sumer*, 11 (1955), 14 ff.
7. Solecki, R. S. 'Shanidar Cave, a Palaeolithic Site in Northern Iraq.' *Smithsonian Report*, Washington, D.C., 1954, 389 ff.
8. Solecki, R. S. 'Early Man in Cave and Village at Shanidar, Kurdistan, Iraq.' In *Trans. N.Y. Acad. Sci.* 21 (1959), 712 ff.
9. Wright, H. E., Jr. and Howe, B. 'Soundings at Barda Balka.' In *Sumer*, 7 (1951), 107 ff.

A. ADDENDUM

EGYPT

1. Hayes, W. C. *Most Ancient Egypt.* Chicago, 1965.

MESOLITHIC TIMES

VIII. NEOTHERMAL ENVIRONMENT AND ITS IMPACT

1. Bate, D. M. A. 'The Fossil Antelopes of Palestine in Natufian (Mesolithic Times).' In *Geol. Mag.* 77 (1940), 418 ff.
2. Clark, J. G. D. 'A Survey of the Mesolithic Phase in the Prehistory of Europe and South-west Asia.' In *Atti del VI Congr. Inter. delle Scienze Preistoriche e Protoistoriche* (Rome, 1962), 97 ff.
3. Donner, J. and Kurtén, B. 'The Floral and Faunal Succession of "Cueva del Toll", Spain.' In *Eiszeitalter und Gegenwart*, 8 (1957), 72 ff.

4. Firbas, F. *Spät- und nacheiszeitliche Waldgeschichte Mitteleuropas nördlich der Alpen.* Jena, 1949.

5. Godwin, H. *The History of the British Flora.* Cambridge, 1956.

6. Godwin, H. 'Coastal Peat-beds of the North Sea Region, as Indices of Land and Sea-level Changes.' In *New Phytologist*, 44 (1945), 29 ff.

7. Godwin, H. and Willis, E. H. 'Radiocarbon Dating of the Late-glacial Period in Britain.' In *Proc. Roy. Soc.* ser. B, 150 (1959), 199 ff.

8. Higgs, E. S. 'Some Pleistocene Faunas of the Mediterranean Coastal Areas.' In *P.P.S.* 27 (1961), 144 ff.

9. Iversen, J. 'The Late-glacial Flora of Denmark and its Relation to Climate and Soil.' In *Studies in Vegetational History in honour of Knud Jessen* (Copenhagen, 1954), 87 ff.

10. Mitchell, G. F. 'Studies in Irish Quaternary Deposits: no. 7.' In *Proc. R.I.A.* 53, sect. B (1951), 192 ff.

11. Mitchell, G. F. and Parkes, H. M. 'The Giant Deer in Ireland.' In *Proc. R.I.A.* 52, sect. B (1949), 291 ff.

12. Munthe, H. *Om Nordens, främst Baltikums, Senkvartära.* Stockholm, 1940.

13. Solecki, Ralph S. 'Palaeoclimatology and Archaeology in the Near East.' In *Ann. N.Y. Acad. Sci.* 95 (1961), 729 ff.

IX. THE MESOLITHIC SETTLEMENT OF NORTHERN EUROPE

1. Althin, C.-A. *The Chronology of the Stone Age Settlement of Scania, Sweden*, 1. Lund, 1954.

2. Bøe, J. and Nummedal, A. *Le Finnmarkien. Les origines de la civilisation dans l'extrême-nord de l'Europe.* Oslo, 1936.

3. Brøndsted, J. *Danmarks Oldtid.* 1, *Stenalderen.* Copenhagen, 1957.

4. Chmielewska, M. 'A Tardenoisian Grave at Janisławice, Skierniewice Admin. District.' In *Wiad. Arch.* 20 (1951), 23 ff.

5. Clark, J. G. D. *The Mesolithic Settlement of Northern Europe.* Cambridge, 1936.

6. Clark, J. G. D. *Prehistoric Europe: the Economic Basis.* London, 1952.

7. Clark, J. G. D. *Excavations at Star Carr. An Early Mesolithic Site at Seamer, Yorkshire.* Cambridge, 1954.

8. Clark, J. G. D. 'A Microlithic Industry from the Cambridgeshire Fenland.' In *P.P.S.* 21 (1955), 3 ff.

9. Clark, J. G. D. 'Neolithic Bows from Somerset, England, and the Prehistory of Archery in North-western Europe.' In *P.P.S.* 29 (1963), 50–98.

10. Clark, J. G. D. and Rankine, W. F. 'Excavations at Farnham, Surrey (1937–1938), the Horsham Culture and the Question of Mesolithic Dwellings. In *P.P.S.* 5 (1939), 61 ff.

11. *Danske Oldsager.* 1, *Aeldre Stenalder.* Copenhagen, 1948.

12. Degerbøl, M. 'On a Find of a Preboreal Domestic Dog (*Canis familiaris*, L.) from Star Carr, Yorkshire, with Remarks on Other Mesolithic Dogs.' In *P.P.S.* 27 (1961), 35 ff.

13. Degerbøl, M. 'Om Kannibalisme i Danmarks Stenalder.' In *Dyr i Natur og Museum*, 1941, 25 ff.

14. Freundt, E. A. 'Komsa-Fosna-Sandarna.' In *Acta Arch.* 19 (1948), 1 ff.

15. Higgs, E. S. 'The Excavation of a Late Mesolithic Site at Downton, near Salisbury, Wilts.' In *P.P.S.* 25 (1959), 209 ff.

16. Jorgensen, Svend. 'Kongemosen. Endnu en Aamose-Boplads fra Aeldre Stenalder.' In *Kuml*, 1956, 23 ff.

17. Lacaille, A. D. *The Stone Age in Scotland*. London, 1954.
18. Madsen, A. P. *et al. Affaldsdynger fra Stenalderen i Danmark*. Copenhagen, 1900.
19. Mathiassen, T. *et al. Dyrholmen. En Stenalderboplads paa Djursland*. Copenhagen, 1942.
20. Mitchell, G. F. 'The "Larnian" Culture: A Review.' In *J.R.S.A. Ireland*, 79 (1949), 170 ff.
21. Movius, Hallam. *The Irish Stone Age*. Cambridge, 1942.
22. Rust, A. *Die alt- und mittelsteinzeitlichen Funde von Stellmoor*. Neumünster, 1943.
23. Schuldt, E. 'Ein mittelsteinzeitlicher Siedlungsplatz von Hohen Viecheln, Kreis Wismar.' In *Jahrb. f. Bodendenkmalpflege in Mecklenburg*, 1955, 7 ff.
24. Schwabedissen, H. *Die Federmesser-Gruppen des nordwesteuropäischen Flachlands*. Neumünster, 1954.
25. Troels-Smith, J. 'Ertebøllekultur-Bondekultur.' In *Aarbøger*, 1953, 5 ff.
26. Wainwright, G. J. 'The Microlithic Industries of Wales.' In *P.P.S.* 29 (1963), 99–132.
27. Zeist, W. van. 'Die mesolithische boot van Pesse.' *Nieuwe Drentsche Volksalmanak*, 1957, 4 ff.

X. SOUTH-WEST EUROPE AND NORTH AFRICA

1. Almagro, M. in *Historia de España* (ed. R. Menéndez Pidal), vol. I, chs. V, VI. Madrid, 1946.
2. Almagro, M. *Manual de Historia Universal*. T. I, *Prehistoria*, ch. VIII. Madrid, 1960.
3. Balout, L. *Préhistoire de l'Afrique du Nord*. Paris, 1955.
4. Blanc, A. C. 'Dei microbulini e della precoce comparsa del mesolitico in Italia.' In *Riv. di Antropol.* 32 (1939), 1–38.
5. Breuil, H. *Les peintures rupestres schématiques de la Péninsule Ibérique*, II. Lagny, 1933.
6. Breuil, H. and Zbyszewski, G. 'Révision des industries mésolithiques de Muge et de Magos.' In *Com. dos Serviços Geológicos de Portugal*, 28 (1947), 149 ff.
7. Cerdán Marquez, C., Leisner, G. and V. *Los Sepulcros megalíticos de Huelva*. Madrid, 1952.
8. Clark, J. G. D. 'Blade and Trapeze Industries of the European Stone Age.' In *P.P.S.* 24 (1958), 24 ff.
9. Coulanges, L. *Les gisements préhistoriques de Sauveterre la Lémance. Arch. de l'Inst. de Paléont. hum.*, Mém. 14. Paris, 1935.
10. Daniel, M. and R. 'Le Tardenoisien classique du Tardenois.' In *L'Anthropologie*, 52 (1948), 411 ff.
11. Lacam, R., Niederlander, A., and Vallois, H.-V. *Le gisement mésolithique du Cuzol de Gramat. Arch. de l'Inst. de Paléont. hum.*, Mém. 21. Paris, 1944.
12. Leisner, G. 'Die Malereien des dolmen Pedra Coberta.' In *Ipek*, 1934, 23 ff.
13. Leisner, G. and V. *Antas do Concelho de Reguengos de Monsaraz*. Lisbon, 1951.
14. McBurney, C. B. M. *The Stone Age of Northern Africa*. London, 1960.
15. Obermaier, H. *Fossil Man in Spain*, ch. X. New Haven, 1925.
16. Péquart, M. and S.-J., Boule, M. and Vallois, H. *Téviec: station-nécropole mésolithique du Morbihan. Arch. de l'Inst. de Paléont. hum.*, Mém. 18. Paris, 1937.

17. Péquart, M. and S.-J. *Hoëdic: deuxième station-nécropole mésolithique côtier Armoricain.* Antwerp, 1954.
18. Pericot, L. *La Cueva del Parpalló.* Madrid, 1942.
19. Pericot, L. 'La Cueva de la Cocina (Dos Aguas).' In *Arch. de Prehistoria Levantina,* 2 (1945), 33 ff.
20. Pericot, L. *La España Primitiva.* Madrid, 1950.
21. Radmilli, A. M. and Tongiorgi, E. 'Gli scavi nella grotta La Porta di Positano. Contributo alla conoscenza del mesolitico italiano.' In *Riv. di Sci. Preist.* 13 (1958), 91 ff.
22. Roche, Abbé J. *L'industrie préhistorique du Cabeço d'Amoreira (Muge).* Porto, 1951.
23. Roche, Abbé J. *Le gisement mésolithique de Moita do Sebastião.* Lisbon, 1960.
24. Thompson, M. W. 'Azilian Harpoons.' In *P.P.S.* 20 (1954), 193 ff.
25. Vaufrey, R. *L'art rupestre nord-africain. Arch. de l'Inst. intern. de Paléont. hum.,* Mém. 20. Paris, 1939.
26. Vilaseca, S. *La Estación Taller de Silex de L'Areny.* Madrid, 1961.

XI. CENTRAL AND EASTERN EUROPE

1. Bandi, H.-G. and Lüdin, C. 'Birsmatten-Basishöhle.' In *Jahrb. des Berni-schen Hist. Mus. in Bern,* 34 (1954), 193 ff.
2. Barta, J. 'Pleistocénne piesočné duny pri Sered a ich paleolitické a mezolitické osídlenie.' In *Slovenska Archeologia,* 5 (1957), 5 ff.
3. Bodmer-Gessner, V. 'Provisorische Mitteilungen über die Ausgrabung einer mesolithischen Siedlung in Schötz ("Fischerhausern") Wauwilermoos, Kt. Luzern, durch H. Reinerth im Jahre 1933.' In *Jahrb. der schweiz. Ges. f. Urgeschichte,* 50 (1949/50), 108 ff.
4. Boriskovskii, P. I. *Paleolit Ukrainy.* In *Mat. i Issled. po Arkheol. S.S.S.R.,* no. 40 (1953).
5. Chmielewska, M. *Huttes d'inhabitation épipaléolithique de Witów, distr. de Łeczyca.* Łódz, 1961.
6. Chmielewska, M. and Chmielewski, W. 'Stratigraphie et chronologie de la dune de Witów, distr. de Łeczyca.' In *Biul. Peryglacjalny,* 8 (1960), 133 ff.
7. Formazov, A. A. 'Periodization of Mesolithic Sites in the U.S.S.R. in Europe.' In *Sovetskaya Arkheologiya,* 21 (1955), 38 ff.
8. Gersbach, E. 'Das mittelbadische Mesolithikum.' In *Badische Fundberichte,* 19. Jhg. (1951), 15 ff.
9. Gersbach, E. 'Ein Harpunenbruchstück aus einer Grube der jüngeren Linearbandkeramik.' In *Germania,* 34 (1956), 266 ff.
10. Gimbutas, M. *The Prehistory of Eastern Europe.* Part 1, *Mesolithic, Neolithic and Copper Age cultures in Russia and the Baltic Area.* Cambridge, Mass., 1956.
11. Gumpert, K. 'Eine paläolithische und mesolithische Abri-Siedlung an der Steinbergwand bei Ensdorf in der Oberpfalz.' *Mannus Z.V.* 25 (1933), 176 ff.
12. Gumpert, K. 'Die Tardenoisien-Abrisiedlung "Hohlstein in Klumpertal", Ldkr. Pegnitz (Frankische Schweiz).' In *Germania,* 32 (1954), 249 ff.
13. Kostrzewski, J. 'Quelques observations sur le Tardenoisien en Grande Pologne.' In *C.R. XIV Congr. int. d'Anthrop. et d'Arch. préhist.* (Paris, 1931), 400 ff.
14. Krainov, D. A. *The Cave-site Tash-Air as a Basis for Dividing the Late Palaeolithic Crimean Culture into Periods.* In *Mat. i Issled. po Arkheol. S.S.S.R.,* no. 91 (1960).

15. Louis, M. 'Les pointes en forme de feuille et à retouches bifaciales de Lommel.' In C.R. XII Congr. Préhist. de France, XIIe sess. 1936, 412 ff.
16. Nuber, A. H. 'Zur Schichtenfolge des Kleingerätigen Mesolithikums in Württemberg und Hohenzollern', Festschrift f. Peter Goessler. Stuttgart, 1954.
17. Ophoven, M., Saccasyn della Santa, E., and Hamal-Nandrin, J. Utilisation à l'âge de la pierre (Mésolithique) du grès-quartzite dit de Wommersom, 1948.
18. Peters, E. 'Das Mesolithikum der Oberen Donau.' In Germania, 18 (1934), 81 ff.
19. Reinerth, H. Das Federseemoor. Leipzig, 1936.
20. Schmidt, R. R. Die diluviale Vorzeit Deutschlands. Stuttgart, 1912.
21. Schwabedissen, H. Die mittlere Steinzeit in westlichen Norddeutschland. Neumünster, 1944.
22. Szmit, Z. 'Badania osadnictw epoki kamiennej na Podlasiu.' In Wiad. Arch. 10 (1929), 36 ff.
23. Tschumi, O. Urgeschichte der Schweiz. Frauenfeldt, 1947.
24. Vértes, L. 'Die Ausgrabungen in Szekszárd-Palánk und die archäologischen Funde.' In Swiatowit, 24 (1962), 159 ff.
25. Völzing, O. Fundberichte aus Schwabe, N.F. 9 (1935–8), 1 ff.
26. Wyss, R. Beiträge zur Typologie der Paläolithisch-Mesolithischen Übergangsformen im Schweizerischen Mittelland. Basel, 1953.
27. Wyss, R. 'Eine mesolithische Station bei Liesbergmühle (Kt. Bern).' Z. f. schweiz. Archäol. u. Kunstgeschichte, 17 (1951), 1 ff.
28. Wyss, R. 'Zur Erforschung des schweizerischen Mesolithikums.' In Z. f. schweiz. Archäol. u. Kunstgeschichte, 20 (1960), 55 ff.

XII. SOUTH-WEST ASIA

1. Bostanci, Enver Y. 'Researches on the Mediterranean Coast of Anatolia A New Palaeolithic Site at Beldibi near Antalya.' In Anatolia, 4 (1959)· 129 ff.
2. Braidwood, Robert J. and Howe, Bruce. Prehistoric Investigations in Iraqi Kurdistan (S.A.O.C. 31), Chicago, 1960.
3. Coon, C. S. Cave Excavations in Iran 1949. Philadelphia, 1951.
4. Coon, C. S. Seven Caves. London, 1957.
5. Garrod, D. A. E. 'The Palaeolithic of Southern Kurdistan : Excavations in the Caves of Zarzi and Hazar Merd.' In Bull. A.S.P.R. no. 6 (1930), 9 ff.
6. Garrod, D. A. E. 'The Natufian Culture : the Life and Economy of a Mesolithic People in the Near East.' In Proc. Brit. Acad. 43 (1957), 211 ff.
7. Kenyon, Kathleen. 'Earliest Jericho.' In Antiq. 33 (1959), 55 ff.
8. Neuville, René. Le Paléolithique et le Mésolithique du Désert de Judée. Arch. de l'Inst. de Paléont. hum., Mém. 24. Paris, 1951.
9. Perrot, Jean. 'Le Mésolithique de Palestine et les récentes découvertes à Eynan (Aïn Mallaha).' In Antiquity and Survival, 2 (1957), 91 ff.
10. Solecki, Ralph S. 'Prehistory in Shanidar Valley, Northern Iraq.' In Science 139 (1963), 179 ff.

CHAPTER IV

I. LANGUAGE AND HISTORY

1. Arens, H. Sprachwissenschaft: Der Gang ihrer Entwickelung von der Antike bis zur Gegenwart. Munich, 1955.
2. Bloomfield, L. Language. New York, 1933.

3. Chrétien, C. D. 'The Mathematical Models of Glottochronology.' In *Language*, 38 (1962), 11 ff.
4. Cohen, M. *Les langues du monde*, 2nd ed. Paris, 1952.
5. Hockett, C. F. *A Course in Modern Linguistics*. New York, 1958.
6. Hoenigswald, H. 'Internal Reconstruction.' In *Studies in Linguistics*, 2 (1943), 78 ff.
7. Hoenigswald, H. *Language Change and Linguistic Reconstruction*. Chicago, 1960.
8. Hoenigswald, H. 'Are there Universals of Linguistic Change?' In *Universals of Language* (ed. J. H. Greenberg). Cambridge (U.S.A.), 1963.
9. Hoijer, H. 'Linguistic and Cultural Change.' In *Language*, 24 (1948), 335 ff.
10. Hymes, D. H. 'Lexicostatistics so far.' In *Current Anthropology*, 1 (1960), 3 ff.
11. Lees, R. B. 'The Basis of Glottochronology.' In *Language*, 29 (1953), 113 ff.
12. Pedersen, H. *Linguistic Science in the Nineteenth Century*. Cambridge (U.S.A.), 1931.
13. Sapir, E. *Language*. New York, 1921.
14. Sapir, E. 'Language and Environment.' In *Selected Writings of Edward Sapir* (ed. D. G. Mandelbaum), 89 ff. Berkeley, 1951.
15. Swadesh, M. 'Linguistics as an Instrument of Prehistory.' In *Southwestern Journal of Anthropology*, 15 (1959), 20 ff.
16. Weinreich, U. *Languages in Contact*. New York, 1953.

II. THE AFRO-ASIAN (HAMITO-SEMITIC) FAMILY

1. Albright, W. F. 'The Principles of Egyptian Phonological Development.' In *Rec. trav.* 40 (1923), 64 ff.
2. Albright, W. F. 'The Early Alphabetic Inscriptions from Sinai and their Decipherment'. In *Bull. A.S.O.R.* 110 (1948), 6 ff.
3. Albright, W. F. *The Proto-Sinaitic Inscriptions and their Decipherment*. Cambridge (U.S.A.), 1966.
4. Altheim, F. and Stiehl, R. *Die aramäische Sprache unter den Achaemeniden*. Frankfurt, 1960.
5. Aro, J. *Studien zur mittelbabylonischen Grammatik*. Helsinki, 1955.
6. Basset, A. *La langue berbère*. Part 1 of *Handbook of African Languages*. Oxford, 1952.
7. Bauer, T. *Die Ostkanaanäer*. Leipzig, 1926.
8. Bauer, H. and Leander, P. *Grammatik des Biblisch-Aramäischen*. Halle, 1927.
9. Beeston, A. F. L. *A Descriptive Grammar of Epigraphic South Arabian*. London, 1962.
10. Bergsträsser, G. *Hebräische Grammatik*. Leipzig, 1918, 1929.
11. Calice, F. *Grundlagen der ägyptisch-semitischen Wortvergleichung*. Vienna, 1936.
12. Cantineau, J. *Grammaire du palmyrénien épigraphique*. Cairo, 1935.
13. Cantineau, J. *Le nabatéen*, 2 vols. Paris, 1930-2.
14. Dalman, G. *Grammatik des jüdisch-palästinischen Aramäisch*, 2nd ed. Leipzig, 1905.
15. Edel, E. *Altägyptische Grammatik*. Rome, 1955.
16. Erman, A. *Neuägyptische Grammatik*, 2nd ed. Leipzig, 1933.
17. Finet, A. *L'accadien des lettres de Mari*. Bruxelles, 1956.
18. Friedrich, J. *Phönizisch-punische Grammatik*. Rome, 1951.
19. Garbini, G. *L'aramaico antico*. Rome, 1956.
20. Gardiner, A. H. *Egyptian Grammar*, 3rd ed., rev. London, 1957.
21. Gelb, I. J. *La lingua degli Amoriti*. Rome, 1958.
22. Gelb, I. J. *Old Akkadian Writing and Grammar*. Chicago, 1961.

23. Gordon, C. *Ugaritic Manual*. Rome, 1955.
24. Greenberg, J. H. *The Languages of Africa*. Bloomington, 1963.
25. Harris, Z. S. *Development of the Canaanite Dialects*. New Haven, 1939.
26. Hintze, E. 'Die sprachliche Stellung des Meroitischen.' In *Afrikanistische Studien*, pp. 355 ff.
27. Höfner, Maria. *Altsüdarabische Grammatik*. Leipzig, 1943.
28. Huffmon, H. B. *Amorite Personal Names in the Mari Texts*. Baltimore, 1965.
29. Leslau, W. 'South-East Semitic (Ethiopic and South Arabic).' In *J.A.O.S.* 63 (1943), 4 ff.
30. Lexa, F. *Grammaire démotique*. Prague, 1947–51.
31. Moran, W. L. 'The Hebrew Language in its Northwest Semitic Background.' In *The Bible and the Ancient Near East* (ed. G. E. Wright), 57 ff. New York, 1961.
32. Moscati, S. *An Introduction to the Comparative Grammar of the Semitic Languages*. Wiesbaden, 1964.
33. Nöldeke, T. *Kurzgefasste syrische Grammatik*, 2nd ed. Leipzig, 1898.
34. Nöldeke, T. *Mandäische Grammatik*. Halle, 1875.
35. Polotsky, H. 'Egyptian.' In *The World History of the Jewish People*. I. *At the Dawn of Civilization* (ed. E. A. Speiser), 121 ff. and 359 ff. Tel-Aviv, 1964.
36. Polotsky, H. 'Semitics.' *Ibid.* 99 ff. and 357 f.
37. Rabin, C. *Ancient West Arabian*. London, 1951.
38. Rössler, O. 'Der semitische Charakter der libyschen Sprache.' In *Z.A.* 50 (1952), 121 ff.
39. Schulthess, F. *Grammatik des christlich-palästinischen Aramäisch*. Tübingen, 1924.
40. Steindorff, G. *Lehrbuch der koptischen Grammatik*. Chicago, 1951.
41. Thacker, T. W. *The Relationship of the Semitic and Egyptian Verbal Systems*. Oxford, 1954.
42. Till, W. *Koptische Grammatik*. Leipzig, 1955.
43. Tucker, A. N. and Bryan, M. A. *The Non-Bantu Languages of North-Eastern Africa*. Part III of *Handbook of African Languages*. Oxford, 1956.
44. Ullendorff, E. *The Semitic Languages of Ethiopia*. London, 1955.
45. Von Soden, W. *Grundriss der akkadischen Grammatik*. Rome, 1952.
46. Von Soden, W. 'Zur Einteilung der semitischen Sprachen.' In *W.Z.K.M.* 56 (1960), 177 ff.
47. Westermann, D. and Bryan, M. A. *Languages of West Africa*. Part II of *Handbook of African Languages*. Oxford, 1952.
48. Winnett, F. V. *A Study of the Lihyanite and Thamudic Inscriptions*. Toronto, 1937.

III. THE INDO-HITTITE FAMILY

1. Albright, W. F. 'Further Observations on the Chronology of Alalakh.' In *Bull. A.S.O.R.* 146 (1957), 26 ff.
2. Albright, W. F. 'Dunand's New Byblos Volume: A Lycian at the Byblian Court.' In *Bull. A.S.O.R.* 155 (1959), 31 ff.
3. Albright, W. F. 'The Eighteenth-Century Princes of Byblos and the Chronology of Middle Bronze.' In *Bull. A.S.O.R.* 176 (1964), 38 ff.
4. Andronov, M. 'Lexicostatistic Analysis of the Chronology of Disintegration of Proto-Dravidian.' In *Indo-Iranian Journal*, 7 (1964), 170 ff.
5. Austin, W. M. 'Is Armenian an Anatolian Language?' In *Language*, 18 (1942), 22 ff.

6. Blegen, C. W. 'The Geographical Distribution of Prehistoric Remains in Greece.' In *A.J.A.* 32 (1928), 146 ff.
7. Carruba, O. 'Lydisch und Lyder.' In *Mitt. Inst. Or.* 8 (1963), 383 ff.
8. Dyakonov, I. M. 'Phrygians, Hittites and Armenians.' In *Problems of Hitto- and Hurrology* (U.S.S.R. Academy of Sciences). Moscow, 1961.
9. Friedrich, J. *Kleinasiatische Sprachdenkmäler* (*Kleine Texte*, 163). Berlin, 1932.
10. Friedrich, J. *Hethitisches Elementarbuch* (*Indogermanische Bibliothek, Grammatiken*, 23). Heidelberg, 1940.
11. Friedrich, J. *Hethitisches Wörterbuch* (*Indogermanische Bibliothek*). Heidelberg, 1952–7.
12. Goetze, A. 'The Linguistic Continuity of Anatolia as shown by the Proper Names.' In *J.C.S.* 8 (1954), 72 ff.
13. Goetze, A. *Kleinasien* (*Kulturgeschichte des alten Orients*). München, 1957.
14. Goetze, A. 'Cilicians.' In *J.C.S.* 16 (1962), 48 ff.
15. Gusmani, R. *Lydisches Wörterbuch mit grammatischer Skizze und Inschriftensammlung*. Heidelberg, 1964.
16. Hauschild, R. *Die indogermanischen Völker und Sprachen Kleinasiens* (*Sitzungsb. Leipzig*, 109, 1). Berlin, 1964.
17. Kammenhuber, A. *Hippologia Hethitica*. Wiesbaden, 1961.
18. Laroche, E. *Dictionnaire de la langue louvite*. Paris, 1959.
19. Mayrhofer, M. 'Zu den arischen Sprachresten in Vorderasien.' In *Die Sprache*, 5 (1959), 77 ff.
20. Mayrhofer, M. 'Indo-iranisches Sprachgut aus Alalaḫ.' In *Indo-Iranian Journal*, 4 (1960), 136 ff.
21. Mayrhofer, M. 'Der heutige Forschungsstand zu den indo-iranischen Sprachresten in Vorderasien.' In *Z.D.M.G.* 111 (1961), 451 ff.
22. Meriggi, P. *Hieroglyphisch-Hethitisches Glossar*. Wiesbaden, 1962.
23. O'Callaghan, R. T. *Aram Naharaim* (*An. Or.* 26). Rome, 1948.
24. Slonek, R. Review of the two contributions of I. M. Dyakonov to: *Problems of Hitto- and Hurrology*. In *Bi. Or.* 22 (1965), 40 f.
25. Ten Cate, Ph. Th. J. H. *The Luwian Population Groups of Lycia and Cilicia Aspera during the Hellenistic Period* (*Documenta et Monumenta Orientis Antiqui*, 10). Leiden, 1961.
26. Thieme, P. 'The "Aryan" Gods of the Mitanni Treaties.' In *J.A.O.S.* 80 (1960), 301 ff.

IV. SUMERIAN, HURRIAN, URARṬIAN, ELAMITE

1. Albright, W. F. Review of E. A. Speiser, *Mesopotamian Origins*. In *J.A.O.S.* 51 (1931), 60 ff.
2. Benedict, W. C. 'Urartians and Hurrians.' In *J.A.O.S.* 80 (1960), 100 ff.
3. Cameron, G. G. *Persepolis Treasury Tablets* (*O.I.P.* 65). Chicago, 1948.
4. Clauson, G. *Turkish and Mongolian Studies* (*Royal Asiatic Society, Prize Publication Fund*, 20). London, 1963.
5. Clauson, G. 'A postscript to Professor Sinor's "Observations on a new comparative Altaic phonology".' In *Bull. S.O.A.S.* 27 (1964), 154 ff.
6. Delitzsch, F. *Sumerisches Glossar*. Leipzig, 1914.
7. Dyakonov, I. M. 'A Comparative Historical Survey of Urartean and Hurrite.' In *Problems of Hitto- and Hurrology* (U.S.S.R. Academy of Sciences). Moscow, 1961.

8. Edzard, D. O. 'Sumerer und Semiten in der frühen Geschichte Mesopotamiens. In *Genava*, n.s. 8 (1960), 241 ff.
9. Falkenstein, A. *Grammatik der Sprache Gudeas von Lagaš*, I, II (*An. Or.* 28–9). Rome, 1949–50.
10. Falkenstein, A. 'Kontakte zwischen Sumerern und Akkadern auf sprachlichem Gebiet.' In *Genava*, n.s. 8 (1960), 301 ff.
11. Friedrich, J. *Einführung ins Urartäische* (*M.V.A.G.* 37, 3). Leipzig, 1933.
12. Gelb, I. J. *Hurrians and Subarians*. Chicago, 1944.
13. Gelb, I. J., Purves, P. M. and MacRae, A. A. *Nuzi Personal Names* (*O.I.P.* 57). Chicago, 1943.
14. Gelb, I. J. 'Sumerians and Akkadians in their ethno-linguistic relationship.' In *Genava*, n.s. 8 (1960), 258 ff.
15. Hinz, W. 'Zur Entzifferung der elamischen Strichschrift.' In *Iranica antiqua*, 2 (1962), 1 ff.
16. Jacobsen, T. *The Sumerian King List*. Chicago, 1939.
17. Jacobsen, T. 'The Waters of Ur.' In *Iraq*, 22 (1960), 174 ff.
18. Kramer, S. N. *From the Tablets of Sumer*. Colorado, 1956.
19. Kramer, S. N. 'Sumero-Akkadian interconnections: religious ideas.' In *Genava*, n.s. 8 (1960), 272 ff.
20. Kramer, S. N. *The Sumerians*. Chicago, 1963.
21. Labat, R. *La structure de l'Elamite, état présent de la question*. Paris, 1951.
22. Oates, J. 'Ur and Eridu, the Prehistory.' In *Iraq*, 22 (1960), 32 ff.
23. Oppenheim, A. L. 'The Seafaring Merchants of Ur.' In *J.A.O.S.* 74 (1954), 6 ff.
24. Paper, H. H. *The Phonology and Morphology of Royal Achaemenid Elamite*. Ann Arbor, 1955.
25. Parrot, A. and Nougayrol, J. 'Un document de fondation hurrite.' In *R.A.* 42 (1948), 1 ff.
26. Poebel, A. *Grundzüge der sumerischen Grammatik*. Rostock, 1923.
27. Sinor, D. 'Observations on a New Comparative Altaic Phonology.' In *Bull. S.O.A.S.* 26 (1963), 133 ff.
28. Speiser, E. A. *Mesopotamian Origins*. Philadelphia, 1930.
29. Speiser, E. A. *Introduction to Hurrian* (*Ann. A.S.O.R.* 20). New Haven, 1941.

CHAPTER V

I. AUSTRALOPITHECINES AND PITHECANTHROPINES

1. Arambourg, C. 'A recent discovery in human palaeontology, Atlanthropus of Ternifine (Algeria).' In *Amer. J. phys. Anthrop.* 13 (1955), 191 ff.
2. Clark, W. E. Le Gros. 'The cranial evidence for human evolution.' In *Proc. Amer. Phil. Soc.* 103 (1959), 159 ff.
3. Clark, W. E. Le Gros. *The Fossil Evidence for Human Evolution*. Rev. Ed. Chicago, 1964.
4. Weidenreich, F. 'The brain and its role in the phylogenetic transformation of the human skull.' In *Trans. Amer. Phil. Soc.* 31 (1941), 321 ff.

II. 'HOMO SAPIENS'

1. Brace, C. Loring. 'The fate of the "classic" Neanderthals: a consideration of hominid catastrophism.' In *Current Anthropology*, 5 (1964), 3 ff.
2. Briggs, L. C. 'The Stone Age Races of Northwest Africa.' In *Peabody Museum Bull.* 18. Cambridge, Mass., 1955.

3. Briggs, L. C. and Balout, L. 'Têtes osseuses de Mechta-el-Arbi (fouilles de 1912, 1926–7).' In *Travaux du Laboratoire d'Anthropologie et d'Archéologie Préhistoriques du Musée du Bardo*, 3 and 4. Algiers, 1961.
4. Brothwell, D. R. In *Current Anthropology*, 5 (1964), 20 ff.
5. Ferembach, D., Dastugue, J. and Poitrat-Targowla, M. J. *La nécropole épipaléolithique de Taforalt, Maroc oriental*. Casablanca, 1962.
6. Ferembach, D. 'Squelettes du Natoufien d'Israël, étude anthropologique.' In *L'Anthropologie*, 65 (1961), 46 ff.
7. Genoves, S. 'Sex determination in earlier man.' In *Science in Archaeology*, ed. D. R. Brothwell and E. S. Higgs. London, 1963.
8. Hewes, G. W., Irwin, H., Papworth, M. and Saxe, A. 'A New Fossil Human Population from the Wadi Halfa Area, Sudan.' In *Nature*, 203 (1964), 341 ff.
9. Higgs, E. S. and Brothwell, D. R. 'North Africa and Mount Carmel: recent developments.' In *Man*, 61 (1961), article 166, 138 ff.
10. Oakley, K. P. and Gardiner, Elizabeth. 'Analytical data on the Swanscombe bones.' In *The Swanscombe Skull*, ed. C. D. Ovey. London, 1964.
11. Stewart, T. D. 'A neglected primitive feature of the Swanscombe skull.' In *The Swanscombe Skull*, ed. C. D. Ovey. London, 1964.
12. Vallois, H. V. 'Diagrammes sagittaux et mensurations individuelles des hommes fossiles d'Afalou-bou-Rhummel.' In *Travaux du Laboratoire d'Anthropologie et d'Archéologie Préhistoriques*, 5. Algiers, 1962.

CHAPTER VI

I. EGYPT

1. Albright, W. F. 'An Indirect Synchronism between Egypt and Mesopotamia, c. 1730 B.C.' In *Bull. A.S.O.R.* 99 (1945), 9–18.
2. Arkell, A. J. Review of E. J. Baumgartel, *The Cultures of Prehistoric Egypt* (ed. 2, London, 1955). In *Bi. Or.* 13 (1956), 123–7.
3. von Beckerath, J. 'Die ägyptischen Königslisten des Manetho.' In *O.L.Z.* 54 (1959), 6–11.
4. Borchardt, L. *Quellen und Forschungen zur Zeitbestimmung der ägyptischen Geschichte*, 1–2. Berlin, 1917, 1935.
5. Broecker, W. S. and Kulp, J. L. 'The Radiocarbon Method of Age Determination.' In *American Antiquity*, 22 (1956), 1–11.
6. Daressy, G. 'Les listes des princes du commencement de la XVIIIe Dynastie à Deir el Médineh.' In *Rec. Champ.* (1922), 283–96.
7. Drioton, É. and Vandier, J. *L'Égypte* ('*Clio.*' *Les peuples de l'orient méditerranéen*, 2). Ed. 3, Paris 1952. See especially pp. 10–17 and 627–32.
8. Edgerton, W. F. 'Critical Note on the Chronology of the Early Eighteenth Dynasty (Amenhotep I to Thutmose III).' In *A.J.S.L.* 53 (1937), 188–97.
9. Edgerton, W. F. 'Chronology of the Twelfth Dynasty.' In *J.N.E.S.* 1 (1942), 307–14.
10. Ehrich, R. W. (ed.). *Relative Chronologies in Old World Archaeology*. Chicago, 1954.
11. Farina, G. *Il papiro dei re restaurato* (*Pubblicazioni egittologiche del R. Museo di Torino*). Rome, 1938.
12. Gardiner, A. H. 'Regnal Years and Civil Calendar in Pharaonic Egypt.' In *J.E.A.* 31 (1945), 11–28.
13. Gardiner, A. H. *The Royal Canon of Turin*. Oxford, 1959.

14. Gauthier, H. *Le livre des rois d'Égypte* (*Mém. Miss. fr. Caire*, 17–21). 5 vols. Cairo, 1907–17.
15. Gauthier, H. 'Quatre nouveaux fragments de la pierre de Palerme.' *Le Musée égyptien*, 3, 29–53. Cairo, 1915.
16. Helck, W. *Untersuchungen zu Manetho und den ägyptischen Königslisten* (*Unters.* 18). Berlin, 1956.
17. Kaiser, W. 'Stand und Probleme der ägyptischen Vorgeschichtsforschung.' In *Z.Ä.S.* 81 (1956), 87–109.
18. Libby, W. F. *Radiocarbon Dating*. Ed. 2. Chicago, 1955.
19. Meyer, E. *Aegyptische Chronologie* (*Abh. Berlin*, 1904). Berlin, 1904.
20. Meyer, E. *Nachträge zur aegyptischen Chronologie* (*ibid.* 1907). Berlin, 1908.
21. Meyer, E. *Die ältere Chronologie Babyloniens, Assyriens und Ägyptens* (*Nachtrag zum ersten Bande der Geschichte des Altertums*). Ed. 2. Stuttgart and Berlin, 1931.
22. Montet, P. 'La stèle de l'an 400 retrouvée.' In *Kêmi*, 4 (1931), 191–215.
23. Neugebauer, O. 'Die Bedeutungslosigkeit der "Sothisperiode" für die älteste ägyptische Chronologie.' In *Acta Or.* 17 (1939), 169–95.
24. Neugebauer, O. 'The Chronology of the Hammurabi Age.' In *J.A.O.S.* 61 (1941), 58–61.
25. Parker, R. A. *The Calendars of Ancient Egypt* (*S.A.O.C.* 26). Chicago, 1950.
26. Parker, R. A. 'Sothic Dates and Calendar "Adjustment".' In *Rev. d'égyptol.* 9 (1952), 101–8.
27. Parker, R. A. 'Egypt: Chronology.' In *Encyclopedia Americana*, 10, 14*b–e* (1957).
28. Parker, R. A. 'The Lunar Dates of Thutmose III and Ramesses II.' In *J.N.E.S.* 16 (1957), 39–43.
29. Petrie, W. M. F. 'New Portions of the Annals.' In *Anc. Egypt* (1916), 114–20.
30. Prisse d'Avennes, E. *Monuments égyptiens: Bas-reliefs, peintures, inscriptions, etc., d'après les dessins éxécutés sur les lieux*, 1, pls. 1, 2. Paris, 1847.
31. Rowton, M. B. 'Manetho's Date for Ramesses II.' In *J.E.A.* 34 (1948), 57–74.
32. Rowton, M. B. 'The Date of Hammurabi.' In *J.N.E.S.* 17 (1958), 97–111.
33. Sauneron, S. 'La tradition officielle relative à la XVIIIe Dynastie d'aprés un ostracon de la Vallée des Rois.' In *Chron. d'Ég.* 26 (1951), 46–9.
34. Schaeffer, C. F. A. 'À propos de la chronologie de la XIIe Dynastie égyptienne et des Hyksos.' In *Chron. d'Ég.* 22 (1947), 225–9.
35. Schäfer, H. *Ein Bruchstück altägyptischer Annalen* (*Anhang zu der Abh. Berlin* 1902). Berlin, 1902.
36. Scharff, A. *Grundzüge der ägyptischen Vorgeschichte* (*Morgenland* 12). Leipzig, 1927.
37. Scharff, A. 'Die Bedeutungslosigkeit des sogennanten ältesten Datums der Weltgeschichte und einige sich daraus ergebende Folgerungen für die ägyptische Geschichte und Archäologie.' In *Hist. Z.* 161 (1939), 3–32.
38. Sethe, K. *Beiträge zur ältesten Geschichte Ägyptens* (*Unters.* 3). Leipzig, 1905.
39. Sethe, K. *Die Zeitrechnung der alten Aegypter im Verhaltnis zu der andern Völker* (*Nachr. Göttingen*, 1919, 1920). Göttingen, 1919, 1920.
40. Sethe, K. 'Sethos I. und die Erneuerung der Hundesternperiode.' In *Z.Ä.S.* (1931), 1–7.
41. Smith, W. S. *Ancient Egypt as represented in the Museum of Fine Arts*. Ed. 4. Boston, 1960. See especially pp. 193–9.

42. Smith, W. S. 'Inscriptional Evidence for the History of the Fourth Dynasty.' In *J.N.E.S.* 11 (1952), 113–28.

43. Stock, H. *Studien zur Geschichte und Archäologie der 13. bis 17. Dynastie Ägyptens unter besonderer Berücksichtigung der Skarabäen dieser Zwischenzeit (Ägyptol. Forsch.* 12). Glückstadt, 1942.

44. Stock, H. *Die Erste Zwischenzeit Ägyptens (St. Aeg.* 2 = *An. Or.* 31). Rome, 1949.

45. Waddell, W. G. *Manetho, with an English Translation (The Loeb Classical Library).* London and Cambridge (Mass.), 1940.

II. ANCIENT WESTERN ASIA

1. Albright, W. F. 'Stratigraphic Confirmation of the Low Mesopotamian Chronology.' In *Bull. A.S.O.R.* 144 (1956), 26 ff.

2. Albright, W. F. 'Further Observations on the Chronology of Alalakh.' In *Bull. A.S.O.R.* 146 (1957), 26 pp.

3. Balkan, K. *Kassitenstudien* 1. *Die Sprache der Kassiten (A.O.S.* 37). New Haven, 1954.

4. Balkan, K. 'Observations on the Chronological Problems of the Kārum Kaniš.' In *Türk Tarih Kurumu Yayınlarından,* Ankara, vii/28 (1955).

5. Balkan, K. 'Letter of King Anum-hirbi of Mama to King Warshama of Kanish.' In *Türk Tarih Kurumu Yayınlarından,* Ankara, vii/31a (1957).

6. Balkan, K. 'Kas tarihinin ana hatları.' In *Belleten,* 12 (1948), 723 ff. (in Turkish).

7. Buchanan, B. 'On the Seal Impressions on some Old Babylonian Tablets.' In *J.C.S.* 11 (1957), 45 ff.

8. Cameron, G. G. *History of Early Iran.* Chicago, 1936.

9. Cavaignac, E. 'Les deux listes royales assyriennes: conséquences chronologiques.' In *R.A.* 49 (1955), 94 ff.

10. Cornelius, F. 'Die Chronologie des vorderen Orients im 2. Jahrtausend v. Chr.' In *Arch. f. Or.* 17 (1956), 294 ff.

11. Cornelius, F. 'Chronology, eine Erwiederung.' In *J.C.S.* 12 (1958), 101 ff.

12. Delitzsch, F. *Die Babylonische Chronik.* Leipzig, 1906.

13. Delougaz, F. *et al. Pre-Sargonid Temples in the Diyala Region (O.I.P.* 58). Chicago, 1942.

14. van Dijk, J. J. 'Textes divers du musée de Bagdad, III.' In *Sumer,* 15 (1959), 5 ff.

15. Dossin, G. 'Le royaume d'Alep au XVIII siècle avant notre ère d'aprés les "Archives de Mari".' *Bulletin de l'Académie Royale de Belgique* (classe de lettres), 5e série, 38 (1952), 229 ff.

16. Dossin, G. 'Les archives économiques du palais de Mari.' In *Syria,* 20 (1939), 97 ff.

17. Dossin, G. 'Les noms d'années et d'éponymes dans les "Archives de Mari".' In A. Parrot, *Studia Mariana (Documenta et Monumenta Orientis Antiqui,* iv), Leiden, 1950, 51 ff.

18. Dothan, T. Review of O. Tufnell, *Lachish IV.* In *I.E.J.* 10 (1960), 58 ff.

19. Edel, E. 'Neue keilschriftliche Umschreibungen ägyptischer Namen aus den Boghazköy Texten.' In *J.N.E.S.* 7 (1948), 11 ff.

20. Edel, E. 'Die Stelen Amenophis II aus Karnak und Memphis etc.' In *Z.D.P.V.* 69 (1953), 97 ff.

21. Edel, E. 'Die Abfassungszeit des Briefes K.Bo. I 10 (Hattušil-Kadašman-Ellil) und seine Bedeutung für die Chronologie Ramses' II.' In *J.C.S.* 12 (1958), 130 ff.

22. Edzard, D. O. *Die 'Zweite Zwischenzeit' Babyloniens.* Wiesbaden, 1957. Ch. III: 'Chronologie', 15–29.
23. Edzard, D. O. 'Königsinschriften des Iraq Museums II.' In *Sumer*, 15 (1959), 19 ff.
24. Edzard, D. O. 'Enmebaragesi von Kiš.' In *Z.A.* 53 (1959), 9 ff.
25. Ehrich, R. W. (ed.). *Relative Chronologies in Old World Archaeology.* Chicago, 1954. Contributors include W. F. Albright, H. J. Kantor, R. J. Braidwood, A. Perkins, D. E. McCown.
26. El-Wailly, F. J. *The Political History of the Kassite Period in Mesopotamia*, (unpubl. dissertation, University of Chicago, 1953).
27. Falkenstein, A. *Archaische Texte aus Uruk (Ausgrabungen der Deutschen Forschungsgemeinschaft in Uruk-Warka*, 2). Berlin, 1936.
28. Falkner, M. 'Die Eponymen der spätassyrischen Zeit.' In *Arch. f. Or.* 17 (1954–6), 100 ff.
29. Feigin, S. D. and Landsberger, B. 'The Date List of the Babylonian King Samsu-ditana.' In *J.N.E.S.* 14 (1955), 137 ff.
30. Fine, H. A. *Studies in Middle-Assyrian Chronology and Religion.* Cincinnati, 1955.
31. Finkelstein, J. J. 'The Year-dates of Samsuditana.' In *J.C.S.* 13 (1959), 39 ff.
32. Forrer, E. O. *Forschungen.* Berlin, 1926–29.
33. Frankfort, H. Review of C. L. Woolley, *The Royal Cemetery.* In *J.R.A.S.* (1937), 330 ff.
34. Furumark, A. *The Chronology of Mycenaean Pottery.* Stockholm, 1941.
35. Füye, Allotte de la. 'En-e-tar-zi patesi de Lagaš.' In *Hilprecht Anniversary Volume.* Leipzig, 1909, 121 ff.
36. Füye, Allotte de la. 'En-gil-sa, patesi de Lagaš.' In *Florilegium....M. de Vogüé.* Paris, 1909, 3 ff.
37. Gadd, C. J. *The Early Dynasties of Sumer and Akkad.* London, 1921.
38. Gadd, C. J. 'The Inscriptions from al-'Ubaid and their significance.' In H. R. Hall and C. L. Woolley, *Ur Excavations*, I (Oxford, 19 27),125ff.
39. Gadd, C. J. *History and Monuments of Ur.* London, 1929.
40. Gadd, C. J. 'Entemena: a new incident.' In *R.A.* 27 (1930), 125 ff.
41. Gadd, C. J. 'Tablets from Chagar Bazar and Tall Brak, 1937–38.' In *Iraq*, 7 (1940), 22 ff.
42. Gadd, C. J. 'Une donnée chronologique.' In *Rencontre assyriologique internationale*, II (1951), 70 ff.
43. Gelb, I. J. *A Study of Writing.* Chicago, 1952.
44. Gelb, I. J. 'Two Assyrian King Lists.' In *J.N.E.S.* 13 (1954), 209 ff.
45. Genouillac, H. de. *Fouilles de Telloh*, II. Paris, 1936.
46. Ginzel, F. K. *Handbuch der mathematischen und technischen Chronologie.* 3 vols. Leipzig, 1906–1914.
47. Goetze, A. 'Zur Chronologie der Hethiterkönige.' In *K.F.* I (Weimar, 1930), 115 ff.
48. Goetze, A. 'The Problem of Chronology and Early Hittite History.' In *Bull. A.S.O.R.* 122 (1951), 18 ff.
49. Goetze, A. 'Alalaḫ and Hittite Chronology.' In *Bull. A.S.O.R.* 146 (1957), 20 ff.
50. Goetze, A. 'On the Chronology of the Second Millennium B.C.' In *J.C.S.* 11, (1957), 53 ff.
51. Gurney, O. R. *The Hittites.* London, 1952.
52. Gurney, O. R. 'The Sultantepe Tablets.' In *A. St.* 3 (1953), 15 ff.

53. Güterbock, H. G. 'Die historische Tradition und ihre literarische Gestaltung bei Babyloniern und Hethitern bis 1200.' Pt. I. In *Z.A.* 42 (1934), 1 ff. Pt. II. In *Z.A.* 44 (1938), 45 ff.
54. Güterbock, H. G. 'The Deeds of Suppiluliuma, as told by his Son, Mursili II.' In *J.C.S.* 10 (1956), 41 ff., 75 ff., 107 ff.
55. Hackman, G. G. *Sumerian and Akkadian Administrative texts (B.I.N.* 8). New Haven, 1958, with an introduction by F. J. Stephens.
56. Hallo, W. W. 'Zāriqum.' In *J.N.E.S.* 15 (1956), 220 ff.
57. Hallo, W. W. *Early Mesopotamian Royal Titles (A.O.S.* 43). New Haven, 1957.
58. Harris, R. 'The Archive of the Sin Temple in Khafajah (Tutub).' In *J.C.S.* 9 (1955), 31 ff.
59. Jacobsen, T. 'Documentary Contributions to the History and Religion of Eshnunna.' In *O.I.C.* 13 (1932), 42 ff.
60. Jacobsen, T. *The Sumerian King List (Assyriological Studies* 11). Chicago, 1939.
61. Jacobsen, T. *Cuneiform Texts in the National Museum, Copenhagen.* Leiden, 1939.
62. Jacobsen, T. 'Historical Data.' Ch. v of *The Gimilsin Temple and the Palace of the Rulers at Tell Asmar (O.I.P.* 43). Chicago, 1940.
63. Jacobsen, T. 'The Reign of Ibbi-Suen.' In *J.C.S.* 7 (1953), 36 ff.
64. Jacobsen, T. 'Early Political Developments in Mesopotamia.' In *Z.A.* 52, (1957), 91 ff.
65. Jaritz, K. 'Quellen zur Geschichte der Kaššu-Dynastie.' In *Mitt. Inst. Or.* 6 (1958), 187 ff.
66. Kannenhuber, A. 'Die Hethitische Geschichtsschreibung.' In *Saeculum,* 9 (1958), 136 ff.
67. Kantor, H. J. 'Further Evidence for Early Mesopotamian Relations with Egypt.' In *J.N.E.S.* 11 (1952), 239 ff.
68. Kantor, H. J. 'Syro-Palestinian Ivories.' In *J.N.E.S.* 15 (1956), 153 ff.
69. King, L. W. *Chronicles concerning Early Babylonian Kings.* London, 1907
70. Knudtzon, J. A. *Die El-Amarna Tafeln.* Leipzig, 1915.
71. Kramer, S. N. 'Gilgamesh: some new Sumerian Data.' In P. Garelli (ed.), *Gilgameš et sa légende* (Paris, 1960).
72. Kraus, F. R. 'Nippur und Isin nach altbabylonischen Rechtsurkunden.' In *J.C.S.* 3 (1951). For the chronology of the dynasties of Isin and Larsa, see 4 ff.
73. Kraus, F. R. 'Zur Liste der älteren Könige von Babylonien.' In *Z.A.* 50 (1952), 29 ff.
74. Kraus, F. R. 'Ungewöhnliche Datierungen aus der Zeit des Königs Rim-Sin von Larsa.' In *Z.A.* 53 (1959), 136 ff.
75. Krückmann, O. 'Zu einem Tonnagel Entemenas.' In *An. Or.* 12 (1935), 200 ff.
76. Landsberger, B. 'Jahreszeiten im Sumerisch-Akkadischen.' In *J.N.E.S.* 8 (1949), 248 ff. (for *ṭuppû* see 265 ff).
77. Landsberger, B. 'Assyrische Königsliste und "Dunkles Zeitalter".' In *J.C.S.* 8 (1954), 31 ff. and 106 ff.
78. Langdon, S. *Some Sumerian Contracts.* In *Z.A.* 25 (1911), 205 ff.
79. Laroche, E. *Chronologie Hittite: état des questions, Anadolu* II (= *Études Orientales...Institut Français d'Archéologie de Stamboul,* XIV). (1955), 1–22.
80. Leemans, W. F. 'Le synchronisme Šamši-Addu-Hammurabi d'après certains textes du Louvre.' In *R.A.* 49 (1955), 202 ff.

81. Lehmann-Haupt, C. F. *Zwei Hauptprobleme der altorientalischen Chronologie.* Leipzig, 1898.
82. Lewy, H. Chronological Notes. In *Or.* n.s. 24 (1955), 275 ff.
83. Lewy H. 'On some Problems of Kassite and Assyrian Chronology.' In *Mélanges Isidore Levy (Annuaire de l'Institut de Philologie et d'Histoire Orientales et Slaves* 13) (Brussels, 1955), 241 ff.
84. Lewy, H. 'The Synchronism Assyria-Ešnunna-Babylon.' In *We. Or.* 2, (1959), 438 ff.
85. Lewy, H. 'Miscellanea Nuziana I. An Assyro-Nuzian synchronism.' In *Or.* n.s. 28 (1959), 4 ff.
86. Lewy, H. and J. 'The Origin of the Week and the oldest West Asiatic Calendar.' In *H.U.C.A.* 17 (1943), 1 ff.
87. Lewy J. 'The Assyrian Calendar.' In *Arch. Orient.* 11 (1939), 35 ff.
88. Lewy, J. 'Apropos of a Recent Study in Old Assyrian Chronology.' In *Or.* n.s. 26 (1957), 12 ff.
89. Lewy, J. 'Remarks on the Chronology of the Kültepe Texts.' In *Akten des vierundzwanzigsten internationalen Orientalisten-Kongresses, München* (Wiesbaden, 1959), 128 ff.
90. Libby, W. F. *Radio-carbon Dating.* Ed. 2. Chicago, 1955.
91. Matouš, L. 'Zur Chronologie der Geschichte von Larsa bis zum Einfall der Elamiter.' In *Arch. Orient.*, 20 (1952), 288 ff.
92. Meek, T. J. *Old Akkadian, Sumerian and Cappadocian Texts from Nuzi (Harvard Semitic Series,* 10), 1935.
93. Mercer, S. A. B. *Sumero-Babylonian Year-formulae.* London, 1946.
94. Moscati, S. 'Nuovi aspetti della cronologia dell'antico Oriente anteriore.' In *Relazioni del X Congresso Internazionale di Scienze Storiche,* II (Rome, 1952), 169 ff.
95. Nagel, W. and Strohmenger, E. 'Alalaḫ und Siegelkunst.' In *J.C.S.* 12 (1958), 109 ff.
96. Nassouhi, E. 'Grande liste des rois d'Assyrie.' In *Arch. f. Or.* 4 (1927), 1 ff.
97. Neugebauer, P. V. *Astronomische Chronologie.* Berlin-Leipzig, 1929.
98. Nougayrol, J. *Textes accadiens des archives sud.* Le Palais Royal d'Ugarit, IV (Mission de Ras Shamra, 9). Paris, 1956.
99. O'Callaghan, R. T. *Aram Naharaim (An. Or.* 26). Rome, 1948.
100. Otten, H. 'Zu den Anfängen der hethitischen Geschichte.' In *M.D.O.G.* 83 (1951), 33 ff.
101. Otten, H. 'Die hethitischen "Königslisten" und die altorientalische Chronologie.' In *M.D.O.G.* 83 (1951), 47 ff.
102. Otten, H. 'Die altassyrischen Texte aus Boghazköy,' In *M.D.O.G.* 89 (1957), 68 ff.
103. Otten, H. 'Keilschrifttexte,' In *M.D.O.G.* 91 (1958), 73 ff.
104. Pallis, S. A. *Chronology of the Shub-ad Culture.* Copenhagen, 1941, 235 ff.
105. Pallis, S. A. *The Antiquity of Iraq.* Copenhagen 1956. Ch. VIII: 'Chronology.' 463 ff.
106. Pallis, S. A. 'The Revision of the Hammurabi Chronology.' In *Festskrift til Paul V. Rubow....* Copenhagen, 1956, 30 ff.
107. Parrot, A. *Archéologie Mésopotamienne.* 2 vols. (Paris, 1946, 1953). Vol. II, ch. II, 'Chronologie Mésopotamienne.' 332 ff.
108. Perkins, A. L. *The Comparative Archaeology of Early Mesopotamia (S.A.O.C.* 25). Chicago, 1949; second printing, 1957.
109. Pinches, T. G. Communication. In *P.S.B.A.* 6 (1884), 193 ff.

110. Poebel, A. 'The Assyrian King List from Khorsabad.' In *J.N.E.S.* 1 (1942), 247 ff., 460 ff.; and 2 (1943), 56 ff.
111. Poebel, A. *Miscellaneous Studies (Assyriological Studies* 14). Chicago, 1947. Study v: 'The use of mathematical mean values in Babylonian king list B.' 110 ff.
112. Poebel, A. *The Second Dynasty of Isin according to a new Kinglist Tablet (Assyriological Studies* 15). Chicago, 1955.
113. Pohl, A. 'Zur Frühgeschichte Anatoliens.' In *Or.* n.s. 27 (1958), 203 ff.
114. Rost, P. 'Untersuchungen zur altorientalischen Geschichte.' In *M.V.A.G.* 2, ii (1897).
115. Rowley, H. H. 'A Recent Theory on the Exodus.' In *Donum natalicium H. S. Nyberg oblatum* (Upsala, 1955). 195 ff.
116. Rowton, M. B. 'Mesopotamian Chronology and the Era of Menophres.' In *Iraq,* 8 (1946), 94 ff.
117. Rowton, M. B. 'The Problem of the Exodus.' In *P.E.Q.*, 1953, 46 ff.
118. Rowton, M. B. 'The Date of Hammurabi.' In *J.N.E.S.* 17 (1958), 97 ff.
119. Rowton, M. B. 'Ṭuppū in the Assyrian King Lists.' In *J.N.E.S.* 18 (1959), 213 ff.
120. Rowton, M. B. 'The Background of the Treaty between Ramesses II and Ḫattušiliš III.' In *J.C.S.* 13 (1959), 1 ff.
121. Rowton, M. B. 'Comparative Chronology at the Time of Dynasty XIX.' In *J.N.E.S.* 19 (1960), 15 ff.
122. Rowton, M. B. 'The Date of the Sumerian King-list.' In *J.N.E.S.* 19 (1960), 156 ff.
123. Schaeffer, C. F. A. *Stratigraphie comparée et chronologie de l'Asie occidentale (IIIe et IIe millénaire).* Paris, 1948.
124. Schaeffer, C. F. A. *Ugaritica III (Mission de Ras Shamra VIII).* Paris, 1956.
125. Schmidtke, F. *Der Aufbau der Babylonischen Chronologie (Orbis Antiquus,* Heft 7). Münster, 1952.
126. Schmidtke, F. 'Die Jahresnamen Išbi-Erras von Isin.' In *Z.D.M.G.* 106 (1956), 23 ff.
127. Schubert, K. 'Die altorientalischen Dynastien zur Zeit Hammurabis von Babylon.' In *W.Z.K.M.* 51 (1952), 21 ff.
128. Simmons, S. D. 'Early Old Babylonian Tablets from Harmal and elsewhere.' In *J.C.S.* 13 (1959), 71 ff. 105 ff.
129. Smith, Sidney. *The Early History of Assyria.* London, 1928. Appendix: 'Chronology', 343 ff.
130. Smith, Sidney. *Alalakh and Chronology.* London, 1940.
131. Smith, Sidney. 'Middle Minoan I–II and Babylonian Chronology.' In *A.J.A.* 49 (1945), 1 ff.
132. Smith, Sidney, *The Statue of Idri-mi* (Occasional Publications of the British Institute of Archaeology in Ankara 1). London, 1949.
133. Smith, Sidney. 'Yarim-Lim of Yamḫad.' In *Riv. stud. or.* 32 (1957), 155 ff.
134. Sollberger, E. 'New Lists of the Kings of Ur and Isin.' In *J.C.S.* 8 (1954), 135 f.
135. Sollberger, E. 'Sur la chronologie des rois d'Ur et quelques problèmes connexes.' In *Arch. f. Or.* 17 (1954–6), 10 ff.
136. Stephens, F. J. 'Who was Urukagina's Predecessor?' In *R.A.* 49 (1955), 129 ff.

137. Stubbings, F. H. *Mycenaean Pottery from the Levant*. Cambridge, 1951.
138. Sturm, J. 'Wer ist Pipḫururiaš?' In *R.H.A.* 2 (1933), 161 ff.
139. Swift, G. F. *The Pottery of the 'Amuq Phases K to O, and its historical relationships* (thesis, University of Chicago, 1958).
140. Tadmor, H. 'Historical Implications of the Correct Rendering of Akkadian *dâku.*' In *J.N.E.S.* 17 (1958), 129 ff.
141. Thureau-Dangin, F. *Die Sumerischen und Akkadischen Königsinschriften.* Leipzig, 1907.
142. Thureau-Dangin, F. 'Statuette d'un petit-fils de Lugal-kisal-si roi d'Uruk.' In *R.A.* 20 (1923), 3 ff.
143. Thureau-Dangin, F. 'La chronologie de la première dynastie babylonienne.' In *Mém. Ac. Inscr. B.-L.*, XLIII/2 (1942), 229 ff.
144. Van der Meer, P. *The Chronology of Ancient Western Asia and Egypt*. Ed. 2. Leiden, 1955.
145. Van der Meer, P. 'The Chronological Determination of the Mesopotamian Letters in the El-Amarna Archives.' In *J.E.O.L.* 15 (1957–8), 74 ff.
146. Unger, E. 'Königslisten, assyrische Jahresintervalle, und Hammurabi seit 1840 v. Chr.' In *Sumer*, 9 (1953), 189 ff.
147. Ungnad, A. 'Untersuchungen zu den...Urkunden aus Dilbat,' In *B.A.* 6, Heft 5 (1909).
148. Ungnad, A. 'Eponymen.' In *R.L.A.* 2 (1938), 412 ff.
149. Weidner, E. 'Studien zur assyrisch-babylonischen Chronologie und Geschichte auf Grund neuer Funde.' In *M.V.A.G.* 20/4 (1915).
150. Weidner, E. 'Die Könige von Assyrien.' In *M.V.A.G.* 26/2 (1921).
151. Weidner, E. *Politische Dokumente aus Kleinasien*. Leipzig, 1923.
152. Weidner, E. 'Die grosse Königsliste aus Assur.' In *Arch. f. Or.* 3 (1926), 66 ff.
153. Weidner, E. 'Die neue Königsliste aus Assur.' In *Arch. f. Or.* 4 (1927), 11 ff.
154. Weidner, E. 'Der altassyrische Kalender.' In *Arch. f. Or.* 5 (1928–9), 184 ff.
155. Weidner, E. 'Die Annalen des Konigs Aššurbelkala von Assyrien.' In *Arch. f. Or.* 6 (1930–1), 75 ff.
156. Weidner, E. 'Aus den Tagen eines assyrischen Schattenkönigs.' In *Arch. f. Or.* 10 (1935–6), 1 ff.
157. Weidner, E. 'Studien zur Zeitgeschichte Tukulti-Ninurtas I.' In *Arch. f. Or.* 13 (1939–41), 109 ff.
158. Weidner, E. 'Die Assyrischen Eponymen.' In *Arch. f. Or.* 13 (1939–41), 308 ff.
159. Weidner, E. 'Bemerkungen zur Königsliste aus Chorsabad.' In *Arch. f. Or.* 15 (1945–51), 85 ff.
160. Weidner, E. 'Die Bibliothek Tiglatpilesers I.' In *Arch. f. Or.* 16 (1952–3), 197 ff., especially 'Die Eponymen der Zeit Tiglatpilesers I.', 213 ff.
161. Weidner, E. *Die Inschriften Tukulti-Ninurtas I und seiner Nachfolger* (*Arch. f. Or.* Beiheft 12). Graz, 1959.
162. Welker, M. *The Painted Pottery of the Near East in the Second Millennium B.C. and its chronological background* (*Transactions of the American Philosophical Society*, New Series 38, pt. 2). Philadelphia, 1948.
163. Wiseman, D. J. 'Abban and Alalaḫ.' In *J.C.S.* 12 (1958), 124 ff.
164. Wiseman, D. J. *The Alalaḫ Tablets* (Occasional Publications of the British Institute of Archaeology at Ankara, no. 2). London, 1953.
165. Winckler, H. *Altorientalische Forschungen*. Leipzig, 1893–1901.

166. Wolski, J. 'Le problème de la chronologie orientale aux IIIe et IIe millénaires avant notre ère.' In *Archeologia*, 6 (1954), 54 ff. (Warsaw, 1956).
167. Woolley, Sir L. *Alalakh* (Reports of the Research Committee of the Society of Antiquaries of London, 18). Oxford, 1955.
168. Yadin, Y. In *Bi. Ar.* 22/1 (1959), 2 ff.
169. Yadin, Y. *Hazor*. 2 vols. Jerusalem, 1958, 1960.

III. THE AEGEAN BRONZE AGE

1. Apollodorus, *Bibliotheca*, 2, 8, 2.
2. Bérard, J. 'Recherches sur la chronologie de l'époque mycénienne.' In *Mém. Ac. Inscr. B.-L.* 15 (1950), pt. 1.
3. Bérard, J. 'Les Hyksos et la légende d'Io.' In *Syria*, 29 (1952), 1 ff.
4. Childe, V. G. 'On the Date and Origin of Minyan Ware.' In *J.H.S.* 35 (1915), 196 ff.
5. Clement of Alexandria, *Stromata*, 1, xxi.
6. Diodorus Siculus, *Bibliotheca Historica*.
7. Eusebius, *Chronikon*.
8. Evans, A. J. *The Palace of Minos*, 1. London, 1921.
9. Forsdyke, J. *Greece before Homer*. London, 1956.
10. Furumark, A. *The Chronology of Mycenaean Pottery*. Stockholm, 1941.
11. Furumark, A. 'The Settlement at Ialysos and Aegean History.' In *A.I.R.R.S.* 15 (1950), 150 ff.
12. Herodotean *Life of Homer, ad fin.*
13. Herodotus, II, 145.
14. Jacoby, F. *Das Marmor Parium*. Berlin, 1904.
15. Pausanias, I, xli.
16. Pendlebury, J. D. A. *Aegyptiaca*. Cambridge, 1930.
17. Pendlebury, J. D. A. 'Egypt and the Aegean in the Late Bronze Age.' In *J.E.A.* 16 (1930), 75 ff.
18. Schaeffer, C. F. A. *Stratigraphie comparée et chronologie de l'Asie occidentale*. London, 1948.
19. Smith, S. *Alalakh and Chronology*. London, 1940. Reviewed by W. F. Albright in *A.J.A.* 47 (1943), 491 ff.
20. Smith, S. 'M.M. I–II and Babylonian Chronology.' In *A.J.A.* 49 (1945), 1 ff.
21. Wace, A. J. B. and Blegen, C. W. 'The Pre-Mycenaean Pottery of the Mainland.' In *B.S.A.* 22 (1916–18), 175 ff.
22. Weinberg, S. 'Aegean Chronology: Neolithic Period and Early Bronze Age.' In *A.J.A.* 51 (1947), 165 ff.
23. Weinberg, S. 'The Relative Chronology of the Aegean in the Neolithic Period and the Early Bronze Age.' In Ehrich, R. W., *Relative Chronologies in Old World Archaeology* (Chicago, 1954).

A. ADDENDA

EGYPT

1. Hornung, E. *Untersuchen zur Chronologie und Geschichte des Neuen Reiches* (*Ägyptol. Abh.* 11). Wiesbaden, 1964.
2. Hornung, E. 'Neue Materialien zur ägyptischen Chronologie.' In *Z.D.M.G.* 117 (1967), 11–16.

3. Kitchen, K. A. 'On the Chronology and History of the New Kingdom.' In *Chron. d'Ég.* 40, no. 80 (1965), 310–22.
4. Redford, D. B. 'The Coregency of Tuthmosis III and Amenophis III.' In *J.E.A.* 51 (1965), 107–22.
5. Redford, D. B. *History and Chronology of the Eighteenth Dynasty of Egypt.* Toronto, 1967.

ANCIENT WESTERN ASIA

6. Albright, W. F. 'Further Light on the History of Middle-Bronze Byblos.' In *Bull. A.S.O.R.* 179 (1965), 38 ff.
7. Ehrich, R. W. (ed.). *Chronologies in Old World Archaeology.* Chicago, 1965. Contributors include W. F. Albright, D. F. Brown, Kwan-Chih Chang, G. F. Dales, R. H. Dyson, Jr., R. W. Ehrich, M. Gimbutas, D. P. Hansen, H. J. Kantor, M. J. Mellink, E. Porada, H. L. Thomas, P. J. Watson, S. S. Weinberg. (Supersedes §11, 25 above.)
8. Goetze, A. 'The Kassites and Near Eastern Chronology.' In *J.C.S.* 18 (1964), 97 ff.
9. Reiner, E. 'The Year-dates of Sumu-Yamutbal.' In *J.C.S.* 15 (1961), 121 ff.
10. Rowton, M. B. 'The Material from Western Asia and the Chronology of the Nineteenth Dynasty.' In *J.N.E.S.* 25 (1966), 240 ff.
11. Rowton, M. B. 'Mesopotamian Comparative Chronology and the Date of the Destruction of Ugarit.' Not yet published.
12. Weidner, E. 'Die älteren Kassiten-Könige.' In *Arch. f. Or.* 19 (1959–1960), 138.
13. Weidner, E. 'Assyrische Epen über die Kassiten-Kämpfe.' In *Arch. f. Or.* 20 (1963), 113 ff.

THE AEGEAN BRONZE AGE

14. Kohler, E. L. and Ralph, E. K. 'C-14 dates for sites in the Mediterranean area.' In *A.J.A.* 65 (1961), 357 ff.
15. Ninkovich, D. and Heezen, B. C. 'Santorini Tephra.' In *Colston Papers,* 17 (1965), 413 ff.
16. Weinberg, S. 'The Relative Chronology of the Aegean in the Stone and Early Bronze Ages.' In Ehrich, R. W., *Chronologies in Old World Archaeology,* 285 ff. Chicago, 1965.

CHAPTER VII (a)

I. GEOGRAPHY, TERMINOLOGY AND CHRONOLOGY

1. Mellaart, J. *Earliest civilisations of the Near East.* London, 1965.
2. Nagel, W. *Die Bauern- und Stadtkulturen im vordynastischen Vorderasien* (with extensive bibliography). Berlin, 1964.
3. Reed, Ch. 'Osteological evidences for prehistoric domestication in south-west Asia.' In *Zeitschrift für Tierzüchtung,* 76 (1961), 31 ff.

II. THE ZAGROS ZONE OF NORTHERN IRAQ

1. Braidwood, R. J. and Howe, Bruce. *Prehistoric investigations in Iraqi Kurdistan* (*S.A.O.C.* no. 31). Chicago, 1960.
2. Mellink, M. J. 'Archaeology in Asia Minor: Urfa-Diyarbakir area.' In *A.J.A.* 69 (1965), 133 ff.

3. Solecki, R. L. 'Zawi Chemi Shanidar, a post-Pleistocene village site in North-ern Iraq.' In *Report of the VIth Intern. Congress on Quaternary*, *Warsaw*, *1961*, vol. IV, 405 ff. Lodz, 1964.

4. Solecki, R. S. 'Shanidar cave, a late Pleistocene site in Northern Iraq.' *Ibid.* 413 ff.

5. Solecki, R. S. 'Prehistory in Shanidar valley, North Iraq.' In *Science*, 18 (1963), 179 ff.

III. THE ZAGROS ZONE OF SOUTHERN IRAN

1. Braidwood, R. J., Howe, Bruce and Reed, C. A. 'The Iranian prehistoric project.' In *Science*, 133 (1961), 2008 ff.

2. Hole, F. and Flannery, K. V. 'Excavations at Alikosh, Iran, 1961.' In *Iranica antiqua*, 2 (1962), 97 ff.

3. Hole, F., Flannery, K. V. and Neely, J. 'Early agriculture and animal hus-bandry in Deh Luran, Iran.' In *Current Anthropology*, 6 (1965), 105 f.

4. Meldgaard, J., Mortensen, P. and Thrane, H. *Excavations at Tepe Guran, Luristan* (= *Acta Arch.* 34), pp. 110–21. Copenhagen, 1964.

IV. SYRIA AND LEBANON IN THE SEVENTH AND SIXTH MILLENNIA

1. Braidwood, R. J. and Braidwood, L. S. *Excavations in the plain of Antioch*, I (*O.I.P.* LXI). Chicago, 1960.

2. Cauvin, J. 'Les industries lithiques du tell de Byblos.' In *L'Anthropologie* 66 (1962), 488 ff.

3. Cauvin, J. 'Le néolithique de Moukhtara.' In *L'Anthropologie*, 67 (1963), 489 ff.

4. Contenson, Henri de. 'Remarques sur la sédentarisation au Proche-Orient.' In *Berlin Jahrbuch für Vor- und Frühgeschichte*, 5 (1965), 207 ff.

5. Contenson, Henri de, 'New correlations between Ras Shamra and Al 'Amuq.' In *Bull. A.S.O.R.*, 172 (1963), 35 ff.

6. Contenson, Henri de and Van Liere, W. J. 'Sondages à Tell Ramad en 1963.' In *Ann. Arch. de Syrie*, XIV (1964), 109 ff.

7. Dunand, M. 'Rapport préliminaire sur les fouilles de Byblos, 1950–52.' In *Bulletin M.B.*, 12 (1955), 7 ff.

8. Dunand, M. 'Rapport préliminaire sur les fouilles de Byblos, 1957–59.' In *Bulletin M.B.*, 16 (1961), 69 ff.

9. Garstang, J. 'Excavations at Sakje-geuzi in North Syria.' In *Ann. Arch. Anthr.* 24 (1937), 132 f.

10. Schaeffer, C. F. A. *et al.* *Ugaritica* IV. Paris, 1962.

11. Van Liere, W. J. and Contenson, Henri de. 'A note on five early neolithic sites in inland Syria.' In *Ann. Arch. de Syrie*, 13 (1963), 175 ff.

12. Van Liere, W. J. and Contenson, Henri de. 'Holocene environment and early settlement in the Levant.' In *Ann. Arch. de Syrie*, XIV (1964), 125 ff.

V. THE MESOPOTAMIAN PLAIN

1. Braidwood, R. J. and L. S. *et al.* 'Matarrah.' In *J.N.E.S.* 11 (1952), 2 ff.

2. Buisson, Comte Mesnil du. *Baghouz.* Leyden, 1948.

3. Herzfeld, E. *Die vorgeschichtlichen Töpfereien von Samarra.* Berlin, 1930.

4. Lloyd, Seton and Safar, F. 'Tell Hassuna.' In *J.N.E.S.* IV (1945), 253 ff.

5. Mortensen, P. 'On the chronology of early farming communities in Northern Iraq.' In *Sumer*, 18 (1962), 73 ff.

VI. THE HALAF CULTURE

1. Dirvana, S. 'Cerablus civarinda Yunus'ta bulunan Tel Halef keramikleri.' In *Belleten*, 8 (1944), 403 ff.
2. Mallowan, M.E.L. and Cruikshank Rose, J. *Prehistoric Assyria. The excavations at Tell Arpachiyah* (= *Iraq*, 11, 1). London, 1935.
3. Schmidt, H. *Tel Halaf*, 1. Berlin, 1943.

VII. THE HALAF PERIOD IN SYRIA AND LEBANON

1. Mellaart, James. *Chalcolithic and Early Bronze Age in the Levant and Anatolia*. Beirut (Khayats), 1966.
   See also bibliography to section IV.

VIII. SUSIANA AND SOUTHERN MESOPOTAMIA

1. Le Breton, L. 'The early periods at Susa: Mesopotamian relations.' In *Iraq*, 19 (1957), 79 ff.
2. Lloyd, Seton and Safar, F. 'Eridu.' In *Sumer*, IV (1948), 115 ff.
3. Oates, J. 'Ur and Eridu.' In *Iraq*, 22 (1960), 32 ff.
4. Stronach, D. B. 'Excavations at Ras' al 'Amiya.' In *Iraq*, 23 (1961), 95 ff.
5. Ziegler, Ch. *Die Keramik von der Qal'a des Haǧǧi Mohammed*. Berlin, 1953.

IX. THE IRANIAN PLATEAU

1. Brown, T. Burton, 'Excavations in Shahriyar, Iran.' In *Archaeology*, 15 (1962), 27 ff.
2. Burney, C. A. 'Excavations at Yanik Tepe, Azerbaijan.' In *Iraq*, 26 (1964), 54, ff.
3. Contenau, G. and Ghirshman, R. *Fouilles du Tépé Giyan, près de Nihavend, 1931, 1932.* Paris 1935.
4. Ghirshman, R. *Fouilles de Sialk près de Kashan, 1933, 1934, 1937.* Paris, 1938.
5. Wertime, Th. A. 'Man's first encounter with metallurgy.' In *Science*, 146 (1964), 1257 ff.
6. Young, T. C., Jr. 'Sixth and fifth millennium settlements in Solduz Valley, Iran.' In *Ill. Ldn News*, 3 Nov. 1962.
7. Young, T. C., Jr. 'Dalma painted ware.' In *Expedition*, 1 (1963), 30 f.

X. SOUTHERN TURKESTAN

1. Coon, C. S. *Cave exploration in Iran, 1949.* Philadelphia, 1951.
2. Dupré, L. 'Prehistoric archaeological surveys and excavations in Afghanistan, 1959–60 and 1961–63.' In *Science*, 146 (1964), 638 ff.
3. Khlopin, I. N. *Eneolit yochikh oblastei Srednei Asii*, 1. Moscow–Leningrad, 1963.
4. Masson, V. M. *Eneolit yochikh oblastei Srednei Asii*, 11. Moscow–Leningrad, 1962.
5. Masson, V. M. *Srednaya Asiya i drevniye vostok* (with extensive bibliography). Moscow–Leningrad, 1964.
6. Masson, V. M. 'The first farmers in Turkmenia.' In *Antiq.* 30 (1961), 203 ff.

CHAPTER VII (*b*)

XI. GEOGRAPHICAL INTRODUCTION

1. Blegen, C. W. 'The Royal Bridge.' In *The Aegean and the Near East, Studies presented to Hetty Goldman*. New York, 1956.
2. Brice, W. C. 'The Turkish Colonization of Anatolia.' In *Bull. Ryl. Libr.* 38 (1955), 18 ff.
3. Planhol, F. X. de. 'Limites antique et actuelle des cultures arbustives méditerranéennes en Asie Mineure.' In *Bulletin de l'Association de géographes français*, nos. 239, 240 (1954), 4 ff.
4. Planhol, F. X. de. *De la plaine pamphylienne aux lacs pisidiens: Nomadisme et vie paysanne*. Paris, 1958.

XII. 'NEOLITHIC' ANATOLIA

1. Bittell, K. 'Fikirtepe kazısı.' In *V-inci Türk Tarih Kongresi* (Ankara, 1960), 1 ff., pls. III–IX.
2. Bordaz, J. Suberde Excavations. In *A. St.* 15 (1965), 30 ff.
3. Bostanci, E. Y. 'Researches on the Mediterranean coast of Anatolia: A new Palaeolithic site at Beldibi near Antalya.' In *Anatolia*, 4 (1959), 129 ff.
4. Bostanci, E. Y. 'The Belbaşi industry.' In *Belleten*, 26, no. 102 (1962), 253 ff.
5. Esin, U. and Benedict, P. 'Recent developments in the prehistory of Anatolia.' In *Current Anthropology*, 4, 4 (1963), 339 ff.
6. French, D. H. 'Early pottery sites from Western Anatolia.' In *Bulletin of the Institute of Archaeology*, 5 (1965), 15 ff.
7. Furness, A. 'Some early pottery of Samos, Kalimnos, and Chios.' In *P.P.S.* 22 (1956), 173 ff.
8. Garstang, J. *Prehistoric Mersin*. Oxford, 1953.
9. Goldman, H. and Mellink, M. *Excavations at Gözlü Kule, Tarsus*, II. Princeton, 1956.
10. Helbaek, H. 'First impressions of the Çatal Hüyük plant husbandry.' In *A. St.* 14 (1964), 121 ff.
11. Kökten, K. I. 'Tarsus-Antalya arası sahil şeriti üzerinde ve Antalya bölgesinde yapılan tarihöncesi araştırmaları hakkinda.' In *Türk Arkeoloji Dergisi*, 8 (1958), 10 ff.
12. Mellaart, J. 'Preliminary Report on a survey of Pre-classical remains in Southern Turkey.' In *A. St.* 4 (1954), 175 ff.
13. Mellaart, J. 'Some Prehistoric sites in Northwestern Anatolia.' In *Istanbuler Mitt.* 6 (1955), 53 ff.
14. Mellaart, J. 'The Neolithic obsidian industry of Ilıcapınar and its relations.' In *Istanbuler Mitt.* 8 (1958), 82 ff.
15. Mellaart, J. 'Excavations at Hacılar: First Preliminary Report.' In *A. St.* 8 (1958), 127 ff.
16. Mellaart, J. 'Excavations at Hacılar: Second Preliminary Report.' In *A. St.* 9 (1959), 51 ff.
17. Mellaart, J. 'Excavations at Hacılar: Third Preliminary Report.' In *A. St.* 10 (1960), 83 ff.
18. Mellaart, J. 'Excavations at Hacılar: Fourth Preliminary Report.' In *A. St.* 11 (1961), 39 ff.
19. Mellaart, J. 'Early cultures of the South Anatolian Plateau.' In *A. St.* 11 (1961), 159 ff.

20. Mellaart, J. 'Excavations at Çatal Hüyük: First Preliminary Report, 1961.' In *A. St.* 12 (1962), 41 ff.
21. Mellaart, J. 'Excavations at Çatal Hüyük: Second Preliminary Report, 1962.' In *A. St.* 13 (1963), 43 ff.
22. Mellaart, J. 'Excavations at Çatal Hüyük: Third Preliminary Report, 1963.' In *A. St.* 14 (1964), 39 ff.
23. Mellaart, J. 'Excavations at Çatal Hüyük: Fourth Preliminary Report, 1965.' In *A. St.* 16 (1966), 165 ff.
24. Mellaart, J. *Earliest Civilization of the Near East.* London, 1965.
25. Mellaart, J. *Çatal Hüyük: a neolithic city in Anatolia.* London, 1966.
26. Solecki, R. S. 'The artifacts from Görüklük Tepe, Suberde.' In *Türk Arkeoloji Dergisi*, 13, 1 (1964), 134 f.
27. Solecki, R. S. 'Cave-art in Kürtün Ini, a Taurus Mountain site in Turkey.' In *Man* (1964), 87 f.
28. Theocaris, D. R. Ἐκ τῆς προϊστορίας τῆς Εὐβοίας καὶ τῆς Σκύρου. In *Archeion Euboikôn Meletôn*, 6 (1959), 179 ff.
29. Todd, I. A. 'The obsidian industry of Avla Dağ.' In *A. St.* 15 (1965), 95 ff.
30. Todd, I. A. 'Surface finds from various sites.' In *A. St.* 15 (1965), 34.
31. Todd, I. A. 'Central Anatolian Survey.' In *A. St.* 16 (1966), 14.

XIII. THE EARLY CHALCOLITHIC PERIOD

1. Mellaart, J. 'Early Chalcolithic Pottery from Çatal Hüyük'; part of article 'Early Cultures of the South Anatolian Plateau'. In *A. St.* 11 (1961), 177 ff.

XIV. THE LATE CHALCOLITHIC PERIOD

1. Braidwood, R. J. 'Near Eastern Prehistory.' In *Science*, 127 (1958), 1419 ff.
2. French, D. H. 'Late Chalcolithic Pottery in Northwestern Turkey and the Aegean.' In *A. St* 11 (1961), 99 ff.
3. Mellaart, J. 'Excavations at Beycesultan, 1958. II. The Chalcolithic Sounding.' In *A. St.* 9 (1959), 35 ff.
4. Mellink, M. Review of Garstang, J., *Prehistoric Mersin.* In *Bi. Or.* 11 (1954), 13 ff.
5. Stronach, D. B. 'Excavations at Beycesultan, 1958. III. An Early Metal Hoard from Beycesultan.' In *A. St.* 9 (1959), 47 ff.

CHAPTER VIII

I. BABYLONIA AND MESOPOTAMIA

1. Amiet, P. *La Glyptique mésopotamienne archaïque.* Paris, 1961.
2. Andrae, W. *Das wiedererstandene Assur.* Leipzig, 1938.
3. Andrae, W. *Die archaischen Ischtar-Tempel in Assur.* Leipzig, 1922.
4. Braidwood, R. J., Braidwood, L., Smith, J. G., Leslie, C. 'Matarrah, a Southern Variant of the Hassunan Assemblage, excavated in 1948.' In *J.N.E.S.* 11 (1952), 1 ff.
5. Braidwood, R. J. and Howe, B. *Prehistoric Investigations in Iraqi Kurdistan* (*S.A.O.C.* 31). Chicago, 1960.
6. Buren, E. D. van. 'Places of Sacrifice (Opferstätten).' In *Iraq*, 14 (1952), 76 ff.
7. Childe, V. G. 'Eurasian Shaft-hole Axes.' In *Eurasia Septentrionalis Antiqua*, 9 (1934), 159 ff.

8. Coon, C. S. 'The Eridu Crania—a preliminary report.' In *Sumer*, 5 (1948–9), 103 ff.
9. Delougaz, P. *The Temple Oval at Khafajah* (*O.I.P.* 53). Chicago, 1940.
10. Delougaz, P. and Lloyd, S. *Pre-Sargonic Temples in the Diyala Region* (*O.I.P.* 58). Chicago, 1942.
11. Driver, G. R. *Semitic Writing*. London, 1948.
12. El Wailly F. 'Tell es-Sawwan.' In *Sumer*, 19 (1963), 1 ff.
13. Falkenstein, A. 'La Cité-Temple sumérienne.' In *Cah. H.M.*, 1 (1954), 784 ff.
14. Hall, H. R. *A Season's Work at Ur*. London, 1930.
15. Hall, H. R. and Woolley, C. L. *Al-'Ubaid* (*U.E.*, 1). Oxford, 1927.
16. Heidel, A. *The Babylonian Genesis*. Ed. 2. Chicago, 1951.
17. Helbaek, H. 'Ecological Effect of Irrigation in Ancient Mesopotamia.' In *Iraq*, 22 (1960), 186 ff.
18. Herzfeld, E. E. *Die Ausgrabungen von Samarra*. v. *Die vorgeschichtlichen Töpfereien von Samarra*. Berlin, 1930.
19. Jacobsen, T. 'Early Political Development in Mesopotamia.' In *Z.A.* 52 (1957), 91 ff.
20. Jacobsen, T. *The Sumerian King-list* (*Assyriological Studies*, no. 11). Chicago, 1939.
21. Lloyd, S. 'Ur–Al 'Ubaid, Uqair and Eridu.' In *Iraq*, 22 (1960), 23 ff.
22. Lloyd, S. and Safar, F. 'Eridu. A Preliminary communication on the Second Season's Excavations 1947–8.' In *Sumer*, 4 (1948), 115 ff.
23. Lloyd, S. and Safar, F. 'Tell Uqair. Excavations by the Iraq Government Directorate of Antiquities in 1940 and 1941.' In *J.N.E.S.* 2 (1943), 131 ff.
24. Mackay, E. *Report on Excavations at Jemdet Nasr, Iraq* (*Field Museum of Natural History, Anthropological Memoirs*, vol. 1, no. 3). Chicago, 1931.
25. Mallowan, M. E. L. 'Excavations at Brak and Chagar Bazar.' In *Iraq*, 9 (1947), 1 ff.
26. Mallowan, M. E. L. 'Noah's Flood Reconsidered.' In *Iraq*, 26 (1964), 62 ff.
27. Mallowan, M. E. L. and Rose, J. C. 'The Excavations at Tell Arpachiyah.' In *Iraq*, 2 (1935), 1 ff.
28. Oates, J. 'Ur and Eridu; the Prehistory.' In *Iraq*, 22 (1960), 32 ff.
29. Otten, C. M. 'Note on the Cemetery of Eridu.' In *Sumer*, 4 (1948), 125 ff.
30. Perkins, A. L. *The Comparative Archaeology of Early Mesopotamia* (*S.A.O.C.* 25). Chicago, 1949.
31. Preusser, C. *Die Wohnhäuser in Assur*. Berlin, 1954.
32. Safar, F. 'Third Season of Excavations at Eridu 1948–9.' In *Sumer*, 5 (1949), 159 ff.
33. Speiser, E. A. *Excavations at Tepe Gawra I*. Philadelphia, 1935.
34. Starr, R. F. *Report on the Excavations at Yorgan Tepe near Kirkuk*. Cambridge (Mass.), 1937–9.
35. Stronach, D. 'Excavations at Ras el 'Amiya.' In *Iraq*, 23 (1961), 95 ff.
36. Tobler, A. J. *Excavations at Tepe Gawra II*. Philadelphia, 1950.
37. *U.V.B. Vorläufige Berichte über die…in Uruk-Warka…Ausgrabungen*. In progress, beginning Berlin, 1930.
38. Woolley, C. L. *The Early Periods* (*U.E.*, iv). London and Philadelphia, 1955.
39. Woolley, C. L. 'Excavations at Ur, 1929–30.' In *A.J.* 10 (1930), 315 ff.
40. Ziegler, C. *Die Keramik von der Qal'a des Ḥaǧǧi Moḥammed*. Berlin, 1953.

II. ASSYRIA

1. Andrae, W. *Die Ionische Säule*. Berlin, 1933.
2. Childe, V. G. *New Light on the Most Ancient East*. London, 1952.
3. Creswell, K. A. C. *Early Muslim Architecture*, part II. Oxford, 1940.
4. Egami, N. *Telul eth Thalathat, the Excavation of Tell II*. Tokyo, 1959.
5. El Amin, M. and Mallowan, M. E. L. 'Soundings in the Makhmur Plain.' In *Sumer*, 5 (1949), 145 ff.
6. El Amin, M. and Mallowan, M. E. L. 'Soundings in the Makhmur Plain.' In *Sumer*, 6 (1950), 55 ff.
7. Lloyd, S. 'Bronze Age Architecture of Anatolia.' In *Proc. Brit. Acad.*, 49 (1963), 163 ff.
8. Lloyd, S. 'Iraq Government Soundings at Sinjar.' In *Iraq*, 7 (1940), 13 ff.
9. Lloyd, S. 'Some Ancient Sites in the Jebel Sinjar District.' In *Iraq*, 5 (1938), 123 ff.
10. Lloyd, S. and Safar, F. 'Tell Hassuna. Excavations by the Iraq Government Directorate of Antiquities in 1943 and 1944, with prefatory remarks by Robert J. Braidwood.' In *J.N.E.S.* 4 (1945), 255 ff.
11. Mallowan, M. E. L. 'The Excavations at Tall Chagar Bazar and an Archaeological Survey of the Habur Region, 1934–5.' In *Iraq*, 3 (1936), 1 ff.
12. Safar, F. 'Pottery from Caves of Baradost.' In *Sumer*, 6 (1950), 118 ff.
13. Thompson, R. C., and Mallowan, M. E. L. 'The British Museum Excavations at Nineveh, 1931–2.' In *Ann. Arch. Anthr.* 20 (1933), 71 ff.

III. SYRIA

1. Braidwood, R. J. *Mounds in the Plain of Antioch. An Archaeological Survey* (*O.I.P.* 48). Chicago, 1937.
2. Braidwood, R. J. and L. S. *Excavations in the Plain of Antioch* (*O.I.P.* 61). Chicago, 1960.
3. Dunand, M. *Fouilles de Byblos*, 1, 1926–32. Paris, 1939.
4. Dunand, M. 'Chronologie des plus anciennes installations de Byblos.' In *Rev. bibl.* 57 (1950), 583 ff.
5. Fischer. *Weltgeschichte: Die altorientalischen Reiche*, 1. Frankfurt and Hamburg, 1965.
6. Himadeh, S. B. *Economic Organization of Syria*. Beirut, 1936.
7. Hood, S. 'Excavations at Tabara el Akrad.' In *A.S.* 1 (1951), 113 ff.
8. Ingholt, H. *Rapport Préliminaire sur Sept Campagnes de Fouilles à Hama en Syrie*. Copenhagen, 1940.
9. Le Breton, L. 'The Early Periods at Susa: Mesopotamian Relations.' In *Iraq*, 19 (1957), 79 ff.
10. Mackay, E. *Report on the Excavation of the 'A' Cemetery at Kish, Mesopotamia* (*Field Museum of Natural History, Anthropological Memoirs*, vol. 1, no. 1). Chicago, 1925.
11. Mallowan, M. E. L. 'The 'Amuq Plain.' In *Antiq.* 37 (1963), 185 ff.
12. Mallowan, M. E. L. 'The Excavations at Tall Chagar Bazar and an Archaeological Survey of the Habur Region. Second Campaign, 1936.' In *Iraq*, 4 (1937), 91 ff.
13. Mallowan, M. E. L. *Twenty-five Years of Mesopotamian Discovery*. London, 1959.
14. Mallowan, M. E. L. 'Excavations in the Baliḫ Valley, 1938.' In *Iraq*, 8 (1946), 111 ff.

15. Maxwell-Hyslop, R., Taylor, J. du Plat, Seton-Williams, M. V. and Waechter, J. D'A. 'An Archaeological Survey of the Plain of Jabbul, 1939.' In *P.E.Q.* (1942), 8 ff.
16. Pottier, E., de Morgan, J., de Mecquenem, R. 'Recherches Archéologiques, Céramique Peinte de Suse et Petits Monuments.' (*Mém.D.P.* 13.) Paris, 1912.
17. Schaeffer, C. F. A. *Ugaritica IV*. Paris, 1962.
18. Thureau-Dangin, F. et Dunand, M. *Til Barsib*. Paris, 1936.
19. Woolley, Sir L. *A Forgotten Kingdom*. London, 1953.
20. Woolley, C. L. 'The Prehistoric Pottery of Carchemish,' In *Iraq*, 1 (1934), 146 ff.
21. Woolley, C. L. and Barnett, R. D. *Carchemish: report on the excavations at Jerablus on behalf of the British Museum*, part III. London, 1952.

IV. IRAN

1. Arne, T. J. *Excavations at Shah Tepe, Iran. The Sino-Swedish Expedition*. Stockholm, 1945.
2. Braidwood, R. J. 'The Iranian Prehistoric Project, 1959–60.' In *Iranica Antiqua*, 2 (1961), 3 ff.
3. Burney, C. A. 'Excavations at Yanik Tepe, Azerbaijan.' In *Iraq*, 24 (1962), 134 ff.
4. Burney, C. A. 'Excavations at Yanik Tepe, Azerbaijan.' In *Iraq*, 26 (1964), 54 ff.
5. Burton-Brown, T. *Excavations in Azerbaijan, 1948*. London, 1951.
6. Casal, J.-M. *Fouilles de Mundigak*. Paris, 1961.
7. Contenau, G. et Ghirshman, R. *Fouilles du Tepe-Giyan près de Nehavend, 1931–2*. Paris, 1935.
8. Coon, C. S. *Seven Caves. Archaeological Exploration in the Middle East*. London, 1957.
9. de Cardi, B. 'New wares and Fresh Problems from Baluchistan.' In *Antiq.*, 33 (1959), 15 ff.
10. Delougaz, P. *Pottery from the Diyala Region* (*O.I.P.* 63). Chicago, 1952.
11. Dyson, R. H. and Young, T. C. 'The Solduz Valley, Iran: Pisdeli Tepe.' In *Antiq.*, 34 (1960), 19 ff.
12. Egami, N. and Masuda, S. *Marv-Dasht*. I. *The Excavation at Tall-i-Bakun 1956*. Tokyo, 1962.
13. Egami, N. and Sono, T. *Marv-Dasht*. II. *The Excavation at Tall-i-Gap 1959*. Tokyo, 1962.
14. Erlenmeyer, M. L. and H. 'Frühiranische Stempelsiegel, I.' In *Iranica Antiqua*, 4 (1964), 85 ff.
15. Fairservis, W. A. 'Preliminary Report on the Prehistoric Archaeology of the Afghan-Baluchi Areas.' *American Museum Novitates*, no. 1587 (1952).
16. Frankfort, H. 'Studies in Early Pottery of the Near East. I. Mesopotamia, Syria and Egypt and their earliest interrelations.' *Royal Anthropological Institute of Great Britain and Ireland, Occasional Papers*, no. 6 (1924).
17. Gautier, J.-E. and Lampre, G. 'Fouilles de Moussian.' In *Mem.D.P.* 8 (1905), 59 ff.
18. Ghirshman, R. *Fouilles de Sialk près de Kashan. I. 1933, 1934, 1937*. Paris, 1938. *II. Ibid.* 1939.
19. Goff, C. 'Excavations at Tall-i-Nokhodi.' In *Iran*, 1 (1963), 43 ff.
20. Goff, C. 'Excavations at Tall-i-Nokhodi.' In *Iran*, 2 (1964), 41 ff.

21. Herzfeld, G. *Iran in the Ancient East*. London, 1941.
22. Hole, V. and Flannery, K. V. 'Excavations at Ali Kosh.' In *Iranica Antiqua*, 2 (1961), 97 ff.
23. Hole, V., Flannery, K. V., Neely, J. 'Early Agriculture and Animal Husbandry in Deh Luran, Iran.' In *Current Anthropology*, 6, no. 1 (1965), 105 ff.
24. Langsdorff, A. and McCown, D. E. *Tall-i-Bakun, A Season of 1932* (*O.I.P.* 59). Chicago, 1942.
25. McBurney, C. B. M. 'Preliminary Report on the Stone Age Reconnaissance in North-eastern Iran.' In *P.P.S.* 30 (1964), 382 ff.
26. McCown, D. E. *The Comparative Stratigraphy of Early Iran* (*S.A.O.C.* 23). Chicago, 1941.
27. McCown, D. E. 'The Iranian Project of the Oriental Institute of the University of Chicago.' In *A.J.A.* 53 (1949), 54 ff.
28. Masson, V. M. 'The First Farmers in Turkmenia.' In *Antiq.* 35 (1961), 203 ff.
29. Meldgaard, J., Mortensen, P., Thrane, H. 'Excavations at Tepe Guran, Luristan. The Danish Archaeological Expedition to Iran 1963.' In *Acta Arch.* 34 (1964), 97 ff.
30. Piggott, S. *Prehistoric India to 1000 B.C.* Penguin Books, Harmondsworth, 1950.
31. Pumpelly, R. *Prehistoric Civilizations of Anau*. Washington, 1908.
32. Schmidt, E. F. *Excavations at Tepe Hissar Damghan*. Philadelphia, 1937.
33. Stein, A. 'An Archaeological Tour in Ancient Persis.' In *Iraq*, 3 (1936), 111 ff.
34. Stein, A. *Archaeological Reconnaissances in North-western India and South-eastern Iran*. London, 1937.
35. Stein, A. *Old Routes of Western Iran*. London, 1940.
36. Upham Pope, A. 'A Note on Some Pottery from the Holmes Luristan Expedition of the Institute.' In *Bulletin of the American Institute for Persian Art and Archaeology*, IV, no. 3, 120 ff.
37. Vanden Berghe, L. *Archéologie de l'Iran Ancien*. Leiden, 1959.
38. Woolley, C. L. 'The Painted Pottery of Susa.' In *J.R.A.S.* (1928), 35. ff.
39. Wulsin, F. R. 'Excavations at Tureng Tepe near Asterabad.' Supplement to the *Bulletin of the American Institute for Persian Art and Archaeology*, II, no. 1 *bis* (1932).
40. Wulsin, F. R. 'The Early Cultures of Asterabad (Tureng Tepe).' In A. Upham Pope, *A Survey of Persian Art*, 1 (Oxford, 1938), 163–7.

CHAPTER IX (*a*)

G. GENERAL

1. Alimen, H. *The Prehistory of Africa* (translated by A. H. Brodrick). London, 1957.
2. Bachatly, C. *Bibliographie de la préhistoire égyptienne (1869–1938)*. Cairo, 1942.
3. Baumgartel, E. J. *The Cultures of Prehistoric Egypt*. 2 vols. (vol. I, ed. 2). Oxford, 1955, 1960.
4. Capart, J. *Primitive Art in Egypt*. London, 1905.
5. Childe, V. Gordon. *New Light on the Most Ancient East*. Ed. 4. London, 1952.
6. Forde-Johnston, J. L. *Neolithic Cultures of North Africa*. Liverpool, 1959.

7. Huzayyin, S. A. *The Place of Egypt in Prehistory*. Cairo, 1941.
8. Kaiser, W. 'Stand und Probleme der ägyptischen Vorgeschichtsforschung.' In *Z.Ä.S.* 81 (1956), 87–109.
9. Lucas, A. *Ancient Egyptian Materials and Industries*. Ed. 3. London, 1948.
10. MacBurney, C. B. M. *The Stone Age of Northern Africa* (*Penguin Books*). Harmondsworth, 1960.
11. Massoulard, E. *Préhistoire et protohistoire d'Égypte*. Paris, 1949.
12. Morgan, J. de. *Recherches sur les origines de l'Égypte*. 2 vols. Paris, 1896–7.
13. Morgan, J. de. *La préhistoire orientale*, tome II. Paris, 1926.
14. Petrie, W. M. F. *Prehistoric Egypt*. London, 1920.
15. Petrie, W. M. F. *Prehistoric Egypt Corpus*. London, 1921.
16. Petrie, W. M. F. *The Making of Egypt*. London, 1939.
17. Quibell, J. E. *Archaic Objects* (*C.C.G.* nos. 11001–12000, 14001–14754). Cairo, 1905.
18. Scharff, A. *Die Altertümer der Vor- und Frühzeit Ägyptens*. 2 vols. Mitt. aus der ägypt. Samm. IV, 1; V. Berlin, 1929, 1931.
19. Scharff, A. *Grundzüge der ägyptischen Vorgeschichte* (Morgenland, Heft 12). Leipzig, 1927.
20. Vandier, J. *Manuel d'archéologie égyptienne*, vol. I, part I. Paris, 1952.

I. INTRODUCTION

1. Butzer, Karl W. *Studien zum vor- und frühgeschichtlichen Landschaftswandel der Sahara. III. Die Naturlandschaft Ägyptens während der Vorgeschichte und der Dynastischen Zeit*. In *Abh. Mainz, Math.-Naturwiss. Kl.* Jahrg. 1959, Nr. 2.
2. Kaiser, W. 'Zur inneren Chronologie der Naqadakultur.' In *Archaeologia Geographica*, Jahrg. 6 (1957), 69–77.
3. Kantor, Helene J. 'The Chronology of Egypt and its Correlation with that of Other Parts of the Near East in the Periods before the Late Bronze Age.' In R. W. Ehrich, *Relative Chronologies in Old World Archaeology* (Chicago, 1954), 1–27.
4. Petrie, W. M. F. 'The Peoples of Egypt.' In *Anc. Egypt*, 1931, 77–85.

II. THE PREDYNASTIC CIVILIZATIONS

1. Arkell, A. J. *Early Khartoum*. Oxford, 1949.
2. Arkell, A. J. *Shaheinab*. Oxford, 1953.
3. Arkell, A. J. 'The Sudan Origin of Predynastic "Black Incised" Pottery.' In *J.E.A.* 39 (1953), 76–9.
4. Arkell, A. J. 'The Relations of the Nile Valley with the Southern Sahara in Neolithic Times.' In *Actes Congrès panafricain de préhistoire, IIe Session Alger 1952* (Paris, 1955), 345–6.
5. Arkell, A. J. 'Early Shipping in Egypt.' In *Antiq.* 33 (1959), 52–3.
6. Ayrton, E. R. and Loat, W. L. S. *Predynastic Cemetery at El Mahasna*. London, 1911.
7. Barnett, R. D. 'Early Shipping in the Near East.' In *Antiq.* 32 (1958), 220–30.
8. Bates, O. and Dunham, D. *Excavations at Gammai* (*Harvard African Studies*, VIII, 1–121). Cambridge (Mass.), 1927.
9. Baumgartel, E. J. 'Some Notes on the Origins of Egypt.' In *Arch. Orient.* 20 (1952), 278–87.

10. Baumgartel, E. J. 'Tomb and Fertility.' In *Jahrb. für kleinasiatische Forschung*, 1 (1950–51), 56–65.
11. Brunton, G. *Mostagedda and the Tasian Culture*. London, 1937.
12. Brunton, G. *Matmar*. London, 1948.
13. Brunton, G. and Caton-Thompson, G. *The Badarian Civilisation*. London, 1928.
14. Case, H. and Crowfoot Payne, J. 'Tomb 100: The Decorated Tomb at Hierakonpolis.' In *J.E.A.* 48 (1962), 5–18.
15. Debono, F. 'El Omari (près d'Hélouan).' In *Ann. Serv.* 48 (1948), 561–9.
16. Debono, F. 'La nécropole prédynastique d'Héliopolis (fouilles de 1950).' In *Ann. Serv.* 52 (1954), 625–52.
17. Debono, F. 'La civilisation prédynastique d'El Omari (Nord d'Hélouan). Nouvelles données.' In *Bull. Inst. d'Ég.* 37 (1956), 329–39.
18. Engelbach, R. and Gunn, B. *Harageh*. London, 1923.
19. Garstang, J. *Mahasna and Bet Khallaf*. London, 1902.
20. Glanville, S. R. K. 'Egyptian Theriomorphic Vessels in the British Museum.' In *J.E.A.* 12 (1926), 52–69.
21. Junker, H. *Bericht über die Grabungen ... auf dem Friedhof in Turah* (*Denksch. K. Akad. Wiss. Wien*, 56). Vienna, 1912.
22. Junker, H. *Bericht über die von der Akademie der Wissenschaften in Wien nach dem Westdelta entsendete Expedition*. Vienna, 1928.
23. Junker, H. 'Vorläufiger Bericht über die Grabung der Akademie der Wissenschaften in Wien auf der neolithischen Siedelung von Merimde-Benisalame (Westdelta).' In *A.A.W. Wien* (1929–40), 6 reports.
24. Kantor, H. J. 'The Early Relations of Egypt with Asia.' In *J.N.E.S.* 1 (1942), 174–213.
25. Kantor, H. J. 'The Final Phase of Predynastic Culture, Gerzean or Semainean?' In *J.N.E.S.* 3 (1944), 110–36.
26. Kantor, H. J. 'Further Evidence for Early Mesopotamian Relations with Egypt.' In *J.N.E.S.* 11 (1952), 239–50.
27. Keimer, L. 'Le Musa Ensete.' In *Chron. d'Ég.* 28, Nr. 55 (1953), 107–8.
28. Larsen, Hjalmar. 'Eine eigenartige Tongefäss-Scherbe aus Merimde.' In *Or. Suecana*, 6 (1958), 3–8.
29. Larsen, Hjalmar. 'Verzierte Tongefässscherben aus Merimde Benisalame in der ägyptischen Abteilung des Mittelmeermuseums in Stockholm.' In *Or. Suecana*, vii (1959), 3–53.
30. Larsen, Hjalmar. 'Knochengeräte aus Merimde in der ägyptischen Abteilung des Mittelmeermuseums.' In *Or. Suecana*, ix (1960), 28 ff.
31. Larsen, Hjalmar. 'Die Merimdekeramik im Mittelmeermuseum Stockholm.' In *Or. Suecana*, xi (1962), 3 ff.
32. Menghin, O. 'Die Grabung der Universität Kairo bei Maadi (Drittes Grabungsjahr).' In *Mitt. deutsch. Inst. Kairo*, v (1934), 111–18.
33. Menghin, O. and Amer, M. *The Excavations of the Egyptian University in the Neolithic Site at Maadi*. 2 parts. Cairo, 1932, 1936.
34. Moller, G. *Die anthropologischen Ergebnisse des vorgeschichtlichen Gräberfeldes von Abusir el-Meleq*. Leipzig, 1915.
35. Mond, R. and Myers, O. H. *Cemeteries of Armant*. 2 parts. London, 1937.
36. Peet, T. E. *The Cemeteries of Abydos*, part ii. London, 1914.
37. Peet, T. E. and Loat, W. L. S. *The Cemeteries of Abydos*, part iii. London, 1913.
38. Petrie, W. M. F. *Diospolis Parva*. London, 1901.
39. Petrie, W. M. F. and Quibell, J. E. *Naqada and Ballas*. London, 1895.

40. Petrie, W. M. F., Wainwright, G. A. and Mackay, E. *The Labyrinth, Gerzeh and Mazghuneh.* London, 1912.
41. Rizkana, I. 'Centres of Settlement in Prehistoric Egypt in the Area between Helwan and Heliopolis.' In *Bull. Inst. Fouad I du Désert*, II (1952), 117–30.
42. Randall-Maciver, D., Mace, A. C. and Griffith, F. Ll. *El Amrah and Abydos.* London, 1902.
43. Reisner, G. A. and others. *The Archaeological Survey of Nubia (Reports for 1907–8; 1908–9; 1909–10; 1910–11).* Cairo, 1901–27.
44. Scharff, A. *Die archäologischen Ergebnisse des vorgeschichtlichen Gräberfeldes von Abusir el-Meleq.* Leipzig, 1926.
45. Schott, S. 'Vorgeschichtliche Handelswege in Ägypten, Ur- und Frühgeschichte als historische Wissenschaft.' In *Festschrift E. Wahle* (Heidelberg, 1950), 308–21.
46. Täckholm, V. Laurent. 'The Plant of Naqada.' In *Ann. Serv.* 51 (1951), 299–311.
47. Caton-Thompson, G. and Gardner, E. W. *The Desert Fayum.* 2 vols. London, 1934.
48. Wainwright, G. A. 'The Red Crown in Early Prehistoric Times.' In *J.E.A.* 9 (1923), 26–33.

A. ADDENDA

1. Baumgartel, E. J. 'What Do We Know about the Excavations at Merimda?' In *J.A.O.S.* 85 (no. 4, 1965), 502–11.
2. Hayes, W. C. *Most Ancient Egypt.* Chicago, 1965.

CHAPTER IX (*b*)

G. GENERAL

1. Albright, W. F. *The Archaeology of Palestine* (Penguin Books). Harmondsworth, 1960.
2. Anati, E. *Palestine Before the Hebrews.* London, 1963.
3. Crowfoot, J. 'Notes on the Flint Implements of Jericho, 1936.' In *Ann. Arch. Anthr.* 24 (1937), 35 ff.
4. Garstang, J. 'Jericho: City and Necropolis'. In *Ann. Arch. Anthr.* 22 (1935), 143 ff.; 23 (1936), 67 ff.
5. Kenyon, K. M. 'Excavations at Jericho.' In *P.E.Q.* 84 (1952), 63 ff.; 85 (1953), 81 ff.; 86 (1954), 45 ff.; 87 (1955), 108 ff.; 88 (1956), 67 ff.; 89 (1957), 101 ff.; 92 (1960), 88 ff.
6. Kenyon, K. M. *Archaeology in the Holy Land.* London, 1960.
7. Perrot, J. 'Palestine–Syria–Cilicia.' In R. J. Braidwood and G. R. Willey, *Courses Toward Urban Life*, 147 ff. Chicago, 1962.
8. Vaux, R. de. 'Les fouilles de Tell el-Fârʿah.' In *Rev. bibl.* 54 (1947), 394 ff.; 55 (1948), 544 ff.; 56 (1949), 102 ff.; 58 (1951), 566 ff.; 59 (1952), 551 ff.; 62 (1955), 541 ff.; 64 (1957), 552 ff.; 68 (1961), 557 ff.; 69 (1962), 212 ff.
9. Zeuner, F. *History of Domesticated Animals.* London, 1963.

V. THE FIRST SETTLEMENTS

HUNTERS AND FARMERS

1. Anati, E. 'Prehistoric Trade and the Puzzle of Jericho.' In *Bull. A.S.O.R.* 167 (1962), 25 ff.
2. Braidwood, R. J. 'Jericho and its Setting in Near Eastern History.' In *Antiq.* 31 (1957), 73 ff.
3. Braidwood, R. J. 'Near Eastern Prehistory.' In *Science*, 127 (1958), 1419 ff.
4. Braidwood, R. J. and Howe, B. *Prehistoric Investigations in Iraqi Kurdistan* (*S.A.O.C.* 31). Chicago, 1960.
5. Buzy, D. 'Une industrie mésolithique en Palestine.' In *Rev. bibl.* 37 (1928), 558 ff.
6. Childe, V. G. 'Civilization, Cities and Towns.' In *Antiq.* 31 (1957), 36 ff.
7. Contenson, H. de. 'New Correlations between Ras-Shamra and Al-'Amuq.' In *Bull. A.S.O.R.* 172 (1963), 35 ff.
8. Contenson, H. de, and Van Liere, W. J. 'Sondages à Tell Ramad. 1963.' In *Ann. Arch. de Syrie*, 14 (1964), 109 ff.
9. Cornwall, I. W. 'The Pre-Pottery Neolithic Burials, Jericho.' In *P.E.Q.* 88 (1956), 110 ff.
10. Dikaios, P. *Khirokitia* (*Monographs of the Depart. of Ant. of Cyprus*, 1). Oxford, 1953.
11. Dikaios, P. 'The Stone Age.' In *The Swedish Cyprus Expedition*, IV, 1 A, 1 ff. Lund, 1962.
12. Gonzalez Echegaray, J. 'Excavaciones en la terraza de "El Khiam" (Jordania), II.' Madrid, 1966.
13. Kenyon, K. M. *Digging up Jericho*. London, 1957.
14. Kenyon, K. M. 'Reply to Professor Braidwood.' In *Antiq.* 31 (1957), 82 ff.
15. Kenyon, K. M. 'Some Observations on the Beginning of the Settlement in the Near East.' In *J.R.A.I.* 89 (1959), 35 ff.
16. Kirkbride, D. 'Notes on a Survey of Pre-Roman Archaeological Sites near Jerash.' In *Bull. Inst. Arch. London*, 1 (1958), 9 ff.
17. Kirkbride, D. 'A Brief Report on the Pre-Pottery Flint Cultures of Jericho.' In *P.E.Q.* 92 (1960), 114 ff.
18. Kirkbride, D. 'The Excavation of a Neolithic Village at Seyl Aqlat, Beidha, near Petra.' In *P.E.Q.* 92 (1960), 136 ff.
19. Kirkbride, D. 'Five Seasons at the Pre-Pottery Neolithic Village of Beidha in Jordan.' In *P.E.Q.* 98 (1966), 8 ff.
20. Mellaart, J. 'Excavations at Hacilar.' In *A. St.* 11 (1961), 39 ff.
21. Mellaart, J. 'Excavations at Çatal Hüyük.' In *A. St.* 12 (1962), 41 ff.; 13 (1963), 43 ff.; 14 (1964), 39 ff.
22. Mellaart, J. 'Chatal-Huyuk.' In *Ill. Ldn News*, 244 (1964), 158 ff., 194 ff., 232 ff. 272 ff.
23. Perrot, J. 'La terrasse d'El-Khiam.' In Neuville, R., *Le Paléolithique et le Mésolithique du Désert de Judée* (*Arch. de l'Inst. de Paléont. hum.* 24), 134 ff. Paris, 1951.
24. Perrot, J. 'Têtes de flèches du Natoufien et du Tahounien (Palestine).' In *Bull. Soc. préh. fr.* 49 (1952), 443 ff.
25. Perrot, J. 'Le Néolithique d'Abu-Gosh.' In *Syria*, 29 (1952), 119 ff.
26. Perrot, J. 'Excavations at 'Eynan ('Ein Mallaha).' In *I.E.J.* 10 (1960), 14 ff.
27. Perrot, J. ''Eynan ('Ain Mallaha).' In *Rev. bibl.* 69 (1962), 384 ff.
28. Perrot, J. 'Munhata.' In *Rev. bibl.* 70 (1963), 560 ff.

29. Perrot, J. 'Les deux premières campagnes de fouilles à Munḥatta.' In *Syria*, 41 (1964), 323 ff.; 'La troisième campagne ...' In *Syria*, 43 (1966), 49 ff.

30. Prausnitz, M. W. 'The First Agricultural Settlements in Galilee.' In *I.E.J.* 9 (1959), 166 ff.

31. Prausnitz, M. W. 'Tell 'Ely (Kh. Sheikh 'Ali).' In *Rev. bibl.* 67 (1960), 389 ff.

32. Prausnitz, M. W. 'Tell 'Ely (Kh. Sheikh 'Ali).' In *I.E.J.* 10 (1960), 119 f.

33. Rhotert, H. *Transjordanien. Vorgeschichtliche Forschungen.* Stuttgart, 1938.

34. Cl. F. Schaeffer, *Ugaritica*, IV (*Mission de Ras Shamra*, xv). Paris, 1962.

35. Stekelis, M. 'Excavations at Naḥal Oren.' In *I.E.J.* 13 (1963), 1 ff.

36. Tzori, N. 'Neolithic and Chalcolithic Sites in the Valley of Beth-Shan.' In *P.E.Q.* 90 (1958), 44 ff.

37. Waechter, J. d'A. and Seton-Williams, V. M. 'The Excavations at Wādi Dhobai, 1937–1938, and the Dhobian Industry.' In *J.P.O.S.* 18 (1938), 172 ff.

38. Zeuner, F. 'The Goats of Early Jericho.' In *P.E.Q.* 87 (1955), 70 ff.

39. Zeuner, F. 'Dog and Cat in the Neolithic of Jericho.' In *P.E.Q.* 90 (1958), 52 ff.

VI. FARMERS AND POTTERS

1. Benoit, P., Milik, J. T. and de Vaux, R. *Les Grottes de Murabba'ât* (*Discoveries in the Judaean Desert*, ii). Oxford, 1961.

2. Cauvin, J. 'Les industries lithiques du Tell de Byblos.' In *L'Anthropologie*, 66 (1962), 488 ff.

3. Contenson, H. de. 'La chronologie du niveau le plus ancien de Tell esh-Shuna (Jordanie).' In *M.U.S.J.* 37 (1960), 57 ff.

4. Contenson, H. de. 'Three Soundings in the Jordan Valley.' In *Ann. D.A.J.* 4–5 (1960), 12 ff.

5. Fitzgerald, G. 'Excavations at Beth-Shan in 1933.' In *P.E.F.Q.S.* 1934, 123 ff.

6. Fitzgerald, G. 'The Earliest Pottery of Beth-Shan.' In *M.J.* 24 (1935), 5 ff.

7. Kaplan, J. 'Excavations at Wadi Rabah.' In *I.E.J.* 8 (1958), 149 ff.

8. Kaplan, J. 'Excavations at Teluliot Batashi in the Vale of Sorek.' In *Eretz-Israel*, 5 (1958), 9 ff.

9. Kaplan, J. 'The Neolithic Pottery of Palestine.' In *Bull. A.S.O.R.* 156 (1959), 15 ff.

10. Kaplan, J. 'The Relation of the Chalcolithic Pottery of Palestine to Halafian Ware.' In *Bull. A.S.O.R.* 159 (1960), 32 ff.

11. Loud, G. *Megiddo* ii. *Seasons of 1935–39* (*O.I.P.* 62). Chicago, 1948.

12. Mellaart, J. 'The Neolithic Site of Ghrubba.' In *Ann. D.A.J.* 3 (1956), 24 ff.

13. Perrot, J. 'Hazoréa, Tell Turmus, Ben Shemen.' In *Rev. bibl.* 70 (1963), 559 f.

14. Shipton, G. M. *Notes on the Megiddo Pottery of Strata VI–XX* (*S.A.O.C.* 17). Chicago, 1939.

15. Stekelis, M. 'A New Neolithic Industry: the Yarmukian of Palestine.' In *I.E.J.* 1 (1950–51), 1 ff.

16. Stekelis, M. 'On the Yarmukian Culture.' In *Eretz-Israel*, 2 (1953), 98 ff.

17. Stekelis, M. 'The Stratigraphy of the Yarmukian Culture.' In *Bull. I.E.S.* 18 (1954), 185 ff.

18. Toombs, L. E. and Wright, G. E. 'The Third Campaign at Balâṭah (Shechem).' In *Bull. A.S.O.R.* 161 (1961), 11 ff.

19. Tufnell, O. *Lachish*. IV. *The Bronze Age*. Oxford, 1958.
20. Wright, G. E. 'An Important Correlation Between the Palestinian and Syrian Chalcolithic.' In *Bull. A.S.O.R.* 122 (1951), 52 ff.

VII. FARMERS, POTTERS AND METALWORKERS

1. Aharoni, Y. 'The Expedition to the Judean Desert, 1960. Expedition B.' In *I.E.J.* 11 (1961), 11 ff.
2. Aharony, Y. 'The Caves of Naḥal Ḥever.' In *'Atiqot*, 3 (1961), 148 ff.
3. Aharoni, Y. 'The Expedition to the Judean Desert, 1961. Expedition B.' In *I.E.J.* 12 (1962), 186 ff.
4. Albright, W. F. 'A Survey of the Archaeological Chronology of Palestine from Neolithic to Middle Bronze.' In Ehrich, R. W., *Relative Chronologies in Old World Archaeology*, 28 ff. Chicago, 1954.
5. Amiran, R. 'Two Notes on the Repertory of the Chalcolithic Pottery of Palestine.' In *Bull. A.S.O.R.* 130 (1953), 11 ff.
6. Amiran, R. 'The "Cream Ware" of Gezer and the Beersheba Late Chalcolithic.' In *I.E.J.* 5 (1955), 240 ff.
7. Amiran, R. *The Ancient Pottery of Eretz-Yisrael* (in Hebrew). Jerusalem, 1963.
8. Anati, E. 'Subterranean Dwellings in the Central Negev.' In *I.E.J.* 5 (1955), 259 ff.
9. Angress, S. 'Mammal Remains from Ḥorvat Beter (Beersheba).' In *'Atiqot*, 2 (1959), 53 ff.
10. Avigad, N. 'The Expedition to the Judean Desert, 1960. Expedition A.' In *I.E.J.* 11 (1961), 6 ff.
11. Avigad, N. 'The Expedition to the Judean Desert, 1961. Expedition A.' In *I.E.J.* 12 (1962), 169 ff.
12. Baillet, M., Milik, J. T. and de Vaux, R. *Les 'Petites Grottes' de Qumrān* (*Discoveries in the Judaean Desert of Jordan*, III). Oxford, 1962.
13. Bar-Adon, P. 'The Expedition to the Judean Desert, 1960. Expedition C.' In *I.E.J.* 11 (1961), 25 ff.
14. Bar-Adon, P. 'The Expedition to the Judean Desert, 1961. Expedition C.' In *I.E.J.* 12 (1962), 215 ff.
15. Callaway, J. A. 'The Gezer Crematorium Re-examined.' In *P.E.Q.* 94 (1962), 104 ff.
16. Contenson, H. de. 'La céramique chalcolithique de Beersheba, étude typologique.' In *I.E.J.* 6 (1956), 163 ff., 226 ff.
17. Contenson, H. de. 'Remarques sur le Chalcolithique Récent de Tell esh-Shune.' In *Rev. bibl.* 68 (1961), 546 ff.
18. Crowfoot, G. M. 'Mat Impressions on Pot Bases.' In *Ann. Arch. Anthr.* 25, (1938), 3 ff.
19. Dothan, M. 'Tell Asawir.' In *I.E.J.* 3 (1953), 263.
20. Dothan, M. 'Affuleh.' In *'Alôn (Bull. of the Department of Antiquities in Israel)* (in Hebrew), 5–6 (1957), 22 f.
21. Dothan, M. 'Excavations at Meṣer.' In *I.E.J.* 7 (1957), 217 ff.; 9 (1959), 13 ff.
22. Dothan, M. 'Some Problems of the Stratigraphy in Megiddo XX.' In *Eretz-Israel* 5 (1958), 38 ff.
23. Dothan, M. 'Excavations at Ḥorvat Beter (Beersheba)'. In *'Atiqot* 2 (1959), 1 ff.
24. Dothan, M. 'Excavations at Azor.' In *I.E.J.* 11 (1961), 171 ff.

25. Engberg, R. M. and Shipton, G. M. *Notes on the Chalcolithic and Early Bronze Age Pottery of Megiddo* (*S.A.O.C.* 10). Chicago, 1934.

26. Ferembach, D. 'Le peuplement du Proche-Orient au Chalcolithique et au Bronze Ancien.' In *I.E.J.* 9 (1959), 221 ff.

27. Glueck, N. *Explorations in Eastern Palestine.* IV. Part II. *Pottery Notes and Plates* (*Ann. A.S.O.R.* 25–8). New Haven, 1951.

28. Guy, P. L. O. *Megiddo Tombs* (*O.I.P.* 33). Chicago, 1938.

29. Jirku, A. *Die ältere Kupfer-Zeit Palästinas und der bandkeramische Kulturkreis.* Berlin, 1941.

30. Josien, T. 'La faune chalcolithique des gisements palestiniens de Bir es-Safadi et Bir Abu Matar.' In *I.E.J.* 5 (1955), 246 ff.

31. Kantor, H. 'The Early Relations of Egypt with Asia.' In *J.N.E.S.* 1 (1942), 174 ff.

32. Kantor, H. 'The Chronology of Egypt and its Correlation with that of the other Parts of the Near East in the Period Before the Late Bronze Age.' In Ehrich, R. W., *Relative Chronologies in Old World Archaeology*, 1 ff. Chicago, 1954.

33. Kaplan, J. 'Two Chalcolithic Vessels from Palestine.' In *P.E.Q.* 86 (1954), 97 ff.

34. Kaplan, J. 'Kfar Gil'adi.' In *I.E.J.* 8 (1958), 274.

35. Kaplan, J. 'The Connections of the Palestinian Chalcolithic Culture with Prehistoric Egypt.' In *I.E.J.* 9 (1959), 134 ff.

36. Kaplan, J. 'The Skin-Bag and its Imitations in Pottery.' In *Bull. I.E.S.* 27 (1963), 260 ff.

37. Kaplan, J. 'Excavations at Benei Baraq 1951.' In *I.E.J.* 13 (1963), 300 ff.

38. Kenyon, K. M. 'Some Notes on the Early and Middle Bronze Age Strata of Megiddo.' In *Eretz-Israel*, 5 (1958), 51* ff.

39. Kenyon, K. M. *Excavations at Jericho.* I. *The Tombs Excavated in 1952–54.* II. *The Tombs Excavated in 1952–58.* London, 1960, 1965.

40. Koeppel, R. 'Ma'adi und Ghassul.' In *Biblica* 18 (1937), 443 ff.

41. Koeppel, R. *Teleilat Ghassul. II. Compte rendu des fouilles de l'Institut Biblique Pontifical 1932–1936.* Rome, 1940.

42. Kurth, G. 'Vorbericht über anthropologische Beobachtungen bei der Jerichograbung.' In *Homo*, 1955, 145 ff.

43. Macalister, R. A. S. 'Report on the Excavations of Gezer.' In *P.E.F.Q.S.* 34 (1902), 317 ff.

44. McCown, C. C. *Tell en-Naṣbeh.* I. *Archaeological and Historical Results.* Berkeley and New Haven, 1947.

45. Macdonald, E. *Beth-Pelet.* II. *Prehistoric Fara* (*B.S.A.* Egypt, 52). London, 1932.

46. Maisler, B. and Stekelis, M. 'The Excavations at Beth Yerah (Khirbet el-Kerak).' In *I.E.J.* 2 (1952), 165 ff., 218 ff.

47. Mallon, A., Koeppel, R. and Neuville, R. *Teleilāt Ghassul. I. Compte rendu des fouilles de l'Institut Biblique Pontifical 1929–1932.* Rome, 1934.

48. Marquet-Krause, J. *Les fouilles de 'Ay (Et-Tell), 1933–1935* (*Bibl. Arch. et Hist.* 45). Paris, 1949.

49. Naveh, J. 'Chalcolithic Remains at 'Ein Gedi.' In *Bull. I.E.S.* 22 (1958), 46 ff.

50. Negbi, M. 'The Botanical Finds at Tell Abu-Matar, near Beersheba' In *I.E.J.* 5 (1955), 257 f.

51. Neuville, R. and Mallon, A. 'Les débuts de l'âge des métaux dans les grottes du Désert de Judée.' In *Syria*, 12 (1931), 24 ff.

52. North, R. *Ghassul 1960 Excavation Report* (*An. Biblica*, 14). Rome, 1961.
53. Ory, J. 'A Chalcolithic Necropolis at Benei Baraq.' In *Q.D.A.P.* 12 (1946), 43 ff.
54. Parr, P. 'A Cave at Arqub el Dhahr.' In *Ann. D.A.J.* 3 (1956), 61 ff.
55. Perrot, J. 'A propos du Ghassoulien.' in *Syria*, 29 (1952), 403 ff.
56. Perrot, J. 'The Excavations at Tell Abu-Matar, near Beersheba.' In *I.E.J.* 5 (1955), 17 ff., 73 ff., 167 ff.
57. Perrot, J. 'Bir es-Safadi.' In *I.E.J.* 9 (1959), 141 f.
58. Perrot, J. 'Statuettes en ivoire et autres objets en ivoire et en os provenant des gisements préhistoriques de la région de Béershéba. 'In *Syria*, 36 (1959), 8 ff.
59. Perrot, J. 'Une tombe à ossuaires du IVe millénaire à Azor près de Tel Aviv.' In *'Atiqot*, 3 (1961), 1 ff.
60. Perrot, J. 'Gat-Govrin.' In *Rev. bibl.* 69 (1962), 387 f.
61. Perrot, J. 'Nahal Besor.' In *Rev. bibl.* 69 (1962), 388 ff.
62. Perrot, J. 'Review of R. North, *Ghassul 1960 Excavation Report*.' In *Or.* 32 (1963), 140 ff.
63. Prausnitz, M. W. 'Alumoth–Sheikh 'Ali.' In *I.E.J.* 5 (1955), 271.
64. Prausnitz, M. W. 'Kabri.' In *Rev. bibl.* 67 (1960), 390 f.
65. Pritchard, J. B. *The Excavations at Herodian Jericho 1951* (*Ann. A.S.O.R.* 32–3). New Haven, 1958.
66. Stekelis, M. *Les monuments mégalithiques de Palestine* (*Arch. de l'Inst. de Paléont. hum.* 15). Paris, 1935.
67. Stekelis, M. 'An Obsidian Core Found at Kibbutz Kabri.' In *Eretz-Israel*, 5 (1958), 35 ff.
68. Sukenik, E. L. 'A Chalcolithic Necropolis at Ḥederah.' In *J.P.O.S.* 17 (1937), 15 ff.
69. Sukenik, E. L. 'Archaeological Investigations at 'Affûla.' In *J.P.O.S.* 21 (1948), 1 ff.
70. Vincent, L. H. *Jérusalem sous terre. Les récentes fouilles de l'Ophel.* London, 1911.
71. Wampler, J. C. *Tell en-Naṣbeh.* II. *The Pottery.* Berkeley and New Haven, 1947.
72. Wright, G. E. *The Pottery of Palestine from the Earliest Times to the End of the Early Bronze Age.* New Haven, 1937.
73. Wright, G. E. 'The Problem of the Transition Between the Chalcolithic and Bronze Ages.' In *Eretz-Israel*, 5 (1958), 37* ff.
74. Wright, G. E. 'The Archaeology of Palestine.' In *The Bible and the Ancient Near East: Essays in Honor of W. F. Albright*, 73 ff. New York, 1961.
75. Yeivin, E. 'The Flint Implements from Ḥorvat Beter (Beersheba).' In *'Atiqot*, 2 (1959), 43 ff.
76. Zaitchek, D. V. 'Remains of Cultivated Plants from Ḥorvat Beter (Beersheba).' In *'Atiqot*, 2 (1959), 48 ff.

VIII. THE 'MEGALITHIC CULTURE'

1. Broome, E. C. 'The Dolmens of Palestine and Transjordania.' In *J. Bibl. Lit.* 59 (1940), 479 ff.
2. Gilead, D. 'Burial Customs and the Dolmen Problem.' In *P.E.Q.* 1968, 16 ff.
3. Horsfield, G. 'Dolmen-field in Transjordania.' In *Antiq.* 7 (1933), 471 ff.
4. Neuville, R. 'La nécropole mégalithique d'El-'Adeimeh.' In *Biblica*, 11 (1930), 249 ff.
5. Turville-Petre, F. 'Dolmen Necropolis near Kerazeh, Galilee.' In *P.E.F.Q.S.* 1931, 155 ff.

CHAPTER IX (*c*)

G. GENERAL

1. Buxton, L. H. D. 'The Anthropology of Cyprus.' In *J.R.A.I.* 50 (1920), 183–235.
2. Casson, S. *Ancient Cyprus.* London, 1937.
3. Catling, H. W. 'Patterns of Settlement in Bronze Age Cyprus.' In *Op. Ath.* IV (1963), 129–69.
4. di Cesnola, L. P. *Cyprus: its Ancient Cities, Tombs and Temples.* London, 1877.
5. di Cesnola, L. P. *A Descriptive Atlas of the Cesnola Collection of Cypriote Antiquities in the Metropolitan Museum of Art, New York*, I–III. Boston; New York, 1885–1903.
6. Charles, R.-P. *Le Peuplement de Chypre dans l'antiquité. Étude anthropologique* (Études Chypriotes, II). Paris, 1962.
7. Cullis, C. G. and Edge, A. B. *Report on the Cupriferous Deposits of Cyprus.* London (Crown Agents), 1927.
8. Dikaios, P. *A Guide to the Cyprus Museum*, 3rd ed., Nicosia, 1961.
9. Gjerstad, E. and others. *The Swedish Cyprus Expedition. Finds and Results of the Excavations in Cyprus 1927–1931*, I–III. Stockholm, 1934–37.
10. Hill, Sir George F. *A History of Cyprus*, I. Cambridge, 1940.
11. Karageorghis, V. 'Chronique des fouilles et découvertes archéologiques à Chypre.' In *B.C.H.* 83 (1959), 336–61; 84 (1960), 242–99; 85 (1961), 256–315; 86 (1962), 327–414; 87 (1963), 325–87; 88 (1964), 289–379.
12. Karageorghis, V. *Treasures in the Cyprus Museum.* Nicosia, 1962.
13. Myres, J. L. and Ohnefalsch-Richter, M. *A Catalogue of the Cyprus Museum.* Oxford, 1899.
14. Myres, J. L. *Handbook of the Cesnola Collection of Antiquities from Cyprus.* New York, 1914.
15. Oberhummer, E. *Die Insel Cypern*, I. Munich, 1903.
16. Oberhummer, E. 'Kypros.' In Pauly-Wissowa, *Real-Encyclopädie*, XII. Stuttgart, 1925.
17. Ohnefalsch-Richter, M. *Kypros, the Bible and Homer.* 2 vols. London, 1893.
18. Peristianis, H. K. Γενικὴ Ἱστορία τῆς νήσου Κύπρου. Nicosia, 1910.
19. Schaeffer, C. F. A. *Missions en Chypre, 1932–1935.* Paris, 1936.
20. Storrs, R. and O'Brien, B. J. *Handbook of Cyprus.* London, 1930.
21. Trendall, A. D., Stewart, J. R. and others. *Handbook to the Nicholson Museum*, 2nd ed. Sydney, 1948.

X. THE EARLIEST SETTLERS IN CYPRUS

1. Catling, H. W. 'Neolithic Settlement Discovered.' In *Cyprus Pictorial*, I, no. 5, 5 April 1957.
2. Dikaios, P. *Khirokitia.* Oxford, 1953.
3. Dikaios, P. 'The Stone Age.' In *The Swedish Cyprus Expedition*, IV, part I*a* (Lund, 1962), 1–204.
4. Gjerstad, E. 'The Stone Age in Cyprus.' In *A.J.* VI (1926), 54–8.

XII. CYPRUS IN THE NEOLITHIC II PERIOD

1. Dikaios, P. *Sotira.* Philadelphia, 1961.

XIII. CHALCOLITHIC CYPRUS

1. Dikaios, P. 'Some Neolithic Sites in Cyprus.' In *R.D.A.C.* 1935 (Nicosia, 1936), 11–13.
2. Dikaios, P. 'The excavations at Erimi, 1933–1935: Final Report.' In *R.D.A.C.* 1936 (Nicosia, 1938), 1–81.
3. Goldman, H. *Excavations at Gözlü Küle, Tarsus,* II. Princeton, 1956.
4. Schaeffer, C. F. A. *Ugaritica,* IV (Mission de Ras Shamra, XV). Paris, 1962.

CHAPTER X

G. GENERAL

1. Childe, V. G. *The Dawn of European Civilization* (6th ed.). London, 1957.
2. Childe, V. G. *Prehistoric Migrations in Europe* (Instituttet for sammenlignende Kulturforskning. Series A: Forelesninger XX). Oslo, 1950.
3. Childe, V. G. 'The Relations between Greece and Prehistoric Europe.' In *Proceedings of the Second International Congress of Classical Studies* (Copenhagen, 1954), vol. I, General Part, 293–316. Copenhagen, 1958.
4. Childe, V. G. 'The Significance of the Sling for Greek Prehistory.' In *Studies Presented to David M. Robinson* (George E. Mylonas, ed.), vol. I, 1–6. St Louis, 1951.
5. Clark, J. G. D. 'Blade and Trapeze Industries of the European Stone Age.' In *P.P.S.* 24 (1958), 24–42.
6. Delvoye, C. 'Remarques sur la seconde civilisation néolithique du continent grec et des îles avoisinantes.' In *B.C.H.* 73 (1949), 29–124.
7. Ehrich, R. W. (ed.). *Relative Chronologies in Old World Archeology.* Chicago, 1954; 2nd ed., 1965.
8. Frankfort, H. *Studies in Early Pottery of the Near East. II. Asia, Europe and the Aegean, and their Earliest Interrelations* (Royal Anthropological Institute. Occasional Papers, no. 8). London, 1927.
9. Grundmann, K. 'Figürliche Darstellungen in der neolithischen Keramik Nord- und Mittelgriechenlands.' In *Jahrb. des d. arch. Inst.* 68 (1953), 1–37.
10. Kaschnitz-Weinberg, G. 'Zur Herkunft der Spirale in der Ägäis.' In *Praehist. Zeitschr.* 34/35 (1949/50), 193–215.
11. Marinatos, S. ''Η Στεατοπυγία ἐν τῇ Προϊστορικῇ 'Ελλάδι.' In Πρακτικὰ τῆς 'Ελληνικῆς 'Ανθρωπολογικῆς 'Εταιρείας (1945), 1–8.
12. Milojčić, V. *Chronologie der jüngeren Steinzeit Mittel- und Südosteuropas.* Berlin, 1949.
13. Milojčić, V. 'Zur Chronologie der jüngeren Steinzeit Griechenlands.' In *Jahrb. des d. arch. Inst.* 65/66 (1950/51), 1–90.
14. Montelius, O. *La Grèce Préclassique.* Stockholm, 1924 and 1928.
15. Mylonas, G. E. 'Η Νεολιθικὴ 'Εποχὴ ἐν 'Ελλάδι. Athens, 1928.
16. Perkins, A. and Weinberg, S. S. 'Connections of the Greek Neolithic and the Near East.' In *A.J.A.* 62 (1958), 225.
17. Schachermeyr, F. *Das ägäische Neolithikum* (Studies in Mediterranean Archaeology, VI). Lund, 1964.
18. Schachermeyr, F. *Die ältesten Kulturen Griechenlands.* Stuttgart, 1955.
19. Schachermeyr, F. 'Prähistorische Kulturen Griechenlands.' In *P.W.* 22, 2, cols. 1351–548.
20. Valmin, N. *Das adriatische Gebiet in Vor- und Frühbronzezeit* (Lunds Universitets Årsskrift, N.F., Avd. 1, Bd. 35. No. 1). Lund, 1939.

21. Vogel, J. C. and Waterbolk, H. T. 'Groningen Radiocarbon Dates IV.' In *Radiocarbon*, 5 (1963), 163–202.
22. Weinberg, S. S. 'Aegean Chronology: Neolithic Period and Early Bronze Age.' In *A.J.A.* 51 (1947), 165–82.
23. Weinberg, S. S. 'Ceramics and the Supernatural—Cult and Burial Evidence in the Aegean World.' In *Ceramics and Man* (F. Matson, ed.). (Viking Fund Publications in Anthropology, no. 41). Chicago, 1965.
24. Weinberg, S. S. 'The Chronology of the Neolithic Period and the Early Bronze Age in the Aegean.' In *A.J.A.* 46 (1942), 121.
25. Weinberg, S. S. 'Halafian and Ubaidian Influence in Neolithic Greece.' In *Bericht über den V. internationalen Kongress für Vor- und Frühgeschichte, Hamburg, 1958*, 858. Berlin, 1961.
26. Weinberg, S. S. 'Neolithic Figurines and Aegean Interrelations.' In *A.J.A.* 55 (1951), 121–33.
27. Weinberg, S. S. 'The Relative Chronology of the Aegean in the Neolithic Period and the Early Bronze Age.' In *Relative Chronologies in Old World Archeology* (R. W. Ehrich, ed.), 86–107. Chicago, 1954.
28. Yeoryiades, A. N. *"Ἔρευνα ἐπὶ τῶν ἑλληνικῶν ὀψιδιανῶν.'* In Πρακτικὰ τῆς Ἀκαδημίας Ἀθηνῶν, 31 (1956), 150–63.
29. Zervos, C. *Naissance de la civilisation en Grèce*. Paris, 1962–63.

I. MACEDONIA AND THRACE

1. Heurtley, W. A. *Prehistoric Macedonia*. Cambridge, 1939.
2. Higgs, E. S. 'A Hand Axe from Greece.' In *Antiq.* 38 (1964), 54.
3. Kokkoros, P. and Kanellis, A. 'Découverte d'un crane d'homme paléolithique dans la péninsule chalcidique.' In *L'Anthropologie*, 64 (1960), 438–46.
4. Mylonas, G. E. *Excavations at Olynthos. Part I. The Neolithic Settlement* (The Johns Hopkins University Studies in Archaeology, no. 6). Baltimore, 1929.
5. Mylonas, G. E. 'The Site of Akropotamos and the Neolithic Period of Macedonia.' In *A.J.A.* 45 (1941), 557–76.
6. Mylonas, G. E. and Bakalakis, G. *"Ἀνασκαφαὶ νεολιθικῶν συνοικισμῶν Ἀκροποτάμου καὶ Πολυστύλου.* In *Praktika* (1938), 103–11.
7. Rodden, Robert J. 'Excavations at the Early Neolithic Site at Nea Nikomedeia, Greek Macedonia (1961 Season).' In *P.P.S.* 28 (1962), 267–88.
8. Rodden, R. J. 'A European Link with Chatal Huyuk: Uncovering a 7th Millennium Settlement in Macedonia. Part I. Site and Pottery.' In *Ill. Ldn News* (11 April 1964), 564–7.
9. Rodden, R. J. 'A European Link with Chatal Huyuk: Uncovering a 7th Millennium Settlement in Macedonia. Part II. Burials and the Shrine.' In *Ill. Ldn News* (18 April 1964), 604–7.

II. THESSALY

1. Biesantz, H. 'Bericht über Ausgrabungen in Thessalien 1958: II. Die Ausgrabung bei der Soufli-Magula.' In *Arch. Anz.* (1959), 56–74.
2. Grundmann, K. 'Aus neolithischen Siedlungen bei Larisa.' In *Ath. Mitt.* 57 (1932), 102–23.
3. Grundmann, K. 'Magula Hadzimissiotiki: Eine steinzeitliche Siedlung im Karla-See.' In *Ath. Mitt.* 62 (1937), 56–69.
4. Hansen, Hazel D. *Early Civilization in Thessaly* (The Johns Hopkins University Studies in Archaeology, no. 15). Baltimore, 1933.

5. Milojčić, V. 'Ausgrabungen in Thessalien.' In *Neue deutsche Ausgrabungen im Mittelmeergebiet und im Vorderen Orient* (Boehringer, E., ed.; Deutsches Archäologisches Institut), 225–36. Berlin, 1959.

6. Milojčić, V. 'Bericht über die Ausgrabungen auf der Gremnos-Magula bei Larisa 1956.' In *Arch. Anz.* (1956), 141–83.

7. Milojčić, V. 'Bericht über die Ausgrabungen und Arbeiten in Thessalien im Herbst 1959.' In *Arch. Anz.* (1960), 150–78.

8. Milojčić, V. 'Die neuen mittel- und altpaläolithischen Funde von der Balkan-halbinsel.' In *Germania*, 36 (1958), 319–24.

9. Milojčić, V .'Ergebnisse der deutschen Ausgrabungen in Thessalien, 1953–1958.' In *Jahrb. des röm.-germ. Zentralmuseums Mainz*, 6 (1959), 1–56.

10. Milojčić, V. 'Vorbericht über die Ausgrabungen auf der Otzaki-Magula 1954.' In *Arch. Anz.* (1955), 157–82.

11. Milojčić, V. 'Vorbericht über die Ausgrabungen auf den Magulen von Otzaki, Arapi und Gremnos bei Larisa 1955.' In *Arch. Anz.* (1955), 182–232.

12. Milojčić, V., Boessneck, J. and Hopf, M. *Die Deutschen Ausgrabungen auf der Argissa-Magula in Thessalien. I. Das präkeramische Neolithikum sowie die Tier- und Pflanzenreste (Beiträge zur ur- und frühgeschichtlichen Archäologie des Mittelmeer-Kulturraumes*, Band 2). Bonn, 1962.

13. Papadopoulou, Maria G. 'Μαγουλίτσα. Νεολιθικὸς συνοικισμὸς παρὰ τὴν Καρδίτσαν.' In *Thessalika*, 1 (1958), 39–49.

14. Theochares, D. R. 'Αἱ ἀρχαὶ τοῦ πολιτισμοῦ ἐν Σέσκλῳ.' In Πρακτικὰ τῆς Ἀκαδημίας Ἀθηνῶν, 32 (1957), 151–9.

15. Theochares, D. R. 'Ἀρχαιότητες καὶ μνημεῖα Θεσσαλίας.' In *Arch. Delt.* 17 (1961/2), Chronikà, 170–9.

16. Theochares, D. R. 'Ἐκ τῆς προκεραμεικῆς Θεσσαλίας. Προσωρινὴ ἀνασκαφικὴ ἔκθεσις.' In *Thessalika*, 1 (1958), 70–86.

17. Theochares, D. R. 'Νεολιθικὰ ἐκ τῆς περιοχῆς τῆς Ἰολκοῦ.' In *Thessalika*, 1 (1958), 3–15.

18. Theochares, D. R. 'Πύρασος.' In *Thessalika*, 2 (1959), 29–68.

19. Theochares, D. R. 'Σέσκλον.' In *Ergon* (1962), 39–48.

20. Theochares, D. R. 'Σέσκλον.' In *Ergon* (1963), 27–35.

21. Tsountas, C. Αἱ προϊστορικαὶ ἀκροπόλεις Διμηνίου καὶ Σέσκλου. Athens, 1908.

22. Wace, A. J. B. 'Thessaly and Tripolje.' In *E.S.A.* 9 (1934), 123–34.

23. Wace, A. J. B. and Thompson, M. S. *Prehistoric Thessaly*. Cambridge, 1912.

III. CENTRAL GREECE

(Phocis, Locris, Boeotia, Euboea, Attica, Aegina, Megarid)

1. Bulle, H. *Orchomenos. I. Die älteren Ansiedlungsschichten (Abh. München*, philos.-philol. Kl., 24, 2). Munich, 1909.

2. Caskey, John L. 'Neolithic Sherds from Thespiai.' In *Hesperia*, 20 (1951), 289–90.

3. Caskey, J. L. and Caskey, E. G. 'The Earliest Settlements at Eutresis: Supplementary Excavations, 1958.' In *Hesperia*, 29 (1960), 126–67.

4. Kunze, E. *Orchomenos. II. Die neolithische Keramik (Abh. München*, phil.-hist. Abt., n.F. 5). Munich, 1931.

5. Levi, D. 'Abitazioni preistoriche sulle pendici meridionali dell'Acropoli.' In *Ann. della R. Scuola archeol. di Atene*, 13–14 (1930/31), 411–98.

6. Markovits, A. 'Die Zaïmis-Höhle (Kaki-Skala, Megaris, Griechenland). I. Mitteilungen: Lage, Morphologie, Genesis und Höhleninhalt.' In *Speläologischen Jahrb.* 13–14 (1932/33), 133–46.

7. Markovits, A. 'Περὶ τῶν μέχρι σήμερον ἐρευνῶν ἐπὶ τῆς λιθικῆς περιόδου τῆς Ἑλλάδος.' In Πρακτικὰ τῆς Ἑλληνικῆς Ἀνθρωπολογικῆς Ἑταιρείας (1928), 114–34.
8. Soteriades, G. 'Fouilles préhistoriques en Phocide.' In R.E.G. 25 (1912), 253–99.
9. Soteriades, G. 'Προϊστορικὰ ἀγγεῖα Χαιρωνείας καὶ Ἐλατείας.' In Arch. Eph. (1908), 63–96.
10. Stampfuss, R. 'Die ersten altsteinzeitlichen Höhlenfunde in Griechenland.' In Mannus, 34 (1942), 132–47.
11. Theochares, D. R. ''Εκ τῆς προϊστορίας τῆς Εὐβοίας καὶ τῆς Σκύρου.' In Ἀρχεῖον Εὐβοικῶν Μελετῶν, 6 (1959), 279–328.
12. Theochares, D. R. 'Nea Makri. Eine grosse neolithische Siedlung in der Nähe von Marathon.' In Ath. Mitt. 71 (1956), 1–29.
13. Theochares, D. R. 'Προϊστορικαὶ ἔρευναι ἐν Σκύρῳ καὶ Εὐβοίᾳ.' In Arch. Eph. (1945–7), Arch. Chron. 1–12.
14. Weinberg, S. S. 'Excavations at Prehistoric Elateia, 1959.' In Hesperia, 31 (1962), 158–209.
15. Welter, G. 'Aiginetische Keramik.' In Arch. Anz. (1937), 19–26.

IV. WESTERN GREECE

(Epirus, Acarnania, Aetolia, Ionian Islands)

1. Benton, S. 'Hagios Nikolaos near Astakos in Akarnania.' In B.S.A. 42 (1947), 156–83.
2. Dörpfeld, W. Alt-Ithaka. Munich, 1927.
3. Higgs, E. S. 'A Middle Palaeolithic Industry in Greece: Preliminary Report.' In Man, 63 (1963), 2–3.
4. Marinatos, S. 'Λίθινα ἐργαλεῖα ἐκ Κεφαλληνίας.' In Arch. Delt. 16 (1960), 41–5.
5. Petrocheilos, I. 'Σπηλαιολογικαὶ ἔρευναι εἰς Κεφαλληνίαν.' In Δελτίον Ἑλληνικῆς Σπηλαιολογικῆς Ἑταιρίας, 5 (1959), 49–54.
6. Zapfe, H. 'Spuren neolithischer Besiedlung auf Zante.' In W.P.Z. 24 (1937), 158–63.

V. PELOPONNESE

1. Bialor, P. A. and Jameson, M. H. 'Palaeolithic in the Argolid.' In A.J.A. 66 (1962), 181–2.
2. Blegen, C. W. 'Gonia.' In Metr. Mus. Studies, 3 (1930), 55–80.
3. Blegen, C. W. 'Excavations at Nemea 1926.' In A.J.A. 31 (1927), 421–40.
4. Blegen, C. W. Prosymna: The Helladic Settlement preceding the Argive Heraeum. Cambridge, 1937.
5. Caskey, J. L. 'Excavations at Lerna, 1956.' In Hesperia, 26 (1957), 142–62.
6. Caskey, J. L. 'Excavations at Lerna, 1957.' In Hesperia, 27 (1958), 125–44.
7. Caskey, J. L. 'Activities at Lerna, 1958–1959.' In Hesperia, 28 (1959), 202–7.
8. Caskey, J. L. and Eliot, M. 'A Neolithic Figurine from Lerna.' In Hesperia, 25 (1956), 175–7.
9. Furst, C. M. Über einen neolithischen Schädel aus Arkadien (Lunds Universitets Årsskrift, N.F., Avd. 2, Bd. 28, Nr. 13). Lund, 1932.
10. Holmberg, E. J. The Swedish Excavations at Asea in Arcadia (Skrifter utgivna av svenska institutet i Rom, xi). Lund, 1944.
11. Kosmopoulos, L. W. The Prehistoric Inhabitation of Corinth. Munich, 1948.

12. Leroi-Gourhan, A., Chavaillon, J. and Chavaillon, N. 'Paléolithique du Péloponnèse.' In *Bull. Soc. préhist. fr.* LX (1963), 249–65.
13. McDonald, W. A. and Hope Simpson, R. 'Prehistoric Habitation in South-western Peloponnese.' In *A.J.A.* 65 (1961), 221–60.
14. Robinson, H. S. and Weinberg, S. S. 'Excavations at Corinth, 1959.' In *Hesperia,* 29 (1960), 225–53.
15. Servais, J. 'Outils paléolithiques d'Élide.' In *B.C.H.* 85 (1961), 1–9.
16. Valmin, M. N. *The Swedish Messenia Expedition.* Lund, 1938.
17. Waterhouse, H. 'Prehistoric Laconia: A Note.' In *B.S.A.* 51 (1956), 168–71.
18. Waterhouse, H. and Hope Simpson, R. 'Prehistoric Laconia: Part I, Part II.' In *B.S.A.* 55 (1960), 67–107; 56 (1961), 114–75.
19. Weinberg, S. S. 'A Cross-section of Corinthian Antiquities.' In *Hesperia,* 17 (1948), 197–241.
20. Weinberg, S. S. 'Remains from Prehistoric Corinth.' In *Hesperia,* 6 (1937), 487–524.

VI. ISLANDS OF THE AEGEAN
(except Aegina and Crete; for Scyros see also Euboea)

1. Caskey, J. L. 'Excavations in Keos, 1960–61.' In *Hesperia,* 31 (1962), 263–83.
2. Caskey, J. L. 'Excavations in Keos, 1963.' In *Hesperia,* 33 (1964), 314–35.
3. Furness, A. 'Some Early Pottery of Samos, Kalimnos and Chios.' In *P.P.S.* 22 (1956), 173–212.
4. Heidenreich, R. 'Vorgeschichtliches in der Stadt Samos. Die Funde.' In *Ath. Mitt.* 60/61 (1935–36), 125–83.
5. Renfrew, C. and Belmont, J. S. 'Two Prehistoric Sites on Mykonos.' In *A.J.A.* 68 (1964), 395–400.

VII. CRETE

1. Alexiou, S. 'Ἀνασκαφαὶ ἐν Κατσαμπᾷ.' In *Praktika* (1954), 369–76.
2. Dawkins, R. M. 'Excavations at Palaikastro. IV.' In *B.S.A.* 11 (1904/5), 258–92.
3. Evans, A. J. *The Palace of Minos at Knossos.* I–IV. London, 1921–35.
4. Evans, J. D. 'Excavations in the Neolithic Mound of Knossos, 1958–60.' In *Bull. Inst. Arch. London,* No. 4 (1964), 34–60.
5. Evans, J. D. 'Excavations in the Neolithic Settlement of Knossos, 1957–60. Part I.' In *B.S.A.* 59 (1964).
6. Furness, A. 'The Neolithic Pottery of Knossos.' In *B.S.A.* 48 (1953), 94–134.
7. Hutchinson, R. W. 'Cretan Neolithic Figurines.' In *Ipek,* 12 (1938), 50–7.
8. Hutchinson, R. W. *Prehistoric Crete.* Harmondsworth, 1962.
9. Levi, D. 'Gli scavi a Festòs nel 1956 e 1957.' In *Ann. della R. Scuola archeol. di Atene,* n.s. 19–20 (1957/58), 193–361.
10. Levi, D. 'Gli scavi a Festòs negli anni 1958–1960.' In *Ann. della R. Scuola archeol. di Atene,* n.s. 23–24 (1961/62), 377–504.
11. Levi, D. 'New Discoveries at one of the greatest of Minoan Sites: The Palace of Phaistos and the Tholos Tomb of Kamilari. Part I.' In *Ill. Ldn News* (27 July 1963), 134–8.
12. Mackenzie, D. 'The Pottery of Knossos.' In *J.H.S.* 23 (1903), 157–205.
13. Marinatos, S. 'Ἀνασκαφαὶ ἐν Κρήτῃ.' In *Praktika* (1929), 94–104; (1930), 91–9.
14. Marinatos, S. 'Funde und Forschungen auf Kreta.' In *Arch. Anz.* (1933), 287–314.
15. Matz, F. *Forschungen auf Kreta, 1942.* Berlin, 1951.

16. Mosso, A. 'Ceramica neolitica de Phaestos e vasi dell'epoca minoica primitiva.' In *Mon. Ant.* 19 (1908), 141–218.
17. Pendlebury, J. D. S. *The Archaeology of Crete.* London, 1939.
18. Pendlebury, H. W., Pendlebury, J. D. S. and Money-Coutts, M. B. 'Excavations in the Plain of Lasithi. I. The Cave of Trapeza.' In *B.S.A.* 36 (1935/36), 5–131.
19. Zervos, C. *L'Art de la Crète néolithique et minoenne.* Paris, 1956.

VIII. SOUTH-EAST EUROPE

1. Benac, A. 'Crvena Stijena (L'Abri rouge)—1955 (I–IV Stratum).' In *Glasnik zem. muz. Sarajevu,* Arheologija, n.s. 12 (1957), 19–50.
2. Benac, A. 'Zelena Pecina (L'Abri vert).' In *Glasnik zem. muz. Sarajevu,* Arheologija, n.s. 12 (1957), 61–92.
3. Benac, A. and Brodar, M. 'Crvena Stijena (L'Abri rouge)—1956.' In *Glasnik zem. muz. Sarajevu,* Arheologija, n.s. 13 (1958), 21–64.
4. Berciu, D. 'Neolitic Preceramic în Balcani.' In *Studii și cerc. Ist. veche,* 9 (1958), 91–100.
5. Brodar, M. 'Crvena Stijena (L'Abri rouge)—1955 (V Stratum).' In *Glasnik zem. muz. Sarajevu,* Arheologija, n.s. 12 (1957), 51–5.
6. Čović, B. 'Rezultati sondiranja na preistoriskom naselje u Gornjoj Tuzli.' In *Glasnik zem. muz. Sarajevu,* Arheologija, n.s. 15/16 (1960/61), 79–139.
7. Fewkes, V. J., Goldman, H. and Ehrich, R. W. 'Excavations at Starcevo, Yugoslavia, Seasons 1931 and 1932.' In *B.A.S.P.R.* 9 (1933), 33–54.
8. Garašanin, M. V. 'Neolithikum und Bronzezeit in Serbien und Makedonien.' In *B.R.G.K.* 39 (1958), 1–130.
9. Garašanin, M. V. 'Zur Chronologie und Deutung einiger frühneolithischer Kulturen des Balkans.' In *Germania,* 39 (1961), 142–6.
10. Garrod, D. A. E., Howe, B. and Gaul, J. M. 'Excavations in the Cave of Bacho Kiro, North-east Bulgaria.' In *B.A.S.P.R.* 15 (1939), 46–126.
11. Gaul, J. H. *The Neolithic Period in Bulgaria: Early Food-Producing Cultures of Eastern Europe (B.A.S.P.R. 16).* Cambridge, Mass., 1948.
12. Korošec, J. *The Neolithic Settlement at Danilo Bitinj: The Results of Excavations Performed in 1953.* Zagreb, 1958.
13. Milojčić, V. 'Präkeramisches Neolithikum auf der Balkanhalbinsel.' In *Germania,* 38 (1960), 320–35.

IX. TROAD AND ANATOLIA

1. Bittel, K. 'Einige Idole aus Kleinasien.' In *Praehist. Zeitschr.* 34/35 (1949/50), 135–44.
2. Blegen, C. W. *Troy and the Trojans.* London, 1963.
3. Blegen, C. W., Caskey, J. L., Rawson, M. and Sperling, J. *Troy. I. General Introduction. The First and Second Settlements.* Princeton, 1950.
4. French, D. H. 'Excavations at Can Hasan. Second Preliminary Report, 1962.' In *A.St.* 13 (1963), 29–42.
5. French, D. H. 'Late Chalcolithic Pottery in North-West Turkey and the Aegean.' In *A.St.* 11 (1961), 99–141.
6. Goldman, H. and Garstang, J. 'A Conspectus of Early Cilician Pottery.' In *A.J.A.* 51 (1947), 370–88.
7. Koşay, H. and Akok, M. *Ausgrabungen von Büyük Güllücek.* (Türk Tarih Kurumu Yayinlarindan, v. seri, No 16). Ankara, 1957.

8. Koşay, H. and Sperling, J. '*Troad*' *da dört yerleşme yeri*. Istanbul, 1936.
9. Lamb, W. 'Schliemann's Prehistoric Sites in the Troad.' In *Praehist. Zeitschr.* 23 (1932), 111–31.
10. Lloyd, S. and Mellaart, J. *Beycesultan. I. The Chalcolithic and Early Bronze Age Levels* (Occasional Publications of the British Institute of Archaeology at Ankara, no. 6). London, 1962.
11. Mellaart, J. *Anatolia before c. 4000 B.C. and c. 2300–1750 B.C.* (*C.A.H.* I [3rd ed.], ch. VII, sect. XI–XIV; ch. XXIV, sect. I–VI). Cambridge, 1964.
12. Mellaart, J. *Anatolia, c. 4000–2300 B.C.* (*C.A.H.* I [3rd ed.], ch. XVIII). Cambridge, 1962.
13. Mellaart, J. 'Excavations at Çatal Hüyük. First Preliminary Report, 1961.' In *A.St.* 12 (1962), 41–65.
14. Mellaart, J. 'Excavations at Çatal Hüyük, 1962. Second Preliminary Report.' In *A.St.* 13 (1963), 43–103.
15. Mellaart, J. 'Excavations at Hacilar. Third Preliminary Report, 1959.' In *A.St.* 10 (1960), 83–104.
16. Mellaart, J. 'Excavations at Hacilar. Fourth Preliminary Report, 1960.' In *A.St.* 11 (1961), 39–75.
17. Mellaart, J. 'Notes on the Architectural Remains of Troy I and II.' In *A.St.* 9 (1959), 131–62.

X. THE NEAR EAST AND CYPRUS

1. Braidwood, R. J. 'The Agricultural Revolution.' In *Scientific American*, 203 (Sept. 1960), 130–48.
2. Braidwood, R. J. 'Discovering the World's Earliest Village Community: The Claims of Jarmo as the Cradle of Civilisation.' In *Ill. Ldn News* (15 Dec. 1951), 992–5.
3. Braidwood, R. J. and Howe, B. *Prehistoric Investigations in Iraqi Kurdistan* (Studies in Ancient Oriental Civilization, no. 31). Chicago, 1960.
4. Burton-Brown, T. *Excavations at Azarbaijan, 1948.* London, 1951.
5. Dikaios, P. *Khirokitia. Final Report on the Excavations of a Neolithic Settlement in Cyprus on behalf of the Department of Antiquities, 1936–1946.* London, 1953.
6. Garstang, J. *Prehistoric Mersin: Yümük Tepe in Southern Turkey.* Oxford, 1953.
7. Herzfeld, E. *Die vorgeschichtlichen Töpfereien von Samarra (Die Ausgrabungen von Samarra, v).* Berlin, 1930.
8. Kenyon, K. *Archaeology in the Holy Land.* New York, 1960.
9. Kenyon, K. *Digging up Jericho.* London, 1957.
10. Kenyon, K. 'Jericho and its Setting in Near Eastern History.' In *Antiq.* 30 (1956), 184–93.
11. Lloyd, S. and Safar, F. 'Tell Hassuna. Excavations by the Iraq Government Directorate General of Antiquities in 1943 and 1944.' In *J.N.E.S.* 4 (1945), 255–89.
12. Schmidt, H. *Tell Halaf. I. Die prähistorischen Funde.* Berlin, 1943.
13. Stekelis, M. and Yizraely, T. 'Excavations at Nahal Oren: Preliminary Report.' In *I.E.J.* 13 (1963), 1–12.

A. ADDENDA

1. Bakalakis, G. Ἀρχαιολογικὲς ἔρευνες στὴ Θράκη, 1959–1960. Thessaloniki, 1961.
2. Bakalakis, G. Προανασκαφικὲς ἔρευνες στὴ Θράκη. Thessaloniki, 1958.
3. Batović, Š. 'Neolitsko nalazište Smilčić. Prethodni izvještaj uz iskapanja 1957–1959.' In Radovi Instituta Jugoslavenske akademije znanosti i umjetnosti u Zadru, 10 (1963), 89–138.
4. Batović, Š. 'Neolitsko nalazište u Smilčiću.' In Diadora, 2 (1960–1), 31–115.
5. Batović, Š. 'Neolitsko naselje u Smilčiću.' In Diadora, 1 (1959), 5–26.
6. Batovič, Š. 'Stariji neolit u Dalmaciji.' In Societas archaeologica Jugoslaviae. Museum Archaeologicum Zadar. Dissertationes. Tome II. Zadar (1966).
7. Benac, A. 'Tragovi kultnog sahranjivanja u neolitu Jadranske oblasti.' In Diadora, 2 (1960–1), 5–11.
8. Cann, J. R. and Renfrew, C. 'The Characterization of Obsidian and its Application to the Mediterranean Region.' In P.P.S. 30 (1964), 111–33.
9. Caskey, J. L. 'Excavations in Keos, 1964–1965.' In Hesperia, 35 (1966), 363–76.
10. Chavaillon, N. and J. and Hours, F. 'Une industrie paléolithique du Péloponnese: Le Moustérien de Vasilaki.' In B.C.H. 88 (1964), 616–22.
11. Dakaris, S. I., Higgs, E. S. and Hey, R. W. 'The Climate, Environment and Industries of Stone Age Greece: Part I.' In P.P.S. 30 (1964), 199–244.
12. Demakopoulou, K. K. 'Προϊστορικὴ κεραμεικὴ νοτίως τῆς Ἀκροπόλεως.' Arch. Delt. 19 (1964), pt. 1, 62–72.
13. Deshayes, J. and Garasanin, M. 'Note sur la céramique de Galepsos.' In B.C.H. 88 (1964), 51–66.
14. Evans, J. D. 'Knossos and the Neolithic of Crete.' In Atti del VI Congresso Internazionale delle Scienze Preistoriche e Protostoriche. II, Comunicazione. Sezioni I–IV. Florence (1965), 220–4.
15. French, D. H. 'Excavations at Can Hasan; Second Preliminary Report, 1962.' In A. St. 13 (1963), 29–42.
16. French, D. H. 'Excavations at Can Hasan; Third Preliminary Report, 1963.' In A. St. 14 (1964), 125–37.
17. French, D. H. 'Excavations at Can Hasan; Fourth Preliminary Report, 1964.' In A. St. 15 (1965), 87–94.
18. French, D. H. 'Prehistoric pottery from Macedonia and Thrace.' In Praehist. Zeitschr. 42 (1964), 30–48.
19. Higgs, E. S. 'Asprochaliko.' In Antiq. 40, no. 157 (March 1966), 55–6.
20. Higgs, E. S. 'Search for Greece of the Stone Age.' In Natural History, 74, no. 9 (Nov. 1965), 18–25.
21. Higgs, E. S. and Vita-Finzi, C. 'The Climate, Environment and Industries of Stone Age Greece: Part II.' In P.P.S. 32 (1966), 1–29.
22. Holmberg, E. J. 'The Appearance of Neolithic Black Burnished Ware in Mainland Greece.' In A.J.A. 68 (1964), 343–8.
23. Holmberg, E. J. The Neolithic Pottery of Mainland Greece (Göteborgs Kungl. Vetenskaps- och Vitterhets-Samhälles Handlingar, Sjätte följden, Ser. A, Band 7, no. 2). Göteborg, 1964.
24. Hood, S. 'Excavations at Emporio, Chios, 1952–1955.' In Atti del VI Congresso Internazionale delle Scienze Preistoriche e Protostoriche. II. Comunicazioni. Sezioni I–IV. Florence (1965), 224–8.
25. Kalicz, N. Die Péceler (Badener) Kultur und Anatolien. (Publicationes Instituti Archaeologici: Studii Archaeologica II.) Budapest, 1963.

26. Korošec, J. *Danilo in danilska kultura*. (Univerza v Ljubljana, Arheološki oddelek filozofske fakultete.) Ljubljana, 1964.
27. Korošec, J. 'Neka pitanja oko neolita u Dalmaciji.' In *Diadora*, 2 (1960–61), 13–30.
28. Leroi-Gourhan, A. 'Découvertes paléolithiques en Élide.' In *B.C.H.* 88 (1964), 1–8.
29. Leroi-Gourhan, A., Chavaillon, J. and N. 'Premiers résultats d'une prospection de divers sites préhistoriques en Élide occidentale.' In *Annales géologiques des pays helléniques*, 14 (1963), 324–9.
30. *L'Europe à la fin de l'âge de la pierre. Actes du Symposium consacré aux problèmes du Néolithique européen*. Praha, 1961.
31. Levi, D. 'Le varietà della primitive ceramica cretese.' In *Studi in onore de Luisa Banti*. Rome, 1965, 223–39.
32. Markotić, V. 'Archaeology.' In *Croatia* (Eterovich, F. H. and Spalatin, C. eds.). Toronto, 1964, 20–75.
33. Mellaart, J. *Çatal Hüyük. A Neolithic Town in Anatolia*. New York, 1967.
34. Mellaart, J. 'Excavations at Çatal Hüyük, 1963; Third Preliminary Report.' In *A. St.* 14 (1964), 39–119.
35. Mellaart, J. 'Excavations at Çatal Hüyük, 1965.' In *Arch. Anz.* (1966), 1–15.
36. Mellaart, J. 'Excavations at Çatal Hüyük, 1965; Fourth Preliminary Report.' In *A. St.* 16 (1966), 165–91.
37. Mellaart, J. 'Çatal Hüyük West.' In *A. St.* 15 (1965).
38. Mellaart, J. *The Earliest Settlements in Western Asia, from the Ninth to the End of the Fifth Millennium B.C.* (*C.A.H.* 1 (3rd ed.), ch. VII). Cambridge, 1967.
39. Milojčić, V. Samos. I. *Die prähistorische Siedlung unter dem Heraion von Samos. Grabung 1953 und 1955*. Bonn, 1961.
40. Pašić, R. 'Neolithic Finding-places in Ohrid.' In *Year-Book of the Popular Museum in Ohrid*, 1 (1957), 115–21.
41. Renfrew, C. *The Neolithic and Early Bronze Age Cultures of the Cyclades and their External Relations*. Doctoral thesis at the University of Cambridge. April, 1965.
42. Rodden, R. J. 'Recent Discoveries from Prehistoric Macedonia.' In *Balkan Studies*, 5 (1964), 109–24.
43. Säflund, G. *Excavations at Berbati, 1936–1937*. (Stockholm Studies in Classical Archaeology.) Stockholm, 1965.
44. Smith, H. S. 'Egypt and C 14 Dating.' In *Antiq.* 38 (1964), 32–7.
45. Sordinas, A. 'Προϊστορικὴ ἔρευνα στὴν Κέρκυρα κατὰ τὸ 1965.' In *Kerkyraïkà Chronikà*, 11 (1966), 141–8.
46. Syriopoulou, K. Th. Ἡ Προϊστορία τῆς Πελοποννήσου. Athens, 1964.
47. Theochares, D. R. ''Ἀπὸ τὴ νεολιθικὴ Θεσσαλία: I.' In *Thessalika*, 4 (1962), 63–83.
48. Theochares, D. R. 'Σέσκλον.' In *Ergon* (1965), 5–9.
49. Weinberg, S. S. 'Chronology of the Neolithic Period in the Aegean and the Balkans.' In *Atti del VI Congresso Internazionale delle Scienze Preistoriche e Protostoriche*. II. Comunicazioni. Sezioni I–IV. Florence, 1965, 228–32.
50. Weinberg, S. S. 'The Relative Chronology of the Aegean in the Stone and Early Bronze Ages.' In *Chronologies in Old World Archaeology* (R. W. Ehrich, ed.), 285–320. Chicago, 1966.

INDEX TO MAPS

The Arabic definite article (Al-, El- etc.) has been disregarded as an element in the alphabetical arrangement of place-names. For example Al-'Ubaid is to be found under 'U'.

GENERAL INDEX

The Arabic definite article (Al-, El- etc.) has been disregarded as an element in the alphabetical arrangement of place-names. For example, Al-'Ubaid is to be found under 'U'.

alder, 52, 91, 93

Aleppo, in N. Syria (Map 8), 412, 414, 416; chronology and rulers, 210, 212–14, 230

Alexandretta, in Turkey, 414; Gulf of, 540

Alföld of Hungary, 38

Algeria, 108, 114, 166; Algerian Sahara, 6

Aliābād, in Khūzistān, 425; scarlet ware, 426

Ali Āghā, near Nineveh (Maps 8 (38), 11 (10)), pottery, 259

Ali Beg, in Kurdistān, 403

Ali-Kūsh, in Khūzistān (Map 11 (40)), 253, 259, 260–1, 289, 296, 423–4, 425, 428; Bus Mordeh phase, 260, 423; Ali-Kūsh phase, 260, 423–4; Muḥammad Ja'far phase, 261, 270, 284, 424; domestic plants, 249, 423, 432

Alişar Hüyük, in central Anatolia (Map 10 (77)), 170, 212

Alīshtar, in Luristān (Map 11 (45)), 434, 438

Alkım, B., 304 n. 1

Allerød oscillation, 90; climate, 91

alleys, 296, 314

alluvial plains and deposits, 25, 38–9, 42, 56, 74, 75–6, 250, 541; of Anatolia, 306, 307, 309; of Dead Sea, 32; of Mesopotamia, 38–9, 42, 57–9, 250, 354, 366; of S. Mesopotamia, 260, 261, 284, 289; of Nile, 38, 42, 59, 62, 65–6, 71; clay, 309, 354; gravels, 54, 56; river alluvium, 15, 66, 541; alluvial valleys, 36; alluviation, 38–9, 64

almond, 266, 285, 309, 424

Alonia district of Cyprus, 556

Alpera, Murcia, Spain, rock-paintings, 113

alphabet, 136; Greek, 134

Alps: formation of, 2, 13, 17 (fig. 1), 19, 22–3, 26–8, 36; Austrian Alps, 18–20, 27; Bavarian, 13; Carnic, 18; Dinaric (Dinarides), 16–19; Julian, 13; Pennine, 13, 19, 22; Swiss, 14; Transylvanian (Map 1), 26, 27, 30; Viennese, 20; alpine zone, 49–50; alpine race, 533

Altaic languages, 129

Altaides, 10 n. 1

Altamira, in N. Spain, cave paintings, 249

altars: at Eridu, 286, 288, 336–7, 338, 339, 346; at Telūl eth-Thalathat, 406; at Tepe Gawra, 380, 385; at 'Uqair, 370; on seal, 392

Altın-Köprü, on lesser Zab, 374, 403

Altithermal phase, 90–1, 93, 103, 117

Amalias, in Elis, 559

Amanus range of N.W. Syria, 304, 540

Amara in Iraq, tribes of, 423

Amari district of Crete, 618

El-Amarna, in Egypt, 136, 245

Amarna period, 196, 205, 215, 237, 239; Amarna kings of Egypt, 188

Amarna Letters, 128, 135, **136**, 143–4, 152, 205–7; no. 1: 12, 207 n. 2; nos. 6–9 and 11 ff., 206 n. 1; no. 9: 19 ff., 207 n. 4; no. 10: 8 ff., 207 n. 3; nos. 15 and 16, 206 n. 4; no. 29 (16–18), 188 n. 8; no. 41, 215 n. 5

Amar-Sin of Ur III, 202, 333

amazonite, 356

Ambelikou, in Cyprus, 556

amber, 100, 102 (fig. 9)

Amenmesses of Egypt, 190

Amenophis I of Egypt, 183, 187

Amenophis II of Egypt, 188, 229, 230 and n. 4

Amenophis III of Egypt, 188 and n. 8, 189, 206–7, 215 and n. 5, 230, 245

Amenophis IV (Akhenaten, q.v.) of Egypt, 189

America: in geological ages, 7–8, 11; Two Creeks stage, 90; domestication of plants, 44 n. 2; Palaeo-American culture and language, 131; American Indian languages, 130; archaeologists, 254, 423, 441, and see Chicago, Pennsylvania, Philadelphia, Washington

Amessis of Egypt, 188

Amharic, official language of Ethiopia, 138

Amiran, R., 520, 535

Ammenemes I of Egypt, 182, 189

Ammenemes III of Egypt, 182 n. 7

Ammiditana of Babylon, 211, 213

Ammiṣaduqa of Babylon, 208, 213, 231, 232 n. 2, 234 and n. 1

Ammishtamru II of Ugarit, 216, 238

Ammitaqum of Alalakh, 213–15

Ammunash, Hittite king, 215 and n. 2

Amnisus, in Crete (Map 17 (137)), 618

Amorite language, **128**, 135–6

Amosis of Egypt, 183, 185

amphibians, 2

El-Amra, in Egypt, 484, 486; tomb B 230, 485–6

Amratian culture of Egypt, 464–5

Amschler, J. W., 460 and n. 4

Amū Daryā, see Oxus

Amud Cave, Lake Tiberias, 163

amulets: from Arpachiyah (Halaf), 278, 359; Crete, 610; Cyprus, 546, 554; Egypt, 469–70, 485, 494, 496; Jeitun, 298; Maglemosian, 100; Syria, 393, 409; Tepe Gawra, 389, 392; 'Ubaid seal amulets, 392, 411

burins (*cont.*)

84; micro-burin technique, **108–10**, 118; scarcity or absence of, 262, 311; illustrations, 85, 88, 98, 107

Burma, 19, 129

Burnaburiash I of Babylon, 196, 203, 207–8, 233

Burnaburiash II of Babylon, 205–7 and n. 1, 231

Burney, C. A., 304 n. 1

Burnham, H., 310 n. 3

burning bush (*Rubus sanctus*), 58

burnished ware, 263, 279, 281, 293, 307, 368, 417, 435, 595; black, 321–2, 324, 579, 598–600, 611, 613; buff, 273, 315, 437; cream, 267, 291, 310; dark, 266–8, 270, 272, 310, 313, 316, 326; dark-faced, 511, 514–15, 600; grey, 315, 371, 401–2, 404, 532, 533–6; grey-black, 597–600, 606; red, 259, 264, 301, 310, 315, 416, 436–7, 532, 534–6, 613; with incision, 273, 413, 618; pattern-burnished, 268–9, 277, 282–3, 596, 598, 606–7, 614, 618; polished, 583, 585; burnished slip, 263, 279, 283, 471, 511; unburnished, 275, 512, 612

burnishing of lime plaster, 265, 308

Bursa, in N.W. Anatolia (Map 10), 305

Bushire, on Persian Gulf, 478

Bus Mordeh (Ali-Kush, q.v.), 253, 260; Bus Mordeh phase, 256–7, 423

butchering tools, 260, 424

butter, 522

butterflies in wall-paintings, 312; on pottery, 602

buttons: copper, 292, 391; gold, 390; button seals, 392, 431, 438, 442, 447, 449, 458

buttresses in fortifications, 319, 320; in houses, 256, 273–4, 578, 590, 593, 613; in shrines and temples, 286, 378–9; of temple façades, 287–8, 336–7, 339, 370, 382, 384–6, 397; cruciform, 337; stepped, 379, 382

Buzàul, river of Romania, 30

Byblos, in Lebanon, N. of Sidon, 253, **266–8, 283–4, 420–1, 515–17,** 519, 521; Early Neolithic, 251, 266–8, 313, 515–16; Middle (Byblos I), 283, 516–17; Late, 284, 516; Byblos B (Énéo-lithique B, level 2), 414, 421; princes of Byblos, 141, 184; Byblian Phoeni-cian, 137; radiocarbon dates, 516, 519

Byzantine period, 39, 143, 524

C-14 dating, *see* radiocarbon

Cadmus, 244

Caetani, L., 139

Caicus, river of Anatolia, 305

Cainozoic, *see* Tertiary

Cairo, 70, 467

Cairo Museum: fragments of Egyptian Annals tablet (Palermo Stone), 175; ostracon, 191; Naqāda II material: 14516, 485 and n. 4; Hamra Dōm silver dagger (14514), 486 and n. 5; El-Amra silver dagger, 485–6

Calabria, district of Italy, 19

calcite, 310

Caledonian orogeny, 2; geosyncline, 2; Caledonides, 10

calendar: Assyrian, 229, 232; Babylonian, 229; Egyptian civil, 173 and nn. 2–3, 182–3

Calimani range of Transylvania, 25, 30

calotte, 162

calves, 518

Calycadnus valley in Anatolia, 305, 325

Cambrian system, 1–3; Pre-Cambrian, 1, 2, 4, 6, 17 (fig. 1); Post-Cambrian, 1, 5, 12

camels, domestication of, 140 and n. 1, 145, 460

camel-thorn, 331

Cameron, G. G., 217–18, 234

camp-sites, *see* encampments

Canaanite era and cities, 237–9, 505; lan-guage, 128, 135–6; Canaanean blades, 414, 532

Canada, 46

canals: in Egypt, 482; in Iran, 423, 425, 434; in Mesopotamia, 327, 332, 350, 354, 368, 373–4, 440; in N. Meso-potamia, 375

Can Hasan culture of S. Anatolia (Map 10 (68)), 252, 253, 281, 318, **325–6**; houses (level 2 *b*), 590, 593

Canis sp., 440; *Canis familiaris*, 445, 455

cannibalism, 103–4

canoe, 98 (fig. 8)

Cantabric region of N. Spain, 106

Cantal, mountains of Auvergne, 24

Cape of Good Hope, 8

caper, 271

Cappadocia, district of central Anatolia, 134, 140, 142–3 *and see* Kültepe

Capra sp., 440; *Capra aegagrus*, 455; *Caprini*, 95; caprids on pottery, 430 (fig. 37), 457 (fig. 42)

Capsian culture of N. Africa (Map 9), 71, 114, 166

carbon-14, *see* radiocarbon

figurines (*cont.*)
Iran, 291, 435; clay, 262, 264, 436, 440, 444; sun-dried, 423; unbaked, 260
Mesopotamia, 274, 351, 358, 364, 369, 376; terracotta, **347–8**, 352, 359, 388
Palestine, 504, 525
Syria and Lebanon, 265, 269, 283; clay, 268, 411–12
S. Turkestan (clay), 298, 300–3; N. Zagros, 257, 259; alabaster, 291; bone, 525, 612; clay, 313, 369, 407, 496, 504 *and see sub-headings* Crete, Greece, Iran, Syria, S. Turkestan *above*; lightly baked, 257, 264; unbaked, 260, 274; sun-dried, 259, 392–3, 423; ivory, 494, 496, 525; pebble, 283; slate, 496; stone or marble, *see* Crete, Greece *above*; terracotta, 392–3, 612 *and see* Mesopotamia *above*; Halaf, 283, 393; 'Ubaid, 303, **347–8**, 352, 359, 364, 376, 388, **392–3**, 411–12; absence of, 255, 616; *see also* animals (representations of), lizard-headed figures (*s.v.* lizards), Mother Goddess
Fikirtepe, in N.W. Anatolia (Map 10 (21)), 316, 318
finger bones, models of, 278; prints and impressions on pottery, 524, 586
Finland, 9; Gulf of, 99; Finnish language, 129
Finnmark (Map 9), 94, 104
Finno-Ugrian languages, 129, 152
fir, 41; used for wooden vessels, 310
fire, destruction by, 290, 309, 412, 415, 609; at Grai Resh, 406; Hacılar, 320–1, 323; Mersin, 323, 324; Ras Shamra, 419; Sotira, 549; Tepe Gawra, 382, 395
fireplaces, 100, 255, 435, 445 *and see* hearth; firedogs, 442
firestones, flint, 311
firing: of bricks, 610–11; of pottery, 279, **430**, 512, 522, **583**, **597**, 601, 611–12; hard-fired ware, 267, 594; over-firing, 327; poor firing, 291, 346; effect on colour, 322, 365, 488, 584; to produce gloss, 287–8, 340; soft-baked, 295
Fischer, Henry G., 181 n. 1
fish, 64–5, 98–9, 110, 423; bones, 99, 338, 346, 396, 473; offerings, 332, 337, 346, 364; on pottery, 369, 430, 443; amulets, 496; fish-scale pattern, 280; fish-tails, flint, 478
fish-hooks: bone, 98, 100, 105 (fig. 10), 121, 568, 582; copper, 356
fishing: in Anatolia, 309; Cyprus, 553; Egypt and Nile Valley, 65, 473, 480;

Greece, 570; Iran, 423; Mesopotamia, 331–2, 347, 349; Palestine, 56, 499, 514; Syria, 411, 415; S. Turkestan, 295; *see also* hunter-fishers
fishing nets, *see* nets
fish-kettles, *see s.v.* hole-mouthed vessels
fish-spear, *see* harpoons
fjords, 91
flake industries and artifacts: Anatolia, 86, 309; Assyria, 391; Crimea, 117; Egypt, 71–3, 480, 491; N. and W. Europe, 97, 101, 103–4, 105 (fig. 10), 160, 162; Greece, 558–64 *passim*, 582; Iran and Zagros zone, 87, 436; Levant, 76, 78, 81, 83–4; S. Mesopotamia, 359; microlithic (q.v.), 72; micro-flakes, 101; bone flakers, 256; flake-scars, 101; flat flaking, 103, 110; radial, 103; steep, 121; *see also* Levalloiso-Mousterian *and* pressure-flaking
flame patterns on pottery, 592, 597
flanges on pottery, 407
flat-based vessels, 444 (fig. 39), 490, 513, 526, 591, 602, 605 *and see s.v.* bowls *and* jars
flax, 279, 285, 310, 350, 424, 431–2
flint industries and artifacts: N. Africa, 108, 114; Anatolia, 313; W. Asia, 118–19, 255, 296; British Isles, 104–6; Crete, 609–10, 613; Crimea, 117; Cyprus, 545–6, 554; Egypt, 72, 467, **472**, 476, 478–9, 484, 490–1, **495**; Central Europe, 115–16; S.W. Europe, 106–8, 110, 112; Greece and Ionian Islands, 559, 561–5; Iran, 426, 436; Maglemosian (q.v.), 100, 105; Palestine, 499, 501, 507–8, 511–13, 526 *and see* Natufian; Syria and Lebanon, 75–6, 78, 256, 268–70, 412, 415, 418; Zagros zone, 257, 262; chipped flint, 97, 255, 258; microlithic (q.v.), 116, 559, 561, 563; tabular, 307, 522; knapping, 550; mining, 478, 480; trade in, 269, 310; bifaces (q.v.), 75, 268, 484, 499, 501; blades (q.v.), *see* knives, sickle-blades; cores, 76, 260, 391, 432, 472, 479, 582; flakes, 545, 559; tools, 256, 260–1, 311, 424, 499, 504, 513, 517, 522 *and see* adzes, axes, hoes, scrapers; weapons, 261, 311 *and see* arrowheads; illustrations, 98, 105, 107, 560
float, wooden, 346
floating islands, 66
Flood, the, 330, **353–4**; Flood Pit F, 351, 353–5; Flood-bank, 355
flooding, 23, 93 *and see* marine transgression

Hacılar (*cont.*)
painted pottery, 273, **315–17**, 318, 321, **322–3**, 602; domestic plants, 249; radiocarbon dates, 313, 317, 320, 588; levels: I (*a–d*), 280–1, 317–18, 320–6 *passim*; II, **319–20**, 321, 323; II*b*, 317; III, IV, 319; V, 317, 319, 323; V–I, 315, 317–18; V–II, 314, 321, 323; V–III, 320; VI, 314, **315–17**, 319; VI–II, 323; IX–VI, 313, 318

hackberry, 309, 314

Ḥadhramaut, district of S. Arabia, 62; Wādi Ḥadhramaut, 9

Ḥadramī, Semitic dialect, 138

haematite, 310, 314, 389, 413, 525, 527

Hageorgitika (Ayioryitika), in Peloponnese (Map 15 (31)), 593–4

Hagia (Ayia) Triada, in Crete (Map 17 (130)), chamber tomb, 245

hair, human, 168; hair-styles, 316, 477

Hajji Fīrūz, in N. Iran (Maps 8 (42), 11 (17), 13 (4)), 253, **290–1**, 292–3, 312, 440–1

Hajji Muḥammad (Qalʿat Ḥajji Muḥammad), near Warka in S. Iraq (Map 11 (31)), 287, **364–6**; pottery, 327, 341 (fig. 26), 365–6, 368, 425

Hajji Muḥammad ware, **288–9**, 340, **342** (and fig. 27), 350, 358, 363, **365–6**, 368, 372; and Assyria, 396–7; and Iran, 264, 286, 350, 428, 436, 437; culture, 253, **287–9**, 366; temples, 287–8

Halabja, in Sulaimaniyyah province of Iraq, 374

Halaf period and culture, 58, 252, 253, 269, **276–84**, 301, 318; architecture, **277–8**, 281, 300, 378, 385, 591; metallurgy, 279; pottery, 269, 277, **279–81**, 322, 340, 366, 374, **393–4**, 426, 428, 438, 602; motifs and design, 286, 365, 368, 408, 411; and Hassūnah, 269, 595; and Sāmarrā, 58, 275, 276–7, 328; and ʿUbaid, 365, 397, 409; finds at Arpachiyah, 359, 366, **368**, 392, 393–4; and Anatolia, 324, 325, 599; and Greece, 580, 591, 596, 600, 602; and Palestine, 517, 530; and Sialk, 292–3, 295, 299, 448; and Syria and Lebanon, **282–4**, 409–10, 411–12, 415–16; and Tepe Gawra, 345, 366, 385–6, 393, 396–7; chronology, 58, 269, 276, 291, 318, 600; pre-Halaf, 448, 590, 600; Early Halaf, 277, 280–1, 600; Middle, 277, 280, 281; Late, 277, 280, 284, 590, 603; *and see* Tell Halaf

halfa-grass, 67

Haliacmon Valley, in W. Macedonia, 592

Haliartus, in Boeotia (Map 17 (59)), 557

Halicarnassus, in W. Anatolia, 305

Hall, H. R., 327, 333

von Haller, A., 362 n. 1

Hallstatt, Iron Age burial ground in Austria, 171

Halys, river of Anatolia, 38

Hama, on Orontes (Map 8), 266, 414–15, **416–17**; stratum K, 414, 416–17; L, M, 416–17

Hamadān, in N.W. Iran (Map 13), 438

Hamitic languages, 131, 132, 481; Hamito-Semitic family, 129, **132–8**

hammada (rocky desert), 39

El-Hammāmīya, in Egypt, stratified excavation, 465, **467–8**, 470, **472–3**, **474–5**, 476, 484

hammers: bone, 568; copper, 446; black marble, 391; stone, 352, 442, 545, 550; socketed, 432; hammer-axe, 369; hammer-stones, 255, 581; hammer-shaped heads of figurines, 352; hammered work, *see* copper

Hammond, E. H., 36 n. 1, 37 (Map 2)

Hammurabi of Alalakh, 213–15

Hammurabi I of Aleppo, 210, 213 and n. 2, 214

Hammurabi II of Aleppo, 213–14

Hammurabi of Babylon, 134, 198, 199, 210, 212–14, 218, 232, 234–5, 243; capture of Larsa, 208

Hamra Dōm, Gebel et-Tārif, finds in Cairo Museum, 485, 486 and n. 5

Hamun Lake, on Irano-Afghan border, 52

handles of ladles, 470, 613

handles of pottery, 272, 275, 322, 324, 516, 522, 532, 553, 583; band, 591, 601–2, 605; basket, 315, 322, 598; flap and wishbone, 612, 613; 'Hacılar', 323; horizontal, 526, 532; ledge, 534, 595; loop, 283, 323, 512, 516, 535; lug, *see s.v.* lugs; pronged, 613; ring, 344, 612; single, 534, 591, 606; twisted cord, 433; wavy, 464, 472, 489

handles of stone vessels, 545

handles of tools and weapons, 121, 369; bone, 255, 256, 311, 568, 582; gold, 491; horn, 479; ivory, 479, 486, 491; wood, 258, 272, 274, 568, 582

hands: in wall-paintings, 312; on pottery, 323, 443

Hapus Tepe, in Göksür oasis, 303

Haram, mountain in N.W. Iran, 32

Harappā culture of Indus valley, 155 and n. 4

Harari, spoken in Ethiopia, 138

23-2

houses (*cont.*)
approximate sizes, 296, 300, 578, 611, 613; examples from Anatolia, 311, 319; Greece, 549–50, 552, 576–8; Iran, 423–4, 435, 442; S. Mesopotamia, 332–3; Palestine, 265, 506–8, 519; Zagros zone, 258, 263; models of houses, 278, 484, 528; ground plans, 302, 405, 577, 590; *see also* doors, floors, rooms, stone foundations, walls, windows; pit-dwellings *s.v.* pits

Howe, B., 254

Howell, F. Clark, 77 and n. 3, 88

Hoxnian Interglacial fauna, 160

Hrdlička, A., 533 n. 11

Hrihor, priest-king at Thebes in Egypt, 191–2

Hulailan, in S. Iran, 262

Ḥūleh, lake in N. Palestine, 75, 249, 499

Hull Valley, in Yorkshire, 99

humidity, 6, 33, 42, 51

Hungarian language, 129

Hungary, 23, 24–5, 38, 42, 47; settlements, 38, 114–15; Upper Palaeolithic man, 166; and Near Eastern culture, 295; Aceramic Neolithic, 570

Huni of Egypt, 177, 193

hunter-fishers: of Europe, **90–106** *passim*, 118; of N. Africa, 90, 108, 114; of S.W. Asia, 121; of W. Asia, 90, 95, **118–21**

hunting, hunters, 167, 248–9, 498; in Anatolia, 308, **309**; in S.W. Asia, 53, 57; in Egypt, 63–4, 68, 74, 473, 480; in Europe, 93–4, 112–13, 117; in Greece, 561, 570, 587; in Iran, 292, 424, 445; in Palestine, 57, 499, 503–4, 507, 509, 514, 523, 526; in Syria and Lebanon, 266, 270; in S. Turkestan, 295–6; in Zagros zone, 255, 258, 260, 263, 289; paintings of, 113 (fig. 14), 312, 495–6; on pottery, 280, 430 (and fig. 37), 489, 494, 495; hunting charms, 470; *see also* hunter-fishers *above*

Huntington, Ellsworth, 139

Hurmuz, Old, in S.W. Iran, 478

Hurrian language, 128, 129, 135, 148, **152–4**; tablets and texts, 152

husking-trays, 268, **273**, 274, 287, 595

huts, 248, 257, 281, 500, 519, 526, 536, 544; circular, 249, 255, 258, 281, 380, 421, 474–5, 509, 512, 556; horseshoe-shaped, 483, 549; irregular, 100, 549; oval, 249, 483; semicircular, 112; sunken, 100, 510–11, 526, 548, 552, 567 *and see* pit-dwellings; brushwood,

448; reed, 262, 332–3, 351, 363, 380, 448; wooden, 263, 435, 436; hut floors, 308, 332–3, 421, 548, 567; hut symbols, 393

Hūtū Cave (Ghār-i-Hūtū), in N. Iran (Maps 12 (6), 13 (16)), 166, 294–5, 441

Huwayiz, in N.W. Syria (Map 8 (14)), 283

Huzayyin, S. A., 72

hybridization, 83, 165, 166–7, 170–1

hyena, 56, 67; spotted hyena, 55, 64

Hyksos Period, *see* Egypt, Dynastic

Iakhdunlim, king of Mari, 210

Iamkhad, kingdom in N. Syria, 210 and n. 7, 212, 213 n. 2; *see also* Aleppo

Iarimlim of Alalakh, 213 and n. 2

Iarimlim of Aleppo, king of Iamkhad, 210

Iarimlim II of Aleppo, 213–14

Iarimlim III of Aleppo, 213–15

Iasmakh-Adad, Assyrian ruler of Mari, 210

Ibalpiel II of Eshnunna, 210

Ibbi-Ishtar of Kish, 223 and nn. 5 and 6

Ibbi-Sin, last king of Ur III, 209, 219

Iberia, Iberian peninsula, 110, 112–14, 168

Ibero-Maurusian (Capsian) culture, 166

Ibero-Maurusian (Oranian) culture, 166

ibex, 309, 541; drawings of, 67; paintings of, 113 (fig. 14), 308; on pottery, 315, 431, 443, 451 (fig. 40), 452, 457; on seals, 392, 401, 416

Ibrāhīm Bayis, site near Makhmur (q.v.), 403

Ibscher, Hugo, 174 n. 2

ice, ice-sheets, 2, 7, 49, 51, 54, 90–1, 93; Ice Age and human settlement, 90, 249, 252; *see* glaciation

Iceland, 2, 12

ideography, 226 n. 4

idiolect deviation in language, 123

Idlib in N.W. Syria (Map 8 (13)), 283

idols: spectacle idols, 393, 405, 409, 417; eye idols, 393, 409

Idrimi of Alalakh, 215, 230

Iğdeli Çeşme, in central Anatolia, 307

igneous rocks, 12, 15, 22–3; deposits, 541

Ikunum of Assyria, 211–12

Île-de-France (Map 9), 110

Ili-man of the Sea Country, 211 n. 2

Ilimilimma of Alalakh, 215, 230

Iluma-ilu of the Sea Country, 211 and n. 2

Ilum-sharma (Ilum-sharrumma) of Assyria, 212 and n. 1

imports: of amazonite, 356; building stone, 363; copper, 473, 487; cowries and other shells, 264, 298, 310, 389, 473, 480, 504; figurines, 243; flint, 269, 311; glazed beads, 473, 480; green-

Mayebre Sheshi of Egypt, 185
Māzanderūn district of N. Iran, 441
McBurney, C. B. M., 441
McCown, D. E., 438
McCown, T. D., 83
Mecca, 6
Media, Iranians in, 145
median mass (*Zwischengebirge*), 16, 17 (fig. 1), 18
medical papyrus, 183
Medīnet Habu, temple of Ramesses III, 191
Mediterranean Sea (Maps 1–4 and 6), 2, 12, 16, 18, **21–3**, 25, 30–1, 33–4, 50, 70, 73; source of sea-shells, 310, 315, 525; climate and vegetation, 39–44, 53–4, 74, 77, 95, 250; race, 114, 170–1, 533; Proto-Mediterranean, 309, 533
Medithermal phase, 91
Megaceros giganteus, 94
megalithic tombs, 112–13, 537–8; walls, 504; Megalithic peoples of Britain, 169–70
Megalopolis, in Peloponnese, 559
Meganthropus, 159
Megarid, district of Greece, 564–5
megaron, 383 and n. 2, 591, 593, 600, 601–6 *passim*
Megiddo, in plain of Esdraelon (Map 14), 518, 521, **531**, **533**, 534, 536; tombs 9, 903, 1103, 1106, 1126 and 1127, 531 n. 1
    levels V–VI, 533; V–VII, 531; VII*b*, 238 n. 5; XIX–XX (mixed), 529, 531, 533; XX, 514
Mehmeh, *see* Ṭīb
Mehrī, modern dialect of Semitic, 138
Meiklewood, Stirling, Scotland, 105 (fig. 10)
Meissner, mts. in Germany, 24
Melamanna of Uruk, 236
Melanesian islands, 130
Melendiz Daǧ, mountain in Turkey, 32, 306
Mellaart, J., 304 n. 1, 515, 605
Melos, Aegean island, 30, 242, 243; source of obsidian, 571, 582, 587
Memphis, in Lower Egypt, 149–50, 174 n. 2, 183, 487; Memphite rulers of Egypt, 179–81; table of Memphite priests, 185
Menes of Egypt, founder of First Dynasty, 174, 482, 491
Menghin, O., 465, 488
Menkare, throne-name in Abydos List, 179
Menkauhor of Egypt, 178
Menkaure Senaayeb of Egypt, 184 n. 2
Menteşe, in N.W. Anatolia (Map 10 (25)), 296, 316, 318

Mentuemsaf, 184 n. 2
Mentuhotpe I of Egypt, 182
Mentuhotpe II of Egypt, 181–2
Mentuhotpe III of Egypt, 182
Mentuhotpe IV of Egypt, 182
Mentuhotpe VI of Egypt, 186
Meotian Basin, 2, 25
Merbat Abu Khanajer, in Daquq area of Iraq, 374
merchant colonies, Arabian, 138; Assyrian, 134, 140–1, 211–12
Mereijeb, site near Ur, 359–60
Merenre I of Egypt, 179
Merenre Antyemsaf II of Egypt, 179
Mereruka, tomb of, at Saqqara, 67
Merhetepre Ini of Egypt, 187
Merimda Beni Salāma, on Nile delta, 60, 465, 467, 475, **483–4**
Merj ʿAyūn, pass into Jordan valley, 518
Merneptah of Egypt, 190, 238–9
Merneptah Siptah of Egypt, 190
Meroe, in Nubia, inscriptions and language, 132
Mersin, in Cilicia (Map 10), 251–3, 267, 278, 415; radiocarbon dates, 324, 516; Neolithic, 307, 313, 318; Proto-Chalcolithic, 317, 588; Early Chalcolithic, 251, 317–19, **321–3**, 517; Late Chalcolithic, 318, **324–6**; fortress, 324–5; Halaf ware, 280, 324, 517; cream-slipped ware, 324; metal, 521, 529–30
    levels: XIII, 404; XVI, 283, 318, 324–6; XVII, 283, 324; XVIII, 324; XIX–XVI, 278; XIX–XVII, 318, 324–5; XIX, 282, 324; XXI, 317, 322; XXII, 321; XXIII, 322; XXIV–XX, 317–19; XXIV–XXII, 322; XXV–XXIV, 587, 588; XXV–XXXIII, 318
Merv, in Turkmenia (Map 12), 461
Merv Dasht plain, in S.W. Iran, 441, 445
Meryibre Achthoes I of Egypt, 180
Mesannipada of Ur I, 222, 224 and n. 2, 226, 235–6
Mesaoria, plain in Cyprus, 541, 551
Meṣer, in N. Palestine (Map 14 (19)), 528, 529, 532–4, 536; level I, 531, 533; level II, 531, 533, 536
MES(?)ḪÉ of Uruk, 236
Meshta el-Arbi, Algeria, 108, 166
Mesilim, Sumerian ruler, 224–5
Meskiag-Nanna of Ur I, 222, 224 and n. 2, 235–6
Meskiagnunna of Ur I, 224 and n. 2, 225, 235–6
Meskigala, *ensi* of Adab, 220
Meskineh, in N. Syria, on Euphrates, 412

Namazga Tepe (*cont.*)
  I, 298–9; II, 295, 299–301; Early, 299–301; Late, 299, 301; III, 301, 303; IV, 303
Namcha Barwa, Himalayan peak, 28
names, personal, **128**, 135, 140, 143–4, 152, 202 n. 3, 227; place, 128, 140, 148–51, 343–4, 480; royal, 142, 223; theophoric, 202 n. 3; year, 197–8 and see *ussa*-years; names of rivers, 148
Namur, Belgium, 163
Nanga Parbat, Himalayan peak, 28
Nanne of Ur I, 224, 235–6
Napata, in Nubia, 132
nappes, 15, 16, 17 (fig. 1), 24
Naqāda, in Upper Egypt, 465, 473–4, 481, 484–5, 491, 497 *and see* Naqāda I *and* Naqāda II *below*; South Town, 476, 478–9, 496; cemeteries, 463–5, 473–80; cranial series, 168, 473; pottery, *see* Naqāda I *and* II *below*; Naqāda F 24 b, 479; seals, 492; derivation of name, 480
  tombs, 492, 497; T. 26, 485; 273, 496 n. 3; 836, 486; 1449, 493; Royal Tomb, 497
Naqāda I period in Egypt, 68, 466–7, **473–80**, 484, 493–4, 497; terminology, 465; radiocarbon dating, 193; flint industry, 478–9; ivories, 496; metallurgy, 480; pottery, 474–5, **477–8**, 489; painted, 488, **495**, 496; white cross-lined, 474, 476, 477, 493
Naqāda II period in Egypt, 68, 467, 475, 477–80 *passim*, **481–92**, 534; terminology, 465; chronology, 193; 228; cemeteries and tombs, 467, 476, 479, 484–5, 492–5; cylinder seals, 492; metallurgy, 485–7; pottery, 474, **487–90**; decorated (painted), 473, 474, 481, 488–90, 493, 495; incised, 472, 489–90; wavy-handled, 489; wall-paintings, 495–6
Naram-Sin, Akkadian ruler, 219
Narbe, 18
Narechi, river in Sulaimān region, 29
Narmer of Egypt, 175; Narmer Palette, 491
Nasi-, cuneiform Hittite, 142
Natufian culture (Map 9), 56–7, 253, 256, 307, 501, 504, 507; Palaeolithic, 86, 166; Mesolithic, 73, 95, 120 (fig. 16), **121**, 251, **499–500**; stage I (Lower Natufian), 500, 503; III–IV, 503; chronology, 50, 56, 89, 255, 264; radiocarbon date, 86; *see* Wādi en-Naṭūf *and* Jericho
natural scientists, 254

naturalistic designs: Halaf, **279–81**, 411; from Assyria, 392; Iran, 285–6, 293, 427, 442–3; Mesopotamia, 275; Syria, 409, 411; S. Turkestan, 298
La Naulette, near Namur, 163
Nauplia, in N.E. Peloponnese, 564
nave, 336–7, 370, 380, 382, 384, **385–6**
Naxos, Aegean island (Maps 10, 17 (120)), 608
Nazareth, 163
Nazibugash of Babylon, 205
Nea Makri, on E. coast of Attica (Maps 15 (21), 16 (41), 17 (89)), Early Neolithic, 576, 580–2, 587–8; Middle, 593
Neanderthal man, 83, 158–9, 161 (fig. 18), **162–6**, 248; type and subspecies, 74, 83, 161, 559, 562
Nea Nikomedeia, in Macedonia (Maps 15 (1), 17 (26)), 574, **577–82**, 600; lay-out of village, 268, 296, **577** (and fig. 43), **578**; chronology and radiocarbon date, 572 n. 2, 577, 587–8
Near East, geography and climate, **35–69**, 139; and beginnings of civilization, 247–54, 566; and Crete, 615–17; and Cyprus, 555; and Greece, 566–71 *passim*, 580–1, 588, 590–6 *passim*, 600–1, 602–3, 608
Nebekian industry at Jabrud, 84
Nebhepetre Mentuhotpe II of Egypt, 181–2
Nebiryerawet I of Egypt, 186–7
Nebka of Egypt, 177
Nebkaure Achthoes II of Egypt, 180
Nebmare Ramesses VI of Egypt, 191
Nebpehtyre (Amosis, q.v.) of Egypt, 185
Nebtowyre Mentuhotpe IV of Egypt, 182
necklaces, 111, 256, 392, 486, 546; links for, 278, 392
needles: bone, 298, 311, 315, 368, 469, 546, 568, 582; copper, 292, 326, 356, 458, 486; netting, 100, 102 (fig. 9)
Neferefre of Egypt, 178
Neferhotep I of Egypt, 184
Neferhotep III of Egypt, 184 n. 2
Neferirkare of Egypt, 178
Neferkahor of Egypt, 180
Neferkare of Egypt, 180 and n. 1
Neferkare 'the Younger' of Egypt, 180
Negeb, S. Palestine, 57, 509, 531; Ghassūl-Beersheba culture, 521, 525–30, 538
Negro languages, 130; negroid physical type, 168, 533
Neith, Egyptian goddess, 493
Nemea, near Corinth (Maps 15 (27), 16 (47), 17 (98)), 564, 579, 585
Nemrut, mountain in E. Turkey, 32
Nenzlingen, Switzerland, 115

shrines: in Babylonia, 148–9; in S. Turkes-
tan, 298; at Arpachiyah, 278; at
Eridu, 286–7, 288, 336, 349, 380, 385;
at Çatal Hüyük, 309, 311–13, 314,
316; at Hacılar, 316, **319–20**; at Tepe
Gawra, 379; at Nea Nikomedeia, 580;
on boats, on Egyptian pottery, 489,
493–6; on seals, 392
shrubs (Map 3), 42, 67
Shubat-Enlil, city of Mesopotamia, 210
Shu-Durul, Akkadian ruler, 219 n. 4
Shu-ilishu of Isin, 209 and n. 1
Shukbah, Wādi en-Naṭūf, 163
Shulgi of Ur III, 225 nn. 3 and 5, 331
Shūneh, in Jordan valley (Map 14 (15)),
531, 533–4; level I, 514
Shūr, river of Fārsistān, 29
Shuruppak (Tell Fārah), city of S. Baby-
lonia, 145 and n. 2, 354, 373; see
Fārah texts
Shu-Sin of Ur III, 218
shuttles, 522, 532, 613, 615
Sialk, see Tepe Sialk
Siberia, 11, 47
Sicily, 18–19, 22; Sicilian straits, 33; skulls,
170
sickles, sickle-blades: from Anatolia, 307,
311, 314; Assyria, 272, 274, 401, 407;
Cyprus, 545–6; Egypt, 490 *and see*
sickle-stones; Greece, 568, 582; Iran,
119, 260–1, 263, 292, 442, 445; Mesopotamia, 359, 368 *and see* clay *below*;
Palestine, 499, 501, 504, 507, 509,
512–14, 516, 522; Syria and Lebanon,
265–6, 268, 269–70, 419; S. Turkestan, 295–7; N. Zagros, 255–6, 258;
denticulated, 266, 268; deeply serrated,
512–13, 516; straight, 297; with silica
sheen, 249, 257, 265; antler, 314; bone,
255–6, 292, 296, 311; clay ('Ubaid),
288, 332–3, 343, 350, 356, 365, 369,
372, **401**; disappearance or absence of,
262, 270, 503; models of, 278
sickle-stones, 472, 479, 490
Sidari, on Corfu (Map 15 (45)), 566, 572,
575
sidereal (Sothic) dates, see *s.v.* Sothis
Sidon (Map 14), 518
signets, Minoan, 243
Sihornedjheryotef, 184 n. 2
Siirt, in S.E. Turkey, 277
la Sila, mt. in Calabria, 19
silica sheen, 249, 265
siliceous gravels (*Augensteine*), 27; organic
oozes, 12
Ṣilli-Sin of Eshnunna, 210 and n. 3
silos, 407, 523–4; domed, 318

silts, 23–4, 38, 56, 58, 571; of Nile, 38,
63–5, 70–1
Silurian system, 1, 2, 6; Siluro-Devonian
rocks, 6
silver, 310, 439, **485–6**; beads, 421, 485;
foil, 485; rings, 326, 421
Simashki, Elamite country, 217–18; *sukkal*
of, 234
Sin, Moon-god, 147; Sin Temples, *see*
Khafājī
Sinai Peninsula, 6, 8, 31, 57, 482; Proto-
Sinaitic inscriptions, 136; rock-en-
gravings, 509; mining of copper, 136;
source of turquoise, 136, 504, 525
Sind, province in lower Indus valley, 455
Singapore, 5
Sin-iqisham of Larsa, 209
Sinjār, *see* Beled Sinjār *and* Jebel Sinjār
sinkers, *see s.v.* nets
Sin-muballiṭ of Babylon, 233
Sino-Tibetan languages, 129
Siptah of Egypt, 190
Sirius, *see* Sothis
Sīstān, district of E. Iran and S.W.
Afghanistān, 445, 455
de Sitter, L. U., 18–19, 22–3
Siut, *see* Asyūt
Siwa Oasis, in N.W. Egypt, 132
Siwalik ranges of Himalaya, 26
Siwepalarkhuppak of Elam, 218, 234
skeletal remains, 101, 103–4, 111 (fig. 13),
113–14, 158, 169, 505–6; Neanderthal,
165; Swanscombe, 159–60; Upper
Palaeolithic, 165–6, 312; *see* burial *and*
burial customs
skeuomorphic origin of pottery design, 394
Skiemiewice, in central Poland, 103
skins, 421, 568, 569; used for clothing, 111,
311, 469, 476; for wrapping dead, 469;
for making boats, 95, 106
skirts, 469; of beads (q.v.), 347, 424
skulls, **156–72**, *and see* brachycephalic,
mesocephalic, dolichocephalic, Neanderthal *and* physical types; broad-
based, low-vaulted, 165; high-vaulted,
114, 169–70; keeled, 114; Galilee skull,
78, 81; of modern man, 83, 166; cranial
capacity and deformation, *see s.v.*
crania; illustrations, 111, 157, 161, 164;
painted skulls, 265, 505; plastered,
265–6, 505–6, 508, 580; on floors, 308;
skull-burials and cult, **116, 505–6,**
507–8; *see* ancestor-worship; skulls of
animals, etc., 99, 312
Skyros, Aegean island (Map 15 (39)), 317
slate, 256, 391, 496; slate palettes, 470, 472,
476–7, 489, 494, 496

VERMONT COLLEGE
MONTPELIER, VERMONT.

GARY LIBRARY
VERMONT COLLEGE
MONTPELIER, VT.